Social Problems
Causes, Consequences, Interventions

Second Edition

Jack Levin
Northeastern University

Kim Mac Innis
Bridgewater State College

Walter F. Carroll
Bridgewater State College

Richard Bourne
Professor Emeritus, Northeastern University

Roxbury Publishing Company
Los Angeles, California

A *website* for this text is available at http://www.bridgew.edu/~wcarroll/ socialproblems.htm. An *instructor's resource guide/testing program* is also availabe in book form or on disk.

Library of Congress Cataloging-in-Publication Data

Social problems: causes, consequences, interventions
  Jack Levin [et al.]. ——2nd ed.
p. cm.
Rev. ed. of: Social problems / Richard Bourne. Jack Levin. 1983. Includes bibliograph‑
ical references and index.
ISBN 0-935732-96-9
1. Sociology 2. Social problems. I. Levin, Jack, 1941– . II. Bourne, Richard, 1940–
Social problems.
HM51.S6619   2000
301—dc21   97-40027
                                                                 CIP

Social Problems: Causes, Consequences, Interventions (Second Edition)

Publisher: Claude Teweles
Supervising Editor: Dawn VanDercreek
Developmental Editor: Arlyne Lazerson
Production Editor: Renée M. Burkhammer
Typography: Synergistic Data Systems
Cover Design: Marnie Kenney

Printed on acid-free paper in the United States Of America. This paper meets the standards for recycling of the Environmental Protection Agency.

ISBN 0-935732-96-9

Roxbury Publishing Company
P.O. Box 491044
Los Angeles, California 90049-9044
Tel: (310) 473-3312 • Fax: (310) 473-4490
Email: roxbury@crl.com

This book is dedicated to
Flea, Andrea, Bonnie, and Michael
Dave, Keaghan, and Kylie
Robin, Becca, Matt, and David
and
Carol, Michael, and Steven

Contents

Preface

We wrote *Social Problems: Causes, Consequences, Interventions* to serve as an introduction to a wide range of social problems. We have organized the chapters in a consistent format, beginning with the definition and prevalence of the social problem covered, followed by levels of causation, consequences, and interventions. Each chapter also includes a discussion of the future of the social problem and a summary of its major substantive issues. Concluding each chapter are discussion questions, references, and a list of relevant World Wide Websites.

An *Instructor's Resource Guide/Testing Program* (available in book form or on disk) and a website for the text are also available (http://www.bridgew.edu/~wcarroll/socialproblems.htm). The website includes updated data, additional teaching resources, and suggested student projects.

We have tried to make this a lively, readable text that introduces students to a variety of sociological viewpoints on social problems. We analyze every topic from individual, cultural, and structural viewpoints. This allows an instructor to compare explanations which incorporate such structural factors as social class and economic structure to those which focus on cultural factors or on biological and psychological characteristics of the individual. Although *Social Problems* is eclectic, it emphasizes the importance of class, gender, and race for understanding social problems. The text focuses on the United States, but incorporates comparative, cross-cultural material when appropriate.

Unique features of this book include:

- A consistent approach that offers possible solutions to social problems, not just explanations.

- Full chapters on cities and urban decline, and on food and population.

- Coverage of such contemporary issues as: the criminalization of pregnancy, domestic violence as a health issue, age discrimination, and sexual orientation and homophobia.

To stimulate student interest, we begin each chapter with an "In the News" section drawing on recent newspaper articles related to the social problem covered in the chapter. The discussion of newspaper articles for this purpose illustrates the everyday occurrence of social problems and helps students link abstract ideas to the concrete circumstances of everyday life.

Every chapter also includes "Closer Look" inserts to heighten student interest by describing ongoing efforts to resolve current social issues. Some inserts highlight the impact of social policy, while others summarize research which has historical importance or challenges traditional, or "common sense" assumptions. We hope that the "In the News" and "Closer Look" sections stimulate discussion and debate on controversial aspects of social problems.

We have sought to provide a book that offers a broad representation of topics, but is not an encyclopedic social problems text. However, the text is comprehensive enough to serve as the sole text for a semester or quarter course. Because many instructors prefer not to rely on a single text, the book is concise enough that an instructor may supplement it with additional materials.

To the Student

We hope you learn a lot from this book, but even more, we hope it stimulates your own thinking and provokes your curiosity. The problems covered are among the most important facing our society today.

In writing this book we tried not to make too many assumptions about who you are. Of course we know you're smart and curious or you wouldn't be taking a social problems course. Beyond that, we did not make assumptions about your age, gender, ethnicity, race, sexual orientation, or type of school. Some of you are 18–22 years old, but many fall into other age categories. Some of you attend community colleges, while others are enrolled in four-year colleges and large universities. The increasing diversity of American society and of American higher education should be reflected in texts, which do not leave any groups of students feeling left out. Please let us know what you think about this or any other aspects of the text, by emailing either Walter Carroll (wcarroll@bridgew.edu) or Kim Mac Innis (kmacinnis@bridgew.edu). We would appreciate receiving your comments, criticism, praise, or suggestions.

Acknowledgments

In writing this text we incurred numerous debts to family, friends, and colleagues. We appreciate their support and learned much from their criticisms and suggestions.

Kim Mac Innis wishes to thank Don Austin and Kevin Borgeson for their research contributions; and Margie Mac Innis, Skip Mac Innis, Joe Mac Innis, Susan Mac Neil, Craig Mac Innis, Rebecca Chin, and Steven Austin. Thanks to Julie Wyman, Cathy Rogers, Lori Zonfrelli, Pam Arrighi, and John Gillies for their continued support and ideas. Janet Fender, Jennifer Stoll, and Jack Lang made important contributions to the chapters on child abuse and battered women. Finally, thanks to Tracey Mac Innis-Holick, Shelley Campbell, Leslie Campbell, Mary Burt, Cheryl Bandera, and Kim Notarangelo for their contributions to the chapter on gender inequality.

Walter Carroll thanks Robin Roth for her unwavering support, editorial acumen, and sociological insight. He is also grateful to Bob Sutherland, his colleague as CART coordinator, for his support, patience, and publishing expertise.

We also wish to thank Ronnie Elwell for her help on the health care chapter, Bill Levin for his assistance on the aging chapter, and Patricia Fanning for writing the Instructor's Resource Guide/Testing Program. Jack Levin and Richard Bourne renew their thanks to those who helped with the First Edition of the book. We are grateful to Claude Teweles, Publisher of Roxbury Publishing Company, for his patience and encouragement during the longer than anticipated preparation of the manuscript. Members of the Roxbury staff also helped us in numerous ways.

We are grateful to the following reviewers. We learned a lot from them and incorporated many of their insightful criticisms and valuable suggestions into the book: Deborah A. Abowitz, Philadelphia College of Textiles; Russell Buenteo, University of South Florida; Lee Frank, Community College of Allegheny County; John Linn, Gustavas Adolphus College; Frank Scarpitti, University of Delaware; William Schwab, University of Arkansas; Scott Sernau, Indiana University at South Bend; Mark A. Winton, University of Central Florida; Morrison Wong, Texas Christian University; Harry Mersmann, Chapman University; Kathleen Tiemann, University of North Dakota; Valerie Jenness, University of California, Irvine; Peter Kivisto, Augustana College; Kurt Cylke, Jr., SUNY Geneseo; Peter Stein, William Patterson College; and Julia Hall, Drexel University.

We also wish to thank the following scholars, who reviewed the proposal for this book: Nijole Benokraitis, University of Baltimore; Julia Hall, Drexel University; John Stratton, University of Iowa.

Finally, we especially would like to thank our families for their love, support, and patience. Jack Levin thanks Flea. Kim Mac Innis is grateful to Dave, Keaghan, and Kylie. Walter Carroll thanks Robin, Rebecca, Matt, and David. Richard Bourne thanks Carol.

Jack Levin
Kim Mac Innis
Walter F. Carroll
Richard Bourne

About the Authors

Jack Levin, Ph.D., is the Brudnick Professor of Sociology and Criminology at Northeastern University, where he directs its Center on Violence and Conflict. He teaches courses on criminal homicide, social psychology, and the sociology of violence. Levin has written widely in these fields, having authored or co-authored 20 books, including *Mass Murder: America's Growing Menace*, and *Killer on Campus*. He has also authored and co-authored some 150 articles in professional journals and newspapers. He has appeared on numerous national television programs and has served as an expert witness or consultant in a number of trials. He was recently honored as Professor of the Year in Massachusetts by the Council for Advancement and Support of Education. In November 1997, he spoke at the White House Conference on Hate Crimes.

Walter F. Carroll, Ph.D., is Professor of Sociology and a coordinator of the Center for the Advancement of Research and Teaching at Bridgewater State College in Massachusetts. He chaired the Department of Sociology and Anthropology from 1991–1997. Carroll teaches courses on social problems, urban sociology, East Asian societies, social theory, and social data analysis. He authored a previous book, *Brockton: From Rural Parish to Urban Center*.

Kim Mac Innis, Ph.D., is Assistant Professor of Sociology at Bridgewater State College. She teaches courses on family violence, women and crime, criminology, gender roles, feminist theory, and social theory. She has done extensive research on family violence, including work on undocumented, abused immigrant women.

Richard Bourne, Ph.D., former Associate Professor of Sociology at Northeastern University, is an attorney in the General Counsel's Office at Children's Hospital in Boston. He has done extensive research on family violence, and co-edited *Unhappy Families*.

CHAPTER ONE

Introduction: Understanding Social Problems

In the News: An End to Social Problems?

The First Edition of this book, published in 1983, started with a newspaper article entitled "President declares all problems solved." According to the article, which was dated July 4, 2107, the President of the United States had commemorated the Fourth of July by declaring an end to all social problems. "Poverty, inequality, and deviance—so prevalent during the 1980's—no longer existed." The minister of mental health released studies showing that "our citizens have never been so happy." The last paragraph of the bogus article did introduce a somber note: "Later in the day, President Ryder also announced that all chronic complainers have been summarily shot."

The year 2107 is still a long way off, but the economic news in the United States in the late 1990s seems good. Unemployment and inflation are both down, and other indicators of economic well-being are rising. Certainly, at least on some counts, the United States economy seems healthy. What about the society? How healthy is it? Does improving economic health suggest that social problems in the United States have been solved? How close are we to solving our major social problems?

According to a New York Times *article, a "report says health of society lags behind that of economy" (Kannapell 1997). Since 1985, the Fordham Institute for Innovation in Social Policy has produced the Index of Social Health. In compiling the Index, the Fordham Institute combines statistics on sixteen areas of social life. The statistics used include measures of drug abuse, average wages, the percentage of children in poverty, teenage suicide, poverty among the elderly, and the gap between rich and poor.*

The Index does indicate that the nation's social health is improving. However, Marc L. Miringoff, the institute's director, did not find the overall picture in the 1990s very encouraging. "Of the eight worst years since 1970, six have been in this decade. The social health of the nation has not kept up with the recovery of the economy." Another recent survey of social conditions found the United States ranking 27th of 160 countries. This report was based on 45 measures in 10 areas of social development, including health, education, and social conflict. Richard J. Estes, a professor of social work at the University of Pennsylvania, conducted the study. He noted that the "relatively low" standing of the United States was due to the "persistence of poverty among 37 million Americans, as well as deteriorating cities, racism, stagnation in social progress for women, and growing hostility toward the poor, the elderly, and recent immigrants" (McDonald 1997).

These surveys raise many questions about social problems in the United States. Although social conditions have clearly been improving, the "end of social problems" does not seem to be in sight. To understand social problems we can start by considering what a social problem is and how it is defined.

What Is a Social Problem?

At first glance, the definition of a **social problem** may appear obvious. Violent crime, poverty, teenage suicide, drug abuse, divorce—these issues are commonly mentioned as concerns of the American people and could be considered social problems. Several difficulties, however, arise in defining what is, and what is not, a social problem.

One difficulty is *who* decides whether a problem exists. While some individuals or groups may view a condition as a problem, others may be indifferent or actually view the phenomenon as desirable. Pro-life (anti-abortion) groups, for example, see abortion as the killing of a child while pro-choice (pro-abortion) advocates consider it a humane technique that limits unwanted births and allows women control over their bodies.

No society has a single, unified set of values, and because of differences in perspectives and interests, it is unclear who has, or should have, the power of defining a problem. An environmentalist may express concern over air pollution, while an automobile manufacturer may protest pollution-control regulations. Parents may complain about excessive television violence and ask for a television rating system, while broadcasters challenge programming constraints as assaults on free speech and resist setting up a rating system. Do you accept the position of the anti- or the pro-abortionist? The environmentalist or the industrialist? The media consumer or the producer?

These are some of the tough questions that arise in the sociological study of social problems. You have probably thought about some of these questions. Undoubtedly you have strong opinions on some of them and you may be unsure about others. In reading this book you will learn how sociologists look at and try to understand social problems. More important, you will learn to think systematically about social problems yourself and develop your own perspective on them.

To understand social problems it helps to cultivate what sociologist C. Wright Mills called the **sociological imagination**, which "enables us to grasp history and biography and the relations between the two within society" (Mills 1959:6). This may sound complicated, but it basically means learning to see how your own individual life experience ("biography") is affected by and interrelated with your society and how it changes ("history"). You can use the sociological imagination to place your individual experience in a broader social and historical context.

Sociology is essential for understanding the connections between your own individual experience and the larger structures of your society because it is the scientific study of human social relationships. Those social relationships vary widely in scale, from interaction between two people to global social processes. Sociologists have studied how we cooperate with each other in face-to-face interaction to create a shared, predictable social life (Goffman 1959), what life is like in working-class families (Rubin 1976, 1994), social organization in large corporations (Kanter 1977), the relationships between work and family life (Hochschild 1989), and the creation of a **world system** of societies (Wallerstein 1974).

Regardless of the scale of human social relationships that they study, most sociologists agree with the central insight of sociology: that social interaction and social relationships crucially shape people's lives, their ideas, and their behavior. Scott Sernau (1997) suggests that sociology has essentially two main topics: social interaction and social organization. **Social interaction** tends to be the focus of **micro-sociology**, the study of small-scale interaction; **social organization** refers to the study of larger-scale social units and processes characteristic of **macro-sociology**. Whether sociologists focus on social interaction or on social organization tends to affect how they define social problems and how they decide that a social problem exists.

Some sociologists argue that a social problem exists when a *significant number* of people *believe* that a certain condition is, in fact, a problem (Spector and Kitsuse 1973). By stressing the phrase "significant number," this position makes a distinction between what Mills called a "private trouble"—a problem for an individual or for scattered individuals—and a "public issue"—a condition defined as a problem by large numbers of people (Mills 1959).

This position also focuses on the importance of belief and therefore presents a **subjective view** of social problems. If people believe that a problem exists, it exists; and unless people define a condition as a problem, it cannot be so considered. Sociologists who emphasize social interaction tend to take this point of view and are sometimes referred to as **subjectivists**.

Others reject the view that a significant number of people can define problems by their beliefs. Because the public is frequently uninformed or misinformed, relying on public perceptions may lead to error. The use of crack cocaine, for example, has been seen as a more serious problem than the use of powder cocaine, but much evidence suggests that this is not the case (Reinarman and Levine 1997). Poverty and racism, on the other hand, may be overlooked as social problems because the primary victims lack power or wealth. Should we then not see poverty and racism as social problems?

The position called the objective or **objectivist view** focuses on conditions that experts, such as sociologists, define as problems even though many people are initially unaware that a problem exists. The role of experts or professionals varies depending on whether the perspective is subjective or objective. With a subjective approach, a sociologist's job is to determine which problems are of public concern and how many people are upset. These social problems analysts often study how some condition or social arrangement becomes defined and accepted as a social problem. As an example, consider welfare reform, a topic that has received considerable attention in recent years. A social problems analyst within the subjective tradition might study how people came to perceive flaws in the welfare system and to see it as a social problem in need of reform.

With an objective approach, a sociologist's job is to identify actual or potential problems and to educate the public as to their dangers. The goal is still public awareness of an undesirable condition, but with the objective approach the sociologist helps to create such awareness rather than merely to measure its existence. Another fundamental task for sociologists working within objective approaches is to investigate how some objective condition or social arrangement developed in the first place and why it continues to exist. For example, sociologists using objective approaches would ask how and why the welfare system was created in the first place and why many aspects of it are viewed as problems. Macro-sociologists, who emphasize social organization, are more likely to take an objective approach.

Remember that those who take the subjective approach emphasize that the general public defines social problems. Taking this perspective leads to three troubling questions: (1) What happens if different segments of the public have differing views as to whether a condition is a social problem? (2) How many people must view a condition as undesirable before it becomes a social problem? (3) What occurs if differences of opinion exist between lay people and professional social scientists over whether a condition is a problem.

In addition to the question of *who* determines what is a social problem, there is the question of *how* a condition becomes so defined. According to Robert Merton and Robert Nisbet's (1976) classic discussion, individuals recognize a social problem when a sizable difference exists between the ideals of a society and its actual achievements. That is, Merton and Nisbet suggest that social problems arise because of a *gap* between the way people believe things should be and the way things really are. For example, pollution becomes a public issue when school children at recess cannot play outside because of dirty air. The realization that the environment is becoming unfit for human life shocks people into recognizing environmental concerns. Consider racial discrimination. From this view, discrimination against minorities conflicts so much with American ideals, and with the requirements of law, that racism becomes defined as an intolerable social harm.

Definitions of social problems vary over time. People may view a condition as harmful at one time but not at another. **Sexism** and the exploitation of women, for example, emerged as a public issue in the mid-1960s, although the conditions were present before that time. Some conditions may be seen as problems over long periods of time, but the focus of concern may shift. With **racism**, for example, concern was first expressed over **prejudice** and interpersonal relations between blacks and whites; only later did **institutional racism** and policy disputes over integration and separatism become major areas of conflict. A condition first defined in a positive way—for example, the ability of medical science to keep people alive who would otherwise die—may later be perceived as a problem, evidenced by an increasingly large population of the sick and the suffering.

Using Merton and Nisbet's idea of the gap between ideal and real, how do social problems develop and change? Sociologists, of course, may study the ideals and values of a society and then determine whether such standards are being fulfilled. They would function as the reporters of change in the existence or intensity of a problem. More commonly, perhaps, a social movement such as the Civil Rights movement or the Feminist movement brings the gap to public and professional attention.

Where does this leave us in terms of defining social problems? From the objective perspective a social problem is some objective condition or social arrangement that causes harm to people in a society. From a subjective view a social problem exists only when a collective interpretation defines the objective condition as a problem. "A social problem only arises when the public recognizes it as such" (Carter 1997:ix). Keep these two definitions in mind as you read about the various perspectives that sociologists have developed.

Social Problems Perspectives

Throughout history, human beings have suffered the consequences of such conditions as crime and delinquency, alcoholism, and poverty. Human pain and suffering are nothing new. What is new, however, is the idea that something can and should be done about them. According to sociologist Arnold Green, this idea emerged from humanitarian and interventionist attitudes that arose at the end of the eighteenth century. Specifically, he suggests that four crucial ideas that emerged at that time—(1) equality, (2) humanitarianism, (3) the goodness of human nature, and (4) the modifiability of social conditions—led to the consciousness of social problems as conditions that could be improved in order to alleviate human pain and suffering (Green 1975).

Changing Approaches to American Social Problems

The following are discussions of the major sociological approaches to social problems, in rough chronological order.

Social Pathology Perspective. In American sociology, the earliest way of looking at social problems is represented in the **social pathology perspective**, a point of view that thrived and prospered during the early decades of the twentieth century (Rubington and Weinberg 1995). The social pathologists adopted an organic, or biological model, which they attempted to apply to the behavior of individuals, institutions, and society as a whole. Just as physicians study physical diseases, so the social pathologists sought to examine "social illnesses" in order to treat and cure them. As a result, the social pathology perspective, in its early form, was conservative and simplistic. The present state of society was regarded as healthy while deviations from the status quo were seen as "illnesses," and those who deviated were treated as "sick" or "diseased."

The social pathologists were convinced that "social illnesses" such as crime, alcoholism, and drug abuse could spread through society in much the same manner as physical illness might spread through the human body. Moreover, **institutions** not operating according to moral expectations were thought of as "sick" in the same way as bodily organs might be diseased. Thus, for example, the economic institution might be held responsible for producing persons who are selfish and greedy; or an entire society might be seen as sick if a substantial number of its members deviated from moral expectations.

Social Disorganization Perspective. After World War I, the social pathology perspective declined and was in large part replaced by a concern with social disorganization. During the 1920s, the rapidly growing prevalence of migration, industrialization, and urbanization was accompanied by increases in alcoholism, juvenile delinquency, drug addiction, and mental illness. Rather than viewing social problems as a result of the moral failings of certain individuals and institutions, the social disorganization perspective located the source of social problems in the **social structure**, more specifically, in the effectiveness or ineffectiveness of the rules that guide and regulate social life. In practice, however, the social disorganizationists often did emphasize the shortcomings of the people they studied.

The social disorganizationists viewed society as a social system having a number of interdependent parts, with a change in one part tending to cause changes in other parts. During periods of rapid social change, there may be a breakdown or disruption in the relations between these parts, so that they get out of phase with one another. For example, a sharp rise in women's participation in the labor force (a change in the economic system) contributes to increased rates of separation and divorce (a change in the family).

Value Conflict Perspective. During the 1930s and 1940s, still another perspective gained widespread credibility in the study of social problems. The Depression and World War II served to heighten an awareness that different groups of people in a society often have opposing values and interests and that social problems frequently arise when group values come into conflict.

The **value conflict perspective** recognized that the United States is a pluralistic society, containing a diversity of group values and interests. The assumption was that these values and interests will clash and that there is nothing wrong, or "disorganized," when group members attempt to defend their own interests against the competitive interests of other groups. For instance, according to this view, race conflict occurs when African Americans attempt to organize politically in order to take charge of local institutions and promote the interests of the black community, and class conflict results when welfare funds are withheld from the poor, who then organize on behalf of their own interests (Piven and Cloward 1982).

Deviant Behavior Perspective. The value conflict approach focused squarely on differences between groups in society. After World War II, greater attention was paid to the view that social problems are a form of deviance—behavior that falls outside of socially approved, usually middle-class, norms. According to the **deviant behavior perspective**, mental illness, crime, and alcoholism are problems of individual characteristics and social institutions: deviant behavior is learned through the processes of **socialization**, when individuals are influenced by deviant role models.

The deviant behavior perspective seeks to locate the causes of deviant behavior in factors such as socioeconomic status, family structure, and anomie. According to Merton's (1957) structural strain theory of **anomie** (normlessness) and deviance, for example, lower-class deviant behavior, especially crime and delinquency, occur because of the tremendous emphasis in American culture on the achievement of material success (making lots of money and moving up the corporate ladder), on the one hand, and the absence of socially approved opportunities for material success on the other hand.

Labeling Perspective. During the 1950s, another approach to the study of social problems emerged. According to the labeling, or societal reaction perspective, the cause of a social problem can be found not in the individual characteristics of the so-called deviant person but in the attention given to a problem by the public or by various agents of social control, for example, by the police and the courts. Therefore, it is far more important to analyze social reactions to alleged acts of deviant behavior than to discover their underlying causes. Labeling theorists were less interested in why a particular individual broke a rule, thus becoming a deviant, and more interested in why that particular rule existed at all. From the viewpoint of the labeling perspective, "deviance is not a quality of the act the person commits, but rather a consequence of the application by others of rules and sanctions to an 'offender'" (Becker 1963:9).

The five perspectives discussed above generated fruitful research that helped sociologists increase their understanding of particular social problems or of social problems generally. Some sociologists employed a labeling approach to study alcoholism, drug abuse, and mental illness, while others used the value-conflict perspective to study race relations. Moreover, many aspects of the five perspectives were used in combination and were not mutually exclusive. To understand the problem of poverty in the United States, for example, it was helpful to consider class interests (value conflict), institutional change (social disorganization), reactions of middle-class individuals (labeling), and the absence or presence of opportunity structures (deviant behavior).

Contemporary Perspectives: Social Constructionist and Power-Conflict Approaches

In recent years sociologists have turned to several perspectives that incorporate insights and assumptions from the five earlier perspectives. The social constructionist and power conflict perspectives have become especially important in the study of social problems. Although they are often seen as mutually exclusive, the authors view them as complementary. Social constructionism is a subjectivist perspective; the conflict perspective is objectivist.

Social Constructionist Perspective. In a Presidential Address to the Society for the Study of Social Problems (SSSP), sociologist Peter Conrad (1997:139) suggested that "the emergence of social constructionism over the past three decades has transformed the sociological analysis of social problems." (See "A Closer Look: The Society for the Study of Social Problems.") In his overview of the constructionist perspective, sociologist Joseph Schneider (1985:210) suggests that social constructionism is the only "distinct theory of social problems."

Based on the work of Herbert Blumer (1971) and M. Spector and J. I. Kitsuse (1973, 1977), social constructionism focuses on how people collectively define social problems.

Blumer stated that social problems were products of a process of collective definition rather than a set of independently existing objective social arrangements. Instead of viewing social problems as objectively existing conditions that are harmful to society, sociologists ought to "study the process by which a society comes to recognize its own social problems" (1971:300).

Spector and Kitsuse came up with a similar approach to social problems. They defined social problems as "the activities of groups making assertions of

---

A Closer Look

The Society for the Study of Social Problems (SSSP)

The Society for the Study of Social Problems (SSSP) is the major scholarly association devoted to furthering "the study of vital social problems." Founded in 1951, the SSSP holds annual meetings to discuss research on social problems. The mission of the SSSP is "scholarship in pursuit of a just society" (Roby 1997). The SSSP has seventeen sections, each focusing on a social problems topic. For example, there are sections on crime and juvenile delinquency; the family; and poverty, inequality, and class.

The SSSP publishes the journal *Social Problems*. Your college or university library probably subscribes to it. You might want to take a look at it to get an idea of the topics current in social problems research or to get some sources for writing term papers. If you become especially interested in some area of social problems, you could look for articles on that area. Although some of the articles are tough going, *Social Problems* is a fairly accessible journal.

The SSSP recently published a booklet entitled *Working Toward a Just World: Visions, Experiences and Challenges* (Roby 1997). The booklet contains brief reports from each of the SSSP sections. Each report briefly outlines each section's vision of a just world, describes several demonstration projects relevant to the section's mission, discusses difficulties in achieving the section's mission, and provides a brief list of recommended articles and books for anyone wishing to learn more about the section's topic. The authors of this text have relied on many of those sources. We also draw on some of these reports for information on the social problems covered in this book.

grievances and claims" about some social conditions (1973:145). Claims and claims making are central to this approach. **Claims** represent the demands made by groups in regard to the conditions they view as problems.

According to Spector and Kitsuse, social problems and social movements have an intertwined "natural history" in which each influences developments in the other. This natural history has four basic stages, beginning with *agitation*, in which an individual or a group defines a condition as undesirable in terms of some ideology or because of their self-interest. They attempt to change a private trouble into a public issue, arousing popular opinion through the mass media. Such attempts at transformation may fail because of a lack of popular support; the individual or group uses tactics that are counterproductive; competition exists from more powerful movements; the public perceives the complaints as false or undeserving of concern; or, for some other reason, disinterest keeps the problem from being seen as important or legitimate. The second stage is *legitimation and co-optation*. If popular concern develops, those who are defining the problem become respectable, and governmental and other authorities begin to accept group claims as legitimate. Formal organizations take control of problem management, while government and other institutions attempt to co-opt the movement's policies and leadership. As government departments become more involved, grass-roots participation decreases, intensity and passion decline, and problems of administration begin to outweigh those of goal achievement. These changes lead to the third stage, *bureaucratization and reaction*. Debates may occur over possible causes and solutions of the problem, with conflict developing between bureaucrats and movement partisans. Finally, if the problem remains unsolved, dissatisfaction grows over existing policies and programs. The original movement may regroup, or new movements may arise, with governmental authorities tentatively taking direct and effective action or attempting to "cool out" grass-roots pressure. This is called the *reemergence of the movement*.

The development of a social problem, then, according to Spector and Kitsuse, usually includes the following elements. First, there must be some visible or observable condition—for example, people living with inadequate food and shelter or children suffering serious abuse from parents. Second, some individual or group must become aware of the condition and define it as harmful. The definers, who may or may not have influence in the society, usually see the condition as undesirable because it threatens their values or their interests. Third, the definers and others must view the condition as capable of solution. If conditions are defined as inevitable or as part of the natural order (like earthquakes), then they remain unchangeable and are not considered social problems, even though they might cause such problems. Fourth, in a process similar to the four stages presented above, more and more people, including those with power and influence in the society, come to define the condition as a problem and to suggest possible interventions.

Joseph Schneider (1985:214) suggests that "the most popular topic for constructionist research has been the creation of bureaucratic and professional categories for problematic conditions, conduct and persons." For example, Joseph Gusfield (1981, 1996) carried out research that clarified the definitions, assumptions, and organizational interests underlying the construction of "drunk driving" as a social problem. Joel Best (1990) analyzed the social construction of the child victim in the United States.

Social constructionists have also carried out important and fascinating research on **moral panics**, defined as collective responses, "generated by unsettling social strain and incited and spread by interest groups, toward persons who are actively transformed into folk devils and then treated as threats to dominant social interests and values" (deYoung 1998: 257). For example, Marilyn deYoung studied the satanic day-care moral panic of the 1980s. In this moral panic, day-care providers in over 100 day-care centers were accused of abusing children in satanic rituals. In many cases, the day-care providers received prison terms, but many of the cases have been reversed on appeal. "Drug scares" are examples of moral panics. Reinarman and Levine have investigated the construction of drug scares as moral panics in American society. These drug scares, including the crack cocaine scare of the late 1980s and early 1990s, usually have little relation to the actual seriousness of drug problems (Reinarman 1996; Reinarman and Levine 1997).

The constructionist approach has generated much useful, insightful research, but some social scientists have criticized the approach for suggesting that social problems are real only if they are publicly recognized (Piven 1981; Simon and Henderson 1997). Although the authors favor a more objective approach, we find much value in the constructionist approach, as will be evident in this text. We do not see the two approaches as mutually exclusive; rather, we see them as usefully linked. It is important to understand how a society comes to recognize social problems. However, we also think it essential to investigate harmful social conditions even if they are not yet publicly defined as social problems. We find the conflict approach helpful here.

Conflict Perspective. The conflict approach sometimes referred to as the **power conflict** or **political economy** approach, takes a very different perspective from the constructionist view. From this point of view social problems are socially patterned, objectively harmful, and measurable conditions (Simon and Henderson 1997). More precisely,

> a social problem is a socially patterned condition involving widespread physical, financial, and/or moral harm that is caused by contradictions (permanent conflicts) stemming from the institutional arrangements of a given society. Such harms exist whether or not they have gained the attention of the mass media and politicians. (Simon and Henderson 1997:13)

Rooted in the work of Karl Marx and Max Weber, this approach focuses on the differing and sometimes antagonistic interests of people and groups. Pursuing their own interests can lead groups into competition and conflict. The outcomes of these conflicts often depends on the resources of the people and groups involved. As Joe Feagin (1986) suggests, the powerful people in a society have power over others because they have greater control over important societal resources, such as private property in factories and land, income, and control over police forces. The powerful also play a major role in shaping the prevailing beliefs and ideologies that explain and legitimate the "exploitative and troubled social arrangements of this society" (1986:22).

Feagin (1986:23) stresses the importance of three hierarchies of inequality based on differences in control over basic societal resources. These "three interrelated systems of stratification, domination, and subordination, are central to major social problems" in the United States. The three hierarchies are:

1. a **class** system in which a large working class is dominated by a small capitalist class;

2. a **race** system in which nonwhite groups are generally dominated by white groups; and

3. a **gender** system in which women are generally dominated by men.

Feagin calls these hierarchies "**interlocking oppressions**." They are a major focus of this text.

The conflicts between the powerful and the powerless periodically generate the mobilization of people's movements aimed at solving problems and redistributing power and resources downward (Feagin 1986; Piven and Cloward 1982).

Erik Olin Wright has carried out research using the Marxian concept of social class (1985), while M. Brinton Lykes and her colleagues published *Myths About the Powerless* (1996), a collection of articles using conflict perspectives to examine social inequality. These articles analyzed a variety of social problems, including homelessness, the underclass, poverty, welfare, and gender relations.

Although the authors emphasize social constructionist and conflict approaches, we will draw on other theories when necessary to examine specific social problems. These perspectives help sociologists to answer important questions about social problems: How do we explain the development and/or maintenance of social problems? Why does the crime rate vary over time and place? What accounts for the prevalence of mental illness in our society? What contributes to the declining status of the elderly? Why does alcoholism exist?

Levels of Causation

The perspectives this book has looked at tend to focus on different levels of social life. In addressing important issues such as those listed above, social problems specialists have differed a good deal in their opinions as to the level of causation or explanation of the problems. Analysts have tended to focus on individual, cultural, or structural levels of causation.

Individual

The individual level of causation is the focal point for those whose orientation is either psychological or bio-social. The general public also often accepts **individual-level explanations**. In these cases, social problems are seen as resulting from characteristics of individual human beings. Proponents of the social pathology and deviant behavior perspectives have often emphasized individual causation. Psychologically, these characteristics may reside in the personality, that configuration of habits, expectations, and attitudes that is an enduring part of an individual's orientation to life. For example, racism has been regarded as but one element in the authoritarian personality syndrome that develops because of harsh child-rearing practices during the first years of life.

Biologically oriented explanations typically focus on either the biochemistry or the genetic heritage of an individual. For instance, certain investigators have suggested that violent criminals might possess an extra Y (male) chromosome whose effect is to predispose them to violent criminality.

Similarly, some mental health specialists have shown that there is a genetic predisposition in the development of schizophrenia. More recently, Richard Herrnstein and Charles Murray (1994) argued for a genetic basis for differences in IQ scores.

Cultural

The **cultural** level of explanation, in its most general meaning, focuses on the way of life that is learned and shared by the members of a given society and that they pass from one generation to another. As it has come to be applied to social problems, however, the concept of **culture** refers to a set of ideas, learned and shared by the members of a group within the society, that provide them with guidelines for their behavior. These ideas are commonly known as **values**—abstract conceptions of what is desirable and undesirable—and **norms**—rules of behavior to apply in specific social situations. In U.S. society, for example, the achievement of material success is a value to which almost everyone is expected to subscribe, regardless of **role** or position. However, the particular norms (rules) to be employed in achieving success vary a good deal from one situation to another. Physicians-in-training are expected to achieve high grades and successfully complete several years of medical training, while sales personnel are expected to persuade their customers as to the quality and effectiveness of their goods or services. There are norms for riding in elevators (don't stand too close, don't stare, don't talk with strangers), just as there are norms for eating at the dinner table (knives and forks in America) or for asking questions in a classroom (raise your hand, please).

The cultural level of causation is most likely to be employed by the proponents of labeling, deviant behavior, value conflict, and social constructionist perspectives. We might ask, for example: How does the emphasis on productivity in American culture influence the status of retired people? Is there a culture of poverty? What is the relationship between American value orientations (for example, achievement and future-time orientation) and the status of women?

The levels of causation start at the most micro level, that of the individual, and progressively focus on larger levels of social organization. Sociologists consider the cultural level as a more micro level than the structural level (whose discussion follows) because although they may speak of the cultural system of a whole society, cultural approaches to social problems generally focus on **subcultures** and the attitudes of groups rather than on the culture of a whole society.

Structural

Many sociologists have sought to provide structural, or institutional, rather than individual or cultural, explanations for social problems. At the **structural** or **institutional** level of causation, sociologists emphasize the patterned and stable—that is, structured—aspects of interaction between people: their characteristic, shared, and socially approved ways of dealing with everyday problems and of interacting with each other.

Sociologists using structural approaches may focus on social groups and the kinds of relationships characteristic of different types of groups or on the "relative wealth, power and social position" of individuals and groups in societies (Stark 1996:44). Structural approaches also increasingly move beyond a focus on individual societies and take into account the world, or global level of social organization. They study the global level not only to understand that level of social organization but also to understand how the relationships among societies affect social life and social relationships within societies and, ultimately, how they affect the lives of individuals. World system theorists, for example, study class conflict at the global level to help understand class conflict within societies (Wallerstein 1979).

The structural level of causation is most likely to be represented in the perspectives of social disorganization, value conflict, deviant behavior, labeling, and power-conflict approaches. For example, certain mental illnesses have been associated with lower-class status; violent crime has been linked to racial discrimination; and the declining status of the elderly is frequently blamed on the elements of modernization. Most global level theories are structural theories because they focus on social structure on a world level.

Research on Social Problems: How Do We Know What We Know?

This book examines the perspectives and levels of causation employed by those who seek to understand the nature of social problems. The authors now ask: How do we decide among the various explanations of social problems? What kinds of evidence do we rely on? Where do we get our evidence? How is it possible to collect evidence concerning the causes and characteristics of important social problems? In other words, how do we know what we know?

Since the turn of the twentieth century, social scientists have developed a number of different research methods, methods of scientific inquiry designed to gather information about social problems in a systematic way. In sociology, the most important of these methods are experiments, sample surveys, field research, and the use of available data. We do not expect you to become experts in social research, but we do think it important that you have a general idea of where most of our evidence about social problems comes from.

Experiments

The **experiment** is a method of research by which the investigator actually manipulates the presumably causal, or **independent variable** (the causal variable) being studied, in order to observe its effect on a **dependent variable**. The experiment typically consists of at least two groups of subjects: an *experimental* group, whose members are exposed to the independent variable, and a *control* group, whose members are not exposed to the independent variable. The researcher usually attempts to make the two groups as similar as possible. By a process of careful matching or by randomization (assigning subjects to experimental and control groups by the flip of a coin, for example, so that the groups differ by chance alone), the investigator is able to assume that the only difference between the experimental group and the control group is the presence or the absence of the independent variable being manipulated. Therefore, any difference that emerges between the groups can be regarded as resulting from the independent variable.

Researchers concerned with the effect of violent television on children have frequently taken an experimental approach in their studies. In an old but still compelling study, Albert Bandura (1963), for example, asked nursery-school children to watch a five-minute videotape on a television monitor in which an adult woman was shown aggressively punching and kicking a doll. One-third of the children also saw an additional scene showing the woman being rewarded with candy and soft drinks for her aggressive behavior (Experimental Group 1). Another third of the children saw the same woman kicking and punching the doll, after which she was punished for her aggressive behavior (Experimental Group 2). The remaining one-third of the children saw only the woman's aggressive behavior and did not know whether she was rewarded or punished (Control Group, in which the independent variable was withheld).

After the children viewed the television monitor, all of them were led into a playroom containing a number of toys, including a doll. The experimenter observed and recorded the number of aggressive acts committed by each child. This was a measure of the dependent variable, aggression. Bandura's results indicated that the most aggressive children were those who had seen the television model rewarded; the least aggressive children were those who had seen the model punished. As compared with the control group condition, the independent variables (reward and punishment of aggression) seemed to have an impact on the dependent variable (children's aggressive behavior).

Experimental studies of children's reactions to portrayals of aggressive behavior suggested, among other things, that television dramatic series in which aggressive behavior—such as police detectives beating a suspect in order to secure a confession and solve a case—is routinely rewarded may increase the aggressive behavior of children in the audience. To what extent can these findings be generalized to the "real world" outside of an experimental laboratory? If the research is right, then heavy viewers (especially children who watch lots of violent television) should turn out to be more aggressive than light viewers.

Survey Research

Survey research is the most widely used research technique in sociology. You have probably participated in a survey. Perhaps you have received a phone call from someone asking you if you would answer some questions about political candidates or consumer choices. Or maybe you have been approached in a mall by someone with a clipboard asking you to answer a few questions. You may have read in a newspaper or seen on a television news show reports on public opinion polls. These are all examples of survey research.

Survey researchers ask people questions about themselves and their attitudes, beliefs, or values. This is typically done by obtaining verbal or written reports from a set of respondents. Written reports are usually obtained by means of a self-administered questionnaire; verbal reports come from an interview in which a trained interviewer asks questions and records responses. Computer-assisted telephone interviewing (CATI), in which an interviewer asks questions over the telephone and enters the responses directly into a computer, is increasingly common.

Survey researchers typically study only a sample of the people they are interested in, so surveys are often referred to as **sample surveys**. A **sample** is a subgroup, or smaller number of individuals, who are more or less representative of a larger population. The A. C. Nielson television ratings, for example, generalize their findings to the entire television audience—millions of households—based on only a thousand systematically sampled American homes.

Accurate generalizations from sample to population are possible because survey researchers often employ random sampling, whereby each and every member of the population has the same chance to become part of the sample. For example, a survey researcher who seeks to study the entire population of a large university might ask the registrar for an official list of students. From this list, a relatively small sample of students (say, a few hundred) could be selected at random to answer a questionnaire or be interviewed (say, every tenth name on the list).

McIntyre and Teevan (1972) studied the relationship between television-viewing behavior and aggression in a sample survey of 2,300 teen-aged boys and girls. All the youngsters in their sample were asked to indicate their favorite television programs and also to report any of their antisocial behaviors (such as serious fights at school, vandalism, trespassing, and so on). Not surprisingly, perhaps, McIntyre and Teevan found that the teenagers whose favorite programs were very violent were also more likely to commit antisocial acts.

Field Research

Field research, also known as participant observation or ethnography, is another widely used method for the study of social problems. In field research the researcher goes out "to observe people as they engage in the activities the social scientist wants to understand" (Stark and Roberts 1996:127). Field researchers sometimes engage in covert observation, when the people they observe are unaware of being observed.

Anthropologist Carol Stack (1974) carried out an ethnographic study of poor African-American families in a Midwestern city. In her book *All Our Kin*, she reported on how reciprocal obligations within extended families and informal social support networks ensured the survival of those in the network. Because of their poverty and the irregular flow of resources, each individual household found it difficult to survive on its own. By pooling resources and establishing reciprocal exchange of a wide variety of resources, the households enhanced their likelihood of survival. Women in the networks were usually responsible for child care and household work, so ties between the women formed the core of the networks. Stack's research presents a rich, nuanced picture of these lives and, in the process, demolishes several **stereotypes** about poor families.

More recently, sociologist Martin Jankowski carried out an ethnographic study of urban street gangs. He studied inner city neighborhoods in Boston, Los Angeles, and New York City so that he could compare gangs on the East and West Coasts. This research enabled him to get close to the gang members and obtain information that would have been impossible to gather with any other research method. However, it entailed some costs. For example, during the course of his research he was held up about 20 times. Jankowski reached conclusions that have disconcerted some critics, because he did not demonize the gang member. He compared some aspects of gang organizations to other kinds of organizations such as fraternities (Jankowski 1991).

Use of Available Data

The use of **available data**, which is increasingly important in social research, actually comprises several types of research. What these types of research have in common is the use of data or content that has already been collected. Researchers may use **content analysis** to analyze the text. The text is "anything written, visual, or spoken that serves as a medium for communication" (Neuman 1997:272-273). Melissa Barlow, David Barlow, and Theodore Chiricos (1995) used content analysis to study the relationships between economic conditions in society and how crime was portrayed in the news.

Another important use of available data is the **secondary analysis of sample surveys**. In this approach researchers use surveys designed and carried out by others. Andrew Cherlin and his colleagues (1991) used two existing surveys to study the effects of divorce on children. By using the National Child Development Study, from Great Britain, and the National Survey of Children, from the United States, they carried out important research much more quickly and cheaply than would have been possible by designing their own survey.

Social scientists also use **existing statistics** in their research. Numerous compilations of existing statistics are available. One of the most comprehensive is the *Statistical Abstract of the United States*, published by the United States government. The Annie E. Casey Foundation publishes the *Kids Count Data Book* (1994), which provides extensive information on the well-being of children in the United States. The *Statistical Abstract*, the *Kids Count Data Book*, and the numerous other sources of statistical information are treasure troves of data for researchers.

With the increasing availability of statistical information comes the necessity to be alert for misuses of data and distortions of statistical evidence. Author Michael Lind provides an excellent illustration of this, noting that one of the factors leading to welfare reform in the United States was "a widespread consensus that an overly generous welfare state encourages an ever-rising rate of illegitimacy among the urban poor" (Lind 1996:D1). Many conservative analysts and writers pointed to increases in the proportion of births to unmarried women. Specifically, "the proportion of out-of-wedlock births to black women has increased dramatically, from 23 percent in 1960, to 28 percent in 1969, to 45 percent in 1980, to 62 percent beginning in the 1990s" (Lind 1996:D1). Think about this for a moment. The proportion of out-of-wedlock births to unmarried black women did increase, but what does this actually mean? Does it mean an increase in the numbers of babies born to unmarried African American women? Not really. The increase in illegitimacy is largely a statistical illusion due to married, employed African American women having fewer children. In fact, four-fifths of the increase in the proportion of illegitimate births in the black community is due to this change, rather than to increasing numbers of illegitimate births (Lind 1996). Public discussion and debate over important social issues is unfortunately often characterized by such distortions of the evidence.

Many people respond to discussions of statistics and their misuse by stating that you "can prove anything with statistics" and ignoring statistical data.

The authors do not recommend that approach. So much of the information presented to us today is quantitative and important decisions are often based on that information. We suggest using and interpreting statistical data carefully, to make it more difficult for anyone to lie with statistics (Huff 1954).

One exciting development for anyone carrying out social research is the expansion of the World Wide Web (WWW) as part of the Internet. Websites offer an incredible variety of data and other information, and we encourage you to use the web in your study of social problems. It is important to critically evaluate the validity of information on websites, however, because much of the information on the web is inaccurate. Several excellent books on Internet resources for sociologists are now available, and they will help you learn to evaluate web sources (Ferrante 1997; Ferrante and Vaughn 1997; Thompson and Rivard 1998). In addition to listing three or four websites for each chapter, we have also included a brief introduction to a specific website as one of the Closer Looks in each chapter. (See "A Closer Look: Using the World Wide Web.")

Social Problems and Values

Early American sociologists, such as Jane Addams, Albion Small, and Lester Ward, were concerned about social problems. Often coming from religious and rural backgrounds, they distrusted industrialization and saw the cities as sources of crime, mental illness, and social conflict. Their goals were to understand urban problems and then to solve them.

It is clear that personal values inevitably influence an individual sociologist's choice of social problems and the remedies selected for resolution. And yet much discussion continues over two issues: Is it possible to select and study topics without bias? And, if it *is* possible, is neutrality desirable? Sociologists often ask whether sociology can be value free.

The authors feel that background, experience, and social position almost always affect outlook, even a scientist's. A white man, for example, might approach such topics as racism and sexism differently from an African American woman. Empathy and understanding would vary, as might the priority given each topic. As a scientist, however, any researcher would feel an obligation to analyze and present all pertinent data and findings—to *strive* for objectivity.

For a long time, social scientists argued that they were unbiased. And yet a history of the relations between whites and Native Americans in the United States would depict Custer's Last Stand as a massacre, whereas to the Native Americans it was a war victory. Many refer to Columbus "discovering" America, but the historian Francis Jennings (1975) calls the European incursion into this continent the "Invasion of America." Some people see immigrants as a threat to the well–being of the United States, while others think that immigration continues to contribute to the vitality and diversity of the society. Social scientists also take sides on these kinds of issues.

The authors think that having a point of view is not only inevitable but also, in a certain sense, desirable. To study racism, poverty, and child abuse without empathy and identification with their victims is morally questionable. Should even a scientist be objective about injustice? All of us have, and should have, opinions about controversial issues.

A Closer Look

Using the World Wide Web

The amount of information available on the World Wide Web is truly staggering. Websites give you access to detailed, up-to-date data on a rich variety of social topics. For example, the U.S. Bureau of the Census maintains websites providing extensive information valuable for investigating social problems. To access the web, you use *web browser* software. The two most popular web browsers are Netscape and Microsoft Explorer.

The address of a website is called a Uniform Resource Locator (URL). For example, the URL for the U.S. Census Bureau is .census.gov. The URL for the Income page of the Census Bureau is .census.gov/hhes/www/income.html. Knowing what kind of site you are on can also be helpful. After the word "census" in the Census Bureau URL is the three-letter word "gov," which stands for government. Other three-letter identifiers are "com"—commercial; "edu"—educational; "mil"—military; "net"—internet service provider; and "org"—nonprofit organization.

You need to be careful in using information from the World Wide Web. Not all of the information is equally useful or accurate. In assessing the accuracy and reliability of information on the web, you should keep the following criteria in mind: (1) Who created the website? If the website was created by an individual, does the website tell you who he or she is and give the individual's credentials? Similarly, websites created by organizations or associations should clearly identify the organization and its goals. (2) What are the sources for the information on the site? Many websites do not clearly reveal the sources of their information. Try to be sure that information comes from authoritative sources. (3) How up to date is the information? Check to see when the information was posted and if it has been updated. (4) Who is the target audience for the website? Some of the websites listed in this book are aimed at professional sociologists, but we have only listed sites that would also be valuable for students and that include links to other useful sites. Be careful as you link to other sites from your initial site. The initial site may be a reliable one with accurate, authoritative information. You may link to another site that is much less reputable. Keep track of where you are.

Having argued, then, that sociology is not value free and that neutrality is not always desirable, it is important to stress two points: first, the importance of presenting all viewpoints, even if they conflict with one's own position or values; second, the importance of letting the reader know one's biases so that these can be taken into account when studying textual materials.

We, the authors, have our own biases. As sociologists we emphasize the importance of the social structure in understanding social problems. That is, we generally place individual behavior and attitudes in a specific environment or setting. We also favor social arrangements that expand human choices and maximize the potential for human development unfettered by age, class, gender, race and ethnicity, or sexual orientation.

The French sociologist Emile Durkheim (1951 [1897]) stressed the role of **social facts** in explaining an individual's suicide. What could be a more individual act than a person taking his or her own life? Yet Durkheim showed that social factors played a major role in suicide. Durkheim showed that Catholics were less likely to commit suicide than Protestants. Religious background, and the sense of community of particular religions, influence the person.

Social structure, then, has individual consequences. We are not saying that psychological (individual) factors are unimportant in explaining behavior or that particular environments always lead to similar results. We are saying that institutions are a source of social problems and that one must never

focus exclusively on persons. Social forces *shape* human behavior. If a child   ❖ ❖ ❖ ❖
becomes truant from school, the school might be at fault rather than just the
child. If a person commits a crime, we need to consider the role of economic
and social conditions rather than just focus on the individual's shortcomings.

If we emphasize social structure as a cause of social problems, we also
tend to sympathize with those who suffer structural and social consequences.
Obviously, how you view those on welfare, the mentally ill, and the aged may
influence your analysis. Do people cause their own misfortune or are they en-
meshed in cultural and social forces beyond their control, forces that victimize and punish them for their status? Emphasizing the environment and social facts that influence behavior minimizes the likelihood of victim-blaming.

Finally, as sociologists, we adopt a questioning stance. We try to discover
what is really taking place rather than what seems to be occurring. In a famous study (Roethlisberger and Dickson 1939), sociologists were attempting
to discover the relationship between productivity and levels of lighting in the
workplace. The hypothesis was that the brighter the lighting in a workplace,
the greater the workers' output and efficiency. Every time the lighting was increased so did worker output. It appeared that the hypothesis was proven.
Then, an especially sensitive researcher decided to decrease the illumination
to see whether production would fall. Instead of falling, it continued to grow.
Employees were so pleased that researchers were paying attention to them—
asking them questions, making them feel important—that the study itself led
to increased efforts. The impact of illumination was not as it had appeared.
Named for the plant in which the study was carried out, this effect is called
the Hawthorne Effect.

In this book we also ask: Who really has power in American society? Who,
if anyone, benefits from poverty, pollution, and other social problems? Does
individual and social gain affect people's ability to eliminate harmful conditions? It is important to ask why those on welfare are characterized as cheat-
ers; why elderly people are seen as children, without social value or worth;
why marijuana is illegal and alcohol legal, despite the possible greater dangers of alcohol. As with the illumination study, the answers are neither clear
nor simple. It is an obligation of sociologists to try to explain social patterns
and social problems, often by challenging common assumptions and beliefs
about social behavior. We should also remember that the Hawthorne study
was carried out to find a way to boost workers' productivity. That in itself is a
reflection of power relationships in the United States (Roethlisberger and
Dickson 1939).

Intervention and Social Policy

Controversy exists over whether sociologists should merely study issues
or actually prescribe what society ought to do about its social problems. Is the
task of sociology to analyze the causes and consequences of social problems
or also to evaluate various intervention strategies and recommend reforms?
If sociologists become a force for social change, then they engage in **social
policy**, applying the findings of science and advocating positions in the political arena.

Because disagreement exists over the nature of social problems and their
solution, the sociologist as advocate is often pictured as biased, nonscientific,
and political. We have argued, however, that even objective analysis is value

laden. To deny social science opinions to policy makers is itself political and may hinder society's ability to cope with its serious issues.

The definition of a social problem includes the assumption that a harmful condition can be solved by human intervention. The type of solution usually corresponds to the view of causation. If individual people are seen as the cause of social problems, then the intervention will emphasize changing the person—through punishment, treatment, or some combination of the two.

The more intentional or deliberate the commission of a harmful act, the more likely it is that an attempt will be made to change the person through punishment. A "sick" person, on the other hand, or a person seen as not responsible for his or her own behavior, receives treatment. An adult criminal, for example, considered to have chosen a life of crime, goes to jail, while a young offender or delinquent undergoes counseling. The amount of responsibility that people are seen as having over their actions influences how these actions are viewed—whether as sinful, criminal, or sick—and determines the preferred intervention. If the social structure or "system" is held responsible for social problems, then the focus may shift to changing the environment in which people live. In the case of delinquency, for example, interventions might include an attempt to eliminate poverty or to create a sense of community in high-crime neighborhoods.

The desire to control social problems does not necessarily guarantee the ability to control them. Sociologists and other experts lack the necessary knowledge and research to fully understand, much less to control, many social problems. Even were we to possess the necessary information, the money available to solve problems is limited, and advocates of various programs must compete with one another for funds. Society may not be willing to intervene because of a fear that the solutions themselves might create problems. Expensive forms of pollution control, for example, might mean reductions in our level of affluence and use of technology; prohibition of alcohol might trigger lawlessness and the rise of organized crime.

What is a problem for some people may be a source of profit and advantage for others. Drugs, pornography, and prostitution have rewards for many individuals and may even serve valued social goals. Attempts at control or elimination engender resistance.

If one believes that adolescent rebellion may be mislabeled delinquency, that government invasion of family privacy is more detrimental to families than are the consequences of poor parenting, that police crackdowns on marijuana use are a waste of resources, then certain activities become accepted or their meaning reinterpreted, and nonintervention emerges as a reasonable strategy. That is, intervention may occur on an individual or a social level, but if the problem is redefined or the costs of change are excessive, then no intervention may be desired or implemented.

These are some issues and questions to keep in mind as you read and think about the social problems in this book. You are undertaking a challenging and yet vital task. Read and think critically and consider the kinds of evidence you might want to help you understand social problems.

About This Book

Each of the next 15 chapters in this book focuses on a particular social problem or related set of problems. We chose the specific problems because

❖ ❖ ❖ ❖

they help us to understand the United States on the threshold of the twenty-first century. The chapters are organized in a consistent format, including definition and prevalence, levels of causation, consequences, and interventions. Each chapter also includes a discussion of the future of the social problem and a summary of its major substantive issues. Each chapter begins with an "In the News" section drawing on recent newspaper articles related to the social problem covered in the chapter. We hope the "In the News" sections help you see how social problems are related to your own life.

Each chapter also includes boxed inserts to give you "A Closer Look" at social problems. The inserts will give you a different perspective on current social issues and efforts to resolve them. Some inserts highlight the impact of social policy. Others summarize research results that either have historical importance or challenge traditional or "common sense" assumptions. One "Closer Look" insert in each chapter introduces you to a useful website. The "In the News" and "Closer Look" boxes are also intended to stimulate debate and discussion.

We conclude each chapter with discussion questions, references, and a list of relevant World Wide Web (WWW) sites. We have also provided a website for this book. The website gives you a chance to comment on the book and to make suggestions or criticisms. We hope you will take advantage of it. The address is http://www.bridgew.edu/~wcarroll/socialproblems.htm.

Discussion Questions

1. Think about some condition or social arrangement that you consider a social problem but that is not widely defined as such. What leads you to see it as a social problem? Why do you think it is not defined as a social problem in society?

2. Now we would like you to reverse your approach from the first question. Is there some social condition considered a problem that you do not think is a social problem? Why don't you see the condition or social arrangement as a social problem?

3. Take a look at the Table of Contents for this book. Do you see any topic(s) that you feel very strongly about, that you may have strong emotional feelings about? Do you think those feelings might hinder your ability to think logically and objectively about that topic? How could you take your feelings into account so that you could be objective about the topic?

4. We discussed subjective and objective approaches to social problems. Given what you know right now, which would you tend to favor? Why?

5. Think about what you hope to gain from this book. Are there any specific social problems that you hope to learn more about and perhaps understand better as a consequence of reading this book and taking this course?

References

Annie E. Casey Foundation. 1994. *Kids Count Data Book*. Greenwich, Connecticut: Annie E. Casey Foundation.

Bandura, Albert. 1963. "What TV Violence Can Do to Your Child." *Look*, October, 46-52.

Barlow, Melissa Hickman, David E. Barlow, and Theodore G. Chiricos. 1995. "Economic Conditions and Ideologies of Crime in the Media: A Content Analysis of Crime News." *Crime & Delinquency* 41:3-19.

Becker, Howard S. 1963. *Outsiders: Studies in the Sociology of Deviance*. Glencoe, Illinois: Free Press.

Best, Joel. 1990. *Threatened Children: Rhetoric and Concern About Child-Victims*. Chicago: University of Chicago Press.

Blumer, Herbert. 1971. "Social Problems as Collective Behavior." *Social Problems* 18:298-306.

Carter, Gregg Lee, ed. 1997. *Perspectives on Current Social Problems*. Boston: Allyn and Bacon.

Cherlin, Andrew J., et al. 1991. "Longitudinal Studies of Effects of Divorce on Children in Great Britain and the United States." *Science* 252:1386-89.

Conrad, Peter. 1997. "Public Eyes and Private Genes: Historical Frames, News Constructions, and Social Problems." *Social Problems* 44:139-54.

deYoung, Marilyn. 1998. "Another Look at Moral Panic: The Case of Satanic Day-care Centers." *Deviant Behavior*, 19:257–278.

Durkheim, Emile. 1951[1897]. *Suicide*. Glencoe, Illinois: Free Press.

Feagin, Joe R. 1986. *Social Problems: A Critical Power-Conflict Perspective*. Second edition. Englewood Cliffs, New Jersey: Prentice-Hall.

Ferrante, Joan. 1997. *Sociology.Net: Sociology on the Internet*. Belmont, California: Wadsworth.

Ferrante, Joan, and Angela Vaughn. 1997. *Let's Go Sociology: Travels on the Internet*. Belmont, California: Wadsworth.

Goffman, Erving. 1959. *The Presentation of Self in Everyday Life*. Garden City, New York: Doubleday.

Green, Arnold. 1975. *Social Problems: Arena of Conflict*, New York:McGraw-Hill.

Gusfield, Joseph R. 1981. *The Culture of Public Problems: Drinking, Driving and the Symbolic Order*. Chicago: University of Chicago Press.

——. 1996. *Contested Meanings: The Construction of Alcohol Problems*. Madison: University of Wisconsin Press.

Herrnstein, Richard J., and Charles C. Murray. 1994. *The Bell Curve: Intelligence and Class Structure in American Life*. New York: Free Press.

Hochschild, Arlie, with Anne Machung. 1989. *The Second Shift*. New York: Viking.

Huff, Darrell. 1954. *How to Lie with Statistics*. New York: W. W. Norton.

Jankowski, Martin Sánchez. 1991. *Islands in the Street: Gangs and the American Urban Society*. Berkeley and Los Angeles: University of California Press.

Jennings, Francis. 1975. *The Invasion of America: Indians, Colonialism, and the Cost of Conquest*. New York: W. W. Norton.

Kannapell, Andrea. 1997. "Report Says Health of Society Lags Behind That of Economy." *New York Times*, October 12, 34.

Kanter, Rosabeth Moss. 1977. *Men and Women of the Corporation*. New York: Basic Books.

Lind, Michael. 1996. "A 'Crisis' of Illegitimacy? Try Hoax Instead." *Boston Sunday Globe*. August 11, D1.

Lykes, M. Brinton, Ali Banuazizi, Ramsay Liem, and Michael Morris, eds. 1996. *Myths About the Powerless: Contesting Social Inequalities*. Philadelphia: Temple University Press.

McDonald, Kim A. 1997. "Denmark Best in Survey of Social Conditions." *Chronicle of Higher Education*, September 12, A24.

McIntyre, J. J., and J. J. Teevan. 1972. "Television Violence and Deviant Behavior." In *Television and Social Behavior*. Vol. 3, edited by G. A. Comstock and E. A. Rubington. Washington, D.C.: U.S. Government Printing Office.

Merton, Robert K. 1957. *Social Theory and Social Structure*. New York: Free Press.

Merton, Robert K., and Robert Nisbet. 1976. *Contemporary Social Problems*. New York: Harcourt Brace Jovanovich.

Mills, C. Wright. 1959. *The Sociological Imagination*. New York: Oxford University Press.

Neuman, W. Lawrence. 1997. *Social Research Methods: Qualitative and Quantitative Approaches*. Third edition. Boston: Allyn and Bacon.

Piven, Frances Fox. 1981. "Deviant Behavior and the Remaking of the World." *Social Problems* 28:489–508.

Piven, Frances Fox, and Richard A. Cloward. 1982. *The New Class War*. New York: Pantheon.

Reinarman, Craig. 1996. "The Social Construction of Drug Scares." Pp. 230–239, edited by Jack Levine and Arnold Arluke. *Sociology: Snapshots and Portraits of Society*. Thousand Oaks, California: Pine Forge Press.

Reinarman, Craig, and Harry G. Levine, eds. 1997. *Crack in America: Demon Drugs and Social Justice*. Berkeley: University of California Press.

Roby, Pamela, ed. 1997. *Working Toward a Just World: Visions, Experiences and Challenges*. Knoxville: Society for the Study of Social Problems.

Roethlisberger, F. J., and W. J. Dickson. 1939. *Management and the Worker*. Cambridge: Harvard University Press.

Rubin, Lillian. 1976. *Worlds of Pain: Life in the Working-Class Family*. New York: Basic Books.

——. 1994. *Families on the Fault Line*. New York: HarperCollins.

Rubington, Earl, and Martin S. Weinberg, eds. 1995. *The Study of Social Problems: Seven Perspectives*. Fifth edition. New York: Oxford University Press.

Schneider, Joseph W. 1985. "Social Problems Theory: The Constructionist View." *Annual Review of Sociology* 11:209-29.

Sernau, Scott. 1997. *Critical Choices: Applying Sociological Insight in Your Life, Family, and Community*. Los Angeles: Roxbury Publishing.

Simon, David R., and Joel H. Henderson. 1997. *Private Troubles and Public Issues: Social Problems in the Postmodern Era*. Fort Worth: Harcourt Brace.

Spector, M., and J. I. Kitsuse. 1973. "Social Problems: A Reformulation." *Social Problems* 21:145-59.

——. 1977. *Constructing Social Problems*. Menlo Park, California: Cummings.

Stack, Carol. 1974. *All Our Kin: Strategies for Survival in a Black Community*. New York: Harper and Row.

Stark, Rodney. 1996. *Sociology*. Sixth edition. Belmont, California: Wadsworth.

Stark, Rodney, and Lynne Roberts. 1996. *Contemporary Social Research Methods*. Bellevue, Washington: MicroCase.

Thompson, Robert, and Joseph D. Rivard. 1998. *Allyn and Bacon Quick Guide to the Internet for Sociology*. Boston: Allyn and Bacon.

Wallerstein, Immanuel. 1974. *The Modern World-System: Capitalist Agriculture and the Origins of the European World-Economy in the Sixteenth Century*. New York: Academic Press.

——. 1979. *The Capitalist World Economy*. Cambridge England: Cambridge University Press.

Wright, Erik Olin. 1985. *Classes*. London: Verso.

Websites

http://www.asanet.org/

American Sociological Association (ASA). This site includes information about the ASA and sociology in general. Although it is aimed primarily at professional sociologists, it does include material of interest to students. Browse through the site and see what you find.

http://www.runet.edu/~lridener/dss/deadsoc.html

Dead Sociologists' Society. We love the name of this site. It is exceptionally useful with extensive information on important—dead—sociologists. Dr. Larry Ridener, of Radford University in Virginia, created this invaluable site.

http://www.trinity.edu/~mKearl/

A Sociological Tour Through Cyberspace. Dr. Michael Kearl of Trinity University in San Antonio created and maintains this site. We regard it as the single most useful sociology website, and we refer to it several times throughout this book.

http://www.socioweb.com/~markbl/socioweb/overview.html

The Socioweb. This site was constructed by Mark Blair, who graduated in sociology from Sonoma State University in California. The Socioweb is an independent guide to sociological resources on the web and has links to lots of useful sites.

CHAPTER TWO

Inequality and Poverty

In the News: Children and Poverty

Children represent two-thirds of the nation's welfare caseload. If many Americans become aware of the negative effects that welfare reform may have on those children, they might change their views of poverty and welfare reform in the United States. The typical welfare recipient in the United States is 7.5 years old. In Massachusetts, the typical welfare recipient is a white child living with a single mother and one sibling.

The Boston Globe *recently ran an occasional series of articles on "Retooling Welfare." One article entitled "A Child Bears the Brunt of Overhaul," looked at one such child and her family in the context of a broader examination of children and poverty (Jacobs 1997). The family lives on about $525 a month from welfare benefits. In Massachusetts, there is now a two-year time limit on receiving welfare. This may mean that many families will lose monthly income as well as housing subsidies, leading to continuing poverty and even homelessness.*

One in every five children under 18 lives below the poverty line in the United States. This is close to the rate in 1965, when the War on Poverty began. Since then the number of children receiving welfare tripled from 3.3 million to 9.6 million in 1994. (See "A Closer Look: Websites on Children and Child Poverty" for data sources.)

People disagree sharply over welfare reform. Many argue that forcing people to work provides children with healthy role models. Others argue that forcing people to take low-paying jobs with the hope of financial improvement within two years is unrealistic and stressful. Acting on this conviction, a coalition of 68 churches, synagogues, and nonprofit organizations in New York City refuses to hire welfare recipients for workfare programs. According to a New York Times *article, the coalition argues that workfare is morally unjust and similar to slavery (Greenhouse 1997).*

Recently, the number of people on the welfare rolls is definitely declining, however it is not clear that this signals a reduction in poverty. In fact, some commentators suggest that welfare reform may lead to increasing poverty and homelessness for many Americans. Children, in particular, may be sacrificed to welfare reform.

Definition and Prevalence

Think about **poverty**. What images come into your mind? The term *poverty* may generate images of dilapidated housing, understaffed schools and hospitals, slum landlords, and rampant street crime. Think about the poor. Who or what do you think of? Poor people lack command over economic resources; they have low incomes and little money to spend on goods and services; and they are often seen as different in some basic way from other people. Some social scientists and commentators have suggested that at least some of the poor have a distinct way of life—a different culture—which prevents them from getting out of poverty. Other social scientists argue that we should focus on persistent poverty itself rather than on the characteristics of poor people.

Despite their disagreements on many aspects of inequality and poverty, most sociologists would probably agree that inequality and poverty are at the "root of many of society's most troubling and insoluble problems," in

addition to being significant social problems themselves (Howard 1998: 9).   ❖ ❖ ❖ ❖
People's access to resources profoundly affects numerous areas of their lives,
including their education, health, and overall well-being. Sociologists refer to
these as **life chances**. Looking at the distribution of resources in American
society will help us define and determine the prevalence of inequality and
poverty.

That takes us to the study of **social stratification**, which focuses on
structured social inequality in access to socially valued rewards, usually related to wealth, power, and status. "Social stratification means that inequality has been hardened, or *institutionalized* and there is a system of *social relationships* that determines who gets what, and why" (Kerbo 1996:11). Structured social inequalities are patterned, stable inequalities among groups that
persist over long periods of time. Another useful definition emphasizes the
dynamic aspect of stratification. Stratification is a "social process through
which rewards and resources such as wealth, power, and prestige are distributed systematically and unequally within and among societies" (Johnson
1995:283).

In any society, groups of people are ranked in ways that determine their
access to valued resources, such as income, **wealth**, or **prestige**. Many important social thinkers have realized that access, or lack of access, to those resources has important consequences in many areas of social life. We mentioned several such areas above. Position in the social stratification scheme
of a society also shapes people's beliefs, attitudes, and values.

Karl Marx emphasized the importance of social class and class conflict
for understanding human societies. By "social class" Marx referred to people's overall economic position in terms of a society's resources, or **productive property**. Productive property, also called the **means of production**, refers to property that can be used to produce goods and services. Those who
own and control the productive property of a society have great economic
power and often also have much political power. Another way of putting this
is that those who own and control the productive property of a society, actually own the society.

Max Weber agreed with Marx about the importance of people's economic
position in society, but he also suggested that there were important additional dimensions of stratification. He developed a three-part stratification
scheme which included economic power (class), prestige or honor (status),
and political power (party). "Weber viewed people with similar life chances
and economic conditions—such as property ownership, income, education,
and skill—as sharing class positions (Rubin 1996: 13). We use "class" in ways
basically similar to Marx's and Weber's approaches.

Social scientists have developed various ways of defining the class structure of American society. For example, Harold Kerbo suggests that there are
five classes in American society: the upper class, the corporate class, the middle class, the working class, and the lower class. These classes are defined
based on their positions in hierarchies of occupation, bureaucratic authority,
and property (Kerbo 1996).

Dennis Gilbert and Joseph Kahl (1993) suggest that there are six classes
in the United States: the capitalist class, upper middle class, middle class,
working class, working poor, and underclass. The *capitalist class* includes
high-level corporate managers, executives, and those with inherited wealth.
Often educated at prestigious universities, and with incomes of more than
$750,000, this group derives most of its wealth from assets such as corporate

stocks and bonds. (See "A Closer Look: The Richest People: 'Born on Third Base?'") The *upper-middle class* includes high level managers, professionals, and owners of medium-sized businesses. This group usually has a college education and often holds advanced degrees. They would have 1990 family incomes of at least $70,000. The *middle class* includes lower-level managers, semiprofessionals, some sales people and skilled-craftspeople, and some supervisors. They may have some college or technical training and incomes of about $40,000. The *working class* are high-school educated clerical, factory, sales, and blue-collar workers, with family incomes of about $25,000. The *working poor* are poorly paid service workers, clerical workers, laborers, and operatives with some high school education and family incomes of below $20,000. Following Gilbert and Kahl, Sernau defines the *underclass* as "persons with erratic job histories and weak attachments to the formal labor force, unemployed, or only able to find seasonal or part-time work, dependent on temporary or informal employment or some type of social assistance" (Sernau 1997: 93). Some sociologists argue that the "underclass" is not a useful category and tends to emphasize pathologies of the poor (Gans 1995).

Regardless of how we might explain how social inequalities arise, there's not much question that substantial inequality exists in most societies. Of the industrial societies, the United States is one of the most unequal and has become even more unequal since the 1980s. In spite of the apparently improving economic health of the United States, during the 1980s and 1990s inequality increased. In fact, some analysts have suggested this period has seen

---

A Closer Look

The Richest People: 'Born on Third Base'?

Every year *Forbes Magazine* publishes their list of the world's richest people. Now *Forbes* even provides an internet database of international billionaires. *Forbes* tends to emphasize that the world's wealthiest individuals became rich through their own efforts. United for a Fair Economy (UFE), a Boston-based organization, thought it would be interesting to analyze the Forbes list to find out which people inherited their way onto the list and which ones actually made it on their own.

United for a Fair Economy analyzed the 400 individuals and 50 families on the Forbes 400 list for 1997. They divided the list into five categories based on baseball. If people inherited their wealth they were "born on home plate." At the other end, those who started in the batter's box were individuals and families whose parents did not have much wealth or did not own more than a small business. United for a Fair Economy points out that "at the same time that the wages of average Americans continue to stagnate, the number of billionaires in the United States has jumped from 135 to 170 in just one year" (United for a Fair Economy 1997). How did those at the top get there? Was it largely through their own individual efforts, or was their wealth inherited?

United for a Fair Economy argues that *Forbes* overstated the percentage of the richest who made it to the top through their own efforts. The organization's study indicated that 55 percent of those on the Forbes 400 list inherited their way onto the list, inherited substantial and profitable companies, or received important start-up capital from a family member. United for a Fair Economy concluded that while a growing number of Americans have stagnating incomes, declining savings, and limited retirement options, assets held by those at the top of the social and economic structure have been increasing. Charles Collins, Executive Director of UFE suggests that "it is time to correct the imbalance" (United for a Fair Economy 1997).

the largest transfer of wealth from lower to upper groups in the country's history (Phillips 1991; Wolff 1996). Denny Braun points out that today there are more poor people in the United States than in any year since 1961. Between 1979 and 1993 the proportion of the very poorest families increased by 63 percent (Braun 1997). Clearly, during a period when the American economy was improving, the situation for many became worse.

This growing inequality has undermined many people's belief in the American dream, "the hope that one's lifestyle can be improved and that following generations will share even greater success than their parents." Charles Howard points out that for many Americans, equal opportunity is a myth. "Factors such as race, gender, ethnicity, age, education, and economic status divide the population and deter some segments from achieving the success of their fellow citizens" (Howard 1998:9). Table 2-1 provides an overview of differences in income among Americans of different characteristics. Do not try to remember the whole table, but look at some of the overall differences and consider it a reference on equality. What kinds of households tend to have higher median income? Does race or country of origin make a difference? What about age or gender? Do you see any interesting patterns emerging from the table?

Table 2-1 Median Income by Selected Characteristics, 1996

Characteristic	Number (in 1,000s)	Median Income (dollars)
Households		
All households	101,018	35,492
Type of Household		
Family households	70,241	43,082
Married-couple		
Families	53,604	49,858
Female householder, no husband present	12,790	21,564
Male householder, no wife present	3,847	35,658
Nonfamily households	30,777	20,973
Female householder	17,070	16,398
Male householder	13,707	27,266
Race and Hispanic Origin of Householder		
White	85,059	37,161
White, not Hispanic	77,240	38,787
Black	12,109	23,482
Asian and Pacific Islander	2,998	43,276
Hispanic origin	8,225	24,906
Age of Householder		
15–24 years	5,160	21,438
25–34 years	19,314	35,888
35–44 years	23,823	44,420
45–54 years	18,843	50,472
55–64 years	12,469	39,815
65 years and older	21,408	19,448
Birthplace of Householder		
Native born	90,585	36,092
Foreign born	10,433	30,008
Not a citizen	5,791	25,560 ☞

Table 2-1 Median Income by Selected Characteristics, 1996 (continued)

Characteristic	Number (in 1,000s)	Median Income (dollars)
Region		
Northeast	19,724	37,406
Midwest	23,972	36,579
South	35,693	32,422
West	21,629	37,125
Earnings of Year-Round Full-Time Workers		
Male	53,787	32,144
Female	36,430	23,710
Per Capita Income		
All Races	266,792	18,136
White	220,070	19,181
Black	34,218	11,899
Asian and Pacific Islander	10,071	17,921
Hispanic origin (Can be of any race)	29,703	10,048

Source: U.S. Bureau of the Census.1997. *March Current Population Survey.*

Table 2-1 reported data on median income. Although there are millions of wealthy people in the country, the United States exhibits substantial economic inequalities. For example, the richest 20 percent of the population earns nearly 45 percent of the nation's total income. In contrast, the poorest 20 percent has only about 4 percent of the national income. Income inequality in the United States is the most pronounced in the industrialized world. Table 2-2 shows how the distribution of share of income has changed since 1970.

Table 2-2 Trends in Inequality: Percentage Distribution of Aggregate Household Income

	1970	1980	1990	1996
Lowest 20%	4.1	4.2	3.9	3.7
Second 20%	10.8	10.2	9.6	9.0
Third 20%	17.4	16.8	15.9	15.1
Fourth 20%	24.5	24.8	24.0	23.3
Highest 20%	43.3	44.1	46.6	49.0
Top 5%	16.6	15.8	18.6	21.4

Source: U.S. Bureau of the Census. 1997. *March Current Population Reports, Historical Income Tables*. http://www.census.gov/hhes/income/histinc/h02.html.

Wealth—which represents an individual's or a family's overall assets—is more difficult to study than income distribution. Along with power and prestige, wealth is one of the most important bases of stratification in the United States. Over the period 1983–1989, the increase in wealth inequality in the United States was almost unprecedented, so that there is a much higher concentration of wealth in the United States than in Europe (Wolff 1995).

Power—the ability to control the behavior of others—is associated with wealth. The wealthy are more likely than the nonwealthy to have power. Top government positions are dominated by the wealthy while the nonwealthy often feel powerless to influence major political decisions. Many sociologists argue that a very small number of people hold most of the power in the United States (Kerbo 1996).

The final basis of social stratification is prestige, also called honor or social status. This kind of stratification is usually referred to sociologically as a status system. In this system, people are stratified according to social prestige, often tied to occupation. Occupations that require more education and provide higher income than others are generally seen as more prestigious.

Another important aspect of inequality and stratification consists of beliefs, attitudes, and values, or—more broadly—an **ideology**. An ideology is a set of strongly held beliefs and myths that help people understand the society around them and their place in it. Social stratification is influenced by an ideology that suggests that in the United States everyone has an equal opportunity for success and that those with ability, who really try, have a better chance of succeeding than those who do not try. The ideology of a stratification system explains and vindicates the distribution of rewards in society and contains both normative and existential statements about the way things ought to be and the way things really are. People in the United States are generally brought up to believe that anyone can "make it" as long as he or she works hard, so if someone does not make it, he or she is usually blamed for the failure.

Some major social changes may be eroding the possibility of realizing the American Dream. That could have important consequences for the continued legitimacy of the American stratification system. One such transformation is **globalization**, the increasing interdependence of national economies and societies and their incorporation into a global economy. Among the possible consequences of globalization are increasing inequality, polarization, and poverty both among and within societies. (See "A Closer Look: The Shifting Social Contract and the American Dream.")

Social scientists typically agree that any definition of poverty should reflect a lack of resources as indicated by low income and assets. There has been much debate, however, as to whether poverty should be defined more broadly to include social and cultural as well as economic considerations.

Even the economic component has been difficult to pinpoint. Should poverty be indicated by low absolute income or by low relative income? **Absolute poverty** refers to an inability to meet a level of basic needs needed to live. **Relative poverty** indicates that people are poor in relation to the overall standard of living in their society. Are the poor those people whose income does not permit them to satisfy their basic needs? Or is poverty best viewed as the inability to satisfy the needs that result from living in a particular society? Using both an **absolute poverty line** and relative dimensions of poverty seems to be the most complete way to understand poverty.

Creating a poverty line based on a family's needs for minimum subsistence involves identifying a minimum subsistence level based on estimates of what families of different sizes and location must pay for food, housing, clothing, and other necessities (Kerbo 1996). The U.S. Bureau of the Census reports that the poverty line for an urban family of four rose from $6,200 annually in 1978 to $15,600 in 1996. For 1992, the Census Bureau estimated that 14.5 percent of all Americans were living below the poverty line (U.S. Bureau of the Census 1993). This represents considerable improvement from the early 1960s, when some 22. 2 percent (40 million persons) were officially

The Shifting Social Contract and the American Dream

Belief in the American Dream has long been an important aspect of American society and culture. Sociologist Beth Rubin suggests that the American Dream refers to belief in a free society "in which anyone, regardless of family background, ethnicity, or race, can 'make it'" (Rubin 1996:7–8). "Making it" means that through education, hard work, luck, and motivation, a person can get a good job, have a home, a happy family, and leisure time (Rubin 1996). The American Dream also includes the belief that each generation will do better economically than its parents. Underlying the American Dream are assumptions about how people succeed. If people work hard, get enough education, and have the right values, they will succeed.

But the American Dream may be fading. In *Shifts in the Social Contract*, Rubin suggests that American society is undergoing "massive social change" in social structures, social relationships, and social institutions. She argues that "contemporary American society is changing from a social world characterized by *long-term, stable relationships* to one characterized by *short-term, temporary relationships*" (Rubin 1996:4) (Emphasis in original). These transformations change the social contract, "the underlying shared social understandings that structure cooperation within a world of self-interested people possessing unequal resources" (Rubin 1996:4). According to Rubin, market societies work because of both explicit and implicit social contracts underlying them. Achieving the goals that make up the American Dream may become increasingly difficult with the social and economic transformations shifting the social contract. The globalization of economic and political relationships is one of the most important processes driving the social transformations that produced the shift in the social contract and the post-war accord between capital and labor which enabled many American workers to achieve the American Dream (Rubin 1996).

In *The Breaking of the American Social Compact*, Frances Piven and Richard Cloward also analyze the basic transformations occurring in American society (1997). They discuss the social compact, or agreement, between business and labor that emerged after World War II. Big business and big labor negotiated an agreement which guaranteed stability to business and increased wages and benefits for many workers, making it possible for them to live the American Dream. But many were excluded from the compact and the promise of the American Dream. Workers in nonunionized sectors and, especially, African Americans were excluded from the compact. "Now in the late 1990s, the compact is under attack: the unions are on the ropes, their membership decimated; welfare state programs are being rolled back; and income and wealth inequalities have widened to historic extremes" (Piven and Cloward 1997:4). Piven and Cloward note that the breaking of the social compact amounts to an attack on the working class. It can also be seen as an attack on the poor.

Rubin's analysis of shifts in the social contract and Piven and Cloward's focus on the breaking social compact both identify changes in American society that threaten the living standards of many Americans and may ultimately threaten belief in the American Dream. Both also focus on globalization. Piven and Cloward take pains to point out that although globalization is often seen as some autonomous process automatically bringing about major social changes, it is, in fact, the outcome of human decision making and needs to be seen as such.

regarded as poor. The poverty level gives us some useful information, but in itself it is not enough to give a complete picture of the extent of poverty. Numerous criticisms have been directed at the determination of the poverty level.

One basic criticism of the official poverty level is that it is very low. The poverty level is based on food costs for families of various sizes and compositions. It is assumed that food costs amount to one-third of a family's budget. Therefore, food costs are multiplied by three to arrive at the poverty-level budget. That is a conservative estimate, which probably leads to an undercount of those who are poor (Kerbo 1996). The 1998 poverty threshold for a family of four is $16,450, which is supposed to represent the same purchasing power as the level set in 1963, when the poverty threshold was set (Institute for Research on Poverty 1998).

To get a sense of changes in American poverty in recent years, look at Figure 2-1, which traces changes in the number of people in poverty and the poverty rate from 1959 to 1996. After a marked drop in the number of the poor from about 1965, when President Johnson launched the War on Poverty, the numbers began increasing in the 1980s and by 1996 were at 35.5 million. Note also the fluctuations in the poverty rate and remember that 13.7 percent in 1996 is almost certainly a conservative figure. The real percentage of those in poverty is probably higher.

Figure 2-1   Poverty in the United States: 1959–1996

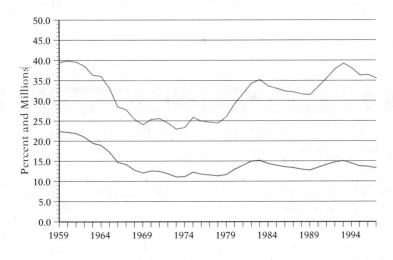

Source: U.S. Bureau of the Census . 1997. *March Current Population Survey.*

Child poverty is also extremely important. Poverty affects a child's life in childhood as well as profoundly influencing his or her life chances in the future. Poverty exacts a terrible toll on children and on the future of society. Figure 2-2 shows you the changing percentage of children in poverty. The lines on the figure represent children living in different types of households. Note how high the line is for children living in female-headed families. In later chapters we will return to this issue.

In contrast to the absolute subsistence level, relative poverty lines vary depending upon changes in the standard of living of a society. Using a relative measure, poverty is a result of relative deprivation. A frequently employed relative poverty line equals 50 percent of the median family income (Williamson and Hyer 1975). For example, if the median family income is $30,000, then, on this definition, the poverty line would be a family income of $15,000. In 1994, the median family income was $32,264; the poverty line would have been $16,132.

Figure 2-2 Pecent of Children Under Age 18 in Poverty by Type of Family

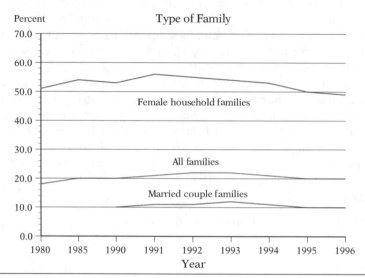

Source: Interagency Forum on Child and Family Statistics. 1998. *America's Children 1998*. <http://www.childstats.gov/ac1998/>.

A Closer Look

Websites on Children and Child Poverty

The two websites described below give you access to important information on children and on child poverty. The National Center for Children in Poverty, at Columbia University, aims to "identify and promote strategies that reduce the number of young children living in poverty in the United States, and that improve the life chances of the millions of children under six who are growing up poor" (National Center for Children in Poverty 1996). The Center (http://cpmcnet.columbia.edu/dept/nccp/) runs projects on a variety of child-related topics, including early childhood care and education, child and family health, family and community support, and research to evaluate the success of programs. Not much appears to have been added to this site recently, but it is still quite useful.

The Children's Defense Fund (CDF) (http://www.childrensdefense.org/index.html) "exists to provide a strong and effective voice for all the children of America, who cannot vote, lobby, or speak for themselves" (Children's Defense Fund 1998). Access this website and click on "What's new!" to get information on child–care bills pending in Congress, the President's child–care initiative, and proof that after-school programs work. Interested in finding out about other related organizations? Click on "Links for child advocates" to get links to other organizations, data sources, and government agencies. If you click on "Issues," you will have access to CDF's information on giving every child a Healthy Start, a Head Start, a Fair Start, a Safe Start, and a Moral Start. Give this site a try to find additional information on children's issues.

Whatever the measure employed, poverty is undoubtedly more than a condition of low income, for it frequently includes few assets, low occupational status, and public dependency, as well as chronic unemployment. But poverty has many faces. Most obvious, perhaps, is the plight of the poor in the cities of our land—the urban underclass who populate the black, Hispanic, or white working-class neighborhoods of every major city.

The syndrome of urban poverty is a familiar one. Less familiar to many Americans is the plight of the rural poor, who also reside in dilapidated housing, who frequently experience unemployment on a seasonal basis, and who are every bit as malnourished and poverty stricken as their urban counterparts. Rural poverty is often hidden and thus less noticeable.

Levels of Causation

Kerbo (1996) suggests four categories of poverty theories: (1) a popular view, based on blaming the poor as individuals; (2) **culture of poverty** views, (3) situational views, and (4) structural views.

Individual

The popular view of the causes of poverty focuses on the supposed negative characteristics of the poor, such as low "moral character" or lack of intelligence. Many people think "the poor are poor because they are lazy, waste their time and money, and simply do not have the self-control to succeed" (Kerbo 1996:263).

In 1971, the late psychologist Richard Herrnstein argued in a controversial article in *The Atlantic Monthly* that social class membership may be based on inherited differences in intelligence. Citing studies which show that IQ increases with socioeconomic status, he contended that smarter individuals are more likely to occupy upper-class positions. Herrnstein, together with conservative policy analyst, Charles Murray, went on to suggest that there are genetically-based differences in intelligence (Herrnstein and Murray 1994). Most social scientists disagree with their approach, which we discuss more completely in Chapter 3.

In spite of the evident wide acceptance of the popular view, most social scientists do not accept it. Some social scientists do support a more sophisticated view of the causes of poverty, which also puts the responsibility for poverty on the poor. However, this approach emphasizes the culture of the poor.

Cultural

Explanations for poverty at the cultural level argue that a population whose members have been economically deprived for a long period of time will develop a distinct subculture, a set of values that is at variance with those of the dominant (middle-class) culture and that perpetuates itself from generation to generation.

The culture of poverty is frequently conceived to be disorganized and pathological, resulting in such characteristics as a dominant one-parent family structure, crime and delinquency, and urban decay. More important, the poverty subculture is regarded as self-perpetuating, its roots being passed from generation to generation in a never-ending vicious cycle.

The culture-of-poverty explanation locates the causes of poverty in the lifestyle and values of the poor themselves. It is argued, for example, that poor people are unable to defer gratification so that they cannot save money or stay in school long enough to get a decent job. This argument may lead to the position that the poor get exactly what they deserve: they are poor because of their own psychological and cultural shortcomings.

Three questions that have dominated the study of poverty have tended to lead to culture-of-poverty explanations. The questions are, "(1) Are the poor different from other people? (2) If so, how different are the poor? And (3) How deep are these differences?" (Kerbo 1996:265-266). These questions have deflected research interest away from societal structures and processes that may cause poverty and have led to emphasis on how the poor differ from others.

Social scientists have made numerous criticisms of culture-of-poverty approaches. It is not clear that the values of the poor differ from those of the rest of society. Moreover, the poor are not a homogenous group. Lifestyle and behavioral differences in the poor may reflect class position and poverty rather than cause them. Despite criticisms of the culture of poverty approach, it continues to be popular. (See "A Closer Look—The Culture of Poverty Once Again.")

Poverty and lack of affordable housing in the United States have led to increasing homelessness which continues to be a problem for many single people.—*Photo: Copyright 1998 by Neil Garcia. All rights reserved.*

Structural

In sharp contrast to the culture of poverty standpoint, structural explanations pinpoint the roots of poverty not in characteristics of the poor, but in the wider society—specifically, in the nature of capitalism; in discrimination based on race, sex, and age; or in unequal education and tax structures that favor the wealthy members of society.

A Closer Look

The Culture of Poverty Once Again

Many social scientists who had assumed that culture of poverty arguments had been discredited have been dismayed by their reappearance and acceptance. Much of the 'welfare reform' of the mid and late 1990s has been based on culture-of-poverty assumptions. Making the assumptions explicit and openly discussing them may be helpful in understanding the nature of welfare reform and attitudes towards the poor. One way such approaches continue to be legitimated is through media reporting and opinion pieces based on social science research but often oversimplifying or distorting the research. A 1997 *Newsweek* column is a good example of oversimplifying research (Samuelson 1997).

In the column, "The Culture of Poverty," Robert J. Samuelson, an influential economics columnist for both the *Washington Post* and *Newsweek*, discusses *What Money Can't Buy*, a recent book by economist Susan Mayer (Mayer 1997). The headline under the column's title insists that "we can't change it despite the overwrought rhetoric of the debate on welfare reform." "It" is apparently either poverty or the culture of poverty. For Samuelson, Mayer's book carries the somber message that "as a society, we are fairly helpless to correct the worst problems of child poverty" (Samuelson 1997:49).

Although Samuelson uses Mayer's work to draw conclusions about the impact of welfare reform—it won't have much—he notes that Mayer does not actually write about welfare reform. She asks a basic question: "How important is money in enabling families to help their children escape poverty?" To her surprise, Mayer's research indicated that the personal characteristics of parents seemed to be more important in improving children's life chances than parents' income. Mayer is a respected economist and *What Money Can't Buy* is based on sound research, but in suggesting that the "thrust of Mayer's grim analysis is to support the existence of a permanent 'culture of poverty,'" Samuelson asks one study to carry too much weight.

Giving credit to political scientist Edward Banfield for introducing the notion of a permanent culture of poverty in the American context in his book *The Unheavenly City* (1970), Samuelson sees Mayer's research as supporting Banfield's theory. Banfield divided the poor into two groups: some had middle class values and simply lacked money; the other group was the "true lower class." Not only did they lack money, they also lacked the middle-class values that would enable them to rise from poverty. Samuelson, who studied with Banfield, notes that the "Banfield theory ignited outrage," because it implied that beyond a certain point poverty could not be eliminated (Samuelson 1997).

Banfield's book certainly elicited outrage and disbelief from many social scientists, and for some it may have been because of his suggestion that poverty could not be eliminated. A revised version of the book has been published, so that those who are interested can examine Banfield's analysis and evidence (Banfield 1990[1974]). Banfield himself attributes the controversy over his work to its subversive qualities in terms of liberal views on poverty. However, many social scientists objected to *The Unheavenly City* not because of its 'unpopular' stance. In fact, it fits into a long line of work deploring the cultural characteristics of the poor and distinguishing between the 'deserving' and the 'undeserving' poor. Some social scientists find this approach useful, but many see culture-of-poverty arguments as inaccurate and misleading explanations for poverty. It seems prudent to ponder Mayer's research but not to jump to conclusions about whether it proves that we can do little about child poverty.

Historically, most societies that have produced an economic surplus have also generated huge economic inequalities. In such societies, a small ruling class typically controlled most of the surplus, giving its members a disproportionately large share of power, status, and wealth. This was true of societies organized around feudalism and slavery, as well as traditional forms of precapitalism. According to this view, the vast productive capacity of capitalist societies has generated a huge economic surplus and economic inequalities as well.

The situational theory suggests that to the extent that the poor may behave differently or have different lifestyles, it is due to their situations. The poor adapt to the situations in which they find themselves. Although the situational view differs markedly from the culture-of- poverty view, both views do have an important similarity: they both focus on individual characteristics of the poor (Kerbo 1996).

The structural view goes beyond the situational approach by specifying the social and economic conditions and forces that are the most important causes of poverty (Kerbo 1996). This view suggests that the social and economic structures of capitalism generate poverty.

Karl Marx is probably the most well known theorist of class inequality. Marx focused on **capitalism** as it existed in the industrialized world. He defined three classes as existing in industrialized societies: the bourgeoisie were known as capitalists; the proletariat as workers; and the petite bourgeoisie as small capitalists. Capitalists own the means of production and hire workers. Workers do not own the means of production or hire others. In a sense, they are forced to work for capitalists. Small capitalists own the means of production but do most of the work themselves.

The two major classes Marx wrote about were capitalist and proletariat. Marx believed small capitalists would eventually be taken over by giant corporations. Marx believed capitalists force workers to work long hours for little pay. Capitalists are bent on maximizing profits. Exploitation basically characterizes the relationship between these two classes. Marx believed that eventually workers might realize their common class interests and revolt against capitalists. This revolution has not yet occurred and it does appear that the exploitation of workers has eased since Marx's time, at least in the United States.

Other sources of poverty have been found in the institutional forms of discrimination against minorities, the elderly, and women. Relatively few African Americans and Latinos are found at the middle and upper levels of society; instead, they have been disproportionately represented among the poor and powerless. We will examine these sources of poverty in other chapters.

Consequences

Poverty has serious consequences. Poverty affects women more than men, creating a social phenomenon sociologists call the feminization of poverty. The **feminization of poverty** is a process by which the poverty population in the United States has become comprised increasingly of women, irrespective of race or age. Over time, poverty has become a female problem. Women are consistently more likely to experience poverty than men. In the last forty years, the overall poverty rate has gone down, but those escaping poverty have primarily been men and their families (Starrels, Bould, and Nicholas 1994).

Why are women poor? There are several possible answers to this question. One is that women do not earn as much as men. Women's labor market earnings are a function of both their hours of work and their wage rates.

Among full-time, year-round workers, women earn 70.6 percent of what men earn. The gap in earnings is usually attributed to differences in worker characteristics and job characteristics. More men than women work full-time in the United States. Women earn less than men and their lower wages are due to a combination of not working full-time and being segregated into lower-paying, female-dominated jobs (Starrels, Bould, and Nicholas 1994).

A second possible answer to the above question is that more women than men are single parents. A high percentage of fathers do not pay child support. Since 1975, the federal government has attempted to collect child support from absent fathers for women receiving welfare. The initial emphasis was on recovering the funds spent on welfare. Now the emphasis appears to be on making absent fathers responsible for their children.

In addition to not receiving support, women with children may not be able to work because they cannot afford child care. In a sense, they are excluded from employment. Minority women are disproportionately represented among the poor because of their minority status and a higher risk of single parenthood.

Education is another contributing factor to female poverty in the United States. About 63 percent of all female householders with children under the age of 18 years do not complete high school (Starrels, Bould, and Nicholas 1994). And because of their lower socioeconomic status, many racial and ethnic minorities receive less education than whites. Other predictors of female poverty include unemployment, divorce, loss of higher-paying manufacturing jobs, domestic responsibilities including child and elder care, the lack of affordable child care, and lower wages (Starrels, Bould, and Nicholas 1994).

The poverty rate for children depends primarily on the type of family in which the children live. For children living in female-headed families, poverty rates are high. Poverty for children in female-householder families relative to married-couple families is about five times higher for whites; 3 1/2 times higher for blacks, Puerto Ricans and other Hispanics; and twice as high for Mexican-Americans. Even when husbands did not work at all, their poverty rate was significantly lower than that of nonemployed female householders with children under age 6 (Starrels, Bould, and Nicholas 1994).

Poverty and the poor may have a number of *positive* consequences for certain nonpoor groups in U.S. society. This is not to say that poverty benefits society as a whole, and it certainly does not benefit the poor. Poverty has its dysfunctions as well as its functions. For example, it creates the conditions giving rise to crime, political protest, social disorder, disease, and high rates of infant mortality.

In order to understand poverty, however, we must also recognize that it may benefit certain subgroups in society. Herbert Gans, somewhat ironically, identified a number of positive functions of poverty:

1. Poor people do dirty work at low cost; they perform those jobs considered to be dangerous, physically dirty, undignified, or menial by the rest of society.

2. By virtue of the low wages they receive, poor people subsidize many activities benefiting the nonpoor. For example, the low wages paid to domestics make life easier for their employers and free affluent women to engage in other activities (such as civic, social, or professional activities). What is more, because of regressive state income taxes and local property and sales taxes,

the poor tend to pay a greater share of their income in taxes than the rest of the population. This helps to subsidize government programs that serve the wealthier members of society.

3. The poor provide "clients" for a number of occupations and professions (for example, the peacetime army, the sale of heroin, and Pentecostal ministers).

4. The poor buy goods that the nonpoor do not want (for example, used automobiles, deteriorating buildings, day-old bread, and so on).

5. The poor serve as a reliable and relatively permanent "measuring rod" for status comparisons made by members of the working class, who are eager to maintain status distinctions between themselves and the poor. In a stratified society—especially where class boundaries are fuzzy—this lets people know where they stand.

6. The poor can be punished as deviants in order to maintain or strengthen the legitimacy of middle-class norms. Thus, accusations against those who are regarded as lazy, dishonest, and promiscuous serve to justify hard work, thrift, and honesty. Deviance assures the respectability of the dominant members of society. (Gans 1972)

If the presence of the poor serves some important consequences for the nonpoor groups in U.S. society, then we might expect that poverty is likely to persist. As Gans suggests, "phenomena like poverty can be eliminated only when they either become sufficiently dysfunctional for the affluent or when the poor can obtain enough power to change the system of social stratification" (Gans 1972: 288).

Some social scientists have argued that poverty can never be eliminated. Kingsley Davis and Wilbert Moore suggested that social inequality exists universally because it performs a universally necessary function: to make sure that society's most important positions are competently filled by its most qualified members (Davis and Moore 1945). Specifically, social inequality provides the monetary and prestige rewards capable of motivating talented individuals to train themselves for important roles and to perform their role obligations with skill and determination. By the same token, the wretched lifestyle characterizing the poor is seen as the result of the unimportant positions that they occupy in society. For example, physicians receive a great deal more money for their services than garbage collectors do, because physicians are so much more important to our survival.

The functional view of social inequality has been widely debated. Detractors point out, for example, that social inequality may not be universal at all: some societies seem to distribute status on an equal basis to all of its members. What is more, it is difficult, if not impossible, to specify objectively the importance of a role. During a garbage strike, for instance, the role of garbage collectors may suddenly seem to be more important than that of physicians. And finally, some apparently insignificant roles are disproportionately well rewarded. Entertainers, singers, and athletes may not be important to the survival of society, but they are nevertheless among the highest status, best paid of its members.

Interventions

❖ ❖ ❖ ❖

Most strategies seeking to reduce or eliminate poverty have focused on changing institutions or characteristics of poor individuals. As noted earlier, Gans contended that poverty survives in part because it is useful to a number of nonpoor groups and individuals in society. He recognized the existence of some alternatives for many of the functions served by the poor. For example, society's dirty work might be automated or wages might be raised. On the other hand, given the hierarchical nature of our society and its basis in a relativistic conception of rich and poor, it is difficult, if not impossible, to suggest substitutes for all of the functions of poverty. From this point of view, then, poverty can be eliminated either by changing the social structure itself—the basic nature of society—or by increasing the power of the poor (Gans 1972).

Many sociologists have proposed that the poor must organize in order to develop their political power. During the 1960s, considerable headway was made in mobilizing the activities of poor people's organizations to influence public policy and public officials.

Poverty continues to be a serious problem for families in the United States, especially single mothers and their children. Many sociologists argue that the welfare reforms of the 1990s put these families at greater risk. —*Photo courtesy of the Open Door Mission—Omaha, Nebraska.*

Despite a major decline in efforts to organize the poor since the early 1970s, a number of social policy writers continue to stress the importance of collective action on the part of the poor themselves. The welfare explosion of the 1960s was seen by Piven and Cloward as a political response to the civil disorder of black Americans. These authors suggest that the relief rolls were not automatically increased when the number of people eligible for relief grew. In addition to need, political pressures at the local level were necessary to cause the explosion in welfare caseloads (Piven and Cloward 1993).

The Future of Poverty

High rates of inflation have eroded purchasing power and caused more people to live in poverty. (See "A Closer Look: Counting the Homeless.") What is more, recent periods of economic recession have produced sizable increases in unemployment, especially among minority segments of the population whose members were already vastly overrepresented among the poor.

A Closer Look

Counting the Homeless

Have you ever wondered how many people are homeless? Counting the homeless would seem to be a daunting task. People frequently call the National Coalition for the Homeless (NCH) to find out how many people are homeless. The NCH notes that there is no easy answer to this question and that the question is actually misleading. Asking how many homeless people there are implies that homelessness is a permanent condition, but for most people it is temporary. "A more appropriate measure of the magnitude of the homeless is therefore how many people experience homelessness, not how many people 'are' homeless" (National Coalition for the Homeless 1997:1).

Methodological and financial constraints limit most studies to people in shelters or on the streets. As difficult as it is to count all of the homeless on the streets, there are additional problems with this type of census. NCH suggests that this approach gives useful information on how many people use services like shelters, but it can underestimate homelessness. Many people who need shelter cannot gain access to shelters because the shelters are full. For example, the U.S. Conference of Mayors 13th Annual Survey of Hunger and Homeless found that in the 29 cities surveyed in 1997, an average of 27 percent of the demand for emergency shelter was unmet. In 84 percent of the cities, shelters may have to turn people away (United States Conference of Mayors 1997). The demand for shelter exceeds the available space. The lack of resources in cities and the paucity of shelters in rural areas means that many people may be forced to live with relatives and friends, usually in crowded, unsanitary settings. Such people would not be counted as homeless, but their living conditions are unstable and they certainly do not have permanent homes. NCH suggests that they are experiencing a kind of homelessness.

Researchers generally use one of two approaches to counting the homeless. They may attempt to count everyone who is homeless on a given day or a given week. These are point-in-time counts. The period prevalence counts approach counts the number of people who are homeless over some given period of time.

The best known estimate of homelessness generated by a point-in-time study is 500,000 to 600,000 during one week in 1988 (Burt and Cohen 1989). Recent research has indicated that more people than had been expected have experienced homelessness for some period of time. A 1994 study found that 6.5 percent (12 million adults) had been literally homeless at some point in their lives. Between 1989 and 1994, 3.9 percent of adults had been literally homeless or living with friends or family (Link, et al. 1995).

NCH notes that, although it is difficult to measure homelessness with complete accuracy, it is clear that there is more homelessness than had been expected. Although counting the homeless is important, NCH correctly emphasizes that ending homelessness is the most important task.

Cutbacks in social programs at the federal level are likely to generate even more poverty, at least over the short run. But the long-term prospects are more difficult to assess. Government measures that effectively reduce unemployment and inflation or that improve economic growth also help to reduce the number of people requiring welfare assistance. Will conservative politics prevail? Or, will we see a backlash of the disaffected left or minority interests creating renewed public sentiment for government spending to reduce poverty?

One approach to welfare reform might be to move more poor people away from need-entitlement programs such as the now defunct Aid for Families with Dependent Children (AFDC) and its successor Temporary Assistance to Needy Families (TANF), toward universal programs that do not require proof of eligibility and therefore do not stigmatize. They are also

frequently less expensive to administer than the entitlement programs they
replace. As is the case in almost all other industrialized nations, for example,
the United States might decide to implement a universal children's allowance
which provides a monthly payment per child for all families whether rich or
poor. This measure would give large poor families additional assistance without their applying to welfare programs such as AFDC or TANF, which require
proof of eligibility.

On a larger scale, a general allowance to all poverty households in the
form of a negative income tax or guaranteed annual income might actually
reduce the costs of administering welfare and would decrease the stigma
presently associated with programs such as TANF, which require proof of
eligibility.

Under such general programs, a poor family would be guaranteed a minimum allowance even if there were no other family income. Payments would
decrease as family income increased, tax rates varying by income to give incentive to work. When family income reached a predetermined level, payments would totally cease.

The acceptance (or lack of acceptance) of various proposals for welfare
reform may be influenced at least in part by the strength or weakness of certain cultural themes. On the one hand, individualism and laissez-faire economic activity have been part of the American culture since the eighteenth
century. According to this cultural theme, "the government that governs least
governs best," and individuals are expected to "pull themselves up by their
bootstraps." On the other hand, twentieth-century public opinion in western
Europe, and to some extent in the United States as well, has supported some
measure of state assistance and regulation of certain industries (for example,
the Chrysler Corporation and public utilities) and welfare assistance to the
poor. Under a cultural value stressing collective responsibility, many individuals agree that the state has a responsibility to meet the basic needs of all its
citizens through disability payments, pensions, health insurance, and the
like. Social policy in the future is likely to continue to reflect individualism
and collective responsibility in some uneasy mix determined more precisely
by the state of the economy as well as by the course of international events.

Summary

Social scientists generally agree that poverty includes a lack of command
over economic resources. There is some disagreement, however, as to
whether poverty should be conceptualized and measured in absolute or relative terms. Those who conceive of poverty as low absolute income usually
identify a minimum subsistence level; those with a relative notion employ a
relative poverty line that varies depending upon changes in the standard of
living. Whatever the measure employed, poverty has many faces, including
the plight of the poor in cities, the rural poor, and the poverty of the very
young and the very old.

Some observers have attempted to explain poverty in terms of a culture of
poverty. They argue that a population whose members are deprived for long
periods of time will develop its own subculture, which perpetuates itself from
generation to generation. From this standpoint, escape from poverty is permanently blocked.

In contrast to the culture-of-poverty view, institutional explanations have located the roots of poverty in the wider society, especially in the nature of capitalism, discrimination, and unequal education and taxes that favor the rich.

In order to understand poverty, we must recognize that it may benefit certain nonpoor groups and individuals in U.S. society. Moreover, some sociologists have suggested that inequality exists universally because it makes sure that society's most important positions are competently filled by its most qualified members.

Many sociologists have proposed that the poor must organize to develop their political power. Some argue for the formation of alliances among disparate elements of the working class; others contend that coalition politics represents an unrealistic strategy for reducing poverty because of the deep divisions that must be overcome.

Certain analysts have contended that the issues of poverty should be cast in terms of social stratification, moving social policy towards the goal of reducing inequality and redistributing income.

Responses to poverty have sometimes sought to change characteristics of the poor rather than that of larger society. Some have suggested that almost any intervention is unwarranted—even harmful—because the amount of poverty in U.S. society has been greatly exaggerated.

Discussion Questions

1. Were you surprised to find out how much inequality exists in American society? Why or why not?

2. Can you think of any ways that poverty affects your life?

3. Have you seen homeless people? How did you react to them?

4. If you were redesigning the U.S. welfare system, what changes would you make? How would you deal with child poverty?

5. Has globalization affected you or anyone you know in any way? How?

References

Banfield, Edward C. 1970. *The Unheavenly City*. Boston: Little, Brown.

——. 1990 [1974]. *The Unheavenly City Revisited*. Prospect Heights, Illinois: Waveland Press.

Braun, Denny. 1997. *The Rich Get Richer: The Rise of Income Inequality in the United States and the Third World*. Second edition. Chicago: Nelson-Hall.

Burt, Martha, and Barbara Cohen. 1989. *America's Homeless: Numbers, Characteristics, and Programs That Serve Them*. Washington, DC: Urban Institute.

Children's Defense Fund. 1998. "Children's Defense Fund Home Page." In *Children's Defense Fund*. http://www.childrensdefense.org/index.html.

Davis, Kingsley, and Wilbert E. Moore. 1945. "Some Principles of Stratification." *American Sociological Review* 10:242–249.

Gans, Herbert J. 1972. "The Positive Functions of Poverty." *American Sociological Review* 78:278–89.

——. 1995. *The War Against the Poor: The Underclass and Antipoverty Policy*. New York: Basic Books.

Gilbert, Dennis, and Joseph Kahl. 1993. *The American Class Structure: A New Synthesis*. Fourth edition. Belmont, California: Wadsworth.

Greenhouse, Steven. 1997. "Nonprofit and Religious Groups to Fight Workfare in New York." *New York Times*, July 24.

Herrnstein, Richard. 1971. "IQ," *The Atlantic Monthly* 288:43–64.

Herrnstein, Richard, and Charles Murray. 1994. *The Bell Curve: Intelligence and Class Structure in American Life*. New York: Free Press.

Howard, Charles. 1998. "Preface," p. 9. In *Inequality: Opposing Viewpoints in Social Problems*, edited by Lori Shein. San Diego: Greenhaven Publishers.

Institute for Research on Poverty. 1998. *Focus*. Issue on Revising the Measure of Poverty. University of Wisconsin-Madison.

Jacobs, Sally. 1997. "Retooling Welfare: A Child Bears the Brunt of Overhaul." *Boston Globe*, June 30, A1, A8.

Johnson, Allan G. 1995. *The Blackwell Dictionary of Sociology: A User's Guide to Sociological Language*. Oxford: Blackwell.

Kerbo, Harold R. 1996. *Social Stratification and Inequality: Class Conflict in Historical and Comparative Perspective*. Third edition. New York: McGraw-Hill.

Link, Bruce, et al. 1995. "Life-Time and Five-Year Prevalence of Homelessness in the United States: New Evidence on an Old Debate." *American Journal of Orthopsychiatry* 65:347–54.

Mayer, Susan. 1997. *What Money Can't Buy*. Cambridge: Harvard University Press.

Mink, Gwendolyn, editor. 1998. "Disdained Mothers & Despised Others: The Politics & Impact of Welfare Reform." Special Issue of *Social Justice: A Journal of Crime, Conflict & World Order* 25(1) Spring.

National Center for Children in Poverty. 1996. "National Center for Children in Poverty Home Page (Columbia University)." In *National Center for Children in Poverty*. http://cpmcnet.columbia.edu/dept/nccp/.

National Coalition for the Homeless. 1997. "How Many People Experience Homelessness?" NCH Fact Sheet #2. http://www2.ari.net/home/nch/numbers.html.

Phillips, Kevin. 1991. *The Politics of Rich and Poor*. New York: HarperPerennial.

Piven, Frances Fox, and Richard A. Cloward. 1993. *Regulating the Poor: The Functions of Public Welfare*. Revised edition. New York: Pantheon Books.

——. 1997. *The Breaking of the American Social Compact*. New York: New Press.

Rubin, Beth A. 1996. *Shifts in the Social Contract: Understanding Change in American Society*. Thousand Oaks, California: Pine Forge Press.

Samuelson, Robert J. 1997. "The Culture of Poverty." *Newsweek*, May 5, 49.

Sernau, Scott. 1997. *Critical Choices: Applying Sociological Insight in Your Life, Family, and Community*. Los Angeles: Roxbury Publishing.

Starrels, Marjorie E., Sally Bould, and Leon J. Nicholas. 1994. "The Feminization of Poverty in the United States: Gender, Race, Ethnicity, and Family Factors." *Journal of Family Issues* 15:590–607.

Thio, Alex. 1998. *Sociology*. Fifth edition. New York: Longman.

United for a Fair Economy. 1997. *Born on Third Base*. Boston: United for a Fair Economy.

U.S. Bureau of the Census. 1993. *Statistical Abstract of the United States, 1992*. Washington, D.C.: U.S. Government Printing Office.

United States Conference of Mayors. 1997. "Summary: 13th Annual Survey of Hunger and Homeless." In United States Conference of Mayors Website. http://www.mayors.org/news/press_releases/documents/release.htm.

Williamson, John B., and Kathryn M. Hyer. 1975. "The Measurement and Meaning of Poverty." *Social Problems* 22:652–63.

Wolff, Edward N. 1996. *Top Heavy: The Increasing Inequality of Wealth in America and What Can Be Done About It*. New York: New Press.

Websites

http://www2.ari.net/home/nch/

National Coalition for the Homeless. This organization is a "national advocacy network of homeless persons, activists, service providers, and others committed to ending homelessness through public education, policy advocacy, grassroots organizing, and technical assistance." This is an exceptionally solid website with useful fact sheets, guides to legislation, and links to other sites.

http://www.census.gov/ftp/pub/hhes/www/index.html

U.S. Census Bureau, Housing and Household Economic Statistics. From this web page you can jump to the Census Bureau's Income, Poverty, or Wealth pages. This is a wonderful source of data.

http://epn.org/prospect/inequity.html

The American Prospect Online on inequality in America. *The American Prospect* is a liberal magazine that features in-depth articles on social, economic, and political issues. The website of the online version of the magazine includes numerous articles on inequality in America. Topics covered include lowering standards of living, the unequal distribution of wealth, and immigration issues.

CHAPTER THREE

Racial Inequality

In the News: Who Are We? Census Racial Categories

On July 8, 1997, a federal task force "recommended abandoning the idea of adding a multiracial classification on Census Bureau forms and other government documents and suggested that all people of mixed backgrounds be allowed to describe themselves as members of more than one race" (Holmes 1997). Since 1997, people filling out government forms, especially census questionnaires, have had to identify themselves as black, white, Asian or Pacific Islander, American Indian, or Other. With the year 2000 census, Americans will be able to choose as many racial or ethnic categories as they want from a new set of categories (Vobejda 1997; Yemma 1997).

The new categories are American Indian or Alaska Native, Asian, black or African-American, Native Hawaiian or other Pacific Islander, and white; the Hispanic category will now be called "Hispanic or Latino." There has been a long-standing debate over requiring people to identify themselves as members of only one racial or ethnic group "in the face of high rates of immigration and interracial marriage that have made the nation increasingly diverse" (Vobejda 1997). Many Americans wanted a multiracial category added to the census, but the Task Force argued that a multiracial category might heighten racial tensions and increase the fragmentation of American society (Holmes 1997).

The new categories will complicate the tabulation of people, but the difficulties are not that great. Martha Minow suggests that the responses can be divided by the numbers of people counted: "The resulting fractions will help remind anyone using census information of its source in self-identification and the roughness of its truths" (Minow 1997). However, some government officials and social scientists are concerned about the tabulation issues because more than 100 government programs are based on the percentage of members of a racial group in a particular area. These include programs dealing with affirmative action, school construction, congressional redistricting, voting rights, and illness and disability (Ferrante and Brown 1998).

Debate over changing census racial categories is nothing new, and the categories have often been changed. In the 1880 census, there were four categories for African Americans: black, mulatto, quadroon, and octoroon. Minow notes that these categories "reflected whites' preoccupation with miscegenation and 'racial purity.'" In the 207 years of the census, 26 different racial categories have been used, but Minow notes that the crucial breakthrough was in 1980, when people were allowed to identify their own racial category (Minow 1997).

Although many policy makers see the opportunity to check multiple categories as an important advance, some of the increasing number of mixed-race or multiracial Americans would prefer a separate "multiracial" category; others would prefer no racial categories at all. From 1960 to 1995, the number of interracial marriages increased from 149,000 to 1.4 million. The golfer Tiger Woods—who is of Asian, African American, and Native American ancestry—is a visible symbol of the increasing number of Americans with multiracial heritage. As America continues to become even more diverse, census categories will have to change again to keep up with and reflect that diversity.

Definition and Prevalence

❖ ❖ ❖ ❖

Were you aware of the debate over census racial categories? Has reading about the debate complicated or changed your view of **race**? We often use "race" as if it were a clear and unambiguous term, and many people think that they can easily identify a person's race, but race and race-related issues are complex and ambiguous. In fact, issues related to race and racial inequality have been and continue to be among the most complex, troubling, and persistent in U.S. society. Much of the debate over race centers on changes in the numbers of people of different racial and ethnic groups.

Did you know that the United States is becoming increasingly diverse? Figure 3-1 presents Census Bureau data and projections in the racial and ethnic make-up of the population. The 1990 data is based on the 1990 census. The projections for 2000, 2025, and 2050 are based on what the Census Bureau calls "middle-series projections," estimates that assume little change in fertility, **life-expectancy**, and **net immigration.** Look at the overall patterns of projected changes. The white, non-Hispanic percent is projected to drop from 75.7 in 1990 to 52.5 by 2050. The projections for African Americans and Native Americans, including Eskimos and Aleuts, rise modestly, however, Asian and Pacific Islanders and those of Hispanic origin, who can be of any race, increase dramatically (U.S. Bureau of the Census 1995).

In spite of this increasing diversity, many Americans insist that racial issues and racial inequality have little relevance in contemporary America.

Figure 3-1 Percent of the Population, by Race and Hispanic Origin: 1990, 2000, 2025, 2050

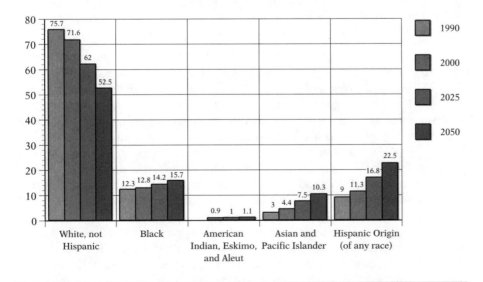

Source: U.S. Bureau of the Census. 1995. *Population Profile of the United States: 1995.* Current Population Reports, Series P-23, 189. Washington, D.C.: U.S. Government Printing Office.

Discussions of racial issues, such as the census race categories, affirmative action, or the legacy of slavery, even irritate some people. Others see racial issues as important and central to the United States today. Before reading further, you might take a moment or two to reflect on your own attitudes and beliefs. As you read this chapter, think about your views and whether the chapter complements or contradicts them. What kinds of evidence support your views? What kinds of evidence cast doubt on your positions? You might start by thinking about the meaning of race.

Defining Racial Inequality

Although we use it widely in everyday conversation, the term "race" is not very useful as a scientific concept. For one thing, it lacks precision. Think about all the groups that have been regarded as races. An amazingly broad range of groups have been called races, including Jews, Indians, English, French, Gypsies, Irish, Scots, Basques, Welsh, Nordic, Eskimos, blacks, Hindus, Latins, and Celts. The term race has been variously applied to the citizens of a particular country, those who speak the same language, a religious group, a local population, and a group having a shared culture and tradition.

Lack of precision is not the only problem with the concept of race. Bryant Rollins, a former *Boston Globe* reporter of mixed racial heritage, suggests that "race does not exist; racism does" (Rollins 1997). Social scientists tend to agree with Rollins. Sociologists stress the social and cultural rather than biological significance of race. A majority of anthropologists believe that "race is not a biological reality at all: It is nothing more than a social, cultural, and political invention" (Chandler 1997). For years physical anthropologists and others created typologies of races, but geneticist Richard Lewontin suggests that these attempts eventually collapsed under their own weight.

> Anthropologists no longer try to name and define races and subraces, because they recognize that there are no 'pure' human groups who have existed since the Creation as separate units. The most striking feature of global human history is the incessant and widespread migration and fusion of groups from different regions. (Lewontin 1995: 113)

The authors are not arguing that there are no differences among people, because that would clearly be untrue. Humans are differentiated along geographic lines, and groups of people from different parts of the world do look different. Rather, we agree with Mark Cohen's view that in understanding human societies and cultures "one of our most significant, dangerous, and blinding assumptions is that misunderstandings, tensions, and inequities among people, as well as the failure and success of groups of people, are based on biology or 'race'" (Cohen 1998:8). Cohen notes the importance of race as a social and political category but argues that the biological differences among people "are *never* 'racial,' because they don't come in the kind of neat clusters or packages that the word 'race' implies" (Cohen 1998:9).

Because of its vague and inconsistent usage and its lack of usefulness as a scientific concept, the term *race* does little to explain group differences and similarities. However, the importance of race as a social and political category rests on people's attribution of social significance to biological attributes and physical differences such as "skin color, the shapes of eyes, noses, or lips, the texture of hair, or the length of limbs" (Cohen 1998:13). For sociologists, race is a socially constructed concept that has social, economic, and political significance. The historical experiences of groups defined as races have been decisively shaped by their treatment as members of those races. Even though the biological definition of race makes little sense, "the idea of race is real if only because its consequences are real" (Ferrante and Brown 1998:xii). Remember that when we use the term "race" in this chapter, we refer to socially defined races. Discussing race and race-related issues often makes students uncomfortable. If you feel uncomfortable, or even if you don't, you may find "A Closer Look: Discussing Race in the Classroom" to be helpful.

As an alternative to the concept of race, the **minority group** concept has provided a valuable frame of reference for understanding the experiences of

A Closer Look

Discussing Race in the Classroom

Discussing race and race-related issues in classes often generates powerful emotional responses, which make students uncomfortable. Psychologist Beverly Daniel Tatum suggests that such discussions can produce responses ranging from guilt and shame to anger and despair (Tatum 1992). Perhaps reading this chapter and discussing racial inequality in class have made you uncomfortable. Such strong emotions and discomfort may lead to resistance, which "can ultimately interfere with the cognitive understanding and mastery of the material. This resistance and potential interference is particularly common when specifically addressing issues of race and racism" (Tatum 1992:2). Understanding why these emotional responses occur can help you deal with them and feel less uncomfortable and anxious about discussing racial inequality.

Tatum identifies "three major sources of student resistance to talking about and learning about race and racism" in predominantly white college classes (Tatum 1992: 5). First, race is seen as a "taboo" topic for discussion, especial in racially mixed classrooms. Second, many Americans, including students, see the United States as a just society and think that individuals succeed or fail on the basis of their individual merit. This perspective makes it hard to consider the possibility that systemic advantages and disadvantages affect individual success or failure. Finally, many students, especially white students, deny that they are prejudiced and do not believe that racism has an impact on their lives.

Discomfort about discussing race and racism may stem from unpleasant, anxiety-provoking experiences in childhood. Young children tend to ask questions or raise issues in very straightforward ways, often embarrassing their parents and leading the parents to quiet them. White children learn not to ask questions about race. Students of color have often experienced name-calling or demeaning episodes when they were young. These experiences cause anxiety and discomfort when discussing racial issues (Tatum 1992). There is no magic solution to this problem, but acknowledging it forthrightly may help you deal with it.

Growing up in the United States usually means learning that we live in a "just" society, a meritocracy in which people's achievements reflect their talents and efforts. When first confronted with evidence of systemic inequalities, students may deny the accuracy of that evidence (Tatum 1992). Try to keep an open mind about the issues discussed in this chapter. Examine your own beliefs to see what they are based on. Are your views based on evidence or are they based on untested assumptions or ideas that others have passed down to you? Test out your ideas and beliefs by trying to find relevant evidence. Ask your instructor to suggest useful sources of evidence.

Finally, students often see themselves as untouched by racism. Learning about racism often produces uncomfortable responses in students of various racial and ethnic groups. As students learn more about racism, they may "start to recognize its legacy within themselves," including their own beliefs, attitudes, and actions, some of which may be based on racial stereotypes (Tatum 1992: 8). If you find yourself uncomfortable discussing or thinking about race and race-related issues, think about these points. You are not alone in your reactions.

groups of people who are excluded from access to resources on the basis of physical or cultural characteristics. According to Louis Wirth's classic definition, a minority group is

> a group of people who, because of their physical or cultural characteristics, are singled out from the others in the society in which they live for differential and unequal treatment, and who therefore regard themselves as objects of collective discrimination. (Wirth 1945:347)

Minority groups have unequal access to society's resources and thus receive fewer of society's rewards. Martin Marger discusses four aspects of the definition of minority groups: (1) social definition, (2) differential power, (3) categorical nature, and (4) sociological and numerical meaning. We have already argued that race is a socially constructed category. Marger emphasizes that minority status itself is socially defined. If minority status is based on physical traits, the group is referred to as a race. Culturally defined groups can also be minorities and are called **ethnic groups**. In this chapter we focus primarily on one racially defined minority group—African Americans—but we do look at the experiences of other groups (Marger 1997).

Marger also emphasizes that minority groups have differential power and occupy subordinate positions in the social structure of a society. Because of their subordinate positions, minority groups lack the power to gain access to valued resources and to end the discrimination against them. Without important social, political, and economic power resources, they are subject to unequal treatment at the hands of powerful majority groups, who are in dominant positions in society. The power dimension is so important that some sociologists think that the concepts **dominant/subordinate** groups are more useful than **majority/minority** groups. The terms *minority group* or *minorities* may also be misleading because they seem to suggest that minorities always comprise a relatively small number of people. The categorical nature of minority groups means that minority status is a group status, not an individual one. A person's individual attributes and achievements are irrelevant for minority status. Denied equal access to educational, occupational, and other opportunity structures, minorities often are relegated to the lowest rungs of the stratification ladders in their societies, no matter what important achievements individuals in the group may have attained.

As we noted above, minority groups are defined sociologically rather than numerically. African Americans make up about 14 percent of the United States population, so they are a numerical minority, but a minority group need not be a numerical minority in a society. Minorities are groups whose members have been assigned a subordinate position in a society by virtue of their race or ethnicity. By contrast, the majority is the group whose members hold a dominant position with respect to wealth, status, and power, because of their race or ethnicity.

Clearly, the concept of a minority group has a distinctly sociological focus informing us that minority group membership is determined by the definitions that society imposes on individuals, regardless of their actual physical characteristics or personal preferences. We can see this clearly if we examine the question of who is "black" in the United States, as F. James Davis does in his book *Who Is Black? One Nation's Definition* (Davis 1991).

The most obvious answer to the question "Who is black?" refers to physical features such as skin color, the texture of hair, and so on. Yet definitions of blackness have varied by time and by place. Other countries define who is

black in different ways. In the United States, laws regarding race identity
have differed from state to state, depending on local custom, regional prejudices, and the proportion of blacks in the local population. We have already
noted the changes in census racial categories. At the societal level, criteria for
determining blackness have varied as well. However, generally any American
possessing even a trace of black ancestry would be referred to as black, regardless of skin color or physiognomy. This is the "one-drop rule." By contrast, individuals in Brazil and Puerto Rico who are not obviously black are
regarded as mulatto or white, regardless of ancestry. In South Africa, before
the end of apartheid, individuals of mixed ancestry had traditionally been regarded as a legally distinct social group, whose members enjoyed fewer privileges than whites but more privileges than blacks. For more on the issue of
defining who is black, see "A Closer Look: Who Is Black?"

Closer Look

Who Is Black?

How does a person get socially and legally defined as black in the United States?
In *Who Is Black*, James Davis looks at the experiences of two well-known African
Americans, singer-actress/beauty pageant winner Vanessa Williams and U.S. con-
gressman Adam Clayton Powell, Jr., to help answer this question (Davis 1991).

For three decades after the first Miss America contest in 1921, black women were
barred from competing. The first black winner was Vanessa Williams from
Millwood, New York, who was crowned Miss America in 1984. The viewing public
loved the musically talented and beautiful Williams, but many people were puz-
zled. Why was she being called black when she appeared to be white? Suzette
Charles, the first runner-up at least looked like many of the "lighter Blacks," so it
seemed okay to call her black. Could these women have won if they were darker or
looked "more black"?

In the words of Roi Ottley, the Rev. Clayton Powell, Jr. "was white to all appear-
ances, having blue eyes, an aquiline nose, and light, almost blond hair" (Davis 1991:
2). Early in his activist career, Powell led 6,000 blacks in a march on New York City
Hall. He was a bold, effective black leader who used his power in Congress to fight
for civil rights legislation and other black causes. In his autobiography, Powell re-
counts some experiences with racial classification. During his freshman year at
Colgate University, his roommate did not know he was black until his father was in-
vited to give a chapel talk on Negro rights, after which the roommate announced
that because Powell was black they could no longer be roommates or friends.

In the United States, a black is defined as a person with any known African-black
ancestry. This definition reflects the long experience with slavery and later with Jim
Crow segregation. In the South, it became known as the "one-drop rule," meaning
that a single drop of black blood makes a person a black (Davis 1991). It is also
known as the "one black ancestor rule," and some courts have called it the "trace-
able amount rule" (Rosenblum and Travis 1996). African Americans had no choice
with regard to this definition. This American cultural definition of who is black
seems to be taken for granted among all groups in the society (Davis 1991).

The arbitrariness of the one-drop rule for African Americans is clear, because it
applies to no other group and it is unique to the United States. In fact, definitions of
who is black vary from country to country. The phenomenon known as "passing as
white" is also unique to the United States. "Passing" is so much more a social phenomenon than a biological one, reflecting the nation's unique definition of what
makes a person black. The black experience with passing as white in the U.S. con-
trasts with the experience of other ethnic minorities. Davis notes that a person who
is one-fourth or less American Indian or Korean or Filipino is not regarded as passing if he or she intermarries and joins fully the life of the dominant community, so
the minority ancestry need not be hidden. ☞

❖ ❖ ❖ ❖

> ☞   Davis argues that it should be apparent that the definition of a black person as one with any trace at all of African ancestry is inextricably woven into the history of the United States. It incorporates beliefs once used to justify slavery and later used to buttress the castelike Jim Crow system of segregation.

Defining a few additional central terms will help you understand racial inequality in the United States. **Prejudice** refers to beliefs, ideas, and attitudes. A prejudiced person "prejudges" an individual or a group on the basis of stereotypes about the group. The prejudgment is usually negative, but even when it is positive it has negative consequences because it denies a person's individuality. An example of this would be assuming that a specific Asian or Asian American student must be good at mathematics.

While prejudice refers to attitudes and beliefs, **discrimination** refers to actions and behaviors. **Individual discrimination** is intentional discrimination that is carried out by individuals or small groups against members of a group and that usually violates the norms of a society (Marger 1997). "The employment manager who refuses to hire Asians, the judge who metes out unusually harsh sentences to blacks, and the homeowners' group that agrees not to sell houses in the neighborhood to Jews are examples of discriminators at this level" (Marger 1997:85). Many people assume that individual discrimination is the only or the most important type of discrimination; however, institutional discrimination plays a major role in generating and maintaining racial inequality.

Discrimination may be legal or expected in a society. For example, there may be laws against minority group members having equal access to education. This is direct institutional discrimination, where the discrimination is built into the social, economic, and political structure of a society. Examples of such direct institutional discrimination include the system of Apartheid which formerly existed in South Africa, as well as the widespread network of legal and customary discrimination against African Americans that existed in the United States until at least the 1960s (Marger 1997).

More difficult to detect and to eliminate is indirect institutional discrimination. This type of discrimination is unintended, but it results from the normal operation of a society's institutions and social structure and it puts members of minority groups at a disadvantage in competing for the society's resources. Past patterns of discrimination may have become "built in" to a society, or direct discrimination in one area of a society may affect behavior in other areas. Marger notes that the creation of new jobs outside of central cities, in suburbs where few minority group members live, operates to deny minority group members access to jobs. Discrimination in the educational system may also work to place minority group members at a disadvantage in other realms of society, including jobs.

When a widespread, long-standing pattern of discrimination is based on membership in racially defined groups, a society is characterized by **racism**. In regard to black-white relations in the United States, William Wilson has defined racism as "an ideology of racial domination or exploitation that (1) incorporates beliefs about a particular race's cultural and/or inherent biological inferiority and (2) uses such beliefs to justify and prescribe inferior or unequal treatment for that group" (Wilson 1973:32). David Wellman's definition of racism as a "system of advantage based on race" also refers to inferior or unequal group treatment (Wellman 1977). Beverly Daniel Tatum notes that people sometimes see prejudice and racism as essentially the same things, but Wilson's and Wellman's definitions clearly allows us to differentiate between prejudice and racism; that differentiation

> allows us to see that racism, like other forms of oppression, is not only a personal ideology based on prejudice, but a *system* involving cultural messages and institutional policies and practices as well as the beliefs and practices of individuals. (Tatum 1997: 7)

Racial Inequality and Minority Groups in the United States

In *A Different Mirror*, his history of multicultural America, Ronald Takaki tells about a taxi driver complimenting him on his English. Takaki, a Japanese American, was born in the United States, as were his parents. In fact, his family has been in the United States for over a hundred years, but the cab driver saw Takaki as *not American*. Americans have often been defined as European and white. But "America has been racially diverse since our very beginning on the Virginia shore, and this reality is becoming increasingly visible and ubiquitous" (Takaki 1993:2).

In this fascinating book, Takaki examines how various groups, including African Americans, Native Americans, Jews, Chicanos, Irish Americans, and Asian Americans created this society and contributed to its rich cultural heritage. Many Americans seem to fear America's diversity. Some see it as opening the United States up to the kind of conflict and warfare that has occurred in many parts of the world in recent years. Takaki argues that those who long for a culturally cohesive and homogeneous America misread or ignore the real history of the society. He asks how "we" Americans should be defined and suggests that "we" have always been a diverse group. Along the same lines, Lawrence Levine argues that

> diversity, pluralism, multiculturalism have been present throughout our history and have acted not merely as the germs of friction and division but as the lines of continuity, the sources for the creation of an indigenous culture, and the roots of a distinctly American identity. (Levine 1996:119-120)

That "distinctly American identity" has been created by a rich mosaic of groups. African Americans are one group that has played a central role in creating American society. As a minority group, blacks have traditionally occupied a subordinate position in American society. From the 1600s, laws governing the enslavement of African Americans permitted separating the children of slaves from their parents and forbade legal marriages between slaves. In the ante-bellum South, African Americans could not own books, learn to read or write, inherit money, or vote. Even in the North, blacks were not permitted to vote or to enter hotels or restaurants, except as servants, and were segregated with respect to schools, and to train, church, and theater seating.

Subordination of blacks did not end with the Civil War. Until recently, blacks were largely restricted to entering the least desirable jobs, and they continued to be segregated from whites in formal education, unions, public accommodations, and housing. Attempting to explain the racial violence of the 1960s, the National Advisory Commission on Civil Disorders noted in 1968 that large numbers of black Americans still failed to receive their share of economic benefits. More specifically, race discrimination was found to persist in employment, education, housing, and the courts. Over the years of their exclusion from important social, economic, and political resources, African Americans made major contributions to the creation of the United States. The cotton from the South, for example, played a major role in the development of the United States into an industrial capitalist society.

Other minority groups have also played important roles in the United States and continue to do so. Hispanic Americans may be of any race, according to the Census Bureau. The Population Reference Bureau estimates that Hispanic Americans will be the society's largest ethnic group by early in the twenty-first century (del Pinal and Singer 1997). Jorge del Pinal and Audrey Singer project that the Hispanic American population will reach 100 million by 2050, at which point it will constitute 25 percent of the population. In 1996, Hispanic Americans made up about 11 percent of the U.S. population.

Use of the term *Hispanic American* or the term *Latino* to refer to this group can be misleading. Hispanic Americans are an incredibly diverse group, many of whom do not consider themselves members of a Hispanic group. Mexican Americans, Cuban Americans, and Puerto Rican Americans are the largest groups within the overall Hispanic group, but others come from Spain and from Central and South America. Figure 3-2 provides a breakdown of Hispanic Americans in 1993. Hispanic Americans come from extremely varied and diverse backgrounds. Peter Winn, for example, notes that the artist Alfredo Jaar, a Chilean of Dutch descent, was "shocked to be regarded as a 'Hispanic' in the United States." Winn emphasizes that the diversity of Latin America and the Caribbean was "the result of immigration patterns as complex as those that formed the United States and Canada" (Winn 1998:207).

Figure 3-2   Persons of Hispanic Origin: 1993

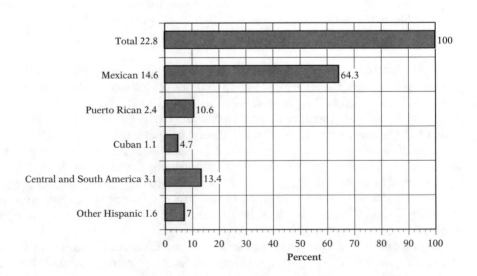

Source: U.S. Bureau of the Census. 1995. *Population Profile of the United States: 1995.* Current Population Reports, Series P23,189. Washington, D.C.: U.S. Government Printing Office.

The Census Bureau estimates that Asian Americans and Pacific Islanders ❖ ❖ ❖ ❖
made up 3.7 percent of the U.S. population in 1996 and will increase to about
10.3 percent of Americans in 2050 (U.S. Bureau of the Census 1995). Japanese Americans and Chinese Americans have long histories in the United
States. Other Asian immigrants have also contributed to American society, and
in recent years increasing numbers of Asian immigrants have come to the
United States from Southeast Asia. These various groups of Asian Americans
have played central roles in the historical development of the United States.

The "Invasion of America," to use historian Francis Jennings' term, ex-
acted an especially heavy toll on Native Americans (Jennings 1975). Arthur
Caswell Parker, a Seneca also known as Gawaso Wanneh, in an article originally published in the *American Journal of Sociology* in 1916, discussed
"seven stolen rights." Parker argued that "the people of the United States
through their governmental agencies, and through the aggression of their citizens have robbed the American Indian" of: (1) freedom of action; (2) economic independence; (3) social organization; (4) intellectual life; (5) moral
standards and racial ideals; (6) a good name among the peoples of the earth;
and (7) a definitive civic status (Parker 1995 [1916]: 241). Parker also called
for the return of the "seven stolen rights."

Most groups came to the United States as immigrants, but "Indians were
already here, blacks were forcibly transported to America, and Mexicans
were initially enclosed by America's expanding border" (Takaki 1993:11). Notice that in this chapter we have referred to blacks and African Americans; to
Hispanics and Latinos; and Takaki refers to Indians, who are also called Native Americans. These language issues are important and should not be dismissed as examples of PC, or political correctness, as is currently likely to
happen. See "A Closer Look: Language, Race, and Political Correctness" for
more discussion of language issues.

A Closer Look

Language, Race, and Political Correctness

The term *Political Correctness,* or PC, became popular in the United States in the
1990s. "Political correctness" refers to what some see as overly heightened sensitivi-
ties on the part of women and members of racial and ethnic groups to language used
to name or describe a group. Mark Cohen suggests that "political correctness" has
become "a pejorative phrase, a put-down used to imply that unwarranted political
pressure is being placed on a marketplace that would supposedly have no politics if
left alone" (Cohen 1998: 291). Cohen is referring to the marketplace of ideas. Those
who complain about "political correctness" sometimes suggest that it has made it
impossible to hold frank, open classroom discussions and that those who try to hold
such discussions are stifled and their academic freedom denied.

Therefore, some may see the authors' careful consideration of what terms to use
for various groups as excessively sensitive or fussy, or even as "politically correct."
We suggest a little experiment. The next time you hear the phrase "political correctness" used as a comment on the use of race, ethnicity, or gender, try substituting the
phrase "common human decency." See if it makes a difference.

In *The Golden Age Is In Us,* Alexander Cockburn quotes Irish writer Fintan
O'Toole's provocative ideas about "political correctness."

> We have now reached the point where every goon with a grievance, every
> bitter bigot, merely has to place the prefix, 'I know this isn't politically cor-
> rect, but . . .' in front of the usual string of insults in order to be not just safe
> from criticism, but actually a card, a lad, even a hero. (1995:396) ☞

> ☞ O'Toole further suggests that anti-PC has become a diversion from serious talk about racial inequality, and argues that "to talk about poverty and inequality, to draw attention to the reality that discrimination and injustice are still facts of life, is to commit the new sin of political correctness" (Cockburn 1995: 396).
>
> The authors think that language is important and that language has often been used to demean some groups of people. So we have thought carefully about how to refer to various groups. In general, we follow Beverly Daniel Tatum's usage, although we differ with her on some points. We refer to people of African descent as both Black and African American. We try to use the terms that other groups use in referring to themselves, although groups often differ in how they refer to themselves. For example, some people of Latin American or Spanish ancestry prefer the term *Hispanic* while others prefer *Latino*. We use both. Everyone may not agree with our usage, but we have thought carefully about these issues and try to use the most preferred terms where possible.
>
> Tatum notes that some people object to using racial categories at all because the terms were developed to help control and oppress groups of people. Along with Tatum, we respect that argument, but we also agree with her that "it is difficult to talk about what is essentially a flawed and problematic social construct without using language that is itself problematic. We have to be able to talk about it in order to change it" (Tatum 1997:17).

Presently, racial minorities in general tend to be seriously over-represented at the bottom of the scale in terms of any measure of material well-being. In the distribution of occupations, whites are substantially overrepresented in the professional and managerial stratum. They are almost twice as likely as blacks (1.71 times) and Latinos (1.97 times) to hold these kinds of jobs. On the other hand, blacks and Latinos are much more concentrated in the lower-paid service sector and in the categories of unskilled and semiskilled operators, fabricators, and laborers. Whereas 27 percent of white employees fall into these combined categories, 47 percent of blacks and 43 percent of Latinos are so categorized. Finally, even though the numbers are relatively small, blacks are more than three times and Latinos more than twice as likely as whites to work as private household servants (Andersen and Collins 1995).

In terms of income distribution, the United States is one of the more unequal of the Western industrial societies. Edna Bonacich argues that the excessive differences in income receive strong ideological justifications. They serve, supposedly, as incentives to impel people to work harder to achieve success. Bonacich argues that such steep inequalities will not act as incentives but may engender hopelessness and despair for those who have no chance of becoming wealthy. Fairly modest inducements can serve as motivators; steep inequalities should not be acceptable. Justifications for inequality are more often rationalizations to preserve privilege than they are a well-reasoned basis of social organization (Bonacich 1980). We will return to these issues when we consider the consequences of racial inequality.

Levels of Causation

Social scientists have differing views of what causes racism; these theories and models generally encompass one of three levels of causation: the individual, the cultural, and the structural.

Individual

❖ ❖ ❖ ❖

Some theories try to explain racial inequality by focusing on the individual psychological or biological characteristics of minority group members. Other theories focus on prejudiced individuals and how prejudice meets their own psychological needs. There has been a great deal of research on the "psychopathology of prejudice." For example, racial inequality has been explained as a result of psychological needs in prejudiced people that are expressed in race discrimination and hostility. One of the best known theories of prejudice is the conception known as the **authoritarian personality**, a configuration of functionally interrelated personality characteristics in which prejudice has a central position (Adorno, et al. 1950).

According to the authoritarian personality theory, prejudice is a psychological pathology that can be traced back to the early socialization experiences of a child. Specifically, race hatred develops as a result of harsh and punitive forms of child-rearing imposed during the first few years of life when the child is most vulnerable and most susceptible to parental influence. The child is expected to be weak and to be submissive to the demands of the parents. In contrast, the parents assume a position of absolute dominance.

The result is a superficial and ambivalent identification of the child with the authoritarian parents. The child actually harbors much latent hostility and resentment towards parental authority, which, as an adult, he or she displaces onto powerless members of society. And so the authoritarian person comes to despise diverse groups, including African Americans, Puerto Ricans, Jews, immigrants, and Catholics. The authoritarian person can bolster his or her self-esteem by comparing himself or herself to allegedly inferior and weak minority members.

The authoritarian personality approach is one approach to understanding racial inequality by examining the causes of prejudice among members of majority groups. It is a subtle, complex theory that links aspects of social structure to individual personality. Nonetheless, this whole approach to understanding racial inequality has serious weaknesses. It does not explain how particular racial and ethnic groups become minorities in the first place. Psychological approaches also tend to explain high levels of prejudice but not moderate levels. Moreover, it is questionable whether prejudice causes discrimination, racism, or racial inequality. This last sentence may not seem to make sense, so bear with us a bit.

Does a person have to be prejudiced against members of a group to discriminate against members of the group? In a classic analysis of the relationships between prejudice and discrimination, sociologist Robert Merton (1949) argued that attitudes and actions towards members of particular ethnic groups may fluctuate within different social contexts. By combining the prejudicial attitudes or lack of such attitudes with the propensity either to engage in discriminatory actions or to refrain from them, Merton suggested four types of people.

First, there are unprejudiced nondiscriminators, whom Merton calls "all-weather liberals." These people accept the idea of social equality and refrain from discriminating against racial or ethnic minorities. The second group is prejudiced discriminators or "active bigots," who do not hesitate to turn their prejudicial beliefs into discriminatory behavior when the opportunity arises. Merton uses the Ku Klux Klan or neo-Nazi parties as examples. The first two types are obvious; however, Merton did not stop there.

Merton called a third type prejudiced nondiscriminators or "timid bigots." These people hold negative beliefs and stereotypes about ethnic minorities but are precluded from acting out these beliefs by situational norms. In a social context where discrimination is frowned on, people with prejudices are less likely to act on those beliefs because of the disapproval their behavior would generate. Finally, Merton identified unprejudiced discriminators, or "fair-weather liberals," who adjust their behavior to meet the demands of particular circumstances. If they are in a social environment where discrimination is approved of, they may discriminate. Or if it is in their own social, economic, or political interests to discriminate they may do so, if the social environment is conducive to it. The essential point of Merton's analysis for us is the recognition that prejudice need not lead to discrimination, and, perhaps more important, discrimination may occur in the absence of prejudice. We return to this when we examine structural levels of causation.

At the individual level, explanations of racial inequality also frequently focus on characteristics of the minority group. From this point of view, racial inequality is a result of some defect in the members of the group that experiences inequality.

This approach can be seen in studies of race and intelligence. In 1969, psychologist Arthur Jensen revised a version of a hypothesis that had been advanced decades earlier to explain the low status of white immigrants to the United States, specifically that their intellectual capacity was genetically limited in comparison to that of the smarter native white population (Jensen 1969; Brigham 1923). Jensen's innovation was to suggest that "genetic factors are strongly implicated in the average Negro-white intelligence difference (1969: 82). This kind of argument can easily be employed to explain racial inequality without making reference to the impact of social structural and institutional factors such as racial discrimination. Jensen's argument was dismissed by most social scientists, but his view, or closely related versions of it, tend to resurface.

A recent example of such an approach is Richard Herrnstein and Charles Murray's *The Bell Curve: Intelligence and Class Structure in American Life* (1994). They argue that intelligence is tied to economic success and that the differences in intelligence, as measured by IQ tests, account for some of the differences in economic success of blacks and whites. *The Bell Curve* received an extraordinary amount of attention, including stories in the major newsmagazines and extensive discussion on radio and television talk shows. You might expect that the book was groundbreaking or an exemplary study to receive such attention. In fact, it is neither groundbreaking nor exemplary. Mark Cohen argues that the book "revived the old argument that class divisions in society reflect the natural biological superiority of some people and the inferiority of others, particularly the poor and black" (1998: 3). This has always been a popular argument among the upper classes, for it seems to legitimate their privileged positions.

The importance of *The Bell Curve* lies not in the strength of its evidence or in the force of its arguments, for both are weak and have been extensively criticized (Fraser 1995; Jacoby and Glaubermann 1995; Fischer, et al. 1996). Nor does it lie in widespread acceptance of its claims, for it has not been widely accepted by social scientists, natural scientists, or policy professionals. However, the attention given to the book may mislead some people into accepting some of its arguments. As many critics have noted, *The Bell Curve* is essentially a political tract masquerading as social science. In his earlier book, *Losing Ground*, Murray (1984) argued that social welfare programs had worsened the situation of the poor and had increased poverty; he recommended their elimination. *The Bell Curve* seems to be an argument for ending affirmative action, although not a very strong argument. In fact, sociologist Michael Nunley (1997) argues that the book is a "fraud."

The shortcomings of *The Bell Curve* illustrate clearly the problems with biological or genetic explanations for racial inequality. Remember that earlier in this chapter we mentioned Cohen's argument that biological differences among people are *never* racial and that the biological differences among people don't come in neat packages called races (Cohen 1998). It is important to be clear on this. "The vast majority of the 50,000–100,000 gene pairs that make up the human blueprint don't seem to have any correlation with the 6–10 gene pairs that are believed to affect skin color" (Cohen 1998: 47). Cohen concludes that race is not a biological reality and that the differential performance of minority group members can therefore not be the result of racial differences. The subordination of some groups and the inequality thus generated come from aspects of American culture.

Cultural

Racial attitudes and beliefs vary widely among people. Commonsense explanations, and even some scientific thought of earlier times, have accounted for out-group antipathy as natural, or innate, patterns of human thought and action. In this view, disliking or fearing those who are different from us is both natural and unavoidable. Today, sociologists generally agree that prejudice and discrimination are not innate human characteristics. We have just seen that psychological and biological theories of racial inequality are inadequate. Sociologists stress situational factors and power structures as the bases of both negative thought and action towards ethnic groups. Basically, racism, which we defined as a "system of advantage" based on race, is part of a society's social and economic structure, including the normative order, to which individuals are socialized and which gives them rules for how to act in various situations (Marger 1997).

Normative theories concentrate primarily on the transmission of ethnic prejudices through the socialization process and on the social situations that compel discriminatory behavior (Marger 1997). Prejudice and discrimination may be explained within the framework of social norms. It is to individuals' social environment—the groups to which they belong, the cultural and political norms operative in their society and community, and the processes of socialization—that prejudice and discrimination can be traced. Prejudice is built into the culture in the form of normative precepts, which define the ways in which members of the group ought to behave in relation to the members of selected out-groups (Marger 1997).

In 1944, Swedish social scientist Gunnar Myrdal proposed that the situation of racial inequality in the United States constituted an "American Dilemma," a basic cultural inconsistency between values emphasizing democracy and general cultural values that include discrimination against black Americans. As Myrdal himself put it, the American dilemma represented

> the ever-raging conflict between, on the one hand, the valuations preserved on the general plane, which we shall call the "American Creed,"

where the American thinks, talks, and acts under the influence of high national and Christian precepts, and, on the other hand, the valuations on specific planes of individual and group living, where personal and local interests; economic, social and sexual jealousies; considerations of community prestige and conformity; group prejudice against particular persons or types of people; and all sorts of miscellaneous wants, impulses, and habits dominate his [sic] outlook. (Myrdal 1944:lxxi)

According to Myrdal, the American dilemma is a continuing source of conflict and tension. Americans discriminate but at some moral and psychological expense to themselves. They must construct justifications that exempt the particular target of discrimination from being included in the general values of the American Creed. As a result, negative stereotypes are developed that portray the minority group members as subhuman (for example, as dirty, sly, shrewd, brutal, lazy, and stupid) and therefore undeserving of treatment accorded the civilized people of the world.

Myrdal's conception emphasizes the cultural basis for equality. Other researchers have focused more directly on the cultural basis for prejudice and discrimination against minority group members. Several researchers contend that the United States is a culture of prejudice and discrimination (Levin and Levin 1982). Cultural prejudices share the following characteristics:

1. *They are learned.* Prejudice is transmitted through socialization, just as are other conceptions of "what ought to be," including ideas about motherhood, patriotism, love of church, and economic achievement. Nobody is born prejudiced; parents, teachers, the mass media, and other agents of socialization teach prejudice.

2. *They are shared widely.* Many studies report that Americans of diverse origin—representing wide differences with respect to education, religion, social class, race, and region—largely agree in terms of their willingness to associate with members of various minority groups; there are important subgroup prejudices as well.

3. *They are enduring.* Prejudices may last for decades, if not centuries.

4. *They include norms governing the relationship between minority and majority members.* As we have seen, from the 1600s, anti-black norms were imposed and rigorously enforced. In addition to the formal rules, blacks were also subjected to a complex system of petty indignities, including prohibitions against interracial dating, social visits by blacks to the homes of whites, sexual relations between black men and white women, and blacks interrupting conversations between whites.

5. *They include a minority role.* Cultural prejudices include a prescribed role that minority members are expected to play. (Levin and Levin 1982)

These cultural prejudices manifest themselves in an elaborate and largely unacknowledged system of **white privilege**. (See "A Closer Look: Whiteness and White Privilege.")

Another culturally based explanation of racial inequality can be found in the notion that minority members are exposed to a never-ending cycle of

A Closer Look

Whiteness and White Privilege

White people in the United States rarely confront the meaning of their own color or racial identity because they rarely need to (Doane 1997). Robert Terry's research on the topic led to the conclusion that *"to be white in America is not to have to think about it"* (Terry 1981:120, emphasis in original). Terry argues that whites rarely think about what it means to be white, and when asked to think about it cite positive attributes. Rarely do respondents suggest anything negative about being white. Terry also questioned whites about whether there were any costs of being white. Their responses fell into two broad categories. One group cited **reverse discrimination** and other forms of supposed preferential treatment occasioned by affirmative action; the other group indicated fears and feelings that they lacked social competency in dealing with people with whom whites have had little contact. In the research by Terry, and others, whites rarely recognized any privileges associated with their racial identity (Terry 1981; Feagin and Vera 1995)

In a classic analysis of "White Privilege and Male Privilege," Peggy McIntosh argues that whites are carefully *taught* not to recognize **white privilege**. She suggests that white children are taught about racism as something that puts others at a disadvantage but are not taught about white privilege, which puts them at an advantage. She compiles a list of advantages often taken for granted by whites (McIntosh 1995). These include assumptions that if a white woman needs to move, she will be able to rent or purchase a home where she wants to and can afford; that her neighbors will be pleasant, or at least neutral, to her; that she can go shopping without thinking about being followed or harassed by store detectives; that she can see white people portrayed positively in the media; and she can take a job with an affirmative action employer and not have co-workers suspect that she got the job because of her race.

McIntosh lists many more white privileges, although she contends that the word *privilege* is misleading. She argues that its connotations are too positive to fit the conditions and behaviors that **privilege systems** produce. People usually think of privilege as being a favored state, whether earned or conferred by birth or luck. Yet some of the conditions described above systematically give excessive power to certain groups. Such privilege confers dominance and gives control because of one's race (1995).

deprivations that perpetuates their economic plight from generation to generation. We discussed this "culture of poverty" approach in Chapter 2. This approach focuses on the alleged defects in the black family and the black community—for example, the failure to provide opportunities for reading books and magazines, the absence of parental support for achievement, and the lack of encouragement for the delayed gratification of advanced education.

William Ryan (1971) coined the term **blaming the victim** for explanations that focus on the individual characteristics and alleged defects of the poor as causes of poverty, and avoid examining the structural causes of poverty and inequality. Ryan's approach has proven so fruitful that other scholars have adopted and extended it (Lykes, et al. 1996).

Much of the original impetus for Ryan's blaming-the-victim approach came from a report on African American families. In 1965, then Assistant Secretary of Labor Daniel P. Moynihan suggested that "at the heart of the deterioration of Negro society is the deterioration of the Negro family." Moynihan, now a senator from New York, argued that slavery and

On April 7, 1968, Dr. Martin Luther King was assassinated in Memphis. This march in Seattle was one of many honoring the slain Civil Rights leader.—*Photo: The Seattle Times Co.*

subsequent impoverishment had created a father-absent, matriarchal family structure among poor blacks, which, in turn, helped to perpetuate a "tangle of pathology" (1965). Moynihan was motivated by genuine concern for the plight of poor African Americans and relied on accepted research in compiling his report. However, other scholars, often without his concern, picked up on Moynihan's work and generated numerous studies critical of African American family structure and culture. Other scholars then carried out studies that cast doubt on the alleged role of black families in creating a tangle of pathology. These studies emphasized that African Americans used various kinds of family strategies to adapt to and survive under conditions of uncertain and limited resources (Gutman 1976; Stack 1974; Susser 1982).

Structural

From the structural view, racial inequality has become incorporated into the fabric of U.S. social institutions, so that the participation of racial minorities is excluded or restricted by conventional rules, regulations, and procedures as well as by personal prejudices. In this sense, social structure generates racial inequality. Underlying these rules, regulations, and procedures are inequalities of power and other resources. Power conflict theories emphasize political economy, stratification, and differential access to power for explaining the origins and continuation of racial and ethnic inequality (Feagin and Feagin 1996).

W. E. B. DuBois was one of the first major theorists to emphasize the links between racial oppression and class inequalities based on capitalism in the United States. He argued that there has never been real democracy for people in all racial groups in the United States. Oliver Cox, a Marxist sociologist, drew on ideas from DuBois. He argued that the economic dimensions of forced slave migration from Africa led to the oppressiveness of later conditions for African American slaves. A search for cheap labor by a profit-oriented capitalist class led to a system of racial subordination. Racial prejudice developed later as an ideology to rationalize this economic subordination of African Americans (Cox 1959[1948]; Hunter and Abraham 1987).

In a classical analysis, Robert Blauner asserts that racial inequality became institutionalized via colonization, a process not unlike that historically experienced by the Third World peoples of Asia and Africa in their dealings with white Europeans. According to Blauner's theory of **internal colonialism**, the United States has existed and prospered by virtue of its ability to colonize subjects on national soil—to conquer Native Americans, defeat Hispanics, and enslave blacks (Blauner 1972).

In this regard, there is a basic distinction between the experiences of immigrants and colonized groups. Most white immigrants entered the United States voluntarily, though they may have left their country of origin because of severe oppression. In most cases, such white immigrants entered as part of a free labor force. Even in the face of extreme prejudice and exploitation, they enjoyed a degree of autonomy, mobility, and choice that was unavailable to those who were colonial subjects of conquest, capture, or slavery. As Blauner notes,

> When living in New York became too difficult, Jewish families moved on to Chicago. Irish trapped in Boston could get land and farm in the Midwest, or search for gold in California. It is obvious that parallel alternatives were not available to the early generations of Afro-Americans, Asians and Mexican-Americans, because they were not part of the free labor force. (1972: 56)

Immigrant groups were also permitted to maintain an independent cultural identity, their assimilation into the mainstream of American society occurring on a voluntary basis. For instance, at the same time that Orthodox Jews were mocked and scorned, they were still permitted the freedom to practice Judaism in their own way. Blauner argues that, by contrast, the cultural heritage of colonized peoples was frequently transformed or destroyed in order to dominate and control them. The independence and integrity of a people as well as its ability to resist outside influences are sustained by the preservation of culture. As a result, colonialism required that new institutions and lifestyles be imposed on those being colonized (Blauner 1972).

The internal colonialism model emphasizes that racial inequality in the United States has an economic component whose importance is difficult to ignore. To illustrate, consider the rate of unemployment in the United States. In 1992, the national unemployment rate was 7.8 percent. Ten million Americans were out of work. The rate for African Americans was almost 15 percent (14.9) and the rate for Hispanics was just over 12 percent (12.1) (Sidel 1994).

A **split labor market theory**, another class-based theory, assesses whether all classes of whites benefit from the labor of people of color or just the dominant class of capitalist employers. Bonacich argues that dominant-group (white) workers do not share the interests of the top political-economic class, the capitalists. Yet both the employer class and the white part of the working class discriminate against the racially subordinated part of the working class. Bonacich emphasizes that because white workers want to protect their own privileges, they discriminate against workers of color (1980).

Michael Omi and Howard Winant have developed a theory of **racial formation**. They argue that racial and ethnic relations are substantially defined by the actions of governments, ranging from the passage of legislation to the imprisonment of groups defined as a threat. They argue that the U.S. Constitution openly defined racial groups and interracial relations in racist terms. For example, the Constitution counted each African-American slave as three-fifths of a person, and the Naturalization Law of 1790 declared that only white immigrants could qualify for naturalization. Japanese and other Asian immigrants were banned by law until the 1950s from becoming citizens. For centuries, the U.S. government officially favored northern European immigrant groups over southern European groups, such as Italians (Omi and Winant 1994).

These structural theories differ from one another in terms of emphases, but they all focus on the political, economic, and social structural bases for racial inequality. Rather than emphasizing individual characteristics or cultural deficiencies, these approaches suggest that structural factors account for pervasive patterns of racial inequality.

Consequences

As a result of discrimination and prejudice, racially-defined groups lack equal access to important societal resources. These resources include jobs, income, wealth, education, and health care. Lack of access to these resources has important consequences for the groups affected. Most fundamentally, constraints on access to economic resources make it more likely that racially-defined groups will be poor. Figure 3-3 gives you a picture of the composition of the poor in the United States. The majority of poor Americans are white, however the percentages of poor people in racially-defined groups are much higher. As you can see from Table 3-1, 8.6 percent of white, non-Hispanic

Figure 3-3 Composition of the Poverty Population

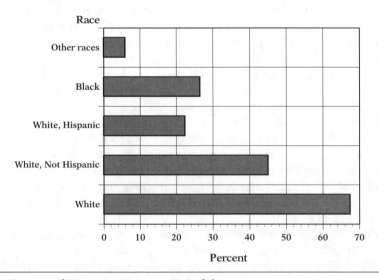

Note: Persons of Hispanic origin are 23.8 of the poor.
Source: Lamison-White, Leatha. 1997. *Poverty in the United States: 1996*. U.S. Bureau of the Census, Current Population Reports, Series P60,198. Washington, D.C.: U.S. Government Printing Office.

Americans were poor in 1996. However, 28.4 percent of blacks, and 29.4 percent of Hispanic origin people fell below the poverty level. The percentages are similar for families. The reason why the majority of the poor are white, even though a smaller percentage of non-Hispanic origin white Americans are poor is simple. There are more non-Hispanic origin white Americans, so even though the percentage of whites in poverty is lower, their absolute numbers of poor people are higher.

Table 3-1 Persons and Families in Poverty, by Race: 1996

| Race | Numbers and Percent Below Poverty Level | | | |
| | Persons | | Families | |
	Number (1,000s)	Percent	Number (1,000s)	Percent
Total	36,529	13.7	7,708	11.0
White	24,650	11.2	5,059	8.6
White, not Hispanic	16,462	8.6	3,433	6.5
Black	9,694	28.4	2,206	26.1
Asian and Pacific Islander	1,454	14.5	284	12.7
Hispanic Origin (may be of any race)	8,697	29.4	1,748	26.4

Source: U.S. Bureau of the Census. 1997. *March Current Population Survey.* <http://www.census.gove/hhes/poverty/poverty96/pv96est1.html>

These statistics and the human realities they reflect have profound consequences for human lives. Here the authors explore those consequences for health, educational attainment, and treatment of racially-defined groups in the criminal justice system.

Among the most important consequences of racial inequality are those related to health and health care. There is a persistent and chronic gap in black and white health in the United States. Drawing on data from the Centers for Disease Control and Prevention, Peter Kilborn notes that black men were the only population group in the United States to have rising cancer rates from 1990 to 1995 and that increasing numbers of black women had breast cancer during that period. More generally,

> African-Americans contract most major diseases sooner than whites and die six or seven years sooner. Government statistics show long-stubborn black-white gaps are getting even bigger for diabetes, maternal mortality, asthma and several forms of cancer. (Kilborn 1998)

A recent study of health differences in the *Journal of the American Medical Association* indicated that African American children watch more television and are less physically active than other children. This leads to greater obesity and assorted health problems associated with it. That this may be a consequence of racial inequality becomes clear when the researchers suggested that the greater propensity of minority children to watch television and avoid physical activity may be related to their parents' fears about crime. Minority parents are twice as likely as other parents to think their neighborhoods are unsafe and thus to keep their children from playing outside (Andersen, et al. 1998).

The health care gap is also visible in the health care coverage and health care status of children. A recent study linked children's health problems to race, ethnicity, parents' education, and parents' employment. Education and employment, of course, are also linked to race and ethnicity. The study found that Hispanic children are more much more likely than other children to be uninsured and to be in fair or poor health. Among the study's specific findings were that 27.7 percent of Hispanic children were uninsured, compared to 17.6 percent of black children and 12.2 percent of non-Hispanic white children; 17.2 percent of Hispanic children lack a health care provider, compared to 12.6 percent of black children and 6 percent of non-Hispanic white children. This study documents additional important consequences of racial and ethnic inequality in the United States (Weinick, et al. 1998; Wiegers, et al. 1998).

Inequalities in educational achievement for minorities are additional, exceptionally important consequences of racial inequality in the United States. Many Americans believe that American society is open and competitive and that poverty or wealth are outcomes of individual inadequacies or strengths. They do not see racial inequality as a result of a system of racial advantages operating together with the distributive mechanisms of a capitalist economy. Education is seen as a primary avenue of upward mobility. American society is seen as open and competitive and giving everyone access to education so they can compete for the society's resources (Mickelson and Smith 1995). However, members of subordinate groups tend to have less education than others, as indicated in Table 3-2.

Table 3-2   Educational Attainment, by Race and Hispanic Origin for Persons 25 and Older

Educational Level	Racial or Ethnic Group	Percentage 1990	Percentage 1995
Completed High School	**Total**	77.6	81.7
	White	79.1	83.0
	Black	66.2	73.8
	Asian/Pacific Islander	80.4	(NA)
	Hispanic (any race)	50.8	53.4
	Mexican	44.1	(NA)
	Puerto Rican	55.5	(NA)
	Cuban	63.5	(NA)
Completed College	**Total**	21.3	23.0
	White	22.0	24.0
	Black	11.3	13.2
	Asian/Pacific Islander	39.9	(NA)
	Hispanic (any race)	9.2	9.3
	Mexican	5.4	(NA)
	Puerto Rican	9.7	(NA)
	Cuban	20.2	(NA)

NA = Not available.

Source: U.S. Bureau of the Census. 1996. *Statistical Abstract of the United States: 1996.* Washington, D.C.: U.S. Government Printing Office. Table 241.

Roslyn Mickelson and Stephen Smith (1995) argue that inequality is so deeply rooted in the structure and operation of the U.S. political economy that, at best, educational reforms can only play a limited role in alleviating such inequality. Considerable evidence indicates that the educational system helps legitimate, if not actually reproduce, significant aspects of social inequality. Take school desegregation for example. The history of race relations in the United States has long suggested that American society has not been based on freedom and equal opportunity. Segregated schools point directly to the shallowness of American claims to equality for all. The school desegregation movement beginning in 1954 was an important attempt to address inequality of educational opportunity and to move away from the "separate but equal" doctrine. That doctrine masked the reality of the educational system in the United States, which was "separate and *very* unequal."

We can look at whether desegregation efforts have actually integrated public schools and whether students' educational opportunities have been enhanced. In fact, progress toward integration has been limited at best. Racial isolation has only diminished, it has not disappeared. In 1968, 77 percent of African American students were in schools with student bodies composed of predominantly nonwhite youths. By 1984, 64 percent of African Americans were in such schools. Moreover, 70.5 percent of Hispanic students attend predominantly minority schools. Furthermore, integrated schools are often resegregated at the classroom level by tracking or ability grouping (Mickelson and Smith 1995). In 1980, the typical black school student attended a public school that was 36.2 percent white. In 1996, the comparable figure was 33.9 percent (Frontline 1998).

Evidence from desegregation research suggests that, overall, minority and majority children benefit academically and socially from well-run integrated programs. Despite these limited but positive outcomes, in the last decade of the twentieth century, most American children attend schools segregated by race, ethnicity, and class. Consequently, educational inequities continue to be important consequences of racial inequality. Forty years of federal interventions aimed at achieving equality of educational opportunity through school desegregation have not achieved that goal; children from different race and class backgrounds continue to receive significantly segregated and largely unequal educations.

When African American or other minority children experience difficulties in school, school authorities often attribute the problems to the children. Educational researcher Lisa Delpit studied cultural conflict in classrooms. She suggests that many academic problems of black children and other children of color result from cultural miscommunications; also, stereotyping of children is widespread. Delpit discusses the "culture of power" in the classroom. The culture of power manifests itself in classrooms in ways that distort the educational process and lead white teachers to make negative judgments about children of color (Delpit 1995).

The consequences of racial inequality are also evident in the American criminal justice system. Sociologists, criminologists, and activists have argued that the criminal justice system displays racial bias in its treatment of minorities through differential arrest, conviction, and sentencing rates. According to the National Criminal Justice Commission, "whites and African Americans live in completely different worlds when it comes to race and the criminal justice system" (Donziger 1996:99). The American Civil Liberties Union (ACLU) argues that the nation's criminal justice system has two tiers, one for blacks and one for whites. According to the ACLU, "beginning with the street level enforcement of state and federal criminal laws, and ending with the meting out of the death penalty, African Americans are disproportionately targeted, stopped, arrested, prosecuted, sentenced to long mandatory prison terms and executed" (American Civil Liberties Union 1996:1).

There are numerous additional areas in which the consequences of racial inequality are clear. We should note, however, that there is a heated debate going on over whether racial inequality has lessened in recent years. Much of the debate focuses on whether African Americans in general are better off today than in the past. Many of those taking part in the debate suggest that the black middle class is "the fastest growing and largest segment within the black community." Some suggest "that the black middle class has doubled and even quadrupled since 1965" (Robinson 1998).

A. J. Robinson points out that many contemporary perspectives on the black middle class are misleading and suggests that there are major problems with current interpretations of data on the black middle class. One basic problem is the lack of a standard definition of the black middle class. Using the income range of $15,000 to $49,999 to indicate middle class status, Robinson notes that in 1970, 11,667,612 black families were middle class, and by 1990, the number grew to 13,309,033. As Robinson suggests, this is "hardly a doubling!"

Interventions

Policies to reduce racial inequality have been institutional or individual in their focus. Institutional interventions to reduce discrimination and its effects include removing restrictions, instituting affirmative action, and providing social programs to redress past wrongs. Some policies of removing restrictions have originated in the courts.

One of the most famous is *Brown v. Board of Education* in May 1954. This Supreme Court decision provided a legal basis for desegregated education on a national level. This decision resulted from the situation of an eight-year-old black girl from Topeka, Kansas, who was required to be bussed to a segregated black school located some distance from her home in order to avoid attending a local neighborhood school that was all white. Partly because of social scientists' evidence about the detrimental impact of segregation on black children, but mostly because of the efforts of black organizations, the court decided that the doctrine of "separate but equal" had no place in the context of public education. Segregation in the public schools was regarded as "inherently unequal" and unconstitutional.

Now forty-five years after the *Brown* decision, African American students still attend largely segregated schools. The culture of power operating in those schools leads to black student behaviors being misunderstood and leads to much negative labeling. Jean Anyon, an education professor, suggests that school reform will not work. She argues that ghetto schools cannot be reformed or eliminated without eliminating the ghetto (Anyon 1997).

Policies of affirmative action can be found in the Civil Rights Act of 1964, which declared that the religion, national origin, race, and color of individuals were not to be used as bases for discrimination or segregation in the areas of employment opportunities, public education, or voting and in the use of public facilities. The act put pressure on employers and educators to take some form of positive action to close the gaps between blacks and whites. Penalties would be imposed when some employer or school district was

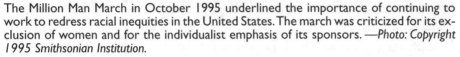

The Million Man March in October 1995 underlined the importance of continuing to work to redress racial inequities in the United States. The march was criticized for its exclusion of women and for the individualist emphasis of its sponsors. —*Photo: Copyright 1995 Smithsonian Institution.*

found to be guilty of discrimination. The act created the Equal Employment Opportunity Commission to help implement decisions with respect to employment. A year after the Civil Rights Act was passed, President Johnson signed Executive Order 11246, which officially created affirmative action and set up enforcement mechanisms.

Affirmative action programs have been at the center of an intense controversy in the 1990s. Proponents argue that programs taking race and gender into account are necessary to promote equal opportunity and to redress past discrimination. Opponents argue that programs using quotas and **reverse discrimination** are unfair to white males. The affirmative action debate raises a number of complex legal, political, and philosophical issues concerning the role the government should play to promote equal opportunity. Most citizens in the 1990s would agree that the government should protect citizens from being discriminated against on the basis of their race, ethnicity, or gender. However, many believe that employment and educational decisions should be made on the basis of the assessments of an individual's skills, abilities, and motivation. Fair decisions would be "color-blind." However, in a society in which past discrimination has conferred a pattern of advantages to one group, and in which racial discrimination still exists, to be "color blind," is to be "blind."

In his provocative *Turning Back: The Retreat from Racial Justice in American Thought and Policy* (1995), sociologist Stephen Steinberg argues that affirmative action policies have been effective at promoting racial justice. He suggests that the increasing disenchantment with affirmative action, as evidenced by California's Proposition 209, is part of an overall retreat from racial justice in American society. Much of the backlash against affirmative action comes out of misunderstandings of the extent of racial inequality and of the policies themselves.

Harry Pachon suggests three reasons for opposition to affirmative action policies. First, in spite of the success of the American economy, many middle-class Americans are uneasy about their futures, and "it's easier to believe affirmative action programs are the root cause of everyday economic problems than it is to admit that the nation is undergoing a wrenching economic transition that makes everyone uncertain about the future" (1996:189). Second, many who oppose affirmative action programs ignore history. "Affirmative action is thirty years old; the problems it attempts to correct are three centuries old" (1996:189). Finally, many critics of affirmative action use anecdotes to support their positions rather than systematic evidence. In the 1990s, there was much rancorous debate over affirmative action on American campuses. For a useful website that discusses affirmative action on campus, see "A Closer Look: Website: *Link: The College Magazine*: Race on Campus."

A Closer Look

Website:
Link: The College Magazine:
Race on Campus

Link: The College Magazine appears in both printed and web versions. The January/February 1998 issue includes "Race Divides," an article that focuses on affirmative action and race on college campuses. The article is a well-informed, fair overview of the debate over affirmative action. The print version includes pictures of students interviewed in the article and is more appealing visually than the web version (Howe 1998a). However, the web version has its own strengths and demonstrates the usefulness of the internet (Howe 1998b, http://www.linkmag.com). For example, the article discusses how the Civil Rights movement drew campus support for Martin Luther King's dream of racial justice. In the web version, rather than just noting the phrase "Martin Luther King Jr.'s dream," the reader can jump to the National Civil Rights Museum website and read King's "I Have a Dream" speech.

Howe argues that although Civil Rights movements "galvanized" student support for civil rights, today "the dream is dividing students instead of harmonizing them, as college communities across the country take sides in ideological warfare over who gets in" (1998a: 19). The article includes a useful abbreviated history of affirmative actions, from the *Plessy v. Ferguson* decision of 1896, which upheld "separate but equal" facilities, to the 1996 passage of California's Proposition 209, which banned state-sponsored affirmative action programs.

Proposition 209 has led Lisa Felipe, who would certainly get into the University of California on the basis of her grades and SAT scores, to decide not to apply to the school. Ms. Felipe feels that Proposition 209 demonstrates that she is not wanted in California public higher education. The article includes interviews with other students with various points of view.

Affirmative action may not have become an issue on your campus yet, but it probably will. Discussions of affirmative action in the press and by politicians often distort the issues involved. For a good start at understanding this complex issue, take a look at this website and follow some of the links it provides. You will receive an instant education on affirmative action and race on campus.

The most controversial of all affirmative action policies are seen as "quotas," that is, programs that reserve certain positions for qualified minority or female candidates. This approach is very unpopular among white Americans, many of whom refer to them as "reverse discrimination." In 1991, for example, more than half the whites in a survey sample opposed laws that would require businesses to hire black and other minority workers in the same proportion as these minorities are represented in the local community. Only 8 percent of the whites said that women and minorities should be given preferential treatment in hiring and college admission, whereas 84 percent said that only test scores should be used. In fact, reverse discrimination is more of a myth than a reality in the United States (Pincus 1994).

There is a widespread belief, especially among whites, that quotas are abundant across the country and that any minority male and almost any female can get a job because they are defined as minorities. White males are perceived to be at a disadvantage, no matter how qualified they are. Fred Pincus argues that government statistics show whites still have the employment advantage, even among the small select group of young college-educated minorities. In 1991, for example, the unemployment rate for 16- to 24-year-old whites with four years of college was 6.4 percent; the rate for comparable blacks was 11.3 percent, and for comparable Hispanics it was 9.2 percent (Pincus 1994).

In sharp contrast to institutional solutions, individual interventions frequently seek to change characteristics of the minority racial group rather than characteristics of American society. Initiated during the 1960s, for example, government programs such as Project Head Start and compensatory education under the Elementary and Secondary Education Act of 1965 sought to eliminate certain alleged educational deficiencies in black children, said to result from a long history of racial deprivation and bigotry. In particular, the gap between the learning achievements of black and white children was to be narrowed by intervening in the early socialization experiences of lower-class black children and by providing them with an educational head start prior to their entrance into the elementary grades.

Another set of interventions centers on interracial dialogue. The most visible example is One America in the Twenty-first Century: The President's Initiative on Race, announced by President Clinton on June 14, 1997. As one aspect of this year-long initiative, the president convened a seven-person Advisory Board. This board and President Clinton held meetings around the country to encourage dialogue on race relations and racial justice. The Advisory Board will also "study critical substantive areas in which racial disparities are significant, including education, economic opportunity, housing, health care and the administration of justice" to suggest concrete actions and policies (White House 1997).

In addition to President Clinton's dialogue on race, Americans across the country have been carrying on interracial dialogue. The Interracial Democracy Program of the Center for Living Democracy carried out a survey to find interracial dialogue groups and to identify the factors that made them successful. Authors of the survey report that in these cross-racial dialogues Americans are engaging in "serious talk—the kind of talk that addresses problems such as institutional racism, racial justice and how to improve race relations; the kind of talk that leads to cross-cultural collaboration in solving community problems" (Du Bois and Hutson 1997:8). Interracial dialogue in itself will not solve America's problems of racial inequality, but it may enable Americans to begin to work together to solve the problems.

You can find out more about these interventions and how you can participate in them to help solve America's racial problems. The Center for Living Democracy has compiled a directory of interracial dialogue groups across America (Interracial Democracy Program 1997). Similarly, the President's

❖ ❖ ❖ ❖

Initiative on Race web pages on the White House website include an extensive list of organizations that have developed promising practices for addressing issues of racial justice and inequality (White House 1997). These are
interventions in which all can participate.

The Future of Racial Inequality

Affirmative action measures and the Civil Rights movement have combined to produce a more sizable black middle class, whose members share
economically in the wealth of our society and serve as role models for upwardly mobile young African Americans. Affirmative action programs, in
general, are one way to deal with intentional discrimination, past and present, on institutional and individual levels. Unfortunately, attacks on affirmative action programs have put their continued viability in doubt. The President's Initiative on Race and the existence of numerous interracial dialogue
groups and grass roots organizations hold out some hope for achieving racial
justice and lessening racial inequality in America.

On the other hand, some recent trends seem to dim hopes for improvements in the immediate future. The types of "welfare reform" policies and the
rollback of affirmative action programs seem to be worsening the situation of
racial minority groups. This retreat has generated conflict among minority
groups. The future of racial inequality in the United States will depend in
large part on our willingness as a society to come to grips with diversity, with
the plight of the urban poor, and with persistent urban poverty.

Summary

Although people use the term *race* widely, it is confusing and ambiguous.
Many consider it as a biological category, but social scientists argue that race
is largely a social and cultural construct. Nevertheless, the consequences of
these social and cultural definitions have important impacts on the defined
groups. As a minority group, African Americans traditionally occupied a subordinate position in American society. From the 1600s, anti-black norms governed their enslavement in the South and their subordination in the North.
Today a focus on racial and ethnic inequality must take account of the rich
mosaic of groups that make up American society, including Hispanics, various groups of Asian Americans, and Native Americans. Incomes of black
Americans and other ethnic minorities continue to fall below those of their
white counterparts.

Explanations for racial inequality have been offered at individual, cultural, and structural levels. At the individual level, explanations often focus
on supposed genetically based differences in intelligence among groups.
These explanations are extremely unconvincing and are accepted by almost
no reputable social scientists. At the cultural level, the situation of race relations in the United States has been regarded as an American Dilemma—a basic inconsistency between values emphasizing democracy and at the same
time discrimination. Those who emphasize the cultural basis for race prejudice argue that it is learned, widely shared, and enduring. Other cultural approaches emphasize aspects of the cultures of minority groups that supposedly explain their lack of resources. Such approaches "blame the victim" for

social structural forces beyond their control. Cultural prejudice also includes norms governing the relationship between minority and majority members and a minority role.

Structural approaches focus on social structural forces, such as labor market structures, discrimination, and entrenched privilege and power, that foster racial inequality. In one well-known approach, Blauner suggests that racial inequality became institutionalized via intranational colonization, a process resembling the one experienced by the third-world peoples of Asia and Africa in their dealings with white Europeans. Other structural approaches also suggest that racial inequality in the United States has an important economic component.

There are numerous consequences of racial inequality. Racial inequality strongly affects the overall life changes of members of racially and ethnically defined groups. Their lives are shorter and their health is worse. Many consequences of racial inequality fall especially heavily on children.

Institutional interventions have typically sought to reduce discrimination and its effects. Affirmative action programs attempted to redress the effects of discrimination, but these policies are under attack. Many argue that the rollback of affirmative action programs and of welfare reform in the United States in the 1990s constitutes a "war on the poor." Some individual interventions have tried to change certain characteristics of the minority group, such as their educational deficiencies. Recent promising interventions include interracial dialogues that can stimulate serious discussion about racial inequality and lead people to learn more about the realities of racial injustice and how to alleviate it. The future of racial inequality will depend, in part, on the success or failure of such interventions.

Discussion Questions

1. You read about the census racial categories. Had you been aware of the controversy over these categories? What do you think about racial categories on the census? Would you favor a separate "multiracial" category? Why or why not?

2. Does discussing race or race-related issues make you uncomfortable? If so, why do you think that is so? Can you recall one or more incidents when you were a child that may help account for any anxieties you may feel?

3. Did you learn anything from this chapter that did not fit your preexisting attitudes, beliefs, or knowledge about racial inequality? What was it?

4. Do you favor or oppose affirmative action policies? Why?

5. Were you familiar with the President's Initiative on Race? How important do you think interracial dialogue is for reducing racial inequality?

References

Adorno, T. W., et al. 1950. *The Authoritarian Personality*. New York: Harper and Row.

American Civil Liberties Union. 1996. "ACLU Says Court Case Exposes America's Dirty Little Secret: The Criminal Justice System Is Racially Biased." In ACLU Press Releases. http://www.aclu.org/news/n022696c.html.

Andersen, Margaret, and Patricia Hill Collins, eds. 1995. *Race, Class and Gender: An Anthology*. Second edition. Belmont, California: Wadsworth.

Andersen, Ross E., et al. 1998. "Relationship of Physical Activity and Television Watching with Body Weight and Level of Fatness Among Children." *Journal of the American Medical Association* 279:938-42.

Anyon, Jean. 1997. *Ghetto Schooling: A Political Economy of Urban Educational Reform*. New York: Teachers College Press.

Blauner, Robert. 1972. *Racial Oppression in America*. New York: Harper and Row.

Bonacich, Edna. 1980. "Class Approaches to Ethnicity and Race." *Insurgent Sociologist* 10.

Brigham, Carl C. 1923. *A Study of American Intelligence*. Princeton: Princeton University Press.

Chandler, David L. 1997. "In Shift, Many Anthropologists See Race as Social Construct." *Boston Sunday Globe*, May 11, A30.

Cockburn, Alexander. 1995. *The Golden Age Is in Us*. New York: Verso.

Cohen, Mark Nathan. 1998. *Culture of Intolerance*. New Haven: Yale University Press.

Cox, Oliver C. 1959 [1948]. *Caste, Class, and Race: A Study in Social Dynamics*. New York: Monthly Review Press.

Davis, F. James. 1991. *Who Is Black? One Nation's Definition*. University Park: Pennsylvania State University Press.

del Pinal, Jorge, and Audrey Singer. 1997. *Generations of Diversity: Latinos in the United States*. PRB Population Bulletin. Washington, D.C.: Population Reference Bureau.

Delpit, Lisa. 1995. *Other People's Children: Cultural Conflict in the Classroom*. New York: New Press.

Doane, Ashley W. 1997. "White Identity and Race Relations in the 1990s." In *Perspectives on Current Social Problems*, edited by Gregg Lee Carter. Boston: Allyn and Bacon.

Donziger, Steven R., ed. 1996. *The Real War on Crime: The Report of the National Criminal Justice Commission*. New York: Harper Perennial.

Du Bois, Paul Martin, and Jonathan Hutson. 1997. *Bridging the Racial Divide: A Report on Interracial Dialogue in America*. Brattleboro, Vermont: Center for Living Democracy.

Feagin, Joe R., and Clairece Booher Feagin. 1996. *Racial and Ethnic Relations*. Fifth edition. New York: Simon and Schuster.

Feagin, Joe R., and Hernán Vera. 1995. *White Racism: The Basics*. New York: Routledge.

Ferrante, Joan, and Prince Brown, Jr. eds. 1998. *The Social Construction of Race and Ethnicity in the United States*. New York: Longman.

Fischer, Claude S., et al. 1996. *Inequality by Design: Cracking The Bell Curve Myth*. Berkeley: University of California Press.

Fraser, Steven, ed. 1995. *The Bell Curve Wars: Race, Intelligence, and the Future of America*. New York: Basic Books.

Frontline. 1998. "The Two Nations of Black America: Vital Signs." PBS, *Frontline Online* February. http://www.pbs.org/wgbh/pages/frontline/shows/race/economics/viyal.html.

Gutman, Herbert. 1976. *The Black Family in Slavery and Freedom, 1750-1925*. New York: Random House.

Herrnstein, Richard J., and Charles C. Murray. 1994. *The Bell Curve: Intelligence and Class Structure in American Life*. New York: Free Press.

Holmes, Steven A. 1997. "People Can Claim One or More Races on Federal Forms." *New York Times*, October 30, A1, A26.

Howe, Jeff. 1998a. "Link Special Report: Race on Campus: Race Divides." *Link: The College Magazine*, January-February, 18–25.

——. 1998b. "Link Special Report: Race on Campus: Race Divides." *Link: The College Magazine*, January-February. http://www.linkmag.com/Link/jan_feb_98/affrmactn. text.html.

Hunter, Herbert M., and Sameer Y. Abraham, eds. 1987. *Race, Class, and the World System: The Sociology of Oliver C. Cox*. New York: Monthly Review Press.

Interracial Democracy Program. 1997. *Interracial Dialogue Groups Across America: A Directory*. Brattleboro, Vermont: Center for Living Democracy.

Jacoby, Russell, and Naomi Glaubermann, eds. 1995. *The Bell Curve Debate: History, Documents, Opinions*. New York: Times Books.

Jennings, Francis. 1975. *The Invasion of America: Indians, Colonialism, and the Cant of Conquest*. New York: W. W. Norton.

Jensen, Arthur R. 1969. "How Much Can We Boost IQ and Scholastic Achievement?" *Harvard Educational Review* 39:1-123.

Kilborn, Peter T. 1998. "Nashville Clinic Offers Case Study of Chronic Gap in Black and White Health." *New York Times*, March 21, A6.

Levin, Jack, and William Levin. 1982. *The Functions of Prejudice and Discrimination*. New York: Harper and Row.

Levine, Lawrence W. 1996. *The Opening of the American Mind: Canons, Culture, and History*. Boston: Beacon Press.

Lewontin, Richard. 1995. *Human Diversity*. New York: Scientific American Library.

Lykes, M. Brinton, et al., eds. 1996. *Myths About the Powerless: Contesting Social Inequalities*. Philadelphia: Temple University Press.

Marger, Martin. 1997. *Race and Ethnic Relations: American and Global Perspectives*. Fourth edition. Belmont, California: Wadsworth.

McIntosh, Peggy. 1995. "White Privilege and Male Privilege: A Personal Account of Coming to See Correspondences Through Work in Women's Studies." Pp. 76–87 in *Race, Class, and Gender: An Anthology. Second Edition*, edited by Margaret L. Andersen and Patricia Hill Collins. Belmont, California: Wadsworth.

Merton, Robert K. 1949. "Discrimination and the American Creed." Pp. 99–126 in *Discrimination and National Welfare*, edited by R. H. MacIver. New York: Harper and Row.

Mickelson, Roslyn Arlin, and Stephen Samuel Smith. 1995. "Education and the Struggle Against Race, Class, and Gender Inequality." Pp. 289–304 in *Race, Class, and Gender: An Anthology*. Second edition, edited by Margaret L. Andersen and Patricia Hill Collins. Belmont, California: Wadsworth.

Minow, Martha. 1997. "Forget 'Multiracial' and Count Each Component." *Los Angeles Times, Commentary*, August 13.

Moynihan, Daniel P. 1965. *The Negro Family: The Case for National Action*. Washington, D.C.: U.S. Department of Labor.

Murray, Charles. 1984. *Losing Ground: American Social Policy, 1950–1980*. New York: Basic Books.

Myrdal, Gunnar. 1944. *An American Dilemma*. New York: Harper and Row.

Nunley, Michael. 1997. "The Bell Curve: Too Smooth to Be True." Pp. 161–68 in *Perspectives on Current Social Problems*, edited by Gregg Lee Carter. Boston: Allyn and Bacon.

Omi, Michael, and Howard Winant. 1994. *Racial Formation in the United States: From the 1960s to the 1990s*. New York: Routledge.

Pachon, Harry P. 1996. "Invisible Latinos: Excluded from Discussions of Inclusion." Pp. 184–90 in *The Affirmative Action Debate*, edited by George E. Curry. Reading, Massachusetts: Addison-Wesley.

Parker, Arthur Caswell. 1995[1916]. "Seven Stolen Rights." Pp. 241–43 in *Native Heritage: Personal Accounts by American Indians 1790 to the Present*, edited by Arlene Hirschfelder. New York: Macmillan.

Pincus, Fred L. 1994. "The Case for Affirmative Action." Pp. 368–82 in *Race and Ethnic Conflict*, edited by Fred L. Pincus and Howard J. Ehrlich. Boulder: Westview Press.

Robinson, A. J. 1998. "The Two Nations of Black America: An Analysis: Percentage of Blacks and Income Group 1970–1994." *Frontline Online* February. http://www.pbs.org/wgbh/pages/frontline/shows/race/economics/analysis.html.

Rollins, Bryant. 1997. "The Meaning of Race." *Boston Sunday Globe*, May 18.

Rosenblum, Karen, and Toni-Michelle Travis. 1996. *The Meaning of Difference*. New York: McGraw-Hill.

Ryan, William. 1971. *Blaming the Victim*. New York: Vintage Books.

Sidel, Ruth. 1994. *Battling Bias: The Struggle for Identity and Community on College Campuses*. New York: Viking Penguin.

Stack, Carol. 1974. *All Our Kin: Strategies for Survival in a Black Community*. New York: Harper and Row.

Steinberg, Stephen. 1995. *Turning Back: The Retreat from Racial Justice in American Thought and Policy*. Boston: Beacon Press.

Susser, Ida. 1982. *Norman Street: Poverty and Politics in an Urban Neighborhood*. New York: Oxford University Press.

Takaki, Ronald. 1993. *A Different Mirror: A History of Multicultural America*. New York: Oxford University Press.

Tatum, Beverly Daniel. 1992. "Talking About Race, Learning About Racism: An Application of Racial Identity Development Theory in the Classroom." *Harvard Educational Review* 62:1-24.

——. 1997. *"Why Are All the Black Kids Sitting Together in the Cafeteria?" And Other Conversations About Race*. New York: Basic Books.

Terry, Robert W. 1981. "The Negative Impact on White Values." Pp. 115–191 in *Impacts of Racism on White Americans*, edited by Benjamin P. Bowser and Raymond G. Hunt. Beverly Hills, California: Sage.

U.S. Bureau of the Census. 1995. *Population Profile of the United States: 1995*. Current Population Reports, Series P23, 189. Washington, D.C.: U.S. Government Printing Office.

Vobejda, Barbara. 1997. "New Forms to Reflect Multiracial U.S." *Boston Globe*, October 30, A3.

Weinick, Robin M., Margaret E. Wiegers, and Joel W. Cohen. 1998. "Children's Health Insurance, Access to Health Care, and Health Status: New Findings." *Health Affairs*, March/April.

Wellman, David. 1977. *Portraits of White Racism*. Cambridge, England: Cambridge University Press.

White House. 1997. "One America: The President's Initiative on Race: Overview." In One America: The President's Initiative on Race. http://www.whitehouse.gov/Initiatives/OneAmerica/overview.html.

Wiegers, M. E., R. M. Weinick, and J.W. Cohen. 1998. *Children's Health, 1996*. MEPS Chartbook No. 1. Rockville, Maryland: Agency for Health Care Policy and Research.

Wilson, William Julius. 1973. *Power, Racism, and Privilege*. New York: Free Press.

Winn, Peter. 1998. "A View from the South: Lands of Immigrants." Pp. 207–210 in *The Social Construction of Race and Ethnicity in the United States*, edited by Joan Ferrante and Prince Brown, Jr. New York: Longman.

Wirth, Louis. 1945. "The Problem of Minority Groups." In *The Science of Man in the World Crisis*, edited by Ralph Linton. New York: Columbia University Press.

Yemma, John. 1997. "Race Debate Simmers Over Who Is What." *Boston Sunday Globe*, May 11, A1, A30.

Websites

http://www.trinity.edu/~mkearl/race.html

Michael Kearl's *Sociological Tour Through Cyberspace*: Resources in Race and Ethnic Studies. As with so many other sociological topics, sociologist Michael Kearl's page on the Trinity University (San Antonio) website, provides an excellent starting point for information on race and ethnic studies. Kearl provides solid information and links to many additional sites.

http://www.whitehouse.gov/Initiatives/OneAmerica/america.html

One America in the Twentieth Century: The President's Initiative on Race. This website for President Clinton's Initiative on Race provides useful information on numerous aspects of racial and ethnic relations in the United States. The Promising Practices is especially interesting because it provides information on important organizations and groups around the country.

http://www.postfun.com/racetraitor/welcome.html

Race Traitor. The guiding principle of Race Traitor is that "treason to whiteness is loyalty to humanity." Race Traitor, which publishes a journal also named *Race Traitor*, emphasizes the social construction of the white race and the privileges that result from being white. This is a provocative website well worth looking at.

http://www.pbs.org/wgbh/pages/frontline/shows/race/main.html

The Two Nations of Black America. This is a website for the Public Broadcasting Service (PBS) Frontline special "The Two Nations of Black America." This site includes audio excerpts, economic and social data on African Americans, fascinating interviews, and links to related sites.

CHAPTER FOUR

Gender Inequality

In the News: Title IX and Women's Athletics

June 2, 1997 marked the 25th anniversary of Title IX. The National Women's Law Center celebrated that anniversary by filing sex discrimination complaints against 25 colleges and universities. Title IX was passed in 1972 to prohibit sex discrimination by schools, colleges, and universities that receive federal money. Title IX has contributed to gender equity in women's sports; however, the complaints filed, if supported, indicate that there is still a long way to go (Leonard 1997; Vogel 1997).

The National Women's Law Center's complaints focus on inequities in sports scholarships awarded to male and female athletes. The complaints, based on 1995 data, were filed with the Civil Rights office of the U.S. Department of Education. Marcia D. Greenberger, co-president of the center, suggested that the schools should "come into compliance with Title IX or lose the millions of taxpayer dollars they benefit from every year" (Vogel 1997).

Interviews with many female student-athletes indicated that they are not surprised at the charges. The athletes are generally aware of inequities and feel that their efforts are not valued as highly as those of men. Some of the athletes had not experienced overt discrimination but noted that their teams seemed to receive less support than men's teams, for example, in terms of transportation to games (MacQuarrie and Dowdy 1997).

In spite of continuing inequities, Title IX has clearly had a major impact on women's sports. In 1972, one in 27 girls played high school sports, but today one in three play. Today, 39 percent of all NCAA athletes are women. Scholarships for women athletes have gone from $100,000 in 1972 to $180 million in 1996. Two women's professional leagues have recently been formed, and Mary Leonard (1997) notes that "Women's professional teams are hot."

Some have responded to Title IX and the growth of women's sports by complaining that men are being forced out of college sports. In fact, Title IX has done little to harm men's collegiate sports. Others complain that colleges and universities will eventually cut scholarships for African American athletes to provide women's programs. Richard Lapchick, director of Northeastern University's Center for the Study of Sport in Society, calls this "a preposterous notion that shows both sexism and racism are alive and well in academia, just as in the corporate world" (Leonard 1997).

Deborah Brake, senior counsel of the National Women's Law Center, sees the current situation in women's athletics as very disappointing. "After 25 years, Title IX has made things better than they used to be but not as good as they should be." And Patricia Viverito, chair of the NCAA Committee, cautions that "before we break our arms patting ourselves on the back about Title IX, let's note that there are horrible injustices and great disparities in spending on women's collegiate sports" (Leonard 1997).

Definition and Prevalence

Male supremacy was probably the earliest form of discrimination against one group by the members of another. Throughout much of human history, gender inequality worked in favor of men, who enjoyed the privileges of membership in a superordinate group and against women, who played a subordinate role in the family, religion, politics, and at work. Psychologist Carol Tavris has shown how, in the social sciences, medicine, law, literature, art, and history, man has usually been the "measure of all things," and women have generally been found wanting. Tavris argues that "despite women's gains in many fields in the last twenty years, the fundamental belief in the normalcy of men, and the corresponding abnormality of women, has remained virtually untouched" (Tavris 1992:17).

Journalist Susan Faludi also acknowledges the changes in women's roles in recent years.

> To be a woman in America at the close of the 20th century—what good fortune. That's what we keep hearing anyway. The barricades have fallen, politicians assure us. Women have 'made it,' Madison Avenue cheers. Women's fight for equality 'has largely been won,' *Time* Magazine announces. (Faludi 1992:ix)

And yet Faludi suggests that something *is* wrong. At the same time that women are being told how lucky they are and how far they have come, another message is also being sent. According to this message, women "have never been more miserable" (1992: ix). The cause of this misery: feminism and equality. Examples of the misery included a shortage of men that endangered women's chances for marriage, a marked decline in women's economic status after divorce, and high levels of emotional depression and burnout affecting single women. Faludi points out that these, and other supposed indicators of women's misery—most of which were supported by sociological and psychological studies—were myths. They were aspects of a backlash against feminism and increasing gender equality that amounts to—as Faludi's apt subtitle suggests *The Undeclared War Against American Women* (Faludi 1992).

Women did not get the vote in the United States until 1920. Today women tend to vote in higher numbers than men.—*Photo:photostogo.com.*

An even more disturbing aspect of the backlash is the development during the past few years of what some sociologists and commentators call a culture of hate in the United States. This culture of hate lends legitimacy to bigotry and expressions of hatred. Much of that hatred has been directed against women. Examples include the comedian Andrew Dice Clay, who often insulted women in his stand-up comedy routine. Musical artists, such as Ice-T and NWA (Niggas With Attitude), have expressed violent anti-women themes in their music (Levin 1993).

According to Jack Levin, "the FBI is keeping track of a growing phenomenon that it calls 'hate crimes'" (Levin 1993: 20). Hate crimes are committed

❖ ❖ ❖ ❖   against individuals because they are members of specific groups, such as women. Many sociologists and psychologists suggest that children learn anti-female attitudes very early in life from parents, siblings, friends, teachers, children's books, and television. Some men hold women "responsible for eroding their economic position in society" (Levin 1993:20). Most men who have hate towards women express it vicariously, but some men resort to violence. Many serial killers—including Ted Bundy, the Son of Sam, and the Hillside Strangler—targeted women as their primary victims (Levin 1993).

Underlying patterns of gender inequality, discrimination, and—sometimes— hatred of women is a complex of negative beliefs and attitudes called **sexism**. On a psychological level such beliefs justify the maintenance of male supremacy by excluding women from resources available to men. Sexism emphasizes sexual differences; it suggests that such differences are innate and permanent and, as a result, women ought to be treated differently from men.

In analyzing gender inequality, sociologists distinguish between sex and gender. "Sex more often refers to the biologically determined sex characteristics of male and female; gender, to the culturally and socially defined elements of male and female role expectations" (Giele 1988:294). Those culturally and socially defined role expectations determine what is considered masculine and feminine in a particular society. These gender role expectations and the gender relations linked to them play such a central role in society that we can speak of institutions as "gendered" (Acker 1992).

Margaret Andersen (1997) argues that gender shapes the experiences of all people in the United States. People often use "pictures in their heads" or stereotypes for purposes of interaction. We have all been socialized to expect gender-specific behavior: passive girls and aggressive boys, for example. The reasoning developed in the use of sexist stereotypes is as follows: if women are "gentle" and "sensitive," then they should be assigned to jobs in which their talents can be fully expressed, such as human service occupations and child care. If men are "logical," "competitive," and "dominant," then they should be given preferential treatment in the areas of management, administration, and executive decision making, where their particular talents can best be utilized.

The continuing existence of gender inequality, discrimination, and sexism has generated a relatively permanent set of expectations for the behavior of men and women. These **gender roles** have had important consequences for the individuals in U.S. society who play them, for they have defined the behaviors that are "proper" and "right" for men and women. Gender roles, like all other roles, basically consist of a set of expectations for behavior. They contain prescriptions—what society says is important for the behavior of men and women as contained in its traditions, customs, and norms. Thus, women have traditionally been expected to stay in the home, take care of children, do housework, and be subservient to their husbands. Although most women no longer stay at home full-time, they are still generally responsible for housework and primary child care (Hochschild and Machung 1989; Landau 1994).

Margaret Andersen (1997) explains that categories of race, class, and gender overlap with one another. This overlap results in distinct experiences for members of different groups. Individuals may feel the salience of one or another category at a given time, but their life experiences are shaped by the confluence of all three. For example, black women experience oppression in many ways besides race (Collins 1986). They are simultaneously discriminated against for being black, for being female and, often, for being poor.

In a static society, role prescriptions are widely shared and enduring. If significant social change occurs, however, a good deal of ambiguity is introduced into a society's expectations for individuals. Under conditions of change, what the individual regards as appropriate for himself or herself may differ from the prescribed role that society regards as appropriate. As a result of the women's movement, for example, many women no longer regard the home as their primary domain of influence. Most American women are now in the labor force.

Of 105 million women 16 and older in the United States in 1997, 63 million (approximately 60 percent) were in the paid labor force, that is, working or looking for work (U.S. Department of Labor 1998). The proportion of working women in America has increased considerably since 1900, when they comprised only 18 percent of the labor force (U.S. Bureau of the Census 1996:405). By 1997, women made up 46 percent of the total labor force, and the Department of Labor projects that women will comprise 47 percent of the labor force by the year 2006 (U.S. Department of Labor 1998). This rapid growth in participation has centered almost entirely on white women, while the labor force participation of African American women has remained relatively stable.

Women's participation in paid work varies by age (see Table 4-1), race, ethnicity, marital status, the presence of children, and educational level (see Table 4-2). Women in their late thirties and early forties have the highest participation level, with over 77 percent in the labor force (Herz and Wooton 1996). The more education women have, the more likely they are to be in the labor force and the lower their unemployment rate. Most of the increase in women's labor force participation is due to the increasing number of married women working, with the percentage of married women in the labor force increasing from about 32 percent in 1960 to about 59 percent in 1995 (see Table 4-3) to over 60 percent in 1997.

Table 4-1 Labor Force Participation Rates for Women, by Age Groups, 1997 (percents)

Age Groups	Participation Rates
All women	59.8
16 to 19 years	51.0
20–24	72.7
25–34	76.0
35–44	77.7
45–54	76.0
55–64	50.9
65 and over	8.6

Source: U.S. Department of Labor. 1998. *20 Facts on Working Women*. Women's Bureau, Facts on Working Women No. 98-2, May. <http://www.dol.gov/ dol/wb/public/wb_pubs/ 20fact97.htm>.

Table 4-2 Employment Status of Women, age 25 and over, by Educational Attainment, 1997 (percents)

Educational Attainment	Participation Rate	Unemployent Rate
Less than high school diploma	30.7	9.6
High school graduates, no college	56.8	4.3
College graduates	75.5	2.2

Source: U.S. Department of Labor. 1998. *20 Facts on Working Women*. Women's Bureau, Facts on Working Women No. 98-2, May. <http://www.dol.gov/dol/wb/public/wb_pubs/20fact97.htm>.

Table 4-3 Labor Force Participation of Women by Marital Status: 1960–1995 (percents)

Marital Status	1960	1970	Year 1980	1990	1995
Single	58.6	56.8	64.4	66.7	66.8
Married	31.9	40.5	49.9	58.4	61.0
Total	37.7	43.3	51.5	57.5	58.9

Source: Adapted from U. S. Bureau of the Census. 1996. *Statistical Abstract of the United States, 1996*. Washington, D.C.: U.S. Government Printing Office Table 625, p. 399.

Table 4-4 Labor Force Participation Rates for Women, by Marital Status, March 1997 (percents)

Marital Status	Participation Rates
Divorced	74.5
Never married	66.8
Married, spouse absent	65.3
Married, spouse present	62.1
Widowed	18.2

Source: U.S. Department of Labor. 1997. *20 Facts on Working Women*. Women's Bureau, Facts About Women Workers, No. 98-2, May. >. (Based on unpublished Bureau of Labor Statistics data, March).<http://www.dol.gov/dol/wb/public/wb_pubs/20fact97.htm.

Despite the recent changes in women's work, most women still work in what have been considered "female occupations." The leading occupations of employed women in 1997 were secretaries and cashiers (see Table 4-5). In such traditional women's jobs, women make up the vast majority of workers (see Table 4-6), so that women continue to be overrepresented in secretarial and clerical jobs and underrepresented in higher-paying fields, such as law, accounting, medicine, or corporate management, although their numbers in such fields are growing (Reskin 1993). The **occupational segregation by sex** that produces such differences in the numbers of men and women in different occupations contributes to continuing disparities in men's and women's income.

Table 4-5 Leading Occupations of Employed Women, 1997 (Numbers in Thousands)

Occupation	Number Employed
Secretaries	2,989
Cashiers	2,356
Managers and administrators*	2,237
Registered nurses	1,930
Sales supervisors/proprietors	1,780
Nursing aides, orderlies, and attendants	1,676

*Not elsewhere classified.

Source: U.S. Department of Labor. 1998. *20 Facts on Working Women*. Women's Bureau, Facts About Women Workers, No. 98-2. <http://www.dol.gov/dol/wb/public/wb_pubs/20fact97.htm>.

Table 4-6 Women's Representation in Most Common Women's Jobs: 1995 (Percents)

Occupation	Percent in Occupation Who Are Women
Dental hygienist	99.4
Secretary	98.5
Dental assistant	98.5
Pre-kindergarten and kindergarten teachers	98.2
Dressmaker	98.2
Child-care provider	97.9
Child-care worker/private household	96.8
Receptionist	96.5
Early childhood teacher's assistant	95.8
Licensed practical nurse	95.4

Source: U.S. Department of Labor. 1996. *Employment and Earnings* Volume 43, Number 1 (January): 71-76.

A gender gap in income still exists in the United States, with women earning substantially less than men. Much of the wage gap is due to the segregation of men and women into different occupations. In 1960, women's earnings were 61 percent of men's earnings. Thus, for every $1.00 that a man earned, on average, a woman earned 61 cents. The wage gap decreased over the ensuing years until it reached 74 percent in 1994. Figure 4-1 depicts the wage gap since 1951. Recently, however, "after nearly two decades in which the wage gap between men and women was steadily narrowing, it is now widening again. . . " (Lewin 1997:A1). Lewin points out that economists and women's groups are puzzled by the change.

In looking at these overall trends, remember the "interlocking oppressions" such as class and race, in addition to gender. We noted earlier in the chapter that African American women are often simultaneously discriminated against on the basis of race *and* gender. This discrimination shows up in the occupational distribution of women of different races (see Table 4-7), and if we look more closely at the wage gap (see Table 4-8), you can see that African American and Hispanic women are underrepresented in managerial

Figure 4-1 Wage Gap Between Men and Women: 1951-1996

Percentage of Men's Earnings

Source: U.S. Bureau of the Census. *Current Population Survey,* Various years. (Annual earnings for full-time year-round workers, adjusted for inflation).

and professional jobs and this contributes to disparities in income. White women in 1996 earned 73.3 percent of a white male's wages, but African American and Hispanic women earned, respectively, only 65.1 percent and 56.6 percent of white male median annual earnings. Gender discrimination and gender inequality affect all women, but they do not affect all women equally.

Table 4-7 Occupational Distribution of Employed Women, by Race, 1996 (percents)

Occupation	Total	Asian and Pacific Islander	White	Black	Hispanic
Management & professional specialty	30.3	30.9	31.5	22.8	17.4
Technical, sales, & administrative support	41.4	37.8	41.9	38.4	38.4
Service	17.5	16.6	16.3	25.4	25.0
Precision, production, craft, & repair	2.1	3.3	2.0	2.2	2.9
Operators, fabricators, & laborers	7.6	11.1	6.9	11.0	11.1
Farming, forestry, & fishing	1.2	0.4	1.3	0.2	1.9

Source: U.S. Department of Labor. 1998. *Facts About Asian American and Pacific Islander Women*. Women's Bureau, Facts on Working Women, Number 98-03, June. <http://www.dol.gov/dol/wb/public/wb_pubs/asian97.htm>.

Table 4-8 The Wage Gap by Race and Gender: 1996

Median Annual Earnings for Year-Round, Full Time Workers, by Gender

Men	Women	Wage Gap
$32,144	$23,710	73.8%

Median Annual Earnings by Race and Gender

Race/Gender	Earnings	Wage Ratio
White Men	$32,966	100.0%
White Women	$24,160	73.3%
Black Men	$26,404	80.0%
Black Women	$21,473	65.1%
Hispanic Men	$21,056	63.9%
Hispanic Women	$18,665	56.6%

Source: U.S. Bureau of the Census. 1996. *Money Income in the United States*. Current Population Reports, Consumer Income, P60-197.

Gender inequality takes many forms in the United States. Not everyone agrees on what constitutes discrimination and many argue that men are discriminated against as much as women. Despite this, scientific research on gender roles and behavior consistently indicates that discrimination is levied disproportionately against women. As we noted above, although women's roles have changed and gender equality has increased, there often seems to be a "backlash" against the advances that have been made (Faludi 1992).

Levels of Causation

Individual

Individual explanations of gender differences commonly focus on biological differences between the sexes. For example, Freud traced the different personality structures of men and women to their different genitals and to cognitive and emotional processes that begin when children discover these physiological differences (Lengermann and Niebrugge-Brantley 1992). Alice Rossi (1977, 1984) has given serious attention to the biological foundations of gender-specific behavior. She has linked the different biological functions of males and females to different patterns of hormonally determined development over the life cycle and this, in turn, to sex-specific variation in such traits as sensitivity to light and sound and to differences in left and right brain connections.

Some view the division of labor by sex in human families as based on biological differences in the social dispositions of men and women. In this view, human family arrangements are an extension of family life among primates and other large mammals. Women are seen as naturally better suited to playing the nurturing, affective roles whereas men are seen as better suited to instrumental activities, especially those related to making a living. Some religious groups continue to embrace these ideas, but most social scientists consider them outdated and inaccurate.

Despite their having been largely discarded by scientists, biological explanations of gender differences are commonplace and popular. **Biological**

determinists argue that a given biological condition determines a particular event. For example, they believe that males are naturally more aggressive than females because they have greater amounts of the hormone testosterone. Generally speaking, the arguments of biological determinists do not account for the complexities in patterns of human aggression or for the wide variation in patterns of aggression among and between men and women (Andersen 1997). Biological arguments rest on the assumption that differences between the sexes are natural. Cultural attitudes, on the other hand, influence what we think of as "natural."

Cultural

The distinction between sex and gender is important. **Sex** is ascribed by biology: anatomy, hormones, and physiology. **Gender** is an achieved status: constructed through psychological, cultural, and social means. By about age five, gender certainly appears fixed, unvarying, and static—much like sex. This early age of gender designation lends support to the argument that masculinity and femininity are natural. In Western societies, the accepted cultural perspectives on gender view women and men as naturally defined categories of being. Competent adult members of these societies see differences between the two as fundamental and enduring. Things are the way they are by virtue of the fact that men are men and women are women—a division perceived to be natural and rooted in biology, producing in turn profound psychological, behavioral, and social consequences (Bonvillain 1995).

As children, human beings learn how to behave as girls and boys. We are given roles to play as males and females. From the moment children are born, they are labeled according to their sex. A boy baby is usually dressed in blue and a girl baby, in pink. These colors are important because parents want to ensure that others can identify their baby's gender. In Western societies, people are socialized to react to others on the basis of their sex. Boys are generally treated more aggressively than girls. Boys are generally expected to be rough, independent, competitive, confident, and intelligent, while girls are generally socialized to be passive, emotional, caring, and dependent. Society expects girls to cry but expects boys to hold back their tears. Gender is so much the routine ground of everyday activities that we assume it is bred into our genes. Everyone "does gender" without thinking about it. Most people find it difficult to see how gender is constructed because they take "masculinity" or "femininity" for granted and believe that gender is based on biology or human nature.

Although there have been changes in gender roles over the years, there are still significant traces of tradition. If males behave in ways that are seen to be part of the female role, they are called "sissies," "wimps," or "pansies." Society seems to be more accepting of females behaving in masculine ways if the behavior is not seen as too deviant. If females appear to be too masculine, they are labeled "tomboys" or "butch," and are often seen as undesirable (Freeman 1995).

People are so well conditioned to behave according to their sex that they believe gendered behavior to be natural and immutable. Often boys' aggressive behavior is explained away as natural because they are boys. Girls who play with dolls or play house are described as "natural mothers" because they are girls. Social scientists suggest that children are trained from the day they are born to behave in particular ways according to their sex. According to this view, we are socialized to behave in masculine and feminine ways, but these behaviors are not natural; they are socially constructed. Hillary Lips (1995) argues that children become well aware of "appropriate" gender roles at young ages. For example, when two researchers examined the creative writing of elementary-school children attending a "young authors conference" in Michigan, they made some striking discoveries with regard to gender roles and gender role socialization. Male characters outnumbered female ones in stories written by both boys and girls. The young writers credited male characters with more attributes—both positive, such as courage and determination, and negative, such as meanness and nastiness—than they did female characters. Of 127 occupations assigned by the young authors to their protagonists, 111 (87 percent) were assigned to males and only 16 (13 percent) to females. The occupational assignments clearly reflected the assumption that females' capabilities limited them to gender-stereotypic jobs: the few roles allotted to female characters included those of princess, cook, hula dancer, teacher, baby-sitter, nurse, and housekeeper (Lips 1995).

Lips suggests that children become aware of the message that males are active while females watch from the sidelines, that females are generally less interesting and less important than males are, and that females have narrower horizons and less impact on the world than do males. The often inadvertent bearers of this message include parents, peers, and teachers, with reinforcement from a variety of media sources and cultural institutions. These assumptions about males and females are so well ingrained in society that most people believe them to be inevitable.

Anthropologist Margaret Mead (1963 [1935]) demonstrated that gender behavior in Western society is socially constructed by producing cross-cultural evidence from three tribal groups in New Guinea. In two of these groups, Mead found very few differences between men and women in terms of psychological patterns or social behaviors. Among the Arapesh, both men and women displayed what might be thought of as essentially feminine traits: sensitivity, cooperation, and overall absence of aggression. In contrast, among the Mundugumor, both women and men typically were insensitive, uncooperative, and very aggressive, traits defined as essentially masculine in Western culture. The third group studied by Mead, the Tchambuli, had distinct differences between men and women. Here, the women were defined as the aggressive, rational, capable sex, and men as the emotional, flighty sex. Tchambuli women were socially dominant, assuming primary economic and political roles in the group. Men were socially passive, assuming artistic and leisure roles.

Cultural attitudes relating to gender roles can be damaging to both males and females. For example, Western society puts a lot of pressure on females to be thin. In other words, the thinner a female is, the more attractive she is perceived to be. Although the more muscular male is also perceived to be more attractive, the effects of such attitudes seem to be more detrimental for females in terms of achieving ideal body types. Ninety-five percent of people suffering from anorexia nervosa and bulimia in the United States are female. Hesse-Biber (1996) explores the pressure on women to become "ultrathin" and shows how adherence to the ideal of ultrathinness is linked to eating disorders. She goes beyond that, however, and argues that these pressures are the outcome of a capitalist/patriarchal system that seeks control over women's bodies.

Consider Barbie. Kamy Cunningham (1993) writes that Barbie is an un-
achievable body type in the United States but is also the ideal body type.
Barbie has a very large bosom, a tiny waist, flared hips, and lissome legs. She
is the perfect woman, and television commercials thrust her upon young
girls. Cunningham describes Barbie as the oppressive equation of beauty.
Barbie influences and reinforces cultural norms of beauty that most females
cannot even approximate. Barbie alone brings in about three-quarters of a
billion dollars a year for Mattel. Numerically, there are 2.5 Barbies for every
household in America (Cunningham 1993). The advertising industry is a
powerful educational force in America. The current emphasis on excessive
thinness for women is one of the clearest examples of advertising's power to
influence cultural standards. (See "A Closer Look: Feminist Resistance to
Advertising.")

The dominant culture provides direct and indirect prescriptions for gen-
der-appropriate behavior. The fact that gender is a social phenomenon means

---

A Closer Look

Feminist Resistance to Advertising

Jean Kilbourne (1994) argues that the $130 billion advertising industry is a pow-
erful educational force in America. The average American is exposed to over 1,500
ads every day and will spend a year and a half of his or her life watching television
commercials.

The current emphasis on excessive thinness for women is one of the clearest examples of advertising's power to influence cultural standards. Kilbourne states that
body types go in and out of fashion and are promoted by advertising. She argues
that the ideal body type today is unattainable by most women, even if they starve
themselves. Only the thinnest 5 percent of women in a normal weight distribution
approximate this ideal, which thus excludes 95 percent of American women.

More than half the adult women in the United States are currently dieting, and
over three-fourths of normal-weight American women think they are "too fat"
(Kilbourne 1994). The preoccupation with weight is beginning at ever-earlier ages
for women. J. C. Rosen and J. Gross (1987), in a study of 3,000 adolescents, found
that most of the boys were trying to gain weight but that at any given time, two-
thirds of girls aged 13 to 18 were trying to lose weight. Boys are encouraged to be
bigger and stronger, whereas girls are supposed to be thin and fragile.

Much feminist criticism is directed against advertising's oppressive content, understood as false or inaccurate portrayals of women. Advertising generates many
ideas about women. It gives us clear messages regarding appropriate roles for
women and men. In computer trade magazines, for example, women are
overrepresented as clerical workers and sex objects, while men are overrepresented
as managers, experts, and repair technicians. In most magazines and on television,
women are portrayed as requiring help to slow the aging process. There are hundreds of moisturizers, said to defy the aging process; most, if not all, of the products
are for women. The assumption is that males age in distinguished ways, whereas
women do not. Overall, the demeanor of women in advertising—in the background, on the ground, or looking dreamily into space—makes them appear subordinate and available to men (Andersen 1997).

Advertising conveys images of women that may influence our thinking about
gender in society. These images convey powerful messages about women's roles,
their sexual and gender identities, and their self-concepts. Images of women con-
veyed by the dominant culture are often based on distortions and stereotypes that
legitimate the status quo at the same time that they falsely represent the actual experiences of women in society (Andersen 1997).

that it is learned. We learn at very young ages what it means to be male and fe-male. Gender roles are learned through the process of socialization. Boys and girls are treated differently from infancy. One study by Jeffrey Rubin, Frank Provenzano, and C. T. Hull (1974) documented how gender expectations be-come part of our experience. In this study, first-time parents were asked to describe their babies only 24 hours after the baby's birth. Parents of girls re-ported their babies to be softer, smaller, and less attentive than did parents of boys. Fathers, more than the mothers, described their sons as larger, better coordinated, more alert, and stronger than girls. Also more than the mothers, fathers described their daughters as delicate, weak, and inattentive. Research continues to show that parents treat their infants differently, according to the infant's sex.

Structural

Cultural explanations of gender inequality emphasize the social and eco-nomic position of women in relation to the values shared by the members of a particular society. Structural explanations stress that gender is systemati-cally structured in all social institutions, meaning that it is deeply embedded in the social structure of society. In fact, gender inequality is created within the structure of major social institutions (Andersen 1997). Structural, or in-stitutional explanations, then, focus on the impact of social institutions—such as the family, the mass media, and the economy—on gender and gender inequality.

To make structural explanations of gender inequality clearer, think back to Hesse-Biber's research on the "cult of thinness." She notes that many early theories of eating disorders were based on individual psychology. Newer ap-proaches often examine family dynamics leading to eating disorders. These approaches locate the source of eating disorders within the individual or the family, so they locate solutions for eating disorders. Hesse-Biber notes that "this approach often amounts to 'blaming the victim'" (Hesse-Biber 1996:15). Although not denying that psychological factors play a role in eating disor-ders, Hesse-Biber suggests looking at broader social and economic forces to help understand the cult of thinness and eating disorders.

Hesse-Biber adopts a conflict perspective which looks at how capitalism and patriarchy contribute to the cult of thinness. Rather than asking how women can meet the body ideal promoted in American society, she asks a dif-ferent set of questions: "Who benefits from women's excessive concern with thinness?" and "How is this obsession created, promoted, and perpetuated?" (1996: 32), she also focuses on how the "cosmetic, beauty, diet and health in-dustries, and the mass media benefit from promoting women's body insecu-rity" (1996:119).

Many sociologists emphasize the **division of labor** in the family when discussing gender inequality. Where the husband is the sole or major source of income—which is still the case in many families—equality between hus-band and wife is difficult to maintain. This may be especially true in the rela-tively few families where the husband works full-time and the wife stays home full-time. Decisions affecting family members revolve around the role of breadwinner; the family takes up residence where the man finds work, and the life of the family revolves around the husband. Many in society may argue that this is not so true today, that families are not as traditional concerning gender roles. Some conservatives claim that males are taking more responsibility for their families while emphasizing equality or teamwork between couples. (See "A Closer Look: Promise Keepers or Equality Stealers?")

A Closer Look

Promise Keepers or Equality Stealers?

Since 1990, thousands of men have joined a male-only Christian movement known as Promise Keepers. The Promise Keepers portray themselves as a religious organization dedicated to assisting men to become better husbands and fathers. However, many suggest that their goals include reasserting the privileges of male leadership in and out of the home. The Promise Keepers seek to undermine separation of church and state and they object to abortion, homosexuality, divorce, adultery, and lack of religious faith.

The National Organization for Women (NOW) argues that the Promise Keepers seek to better the position of men at the expense of women. According to NOW, under the guise of Christian piety and devotion to family, the Promise Keepers are engaging in a holy war on the gains made for women's equality (National Organization for Women 1998). Now further argues that the Promise Keepers seek to convince women that they need to be dependent on men and there is no room for the concept of equality between the sexes. Many of the Promise Keepers beliefs are based on rigid gender roles as they exist in the Bible.

Ron Stodghill (1997) states that the Promise Keepers number about 1.1 million. The seven-year old organization boasts annual revenues of $87 million and has 360 paid staff members. Promise Keepers declares that it has no political agenda, despite the fact that it appears to be a sophisticated right-wing political movement with numerous allies on the religious right. For example, Pat Robertson, head of the Christian Coalition, has long been a Promise Keeper supporter. NOW is concerned with not just the promises evoked by this organization but also with what the Promise Keepers fail to say. The group's mission is vague concerning its relationships with women (Stodghill 1997). It calls for men to take "spiritual leadership" over their wives and suggests that women follow. Feminists argue that this is a throwback to the days of women's servitude and oppression (Stodghill 1997). The Promise Keepers wish to retake male responsibility and reestablish male leadership. NOW has described the Promise Keepers as the greatest danger to women's rights.

Women face obstacles in the labor market as well as in the family. First, many married women who hold a job are generally expected to perform the duties of a housewife as well. Arlie Hochschild and Anne Machung (1989) refer to this as "the second shift." Relatively few married men share equally in the household and child-raising chores. According to Hochschild and Machung, woman's second shift is equal to an extra month of twenty-four-hour days every year. Overall, research studies have found the following:

1. Over the last two decades, all women have reduced their time in housework. Employed wives have reduced their time in household work more than unemployed wives, but neither group has reduced it by much.

2. Husbands have not picked up the slack, and husbands of both employed and unemployed women do considerably less housework than their wives.

3. Employed women more often purchase household services than rely on additional assistance from family members. Yet only between 14 and 20 percent of working wives obtained paid housekeeping help on a regular basis. Employed women are no more likely than nonemployed women to have cleaning help. It is a matter of who can afford it.

4. Husbands of employed wives have increased the social time they spend with their children, especially when the children are of preschool age, but not time spent in physical care. Both parents do almost equal amounts of educating and socializing of children, but wives do much more of the day-to-day physical care.

Sharon Harlan and Catherine Berheide (1994) argue that invisible barriers limit women's progress toward employment equity. These barriers extend all the way from the **glass ceiling** at the top of the nation's largest corporations to the "sticky floor" of low-paying, low-mobility jobs at the bottom of the labor market. These barriers are created by a process of exclusionary practices that successively eliminate women. Barriers exist in the structure of work organizations, in the structure of the educational and economic systems, and in the larger social order. Harlan and Berheide focus on five areas presenting formidable structural barriers to women:

1. *Educational systems* that use gender, race, and class to ration access to first-rate education restrict future job opportunities for many women from lower- or working-class backgrounds.

2. *Occupational segregation* results in the overrepresentation of women and minorities in the lowest-paying jobs. Nearly 70 percent of the full-time female labor force works in low-paying occupational categories. Women of color work in jobs in the secondary labor market that are race-and-gender specific segments of the secondary labor market.

3. *Wage differentials by gender and race* are the result of channeling women and minorities into less complex jobs, as well as paying less for female-dominated and minority-designated jobs than the job's characteristics would call for.

4. *The class position* of low-paying jobs in the capitalist labor market is a structural barrier to job advancement. Class-based economic power relationships are closely associated with the sexual and racial division of labor.

5. *The growth of the contingent work force* is creating more part-time and temporary jobs, in which women are overrepresented.

Many women work in low-paying jobs in the informal and secondary sectors of the economy, where opportunities are lacking. The informal sector refers to nonmarket work, which is often not reported to the government for taxes, while jobs in the secondary sector, or labor market, tend to be low-paying, require little skill, have low prestige, have high turnover rates, and offer little opportunity for advancement. The majority of the women employed in the largest and most stable U.S. companies work in clerical, blue-collar, service, and sales jobs at the lower levels of organizational hierarchies. Women in these types of jobs have few opportunities for promotion, and they face many structural and cultural barriers that keep them from earning more money (Harlan and Berheide 1994).

Harlan and Berheide also argue that organizations mirror society's ideas about which groups of workers are appropriate for different kinds of jobs. Hiring and promotion decisions often express informal social expectations about the gender, race, and class of the people best suited for particular positions. Gender and race can often pinpoint one's place in an organizational hierarchy. Individuals who occupy the top positions in a hierarchy have a stake in maintaining traditional rules, which work to their advantage. Social norms, cultural stereotypes, and power and privilege in organizations provide the "invisible foundation" for organizational decisions about which jobs and how much opportunity are suitable for certain types of workers. These decisions determine the ways that complex organizations structure work, creating barriers for women and keeping them from advancing in organizational pipelines (See "A Closer Look: Women in Combat.")

Consequences

Another obstacle facing women can be found in educational institutions, which fail to prepare women for traditionally male-dominated occupations. Tracking in schools places a disproportionately large number of girls into typing and home economics, while the boys are channeled into shop and drafting. Moreover, girls are socialized to believe that they lack the talent for careers in "masculine" fields such as science and mathematics. Mary Fox (1995) states that feminists have always believed that higher education for women would bring widespread political, legal, and economic reform. Women's educational attainment is related to their participation and role in the economy since the more education a woman has, the more likely she is to be employed. Fox argues that men use their educational credentials for initial entry to jobs, then rely on job-related "experience" for advancement. For women, however, formal education remains critical throughout their working lives. Women receive less returns on their education than men do. That is, each additional year of education gives women less additional income than it does for men. Without superlative credentials women often suffer even greater inequality.

Title IX has made some difference for women in terms of enrollment in higher education, but it has had limited effect on the segregation of male and female students into different areas of study. According to Fox (1995), women continue to be restricted, especially in their technical and scientific training, which has profound consequences for their occupational choices. Because they have been diverted from higher-level mathematics courses, many women lack the critical skills necessary for education in the 75 percent of all university majors (business, medicine, science, engineering, and architecture programs) that lead to higher paying jobs.

Employers and co-workers who treat women as sex objects represent another important obstacle. Sexual harassment affects millions of women in the United States. In fact, some feminists claim that every woman has been sexually harassed at least once in her life. Cheryl Bernard and Edit Schlaffer (1997) state that sexual harassment is so normal in the United States that we expect it. For example, on public streets, women "plan our routes and our timing as if we are passing through a mine field" (p. 395). Males often touch,

A Closer Look

Women in Combat

Whether women should be expected to go into combat is hotly debated. Hart (1991) states there is a wide range of arguments on both sides of the issue. Some are based on logic, reality, and facts. Others are emotional, based on cultural and/or traditional beliefs and attitudes. One important point Hart makes is that there has been little in U.S. history textbooks about how women have fought to defend their homes, causes, and countries over the years.

Women have always participated in combat throughout the world. During the classical period, women challenged the Roman warriors in Ireland, Germany, Britain, and the Iberian peninsula. During the medieval period, women were soldiers and commanders of entire armies. Women such as Joan of Arc, Isabella of Spain, and Mary of Hungary are legendary. The British army honored a surgeon for his service from 1815–1865. His exceptional medical skills and frequent fist fights contributed to the illusion of his manhood. When Dr. James Barry died, it was discovered that "he" was a woman and that she had had at least one child (Hart 1991).

There has been much controversy over the issue of women in combat. However, historically women have participated in combat throughout the world. —*Photo courtesy of Sandra L. Bonchin.*

Female military nurses have always been in combat. When the conflict started in Korea, within four days after the first U.S. troops landed, 57 nurses arrived at Pusan to help set up the hospital. During the Vietnam War, nurses worked day and night, with shelling all around them. Besides nurses, other female military personnel have been in combat. For example, the U.S. Army sent 200 women on the 1983 Grenada operation. They went in as part of the air crews, and some of the planes returned with shrapnel holes. On December 20, 1989, Operation Just Cause commenced in Panama. Some 600 women participated in the invasion of the country and the capture of General Manuel Noriega. They found themselves dodging bullets and returning fire (Hart 1991).

Despite past contributions, the debate continues about women in combat. Those who oppose women serving on the front lines argue that women do not have the physical strength or endurance to be in combat; that pregnancy interferes with combat; that masculinity is challenged; that women will be sexually harassed; that men would be reluctant to fight if women were present because they would be more concerned with protecting the women.

There are counterarguments to all these points. First, Hart argues that the question is not how strong women are but how strong they need to be. In addition, we need to acknowledge that not all men are physically capable of some strenuous combat assignments whereas many women are. Second, people in combat jobs do not spend most of their time in combat. Third, having women in combat does challenge masculinity, but so what? Infringing on a traditional male role may be a good thing. Male soldiers place far too much pressure on themselves to be "macho." Having men and women as comrades may change levels of sexism in the military and perhaps in society at large. Finally, women have proved to be aggressive fighters in the past and the present; therefore, men need not be concerned about protecting them. In addition, male soldiers have always been concerned about protecting other male comrades. The feeling of allegiance should not be greater for female soldiers.

Hart contends that the debate over participation of women in combat is clouded by emotional appeals on both sides. The issues extend into societal norms, values, and attitudes and not just the "objective" evidence. Opinion polls show that the majority of Americans are in favor of women in combat.

harass, and comment on women walking along the streets. Public opinion claims women like it—are flattered by it. Advertising agencies actually use this belief to sell their products. The message, according to Bernard and Schlaffer, is that men own the public sphere and women happen to be walking in it. Harassment is a way to ensure that women will not feel at ease, that they will remember their role as sexual beings, available to men.

The legal system has drastically failed women who are victims of violence or are defendants in the U. S. criminal justice system. One out of every two women in the United States will experience violence in a relationship (National Organization for Women 1998). The criminal justice system responds inconsistently to battered women. Male abusers often receive minimal punishment for battering their female partners. Female rape victims are also often treated poorly by the criminal justice system. Rape, battering, and murdering of women are termed forms of femicide by many feminists. Feminists have consistently argued that rape is a direct expression of sexual politics rather than a crime of frustrated attraction or uncontrollable biological urges (Caputi and Russell 1990). Murder is described as the ultimate form of sexist terrorism. The fact that femicide is most likely to be perpetrated by a male demonstrates well the seriousness of sexism in the United States. Ironically, most women are raped, assaulted, or murdered by males they know. The criminal justice system, the public, politicians, and the media fail to protect women from dangerous males.

Gender inequality exists in almost every society. Females are victimized in many ways including sexual harassment, unequal pay, unequal opportunities for success, and violence. Scholars have found many ways in which gender inequality has been justified. According to Richard Edwards, Michael Reich, and Thomas Weisskopf (1986), the development of capitalism as an economic system was influenced, at least in part, by the need to preserve gender inequality. To maintain their dominant position in the family, men discriminated against women in the labor market. As a result, women played a marginal and vulnerable position in the labor force—they were, for example, widely employed in factories beginning with the Industrial Revolution. "Sexism in this way assisted capitalism" (p. 325).

Capitalism also reinforced gender inequality in other ways. The transfer of production and distribution of goods and services from the home to factories reduced the incidence of men and women working together as a productive unit and increased the tendency for men to work separately from women. In this way, women were excluded from areas of production and became even more dependent economically upon men. The capitalist system needed women to stay at home, out of the public sphere. A woman could make sure that everything was taken care of for her male partner, such as laundry, meals, housework, and child care. These responsibilities created leisure time for males and ensured they would be well rested when returning to work. Women produced laborers for capitalism by assuming these responsibilities and by giving birth. By creating this sexual division of labor, capitalism effectively convinced males and females that these roles were "natural" and further created a gendered hierarchy in society, with males in the dominant position. Women's labor in the home was considered of value only in the sense that it profited capitalism. This labor remains unpaid and therefore women who do it do not have equal access to valued resources created and controlled by capitalism.

Interventions

❖ ❖ ❖ ❖

The history of the women's movement in American society predates the Civil War. As early as the 1820s, many women joined the movement to abolish slavery, thereby gaining their first political experience. The Abolitionist movement was the most important direct cause of the growth of the women's movement in the 1830s and 1840s (Deckard 1979).

In 1840, women delegates to the World Anti-Slavery Convention in London were not permitted to take seats on the floor and were instead forced to sit in the gallery. Subsequent discussion of their unequal treatment led these women to finally establish the Women's Rights caucus at Seneca Falls, New York, in 1848. Under the leadership of Susan B. Anthony and Elizabeth Cady Stanton, they discussed various forms of discrimination against women and pledged to use every means at their disposal to end inequality. After lengthy debate, a majority of women finally passed a suffrage resolution—they demanded that women be given the vote.

The Women's Suffrage movement began with the Seneca Falls Convention and ended after more than seven decades of struggle and militancy with the passage of the Nineteenth Amendment to the Constitution in 1920. The spread of sentiment in favor of suffrage could be seen in the explosive growth of membership in the National American Woman Suffrage Association—from 13,000 in 1893 to more than 2 million by 1917 (Deckard 1979).

The hard-won legal changes achieved by women's suffrage did not automatically produce altered attitudes. For some time after the passage of the Nineteenth Amendment, women voted in smaller numbers than men, and a women's bloc vote failed to materialize. In fact, for the women's movement, the period between 1920 and 1960 has been characterized as "forty years in the desert" (Deckard 1979:301).

A resurgence of interest in gender inequality occurred during the 1960s, as the gap between social ideology and social reality widened. The ideology depicted the typical American woman as a happy, contented, and fulfilled housewife. But the reality was that more and more women needed to work in order to support or supplement their family's income, though they continued to be discriminated against with respect to jobs, promotions, and equal pay. What is more, many women who were well educated and could economically afford the luxury of being housewives were dissatisfied with their role. Also during the early and middle 1960s, many young women became more familiar with the organization and rhetoric of protest as

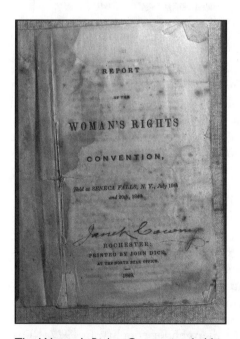

The Women's Rights Convention held in Seneca Falls, New York, in 1848 marked the beginning of the Feminist Movement in the United States. —*Photo: From the archives of the Seneca Falls Historical Society.*

a result of their involvement in the Civil-Rights movement and in anti-war struggles on college campuses. Women in these movements gained increased awareness of their own oppression.

Several interventions with important consequences for gender equality occurred during the 1960s and 1970s. A federal law whose provisions had a profound effect on gender equality was the Equal Pay Act of 1963. This law legally prohibited differential rates of pay for women and men who do equal work, except in certain cases where sex was considered to be a bona fide occupational qualification for the job in question. Title VII of the 1964 Civil Rights Act also had a bearing on gender inequality. This act prohibited an employer from discriminating in hiring conditions and the benefits of work on the basis of

Madeline Albright became the first woman secretary of state during the Clinton administration. However, women are still dramatically underrepresented in positions of political power in the United States.—*Photo courtesy of the U.S. State Department.*

race, color, religion, sex, or national origin. Educational institutions and government employers were exempted. This has since changed. Both acts have met with limited success because of occupational segregation by sex, which leads women and men to be in different occupations.

The Equal Pay Act also created the Equal Employment Opportunity Commission (EEOC), whose powers were limited primarily to the investigation and conciliation of complaints. The Equal Employment Opportunity Act of 1972 expanded the enforcement powers of the EEOC, enabling it to sue an employer in federal court when its conciliation efforts failed, and extended coverage of the act to prohibit government agencies and educational institutions from receiving federal funds if guilty of discrimination based on sex. Also in 1972, the Equal Pay Act was extended to cover discrimination by sex in executive, professional, and administrative jobs.

In 1966, the National Organization for Women (NOW) was formed in response to gender discrimination generally and in particular to the failure of the EEOC to outlaw sex-segregated want ads. With a charter membership of only 300, and with Betty Friedan at its head, NOW stated its central purpose as follows: "To take action to bring women into full participation in the mainstream of American society *now*, exercising all the privileges and responsibilities thereof in truly equal partnership with men" (NOW Statement of Purpose, Organizational Conference, October 29, 1966).

During its early years, NOW set up task forces, filed suit on gender issues, and lobbied government officials to further gender equality. In 1977, NOW adopted the ratification of the Equal Rights Amendment (ERA) as its top priority and fought to get it passed. Written in 1921 by Alice Paul, an important feminist activist, the ERA was first introduced into Congress in 1923 and was finally passed in March 1972. The U.S. Congress overwhelmingly approved

the ERA and by the end of 1973, thirty states had ratified the ERA; it received
widespread public approval as well as the support of such organizations as
the AFL-CIO, the American Bar Association, the NAACP, the League of
Women Voters, and the Common Cause. A few months later, however, there
was already a substantial slowdown in the forward thrust of the ERA. Only
three more states ratified it in 1974; one in 1975; and one more in 1977. Upon
ratification by thirty-eight states, the ERA would have become the twenty-
seventh amendment to the Constitution. Despite the intense lobbying efforts
of the women's movement and a three-year extension by Congress in 1979,
only thirty-five states ratified the amendment and so, in 1982, the ERA failed.

In spite of the ERA having failed ratification over 15 years ago, the authors think it is important to understand the amendment. It has both historical and contemporary significance. What would the ERA have done? Section
1 of the ERA—the substance of the amendment—states that "Equality of
Rights under the law shall not be denied or abridged by the United States or
any state on account of sex." This simple amendment would have rendered
unconstitutional all laws and practices that treat men and women unequally—even those laws designed to "protect" women from physical injury.
Many analysts argued that not only would this have eliminated inequities in
property law, jury service, public education, public employment, job-training
programs, and the armed services, but that ERA would also have invalidated
"advantages" granted to women by law, regulation, and custom. For example,
women would have lost their right to preferential treatment in divorce actions, in the allocation of longer rest periods on the job relative to men, and in
nonparticipation in military service. Symbolically, ratification of the ERA
would have suggested dramatically that U. S. society had moved a substantial
distance towards gender equality since the early decades of the century when
women's suffrage was a central issue.

In spite of the failure of the ERA, efforts to secure protection for women's
rights under the U.S. Constitution continue. NOW has drafted the Constitutional Equality Amendment. This chapter has documented continuing gender inequality and discrimination against women. Discrimination against
women exists in employment and wages; in reproductive rights; in insurance,
pensions, and social security; in lesbian and gay rights; and in education.
NOW and other commentators and analysts suggest that unless laws against
sex-based discrimination have a constitutional foundation, they will remain
ephemeral and can be weakened or repealed (National Organization for
Women 1998).

Among the most important provisions of the draft Constitutional Equality Amendment are those dealing with equal rights and privileges. For example, Section 1 proposes that "women and men shall have equal rights
throughout the United States and every place and entity subject to its jurisdiction; through this article, the subordination of women to men is abolished." Section 2 proposes that "all persons should have equal rights and privileges without discrimination on account of sex, race, sexual orientation,
marital status, ethnicity, national origin, color or indigence." Section 3 prohibits pregnancy discrimination and gives a woman the right to make her
own reproductive decisions (National Organization for Women 1998). Note
that this proposed amendment goes beyond ensuring the rights of women, or
sex-based rights; it aims to promote equality in a broad sense. For more information on many of these topics, see "A Closer Look: The Feminist Majority
Website."

A Closer Look

The Feminist Majority Website

Male and female students will find much useful information on this exciting new website. *The Feminist Majority Foundation Online* is located at http://www.feminist.org/. When you log on to this site, you are presented with news items for the day, highlights of the news, and a calendar of upcoming events. You also see a variety of options to choose. You can click on the *Feminist Research Center* or *Global Feminism*. Each choice gives you additional options. Additional options deal with domestic violence, sex discrimination, and information on breast cancer. Each month the site highlights different issues.

Try clicking on *The Feminist Internet Gateway*, which is a listing of links to other sites that provide feminist information. When you get to the *Feminist Internet Gateway*, you see about 14 choices. Click on *911 for Women* and you will gain access to resources such as domestic violence hotlines and job postings for progressive organizations. You can link to government research and reference sites and to internet search tools, so you can carry out your own searches on the web.

Another option is "Women & Girls in Sports." As the introduction notes, the sites tend to focus on collegiate athletics. At the end of the introduction, you will see the "Mediated List of Internet Resources." Clicking on that list gives you access to numerous websites. One site, *Title IX*, provides the actual language of Title IX. Another site, *Gender Equity in Sports*, is based at the University of Iowa and provides a comprehensive examination of Title IX. This is an especially rich site. You may want to look at it in conjunction with the *In the News* section. You will find lots of additional information on the *Feminist Majority Foundation* site and sites linked to it. Try exploring it for a while.

Presently there exists a Women's Human Rights movement in the United States and across the world. This movement evolved from women organizing on local, national, regional, and international levels around issues that affect their daily lives (Peters and Wolper 1995). Within this movement, women's rights activists attempt to use the human rights framework to promote the achievement of women's rights in the interrelated areas of political, civil, economic, social, and cultural action.

Charlotte Bunch (1990) argues that few governments are committed, in domestic or foreign policy, to women's equality as a basic human right. She further argues that women's human rights are violated in a number of ways, most of which are specifically gender based. The United Nations Universal Declaration of Human Rights, adopted in 1948, defines human rights broadly and symbolizes a world vision of respect for the humanity of all people. Although not much is said about women, Article 2 does entitle all to the rights and freedoms set forth in the declaration. When read from the perspective of women's lives, many violations of women's rights such as rape and battering can readily be interpreted as forbidden under existing clauses such as "No one shall be subject to torture or to cruel, inhuman or degrading treatment or punishment" (Peters and Wolper 1995).

One major issue that women's rights advocates have used to demonstrate how human rights law has excluded women is violence against women. Violence against women lends credence to the claim that changes are needed in human rights law in order to make it truly inclusive of women's experiences. Violations of women's rights are often perpetrated by "private agents"—members of women's communities, from family members such as husbands, to co-workers—and not governments, which are generally targeted by

human rights law. However, advocates for women's rights have made a clear
case that governments, while not directly responsible for private-agent
abuse, can be seen as condoning it—through inadequate prosecutions of
abuse against women, sexual harassment, and rape, for example—and thus
should be held accountable (Peters and Wolper 1995).

The Future of Gender Inequality

Despite the growing presence of women in the labor force, gender inequality will continue to influence the relationship of women to work. Present income figures give little comfort to those who expect further narrowing
of the gap between incomes of men and those of women. Women's earnings
as a proportion of men's are increasing slowly if at all.

In the short term, almost anything can happen. For example, a period of
deep economic recession might temporarily reverse the numbers of women
entering the labor force and higher education; a strong conservative backlash
might reduce support for child-care services and generally increase resistance to further change in gender roles. It is even conceivable that there will
be a reversal in present trends, where the members of society express a preference for sharper differences between the sexes, at least in certain areas of life.

In light of current long-term trends, however, we might reasonably expect even greater blurring of the traditional distinctions between men and
women at home, on the job, and at play. This would mean a more favorable
portrayal of women in children's readers and mass media coverage; larger
numbers of women entering traditionally male occupations; more girls and
women in competitive sports; a further erosion of the double standard by sex
for pre- and extramarital sexual relationships; greater numbers of women at
the upper levels of education, politics, government service, and technical/
professional careers; a convergence of athletic records for men and women;
and larger numbers of women in the armed services.

Assuming that present trends continue, there is likely to be a growing impact of women's work during the decades to come. The participation of
women in the labor force should continue to increase at a very high rate. For
women with young children, much of this movement into the labor force will
be into part-time jobs, as they continue to adjust their work schedules to ac-
commodate family responsibilities. To an increasing extent then, women will
come to regard work as part of the normal course of events in their lives.

Summary

Gender inequality is maintained by a pervasive set of sexual stereotypes
and gender roles, which are employed to justify discrimination against
women and to assign appropriate behavior based on sex. Women continue to
be found in the subordinate positions of the occupational hierarchy. Their
salaries are low relative to those of their male counterparts, and they constitute a major portion of all part-time employees.

From a cultural perspective, gender inequality stems from the value orientations associated with the female sex role. From the institutional point of
view, gender inequality is perpetuated by a family structure that places more

value on males and provides them with more social, economic, and political power.

The history of the Women's movement in American society predates the Civil War. The Women's Suffrage movement ended in 1920 with the passage of the Nineteenth Amendment. Between 1920 and 1960, little more was accomplished with respect to women's rights. Interest in issues of gender inequality increased again during the 1960s, with the birth and rapid growth of the National Organization for Women (NOW). Issues that continue to concern the women's movement include, (1) improving the media portrayal of women, (2) fostering equal opportunity in jobs and schooling, (3) increasing the availability of child-care facilities, (4) improving the status of the homemaker, (5) protecting a woman's right to control her own body, (6) reducing violence against women, and (7) passing the Equal Rights Amendment.

Assuming that present trends continue, we might expect even greater blurring of the traditional distinctions between men and women on the job, at home, and at play. Presently there exists a Women's Human Rights movement in the United States and across the world.

Discussion Questions

1. Think back to your high school experience. In your high school, did male and female athletes receive differential treatment? How about in your college? What do you think about gender equity in athletics?

2. The chapter notes that sex is biologically based but that gender is a cultural and social concept. For men's and women's roles in society, what are the implications of seeing gender as a cultural and social concept?

3. Watch some current television situation comedy in which both men and women are central characters. Then, if you have cable television, watch an episode of a situation comedy from the 1950s or 1960s. Are men and women portrayed differently on the shows? Have the gender roles changed? How?

4. Have there been episodes of violence against women on your campus? What has been the reaction to them? Do you see traditional gender roles leading to violence against women?

5. How do you feel about women in the military, especially in combat roles?

References

Acker, Joan. 1992. "Gendered Institutions: From Sex Roles to Gendered Institutions." *Contemporary Sociology* 21:565–69.

Andersen, Margaret. 1997. *Thinking About Women: Sociological Perspectives on Sex and Gender*. Boston: Allyn and Bacon.

Bernard, Cheryl, and Edit Schlaffer. 1997. "The Man in the Street: Why He Harasses," Pp. 395–98 in *Feminist Frontiers IV*, edited by L. Richardson, V. Taylor, and N. Whittier. New York: McGraw-Hill.

Bonvillain, Nancy. 1995. *Women & Men: Cultural Constructs of Gender*. Englewood Cliffs, New Jersey: Prentice Hall.

Bunch, Charlotte. 1990. "Women's Rights as Human Rights: Toward a Re-Vision of Human Rights." *Human Rights Quarterly* 12:486–98.

Burstein, Paul. 1979. "Equal Opportunity Employment Legislation and the Incomes of Women and Nonwhites." *American Sociological Review* 44:367–91.

Caputi, Jane, and Diana E. H. Russell. 1990. "Femicide: Speaking the Unspeakable." *MS*, September-October.

Collins, Patricia Hill. 1986. "Learning from the Outsider Within: The Sociological Significance of Black Feminist Thought." *Social Problems* 33:14–32.

———. 1990. *Black Feminist Thought: Knowledge, Consciousness, and Empowerment*. Cambridge, England: Unwin and Hyman.

Cunningham, Kamy. 1993. "Barbie Doll Culture and the American Waistland." *Symbolic Interaction* 16.

Deckard, Barbara. 1979. *The Women's Movement*. New York: Harper and Row.

Edwards, Richard C., Michael Reich, and Thomas E. Weisskopf, eds. 1986. *The Capitalist System: A Radical Analysis of American Society*. Third edition. Englewood Cliffs, New Jersey: Prentice Hall.

Faludi, Susan. 1992. *Backlash: The Undeclared War Against American Women*. New York: Doubleday Anchor Books.

Fox, Mary Frank. 1995. "Women and Higher Education: Gender Differences in the Status of Students and Scholars." Pp. 220–37 in *Women: A Feminist Perspective*. Fifth edition, edited by J. Freeman. Mountain View, California: Mayfield Publishing.

Freeman, Jo, ed. 1995. *Women: A Feminist Perspective*. Fifth edition. Mountain View, California: Mayfield Publishing.

Giele, Janet Z. 1988. "Gender and Sex Roles." Pp. 291–323 in *Handbook of Sociology*, edited by N. Smelser. Newbury Park, California: Sage Publications.

Harlan, Sharon, and Catherine Berheide. 1994. *Barriers to Workplace Advancement Experienced by Women in Low-Paying Occupations*. Research report for the Glass Ceiling Commission of the United States Department of Labor. Center for Women in Government: SUNY, Albany.

Hart, Roxine. 1991. "Women in Combat." Defense Equal Opportunity Management Institute, Patrick Air Force Base Website. http://www.pafb.af.mil./DEOMI/cbtwomen.htm.

Herz, D. E., and B. H. Wooton. 1996. "Women in the Workforce: An Overview." Pp. 44–78 in *The American Woman, 1996–1997: Where We Stand*, edited by D. E. Herz and B. H. Wooton. New York: W. W. Norton.

Hesse-Biber, Sharlene. 1996. *Am I Thin Enough Yet?* New York: Oxford University Press.

Hochschild, Arlie, with Anne Machung. 1989. *The Second Shift*. New York: Viking.

Kilbourne, Jean. 1994. "Still Killing Us Softly: Advertising and the Obsession with Thinness." Pp. 395–418 in *Feminist Perspectives on Eating Disorders*, edited by P. Fallon, M. A. Katzman, and S. C. Wooley. New York: Guilford Press.

Landau, Reva. 1994. "On Making Choices." *Feminist Issues* 12:47–72.

Lengermann, Patricia Madoo, and Jill Niebrugge-Brantley. 1992. "Contemporary Feminist Theory." Pp. 308–56 in *Contemporary Sociological Theory*, edited by George Ritzer. New York: McGraw-Hill.

Leonard, Mary. 1997. "Sporting Chance: The Impact of Title IX on Women's Sports." *Boston Sunday Globe*, June, 1, C1, C5.

Levin, Jack. 1993. *Sociological Snapshots: Seeing Social Structure and Change in Everyday Life*. Thousand Oaks, California: Pine Forge Press.

Lewin, Tamar. 1997. "Wage Difference Between Women and Men Widens." *New York Times*, September 15, A1, A12.

Lips, Hillary. 1995. "Gender Role Socialization: Lessons in Femininity." In *Women: A Feminist Perspective*, edited by J. Freeman. Mountain View, California: Mayfield Publishing.

MacQuarrie, Brian, and Zachary Dowdy. 1997. "Female Athletes See Unequal Playing Field." *Boston Globe*, June 4, B1, B8.

Mead, Margaret. 1963 [1935]. *Sex and Temperament in Three Primitive Societies*. New York: William Morrow.

National Organization for Women. 1998. *National Organization for Women (NOW) Home Page*. http://www.now.org/

Peters, Julie, and Andrea Wolper, eds. 1995. *Women's Rights, Human Rights: International Feminist Perspectives*. New York: Routledge.

Reskin, B.F. 1993. "Sex Segregation in the Workplace." *Annual Review of Sociology* 19:241–70.

Rosen, J. C., and J. Gross. 1987. "Prevalence of Weight Reducing and Weight Gaining in Adolescent Girls and Boys." *Health and Psychology* 26: 131–147.

Rossi, Alice. 1977. "A Biosocial Perspective on Parenting." *Daedalus* 106:1–31.

——. 1984. "Gender and Parenthood." Pp. 161–91 in *Gender and the Life Course*, edited by A. Rossi. Hawthorne, New York: Aldine.

Rubin, Jeffrey Z., Frank J. Provenzano, and C. T. Hull. 1974. "The Eye of the Beholder: Parents' Views on Sex of Newborns." *American Journal of Orthopsychiatry* 44:512–19.

Stodghill, Ron. 1997. "God of Our Fathers: The Rise of the Promise Keepers." *Time*, October 6.

Tavris, Carol. 1992. *The Mismeasure of Women*. New York: Simon and Schuster Touchstone.

U.S. Bureau of the Census. 1996. *Statistical Abstract of the United States, 1996–1997*. Washington, D.C.: U. S. Government Printing Office.

U.S. Department of Labor. 1996. *Employment and Earnings*. Vol. 43, no.1, January.

——. 1998. *20 Facts on Working Women*. Women's Bureau, No. 98, 2.

Vogel, Charity. 1997. "Sports Scholarship Bias Alleged." *Boston Globe*, June 3, B1, B6.

Websites

http://www.aauw.org/4000/extlinks.html

American Association of University Women (AAUW): Other Websites of Interest. This website will lead you to many other valuable sites.

http://www.asanet.org/sexgend.htm

American Sociological Association (ASA) Sex and Gender Section. This is the website for the ASA Sex and Gender section.

http://www.dol.gov/dol/wb/public/wb_pubs/wagegap2.htm

U.S. Department of Labor, Women's Bureau. This valuable website provides a wide variety of information on topics related to women and their work. You will find information on child care and educational resources, as well as statistics and data. The site also includes useful links to other sites.

http://now.org/now/nnt

National Organization for Women (NOW). In addition to offering information on NOW, this website also provides information on numerous related topics including violence against women, the Promise Keepers movement, economic equity, and reproductive rights.

CHAPTER FIVE

Age
Discrimination

In the News: Ageless Love

The picture in the Los Angeles Times *is striking. Harold Goodman and his sweetheart Marj Linz are perched on a Harley-Davidson motorcycle. You may recognize Goodman and Linz. They appeared in a Miller Lite beer commercial "groping each other while rolling around on a sofa, teenage style" (Levine 1997: E6). Goodman is 92; Linz is 80. The article also includes a picture of Art Sherman and his wife Florence. They have recently celebrated their first wedding anniversary, and, according to Art Sherman, are "possibly the happiest people on Earth" (Levine 1997: E1). Art Sherman is 79, while Florence Sherman is 81. The article is entitled "Ageless Love" (Levine 1997).*

Were you surprised by the ages of the people pictured in the article? Does it seem wrong somehow that elderly people are involved in intense and giddy romantic and sexual relationships? Like teenagers, the elderly have often been stereotyped and not taken seriously. You will see some examples in this chapter.

Today many people live longer, healthier lives, especially middle- and upper-class Americans. They may divorce late or be widowed at very advanced ages. Many older people are not willing to live the rest of their years alone. They are looking for love. In examining this phenomenon, Bettuane Levine poses three questions:

Do old people have sex?

Do they experience real romantic love?

Do they feel the same romantic yearnings, churnings, giddy desire, agonizing intensity—and the same serene fulfillment when they find the perfect mate—that we usually think of as the exclusive province of the young? (Levine 1997:E1)

The answer is yes to each of the questions. It's time to stop stereotyping the elderly and see them as they really are.

It is especially important to move away from stereotypes of the elderly because the stereotypes are increasingly inaccurate and make it difficult to understand the lives and the problems facing older Americans. Recent studies have shown that older Americans not only live longer, they also live healthier, more active lives. As a Boston Globe *article reporting on research on aging puts it, "living well isn't just the best revenge, it's increasingly the happy fate of older Americans, whose rising life expectancy, scientists say, is giving them not only more years, but more good years" (Foreman 1997).*

Definition and Prevalence

Issues related to aging and the elderly appear often in newspapers and in the media today. Americans—and people around the world—are living longer. For Americans those longer lives are also generally healthier lives, as noted above, but many people express concern about the increasing numbers of the elderly. Ongoing debates over Social Security and extending the retirement age have the potential for provoking generational conflict. The aging of the very large Baby Boom generation worries some younger people, concerned that health care for an increasingly aged population may strain the health care system and drain resources that they may need. In this chapter we look at some of these concerns as we examine age discrimination directed against the elderly. We also briefly look at age discrimination directed against teenagers.

When does old age begin? For sociologists, age is not just the number of years since a person was born; it also involves a set of social definitions regarding what is required of, and appropriate for, people of different ages. Although aging refers to people growing older in terms of their chronological progress, for sociologists it refers primarily to their transitions into new age-related statuses and roles. What we mean by "old age" depends as much on social definition as on biology.

In almost every known society, certain people have been singled out as being aged or old. However, the chronological age at which old age begins has varied a great deal from one society to another. In many preliterate societies, such as the Igbo and the Sidamo of Africa, old age status begins as early as forty or as late as forty-five years of age. In Samoa, old age starts at fifty. In contrast, modern societies identify the sixty-fifth or seventieth year of life with onset of old age. In the United States, for instance, age sixty-five has traditionally been used to determine eligibility for Social Security payments, senior citizen discounts, Medicare, and mandatory retirement.

One of the most important changes related to aging in the United States is the redefinition of what it means to be old. Not only do people live longer, they also live healthier and more active lives.

Societies also vary with respect to their treatment of the elderly. In many preliterate societies, being old means promotion to a position of leadership and respect in the community. Old people are asked to reduce their strenuous physical activities but are not asked to retire. Instead, they assume supervisory or advisory roles that have greater prestige and power than those of their roles earlier in life. A typical example is the Bantu elder who is revered as "the father of his people." Aging has clearly meant different things in various societies (Albert and Cattell 1994).

In colonial America, the elderly enjoyed power and privilege. For this reason, younger people frequently powdered their hair or wore white wigs to look older. When the census taker came, many colonial Americans would misrepresent themselves as older than they actually were. Only 2 percent of Americans lived to the ripe old age of sixty-five; old age was regarded as a special gift from God, a sign of Election (Achenbaum 1978; Fischer 1978).

Institutional retirement of the elderly is very much a creation of modern societies. Before 1800, mandatory retirement by chronological age was virtually unknown. Many of the problems experienced by older Americans increased at the very time that they were becoming a larger segment of the total population. The percentage of elderly in the United States has gradually risen from about 4 percent in the early 1900s to more than 13 percent today (Treas 1995).

The concept of **ageism** helps us understand the position of the elderly in the United States. Ageism refers to systematic discrimination toward the aged. Ageism leads to belittling of the elderly and the perpetuation of negative stereotypes about them. (See "A Closer Look: Belittling the Elderly.") Ageism is generated when older people have decreased social status and diminished contact with younger individuals. Robert Butler defines ageism as

> systematic stereotyping of and discrimination against people because they are old, just as racism and sexism accomplish this with color and gender. Old people are categorized as senile, rigid in thought and manner, old-fashioned in morality and skills. . . . Ageism allows the younger generation to see older people as different from themselves; thus they subtly cease to identify with their elders as human beings. (1989:132)

A Closer Look

Belittling the Elderly

Ageism produces the systematic stereotyping of, and discrimination against, people because they are old. Ageism has been compared to racism and sexism. One of the most pernicious ways of stereotyping and belittling the elderly is the notion of the "second childhood." It is certainly widely represented in popular culture, including television shows and commercials. There are at least five ways in which second childhood is portrayed.

1. Children and old people are often paired with each other. A television commercial for Country-Time Lemonade shows an elderly man with children gathered around him, claiming that the lemonade tastes as good to him as lemonade did when he was young.
2. Old people are given the personality and moods of children. People laugh at elderly people when they get angry or agitated. The elderly are called "honey" and "dear" by people half their age.
3. Old people are often given the dress and appearance of children. Bows may be put in elderly women's hair in an attempt to dress them up.
4. The elderly are given the physical problems of children. A prescription drug ad for a stool softener features a smiling older woman wearing bifocals. The text reads: "Minnie moved her bowels today."
5. Old people are given the activities and playthings of children. Children's board games are common examples. Beanbag tossing is another common activity. The roles of the old and the young are reversed, and the elderly are often treated as if they are helpless or incapable of accomplishing adult-like tasks.

Before going on to look more closely at the lives and status of the elderly, we need to get an idea of how many elderly people there are in the United States and how many there will be in the future. The number of elderly has grown dramatically in this century, especially those over 85—the "oldest old." In fact, the growth rate of the elderly greatly exceeded the growth for the whole population in the twentieth century (U.S. Bureau of the Census 1995).

Figure 5-1 shows the average annual growth rate of the elderly within 20 year periods. The growth rate projection is relatively low for 1990 to 2010, but look at the projection for 2010 to 2030. In those years, the Baby Boom generation will start reaching 65. Figure 5-2 shows what that growth rate will mean in terms of the number of elderly Americans. In 1900, there were 3.1 million Americans over 65. You can see the increases, leading to 33.9 million elderly in 1996, and projected to 69.4 million elderly by 2030.

Figure 5-1 Average Annual Growth Rate of the Elderly Population: 1910-1930 to 2030–2050 (percents)

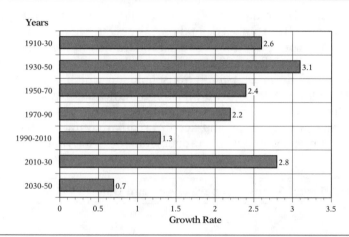

Source: U.S. Bureau of the Census . 1995. *Sixty-Five Plus in the United States*. Economics and Statistics Administration, U.S. Department of Commerce. <http://www.census.gov/socdemo/www/agebrief.html>.

Figure 5-2 Number of Persons 65 and Older: 1900-2030 (in millions)

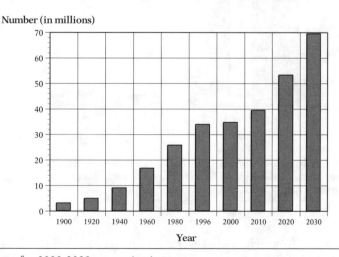

Note: Numbers for 2000-2030 are projections.
Source: Administration on Aging. 1997. *Profile of Older Americans: 1997*. Washington, D.C.: Department of Health and Human Services. Based on Data from the U.S. Bureau of the Census.

The aged are diverse demographically and will become even more so. There are far more elderly women than elderly men in the United States. Life expectancy has improved more for women than for men because of medical advances (Quadagno and Street 1996). Men generally die from heart disease, emphysema, or cancer. Less medical progress has been made in these areas than in areas (childbirth) that have claimed the lives of women. In light of this, women are more likely to be widowed than men. In 1995, 78 percent of men aged 65 to 74 were married and living with their wives compared to only 53 percent of women. Among those over 75, 68 percent of men, but only 25 percent of women were still married (U.S. Bureau of the Census 1997). Besides the fact that women live longer, men who become widowed are three times more likely to remarry than women. Older men have a larger pool of women to choose from since societal norms encourage men to marry younger women. This privilege does not exist for women to the same extent.

The married couple is still the basic family unit among the elderly, but there are also many single-person households in which a widowed man or woman lives alone. (See Figure 5-3.) Although the majority of older persons no longer live in the households of their adult children or with other relatives, they do tend to live close by and keep in regular contact. Table 5-1 clearly shows the differences in living arrangements for elderly men and women.

Figure 5-3 Marital Status of Americans 65 and Older: 1995

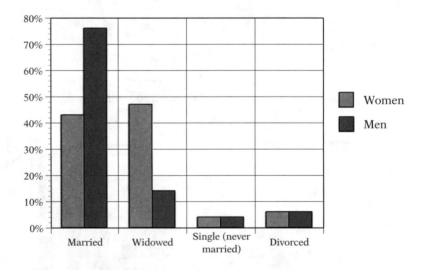

Source: Administration on Aging. 1997. *Profile of Older Americans: 1997*. Washington, D.C.: Department of Health and Human Services. Based on Data from the U.S. Bureau of the Census. <http://pr.aoa.dhhs.gov/aoa/stats/profile/>.

Race and ethnic origin are also major factors to examine when discussing the elderly. In 1990, 8.2 percent of African Americans were elderly. This is projected to rise to 13.6 percent by 2050. African Americans have higher mortality rates over the life course; fewer blacks than whites survive to age 65. Among the reasons for this are that African Americans receive poorer health

care than whites and are more likely to work at jobs that put them at greater
risk of injury and illness (Quadagno and Street 1996). Even larger increases
in the elderly are predicted for other racial and ethnic groups, although the
percentages of elderly among these groups will still be much lower than that
of whites (see Figure 5-4).

Table 5-1 Living Arrangements of Persons 65 and Older, by Sex, 1995 (percents)

Living Arrangements	Men	Women
Living with spouse	77	48
Living with other relatives	4	8
Living alone or with nonrelatives	19	44

Source: Administration on Aging. 1997. *Profile of Older Americans: 1997*. Washington, D.C.:
U.S. Department of Health and Human Services. Based on Data from the U.S. Bureau of
the Census. <http://pr.aoa.dhhs.gov/aoa/stats/profile/>

Figure 5-4 Percent 65 and Older, by Race and Hispanic Origin:1990 and 2050

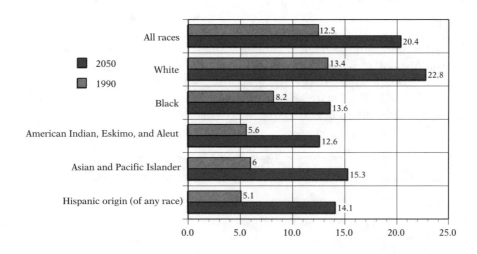

Note: For the Middle Series Projections, the Census Bureau assumes that present population trends in areas such as fertility and mortality will continue.
Source: U.S. Bureau of the Census. 1995. *Population Profile of the United States: 1995*.
Current Population Reports, Series P23, 189. Washington, D.C.: U.S. Government Printing Office.

Illness is a central concern in the lives of the elderly. Many elderly have
some chronic illness, especially heart disease, hypertension, diabetes, and arthritis. These chronic conditions often force them to limit their daily activities. They may be unable to work, keep a house, or participate in recreational
activities. The proportion of people over 65 with chronic illnesses that

severely limit their activities is three or four times greater than the proportion for middle-aged people (Kalish 1970).

Some decline in poverty among the aged has occurred due to government programs such as Social Security—and cost of living adjustments in it—and Medicare. In 1970, 24.6 percent of Americans over 65 had incomes below the poverty level. That figure had dropped to 12.2 percent by 1990 and 10.8 percent by 1996 (Matcha 1997; Administration on Aging 1997). However, another 7.6 percent of the elderly were "near poor" in 1996. Their incomes were between the poverty level and 125 percent of that level, so that "almost one-fifth (18.4%) of the older population was poor or near poor in 1996" (Administration on Aging 1997: 8). In spite of the decline in poverty among the elderly population as a whole, those figures conceal major differences among subgroups of the elderly. In 1996, 9.4 percent of the elderly white population was poor, but 25.3 percent of elderly African Americans and 24.4 percent of elderly Hispanic Americans were poor. The poverty rate for elderly women was 13.6 percent, while for men it was 6.8 percent. The situation of elderly, African American women living alone was the worst: 47.5 percent of them were poor in 1996 (Administration on Aging 1997). Even though the economic position of elderly Americans has improved in recent years, many still live in or near poverty, and some subgroups live in very difficult circumstances.

In spite of the improving economic status of the aged, negative stereotypes about the elderly persist. (See "A Closer Look: Tot Tempters—An Insulting Restaurant Menu.") Over 40 years ago, Tuckman and Lorge (1953) discovered that a majority of the graduate students they studied agreed that old people are "set in their ways," "conservative," " dislike any changes," "have lost most of their teeth," "like to give advice," "are bossy," "like to be waited on," and "like to doze in a rocking chair." In 1975, Harris reported that the majority of adult Americans hold images of the elderly that are far from flattering: They are seen as not very active, not very efficient, and not very alert. William Levin discovered that college students are still very likely to stereotype the elderly in negative ways (1988).

A Closer Look

Tot Tempters—An Insulting Restaurant Menu

The following is excerpted from a real restaurant menu:

Tot Tempters

For all kids under 10 and over 65

HOT DOGGY .99

KIDDIE BURGER .99

PEANUT BUTTER & JELLY SANDWICH .75

FLUFFERJELLYNUTTER CLUB
marshmallow, peanut butter and jelly on untoasted white bread .85

All of the above served with french fries.

Although stereotypes about the aged are decidedly negative and widely shared, their economic position has improved in recent years. The non-institutionalized elderly are better off economically than other Americans. Poverty among the elderly has declined during the 1980s and 1990s, but many elderly still live in very difficult circumstances (U.S. Bureau of the Census 1997). Retirement typically reduces their incomes by half, they must spend a disproportionately large share of their incomes for medical expenses, and—perhaps most important for many—they no longer enjoy a meaningful position within the family. For more information on the elderly, see "A Closer Look: Social Gerontology and the Aging Revolution Website, Trinity University."

A Closer Look

Social Gerontology and the Aging Revolution Website, Trinity University

The Social Gerontology site (http://www.trinity.edu/~mkearl/geron.html) is part of the Sociological Tour Through Cyberspace (http://www.trinity.edu/~mkearl/) created and maintained by Dr. Michael Kearl, of the Department of Sociology and Anthropology at Trinity University in San Antonio, Texas. As valuable and extensive as the Social Gerontology site is, it is just a small part of the overall tour. Kearl's Sociological Tour Through Cyberspace is the most impressive, valuable sociological web site that we have seen. You will find it a gold mine of resources on sociology and the related social sciences.

We can say the same for the materials on social gerontology and the aged. The first link on this site is to the Administration on Aging's "Profile of Older Americans: 1995," which provides you with detailed statistical information on the aged. Kearl has provided an outline of the page, which includes pages on a wide variety of topics, including old age across culture and time, Social Security, aging and the economy, and old age in the mass media. Each of these pages includes solid discussions of the topic as well as links to relevant sites.

Before exploring the levels of causation of age discrimination, we should note that, although we emphasize age discrimination against the elderly, discrimination based on age can be aimed at other groups. For example, social scientist Mike Males argues that America is at war with its adolescents. (For more on this perspective, see "A Closer Look: Scapegoating America's Teenagers: Myths and Realities.")

Levels of Causation

Explanations of age discrimination involve many issues and depend on the level of approach taken by the theorist. Here we discuss explanations at the level of individuals, of cultures, and of structures.

Individual

Those who explain the problems of the aged in U. S. society in terms of their biological or psychological characteristics tend to regard old age as an irreversible disease. At the biological level, the key concept is **senescence**, or

Scapegoating America's Teenagers: Myths and Realities

Age discrimination is not always aimed at the elderly. In *The Scapegoat Generation: America's War on Adolescents*, Mike Males shows that from 1970 to the mid-1990s poverty among the elderly in California has been "virtually eradicated," while child poverty has continued to grow (Males 1996:3). As the subtitle of his book suggests, Males argues that American society is carrying on a war against adolescents in which politicians, private groups, and the media unfairly scapegoat adolescents and blame them for many of America's social problems. In this fascinating, solidly documented book, Males draws extensively on U.S. government data to examine many beliefs about adolescents and adolescent behavior. He argues persuasively that many of the beliefs are myths and he explains the reality distorted by the myths.

In an article focusing more narrowly on the 10 worst myths about America's teenagers, Males argues that teenagers behave like the adult society that raises them. He notes that "they did not land on a meteorite. We raised them. They share our values. They act like us" (1997:12). Myths about teenagers portray them as fundamentally different from adult society, and deviant in some ways. Here we examine three of the most pervasive myths.

Myth #1 is that "teenagers are uniquely violent and crime-prone." Males acknowledges that youths have slightly higher arrest rates than adults for violence. However, he argues that police arrest teenagers in higher proportion than adults for the crimes they commit and suggests that, taking this into account, youths and adults commit crimes at roughly equal rates for their numbers in the population.

Myth #2 is that "the worst danger to youth is 'children killing children' (Males 1997: 12). In fact, 90 percent of children under 12 and 60 percent of teenagers killed, are killed by adults. Teens are unlikely to be killed by those near them in age. . . .

Myth #6 suggests that teenage birth rates are "out of control due to teenage immaturity, lack of information on sex, lack of values, and 'children having children' (Males 1997: 13). In fact, teenage birth trends and rates match those of the adults around them. The single most important factor in predicting whether teenagers would get pregnant is poverty.

Males suggests that we stop scapegoating teenagers. He argues that there is no such thing as "teenage sex," "teenage violence," or "teenage smoking." Rather, these behaviors reflect adult behaviors. He concludes that America should stop destructive attacks on youth and "recognize that adult and teen behaviors are intercon-

physiological deterioration. Old people suffer because of decreased biological viability, increased vulnerability, degeneration of the circulatory and nervous systems, impairment of the respiratory system, reduced muscle tone, and slowed reaction time.

The biological model of declining capacities can also be applied to the psychology of old age. Aging is regarded as a loss of adaptive capacities. Therefore, the aged are viewed as the recipients of impaired sensory and perceptual processes, reduced psychomotor performance, decreased intelligence and learning ability, limited memory, and lack of creativity.

Cultural

The case of modern Japan serves to illustrate the influence of culture on the treatment of the elderly. There is much evidence suggesting that the status of elders is higher in Japan than in any other industrialized society. In contrast to the situation in the United States, the majority of Japanese elders continue to live with their children and to be integrated into their families. Except for voluntary and health reasons, most older Japanese men continue to work. What is more, Japanese elders are given preferential treatment in seating, bathing, and serving. And they are honored in special celebrations such as Respect for Elders Day and on the occasion of their sixty-first birthday.

According to Erdman Palmore and Daisaku Maeda (1985), the relatively high status of Japanese elders is maintained by a tradition of respect for the aged. The basis of this tradition is twofold: (1) a vertical social structure, which obligates younger persons to respect all older persons, and (2) filial piety, which obligates children to honor their own parents and grandparents.

The presence of a vertical social structure indicates that interaction between members of Japanese society is frequently influenced by a hierarchy of relationships involving superiors and inferiors, such as those between parents and children, masters and servants, or teachers and students. In Japan, all relationships—even those between friends and colleagues—become vertical, so that some ranking by seniority almost inevitably occurs. This emphasis on seniority is a basis for the vertical society and, specifically, for the maintenance of the high status of Japanese elders.

Filial piety has its roots in Confucian precepts and ancient ancestor worship. According to Japanese religious beliefs, dead ancestors acquire godlike supernatural powers which determine all earthly events and human actions. The happiness of the living is dependent upon the success with which they respectfully serve the dead. Therefore, the most important thing in the life of the Japanese has been their devotion to dead ancestors. The second most important thing has been respect towards living parents and grandparents, older members of the family who will eventually become dead ancestors. Although the elderly in Japan continue to enjoy higher status than in most other industrialized societies, change has occurred in Japan (Martin 1989). Some Japanese elders have begun to feel "dishonored" and "fearful" (Kristof 1997).

In a similar way, early American settlers believed in a hierarchy of age relations which formed the basis for the authority of the elderly. Respect for the aged was deeply rooted in the Judeo-Christian ethic of colonial America. As noted earlier, old age was regarded as a sign of Election; an individual survived to old age as a result of God's intervention.

David H. Fischer suggests that cultural forces underlying the American War for Independence also formed the basis for profound changes in relations between young and old. According to Fischer, a revolution in attitudes toward age took place between 1770 and 1820, when many hierarchically oriented institutions disintegrated, and the ideal of equality emerged in full force. Equality as applied to legal status, social conditions, cultural manners, and political rights called into question the prevailing hierarchies of sex, race, and age. As a result, the elderly began to lose their privileged status in American society (Fischer 1978).

Fischer argues that the direction of age bias was totally reversed, after a brief period of equality ended. Many changes occurred: preferential seating arrangements for the elderly were abolished; mandatory retirement laws appeared; youthful fashions were preferred; patterns of age preference revealed by census data shifted from old age to youth; and eldest sons lost their inheritance advantage. What resulted was a cult of youth, which developed and spread throughout American society during the nineteenth century and grew rapidly during the twentieth (Fischer 1978).

The shift in attitudes toward the aged was tied to changes in family patterns and ideals. Prior to industrialization, older people generally lived with their children and occupied a very honored position within the family. Carole Haber and Brian Gratton reveal that by the early decades of the twentieth century, scores of social critics were convinced that the nuclear family was the ideal arrangement for family members (1994). Family experts viewed nuclear households as the proper environment for raising children and ensuring their moral upbringing. In addition, welfare advocates were concerned about the economic impact of extended families. Advocates believed that middle-aged adults were faced with choosing between providing for their children's growth and education and caring for their elderly parents.

By the early twentieth century, attitudes towards the elderly had changed dramatically. The elderly were no longer revered or valued as they had been in earlier times. Severe economic dislocation caused by the Great Depression did not help matters. The elderly watched their hard-won assets vanish and with them their hopes for an independent and secure old age. Many had to rely on other family members (Haber and Gratton 1994).

Liberty is another cultural ideal that may have contributed to the declining status of older Americans. The American interpretation of the concept of liberty reduced the authority of old age by destroying its communal ties to the family, church, and the town. The growth of individualism served to loosen the obligations between age groups and instead fostered "a spirit of social atomism" (Fischer 1978).

The low status of the aged in U.S. society has also been linked to cultural values that emphasize future orientation and economic production (Rosow 1974). In contrast to stable, tradition-oriented societies, U. S. culture emphasizes innovation and change. Given a limited heritage of current popular appeal, the aged do not play a valuable role as symbols of historical continuity or respected tradition. What is more, in a society where individuals are rewarded in terms of their economic utility, the limited access of elder Americans to employment opportunities places them at a severe disadvantage with respect to social status (Levin and Levin 1980).

Structural

Sociological theories on aging come from various perspectives, not all of which are actually approaches, which focus on interaction among individuals. However, the authors have included them in this section because they are all sociological approaches, rather than psychological, individual-blaming, or biological approaches. There are many approaches to aging, and we emphasize the major points or contributions of each theory.

First, **structural functionalists** have argued that social behavior is best understood from the perspective of the equilibrium needs of the social system. This approach analyzes social behavior in terms of its function within the structure of society. Structural functionalist influences on the discussion of aging can be seen in formulations regarding disengagement, modernization, and age stratification (Passuth and Bengtson 1988).

Disengagement theory examines the aging process in terms of the needs and requisites of society; individuals are conceived as passive agents of the social system. Patricia Passuth and Vern Bengtson define disengagement as ❖ ❖ ❖ ❖ "the universal, mutual, and inevitable withdrawal of older people from the configuration of roles characteristic of middle age." Disengagement theorists contend that elderly people recognize, as fully socialized members, their readiness to disengage on behalf of society. This process of disengaging is functional for both society and the individual in that society can make room for more efficient young people while allowing the elderly time to prepare for their eventual death. Elders do not withdraw from society completely but their social interaction does decline. This disengagement is mutual—both elders and younger members of society withdraw from each other.

From this point of view, society benefits in at least two ways from the process of disengagement. Disengagement renders the eventual death of the elderly less disruptive to the lives of friends and relatives. It also precludes harmful economic effects of the older workers' increasing incompetence or sudden death, because younger people have already replaced them in the workplace. This theory has been criticized for assuming that the elderly are useless members of society. Critics argue that disengagement may mean losing the talent and expertise of disengaged elders, and it could contribute to poor health, poverty, and loneliness of many elders (Levin and Levin 1980).

Modernization theory attempts to explain variations in age status both historically and across societies. Many gerontologists believe that the status of the aged varies in relation to a complex of societal forces known collectively as modernization. Modernized societies are characterized by advanced levels of industrialization and technology, urbanization, and rapid social change. The status of the elderly seems to decline in modernized societies. Theorists using this approach hypothesize that elements of modernization contribute to the problems of the elderly. These include shifts in (1) education and literacy; (2) retirement; (3) family life; and (4) the economy from agriculture to industry. As modernization produces higher levels of literacy and education, members of society rely less and less on the older generation as a source of knowledge. Modernization created an educational gap between young and old. Because the young are better educated, they hold a competitive advantage over the old with respect to job status and power. Retirement occurs only in modern societies where increased productivity permits a segment of the population to terminate its occupational activities while others continue to work. Unfortunately, retirement usually reduces the standard of living and social status of the aged.

Scholars formerly believed that extended families, including older family members, were prevalent prior to industrialization and modernization, and that families were more likely to be nuclear under the impact of modernization. Although that turned out to be wrong, modernization does seem to have led to more emphasis on nuclear families. In such family arrangements, older members of society are expected to live apart in independent households or to seek institutional care. The shift from a primarily agricultural to an industrial society resulted in a reduction in the economic power of the aged. The older members of society lost control over land and were forced to compete with younger persons for nonagricultural positions.

The **age stratification** perspective suggests that the age structure of roles in a society is organized hierarchically, much like social class. The point is to examine how location within an age structure influences opportunities for societal power and rewards. The location of elders within the age structure does not give them high status. A related theory, derived from the conflict perspective, suggests that older people are treated as an oppressed minority. In other words, they are victims of ageism (Dychtwald 1989).

Activity theory emphasizes the processes of social interaction. Activity theory argues that the more active elderly persons are, the greater their satisfaction with life. With old age comes a loss of roles. The theory suggests that to maintain a positive sense of self, elderly persons must substitute new roles for the old roles that they lose. As opposed to disengagement theory, activity theory argues that the elderly can invest more of their energies in the roles they retain, or in new activities. By keeping active, the elderly are happier, healthier, and able to live longer.

Symbolic interactionism focuses on how people use symbols to communicate with each other and create a shared social world. The basic premise of this theory is that social interactionism is a process through which interacting individuals continually create and recreate a shared world. This perspective also emphasizes how the elderly create meaningful lives and situations for themselves through interaction (Matcha 1997).

Marx's theory of capitalist development has also been applied to the study of old age. It is a conflict perspective sometimes referred to as the **political economy of aging**. This approach explains the situation of the elderly by focusing on their class position and the role of the state and economy in a capitalist society. (Matcha 1997; Passuth and Bengtson 1988). Rather than focusing on aging as causing social problems, this approach emphasizes the importance of examining "aging as a consequence of institutional structures and an unequal distribution of power" (Matcha 1997:60). Theorists of this persuasion examine the effects of government social programs on the elderly. For example, Duane Matcha suggests that although a variety of government programs, such as the War on Poverty in the 1960s, provided significant benefits to meet the social, psychological, and economic needs of the elderly, such programs may also have created a relationship or presumption of dependence. "That is, it is now assumed that if a person is old, he or she is in need of assistance from others. Thus, age has become equated with dependence" (Matcha 1997:50). In fact, people in all age categories need assistance at some time.

Sociological theories of aging are diverse, and yet they have a few important points in common. Increasingly, sociologists have moved away from approaches that stress debilitating biological aspects of aging, and begun to move toward more sociological perspectives. Gerontologists—social scientists who study the social aspects of aging—had often taken a blaming the victim approach to understanding aging and the situation of the aged. Jack Levin and William Levin suggest that the unifying theme of blaming the victim approaches is "that *aging* is something that happens to individuals" (1980:35). Sociological approaches to aging must focus on the social forces that affect aging and the elderly, and on the consequences of those social forces for the life chances of the elderly.

Consequences

As we have seen in this chapter, there have been overall improvements in the well-being of the elderly, including a marked decrease in poverty. Many stereotypes about the elderly are inaccurate, and many elderly Americans lead active, healthy, independent lives. However, many elderly Americans still

lack access to important resources. Stereotypes based on ageism and age dis-   ❖ ❖ ❖ ❖
crimination still have serious consequences for many older people. Those
consequences include hunger and malnutrition, elder abuse and crime, poor
health and lack of access to health care, and loneliness and isolation.

In 1993, an Urban Institute study estimated that "some 5 million elderly
have no food in the house, or worry about getting enough to eat" (Lieberman
1998:12). How can this happen? Health policy analyst Trudy Lieberman
points out that "thousands of elderly men and women too infirm to cook or
even see the flames of the stove are put on ration lists for food in the most
bountiful country in the world" (Lieberman 1998:12). Other studies have established that many elderly Americans face the threat of malnutrition. Researchers at Florida International University point out that "good nutritional
status is vital to helping American's 34 million elders remain independent,
maintain their quality of life and avoid premature nursing home placement"
(Wellman, et al. 1996:1). N. S. Wellman and her colleagues note that while

> hunger, poverty, and malnutrition often take dramatic tolls on elders
> themselves, the ramifications of these three interrelated problems are
> devastating for family members and are unnecessarily costly for
> taxpayers.

Greater public awareness of the extent of hunger and malnutrition
among the elderly can lead to programs to alleviate such hunger, which
would make it easier for elderly Americans to live independently at home and
to remain healthy longer.

Another consequence of ageism is the abuse of the elderly in the home.
Reports of domestic abuse against the elderly increased from 117,000 in 1986
to 241,000 in 1994 (National Center on Elder Abuse 1997). Although not every report of abuse to state or local authorities is substantiated, and some instances of abuse may be self-inflicted, experts on aging believe that the rise in
reported cases illustrates a growing problem of violence and neglect among
the nation's expanding elderly population. The neglect and abuse of old people—including poor care, mistreatment, physical, emotional, or financial
abuse—is not new; however, sociologists have only investigated these types of
abuses since the late 1970s (Glendenning 1997).

In the United States, about 5 percent of elderly people live in institutional
settings. There is chilling evidence that these elderly people are more likely to
be at risk than the 95 percent who live in the community. Frank Glendenning
contends that although the vast majority of the elderly are well cared for at
home, a considerable amount of violence takes place within the family.

Some elders are physically abused. This includes direct beatings, sexual
assault, unreasonable physical restraint, and prolonged deprivation of food
and water. Elders are financially abused. This includes any theft or misuse of
an elder's property or money, by a person in a position of trust with an elder.
Elders are neglected. Care givers have failed to provide adequate care. This
includes failing to assist in personal hygiene or the provision of clothing. Neglect entails the failure to provide medical care for the physical and mental
health needs of an elder. This does not include instances in which an elder refuses treatment. Neglect also entails failure to protect an elder from health
and safety hazards. Elders are emotionally abused and abandoned as well.
Care givers inflict mental suffering. Examples of such abuse are verbal assaults, threats, instilling fear, humiliation, intimidation, or isolation of an

❖ ❖ ❖ ❖   elder. Abandonment constitutes the desertion of an elder by any person having the care and custody of that elder (National Center on Elder Abuse 1997).

The vast majority of elderly Americans are not abused; however, abuse of any significant number of older Americans is clearly of great importance. Such abuse certainly has major consequences for those abused, even beyond the immediate effects of the abuse. A recent study indicated that mistreatment of elderly people was associated with an increased risk of death. During the 13 year period of the study, mistreated elders were over three times more likely to die than those who had not been abused (Lachs, et al. 1998).

In addition to the possibility of abuse in the home, elderly people may also become victims of crime. In fact, one of the biggest worries of older people in the United States is the fear of crime, although crime victimization rates are actually very low among the elderly, especially the rates of the three most serious crimes—murder, rape, and assault. Crimes that are more likely to affect the elderly include purse snatching, fraud, theft of checks from the mail, vandalism, and harassment, especially by teenagers. Older Americans consistently report a high level of fear of crime, even though their crime victimization rates have actually been declining. Persons aged 65 or older report less than 2 percent of all victimizations in the United States, according to the National Crime Victimization Survey (U.S. Department of Justice 1997). The violent crime rate is nearly 16 times higher for persons under age 25 than for persons over 65. However, some of the high level of fear of crime among the elderly may be due to their awareness that crimes against them often have serious consequences.

Elderly victims of violent crime are almost twice as likely as younger victims to be raped, robbed, or assaulted at or near their home. The vulnerability of the elderly to violent crime at or near their home may reflect their lifestyle. They often live alone and do not work. Public opinion surveys conducted over the last 20 years among national samples of persons age 50 or older consistently show that about half of them are afraid to walk alone at night in their own neighborhood and are reluctant to go out after dark. Sometimes the fear of crime can be as harmful as crime itself when it constrains the behavior of the elderly. Older persons understand that they appear vulnerable. They are particularly susceptible to crimes motivated by economic gain. To make matters worse, injured elderly victims of violent crime are more likely than younger victims to suffer a serious injury. In addition, even though the rates of violent crime are low among the elderly, when they are

In the United States today, more people are living into their eighties, nineties and even over 100. Such increasing longevity has led to discussion of its consequences in a variety of areas, especially health care costs.

victimized, the impact of crime is heavy because they often have limited budgets, frequently live in inner-city neighborhoods where crimes are more common, and may be injured more easily in the course of a crime. Physical handicaps, such as a vision or hearing loss, can make the old easy prey. With diminished strength, older people are less able to defend themselves or escape from threatening situations (Matcha 1997; National Institute on Aging 1996; U.S. Department of Justice 1997).

Health problems are of obvious concern to the elderly. These concerns affect men and women differently. American women can expect to outlive men by about seven years. Older women are more likely than older men to suffer from debilitating chronic illnesses including arthritis, high blood pressure, diabetes, allergies, most orthopedic problems, and most digestive and urinary problems. Older women typically have greater mobility limitations than older men and greater difficulties performing various personal care activities such as bathing. Men typically die sooner than women, having experienced fewer or briefer periods of chronic illness and disability (Hatch 1995).

Older women are more likely than older men to spend some portion of their lives in a nursing home and to spend a significant amount of time there prior to death. This is mainly due to a combination of factors including their higher disability levels, greater longevity, and higher rates of living alone. One of the problems with this for women is that the major U.S. health care program for the elderly (Medicare) is intended primarily to meet acute care needs. Medicare covers 44 percent of the health costs of older married couples and only about 33 percent of older single women. The difference may be attributed to the fact that Medicare does not cover the long-term care that is needed by many older women and thus pays a lower proportion of women's health costs than those of men. Given that older women are more likely to be poor than men and less likely to have private health coverage, they are harder pressed to cover out-of-pocket health care costs (Arendell and Estes 1991). In terms of mental health, depression is more common among older women than among older men. This difference is not surprising considering their greater risks for poverty, widowhood, and chronic illnesses. Older men are more likely to be diagnosed with drug and alcohol problems.

Interventions

The status of the aged would be greatly enhanced by a fundamental change in our culture's values that would reduce the emphasis on economic utility, productivity, achievement, and competition. In the context of an alternative status system based on intrinsic human qualities, people could be evaluated and rewarded for their attributes and relationships rather than for their performances. At a cultural level, consciousness raising is most likely to begin with the elderly themselves. Using the experiences of African Americans or of women as a model, we might expect increasing political pressure from the aged as they become more aware of their shared interests.

The aged have reacted to age discrimination in diverse ways. Many have accepted the role assigned them. Frequently with extreme reluctance, they have retired from their occupational roles, collected Social Security payments, and segregated themselves from the younger members of society. Neither acceptance nor avoidance aims at fundamental change. By contrast, increasing numbers of elders are becoming aggressive in their determination to eliminate the role to which they have been assigned. Political organizations such as the Gray Panthers have established a list of priorities including (1) an end to mandatory retirement and other forms of age discrimination, (2) a federally financed system of health insurance for all Americans, and (3) democratic decision making for residents of nursing homes. Organized political associations of old people have successfully lobbied for Medicare and legislation to increase the retirement age.

Steve Scrutton (1990) suggests some general strategies for combating ageism. He believes that legal action must become the major objective. There are no statutory safeguards against ageism, no equivalent of the Race Relations Act or Equal Opportunities legislation. Scrutton cautions that legislation will not end ageism but it will bring the issues into sharper focus. For example, legal protection is needed in the area of employment, and to outlaw discriminatory practices in advertising and filling job vacancies. Scrutton argues that individuals should have the right to choose their own time of retirement. Elderly people also need safeguards to protect their money and property. There should be legislation that protects elderly people against bad practice and abuse in both private and public residential care and nursing homes and in hospitals.

The Future of Age Discrimination

The future of age discrimination and of relations between different age groups in the United States will depend to a large extent on how well the generations know and understand each other. Many young people fear that Social Security and other support programs will not be available for them, and this can generate fear and antagonism towards the elderly. Many younger people also have little idea about the reality of aging and the characteristics of the elderly. A group named *Americans Discuss Social Security* (ADSS) carried out a national survey to investigate the differences between perceptions and realities of old age. The survey led ADSS to conclude that "there are surprises ahead for today's young people." Table 5-2 presents some of the most important results of that survey. Take a look at the table and see if any of the differences surprise you. In many cases the differences are not great, only 46 percent of Americans 18–34 in the survey expect to receive Social Security, while 90 percent of the elderly have received it. Of course, the younger people could be right about their likelihood of receiving Social Security.

Table 5-2 Old Age: Perceptions and Realities

Experiences	Perceptions Percent of Americans 18–34 who expect these things to happen when they get old	Realities Percent of Americans 65 and over who have experienced these things
More travel	77	46
More hobbies	76	56
Less active	69	41
New skills	64	28
More respect	62	53
Less stress	58	50 ☞

Table 5-2 Old Age: Perceptions and Realities (Continued)

Serious illness	48	25
Get Social Security	46	90
Can't drive	47	15
Get Medicare	44	80
Fewer responsibilities	43	50
Trouble walking	41	30
Lose bladder control	38	14
Less sex life	32	37
Become senile	29	2
Dependent on kids	29	5
Be lonely	26	24
Be poor	13	18

Source: *New York Times*. 1998. "Old Age: Perceptions, Realities." OP-ED Page. Advertisement sponsored by Americans Discuss Social Security. Data based on a National Survey conducted by Americans Discuss Social Security. Courtesy: Americans Discuss Social Security.

Many people believe that the Social Security program will eventually "go broke." While this is actually unlikely to happen, there can be little doubt that the social security system will continue to change during the years ahead.

The future of age discrimination is also likely to be influenced by growing numbers of retired persons. Members of the post-World War II Baby Boom generation will reach their sixties during the early decades of the next century. As this cohort makes the transition to retirement, the number of Social Security recipients per worker is expected to increase markedly, placing a much larger financial burden on the employed sector of the economy and increasing potential conflicts between young and old.

With increased awareness, age discrimination can be eliminated. Legislation may be necessary, but cultural attitudes must change. It appears that the poverty rate among the general elderly population has decreased, but the rate among minorities and white women has increased. This discrepancy must be examined.

Summary

Societies differ with respect to their treatment of the aged. In U. S. society, the elderly are negatively stereotyped and suffer more than their share of poverty. The fact of institutionalized retirement by age compounds their problems.

Age discrimination has meant more than impoverishment for millions of people. It has meant massive Social Security payments for the rest of society. The elderly have reacted in diverse ways. Many have accepted their roles. Others have actively sought to avoid the aged status. Elders may themselves attempt to strengthen a subculture, patterned after the consciousness-raising of the women's movement.

Many theories attempt to explain the treatment of the elderly. Symbolic interactionism focuses on interaction and the idea that the elderly hold low status. Marxist interpretations stress the political economy of aging. Disengagement theory has ties to structural functionalism and contends that it is better for society and the individual that the elderly should disengage from society and prepare for death.

Modernization theory attempts to explain variations in age status across societies. The status of the elderly seems to decline in modern societies for a number of reasons, such as education gaps, between the elderly and younger members of society. The age stratification perspective suggest that the age structure of roles in a society is organized much like social class. The location of elders within the age structure does not give them much status. Activity theory emphasizes the processes of social interaction. This theory suggest that the elderly must substitute roles in life in order to keep active and contribute positively to society.

Although there have been overall improvements in the well-being of the elderly, many elderly still lack access to important resources and may be mistreated by family members and acquaintances. Many elderly still experience poverty, health problems, and different forms of abuse. In addition, the elderly may be more vulnerable to certain types of crime.

Changes in cultural attitudes toward the elderly may enhance the status of the aged. Consciousness raising should begin with the elderly themselves. People should be evaluated for their attributes, relationships, and contributions to society regardless of their age. Increasing numbers of elders are taking political action to combat the negative stereotypes attached to their age. Organizations such as the Gray Panthers are active in protecting the elderly and enhancing their status.

The future of age discrimination is likely to be influenced by the growing numbers of elderly people in our society. Legislation may be necessary to combat age discrimination, but cultural attitudes must change. Although the poverty rate among the elderly has generally declined, some elderly Americans, especially women and African Americans continue to experience serious poverty.

Discussion Questions

1. What were your reactions to the "In the News" section on ageless love? What kinds of assumptions do you make about elderly people and their lives?

2. Can you suggest some ways in which we could change our perceptions of aging?

3. Try watching television looking for stereotypes of teenagers or the elderly. What impact do you think such stereotypes have on people's attitudes?

4. The Social Security retirement age is gradually being raised. What are some positive and negative aspects of raising the retirement age?

5. Think of what your life will be like when you are elderly. To what age do you intend to work? What kind of life do you hope to have?

References

Achenbaum, W. Andrew. 1978. *Old Age in the New Land*. Baltimore: Johns Hopkins University Press.

Administration on Aging. 1997. "A Profile of Older Americans:1997." Administration on Aging Website, U. S. Department of Health and Human Services. http://pr.aoa.dhhs.gov/aoa/stats/profile/.

Albert, Steven M., and Maria G. Cattell. 1994. *Old Age in Global Perspective: Cross-Cultural and Cross-National Views*. Social Issues in Global Perspective: Human Relations Area Files. New York: G. K. Hall.

Arendell, Terry, and Carroll L. Estes. 1991. "Older Women in the Post-Reagan Era." In *Critical Perspectives on Aging: Toward a Political and Moral Economy of Aging*, edited by Meredith Minkler and Carroll L. Estes. New York: Baywood.

Butler, Robert N. 1989. "Dispelling Ageism: The Cross-Cutting Intervention." *Annals of the American Academy of Political and Social Sciences* 503:138-47.

Dychtwald, Ken. 1989. *Age Wave: The Challenges and Oportunities of an Aging America*. Los Angeles: Jeremy Tarcher.

Fischer, David Hackett. 1978. *Growing Old in America*. New York: Oxford University Press.

Foreman, Judy. 1997. "Americans' Lives Both Longer and Healthier." *Boston Globe*, October.

Glendenning, Frank. 1997. "What Is Elder Abuse and Neglect?" In *The Mistreatment of Elderly People*, Second edition, edited by Peter DeCalmer and Frank Glendenning. Thousand Oaks, California: Sage Publications.

Haber, Carole, and Brian Gratton. 1994. *Old Age and the Search for Security*. Bloomington: Indiana University Press.

Harris, Louis. 1975. *The Myth and Reality of Aging in America*. Washington, D.C.: National Council on Aging.

Hatch, Laurie Russell. 1995. "Gray Clouds and Silver Linings: Women's Resources in Later Life." In *Women: A Feminist Perspective*. Mountain View, California: Mayfield Publishing.

Kalish, Richard A. 1970. "The Onset of the Dying Process." *Omega*:57-79.

Kristof, Nicholas D. 1997. "Once Prized, Japan's Elderly Feel Dishonored and Fearful." *New York Times*, August 4.

Lachs, Mark S., Christianna S. Williams, Shelley O'Brien, Karl Pillemer, and Mary E. Charlson. 1998. "The Mortality of Elderly Mistreatment." *Journal of American Medical Association* 280: 428-432.

Levin, Jack, and William C. Levin. 1980. *Ageism: Prejudice and Discrimination Against the Elderly*. Belmont, California: Wadsworth.

Levin, William C. 1988. "Age Stereotyping: College Student Evaluations." *Research on Aging* 10 (1988):134-48.

Levine, Bettuane. 1997. "Ageless Love." *Los Angeles Times, Life & Style Section*, August 13, E1, E6.

Lieberman, Trudy. 1998. "Hunger in America." In *Nation*, March 30, 11-16.

Males, Mike A. 1996. *The Scapegoat Generation: America's War on Adolescents*. Monroe, Maine: Common Courage Press.

———. 1997. "Debunking the 10 Worst Myths About America's Teens." *Wingspread Journal* 19(1):12-14.

Martin, L. G. 1989. "The Graying of Japan." In *Population Bulletin* 44 (2), 5-40. Washington, D.C.: Population Reference Bureau.

Matcha, Duane A. 1997. *The Sociology of Aging: A Social Problem*. Boston: Allyn and Bacon.

National Center on Elder Abuse. 1997. *Elder Abuse in Domestic Settings*. NCEA Statistics: Elder Abuse Information Series #1-3. http://www.gwjapan.com/NCEA/Statistics/.

National Institute on Aging. 1996. *NIA Age Page: Crime and Older People*. Gaithersburg, Maryland: Department of Health and Human Services, National Institutes of Health. http://www.nih.gov/nia/health/pub/crime.htm.

Palmore, Erdman, and Daisaku Maeda. 1985. *The Honorable Elders Revisited*. Durham: Duke University Press.

Passuth, Patricia M., and Vern L. Bengtson. 1988. *Emergent Theories of Aging*. New York: Springer Publishing.

Quadagno, Jill, and Debra Street, eds. 1996. *Aging for the Twenty-First Century: Readings in Social Gerontology*. New York: St. Martin's Press.

Rosow, Irving. 1974. *Socialization to Old Age*. Berkeley: University of California Press.

Scrutton, Steve. 1990. "Ageism: The Foundation of Age Discrimination." In *Age: The Unrecognized Discrimination*, edited by Evelyn McEwen. London: Age Concern.

Treas, Judy. 1995. "Older Americans in the 1990s and Beyond." *Population Bulletin* 2.

Tuckman, Jacob, and Irving Lorge. 1953. "Attitudes Toward Old People." *Journal of Social Psychology* 37:249-260.

U.S. Bureau of the Census. 1995. *Population Profile of the United States: 1995*. Current Population Reports, Series P23,189. Washington, D.C.: U. S. Government Printing Office.

U.S. Bureau of the Census. 1997. *Statistical Abstract of the United States: 1996*, Washington, D.C.: U. S. Government Printing Office.

U.S. Department of Justice. 1997. *National Crime Victimization Survey (NCVS)*. Washington, D.C. Bureau of Justice Statistics. http://www.ojp.usdoj.gov/bjs/.

Wellman, N.S., D. O. Weddle, S. Kranz, C. T. Brain. 1996. "Elder Insecurities: Poverty, Hunger and Malnutrition."American Dietetic Association (ADA) HungerLine 6(Spring):1-4. http://www.fiu.edu/~nutreldr/Elder_Insecurities.htm.

Web Sites

http://www-lib.usc.edu/Info/Gero/gerourl.htm

Andrus Gerontology Library, University of Southern California. This website provides links to numerous WWW sources on aging and related topics. The links to sociology and psychology resources are especially useful.

http://pr.aoa.dhhs.gov/aoa/stats/profile

A Profile of Older Americans: 1997, Administration on Aging, Department of Health and Human Services. This government site provides an invaluable statistical profile of elderly Americans.

http://www.mbnet.mb.ca/scip/categ.html

Senior Computer Information Project. This Canadian-based website provides information on many senior issues and includes links to other sites.

CHAPTER SIX

Sexual Orientation and Homophobia

In the News: 'Ellen' Comes out on Prime Time

In one of the most eagerly awaited and heavily watched prime-time television shows of 1997, the title character of the sitcom Ellen *came out as a lesbian. Ellen DeGeneres, the star of the show, also came out in real life as a lesbian. One* Boston Globe *reporter reacted ironically to the show, noting that "once you get past the fact we can't serve openly in the military, can't adopt children in some states, can be discriminated against in employment and housing, and have been demonized by the religious right, it's a great time to be a lesbian" (Graham 1997).*

All over the country, people celebrated as Ellen acknowledged her sexual orientation. The Gay and Lesbian Task Force Against Defamation (GLAAD) held fund-raisers in various cities, while many others celebrated privately. Kristin Esterberg, chairwoman of the Kansas City chapter of GLAAD and professor of sociology and director of the Women's Studies Department at the University of Missouri, Kansas City, suggested that, "television is really where a lot of people get their ideas about other people, so having Ellen come out is very important" (Van Gelder 1997). Many others expressed elation about the show, feeling that it was an important step in the increasing acceptance of homosexuality in the United States. Some watchers emulated Ellen and publicly declared themselves gay.

Not everyone appreciated the episode. WBMA-TV, the ABC affiliate in Birmingham, Alabama, refused to carry it. Organizations around the country protested. In Washington D.C., Americans for the Truth About Homosexuality protested in front of ABC's news bureau. The American Family Association, based in Tupelo, Mississippi, tried to convince sponsors to withdraw their advertising from the show, and some advertisers complied. The Southern Baptist Conference mentioned the coming out episode as one of its reasons for urging a boycott of Disney Enterprises, which owns ABC.

The coming out episode of Ellen *may help change attitudes toward gay men and lesbians. In Hollywood, changing attitudes are evident in the increasing willingness of actors and actresses to play gay characters. A recent* New York Times *article suggested that playing a gay role has gone "from poison apple to plum role" (Weinraub 1997). Tom Hanks, Harry Hamlin, Kevin Kline, Robin Williams, and Nathan Lane have all played gay roles in recent years. Those roles have certainly not hurt their careers.*

The Gallup Poll has documented increasing acceptance of homosexuality and the rights of homosexuals, at least in some areas of American social life. According to a Gallup Poll taken soon after the Ellen episode, about 50 percent of Americans were not bothered by and did not care much about the show, while 37 percent were bothered by it. A Boston Globe *headline suggested that the show provided "the kind of lesbian icon a mother could love" (Graham 1997). Another headline suggested that the episode "makes history and saves sitcom" (Biddle 1997). The episode may have saved the sitcom, but the extent to which it made history is unclear. The Gallup Poll found that only about 7 percent of Americans were actually pleased at Ellen's character being gay (Saad 1997). Most Americans still view homosexuality negatively, despite breakthroughs like* Ellen.

Definition and Prevalence

❖ ❖ ❖ ❖

Think about your own sexual orientation. That is, are you bisexual, a gay male, a lesbian, or straight? Whatever your sexual orientation, what led you to it? If you are heterosexual, sometimes referred to as straight, you may never have considered that question. It may even sound bizarre. That's just the way people are, you may think. If you are gay, lesbian, or bisexual, you probably have thought about your sexual orientation and considered the reasons for it. You may even be familiar with some of the research on why people become homosexuals. If you think about it, that research should also explain how and why people become heterosexual. Of course, the question of how people become heterosexual rarely comes up in research on and discussions of sexual orientation. Heterosexuality is seen as natural and not needing explanation.

Heterosexual indoctrination pervades American society. The Gallup Poll results attest to the continuing strength of **compulsory heterosexuality** (Rich 1980). Almost everyone is socialized to be heterosexual in the United States. Heterosexuality is expected, actually demanded. **Opposite-sex eroticism** is the norm; **same-sex eroticism** is frowned upon. Many people believe that males who are more "masculine" are more attractive to women and that more "feminine" women will be more attractive to men. Sons and daughters are raised to be attractive to the opposite sex, and any resistance is perceived as abnormal (Pogrebin 1980).

Acceptance of lebian, gay, and bisexual life styles has increased in the United States in recent years, although the depth and virulence of homophobia is still troubling. —*Photo: photostogo. com.*

Given the pervasiveness of heterosexuality in American society, it's not surprising that most Americans have a negative view of homosexuality. Nor is it surprising that if you are a heterosexual, you may never have considered why.

Although attitudes continue to change, the Gallup Poll suggests that many Americans believe that **homosexuality**, which refers to sexual attraction to the same sex, and **bisexuality**, which refers to sexual attraction to members of both sexes, are abnormal and morally wrong. However, attitudes about homosexuality differ depending on the area of social life being considered. For example, in a 1996 Gallup Poll, 84 percent of those polled favored equal job opportunities for homosexuals, but only 39 percent supported extending civil rights protections to them. Responding to an April 1996 Gallup survey, 67 percent opposed legalizing same-sex marriages. In 1996, President

Clinton signed into law the Federal Defense of Marriage Act, which denied recognition to same-sex marriages (Golay 1997).

Many heterosexuals continue to stereotype gays, lesbians, and bisexuals. Such stereotyping often leads heterosexuals to see sexual orientation as the dominant aspect of a gay, lesbian, or bisexual person's life. In fact, gays, lesbians, and bisexual men and women are individuals who differ from one another in personality and lifestyle just as do heterosexuals. Gays, lesbians, and bisexuals are no more totally and exclusively sexual than are heterosexuals. To a large degree, the only obvious difference between many homosexuals, bisexuals, and heterosexuals is in the choice of sexual partners. As with heterosexuals, gays, lesbians, and bisexuals may be of any socioeconomic status, occupation, religion, race, educational level, or age.

From a sociological perspective, homosexuality is not deviant or morally wrong. Many Americans may consider homosexuality as a form of **deviance**, but for sociologists deviance is a relative concept. Certain behaviors may be considered deviant in one society but not in another. Some behaviors may be seen as deviant at one time but not at another. The historian Lawrence Stone argues that "over the long history of Western civilization, there has been no such thing as 'normal sexuality'" (1985:37). Stone further notes that sexuality is culturally defined, has changed dramatically over time, and will probably undergo surprising transformations in the future. Other civilizations have also considered a wide variety of sexual behaviors acceptable (Greenberg 1988).

In this chapter we focus on homosexuality, with some reference to bisexuality. In addition to examining the dominant explanations for homosexuality, we also examine the causes and consequences of **homophobia**, the fear, misunderstanding, and hatred of homosexuals. Homophobia, which is virulent and extensive in the United States, can lead to discrimination and violence against gays, lesbians, and bisexuals. For more information, see "A Closer Look: What is Homophobia?"

We initially defined homosexuality as sexual attraction to a person of the same sex, but things are more complicated than that. Some social and natural scientists define homosexuality as an individual choice, while others define it as a biological condition that is beyond an individual's choice (Meier and Geis 1997). The terms *sexual preference* and *sexual orientation* are both used to define a person's sexuality. **Sexual preference** implies a choice, while **sexual orientation** reflects a more deterministic view of homosexuality as a biological condition. "Heterosexuals tend to assume that homosexuality is a matter of sexual preference, while gays and lesbians tend to define their sexuality in terms of sexual orientation" (Eitzen and Zinn 1997:296). The authors see the term *sexual orientation* as broader and more accurate, although we consider that the evidence for a biological basis for homosexuality is inconclusive.

Complications do not end with the distinction between preference and orientation. Homosexuality also has at least three differing connotations: "homosexual behavior, homosexual preference or orientation, and homosexual identity or self-concept" (Meier and Geis 1997:115). These connotations differ from one another and need not overlap in a person's life. For example, a person may define his or her own sexual identity as homosexual yet never engage in a homosexual relationship, perhaps because of fear of exposure and

What Is Homophobia?

The Boston NOW Lesbian Task Force defines homophobia quite clearly in the statements below:

- Looking at a gay male/lesbian and automatically thinking of their sexuality rather than seeing him/her as a whole, complex person.

- Thinking you can "spot one."

- Using the terms "gay, lesbian, queer, fag, homo" as accusatory.

- Thinking that if a gay male/lesbian touches you he/she is making sexual advances.

- Stereotyping gay males/lesbians as promiscuous, "recruiters," separatists, or radicals.

- Feeling repulsed by public displays of affection between gay men or lesbians but accepting the same affectionate displays between heterosexuals as O.K.

- Wondering which one is the "man/woman" in a gay or lesbian couple.

- Feeling that gays and lesbians are too outspoken about gay rights.

- Assuming that everyone you meet is heterosexual.

- Feeling that a gay male or lesbian is homosexual because he/she could not find a heterosexual partner or because they were victims of rape or child sexual abuse.

- Not confronting a heterosexist remark for fear of being identified with gay males/lesbians.

discrimination. Such fears make many people who have had homosexual relationships continue to define themselves as heterosexuals.

These complications, and others, make it difficult to determine the prevalence of homosexuality in American society; prevalence data depend on which definition of homosexuality is used. In one of the most extensive surveys of adult sexual behavior ever conducted, Edward Laumann and his colleagues found that 2.7 percent of the males in their sample and 1.3 percent of the females reported having sex with someone of the same sex during the previous year (Laumann, et al. 1994). Other estimates go as high as 10 percent of the population. To make things even more difficult, we have no reliable data on how many people have a homosexual orientation or self-concept. We tentatively estimate that between 3 and 10 percent of the population are gay or lesbian. Some gay and lesbian activists prefer the higher estimates because they think that makes a stronger case against discrimination. Many other people concerned with human rights argue that discrimination against gays, lesbians, and bisexuals should not be tolerated regardless of their percentage of the population.

Homosexuals do continue to be targets of much discrimination in American society. Many heterosexuals use epithets for homosexuals—queers, fairies, dykes, and fags—words connoting revulsion and hostility. Homosexuals often call themselves gay, a label implying self-acceptance and political liberation. The term *queer* is also increasingly used by gays and lesbians in a positive way. **Gay** is more likely to refer to homosexual men, while homosexual women are referred to as **lesbians**. Robert Meier and Gilbert Geis point out that the prefix "homo" refers to "same," not "male," and thus applies to both male and female homosexuals. They also note that most of the writing and research on homosexuality has focused on male homosexuals (1997).

There is no reliable evidence that the homosexual population is growing, although homosexuality is more visible now than it was in the past. As gay men, lesbians, and bisexuals become more visible, they may appear more numerous to heterosexuals. Growing numbers of openly gay parents are raising children, thereby defining parenthood as a component of their gay identity. Lesbian and gay relationships, long hidden from heterosexual society, are becoming increasingly open and are receiving some legal recognition.

New York's highest court, for example, ruled that gay partners constitute a family for purposes of rent control laws. In 1989, New York Mayor Koch signed a Domestic Partners Law which extended benefits such as funeral leave to gay city employees. The California secretary of state now allows gay families to register as unincorporated nonprofit associations. On February 14, 1991, a domestic partners law took effect in San Francisco. This law creates a legal mechanism for members of an unmarried couple, whether gay or heterosexual, to register their relationship. Despite these significant steps forward for gays and lesbians, there is still a great deal of discrimination against them, much of it based on homophobia (Herek and Berrill 1992).

Levels of Causation

We examine here three different approaches to the origins of sexual orientation: individual (or biological), cultural, and structural.

Individual

Scientific research has generated increasing evidence for a biological basis for homosexuality, and this research has received much media attention (Angier 1993; Gelman 1992; Thompson 1995). Many gays, lesbians, and bisexuals welcome the possibility that their sexuality is biologically based, that they did not choose to be homosexual. For some, a biological base for homosexuality would emphasize its naturalness. Others, fearing that such research could be turned against homosexuality, claim that "such research is necessarily heterosexist and continuous with the oppressive lineage of science that had as its goal the eradication of homoeroticism" (Murphy 1997:5).

There are various strands of research into a biological basis for homosexuality. One of the best known is neuroanatomist Simon LeVay's study of differences in the size of one area of the brain, the hypothalamus, for homosexual and heterosexual men (1991, 1993). Numerous criticisms of this research led Timothy Murphy to see LeVay's work as "suggestive" but certainly not definitive (1997). This research did receive some fairly sensationalist and oversimplified attention in the popular press. LeVay was not pleased with much of the coverage and insisted that he did not prove that "homosexuality is genetic or some such thing" (1993:122).

Another study that received much media attention was that of molecular geneticist Dean Hamer and his colleagues (Hamer et al. 1993; Hamer and

Copeland 1994). The researchers suggested a "strong genetic involvement in homosexual orientation," but Murphy argues that "their study is clear evidence that there *must* be multiple pathways to the same erotic outcome" (1997:34).

Although some gays and lesbians oppose biological research on homosexuality, others suggest that it will not necessarily have negative consequences for gay men, lesbians, and bisexuals. It is important to keep a balanced view of such research. Both LeVay's and Hamer's research received much media attention, including articles in weekly news magazines. These articles and those in newspapers often trumpeted the research as major breakthroughs in understanding the causes of homosexual orientation. They were not; they were important but limited steps toward a more complete understanding of sexual orientation. It is also important not to put too much emphasis on the implications of such research. Biologist Ruth Hubbard notes that "grounding difference in biology does not stem bigotry" (Hubbard and Wald 1993:95). Bigotry toward those who are "different" should be opposed on its own, regardless of the source of the difference.

Homosexuality has also been viewed as a form of psychosexual disorder, equivalent to a disease or illness. However, in 1973, the American Psychological Association asserted that homosexuality was not a mental illness, and the American Psychiatric Association followed suit the next year by dropping homosexuality from its list of mental disorders. Many people still believe that homosexuals can be "cured," but gays and lesbians claim that homosexuality is not a condition that can be cured, any more than heterosexuals can be cured of their attraction to the opposite sex (Angier 1993).

Some individuals and organizations see homosexuality as a mental illness and advocate "conversion" or "reparative" therapy to convert gays to heterosexuality. At its 1997 annual meeting, the American Psychological Association passed a motion calling for conversion therapists to obtain consent before beginning conversion therapy with a gay male or lesbian. To the dismay of many gay and lesbian individuals and groups, the association stopped short of condemning conversion therapy. Supporters of conversion therapy, many of whom are motivated by religious beliefs, condemned the motion for interfering with the therapy (*Boston Globe* August 15, 1997).

Homophobia may also be explained from an individual perspective. Psychoanalytic theory holds that homophobia is the result of repressed homosexual urges that the person is either unaware of or denies. Instead of dealing with these feelings, the individual may react negatively to homosexuality as a way to ensure his or her own heterosexuality. In addition to insecurity about their own sexual identity, some heterosexual men see gay men as feminine. The extreme homophobia exhibited by some men may therefore be "rooted in fear and hatred of women" (Nowak 1993:3).

Heterosexism also plays an important role in generating homophobia. Gregory Herek defines heterosexism "as an ideological system that denies, denigrates, and stigmatizes any non-heterosexual form of behavior, identity, relationship, or community" (Herek and Berrill 1992). Herek argues that **psychological heterosexism**, "the manifestation of heterosexism in individuals' attitudes and actions," may play a role in anti-gay violence by filling psychological functions for those who hold such attitudes.

Cultural

Cultures differ as to whether and under what circumstances they accept homosexuality or find it deviant. Societies define right and wrong by creating values and norms. Failure to follow the norms is considered deviance. American society, with its norms of heterosexuality, stigmatizes homosexuality as deviance. However, not all cultures react negatively to homosexuality. For example, the Siberian Chukchee and the Aleutian Koniaga cultures provide an institutionalized shaman role for male homosexuals. These men adopt feminine dress, activities, and mannerisms; become "wives;" of other men, and assume the "female" role in intercourse. In some societies, among the Keraki and Kiwai of New Guinea, for instance, male homosexuality is an institutionalized feature of puberty rites. All males must engage in homosexual behavior, such practices being seen as essential for growth and strength (Greenberg 1988; Rosenblum and Travis 1996).

Most Western cultures have not built overt homosexual behavior into their accepted and obligatory social roles; indeed, homosexual behavior has long been discouraged. Not only has Judeo-Christian religion taken a strong stand against homosexual behavior, but secular laws have also prohibited and punished acts of sodomy, broadly defined as any sexual practice considered unnatural in a society but usually referring specifically to anal or oral sex. Public opinion in twentieth-century Europe and the United States remains hostile to overt homosexual behavior (Rosenblum and Travis 1996).

In spite of continuing hostility towards gays, lesbians, and bisexuals, there have been important advances. Many European countries allow gays and lesbians to marry, although with some restrictions. In the United States a growing number of corporations and cities provide same-sex partner benefits. Nine states have some form of gay and lesbian rights (American Civil Liberties Union 1997). These changes indicate growing acceptance of gays, lesbians, and bisexuals; however, the Gallup Poll cited earlier suggests that many Americans continue to disapprove of homosexuality. In research for his Middle Class Morality Project, sociologist Alan Wolfe (1998) found that those he interviewed accepted diversity in American society, except when it came to gays, lesbians, and bisexuals.

Larry Gross (1993) notes that sexual acts between members of the same sex occur in all societies, but only in some instances have they become the organizing principle for distinctive subcultures. Gay and lesbian subcultures have become more visible in recent years in Western nations but are not yet accepted as positive attributes of our larger culture. Most people continue to be raised as heterosexuals and see heterosexuality as "normal."

Ironically, Gross suggests that most young gays, lesbians, and bisexuals get their first introduction to what it means to be gay from mainstream mass media. However, the mass media regularly engage in negative stereotyping of gay men and lesbians, so many in the gay movement point to the media as a major source of oppression. The media do play an important role in maintaining cultural beliefs and fostering homophobia. For example, the "In the News" feature for this chapter focused on the "coming out episode" of the television show *Ellen*. That episode seemed to mark increasing openness to homosexuality in television. However, ABC later held back one episode of the show and wanted to give the show a TV-14 rating to indicate that it was unsuitable for children under 14. The reason for the rating was that the leading

❖ ❖ ❖ ❖

character was gay (Bark 1997). Other television shows with milder sexual situations and dialogue did not receive the rating.

There are probably no simple causes of homophobia. People may grow up exposed to more or less the same beliefs about sexuality but, as adults, may hold different attitudes. Personal experiences and feelings combine with social images and models to produce points of view and to inform beliefs in ways that cannot be accurately predicted.

With regard to sex roles, homosexuality is often seen as one of the worst things "to happen" to males. In a patriarchal society such as the United States, men are generally more valued than women, as long as they conform to traditionally established masculine roles. Our society works hard to convince everyone that boys are better. Taunts such as "sissy" or "faggot" imply that a male is a non-boy. One of the worst insults a boy can give to another boy is to call him a girl. Military training instructors and football coaches often refer to their trainees or players as "girls," evidently to encourage them to be "tougher" and "more male." Sexism and homophobia seem to go hand in hand. The homophobic male needs clearly defined gender-role boundaries to help him avoid transgressing to the "other side" and appearing feminine (Pogrebin 1980).

Women seem to be less threatened by homosexuality than men and less obsessed with latent homosexual tendencies or impulses. Letty Pogrebin argues that this may be so because the process of becoming a woman is considered less important to society than the process of proving one's manhood. Not that homosexual women are readily accepted by society. Lesbianism is often viewed as the ultimate crime against traditional norms: a lesbian does not need men at all, so lesbians may be seen as hostile alternatives to heterosexual marriage, family, and patriarchal survival.

Structural

In the past, some social scientists suggested that certain types of family relationships might be linked to the development of homosexuality. One of these scenarios features an overpossessive mother who demasculinizes her son and attempts to form an intimate alliance with him against the father (Bieber 1971). Others have suggested that an overprotective and indulgent mother produces a homosexual son. These studies are unreliable; almost no social scientists accept them today, but they do raise interesting questions. Both positions suggest that mothers cause their sons to become gay. Mothers may be blamed for children "becoming" homosexuals because in traditional gender roles mothers are considered the primary caretakers of their children. Gays, lesbians, and bisexuals are seen as threats to traditional gender roles.

From a sociological viewpoint, the more interesting questions have to do with understanding the causes for the depth and virulence of the prejudice and discrimination directed against homosexuals in the United States. What can account for this hostility to homosexuals in some societies, including this one?

Levin and Levin suggest that prejudice and discrimination may have functions for a society. Robert Merton uses the term *positive function* to describe a consequence that aids in a system's adaptation or adjustment (1968). He also identified the concept of **dysfunction**, a consequence that diminishes or detracts from the adaptation or adjustment of a system. Levin and

Levin argue that if we use Merton's ideas, we can understand why certain behaviors, such as discrimination against gays and lesbians, persist. Discriminating against gays and lesbians reinforces heterosexuality: Because most children are socialized to be heterosexual, discouraging homosexual behavior will help children adapt well to a predominantly heterosexual society. Even if many people do not blatantly discriminate, they effectively promote heterosexuality. The negative side, or dysfunction, of such discrimination would be the emotional and physical harm gays and lesbians suffer simply because they are not heterosexual (Levin and Levin 1982; Merton 1968). Keep in mind that this kind of functionalist language can seem to confer a sense of the usefulness of prejudice and discrimination, but this is not what Levin and Levin and Merton have in mind. In fact, such prejudice and discrimination often constitutes **scapegoating** in which one group is blamed for the troubles of the society or other groups.

Bisexuality also functions as a rejection of the norm of sexuality but becomes even more complicated than homosexuality. People who are bisexual, and not just in transition between heterosexuality and homosexuality, have resisted accommodating completely to either heterosexuality or homosexuality. There appears to be much less tolerance for bisexuality in the United States than there is for homosexuality (Valverde 1987).

It is important to observe that there is a growing tolerance for homosexuality. Emerging homosexual communities in large urban centers and the formation of homophile organizations are not merely a reaction against stigma but reflect radical changes in the attitudes of the public and gays. Being homosexual does not mean that one is unable to function, produce, or create. A deviation from the sexual norms of society does not inevitably entail disastrous consequences.

The functionalist account helps us understand why discrimination against gay men and lesbians is pervasive in a predominantly heterosexual society that enforces norms of compulsive heterosexuality. It does not help with more basic questions—why is the society predominantly heterosexual and why are norms of compulsive heterosexuality so strongly held? Why should reinforcing norms of heterosexism be so important? Here again, examining heterosexism can help us.

Following Herek, we define heterosexism as an ideological system that denies, denigrates, and stigmatizes any nonheterosexual form of behavior, identity, relationship, or community. Like racism, sexism, and other ideologies of oppression, heterosexism is manifested both in societal customs and institutions, such as religion and the legal system, and in individual attitudes and behaviors. The Catholic Church, for example, officially opposed extending civil-rights protection to gay people; this Vatican statement was widely interpreted as condoning anti-gay violence (Herek and Berrill 1992). Judeo-Christian tradition considers homosexual behavior a serious sin. The Old Testament approves of sexual intercourse only within marriage and for the purpose of procreation. Present-day religious denominations have varied in their reactions to homosexuality. Roman Catholicism and right-wing Protestant churches generally condemn homosexuality and have sometimes gone so far as to condone discrimination against homosexuals in employment, housing, and the adoption of children. On the other hand, the Quakers fully accept gays, lesbians, and bisexuals.

The social constructionist perspective has also been widely used in the sociological understanding of gays, lesbians, and bisexuals. The social constructionist perspective emphasizes that sexuality, sexual desire, and sexual orientation—often seen as natural—are socially and culturally variable and complex (Vance 1998). This approach suggests that people develop a gay, lesbian, or bisexual identity through a process of self-definition and labeling in which they go through a series of stages of greater acceptance of their sexual orientation (Troiden 1998).

Consequences

The consequences of being gay, lesbian, or bisexual in a heterosexist, homophobic society range from derogatory comments to horrendous anti-gay violence. Our legal institutions have always discriminated against gays and lesbians in one form or another. Prohibitions against sodomy were universal in the United States until 1961. Since then, many states have repealed their sodomy laws, with twenty-four states still having them. Although many heterosexuals engage in sex acts prohibited by the sodomy laws, the laws have been used and still are used to harass homosexuals, especially gay men (Leonard 1990).

Table 6-1 States Permitting Lesbians and Gay Men to Adopt

California	New Jersey
Connecticut	New Mexico
Illinois	New York
Indiana	Ohio
Iowa	Oregon
Maryland	Pennsylvania
Massachusetts	Rhode Island
Michigan	Texas
Minnesota	Vermont
Nevada	Washington and the District of Columbia

Source: American Civil Liberties Union Fact Sheet. 1997 http://www.aclu.org

Institutional heterosexism gives heterosexuals many privileges. For example, heterosexuals are allowed to marry the person they love. Homosexual couples cannot. Heterosexual couples are entitled to receive all the benefits that the government and the private sector can give to married couples. Homosexual couples cannot be guaranteed these privileges. A heterosexual can legally adopt a child. A homosexual couple either cannot adopt, depending on the state (see Table 6-1), or has an extremely difficult time doing so. In fact, in many jurisdictions, heterosexist laws make being in a homosexual relationship grounds for taking his or her own children away from a homosexual. This happened in the late 1990s to Sharon Bottoms, a mother in Virginia whose child was taken away from her because the judge did not approve of her lesbian relationship. Many people believe that children exposed to homosexuality will either be molested or become homosexual themselves. (See "A Closer Look: Gay and Lesbian Parenting.")

Gay and Lesbian Parenting

The topic of gay parenting usually only surfaces in the context of custody or adoption discussions. Whether or not gays and lesbians make good parents remains a controversial subject even though many nontraditional types of families have been legally recognized throughout the country. For example, in an effort to meet the need for care of so-called unwanted children, many states have allowed adoptions by single parents (Collum 1993). A number of these single parents may be homosexual. Some are open about their sexuality, others are not. Those who are not open rightly fear discrimination and violence; some fear losing custody or visitation rights. Carole Collum estimates that the number of lesbian mothers and gay fathers is well over 2 million and the number of children being raised by them is as high as 6 million. Many of these parents had their children during a past heterosexual relationship; also, many have adopted children outside a traditional heterosexual relationship. A recent "baby boom" among lesbians over the past five years increased the number of children raised by homosexuals substantially. This increase is mainly a result of artificial insemination.

Some states allow gays and lesbians to adopt children—or at least do not have laws against such adoptions. Most of these states apply a "best interest of the child" standard to make a final determination about an adoption (American Civil Liberties Union 1997). As of 1997, only Florida and New Hampshire had specific statutes prohibiting gay and lesbian adoptions. Second-parent adoptions are being granted in other states. They have occurred where the adopting co-parents were the child's natural parent, a heterosexual partner of the parent, and a same-sex partner of the parent. Co-parent adoptions have been granted by judges in Alaska, California, Minnesota, New York, Oregon, Vermont, Washington, and the District of Columbia (Collum 1993).

Many courts have recognized that a parent's sexual orientation is not contrary to the child's best interest. Attorneys have basically argued that children raised by gay parents are no more likely to have psychological problems than those raised by straight parents. Based on such evidence and arguments, many courts have recognized that sexual orientation alone cannot provide the basis for denying custody.

A recent case in Hawaii raised many of these issues. In *Baehr et al. v Miike*, the judge ruled that the state's refusal to grant marriage licenses to gay and lesbian couples violated the state's constitution. His ruling cleared the way for three lesbian and gay couples to marry. One of the central issues in the case was gay and lesbian parenting. Among those testifying for the plaintiffs were sociologist Dr. Pepper Schwartz and psychologist Dr. Charlotte Patterson. Dr. Schwartz and Dr. Patterson both testified that the research on gay and lesbian parenting indicated that gays and lesbians can parent as well as heterosexual parents. Unfortunately, the Hawaii legislature responded to the ruling by passing and sending to the voters a constitutional amendment banning gay and lesbian marriages in the state.

Not all courts agree: In May 1997, the American Civil Liberties Union (ACLU) opened a case against that statute. Florida passed a statute banning gays and lesbians from adopting children. The ACLU argues that the law violates the Florida Constitution's equal protection guarantee. No other group is targeted as ineligible for adopting—even convicted felons (American Civil Liberites Union 1997).

Job security is also a privilege for heterosexuals. Heterosexuals can be sure that they will not be fired from their jobs because of their sexual orientation. In Kansas, people can be fired from jobs simply for being homosexual. With regard to personal security, heterosexuals can walk down the street holding hands without the fear of being verbally or physically assaulted. Homosexual couples cannot, and if they are attacked, they are blamed for "flaunting it" or "bringing it on themselves."

❖ ❖ ❖ ❖

A Closer Look

The National Gay and Lesbian Task Force (NGLTF) Website

The National Gay and Lesbian Task Force (NGLTF) was founded in 1973 to support grassroots organizing and advocacy for lesbian, gay, bisexual, and transgender rights. The NGLTF is a major resource center for grassroots organizations that are working at state and local levels on a variety of initiatives, among which are combating anti-gay violence, defeating anti-gay legislative and ballot measures, and advocating an end to job discrimination based on sexual orientation.

The NGLTF website is located at http://www.ngltf.org. You'll find that the Task Force site offers information on legislative and nonlegislative activities concerning gays and lesbians. Since its inception, NGLTF has been at the forefront of every major initiative for lesbian and gay rights.

This website offers a myriad of information regarding gay and lesbian issues. If you click on the "Main Menu," a table of contents is available with the following choices: General Information, Press Releases, Publications, How to join NGLTF, and Upcoming Events. The "General Information" segment gives a detailed background of NGLTF, its goals, and achievements. If you click on "Publications" you will receive a list of bestsellers concerning gay and lesbian issues as well as a "State of the States Report."

The prevailing attitude toward homosexuals often seems to be revulsion and hostility. This attitude has led to violence directed at gay men and lesbians. The first national study of anti-gay violence was conducted by the National Gay and Lesbian Task Force (NGLTF) (1984). The study sampled 1,420 gay men and 654 lesbians in eight U.S. cities: Boston, New York, Atlanta, St. Louis, Denver, Dallas, Los Angeles, and Seattle. Among those surveyed, 19 percent reported having been punched, hit, kicked, or beaten at least once in their lives because of their sexual orientation; 44 percent had been threatened with physical violence. In addition, 94 percent had experienced some type of victimization (including being verbally abused, physically assaulted, abused by police, assaulted with a weapon, having property vandalized, being spat upon, being chased or followed, or being pelted with objects), and 84 percent knew other gay or lesbian individuals who had been victimized because of their sexual orientation.

Many respondents had been victimized more than once. For example, 92 percent of those who were targets of anti-gay epithets noted that they had experienced such harassment "more than once" or "many times." More than two-thirds (68 percent) of those who had been threatened with violence and nearly half (47 percent) of those who had been physically assaulted reported multiple experiences of such episodes.

The threat of anti-gay violence had a major impact on the attitudes and behavior of those surveyed by the NGLTF: 83 percent of the men and women believed they might be victimized in the future, and 62 percent said they feared for their safety. Also, 45 percent reported having modified their behavior to reduce the risk of attack. For example, they took a self-defense class, avoided certain locations, or avoided physical contact with friends or lovers in public places. It is not just the incidence of anti-gay and anti-lesbian violence that is so disturbing. The cases described in Herek and Berrill's *Hate Crimes: Confronting Violence Against Lesbians and Gay Men* (1992) should never be tolerated in any society.

Gay men and lesbians also remain largely outside the law (Melton 1989). Except in four states (Wisconsin, Massachusetts, Hawaii, and Connecticut) and several dozen municipalities (including San Francisco, New York City, and Chicago), discrimination on the basis of sexual orientation is not prohibited in employment, housing, or services. Gay relationships generally have no legal status, and lesbian and gay male parents often lose legal custody of their own children when their homosexuality becomes known (Falk 1989).

Nearly half of the states outlaw private homosexual acts between consenting adults, and their right to do so was upheld by the U.S. Supreme Court in 1986. Justices Byron White and Warren Burger refused to find a constitutional right for adults to engage privately in consenting homosexual behavior; their arguments were based on the fact that legal proscriptions against sodomy have ancient origins and that condemnation of homosexuality is firmly rooted in Judeo-Christian standards (*Bowers v. Hardwick 1986*).

Herek and Berrill argue that the mass media perpetuate cultural heterosexism. In the past, media portrayals of homosexuality were relatively infrequent, and when they did occur they were typically negative. V. Russo's study of Hollywood films demonstrated that most homosexual characters died before the end of the movie, usually from suicide or murder (1981). Even when gay characters were portrayed positively, in more recent films and television programs, they almost always appeared in the story because they were gay, that is, because their homosexuality was important to the plot (Gross 1993). This policy has changed recently, and gays and lesbians have been portrayed more positively in films and on television.

Homosexuals are vulnerable to exploitation by blackmail and are prey to theft and physical harm. Since the beginning of the modern gay liberation movement in the 1960s, a large body of data on anti-gay violence and other victimization has been developed. Thousands of episodes of violence have been reported to police departments and local and national organizations, including the American Civil Liberties Union and the National Gay and Lesbian Task Force. Thousands and thousands of incidents have gone unreported. Males generally experience higher levels of anti-gay violence than lesbians. Lesbians generally experience higher rates of verbal harassment and report greater fear of anti-gay violence (Herek and Berrill 1992).

Ruth Sidel argues that homosexuals are consistent targets of violence and bias in the United States (1994). The brutal murder of an American sailor highlights the level of hostility felt toward homosexuals by some Americans. On September 30, 1992, Allen R. Schindler, twenty-two, a naval radioman stationed on the USS *Belleau Wood*, told his commanding officer that he was homosexual. A month later, he went to a park near the naval base in Japan and was battered to death against the fixtures of a public toilet. The following day, two other sailors from the ship were arrested.

After admitting to participating in the murder and agreeing to testify for the prosecution, one of the arrested sailors was given a four-month sentence and a bad-conduct discharge. To many, his lenient punishment symbolized the Navy's lack of concern for the murder of one of their own who also happened to be homosexual. The Navy had originally charged the other sailor with premeditated murder, which carries a possible death sentence. However, in May 1993, he was permitted to plead guilty to the lesser charge of murder with intent to commit great bodily harm and was sentenced to life imprisonment.

During the same period as this trial, three marines were acquitted of charges that they had assaulted three men at a Wilmington, North Carolina bar that caters to homosexuals. The three marines allegedly dragged one man out of the bar and beat him while shouting "Clinton must pay," apparently referring to President Clinton's efforts to lift the ban on gay men and lesbian women serving in the military (Sidel 1994).

The military became very defensive when Clinton promised to lift the ban on gays in the U.S. military. Colin Powell, chairman of the U.S. Joint Chiefs of Staff, opposed lifting the ban, claiming that "the presence of homosexuals in the force would be detrimental to good order and discipline" (Nowak 1993:1). In a July 1993 policy statement, President Clinton backed down. He proposed that gays and lesbians be allowed to serve in the military only if they hide their sexual orientation. To aid them in this subterfuge, Clinton proposed that the military cease investigating active-duty personnel and questioning new recruits about their sexual orientation. Despite these changes, anti-gay sentiment pervades the military (Nowak 1993). Interestingly enough, prior to World War II, the U.S. military had never systematically screened homosexuals from entering the service. It was not until 1941 that the army surgeon declared homosexuality to be a disqualifying attribute (see "A Closer Look: Gays and Lesbians in World War II.")

A Closer Look

Gays and Lesbians in World War II

The United States entered World War II in 1941. During the massive wartime mobilization, President Roosevelt agreed to psychological screening for recruits. Eventually 2.5 million soldiers were rejected or discharged from the military for "neuropsychiatric" reasons. Of the men who passed their initial exam, 163,000 were later given "dishonorable" discharges for reasons including psychopathic personality, drug addiction, alcoholism, and homosexuality.

Prior to World War II, the U.S. military had never systematically tried to prevent homosexuals from entering the service. Even at the beginning of World War II, local draft boards were not instructed to screen out homosexuals. By May 1941, the army surgeon general had declared that homosexuality was a disqualifying deviation. How to detect homosexuals was a problem. One suggestion was to ask men to undress and to keep them naked during their entire psychiatric examination. Another was to ask them point-blank whether they had homosexual feelings. Discomfort about being naked or embarrassment when describing sexual experiences were considered clues about the potential for homosexuality. But the surest signs—feminine bodily characteristics and effeminate dress or behavior—had to do with violating gender norms.

Interestingly, women who strayed from their proper roles were not generally treated with the same suspicion. The presence of lesbian soldiers did not seem to pose as great a threat. Any fears about homosexuality proved largely groundless. Few gays or lesbians voluntarily declared their homosexuality. Only a handful of soldiers and sailors were actually rejected in advance of World War II for being homosexual. Gays and lesbians who were discovered after they had already entered the military were perceived as "sick" and placed in psychotherapy or assigned to mental wards in military hospitals (Duberman 1991).

Many heterosexuals fear homosexuality. The reasons for this homophobia are widespread. Among these reasons is the belief that homosexuals attempt to convert heterosexuals. Another possibility is that all individuals have repressed sexual feelings towards members of the same sex and homophobics react by condemning those who overtly express these feelings. They view homosexuality as a threat to social values, family, and home. The tradition of religious fundamentalism encourages homophobia because it views homosexual behavior as sinful (Rosenblum and Travis 1996).

Most gays and lesbians cope with societal stigma by hiding their sexual orientation. Many attempt to "pass" as heterosexuals. This need to be secret and to lead a double life—sometimes including heterosexual marriage and the raising of children—is an additional strain, a fear of revelation and ruin that creates continuing pressure (Herek and Berrill 1992).

Homosexuals may decide to "come out," to reveal their homosexuality to friends, family, or others. Coming out is difficult because it involves the possibility of rejection. Parents may blame themselves for their child's homosexuality. They may deny reality by believing that their child is "in a phase" or "hasn't met the right person of the opposite sex." Coming out may mean a public disclosure, but it may also signify participation in a homosexual subculture or acceptance of a homosexual identity. Coming out is often a sign of self-acceptance. Lesbians do not appear to suffer the same stigma as male homosexuals. In American society, there is a wider range of acceptable female attire and mannerisms and more tolerance towards women embracing in public or living together.

Interventions

There are many intervention strategies used to combat homophobia, just as there are many to oppose homosexuality. Save Our Children Inc., was especially concerned about the growing visibility of homosexuals and the fact that the Metropolitan Dade County (Florida) Commission had legitimized homosexuals' presence "by forcing our private and religious schools to accept them as teachers, by forcing property owners and employers to open their doors to homosexuals no matter how blatant their perverted lives may be."

The repeal of a civil-rights ordinance by Dade County voters was followed by other attempts to restrict gay rights. Proposition 6 in California, for example, stated that homosexuals were not to be hired or retained as educators. Gay teachers, most of whom had kept their sexual orientation secret, were pictured as recruiting impressionable youngsters for homosexuality. Although these specific anti-gay sentiments existed as early as the 1970s, they are very much alive in the nineties. Many people continue to fall back on the stereotypical gay image of homosexuals luring children into sexual deviance or molesting children. The fact remains that 95 percent of adults who sexually molest children are heterosexual (Finkelhor 1994).

Many anti-gay leaders are fundamentalist Christians who see homosexuality as a sin against nature and God. Their goal is to control, and ideally eradicate, homosexuality by means of severe moral and legal condemnation. Criminal laws against homosexuality are also based on the idea that homosexuality is a crime against nature. Though it is not a crime to be homosexual, homosexual acts are still illegal in many states, as mentioned earlier (Herek and Berrill 1992).

One reason for recent hostility towards gays is their visibility. Gay student organizations exist on many college campuses, and there are several organizations established across the country that fight for gay rights, such as the

Increasing numbers of cities, counties, and states have implemented domestic partnership legislation which grants benefits to both homosexual and heterosexual unmarried partners. —*Photo: photostogo.com.*

❖ ❖ ❖ ❖

National Gay Task Force and the Gay Rights National Lobby. Gay newspapers and magazines are also widely displayed. The National Organization for Women is actively involved in fighting for lesbian and gay civil rights.

Herek and Berrill argue that growing tolerance of gays, lesbians, and bisexuals will come from basic changes in attitudes about what is acceptable and unacceptable behavior. Seeing that gays are human beings, more and more people are coming to believe that each individual is entitled to his or her own lifestyle, that in matters of sex and procreation, freedom of choice should exist. Sexual behavior, after all, is only a portion of everyday behavior and should not be the sole basis for judging a person's morality or mental health (Herek and Berrill 1992).

The feminist and gay movements, coupled with struggles for civil rights for racial minorities, have a profound effect on homosexuality and homophobia. Gays and lesbians feel support from these factions and have achieved increasing visibility through community action and by individually coming out. Another goal of the gay movement has been to foster sexual liberation, which requires, in part, the breaking down of rigid gender roles. Although the range of experiences available to each gender may have expanded, the importance of gender conformity seems to have remained relatively unchanged. The traditional equation of homosexuality with gender norm violations does appear weaker. If this trend continues, we may see a decrease in homophobia or more societal tolerance for homosexuality, especially if parents and teachers are less strict in socializing children within the realms of traditional gender roles and expectations (Herek and Berrill 1992).

As heterosexual Americans begin to have more contact with openly gay people, the inaccuracy of the heterosexuals' stereotypes of homosexuals may become clearer. Heterosexuals may continue to dislike men they define as effeminate and women they define as masculine, but they may not equate this with dislike of homosexuals, and may even overcome these aversions (Herek and Berrill 1992).

The Future of Sexual Orientation and Homophobia

Gays, lesbians, and bisexuals will become increasingly visible, but visibility does not necessarily lead to social acceptance. Into the late 1990s, homophobia remains strong. To overcome homophobia, people need to challenge

❖ ❖ ❖ ❖   the cultural climate that tolerates victimization of lesbians and gay men. We cannot understand anti-gay violence and victimization in the United States today apart from cultural heterosexism. Fighting homophobia and anti-gay violence will require public and private agencies to collaborate in developing and implementing programs to reduce prejudice against all minority groups, including gays and lesbians (Herek and Berrill 1992).

Elementary, secondary, and postsecondary schools must be active participants in revising their curricula to educate students about prejudice and oppression. Because the AIDS epidemic is often associated with anti-gay prejudice, school programs should be instituted to teach students, faculty, and staff alike how to respond appropriately to the social challenges of AIDS.

The criminal justice system should treat anti-gay violence seriously. Communities with frequent and serious anti-gay hate crimes might establish special units to prevent, investigate, and respond to such incidents. Boston, New York City, Chicago, and San Francisco have already set up such units. These units may also help prevent harassment and abuse of lesbian and gay crime victims by officials of the criminal justice system (Herek and Berrill 1992).

Support groups for lesbian mothers help counteract the discrimination they have faced from courts and social service agencies. —*Photo: Lesbian Mothers Support Society.*

Summary

A homosexual is a person whose sexual orientation is for individuals of the same sex. Bisexuals are attracted to both men and women. Lesbians and gay men come from all social, economic, racial, ethnic, and religious backgrounds. It is difficult to estimate what percentage of the population is homosexual or bisexual. Although some progress has been made in terms of public awareness, lesbians and gays continue to suffer discrimination and violence.

Culturally defined norms of heterosexuality make it difficult to be gay in a heterosexual world. In such a society, homosexuals often feel isolated and different. Aware of the hostility sometimes directed toward them, homosexuals have to choose between remaining in the closet or coming out. Some become part of a gay subculture, where they gain information and receive support.

Gays, lesbians, and bisexuals have become increasingly militant and organized in recent years. Though discrimination still exists in employment and housing, criminal prosecution of homosexual behavior is lessening. Society seems to be more tolerant toward gays and lesbians. This tolerance is reflected in the growing numbers of openly gay people who are raising families. Some courts have defined gay partners as constituting a family. Despite these changes, homophobia and discrimination against homosexuals is still strong in the United States.

Discussion Questions

1. Did you see the "coming out episode" of *Ellen*? Have you ever seen the show? If you have seen it, how do you feel about the episode or about the show? Why do you think you feel as you do?

2. Some see homosexuality as a choice, while others view it as a biologically based condition or orientation. What difference does it make how you look at it? How did you arrive at your view on this?

3. Research indicates that gay men and lesbians make fine parents. Some people may have trouble accepting this. Why do you think that is so?

4. Have you ever been in a group when someone used slurs about homosexuals or told a homophobic joke? How did you react? How do you think people should react to such slurs and jokes?

5. What kinds of gay and lesbian support groups or organizations does your college or university have? Are they very active?

References

American Civil Liberties Union. 1997. "Lesbian and Gay Rights." *American Civil Liberties Union Website, Lesbian and Gay Rights*. http://www.aclu.org/issues/gay/hmgl.html.

Angier, Natalie. 1993. "Research on Sexual Orientation Doesn't Neatly Fit the Mold." *New York Times*, July 18, 13A.

Bark, Ed. 1997. "Rumors Rise Over Held 'Ellen.'" *Boston Globe*, October 11, B4.

Biddle, Frederic M. 1997. "Television Review: Tonight's Show Makes History, and Saves Sitcom." *Boston Globe*, April 30.

Bieber, Irving. 1971. *Homosexuality: A Psychoanalytic Study*. New York: Basic Books.

Boston Globe. 1997. "'Conversion Therapy' for Gays Debated." August 15.

Collum, Carole S. 1993. "Co-Parent Adoptions: Lesbian and Gay Parenting." *National Adoption Center, Faces of Adoption, Gay and Lesbian Issues Website*. http://www.adopt.org/adopt/gay/gay2.html.

Duberman, Martin. 1991. *About Time: Exploring the Gay Past*. New York: Meridian.

Eitzen, D. Stanley, and Maxine Baca Zinn. 1997. *Social Problems*. Seventh edition. Boston: Allyn and Bacon.

Falk, P. 1989. "Lesbian Mothers: Psychosocial Assumptions in Family Law." *American Psychologist* 44(6).

Finkelhor, David. 1994. "Current Information on the Scope and Nature of Child Sexual Abuse." *Future of Children* 4:31–53.

Gelman, David. 1992. "Born or Bred?" *Newsweek*, February 24, 46–53.

Golay, Michael. 1997. *Where America Stands 1997*. New York: Wiley and Sons.

Graham, Renee. 1997. "On the Arts: What Took the Networks So Long?" *Boston Globe*, April 30.

Greenberg, David F. 1988. *The Construction of Homosexuality*. Chicago: University of Chicago Press.

Gross, Larry. 1993. *Contested Closets: The Politics and Ethics of Outing*. Minneapolis: University of Minnesota Press.

Hamer, Dean H., et al. 1993. "A Linkage Between DNA Markers on the X Chromosome and Male Sexual Orientation." *Science* 261:321–27.

Hamer, Dean H., and Peter Copeland. 1994. *The Science of Desire: The Search for the Gay Gene and the Biology of Behavior*. New York: Simon and Schuster.

Herek, Gregory, and Kevin Berrill. 1992. *Hate Crimes: Confronting Violence Against Lesbians and Gays*. Thousand Oaks, California: Sage Publications.

Hubbard, Ruth, and Elijah Wald. 1993. *Exploding the Gene Myth: How Genetic Information Is Produced and Manipulated by Scientists, Physicians, Employers, Insurance Companies, Educators, and Law Enforcers*. Boston: Beacon Press.

Laumann, Edward O., et al. 1994. *The Social Organization of Sexuality: Sexual Practices in the United States*. Chicago: University of Chicago Press.

Leonard, Arthur S. 1990. "Gay/Lesbian Rights: Report from the Legal Front." *Nation*, July 2, 12–15.

LeVay, Simon. 1991. "A Difference in Hypothalamic Structure between Heterosexual and Homosexual Men." *Science* 251:1034-1037.

———. 1993. *The Sexual Brain*. Cambridge: MIT Press.

Levin, Jack, and William Levin. 1982. *The Functions of Prejudice and Discrimination*. New York: Harper and Row.

Meier, Robert F., and Gilbert Geis. 1997. *Victimless Crime? Prostitution, Drugs, Homosexuality, Abortion*. Los Angeles: Roxbury Publishing.

Melton, G. B. 1989. "Public Policy and Private Prejudice." *American Psychologist* 44(6).

Merton, Robert K. 1968. *Social Theory and Social Structure*, enlarged edition. New York: Free Press.

Murphy, Timothy F. 1997. *Gay Science: The Ethics of Sexual Orientation Research*. New York: Columbia University Press.

National Gay and Lesbian Task Force. 1984. *Anti-Gay/Lesbian Victimization: A Study by the National Gay and Lesbian Task Force in Cooperation with Gay and Lesbian Organizations in Eight U.S. Cities*. Washington, D.C.: National Gay and Lesbian Task Force.

Nowak, Rachel. 1993. "Fear and Loathing in the U.S. Military: Psychological Explanations for Homophobia." *Journal of NIH Research*, September.

Pogrebin, Letty Cottin. 1980. *Growing Up Free: Raising Your Child in the 80s*. New York: McGraw-Hill.

Rich, Adrienne. 1980. "Compulsory Heterosexuality and Lesbian Existence." *Signs* 5(2).

Rosenblum, Karen, and Toni-Michelle Travis. 1996. *The Meaning of Difference*. New York: McGraw-Hill.

Russo, V. 1981. *The Celluloid Closet: Homosexuality in the Movies*. New York: Harper and Row.

Saad, Lydia. 1997. "Majority of Americans Not Fazed by Ellen's Coming Out Episode." *The Gallup Poll Press Releases* April 29. http://www.gallup.com/poll/news/970429~1.html.

Sidel, Ruth. 1994. *Battling Bias: The Struggle for Identity and Community on College Campuses*. New York: Viking Penguin.

Stone, Lawrence. 1985. "Sex in the West: The Strange History of Human Sexuality." *New Republic*, July 8, 25–37.

Thompson, Larry. 1995. "Search for a Gay Gene." *Time*, June 12, 61–62.

Troiden, Richard. 1998. "A Model of Homosexual Identity Formation." Pp. 261–278 in *Social Perspectives in Lesbian and Gay Studies: A Reader*, edited by Peter M. Nardi and Beth E. Schneider. New York: Routledge.

Valverde, Mariana. 1987. *Sex, Power, and Pleasure*. Philadelphia: New Society Publishers.

Vance, Carole S. 1998. "Social Construction Theory: Problems in the History of Sexuality." Pp. 160–170 in *Social Perspectives in Lesbian and Gay Studies: A Reader* edited by Peter M. Nardi and Beth E. Schneider. New York: Routledge.

Van Gelder, Lawrence. 1997. "Celebrations as a TV Lesbian Goes Prime Time." *New York Times*, May 1.

Weinraub, Bernard. 1997. "From Poison Apple to Plum Role." *New York Times*, Arts Section, September 10, B1, B6.

Wolfe, Alan. 1998. *One Nation, After All*. New York: Viking.

Websites

http://www.avert.org/

AIDS Education and Research Trust (AVERT). This very useful site focuses on education about HIV infection, and information for HIV-positive people as well as statistics and news about HIV/AIDS in the United Kingdom and the United States. This website is aimed at young people and includes suggestions on how to talk about homosexuality in secondary schools. It also offers related information on AIDS prevention and safe sex.

http://www.aclu.org/

American Civil Liberties Union (ACLU). The ACLU website presents the American Civil Liberties Union fact sheet on gay and lesbian issues, such as gays in the military and gay parenting.

http://www.hrc.org/

Human Rights Campaign (HRC). This exceptional organization focuses on four main issues: renewing America's commitment to fighting HIV/AIDS; ending workplace discrimination; launching a rapid response to anti-gay hate legislation; and focusing attention on lesbian health issues. On this site you can not only learn about these issues, you can find out how to make your voice heard about them.

CHAPTER SEVEN

Crime and Violence

In the News: Date Rape

A Boston Globe series focused on a disturbing topic: date rape, also called acquaintance rape (Dembner 1997a, Dembner 1997b). Americans became aware of date rape as a serious issue a dozen years ago. Five years ago Congress asked colleges and universities to develop policies that could prevent date rape or at least deal with offenders and victims. Alice Dembner suggests that the way students talk about the issue has changed but that solutions for the problem remain elusive. Numerous surveys indicate that as many as 25 percent of young women may be victims of rape or attempted rape during the years between adolescence and college graduation. "When they can speak anonymously, nearly 10 percent of college men admit to sexual acts that meet the legal definition of rape" (Dembner 1997a).

Northeastern University agreed to serve as a case study for the Boston Globe. *In trying to decrease the incidence of date rape, Northeastern "established new codes of conduct, added rape education to orientation programs and developed protocols for treating victims and disciplining assailants (Dembner 1997a). Between 1990 and 1997, 80 cases of sexual assault or rape were reported to campus police at Northeastern. It seems likely, however, that many rapes occurred that were not reported. Sometimes the victims may feel too humiliated to report the crime. Many of the assaults are tied to excessive alcohol use. Campus police also worry about the spread of Rohypnol, referred to as the date rape drug.*

Despite extensive efforts to educate students about the realities of date rape, both male and female students believe myths about it. Male students believe that there is a high risk of false accusation; in reality, only about 2 percent of rape accusations nationally are shown to be false. Many female students believe that they are more likely to be raped by a stranger; in fact, they are more likely to be raped by someone they know.

Researchers suggest several kinds of changes to reduce date rape. Cutting down on excessive drinking on campuses is one important step. Orientation programs and education efforts should be targeted at men. Many researchers also say that the educational efforts must begin before college, to change the way young men think about women and about sex. Education about date rape must also be continuous and repeated. Without such changes, college campuses will continue to be threatening places for many young women.

Definition and Prevalence

The word **crime** has been used in several different ways. Some equate it with sin or falsehood; others define it as behavior that is harmful to society or that deviates from socially accepted norms. Accepting a legal definition, many sociologists regard crime as any act that violates the criminal law. However, "if crime is defined as violations of law, officials and politicians are permitted to dictate the parameters of an essentially social scientific concept" (Stark 1996:180). Michael Gottfredson and Travis Hirschi have proposed a definition of crime that is separate from legal definitions. Crime refers to "acts of force or fraud undertaken in pursuit of self-interest" (Gottfredson and Hirschi 1990).

As we think about crime in this chapter, consider these definitions and the strengths and weaknesses of each. Although Gottfredson and Hirschi's definition is useful, for most purposes in this chapter we use a legal definition of crime. That is because most of the statistics with which criminologists work come from violations of law known to the criminal justice system and are part of the public record. Moreover, there is no general agreement about what constitutes antisocial behavior or norms defining criminal activity. Even when we use a legal rather than a sociological conception of crime, there are numerous important sociological questions to be asked about crime: Under what conditions do deviant acts become part of the criminal code? What kinds of persons are most likely to be regarded as criminals? What are the costs of crime? And what policies have been proposed to reduce it?

In the legal sense, crime is any act that violates the criminal law. The legal idea of a crime restricts the meaning to those transgressions that a society recognizes in its law. But a number of sociologists contend that legal regulations defining a crime must also reflect the support of public approval and the presence of underlying **mores** or customs that society considers important for its welfare or survival. Walter Reckless suggested that modern statutory regulations that define new offenses must have a basis in public opinion favorable to the regulations and what the regulations stand for (1961:19).

In the Marxian view, crime is a legal definition of human behavior but not a definition reflective of the values and customs of society at large. Instead, definitions of crime tend to reflect the interests of the most powerful in a society. Therefore, particular definitions of crime are created and modified in order to serve the economic interests of the capitalist class, the dominant class, which has the power to translate their interests into policy. Some conflict theorists suggest that definitions are formulated to incorporate behavior that conflicts with dominant class interests. Thus, crimes that aim at taking the property of the wealthy, such as burglary and robbery, are identified and penalized, whereas harms perpetrated by large corporations, such as violations of employees' health and safety standards, are largely ignored and not defined as crimes (Reiman 1998; Beirne and Messerschmidt 1995).

Whether representative of public sentiment, class interests, or both, there does not seem to be anything intrinsically "criminal" about most transgressions. Offenses that are called crimes in some states are permitted by law in others. Acts that once were deemed violations of the criminal code have subsequently been decriminalized. The variation by time and state with respect to penalties for the possession of marijuana provides an appropriate case in point. Some states continue to jail individuals convicted of possession of marijuana, whereas others legally permit possession of small amounts.

Crime statistics must be treated with caution. The most commonly recognized measures of crime are from the *Uniform Crime Reports (UCR)* compiled by the Federal Bureau of Investigation (FBI). These statistics are compilations of crimes regarded as serious—murder, rape, robbery, aggravated assault, burglary, larceny, and motor vehicle theft—as reported to the police across the country (Kappeler, Blumberg, and Potter 1996). The UCR is based strictly on reported crimes and is generally seen as somewhat inaccurate. At one extreme, the UCR homicide count is probably reliable. It is hard to imagine that a great many murders go permanently unreported. At the other extreme, there may be numerous forcible rapes, especially sexual assaults committed by acquaintances, that are never reported to the police and therefore do not get into the UCR count. Victor Kappeler (1996) and his colleagues also argue that crime rates are open to political manipulation. For example, the Nixon administration was accused of bureaucratic manipulation in the reporting of crime by the police. The Nixon administration wanted the crime rate to go down so it could claim success in fighting crime.

One major criticism of UCR data is that they are presented in ways that are far from scientific. The FBI creates gimmicks to exaggerate the incidence of crime and the threat to the public. For example, the crime clock: UCR tell us that one criminal offense occurs every two seconds; one violent crime occurs every sixteen seconds; one forcible rape occurs every five minutes. These rates leave an exaggerated impression of the amount of crime in society. The media play on the fear of crime, and law enforcement agencies are given enough political clout to demand more resources (Kappeler et al. 1996). Interestingly, at the close of 1994, the FBI showed that serious crime reported to the police had declined for the third consecutive year. The decline in crime rates has continued since then (Bureau of Justice Statistics 1997). For a website with data on all aspects of crime and the criminal justice system, see "A Closer Look: Sourcebook of Criminal Justice Statistics Online."

An even better source than the UCR for determining the rate of many crimes is the National Crime Victimization Survey (NCVS). Since 1972, the Department of Justice has conducted an annual survey of 100,000 households across the country, asking respondents if they have been victims of

---

A Closer Look

Sourcebook of Criminal Justice Statistics Online

The U.S. Department of Justice, Bureau of Justice Statistics, publishes the *Sourcebook of Criminal Justice Statistics* every year (Bureau of Justice Statistics 1997). This invaluable compendium brings together data on all aspects of crime and criminal justice in the United States. As valuable as the *Sourcebook* is, the online version is even more useful. *The Sourcebook of Criminal Justice Statistics Online* website is located at http://www.albany.edu/sourcebook/ (Maguire and Pastore 1997). This website includes over 600 tables from more than 100 sources. Based on the print version, the online version is continually updated.

Kathleen Maguire and Ann L. Pastore are project co-directors of the Utilization of Criminal Justice Statistics Project of the Hindelang Criminal Justice Research Center at the University of Albany. In collaboration with the Bureau of Justice Statistics, the project has compiled the *Sourcebook of Criminal Justice Statistics* since 1973. The online version significantly enhances the goal of making criminal justice data available to a wide audience.

Data on the site are divided into six general sections: (1) characteristics of the criminal justice systems; (2) public attitudes toward crime and criminal justice and related topics; (3) nature and distribution of known offenses; (4) characteristics and distribution of persons arrested; (5) judicial processing of defendants; and (6) persons under correctional supervision. The site has search capabilities so that you can locate data on specific topics. Taking a look at one topic will give you a sense of what is available on the site.

In section 2 you will find various tables about public attitudes toward the death penalty. For example, Table 2.65 reports changing attitudes toward the death penalty from 1965 to 1997. Other tables give attitudes toward the death penalty broken down by population groups (Table 2.66), attitudes towards the death penalty for teenagers convicted of murder (Table 2.72), and attitudes toward the death penalty for those convicted of murder when interviewees are given evidence that innocent persons have been sentenced to death (Table 2.73).

crime in the past year. Measuring both reported and unreported crime, these surveys tell us that crime has been decreasing in America for almost two decades. Victimization surveys also tell us that the vast amount of crime that does occur is not the violent predatory crime that we imagine (Kappeler, Blumberg, and Potter 1996).

Figure 7-1 shows trends in serious violent crime over the past 25 years. Note how much the levels differ depending on the measure used. Notice also that crime levels are declining and have been for several years. In fact, crime has declined dramatically over the past six years, although sociologists and criminologists are not sure why. We discuss this further in the Interventions

Figure 7-1 Trends in Violent Crime: Four Measures of Serious Violent Crime: 1973–1996

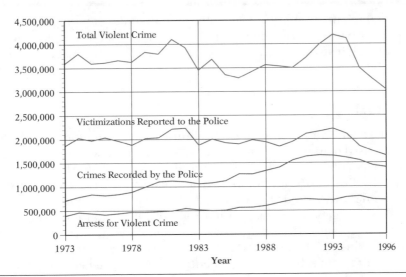

Source: U.S. Department of Justice, Bureau of Justice Statistics. 1998. White House Web Site, Social Statistics Briefing Room. <http://www.whitehouse.gov/>.

section.

People fear crime. Despite the fact that crime is decreasing, the fear of crime is not. There appear to be three main reasons for the persistence of widespread fear. First, the media seriously distort our perceptions of crime and its dangers. Tabloid television presents almost daily reports of crime, mostly violent crime. Local news stations commonly lead with stories concerning murder, rape, and other violent crimes. Murder constitutes only 0.2 percent of all crimes reported to the police, yet it occupies 25 percent of newspaper reports about crime. The media downplay the amount of nonviolent crime which leaves readers and viewers with the impression that crime rates are continually increasing (Kappeler, Blumber, and Potter 1996).

The law enforcement establishment has a vested interest in representing crime as a serious epidemic in our society. Large sums of money and millions of jobs depend on concerns about crime. For example, the "War on Drugs," initiated during the Reagan administration, generated enormous funds and expanded the jurisdiction and police powers of many federal law enforcement agencies.

The politicization of crime also adds to our fear of crime. Opposing crime is a safe political position. Politicians consistently attempt to outdo one another in their concern about crime, especially violent crime. They often take punitive, hard-line positions, attributing high crime rates to human nature, lenient punishment, and excessive self-expression. Elliot Currie points out the contradictions of this "conservative model" of crime control.

> In a world of dramatic national variations in criminal violence, it blames crime on an invariant human nature. In a society that ranks among the most punitive in the developed world, it blames crime on the leniency of the justice system. In a country noted for its harsh response to social deviation, it blames crimes on attitudes of tolerance run wild. (1985:49)

Levels of Causation

Social scientists are primarily interested in understanding the causes of crime as a first step to reducing it. In this section, we look at explanations for crime arising from three different theoretical levels: individual, cultural, and social.

Individual

In the eighteenth and nineteenth centuries, many attempts to understand crime focused on the biological characteristics of offenders (Beirne 1993). In recent years, some studies have offered a genetic explanation for violence and criminality. Despite the attention such approaches have received, they do not seem to offer any serious basis for understanding most crime and violence. Though some genetic predisposition for certain mental illnesses, such as schizophrenia and manic-depressive disorder, may exist, those who suffer from such illnesses do not seem to commit the overwhelming majority of acts of criminal violence. Indeed, the tendency to view violent behavior as a symptom of mental disease may only detract from more effective efforts to locate and understand the environmental bases for crime and violence.

In an effort to locate individual differences in criminal behavior, some researchers have offered psychological explanations of crime. Criminologists have suggested, for example, that most serial killers —those who murder one victim at a time over a period of weeks, months, or years—are actually **sociopaths** (Levin and Fox 1985; Fox and Levin 1994). That is, they are remorseless, lack the capacity to empathize with their victims, and are extremely manipulative in managing the impression that they want others to have of them. In a sense, sociopaths are Erving Goffman's quintessential actors—they are constantly playing a character on the stage of life, convincing others of their goodness, lying to make themselves look good, and performing a role for an audience (1959). Thus, they present a veneer of civility and human warmth, but only a veneer. Inside, they are totally devoid of conscience, caring, or human warmth. As a result, they are able, with moral impunity, to torture, rape, mutilate, and dismember their victims and then are frequently able to convince their friends and family of their total innocence, even in the face of overwhelming evidence to the contrary. Because of the grisly nature of their crimes and their large body counts, the names of some serial killers—Jeffrey Dahmer, Ted Bundy, the Hillside Strangler, Son of Sam, and Charles Manson—have become household words.

Where does sociopathy come from? Most criminologists believe that the environment plays an important role. According to many mental health practitioners, the roots of sociopathic behavior are located in the failure of an individual to bond with a parent or other meaningful individual during early childhood. Some argue that the absence of a human bond and subsequent sociopathy result from profound neglect, abandonment or abuse; others suggest that sociopathic behavior is a consequence of abuse but in combination with repeated head trauma.

Individual differences in criminal behavior may be explained in terms of psychological variables such as sociopathy and abuse. For understanding differences between groups and over time, however, cultural and structural approaches are more helpful.

Cultural

Robert Merton has suggested that certain types of criminal behavior are a response to characteristics of American culture—a culture that emphasizes success without placing equivalent emphasis upon socially acceptable means for achieving that success. Our values, according to Merton, dictate that all members of society should strive to achieve the same lofty goals; the values also say that failure to achieve happens only to those who reduce their ambition and cease striving. These values become translated into everyday rules of behavior; for example: "not to be a quitter," "there is no such word as 'failure,'" and Andrew Carnegie's "Be a king in your dreams. Say to yourself, 'My place is at the top'" (1968).

Such cultural beliefs are important in their sociological implications: they serve to direct blame for failure based on poverty away from the social structure and toward individuals who lack equal access to opportunity for success. Criticism of society is further defused by having individuals from the lower social strata identify themselves with those who are wealthy and successful—those whom they believe they will eventually join.

Cultural emphasis upon success while excluding emphasis upon legitimate opportunities invites what Merton refers to as innovation: an individual accepts the cultural emphasis upon the success goal but rejects the socially acceptable means for its attainment. The result may be that the individual substitutes illegitimate (frequently illegal) but more effective methods of securing wealth and power. Unethical business practices and white-collar crime may frequently reflect this pressure toward innovation. As Merton noted,

> The history of the great American fortunes is threaded with strains toward institutionally dubious innovation as is attested by many tributes to the Robber Barons. The reluctant admiration often expressed privately, and not seldom publicly, of these "shrewd, smart and successful," men is a product of a cultural structure in which the sacrosanct goal virtually consecrates the means. (1968:195–196)

Merton contended that the greatest pressures toward innovation are exerted upon individuals in the lower socioeconomic strata. Despite the open-class ideology, success is an elusive goal for individuals who have little formal education and few economic resources. Regardless of the reality, such individuals are still expected to orient themselves toward the achievement of great wealth, even though they are denied effective opportunities to do so in a socially appropriate manner. The consequence is a high rate of property crime.

Merton views the United States as a society egalitarian in its ideology but unequal in the availability of the means of achieving goals. This gap between the ideology and the reality creates strain for many people. Notice that its focus on the socially structured access to the means of achieving valued goals makes this a structural as well as a cultural theory. Merton identified five responses to these strains:

1. *Conformity*. This is the most common practice. People generally agree with cultural goals such as making money and employ legitimate means to achieve these goals.

2. *Innovation*. Innovative deviant adaptation occurs when conflict exists between culturally defined goals in society and legitimate means to achieve those goals. Innovation is deviant behavior that uses illegitimate means to achieve socially acceptable goals. Merton contended that innovative deviance in the United States is concentrated largely in the skilled and unskilled working class. It is there that the gap between goals and means is most acute.

3. *Ritualism*. In ritualism, a person gives up the struggle to get ahead and concentrates on retaining what has been gained.

4. *Retreatism*. Retreatism is an adaptation that relinquishes culturally prescribed goals and does not conform to institutionalized means. Merton describes retreatism as an escape mechanism that often arises after an individual suffers repeated failure to achieve goals. Examples used by Merton include psychotics, alcoholics, and drug addicts.

5. *Rebellion*. Rebellion involves alienation from legitimate means and values. Rebellion is a collective activity. Examples include anarchists and the Ku Klux Klan.

Structural

Emile Durkheim was one of the founders of sociological criminology. Durkheim rejected definitions of crime that were based on legalistic criteria. He believed that no action was intrinsically criminal. As he argued in *The Division of Labor in Society*, "an act is criminal when it offends the strong, well-defined states of the collective consciousness. . . . We should not say that an act offends the common consciousness because it is criminal, but that it is criminal because it offends that consciousness" (1933[1893]:80–81).

Durkheim also argued that crime had specific positive functions for society. One function is that behavior defined as crime would be punished. The function of punishment is not solely revenge, deterrence, or reformation. The true function is to maintain and strengthen social solidarity. Each time a community or society expresses horror or distaste for an act, its values and beliefs are reaffirmed. Durkheim claimed that crime is normal. Every society has crime. He claimed that crime is inevitable; no society can ever be totally rid of it. Moreover, absolute conformity to rules is impossible because everyone does not agree with all the norms and values. Finally, crime is useful because it may be perceived as a symptom of individual originality. If there were no crimes, then a society would be unhealthy—it would have to be totally controlled, subject to a dangerous level of authoritarianism. In other words, a society with no crime would have to be extremely repressive.

Marxist conflict perspectives on crime take different views. Marx and Engels wrote virtually nothing about criminal behavior; however, they made notable contributions to the study of crime by focusing on criminal law and the criminal justice system. They suggested that law has an ideological basis. Marx argued that both the amount and the types of crime in modern society were produced by the fundamental conditions of a capitalist society.

Marx and Engels focused on three separate dimensions when analyzing the links between crime and capitalism. The first dimension, criminalization as a violation of human rights, was described somewhat moralistically. Marx argued that some laws violate real freedom: for example, censorship violates freedom of expression. The second dimension, crime and demoralization, linked capitalism with massive demoralization. Marx and Engels argued that working conditions under capitalism led to competition among members of the working class. This competition led to massive demoralization and hence to crime. Finally, primitive rebellion was seen as an alternative to demoralization. Marx and Engels did identify certain working-class crime as rebellion but did not look upon it favorably (Beirne and Messerschmidt 1995).

Another theory that was important in explaining crime was **labeling theory**, so named because labeling theorists argue that social groups create deviance or crime by first making the rules whose infraction constitutes deviance and then applying those rules to particular people and labeling them as outsiders (Becker 1963). What is important for labeling theorists is not the actual label but who does the labeling and why. Labeling theorists contend that it is the agents of control, who function on behalf of the powerful in society, who impose the labels on the less powerful.

Several learning theories have sought to explain how people learn to engage in crime. Edwin Sutherland's theory of **differential association** attempted to explain the process by which a given person learns to engage in crime and also the content of what is learned. Sutherland argued that criminal behavior is learned, like all other behavior, within intimate personal groups in an interactive process of communication. The learning of criminal behavior includes instruction in the techniques of crime and the values favorable to committing it. The principle of differential association asserts that a person becomes criminal when definitions favorable to violation of the law exceed definitions unfavorable to violation. Exposure to such definitions vary in frequency, duration, priority, and intensity (1947).

In essence, Sutherland contends that persons who engage in crime do so because they have more associations with pro-criminal patterns than with anti-criminal patterns. His theory is generally well received but has been criticized for assuming that persons become criminal when they associate with criminals.

Ronald Akers (1996) offers explanations of crime using a broader social learning theory than Sutherland's. Akers' theory retains the differential association processes of Sutherland and integrates them with other principles of behavioral acquisition. Akers' social learning theory also retains a strong element of symbolic interactionism, the theory that social interaction is mainly the exchange of meaning and symbols; individuals have the cognitive capacity to imagine themselves in the role of others and integrate such imagined roles into their conceptions of themselves. Akers' development of the theory focused on four major concepts: differential association, definitions, differential reinforcement, and imitation. Differential association is described as Sutherland defined it. Definitions are one's own attitudes or the meanings that one attaches to a given behavior. In social learning theory, these definitions have both general and specific aspects. General beliefs include religious, moral, and other conventional norms that are favorable to conformity and unfavorable to criminal behavior. Specific definitions orient the person to a particular act or series of acts. For example, a person may believe it wrong to steal but okay to smoke marijuana.

Differential reinforcement refers to the balance of anticipated and actual rewards and punishments that follow or are consequences of behavior. Whether individuals will refrain from or commit a crime at any given time depends on the past, present, and anticipated future rewards and punishment for their actions.

Imitation refers to the engagement in behavior after the observation of similar behavior in others. Whether the behavior modeled by others will be imitated is affected by the characteristics of the models, the behavior observed, and the observed consequences of the behavior.

Akers' theory is broad in scope and does not include a general explanation of laws, criminal justice, or the structural aspects of society that have an impact on crime. The theory does explain how the social structure shapes individual behavior. Akers adds that age, race, sex, class, and other characteristics have an impact on an individual's place in the social structure. These characteristics help designate the groups that an individual is likely to be a member of, with whom that person interacts, and how others around the person are apt to respond to his or her behavior. Other structural conditions, such as conflict and social disorganization identified in other theories, can have an impact on one's exposure to criminal associations, models, definitions, and reinforcement.

Traditional criminology has largely ignored the analysis of women. Nicole Rafter and Frances Heidensohn state that criminology has always been the most masculine of all the social sciences (1995). In the late twentieth century many feminists began questioning criminology's male-centered focus. Many feminists argue that female crime cannot be understood using male-centered theories. For example, theories on juvenile delinquency have almost exclusively focused on males, until recently. Women usually commit different crimes than men and for different reasons. (See "A Closer Look: Is Crime Still a Man's World?")

Delinquency and broken homes are often seen as related variables. Recent research has indicated that the relationship between family structure and delinquency is complex. There is evidence that the justice system discriminates on the basis of family structure alone (Reid 1996). The criminal justice system is more likely to intervene in families of adolescents when there is only one parent living in the home. Recent research has, in fact, found some association between adult criminality and family structure. An analysis of female criminality demonstrates this association. More than half of the women serving time for violent crimes report that they were abused sexually, mostly during childhood. Many of those victimizations were by family members.

In addition to focusing on gender, social scientists studying crime have increasingly incorporated race in their approaches. In a classic study, Charles Silberman (1978) argued that violent crime is a result of generations of racial

A Closer Look

Is Crime Still a Man's World?

Are women becoming more violent? Is there a new, more aggressive female criminal? The media might lead us to believe so. In the 1970s, two studies of women and crime seemed to support the idea that the level and types of male and female crimes were becoming alike (Adler 1975; Simon 1975). However, a careful review of the research led Ronald Flowers to reject the "gender equality hypothesis" (1987). In fact, the rate of violent crime among females has remained consistent over the last 30 years (Steffensmeier and Allan 1995). A new dangerous female criminal has not arrived on the scene.

Looking at some crime data helps in dismantling the notion of the new violent female criminal. One crime category where the number of females certainly has increased is larceny, specifically shoplifting. Larceny is categorized as a "serious crime" by the criminal justice system. To use this to claim that more women are becoming serious criminals is shortsighted and misleading. Women do continue to commit traditionally "female crimes" such as shoplifting, check forgery, and petty property crimes. These offenses represent extensions of traditional female domestic and consumer role activities rather than new role patterns. Women are not being arrested for fraud connected to their occupations or for what is considered white-collar crime. Darrell Steffensmeier argues that changes in arrest rates are not so much due to changes in levels of female offending as to less biased or more effective official responses to female criminality. The increase in female larceny–related crimes is exacerbated by the worsening economic position of many women in the United States (Steffensmeier and Allan 1995).

Drug use and addiction may help account for female crime trends. Drug addiction amplifies income-generating crime much more for females than for males. Female involvement in robbery typically occurs after addiction and is likely to be abandoned when drug use stops. Female crime patterns have remained fairly constant, even taking into account female gang activities. Crime, especially violent crime, remains a man's world (Steffensmeier and Allan 1995).

inequality and racism. African Americans are disproportionately represented in violent crime statistics, although this seems to be a class phenomenon as much as a racial one: As groups move into the middle class, their participation in crime declines. Silberman argues that, given the degree to which African Americans have traditionally been persecuted and oppressed, it is remarkable that they have not been even more violent in the past. Our society is not likely to achieve the domestic tranquility desired until the socioeconomic gap between African and European Americans is closed and until African Americans become first-class citizens of American society.

Some social scientists suggest that the criminal justice system itself generates crime and violence in the United States. Michael Tonry, for example, contends that the American criminal justice system is racist. Specifically, he maintains that tough crime measures enacted since 1980 have fallen more harshly on African Americans than on whites. Tonry suggests that this discrepancy has little to do with crime patterns and more to do with two political developments. First, conservative Republicans in national elections "played the race card" by using anti-crime slogans and advertising campaigns aimed at exploiting white fear of crime by African Americans, especially African American males. For example, in the 1988 presidential election, the Bush campaign used the case of Willie Horton to suggest that his opponent, Michael Dukakis, Governor of Massachusetts, was soft on crime. Horton was a murderer, who, while on furlough from a Massachusetts prison, raped a woman. The second development involved conservative politicians of both parties who promoted and voted for harsh crime control and drug policies (Tonry 1995).

For as long as prison population data have been compiled, African Americans have been disproportionately represented as inmates. In addition, since 1980 the black percentage among prisoners has increased sharply. One reason for this may be an inherent bias in arrest proceedings. Using drug use as an example, Tonry argues that blacks are no more likely than whites to use illicit drugs but are arrested and imprisoned for drug violations at a much higher rate. One reason for the discrepancy may have to do with how drugs are dealt. Drug arrests are easier to make in urban areas because drug sales are likely to take place outdoors. In addition, dealers in urban areas will more than likely sell to strangers, who could be undercover police officers. Drug sales in middle- or upper- class environments are likely to take place indoors, and dealers are less likely to sell to strangers. People of color are disproportionately located in urban areas.

Tonry argues that tougher penalties for drug crimes have placed more African Americans and Latinos than European Americans under arrest and in prison. If African Americans and other minorities are more likely to be arrested for drug crimes and other crimes than whites, our society will see an ever-increasing prison population of color (Tonry 1995).

Barbara Price and Natalie Sokoloff (1995) argue that the law is created in large part by and for the dominant class in society. The law determines which groups of people are most likely to be punished. In our society people are most commonly arrested for crimes against property, crimes against the public order, and crimes against persons. Those most likely to be arrested and convicted of these crimes are poor and working-class people, who happen to be disproportionately members of racial/ethnic minority groups.

As stated earlier, the War on Drugs had a great impact on people of color. Sokoloff and Price add that this war also has had a severe impact on women offenders. Since 1989, women are more likely than men to be jailed on drug charges. More than one-third of all women in local jails and about 60 percent of women in federal custody serve sentences for drug offenses. And the majority of these women are poor, African-American women or Latinas. Other state-created drug crimes include the criminalization of women's bodies. Women in at least 24 states have been arrested and prosecuted after their newborn babies tested positive for drugs (Price and Sokoloff 1995). (See "A Closer Look: Criminalizing Pregnancy?")

Class is a key consideration in understanding crime data. People from lower socioeconomic backgrounds are much more likely to be found guilty and to receive harsher sentences than those from higher socioeconomic backgrounds. Minority women, in particular, have unique negative experiences within the criminal justice system. Minority women are treated poorly when arrested, during bail settings, and when they are sentenced. Women prisoners are 46.1 percent African American and 11.7 percent Latina. Yet blacks constitute only 12.3 percent of the general population and Hispanics 8.1 percent. In some states, for example, New York, more than three-fourths of all women arrested are African American and Latina (Price and Sokoloff 1995).

A Closer Look

Criminalizing Pregnancy?

Since 1992, there has been a trend across the country to charge women with abusing their unborn children through illegal drug use during pregnancy. This has led to growing fears of "the criminalization of pregnancy." Some prosecutors are making decisions which threaten to make pregnancy a crime (Reed 1993). In one 1997 case the highest court in South Carolina upheld the criminal conviction of Melissa Crawley. Crawley had used drugs during her pregnancy and her baby was born with cocaine in its system. She was prosecuted on the basis that the fetus was legally a "child" (Herbert 1998; Lewin 1997). Although the highest courts in Florida, Kentucky, Nevada, and Ohio refused to agree with such an interpretation of the law, South Carolina prosecutors have charged over 40 women with this crime since 1989. Chief Justice William Rehnquist of the United States Supreme Court rejected Crawley's emergency request to avoid imprisonment (Associated Press 1998).

Some researchers have suggested that every year, approximately 375,000 babies are born to mothers who use drugs. This claim has been widely reported, but its accuracy is not established (Humphries 1993). Regardless of that estimate, we can agree that maternal drug use has serious consequences for fetal development, is a serious public health problem, and needs to be dealt with. However, criminalizing pregnant women as a way of solving the problem is short-sighted and difficult to justify. Connell argues that "subjecting women to criminal punishment for their substance abuse problems will not protect newborns or their mothers and, in the end, threatens everyone's civil liberties" (Connell 1996:26).

Much of the emphasis on pregnant drug users has focused on those who use cocaine. Humphries notes that

> Cocaine use is of special concern. Not only have estimates of cocaine use spawned a moral panic; the awareness that women, including pregnant women, use cocaine and crack contributes to the medical and legal reactions. (Humphries 1993:132)

The 1990 National Drug Control Strategy Report estimated that 100,000 cocaine babies are born each year (Humphries 1993). Before jumping to unwarranted conclusions, however, we should note two points. First, studies show that the women in question tend to use more than one drug, so tracing most of the newborns symptoms to cocaine is difficult. Some symptoms may be due to drugs other than cocaine or may be due to lack of prenatal or health care. Second, prosecutors tend to ignore studies that do not show cocaine having adverse effects on pregnancy (Humphries 1993; Koren, et al. 1989).

Prosecutors have argued that pregnant women who use drugs are breaking the law and ought to be arrested, prosecuted, and convicted. They want to stop maternal drug use by incarcerating women or forcing them into drug treatment. However, the American Civil Liberties Union (ACLU) argues that such prosecutions criminalize pregnancies. These women are ultimately arrested for becoming pregnant while addicted to drugs. Most women are addicted first and get pregnant later (Reed 1993).

What are the consequences of prosecuting pregnant addicts? One woman from Florida was convicted of trafficking by passing cocaine to her newborn through the umbilical cord. This conviction was appealed on the basis that the fetus is not considered a person under the constitution. Other methods of prosecution center on issues of child abuse. Maternal drug use during pregnancy imposes serious health risks on a developing fetus and can result in postnatal trauma. This type of prosecution is more likely to result in a conviction but such convictions are usually appealed because most states do not have child abuse statutes that refer to prenatal conduct (Humphries 1993). ☞

☞ Civil and women's rights advocates argue that these proceedings are unethical and unconstitutional, and that they are part of a widespread attack on poor women. Prosecutors stretch the law to unreasonable lengths; drug trafficking laws only apply to born persons. Using these laws to convict pregnant women violates due process since there has been no notice that these laws are applicable to this situation. Prosecutors are not always able to prove that the mother's drug use is the cause of postnatal defects, if such defects occur at all. If prosecutors succeed in establishing fetal rights, women will come to be viewed as incubators unable to control pregnancies. In addition, many legal behaviors damage developing fetuses. For example, diabetic or obese women who take medication during pregnancies may cause fetal damage. Prosecutions cannot be limited to illegal behaviors. Poor women who cannot afford health or prenatal care would have to be categorized as fetal abusers. As it is, the overwhelming number of prosecutions involve poor women of color. Drug testing is mandatory in many states but it is generally random and discriminatory. Prosecuting drug-using pregnant women may result in driving these women away from health care systems. Drug programs seem to be a logical answer to this problem but very few programs across the country take pregnant drug addicts or users.

Despite the common belief that it is the white middle and upper classes that are most likely to be victims of street crime, the data show that poor and minority groups living in urban areas are the most common victims of violent crime. The black murder rate is almost six times the rate for whites. Blacks are also 40 percent more likely to be burglarized, 50 percent more likely to be robbed, and 25 percent more likely to be assaulted. For minority women, racism is compounded by sexism. African American women and Latinas are more likely to suffer crimes of violence than white women. Black women are 1.5 times more likely to be raped than other women but are believed less often by the police than white rape victims (Price and Sokoloff 1995).

Consequences

The consequences of crime include heavy economic, social, and psychological costs. Crime can lead to death, serious physical injury, loss of property, addiction to drugs, and emotional trauma. Crime may also undermine a community or society by fostering fear, cynicism, and apathy.

Looking first at the economic costs of crime, we can use sociologist John Conklin's five categories of financial or economic losses from crime (1995). First are direct losses. This category includes buildings lost through arson or vandalism and may also include environmental destruction. Second, are losses stemming from the transfer of property from legal owners to criminals. This category includes bank robbers, car thieves, and employees who steal from their employers. The third category is related to the costs of violent crimes, such as the losses incurred when injured workers cannot work and the costs of medical care for victims of violent crimes. "Fourth are the costs associated with the production and sale of illegal goods and services, that is, illegal expenditures" (Mooney, Knox, and Schacht 1997:112). As Linda Mooney and her colleagues point out, "the expenditure of money on drugs, gambling, and prostitution diverts funds away from the legitimate economy and enterprises and lowers property values in high crime neighborhoods" (1997:112). The fifth category includes the considerable costs of the criminal justice system itself, including policy, courts, and prisons.

Estimates of the economic costs of crime are imprecise. Even accepting such estimates only as crude guidelines, however, it is clear that crime and violence impose enormous economic costs on American society. One estimate puts the cost at over $450 billion dollars a year (National Research Council 1994).

The United States has the highest incarceration rate of any industrialized society. Young African American men are disproportionately likely to be imprisoned. —*Photo: photostogo.com.*

Overall estimates of the costs of crime are useful, but the consequences and costs of crime also depend on the type of crime, so we will look at different types of crime. Conklin suggests that the costs of white- collar crimes are three times higher than the costs of street crime (1995). Sutherland developed the classic definition of white-collar crime, suggesting that white-collar crime is "a crime committed by a person of respectability and high social status in the course of his occupation" (1949: 9). By this definition, white-collar crimes included violations of antitrust laws, embezzlement, price-fixing, industrial safety violations, and misrepresentation in advertising. Some criminologists have recently broadened their conception of white-collar crime to include violations committed by nonphysical means and by concealment or guile, whether or not in the course of an occupation. Sutherland documented the myriad crimes committed by America's largest corporations, including such offenses as price-fixing, tax evasion, misrepresentation in advertising, and such unfair labor practices as the coercion and intimidation of union organizers (Galliher 1989).

The public does not appear to be generally outraged by these crimes because the public is not always the victim of such offenses. Stockholders are usually the victims of corporate embezzlement; employees are the victims of unfair and illegal labor practices. The public is the victim of price-fixing but it is very difficult to demand full prosecution of such offenders.

It is difficult to know exactly how many "members in good standing of American society" commit white-collar crime. White-collar criminals are as varied as the occupations from which they come. They include stockbrokers who make millions through insider trading; members of Congress who take payoffs; and people who cheat on their income taxes like Leona Helmsley. Are their crimes less harmful than street crimes? White-collar criminals cause considerable harm. During the Watergate era, President Nixon and his aides threatened the integrity of the U.S. electoral system. Auto executives have approved design features that have caused fatalities. Managers of chemical companies have allowed the environment to be polluted. The Savings and Loan scandals imposed heavy costs on American taxpayers.

Jeffrey Reiman (1998) argues that we apply criminal labels inconsistently. Killing one's wife or neighbor is termed murder, but when corporations cause the deaths of people in avoidable ways, that is not generally labeled as murder. He cites a mine disaster that killed 26 men because of safety violations. Why is this not termed murder? Calling it a disaster suggests impersonal forces at work. This mine disaster could have been prevented. Reiman argues that we are fooled by the fear of the "typical criminal." We have a better chance of being killed or disabled by an occupational injury or disease, by unnecessary surgery, or by shoddy emergency medical services than by aggravated assault or even homicide. Despite this, the FBI Index of serious crimes does not reflect these realities.

Similarly, the general public loses more money from price-fixing and monopolistic practices, consumer deception, and embezzlement than from all property crimes in the FBI Index combined (Reiman 1998). In essence, the criminal justice system does not simply reflect the reality of crime, it has a hand in creating the reality we see.

D. E. Weisburd and his colleagues (1990) found, in a sample of offenders convicted of federal white-collar crime, that white-collar criminals are often repeat offenders. In addition, white-collar criminals often commit crimes of a nonwhite collar type. Weisburd and his colleagues suggest that it may be useful to develop criminal justice policies for white-collar crime, like those for common crime. White-collar crime appears to be as harmful as street crime.

Organized crime refers to the activities of a group with a hierarchical organization, whose members operate an illegal business or a lawful business using unlawful force. Organized crime is carried out by organizations primarily designed to engage in criminal activity for personal profit (Calavita and Pontell 1990). During the 1920s, the prevalence of organized crime gave criminal violence a special character. In certain American cities, murder became a routine technique for dealing with business rivalries between bootleggers. As early as 1920, Chicago, whose population was one-third the size of London's, had twelve times the number of murders and twenty-two times the number of robberies. Organized crime and a prohibition against the sale of alcoholic beverages only served to increase violent crime during the Roaring Twenties. Today organized crime operates both domestically and internationally. Within the United States, organized crime provides illegal services such as drugs and gambling. Organized crime also extorts money from legal businesses by threatening violence. The drug trade and arms sales are two examples of organized crime on the international level.

The wealthy are weeded out at every stage of the criminal justice system, beginning with the definition of crime and proceeding through investigation, arrest, conviction, and sentencing. The dangerous activities of the rich and powerful are rarely defined by the legal system as crimes, even though such activities may result in hundreds of thousands of deaths and the loss of billions of dollars. Thus, for example, work safety regulations are often not enforced; the medical profession is not closely policed; and clean air standards are rarely met. As a result, the workplace, the medical profession, the air we breathe, and the poverty we refuse to rectify lead to far more human suffering, death, and disability, and take far more dollars from our pockets than the murders, aggravated assaults, and thefts reported annually by the FBI (Reiman 1998).

Acts of elite deviance are typically committed with little risk because legal sanctions are generally lenient relative to those associated with violent crime. Yet many acts of elite deviance pose significant danger and expense to the members of our society. For instance, between 100,000 and 200,000 persons annually die from illnesses and injuries on the job; between 174 and 231 billion dollars are added to the price of goods and services. What is more, elite deviance may promote the growth and maintenance of organized crime; and, most importantly, revelations of elite deviance in high political circles tend to erode public confidence in our institutions. Watergate was an example of this.

The consequences of juvenile crime are of great concern in modern society, especially since it appears to be on the rise. Several states across the country are reacting with frustration to juvenile, or youth, crime. For example, in reaction to increasing and more violent juvenile crime, the Massachusetts House of Representatives voted to require that accused murderers as young as 14 be tried as adults. Tennessee has eliminated any minimum age for trying some youths as adults. Oregon lowered its minimum age from 14 to 12 and Wisconsin put the minimum at 10 (Gest 1996).

This graffiti represents symbols of gang presence and activity. Increasing gang violence has been one aspect of juvenile delinquency. —*Scott H. Decker and Deitrich L. Smith.*

Larry Siegel and Joseph Senna (1997) state that juvenile crime has significantly influenced the nation's crime statistics. For example, in a 10-year period, from 1985 through 1994, the total number of juvenile arrests increased 28 percent; juvenile arrests for violent crime increased 75 percent. The teenage population remained stable during this period, so the increase in juvenile crime cannot be explained by a rising adolescent population.

Numerous acts of teenage aggression seem to be the result of unmotivated, random street violence. Jack Levin and Jack McDevitt argue that some of these incidents have their root cause in hatred or bias (1993). In their analysis of hate-inspired crimes, these authors found that many of the thousands of hate crimes committed each year—offenses directed against individuals because they are different with respect to race, religion, or sexual orientation—are perpetrated by young people and can be classified into three types:

1. **Thrill-seeking hate crimes**. These crimes usually involve juveniles who join forces to have fun or get thrills by bashing minorities or destroying property.

2. **Reactive hate crimes**. Perpetrators of these crimes rationalize criminal behavior as a stand against outsiders who are threatening their way of life.

3. **Mission hate crime**. These crimes are usually motivated by the need to eliminate people who threaten religious beliefs and to seek racial purity.

Levin and McDevitt (1993) estimate that 50,000 hate crimes are committed each year, 70 percent by teens. A growing proportion of such crimes involve the use of a gun. J. F. Sheley and J. D. Wright contend that juveniles want guns and will do what is necessary to get them (1993). All 50 states have firearm laws that apply specifically to juveniles. Many states have toughened penalties for violation of juvenile gun laws. At the federal level, the Youth Handgun Safety Act of 1994 prohibits the possession of handguns by anyone under age 18 and provides criminal penalties of up to 10 years in prison for anyone convicted of providing a handgun to a person under 18. Nevertheless, juveniles now possess handguns in unprecedented numbers. Handguns play a prominent role in violent crime: 62 percent of the homicides committed by juveniles involve firearms. A recent survey of 4,000 juveniles arrested in 11 major cities found that 22 percent of them carried guns all or most of the time (Siegel and Senna 1997).

Teenage gangs are also an area of great concern. There may be more than 500,000 gang members in the United States. A growing number of juveniles who kill do so in groups of two or more; the number of such multiple-offender killings has doubled since the mid-1980s. Related to gangs are teenage substance abusers and drug traffickers. Gangs involved in urban drug trades recruit juveniles because they work cheaply, are immune from heavy criminal penalties, and are daring and willing to take risks (Siegel and Senna 1997).

According to FBI statistics, the rate of serious crimes such as rape, assault, and murder has recently declined, after being on the rise for a number of years. Part of the explanation is demographic: The 76 million Baby Boomers have matured into their thirties and forties and are no longer part of the crime-prone age group. Another factor is a strengthened criminal justice system, which has placed more and more police officers between citizens and criminals. In New York City and Houston, Texas, for example, zero-tolerance policing—in which police do not tolerate any instances of crime or disorder in an area—has taken offenders off the streets and out of the reach of victims. William Bratton, when he was still New York's Police Commissioner, attributed the success of his crime-fighting effort to this zero-tolerance, get tough policy that locks away street criminals for minor offenses long *before* they have had the opportunity to commit serious offenses.

But the most important factor in declining murder rates in U. S. major cities may have nothing to do with population characteristics, get-tough policies, or prisons. Whether we realize it or not, Americans everywhere, at the grass-roots level and up, are just beginning to recognize that they can make a difference in the crime rate. In response to severe cutbacks by state and federal government, they are working to repair the moral, social, and economic damage done to our youngsters and to take the glamour out of destructive behavior. It is too little recognized that many youngsters benefit from destructive, violent behavior—they receive the approval of their peers; they make money if the violence is connected to the drug trade; and they gain a sense of importance.

Compared to other industrialized nations, the United States has high levels of gun violence and weak gun-control laws. Many sociologists suggest that these two phenomena are closely related. —*Photo: photostogo.com.*

In major cities throughout the country, local institutions have sponsored a number of effective programs aimed at providing healthy alternatives to violence in the form of hope, guidance, and supervision for local youngsters— gun-buyback programs and midnight basketball in the churches, conflict resolution and mentoring programs in the public schools, college scholarships, and summer jobs and after-school activities sponsored by local companies. In combination, such programs and policies seem to have a profound preventive effect on children and teenagers who might otherwise have turned to crime.

Interventions

All societies have established institutions for controlling criminal behavior. In U. S. society, such institutions have taken the form of a criminal justice system consisting of the police, courts, and a correctional system, including prisons. Currently, the United States emphasizes punishment. In the past three decades, there has been a dramatic increase in the number of Americans who think that authorities should be tougher on criminals. For example, while a majority of Americans in the 1960s favored the abolition of the death penalty, today more than 70 percent favor its use for certain crimes.

Sociologists have argued that the government must do more than rely on the police, courts, and jails. It must do something about the underlying social roots of crime, especially poverty and racism. This was a very popular argument during the 1970s. By the late 1970s, some sociologists and criminologists were having second thoughts. For example, James Q. Wilson (1985) argued that society's attempts to change social conditions have met with little success, so that locking up criminals remained the best way to deal with the crime problem in the short term. Morgan Reynolds (1999) argues that crime pays because most crimes do not result in significant jail time for criminals.

Reynolds (1999) states that the United States has more crimes per capita than any other developed country. He argues that crime continues in our society because our society is too lenient in terms of punishment. On the average, crimes with the longest expected prison terms are the crimes least frequently committed, comprising only about 10 percent of all serious crime. Reynolds argues that prison terms should be longer and punishment harsher.

Eitzen (1999) argues that long prison terms are not the answer to preventing crime. Currently there are 1.2 million Americans in prisons. Our incarceration rate is 455 per 100,000. The costs of running a prison are enormous. It costs about $60,000 to build a prison cell and $20,000 to keep a prisoner for a year. The overall costs of prisons and jails (federal, state, and local) is $29 billion annually. Eitzen contends that huge amounts of money could be spent on other programs that might prevent crime. He further states that prisons do not rehabilitate. Prison experience tends to increase the likelihood of more criminal behavior. Prisons are overcrowded and brutal places, according to Eitzen, that change people for the worse, not the better. Prisoners are forever stigmatized as ex-convicts and considered suspect and dangerous. They are often driven into a deviant subculture, and about two-thirds are arrested within three years of leaving prison.

Preventive measures are the key solution to fighting crime, according to Eitzen (1999). These measures are out of favor politically but may be the only realistic ways to reduce crime, especially violent crime. Eitzen argues that the problem with the conservative, after-the-fact crimefighting proposals is that while they promote criminal justice, these programs dismantle social justice. Eitzen proposes four preventive measures that could effectively reduce a significant amount of crime:

1. Society should be protected from predatory sociopaths. This means that we should only imprison the most dangerous people. For other criminals, society should provide reasonable alternatives to prison such as house arrest, halfway houses, boot camps, electronic surveillance, job corps, and alcohol/drug treatment.

2. The number of handguns and assault weapons must be significantly reduced by enforcing stringent gun controls at the federal level. The United States currently has 210 million guns in circulation. A special effort must be made to get guns out of the hands of juveniles.

3. The criminal justice system must be reinvented so that race, class, and gender biases are eradicated. There are differences by

race, class, and gender in arrest rates, plea bargain arrangements, sentencing, parole, and the death penalty.

4. Prison should be more humane. More vocational training and rehabilitation should be offered.

What about punishment? Prison unquestionably does deprive offenders of their freedom. By contrast, rehabilitation, resocialization, and even protection seem to be elusive goals, which to a large extent have not yet been achieved. The deterrent effect of punishment, and especially of capital punishment, is hotly debated. Some evidence indicates that *certainty* of punishment does, in fact, deter serious offenses. The *severity* of punishment, however, seems to have no determinable effect on deterrence.

Despite popular conceptions or misconceptions, no compelling evidence suggests that capital punishment reduces the incidence of homicide. If anything, the use of the death penalty may increase murder: it may have a brutalizing effect, in that brutality by the state is sanctioned, and others are encouraged to imitate the destructive behavior. Some studies have shown that homicide rates in states with the death penalty were dramatically *higher* than in states without the death penalty (Bedau 1997). In fact, for a short period of time after an inmate is executed by the state, the homicide rate actually increases. Thus, the state executioner becomes a model for citizens to follow in resolving their own personal problems with other people.

David von Drehle (1995) argues that capital punishment is an expensive government program that does not work. There is a lot of talk about getting rid of government programs that cost too much and produce scant results. It is curious, states von Drehle, that one of the least efficient government programs in America is also among the most popular. In 1994, the death row population exceeded 3,000 people, and by the end of 1994, only 31 had been executed. There are hundreds of prisoners in the United States who have been on death row for more than a decade, and at least one—Thomas Knight of Florida—has been awaiting execution for twenty years (von Drehle 1995).

Many people agree with the death penalty in theory, but very few are aware of its slow, costly process. Every cost study undertaken has found that it is far more expensive, because of legal safeguards, to carry out a death sentence than to imprison someone for life. Capital punishment is the principal burden on the state and federal appellate courts in every jurisdiction where it is routinely practiced (von Drehle 1995).

Originally, capital punishment was a state matter. Federal judges took almost no interest in it. For most of American history, criminals were tried, convicted, and sentenced according to local rules, and executions were generally carried out by town sheriffs. A disproportionate number of people executed under these customs were African American. This was particularly true for the crime of rape. In the 1920s, a coalition of women's clubs began objecting to executions, especially those conducted in public squares. By the 1950s and into the 1960s, opponents of the death penalty were more vocal and urged the federal government to get involved. Many argued that the death penalty violated the Eighth Amendment (which bars cruel and unusual punishment) and the Fourteenth Amendment (which guarantees equal protection under the law).

In 1972, the Supreme Court decided to hear arguments concerning handling of death sentences. Anthony Amsterdam, a Stanford University law professor, delivered arguments against the death penalty. He began by presenting statistical proof that the death penalty in America was overwhelmingly used against the poor and minorities. Next, he argued that the death penalty was imposed randomly; judges and juries meted out their sentences without clear guidelines. In addition, Amsterdam argued that the death penalty was so rarely carried out in the modern United States that it could no longer be justified as a deterrent to crime. The Supreme Court decided to abolish the death penalty as it existed but not to completely abolish it (von Drehle 1995). Despite such evidence and arguments, people still demand the death penalty to deal with a society that they believe is becoming more crime-ridden.

One of the most commonly employed alternatives to confinement in a correctional facility is probation, whereby an offender serves the sentence of a court while remaining at liberty under the supervision of a probation officer. The probation officer sees that the probationer complies with the conditions of his probation. If the conditions of probation are violated, the probation officer can send a probationer to a custodial institution.

Another widespread practice is parole, whereby an offender is conditionally released under the supervision of a parole officer after having served part of his or her sentence in a correctional institution. Parole is granted only when a review board has determined that a prisoner deserves the privilege—specifically, that he or she has shown sufficient progress while in prison to warrant an opportunity for rehabilitation outside of prison. The released prisoner who seeks to reconnect himself to society might be able to find a temporary residence, usually located in the community in which he lived before going to prison. These temporary residences are usually called halfway houses to emphasize their purpose of facilitating the transition between prison and total freedom. Halfway houses have been established by private charitable organizations; they are also operated by state correctional systems in connection with their probation or parole programs or for ex-prisoners who have completed their sentences and have no place to turn for help.

In 1973, the National Advisory Commission on Criminal Justice Standards and Goals emphasized pretrial diversion as an alternative to incarceration when the offender is not dangerous to others and the arrest has already served as a deterrent. By attempting to avoid official processing, diversion minimizes the stigmatizing of the offender and may also provide a means of compensating the victim or society. For example, some judges have waived imprisonment in favor of an alternative sentence of a number of hours of unpaid community work.

Community policing is one of the newest approaches to preventing crime. Crime prevention appears to be as dependent on the community as it is on the criminal justice system. It is not easy to have the police force join with every community. Police and citizens may have a history of not getting along with each other. This may be especially true in disadvantaged neighborhoods. Research that has examined participation in crime prevention programs has revealed that in disadvantaged neighborhoods participation is not easily sustained. Crime and fear stimulate withdrawal from, not involvement in, community life (Skogan 1992).

Society has raised the level of expectations of police agencies. Many police agencies estimate that only 5 to 15 percent of a police department's time is spent actually arresting individuals. Approximately 85 to 95 percent of an officer's time is spent responding to calls for service such as lockouts, animal complaints, landlord disputes, and disturbances.

The Future of Crime

It is popular to blame increased violent crime on the incompetence of our criminal justice system or on shifts in unemployment or on racial tension. Many members of American society are very concerned about crime and violence. We must wonder how serious crime is and how we can prevent crime. The criminal justice system does need work, but it is difficult to determine viable solutions.

It seems that all social institutions need to work together to deal with crime and prevent it. Factors such as poverty, racism, and sexism cannot be ignored. Government programs are needed, but so are grass-roots efforts on the part of members of the local communities in which violent crime is a problem. Although violent crime rates have not increased significantly during the last few years (and may even be on the decline), the United States continues to be seriously crime-ridden.

Summary

Although the word *crime* has been used in several different ways, many sociologists have agreed to accept a legal definition: crime is any act that violates the criminal law. Some argue that legal regulations defining a crime reflect a society's values and customs. Others contend (instead or in addition) that legal definitions of crime are created in order to serve the special interests of the capitalist class.

One way to determine the amount of crime in a society is to analyze crime statistics. They must, however, be treated with caution. Statistics can be biased and open to manipulation.

People generally fear crime. The media play a role in this fear by distorting our perception of crime. Law enforcement agencies add to this distortion by representing crime as a serious epidemic in society. Some have suggested as well that this representation may be exaggerated to justify the maintenance or expansion of police powers.

Robert Merton suggested that criminal behavior may be a response to certain characteristics of our culture, specifically, to the cultural emphasis on success while excluding an emphasis on legitimate opportunities for achieving success. One result may be innovation—deviant behavior whereby the individual substitutes illegal, but more effective, means for securing wealth and power. On the other hand, conflict theorists, such as Marx, argue that the law is created to serve the interests of the ruling class in society.

Institutional responses to crime have received mixed reviews. The criminal justice system is criticized for being racist, classist, and sexist in its response to crime. African Americans, for example, are disproportionately arrested for crimes, as well as prosecuted and convicted, compared to European Americans. The war on drugs has a significant impact on minorities, with a recent emphasis on women. At the same time, fearful Americans seek to strengthen the criminal justice system by expanding its powers and making it more punitive in its approach to crime fighting.

The consequences of crime are difficult to estimate. We do know, however, that organized crime costs our society billions of dollars annually and that crime in general contributes to the high cost of insurance, retail prices, and taxes, as well as to considerable pain and suffering.

Juvenile delinquency is of great concern in our society. Several states are reacting to this type of crime with harsh laws and great frustration. Until very recently, juveniles appeared to be increasingly more violent, especially in the commission of hate crimes. During the last few years, however, perhaps as a result of changing law enforcement policies as well as of grass-root activism on the part of local residents, juvenile violence seems to be somewhat on the decline. This good news is, however, tempered by the fact that crimes committed by teenagers remain at a very high level. Despite some effective efforts to reduce the availability of firearms, handguns continue to play a dominant role in the lives of many teenagers today. Almost half of all high school students report that their schoolmates carry weapons; about 40 percent report that gangs are present in their schools.

There are many sociological perspectives on crime. Durkheim believed crime had many functions in society, some positive, others negative. Marx and Engels, conflict theorists, believed that crime was an inevitable response to capitalism and that capitalists used crime to protect their interests.

Sutherland's theory of differential association attempted to explain the process by which a given person learns to engage in crime and also the content of what is learned. Akers' social learning theory also offers an explanation of crime that draws from social learning principles. In addition, his theory retains a strong element of symbolic interactionism.

With respect to intervention, all societies have established institutions for controlling criminal behavior. U. S. society has developed a criminal justice system consisting of the police, courts, and a correctional system, including prisons. The only function that actually seems to be carried out successfully by our correctional system is that of punishment. By contrast, rehabilitation, re-socialization, and protection functions are not effectively performed.

A number of alternatives to the present approach (long-term incarceration) have been proposed; some have even been attempted. Probation and parole provide the circumstances for offenders to serve some or all of their sentences while remaining at liberty under the supervision of the criminal justice system. Pretrial diversion seeks to avoid the stigma of official processing and may be used to compensate victims as well as society. Community policing, one of the newest approaches in combating crime, emphasizes the police and the community working together as partners.

Discussion Questions

1. Have there been any date rapes or acquaintance rapes on your campus? How were they dealt with? Does your college or university offer programs to reduce the likelihood of date rape?

2. Do you think that juveniles who murder should be tried as adults? Are there any circumstances in which you think juveniles should be treated as adults? On what do you base your opinion?

3. Do you think that your home or your campus is safe? What is being done in your neighborhood or on your campus to make them

safer? How effective are these measures? What additional policies would you try?

4. Where do you stand on the death penalty? What are your reasons
for your position? Try giving strong arguments for the opposing
view.

5. Have there been any hate crimes in your city or on your campus?
What do you think causes such hate crimes? How should they be
dealt with?

References

Adler, Freda. 1975. *Sisters in Crime: The Rise of the New Female Criminal*. New York:
McGraw-Hill.

Akers, Ronald. 1996. *Criminological Theories*. Second edition. Los Angeles: Roxbury
Publishing.

Becker, Howard S. 1963. *Outsiders: Studies in the Sociology of Deviance*. Glencoe, Illinois: Free Press.

Bedau, Hugo Adam, ed. 1997. *The Death Penalty in America: Current Controversies*.
New York: Oxford University Press.

Beirne, Piers. 1993. *Inventing Criminology: Essays on the Rise of "Homo Criminalis."*
Albany: State University of New York Press.

Beirne, Piers, and James Messerschmidt. 1995. *Criminology*. Second edition. Fort
Worth: Harcourt Brace Jovanovich.

Bureau of Justice Statistics. 1997. *Sourcebook of Criminal Justice Statistics 1996*.
Washington, D.C.: Bureau of Justice Statistics Clearinghouse.

Calavita, Kitty, and Henry N. Pontell. 1990. " 'Heads I Win, Tails You Lose': Deregula-
tion, Crime, and Crisis in the Savings and Loan Industry." *Crime and Delinquency*
36:309-341.

Conklin, John E. 1995. *Criminology* Fifth edition. Boston: Allyn and Bacon.

Connell, Colleen K. 1996. "Legal Battleground: The Womb." *Chicago Sun Times*, September 3, 26.

Currie, Elliot. 1985. *Confronting Crime: An American Challenge*. New York: Pantheon.

Dembner, Alice. 1997a. "Efforts by Universities to Curb Date Rape Falling Short."
Boston Sunday Globe, May 18, A1.

Dembner, Alice. 1997b. "Colleges Struggle to Find Answers: School Programs Fail to
Put a Halt to Date Rape." *Boston Globe*, May 19, A1.

Durkheim, Emile. 1933[1893]. *The Division of Labor in Society*. New York: Free Press.

Eitzen D. Stanley. 1999. "Violent Crime: Myths, Facts, and Solutions," pp. 327–333.
Taking Sides: Clashing Views on Controversial Social Issues, edited by Kurt
Finsterbusch. Guilford, Connecticut: Dushkin/McGraw Hill.

Flowers, Ronald Barri. 1987. *Women and Criminality: The Woman as Victim, Offender,
and Practitioner*. Westport, Connecticut: Greenwood Press.

Fox, James A., and Jack Levin. 1994. *Overkill: Mass Murder and Serial Killing Exposed*.
New York: Plenum.

Galliher, John F. 1989. *Criminology: Human Rights, Criminal Law, and Crime*.
Englewood Cliffs, New Jersey: Prentice Hall.

Gest, Ted. 1996. "Crime Time Bomb." *U.S. News and World Report*, March 25.

Goffman, Erving. 1959. *The Presentation of Self in Everyday Life*. Garden City, New
York: Doubleday.

Gottfredson, Michael R., and Travis Hirschi. 1990. *A General Theory of Crime*. Stanford: Stanford University Press.

Herbert, Bob. 1998 "In America: Pregnancy and Addiction." *New York Times*, June 11.

Humphries, Drew. 1993. "Mothers and Children, Drugs and Crack: Reactions to Maternal Drug Dependency," pp. 130–45. *It's a Crime: Women and Justice*, edited by Roslyn Muraskin and Ted Alleman. Englewood Cliffs, New Jersey: Regents/Prentice Hall.

Kappeler, Victor E., Mark Blumberg, and Gary W. Potter. 1996. *The Mythology of Crime and Criminal Justice*. Second edition. Prospect Heights, Illinois: Waveland Press.

Koren, Gideon, Karen Graham, Heather Shear, and T. R. Einarson. 1989. "Bias Against the Null Hypothesis: The Reproductive Hazards of Cocaine." *The Lancet* 8677: 1440–1442.

Levin, Jack, and James A. Fox. 1985. *Mass Murder: America's Growing Menace*. Newbury Park, California: Sage Publications.

Levin, Jack, and Jack McDevitt. 1993. *Hate Crimes: The Rising Tide of Bigotry and Bloodshed*. New York: Plenum.

Lewin, Tamar. 1997. "Abuse Laws Cover Fetus, a High Court Rules." *New York Times*, October 30.

Maguire, Kathleen, and Ann L. Pastore. 1997. *Sourcebook of Criminal Justice Statistics, Online*. http://www.albany.edu/sourcebook.

Merton, Robert K. 1968. *Social Theory and Social Structure*. Enlarged edition. New York: Free Press.

Mooney, Linda A., David Knox, and Caroline Schacht. 1997. *Understanding Social Problems*. Minneapolis/St. Paul: West Publishing.

National Research Council. 1994. *Violence in Urban America: Mobilizing a Response Summary of a Conference*. Washington, D.C.: National Academy Press.

Price, Barbara Raffel, and Natalie J. Sokoloff, 1995. *The Criminal Justice System and Women*. New York: McGraw-Hill.

Rafter, Nicole, and Frances Heidensohn, eds. 1995. *International Feminist Perspectives in Criminology*. Philadelphia: Open University Press.

Reckless, Walter C. 1961. *The Crime Problem*. New York: Appleton-Century-Crofts.

Reed, Susan O. 1993. "The Criminalization of Pregnancy: Drugs, Alcohol, and AIDS." Pp. 93–117 in *It's a Crime: Women and Justice*, edited by Roslyn Muraskin and Ted Alleman. Englewood Cliffs, New Jersey: Regents/Prentice Hall.

Reid, Sue Titus. 1996. *Crime and Criminology*, Eighth edition. New York: McGraw Hill.

Reiman, Jeffrey. 1998. *The Rich Get Richer and the Poor Get Prison: Ideology, Class, and Criminal Justice*. Fifth edition. Boston: Allyn and Bacon.

Reynolds, Morgan. 1995. *Crime and Punishment in America* NCPA Policy Report, 193.

Reynolds, Morgan O. 1999. "Crime Pays, but so Does Imprisonment," pp. 318–326. *Taking Sides: Clashing Views on Controversial Social Issues*, edited by Kurt Finsterbusch. Guilford, Connecticut: Dushkin/McGraw Hill.

Sheley, J. F., and J. D. Wright. 1993. *Gun Acquisition and Possession in Selected Juvenile Samples*. Research in Brief, vol. (December). Washington, D.C.: National Institute of Justice.

Siegel, Larry, and Joseph Senna. 1997. *Juvenile Delinquency*. Sixth edition. New York: West Publishing.

Silberman, Charles E. 1978. *Criminal Violence, Criminal Justice*. New York: Random House.

Simon, Rita J. 1975. *Women and Crime*. Lexington, Massachusetts: D. C. Heath.

Skogan, Wesley G. 1992. *Disorder and Decline: Crime and the Spiral of Decay in American Neighborhoods*. Berkeley: University of California Press.

Stark, Rodney. 1996. *Sociology*. Sixth edition. Belmont, California: Wadsworth.

Steffensmeier, Darrell, and Emilie Allan. 1995. "Gender, Age, and Crime." Pp. 83–113 in *Criminology: A Contemporary Handbook*. Second edition, edited by Joseph Sheley. Belmont, California: Wadsworth.

Sutherland, Edwin H. 1947. *Criminology*. Philadelphia: J. B. Lippincott.

——. 1949. *White-Collar Crime*. New York: Dryden Press.

Tonry, Michael. 1995. *Malign Neglect: Race, Crime, and Punishment in America*. New York: Oxford University Press.

von Drehle, David. 1995. *Among the Lowest of the Dead: The Culture of Death Row*. New York: Random House.

Weisburd, D., E. Chayet, and E. Waring. 1990. "White-collar Crime and Criminal Careers: Some Preliminary Findings" *Crime & Delinquency* 36:342-355.

Wilson, James Q. 1985. *Thinking About Crime*. New York: Vintage.

——. 1997. *Moral Judgement: Does the Abuse Excuse Threaten Our Legal System?* New York: Basic Books.

Websites

http://www.ojp.usdoj.gov/bjs/cvict.htm#ncvs

U.S. Department of Justice, Bureau of Justice Statistics, Crime and Victims Statistics. This website provides information on the National Crime Victimization Survey (NCVS) and the Uniform Crime Reports (UCR).

http://www.crime.org/

Organized Crime. A Crime Statistics Site by Regina Schekall. Schekall plans to develop this site into a one-stop crime statistics, tutorial, and link guide. It is still under construction, but includes some useful tutorials on crime statistics and valuable links to other sites.

CHAPTER EIGHT

Substance Abuse

In the News: Cocaine Sentencing—Crack Versus Powder

Possession of as little as five grams of crack cocaine leads to a mandatory five-year minimum prison sentence; the threshold for the same mandatory minimum sentence for powder cocaine (cocaine hydrochloride) is 500 grams (Holmes 1997). The 100 to 1 disparity in sentencing in Federal courts, established by Congressional legislation in 1986, was justified as a response to widespread voter fears of violence tied to crack dealing. In July 1997 President Clinton recommended reducing the disparity but not eliminating it.

General Barry R. McCaffrey, a retired general who is President Clinton's drug-policy advisor, had wanted to completely eliminate the disparity because the pharmacological effects of the two forms of cocaine are nearly identical. He backed away from his position and endorsed the President's recommendations. The recommended changes would raise the minimum five-year-sentence threshold for crack cocaine to 25 grams. The threshold for powder cocaine would be lowered to 250 grams, thus reducing the disparity from 100 to 1 to 10 to 1.

The Congressional Black Caucus suggested that the White House proposals did not go far enough. Some commentators have suggested that whites are statistically more likely to snort or inject cocaine, while blacks are likelier to smoke cocaine in its cheaper crack form, so that having harsher penalties for crack puts higher numbers of African Americans in jail. In fact, data suggest that African Americans make up 36 to 38 percent of crack users, while white Americans make up 46 to 52 percent of the nation's crack users. In a stark contrast, 88 percent of those convicted under crack laws are black, while 4 percent of those convicted are white (Hatsukami and Fischman 1996).

Dorothy Hatsukami and Marian Fischman's review of the literature on crack cocaine and powder cocaine led them to conclude that a 2 to 1 or 3 to 1 disparity in sentencing might be justified, but not a 10 to 1 disparity (1996). Putting more social and economic resources into poor communities might be even more effective in reducing crack cocaine use. Jackson (1997) argues that current drug laws, even with the proposed modifications in cocaine sentencing, continue to link African Americans with drugs and to produce inequitable sentencing.

Definition and Prevalence

$\mathbf{A}$ **drug** is often defined as any chemical that affects the structure or functioning of a living organism. Even if we exclude food, this is still a broad definition, which includes some substances we do not usually consider to be drugs. Erich Goode (1993) suggests that custom and law, not science or logic, are the sources of that definition and that, in fact, a drug is anything that is defined as a drug. **Drug abuse** or **substance abuse** refers to the use of illegal drugs or the excessive or inappropriate use of legal substances so as to produce physical, psychological, or social harm. **Psychoactive drugs** are chemicals that change the perceptions or moods of those who take them.

In this chapter, we focus on the impact that both illegal drugs and legal drugs have on people's lives. Not everyone agrees on the effects or meaning of these substances. In fact, much controversy exists over which substances are most harmful and which should or should not be legal. We focus on the most controversial illegal substances: marijuana, heroin, and cocaine, as well as on legal substances such as alcohol and tobacco. Many Americans use legal drugs such as caffeine, nicotine, and alcohol and often do not even think of them as drugs.

The social construction and conflict approaches to social problems are both useful in examining substance abuse. Definitions of drugs, drug problems, and substance abuse are all socially constructed. That is, they are based on the social meanings that groups of people attribute to drugs and drug-related behaviors and issues. For example, Craig Reinarman and Harry Levine (1997) argue that American media and politicians succeeded in socially constructing a crack cocaine "epidemic" in 1986. Because drug definitions and issues are socially constructed, members of different societies or groups will disagree about those definitions and issues. Conflict over definitions will occur, and the most powerful groups in any society will most often prevail in imposing their definitions on the rest of society. These powerful groups also usually benefit from having their definitions prevail.

Every society defines some drugs as acceptable and others as unacceptable. Attitudes toward drugs reflect both customs and the power of special interests. Drugs traditionally used by dominant social groups in a society tend to be positively defined. There is often little relationship between how drugs are defined and their harmfulness. Nicotine, for example, is widely used despite its association with cancer. Alcohol does great damage to both individuals and society. Marijuana, although generally less dangerous to users than nicotine or alcohol, is illegal. The distinction between socially acceptable and socially unacceptable drug use has less to do with the pharmacological properties or risks to health of a particular substance, and more to do with threats to the moral order symbolized by the drug and with threats to the power of groups who have investments in its production and distribution (Goode 1993).

In thinking about substance abuse, we need a double awareness. Obviously, many people use illegal substances that can be harmful, such as

Alcohol abuse and underage drinking continue to be serious problems on college campuses. Several alcohol-related fatalities in recent years have led many colleges and universities to rethink their alcohol policies.

cocaine. People also use legal substances that are harmful, such as tobacco. They may also use legal substances, such as alcohol, to excess. However, laws about substance abuse or public awareness of the dangers of substance abuse do not necessarily reflect the most harmful substances or the most harmful types of substance abuse. Government agencies or private groups may launch campaigns to shape public perceptions about substance abuse and may even create drug panics to influence public opinion. These moral entrepreneurs make claims in order to socially construct their definitions and classifications of substance abuse and behaviors related to substance abuse. The creation of a crack cocaine panic, which we mentioned earlier, is a good example of this social construction process. Keep this double awareness in mind when thinking about how drugs are classified and the seriousness of various kinds of substance abuse.

Drugs may be classified along certain overlapping dimensions: legal and illegal; socially acceptable and unacceptable; medical and nonmedical. The distinction between legal and illegal drugs seems artificial because large quantities of legal drugs, such as amphetamines and barbiturates, are diverted from the prescription market into the illegal black market for direct sale to users.

The medical/nonmedical distinction seems to imply that medically approved drugs are good because they are prescribed and thus legitimized by physicians. Medically useful drugs such as Valium, however, are often overprescribed, may be very addictive, and can cause great harm to those who take them inappropriately. It is often difficult to distinguish between drug use and drug abuse. To some, use of a drug for pleasure or recreation always implies abuse. To others, drug use becomes abuse only when it is so compulsive or excessive that it harms a person's health or social functioning or has harmful consequences for society. It is possible to abuse substances that are legal, socially acceptable, or medically functional.

Partly because defining substance abuse is complicated, it is also difficult to accurately assess the extent of use of various drugs. Statistics from official sources often do not reveal those who received no treatment or punishment, the hidden population of drug takers. The Substance Abuse and Mental Health Services Administration (SAMHSA) of the Department of Health and Human Services (HHS) probably provides the most complete and accurate statistical data on substance use and abuse. Figure 8-1 is based on SAMHSA's National Household Survey on Drug Use for 1996. It shows what percentage of people in various age groups reported using illegal drugs during the past month. For those 35 and older, the percentage has been low and stable since 1979. Look closely at the trends for other age groups. All are generally declining. Drug use for those 12 to 17 started increasing in about 1993 but seemed to peak in 1995. You can see that even with the 1993 increase, illicit drug use among teenagers was still lower than it had been in 1979 (SAMHSA 1997). In fact, drug use in general has declined over the past 20 years. Let's take a closer look at specific drugs.

Ever since the discovery that alcoholic beverages cause pleasurable sensations in some drinkers, their use has become common in most cultures. In the United States some 95 million people drink alcohol. A small percentage of drinkers, about 7 percent, become alcoholics, or problem drinkers. For the 9 to 12 million alcoholics in the United States, drinking may disrupt their lives in various ways. Most people can drink normally, however, so the real enemy

Figure 8-1 Percent of Any Age Group That Used Illegal Drugs During the Past Month: 1979–1996

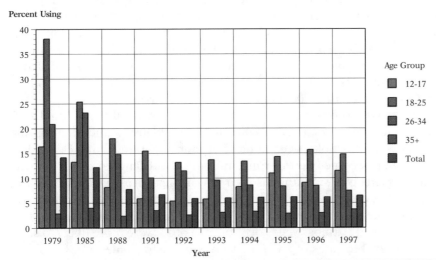

Source: Substance Abuse and Mental Health Services Administration. 1998 *National Household Survey on Drug Abuse*. Department of Health and Human Services. Office of Applied Studies. <http://www.samhsa.gov/oas/nhsda>

is excessive alcohol use, not alcohol itself. Despite this, alcohol is potentially dangerous, and alcoholism remains the most serious drug problem in this country today. In 1996, 109 million Americans age 12 and older (51 percent of the population) had used alcohol at least once. About 32 million engaged in binge drinking, defined as five or more drinks on at least one occasion, and about 11 million were heavy drinkers, defined as drinking five or more drinks per occasion on five or more days in the past 30 days (SAMHSA 1997).

Whites continue to have the highest rate of alcohol use, followed by Latinos and African Americans. Whites are also more likely than African Americans or Latinos to engage in binge drinking. Men drink more than women and are more likely to engage in binge drinking and heavy drinking (SAMHSA 1997). Binge drinking and heavy drinking may lead to **alcoholism**, defined as a chronic behavioral disorder manifested by a dependence on alcohol and by repeated drinking of alcoholic beverages in excess of the dietary and social uses deemed acceptable by the community and to an extent that interferes with the drinker's physical and mental health or social and economic functioning. This definition, similar to one formulated by the World Health Organization (WHO), has several components.

The word *chronic* indicates that alcoholism is a long-term problem. It may take many years for problem drinkers to realize that they are alcoholics. Some organizations suggest that alcoholism is a lifelong problem. Alcoholics Anonymous (AA), for example, teaches that once a person is an alcoholic, he or she is always an alcoholic. Even a problem drinker who has not had a drink for twenty years is still an alcoholic, according to AA, and can never drink normally again. *Dependence* implies that the alcoholic needs alcohol and cannot stop drinking. Loss of control over the amount of alcohol consumed and the occasions on which it is drunk is the crux of the definition.

Focusing on the dietary and social uses of alcohol in the community is important because definitions of normal drinking vary in different contexts.

For example, lumberjacks may drink a lot during those long evenings in the woods. Does this mean that all lumberjacks are alcoholics, or is it only those who drink more frequently or compulsively than the rest? In American society the norms for appropriate drinking are unclear, and different groups have different drinking customs and different reactions to intoxication. In the past, alcoholics were often seen as sinners and alcoholism seen as a moral failing. Today people are more likely to view the alcoholic as sick and alcoholism as a disease. How alcoholism is defined influences the way alcoholism is managed—whether the alcoholic is punished or treated.

Tobacco is probably the most physically harmful of all drugs. Smokers inhale nicotine, coal tars, nitrogen dioxide, formaldehyde, and other harmful substances. Most smokers consume 15 or more cigarettes a day. Dependence on smoking becomes very strong, making it difficult to quit. The well-publicized effects of smoking resulted in warnings on all packs and a ban on radio and television tobacco advertising. In 1996, there were an estimated 62 million smokers in the United States. Blacks are slightly more likely to smoke than whites and Latinos. Males over the age of 17 were more likely to smoke than females, but rates of smoking were similar for males and females between ages 12 and 17 (SAMHSA 1997). Each day, an estimated 3,000 teenagers smoke their first cigarette. That is 995,000 new teenage smokers per year. (Kulnis 1997). Smokers generally begin smoking when they under 18. Nine out of ten of these young smokers continue to smoke regularly as adults. Nicotine is addictive, so consumption increases with age.

Alcohol and tobacco are legal, but in 1996, an estimated 13 million Americans used illegal drugs. This represents little change from the 1995 level estimate of 12.8 million. The number of illicit drug users was at its highest level in 1979, when it reached 25 million. According to the SAMHSA survey, based on a representative sample of the national civilian population 12 years old and older, illicit drug use among those 12 to 17 years of age decreased between 1995 and 1996. Males use illicit drugs more than females. With regard to race, an estimated 9.7 million whites, 1.8 million African Americans and 1.1 million Latinos use illicit drugs. Among young people, the rate is the same for all three groups (SAMHSA 1997).

For all age groups, the rate of cocaine and marijuana use did not change significantly between 1995 and 1996. There was relatively little cocaine use in the United States until the 1970s and 1980s. In 1985, crack cocaine was introduced in the United States, especially in urban areas. Crack cocaine became an attractive alternative to powder cocaine mainly because it can be smoked, not snorted, and as a result, it is more rapidly absorbed into the body. Crack cocaine offers a quick high and is cheaper than powder cocaine. Powder cocaine highs are shorter and require many more doses. Also, crack cocaine is easily hidden (Inciardi, Lockwood, and Pottienger 1993). Although there are as many as 1.75 million cocaine users in the United States, cocaine use appears to be on the decline (Meier and Geis 1997).

Marijuana is the most widely used illicit drug in the United States. Marijuana use in the United States tends to be concentrated in those in their twenties and younger (Goode 1993). According to the SAMHSA survey, there are about 2.4 million marijuana users in the United States; 34 percent of Americans over 12 years of age have used marijuana at some time (Zimmer and Morgan 1997).

Heroin use is rising, according to this survey. In 1995, there were an estimated 141,000 new heroin users. Heroin use has increased since the early 1990s. From 1993 to 1996, for example, the estimated number of heroin users increased from 68,000 to 216,000 (SAMHSA 1997).

It is doubtful that there are more drug addicts now than in the past. In the nineteenth and early twentieth centuries, opium and its derivatives were widely available in over-the-counter patent medicines and in prescriptions. In fact, people could buy heroin cough syrup in the late nineteenth century. Users were not defined as deviant and thus not included in official statistics on drug abuse. Rarely were such addicts recognized, stigmatized, or punished (Duster 1970; Musto 1991).

The current drug scare may be partially due to the entry of middle-class youth into the drug scene and the use of amphetamines, barbiturates, and other substances for recreation and pleasure rather than for medical purposes (Males 1996). For example, some suggested that the growth of a youth counterculture in the 1960s, and of student and inner-city populations alienated from mainstream America, may help to explain those emerging drug patterns, but this is speculative and hard to prove.

Levels of Causation

Individual

Many psychologists have tried to explain substance abuse by investigating users' personalities. This has led to conflict over whether there is an addictive personality. Psychologists also disagree about the characteristics of substance abusers. One theory suggests that alcoholics and drug addicts have weak personalities and low self-esteem, so they turn to substance abuse to deal with their problems. This theory has been criticized for focusing exclusively on the individual with the problem. Personality may play a role in an individual's decision to use alcohol and drugs, but there is no single type of personality that leads to substance abuse.

It is hard to explain why some people become addicted to alcohol or other drugs. Some evidence exists for a physiological basis or a genetic predisposition for alcoholism, but the studies are inconclusive. Though alcohol has negative effects on the body, and the degree of intoxication depends upon the amount of alcohol in the blood, the alcoholic does not have faulty body chemistry. But alcohol is physically as well as psychologically addicting. Using alcohol frequently and in large amounts leads to the body building up a higher tolerance, and withdrawal symptoms may occur if the person stops drinking. The same is true for those addicted to illegal drugs and tobacco. Physiological theories of substance abuse are often based on a post hoc sample; that is, individuals are examined after the heavy substance ingestion and its detrimental consequences have begun. The danger is that the causes of substance abuse will be confused with the effects.

There are many psychological theories of substance addiction. Because the majority of drinkers and drug users do not become addicts, it is presumed that the person is the source of the problem. As is the case with physiological theories, psychological explanations of substance addiction have been difficult to verify. Most psychiatric studies show that the majority of drug users and abusers have no diagnosable mental illness or underlying personality disorder. If psychological problems do exist, they may be results rather than causes of substance abuse.

Cultural

Whether or not a person decides to use substances—legal or illegal—often depends on cultural attitudes. For example, cultural attitudes about drinking influence alcohol use and, probably, the rate of alcoholism. Different groups use and respond to alcohol in radically different ways. For example, drinking has often been viewed as a masculine activity. American women have experienced less pressure to prove themselves through drinking than have men. So it is not surprising that in the past, data seemed to show that there were six male alcoholics for every female. Part of this statistical difference, of course, might be due to women drinking more often at home, where they were less visible than if they were drinking in public. As middle-class women enter the job market in increasing numbers, however, the pressures on them may grow and may lead them to follow men in turning to alcohol to relieve career-related stress. Under these circumstances, alcoholism among women may increase.

Drug taking is a part of American culture. When we do not feel well, we may use aspirins or a laxative; when we want to relax, we drink alcohol or smoke cigarettes. Telling us to avoid pain and seek pleasure, advertising both reflects and shapes this stress on medication. The mass media emphasis on drugs and the adult disposition to medicate create a context in which illegal drug use seems almost culturally acceptable.

Some social scientists, policy makers, and drug experts argue that users of any drug—whether legal or illegal, medical or nonmedical—are statistically more likely to use other drugs. For example, some who study drug use and make policy recommendations argue that using marijuana leads to use of other, harder drugs. Marijuana is thus seen as a gateway to other drugs. Other researchers and policy experts argue that there is little evidence for the **gateway theory**. For a look at two drug information and policy centers that take opposing positions on this issue, as well as many others, (see "A Closer Look: Dueling Drug Centers.")

A Closer Look

Dueling Drug Centers

Columbia University's National Center on Addiction and Substance Abuse (CASA) and the Lindesmith Center are drug-policy research institutes located on the same block in New York City. The centers may be close to each other geographically, but they are worlds apart in terms of their approaches to drug policy. Joseph A. Califano, a former cabinet member and Washington insider, heads CASA, while Dr. Ethan Nadelman, a political scientist, directs the Lindesmith Center.

CASA combines many disciplines to "study and combat all forms of substance abuse—illegal drugs, pills, alcohol and tobacco—as they affect all aspects of society" according to its website (http://www.casacolumbia.org/about/menu1.htm). CASA takes what might be called a "hard line" approach to substance abuse and prevention. The center's goal is to reduce drug use. Many substance abuse researchers and experts criticize the CASA approach and suggest that the center sometimes misuses statistics. Other drug policy experts and researchers praise CASA highly (Shea 1997). ☞

❖ ❖ ❖ ❖

☞ The Lindesmith Center, which is funded by the venture capitalist and philanthropist George Soros, takes a different approach. According to its web page, the Lindesmith Center advocates "drug substitution and maintenance approaches" to substance abuse (http://www.lindesmith.org/). These approaches would provide drug addicts with legal access to drugs that they would otherwise obtain illegally. The rationale underlying these approaches is **harm reduction**. Providing addicts with legal drugs would reduce harm both to the drug users and to society, through the declining risk of overdoses, declining need for addicts to commit crimes to support their drug habit, and greater likelihood that drug users would maintain contact with drug treatment services.

Two specific issues on which the centers differ are the legalization of marijuana for medical use and the validity of the "gateway theory" of drug use. CASA rejects legalizing marijuana while the Lindesmith Center supports it. In fact, Mr. Califano has been harshly critical of those advocating such legalization, even though many respected medical professionals support it and there is substantial evidence for its effectiveness (Grinspoon and Bakalar 1997; Zimmer and Morgan 1997). CASA supports the gateway theory, while the Lindesmith Center rejects it for confusing statistical association with causation.

You might want to explore the websites for these two centers and examine the materials each provides. On some issues you can directly compare their positions. If you get on to the Lindesmith Center website first, they have a link to CASA, so you can jump right over. CASA does not have a link to the Lindesmith Center.

Cultural changes may lead to changes in substance abuse. Increased substance abuse has been attributed to increased anti-social behavior such as alienation, the loss of a sense of community, and the decline of traditional work, family, and religious values. However, it is difficult to define and measure such broad cultural trends or to show their impact on drug use. For example, widespread medical drug taking in the United States dates back to even before the last quarter of the nineteenth century, but nonmedical recreational use for the purpose of getting high was relatively rare until the 1960s (Goode 1993).

Other cultural factors influence substance use. Taking illegal drugs and drinking alcohol often occur in group contexts and are learned behaviors. Almost no one initially uses a drug in isolation. People become turned on to drugs by acquaintances; users learn drug patterns from significant others—from family and peers. As we noted above, America is a drug culture. For adolescents, peer influence is more important than that of parents. For young people to be influenced in drug use by a peer group, they must already have accepted its values to some

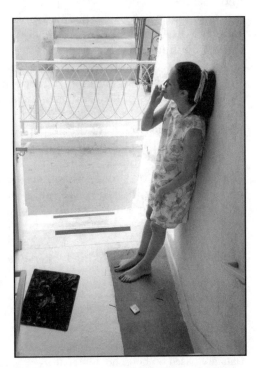

Controversy over marijuana often centers on whether it is a "gateway drug," which leads to use of harder drugs.

extent. Young people are curious, interested, and willing to take risks. Because they also want to be accepted by their peers, they have strong motivations to accept and conform to the expectations and norms of their group (Goode 1993).

A drug subculture may form that teaches individuals the techniques and skills for using drugs, passes on information about drug distribution and supply, and recruits new members—sometimes to sell drugs to support the group's drug buying. Goode (1993: 44) notes that, "differential exposure to drug-using friends, and isolation from those who do not use marijuana or other drugs, is the key explanatory variable causally related to drug experimentation and involvement." The more punitive and judgmental the outside world, such as the family or police become, the more alienated and withdrawn become the members of the subculture, who are already unified by common norms and values.

Drug taking is connected to several additional features of American life. There is a close connection between taking drugs and physical well-being. For example, many people take drugs to fall asleep or to cure a headache or stomach ache. The use of drugs is often associated with social events. Alcohol is an example. For many, drinking is closely associated with all social events, because alcohol is associated with attaining desired moods. Using alcohol and drugs to feel good is almost an unquestionable part of our culture. We can alter our moods with drugs. In this way, our culture comes to view some drugs as functional. Robert Meier and Gilbert Geis (1997) argue that patterns of illegal drug use do not differ much from those of legal drug use. They also argue that there are many similarities between the consumption patterns for alcohol and those associated with such illegal drugs as marijuana, heroin, and cocaine.

Explanations for why people smoke also vary. Anti-smoking forces place much of the responsibility on the advertising campaigns of the tobacco industry, claiming that cigarette ads are directed specifically at younger age groups. Tobacco companies spend nearly 5 billion dollars a year on advertising. The National Cancer Institute reports that teenagers are twice as likely to be influenced to smoke by advertising as they are by peer pressure, although the large increase in teenage smoking in this society has been attributed to peer pressure as well as to the perception by teens that "it is a very cool thing to do" (Kulnis 1997). Many teenagers do not realize how easy it is to become addicted or how hard it is to quit. Growing numbers of teenage women smoke. Getting or staying thin may be a major factor related to their increased smoking. For those 18 and older, more males than females smoke, and this trend has existed since 1988 (see Table 8-1).

Table 8-1   Cigarette Smoking by Persons 18 and Older, by Sex, 1988–1993

Sex	1988	1990	1991	1992	1993
Female	26.0	23.1	23.6	24.8	22.7
Male	30.1	28.0	27.5	28.2	27.5

Data are based on household interviews of a sample of the civilian noninstitutionalized population.
Source: National Center for Health Statistics. 1996. *Health, United States, 1995.* Hyattsville, Maryland: Public Health Service, p.173.

Structural

Sociologists are particularly concerned with the effects of social organization on social problems and deviant behavior. Merton's (1968) **structural strain theory of anomie** has been especially influential. Merton's theory suggests that in a complex society there may be a gap between socially and culturally approved societal goals and the availability of legitimate means for achieving those goals. So the poor are encouraged to work for achievement and success but are not provided with adequate means, such as education or employment, for goal fulfillment. The gap between goals and means may lead to deviant behavior as a means of coping (Akers 1996; Merton 1968).

Substance abusers may become retreatists, who reject socially and culturally approved goals and stop striving to reach those goals. Or they may become innovators, using socially disapproved means—such as drugs or alcohol—to attain approved goals. For example, alcoholics may feel that the false sense of confidence achieved from drinking brings them luck or provides the skills necessary for them to achieve their material desires.

Anomie theory, however, does not adequately explain substance abuse, such as heavy drinking, in America. Even though alcoholism exists among the poor and the alienated, the majority of alcoholics appear to be in the mainstream of American life, where the gap between goals and means is arguably the smallest. **Anomie** indicates the absence of clear-cut rules governing behavior. Interestingly, one of the main features of American drinking practice is the absence of clear-cut rules of normal drinking.

People who use illegal drugs may do so for many of the same reasons people engage in deviant drinking. Illegal drugs are almost as easy to obtain as alcohol. Individuals can obtain drugs because sellers provide them. Promoted by pharmaceutical manufacturers and excessively prescribed by physicians, drug use is encouraged. Barbiturates and tranquilizers for example, usually originate from legitimate drug firms. Other drugs, like heroin, are illegally manufactured and distributed. Organized crime and individual lawbreakers flourish, making much money. They will continue to do so as long as demand and profits remain high.

With marijuana, a vast, loosely structured marketing system moves over 10,000 metric tons a year into the hands of an estimated 16 million steady users. The supply chain generally originates from the smugglers, who bring the marijuana in from Colombia and Mexico in bales. Thereafter, it is packaged and repackaged by an army of anonymous wholesalers, middlemen, and dealers in ever-smaller amounts. These individuals will continue to make big money by supplying user needs as long as distribution of marijuana remains illegal (Kappeler, Blumberg, and Potter, 1996).

Consequences

Substance abuse has a variety of consequences. For example, alcohol abuse has certain physiological effects on the body. As a powerful depressant, it serves to release tensions and inhibitions. It also impairs judgment, harms one's ability to perform complex tasks, and slows down the brain centers that control muscle reaction. It does not have the same physical or social effects on all users; the same user may even react differently at different times.

Alcohol abuse results in economic costs of at least 50 billion dollars annually. This includes lost productivity, where alcohol interferes with work performance; alcohol-related costs in the criminal justice system; and the costs of education and rehabilitation programs. There are other social costs as well. Alcohol abuse contributes to divorce, child abuse, and other family and community problems. In addition, the life expectancy of alcohol abusers is 12 years shorter than that of those who do not abuse alcohol.

One consequence of alcohol use is drunk driving; it is a serious problem in the United States. A driver with an alcohol concentration of 0.10—the legal limit in many states—or greater is seven times more likely to be involved in a fatal motor vehicle crash than is a driver who has not consumed alcoholic beverages (National Center for Injury Prevention and Control 1997).

A Closer Look

The Mothers Against Drunk Driving (MADD) Website

Founded in 1980 by a small group of California women responding to the hit-and-run death of a 13-year-old girl, Mothers Against Drunk Driving (MADD) educates. The driver of the car that killed the little girl was out on bail from another hit-and-run drunk-driving crash and had two previous convictions for drunk driving. MADD focuses on "effective solutions to the drunk driving and underage drinking problems." The organization also offers support to those who have been affected by collisions arising from drunk driving. MADD played a leading role in enacting the Age 21 Law.

Check out the national MADD website at http://www.madd.org/. The website offers a variety of information including current news, information about MADD programs and campaigns, statistics about impaired driving, and links to other resources. You will also find links to the websites for many MADD chapters. MADD's 1997 Summary of Statistics page does not provide tables or graphics, but it does present data from the National Highway Traffic Safety Administration. For example, on this page you learn that 16,189 people in the United States died in alchohol related automobile accidents in 1997.

You can read about the many accomplishments of MADD, such as the fact that judges in more than 200 counties across the United States are now assigning drunk-driving offenders to attend MADD–operated Victim Impact Panels. A panel is composed of crash victims and survivors who tell offenders how drunk driving has affected their lives.

The consequences of excessive alcohol consumption have become especially noticeable on college campuses. Binge drinking during fraternity parties is related to several recent deaths. Other students have also died from what appears to be alcohol-related accidents. Heavy drinking has long been part of college culture. According to a recent newspaper headline, the University of Massachusetts at Amherst has to contend with a "4th R—reveling" (Gover 1997). One student died as a result of a fall through a greenhouse roof at the University of Massachusetts. Colleges are now making greater efforts to control excessive drinking, but it is not clear whether those efforts will succeed, especially since many of the efforts are politically motivated and seem to ignore the reality of campus culture. Prohibiting alcohol on campus will push drinking off campus but probably will not reduce it. It will also deprive the colleges of control over drinking.

A recent Harvard School of Public Health study provides the most complete picture of campus binge drinking available (Wechsler, et al. 1996). In 1993, the researchers collected data from a national sample of about 17,600 students at 140 four-year colleges and universities. "The survey provides an estimate of the extent of binge drinking and a profile of the types of students most prone to alcohol-related problems."

Smoking greatly affects people's health as well. It is responsible for respiratory problems, such as emphysema; blood circulation problems; and elevated blood pressure. Some smokers claim that smoking relaxes them, but this effect may arise from the easing of withdrawal symptoms when the smoker has gone without a cigarette for a long period than usual. Health care costs for smokers at a given age are as much as 40 percent higher than for nonsmokers (Barendregt, et al. 1997). Mortality associated with cigarette smoking is also substantial. (See Table 8-2).

Table 8-2 Cigarette Smoking Related Mortality, 1996

Disease	Male	Female	Overall
Cancers	103, 893	47,429	151,322
Cardiovascular Diseases	118,603	61,117	179,720
Respiratory Diseases	51,788	32,689	84,477
Diseases Among Infants	1,006	705	1,711
Burn Deaths	863	499	1,362
All Causes	276,153	142,439	418,592

Source: Office on Smoking and Health, 1996. *Cigarette Smoking-Related Mortality.* Center for Disease Control (CDC), Tobacco Information and Prevention Source (TIPS). http://www.cdc.gov/nccdphp/osh/mortal.htm.

In 1995, drug, alcohol, and tobacco use triggered some 200 billion dollars in healthcare costs. Across the country, hospitals are overwhelmed with violence caused by drug and alcohol abusers, as well as with cancer, emphysema, and cardiac arrest caused by alcohol, tobacco, cocaine, and other drugs. More than 500,000 newborns each year have been exposed to drugs and/or alcohol during pregnancy. Mothers abusing drugs during pregnancy account for most of the 3 billion dollars that Medicaid spent in 1994 on inpatient hospital care for illness and injury due to drug abuse (National Center on Addiction and Substance Abuse 1996).

Heroin use is associated with crime, mostly property offenses rather than violent crimes against persons. Addicts steal hundreds of millions of dollars in goods each year in order to support habits that can cost a hundred dollars or more per day. If heroin were not illegal and were therefore cheaper and more easily obtained, the relationship between its use and crime might lessen. When drugs are readily available, addiction has a minimal impact on the social functioning of addicts. Drug laws have forced users to support their habits through crime and have given rise to an organized crime industry that controls production and distribution.

A popular perception exists that drug use threatens the moral fabric or work ethic of American society. Marijuana, as opposed to alcohol, supposedly involves a rejection of middle-class values. In fact, there is widespread use of marijuana by respectable middle-class people, who remain productive and functional, while alcoholism has a strong impact on worker efficiency and absenteeism. However, many myths about substance abuse persist. See "A Closer Look: Marijuana Myths and Facts," for myths about marijuana, the most widely used illegal drug in the United States.

A Closer Look

Marijuana Myths and Facts

Marijuana is the most popular illegal drug in the United States, with more than seventy million Americans having tried it. Twenty million Americans have smoked marijuana in the past year alone. Sociologist Lynn Zimmer and pharmacologist John P. Morgan review the scientific evidence about marijuana in *Marijuana Myths, Marijuana Facts* (Zimmer and Morgan 1997). In the foreword to the book, Ethan Nadelman, director of the Lindesmith Center, notes that "it seems obvious that marijuana policies, and the personal decisions people make about the use of marijuana, should be based on scientific information, factual information, and common sense" (Nadelman 1997: ix). Unfortunately, he suggests, this is not always the case. Instead, policies and personal decisions about marijuana are often based on myths.

We will consider five of the 20 myths that Zimmer and Morgan examined. The first myth is that "marijuana's harms have been proven scientifically" and that marijuana is far more harmful than was thought in the 1960s and 1970s. In fact, numerous studies indicate that although marijuana is not completely safe, its dangers have been greatly exaggerated. Some studies recommended that marijuana be decriminalized. The second myth is that marijuana has no value as a medicine. Zimmer and Morgan's review of the scientific evidence does not support this view. Marijuana appears to have many medicinal uses, including lessening the nausea caused by cancer chemotherapy. Lester Grinspoon and James Bakalar (1997) also document marijuana's medicinal uses. A third myth is that marijuana is addictive. On the contrary, most people who smoke marijuana smoke it occasionally. Less than 1 percent of marijuana users smoke it on a daily or near-daily basis, and few ever become dependent on it.

The fourth marijuana myth suggests that marijuana is a **gateway drug**, that is, a drug that leads to the use of more harmful drugs. Even if marijuana itself is not so harmful, the reasoning goes, it leads users to seek out and use harder drugs such as heroin and cocaine. Zimmer and Morgan (1997) argue that "marijuana does not cause people to use hard drugs." Because marijuana is the most popular illegal drug in the United States, people who have used drugs such as heroin and cocaine are also likely to have used marijuana, but this does not indicate that the marijuana use caused them to use harder drugs. As social scientists often point out, association between two things does not mean that they are causally related.

Finally, Zimmer and Morgan address the myth that marijuana offenses are not severely punished. They note that arrests for marijuana use in the United States doubled between 1991 and 1995. Thousands of people have been imprisoned for marijuana offenses, while many others are on probation, have paid fines, or have had their driver's license revoked. A close examination of the data makes it hard to maintain that marijuana offenses are not severely punished

---

The possible effects of a drug on a user depend in part on its chemical properties. Stimulants such as cocaine and amphetamines cause increased alertness, excitation, higher pulse rate and blood pressure, insomnia, loss of appetite, and euphoria. Depressants, on the other hand, may produce slurred speech, disorientation, and drunken behavior; by decreasing central nervous system functioning, they ease the user's tension and anxiety.

Effects are also influenced by the quality or purity of the drug, how it is administered, dosage, and length of use. Prolonged use of heroin, for

❖ ❖ ❖ ❖

example, results in no disease or damage to human organs or tissues but is dangerous because of the possibility of harmful impurities, malnutrition, hepatitis, other infections from unsterilized needles, or the risk of overdose. Hallucinogens usually create a mild to intense distortion of visual and auditory functions, but long-term use may impair judgment and trigger delusions and psychosis (Kappeler, et al. 1996).

The impact of a drug, however, is not simply based on pharmacological factors or chemical attributes. Erich Goode (1993) disputes the **chemicalistic fallacy**, the view that Drug A causes Behavior X and that what we see as behavioral effects of a drug are solely a function of the biochemical properties of that drug. Substance abusers have widely different responses and reactions, even to the same drug. Much depends on the user's personality, prior drug involvement, the conditions under which the drug is used (situational factors), and personal expectations. Street users, for example, experience morphine as pleasurable; most hospital patients do not. The difference in effect may reflect user anticipation and social context (Goode 1993).

The words *addiction* and *dependence* are clearly value laden. Though usually applied to mood-changing substances, they can also be applied to any repeated activity, from work to watching television. A person might be dependent on the attention of his or her spouse. Psychic dependence on drugs has been humorously defined by Goode as repeating something that is pleasurable to the user but that some authorities can't conceive of as being pleasurable (1993). That is, the word *dependence* is used to describe an activity that some people dislike.

The concept of addiction has created certain myths: that users of all drugs will inevitably become addicted; that once in the clutches of addiction a user is powerless to control the situation; and that a single dose of certain drugs will automatically lead to lifelong addiction. As we mentioned before, it is false to believe that use of certain drugs, like marijuana, inevitably leads to use of other, more dangerous drugs. While most heroin addicts probably begin with less powerful substances, most marijuana users never gravitate to anything stronger.

What makes most drugs harmful is inherent not in their chemistry but rather in the context in which they are used or the way in which they are defined. No drug is inherently good or bad, except possibly tobacco, and no substance is completely safe. A crucial question is whether the illnesses and death we commonly see in some users—heroin addicts, for example—are caused by the heroin itself or by factors associated with its use. Being a heroin addict is not incompatible with good physical health. In fact, according to Goode (1993), all the diseases of addicts result from the way they live, that is, from the conditions of street use. When opiate addicts receive a continuous supply of pure drugs in a normal environment, they suffer no more health problems than nonusers. The dangers stem not from the drug itself but from the conditions that its illegality creates. (See "A Closer Look: Why Cocaine Became Illegal.")

Opiate withdrawal, which usually resembles a bad case of the flu, has never been known to be a direct cause of death. Death from overdose, moreover, could be virtually eliminated if controlled and standardized doses of pure heroin could be administered under sterile conditions. Death usually results from the variability of the available doses—when the user cannot judge the drug's strength because of its having been cut by quinine or milk sugar, or because the heroin, interacting with other drugs such as alcohol or

---

A Closer Look

Why Cocaine Became Illegal

As the active ingredient in scores of patent medicines, tonics, and soft drinks, including Coca Cola, cocaine was popular in the United States early in the twentieth century. Freud and others reported on its psychological effects, which they described as "exhilarating" and "lasting euphoria." The medicine industry promoted cocaine as a panacea for a wide variety of physical ills, including asthma, dysentery, vomiting associated with pregnancy, gonorrhea, and syphilis (Musto 1991).

In 1906 alone, more than 21,000 pounds of cocaine were manufactured for a population of less than 90 million. How did this "wonder drug" become illegal? In *Cocaine: The Mystique and the Reality*, Joel Philips and Ronald Wynne (1980) suggest two important reasons for the change: the changing attitudes of physicians and pharmacists and the growing association of coke with crime and minority groups.

Physicians began to see the results of cocaine abuse in their patients. Even the medical use of cocaine entailed risk. In an American Medical Association study, of 43 reported deaths caused by local anesthetics, 26 involved cocaine. Pharmacists, too, became concerned about their role in inducing drug habits. They also wished to limit competition from nonprescription drugs containing cocaine.

The media began to associate cocaine with groups that "threatened the social order," in particular criminals and African Americans. White Southerners feared that the euphoric and stimulating properties of cocaine might cause blacks to attack whites. Myths developed that "cocainized" African Americans became violent, possessed superior marksmanship, and were impervious to police bullets.

In 1887, Oregon became the first state to prohibit the dispensing of cocaine without a prescription. By 1914, forty-six of the forty-eight states had adopted some form of legislation regulating distribution. The federal government responded with the Pure Food and Drug Act of 1906 and the Harrison Act of 1914. These created harsher penalties for violation of cocaine regulations than for violating the opiate rules. The Harrison Act, for example, permitted inclusion of minimal amounts of opium or its derivatives in patent medicines, while no such exceptions were allowed for the cocaine-based products. It also falsely labeled cocaine a narcotic, though it is a central nervous system stimulant rather than a depressant like heroin.

---

barbiturates, produces a dangerous multiplier effect. Barbiturates, in fact, are the primary cause of death resulting from drug overdose.

The consequences for users often depend on how they view the drug; if they think that a drug has certain terrible effects, those expectations may give it such powers. The consequences also depend on how users are viewed by others; shunning and stigmatizing substance abusers may cause trauma. The public sometimes identifies unconventional drug use with the disadvantaged and disliked (heroin use in the ghetto; opium dens in the immigrant Chinese community), and people often stereotype and scapegoat substance abusers, pushing them further into deviant lifestyles rather than providing medical and preventive care.

Interventions

In most of America, alcohol is legal, and its use is seen as acceptable. Drinking excessive amounts of alcohol is usually not stigmatized as much as is the taking of small quantities of heroin. This toleration of alcohol has not always existed. In 1870, the Anti-Saloon League began a political vendetta against alcohol consumption. Coming from fundamentalist Protestant churches and from small rural communities, its members associated drinking with "the wickedness of cities and the laziness and corruption of the ethnic masses that lived in them."

This antidrinking campaign culminated in the passage of the Eighteenth Amendment to the Constitution in 1919, which outlawed the manufacture and sale of alcoholic beverages. Prohibition, an attempt to legislate private morality, was an experiment that failed. Because most Americans desired alcohol, organized crime developed to satisfy the demand. Gangsters like Al Capone controlled and distributed the supply, with speakeasies (illegal saloons) developing in most communities. Drinking did decrease during Prohibition; however, the lack of cultural support for the ban and the inability to enforce anti-liquor laws led to the amendment's repeal in 1933.

Most states resort to disorderly conduct statutes as a means of controlling public drinking. The law does not interfere with drinking in a private residence unless disorderly conduct follows or unless minors are involved. The laws against public drunkenness are almost exclusively applied against lower-class drinkers who may find themselves in jail with fifty to two hundred other inmates. They may be fined or, if they have a previous record, may be sent to a short-term penal institution. Some jurisdictions have detoxification programs where gradual withdrawal from alcohol is supervised. Occasionally, nonpunitive therapy groups, such as Alcoholics Anonymous, are also available.

Alcoholics Anonymous was founded in 1935 as a nonresidential treatment program. Alcoholics Anonymous now has over 14,000 chapters in the United States and Canada, with a membership of over a quarter of a million alcoholics. The association, which is made up entirely of ex-alcoholics, helps members to maintain their sobriety by emphasizing moral and spiritual values and personal reform. The AA program has strong religious overtones, with twelve steps suggested as a prerequisite for recovery. Alcoholics must first acknowledge their helplessness and lack of control over drinking. This admission ends the rationalization and denial that precede AA involvement, and allows the drinker to begin a process of repentance. Group support is the basic therapeutic component of AA, therefore, much emphasis is placed on member compatibility. Chapters may differ by occupation, race, ethnicity, and socioeconomic condition. If a member is weak and has difficulty avoiding the urge to drink, other members will work to prevent relapses by acting as parents, teachers, and supporters through communication and personal example.

Despite the widespread acceptance of AA, and other twelve-step programs that stress abstinence from drinking, some research indicates that other approaches hold much promise. Psychologist Stanton Peele notes that "few clinical trials exist to show that the most popular American treatment for alcoholism, the twelve-step approach, is effective at all." Peele further notes that two major studies "showed that most people who had once struggled with alcohol abuse could later cut down on their drinking—a result that is anathema to the devotees of AA, to the U.S. medical establishment, and to the American way of temperance" (Peele 1998:17). In his controversial book *Heavy Drinking: The Myth of Alcoholism as a Disease* (1988), philosopher Herbert Fingarette also describes the dangers of treating alcoholics as sick and in need of intervention by physicians. In Fingarette's view, this approach leads people to think that they cannot escape alcoholism without the help of a doctor, which is especially troubling for people with limited financial resources.

Many people do not usually think of alcohol as a dangerous drug. Most Americans still view marijuana, cocaine, and heroin as far more serious threats. Users of these substances are seen as drug addicts, whose addiction is illegal and repugnant, a much different orientation from that given alcoholism. And yet alcohol is more destructive, both individually and socially, than these other agents.

This differential perspective might arise from the fact that alcohol is used and abused by a large and heterogeneous group of Americans. It is, in short, a popular drug with broad public acceptance. When representatives of the society—social workers, for example—intervene despite such acceptance, they often do not act consistently or effectively. Lower-status alcoholics, for example, are more likely to be labeled as problems, partly as a result of the greater visibility of their consumption and partly because of society's hesitancy to apply negative categories to those with high status and power. They react by excluding or scolding the alcoholic, which not only fails to limit the users' alcohol consumption but also serves to rationalize continued drinking.

Intervention, whatever the benign intent, may have harmful or unanticipated consequences for both the alcoholic and the society. While providing the resources required for effective prevention and treatment, members of society should understand that any social policy has costs, and they should attempt to lessen those costs as much as possible. Intervention approaches often reflect the goals and concerns of moral entrepreneurs, who have the power of the state to force their morality on others. Control of drug use, for example, has sometimes masked attempts to control drug users. Chinese workers, not opium, were the targets of early anti-opium laws, while Prohibition was partly an effort by rural, native-born Protestants to repress urban Catholic immigrants.

Marijuana use was not defined as a social problem as long as its smoking was confined to jazz musicians and ghetto dwellers. When middle-class children began lighting up, however, programs and treatment strategies rapidly developed. Central to the call for drug prohibition is the idea that drugs are dangerous to users. No one will dispute this. People die of drug overdoses. People also die of lung cancer as a result of smoking and of a variety of diseases related to the consumption of alcohol, even though these drugs are legal. In fact, only about 3,600 people die each year from the consumption of all illegal drugs put together. There are 200,000 alcohol-related deaths each year and an estimated 320,000 deaths related to the consumption of tobacco (Kappeler, et al. 1996).

Interventions aimed at controlling a so-called drug problem in the United States are misleading. The dangers of drug use are exaggerated. Of the 20 million cocaine users in the United States, only about 3 percent become problem users. Kappeler and his colleagues argue that the real danger from cocaine lies in drug laws driving the price of cocaine up and forcing users to seek a cheaper high by smoking the drug rather than snorting it. Most heroin overdoses result from the ingestion of adulterated drugs, not from user misuse or abuse. With regard to marijuana, the available evidence indicates that it is not addictive. In addition, there has never been a death resulting from marijuana consumption (Kappeler, et al. 1996).

Powerful economic interests promote drug laws favorable to them. Tobacco farmers, for example, receive government subsidies despite efforts by other government agencies to educate citizens about the medical dangers of nicotine. Overzealous bureaucrats have acquired a vested interest in the drug problem, using it to expand their funding and power. The intervention approach thus reflects the self-interest of those who adopt it. User characteristics also influence change strategies. It is ironic, given the individual and social costs, that alcoholics are viewed as sick, while heroin addicts are most often defined as criminal. This difference in definition may stem from the fact that so many people drink while relatively few use narcotics and the fact that heroin use is associated with blacks and other stigmatized groups.

There are nevertheless several possible intervention strategies; they are discussed in what follows.

To prohibit use of, or trade in, a particular drug, with criminal laws and police action. The Harrison Narcotics Act of 1914 established a Narcotics Division in the U. S. Treasury Department and prohibited the use and sale of opiate substances. This federal legislation began the process of defining addiction as a criminal problem. A difficulty with these and other criminal sanctions is that they have rarely deterred drug use. E. M. Brecher (1972) reports that as early as the seventeenth century a sultan of Constantinople decreed the death penalty for smoking tobacco, but this did not discourage many of its users. The current "War on Drugs" seems no more effective than these early efforts.

Let us briefly look at the ineffectiveness of prosecuting marijuana users. First of all, some users may smoke to rebel against society, since the illegality of marijuana serves as a lure and a source of excitement. Second, police and criminal justice resources have been diverted from concern with other, socially more dangerous offenses. Third, the number of smokers has continued to increase despite enforcement efforts. Fourth, marijuana smokers—perceiving a disparity between the severity of the sanction and the relative harmlessness of the drug—develop a disrespect and cynicism for law. Fifth, if sanctions are seen as overly severe or as unenforceable because of the extent of use, police will not arrest, prosecutors will not indict, and juries will often refuse to convict. Sixth, if convictions do result, many otherwise law-abiding citizens may go to jail or suffer unnecessary stigma. It is most unhealthy for a society to turn a large percentage of its young people into potential felons. Arrests for marijuana violations, furthermore, may mark the beginning of more serious criminal careers, since a criminal record makes it much more difficult for a youngster to find legitimate employment.

To curtail the drug supply by either reducing or banning production or by choking off drug sources. Several problems exist with this alternative. Diminishing the supply of one drug will often only result in an increase in the intake of other drugs by users and addicts. When the Nixon administration, for example, attempted to stop the flow of marijuana across the Mexican border (Operation Intercept), use of other drugs reportedly increased because of the marijuana shortage. Limiting one source of supply may only generate another. Pressure to curtail opium production in Turkey by subsidizing farmers to refrain from planting opium created a burgeoning heroin business in other parts of the world.

By the same token, the removal, by arrest, of one dealer merely opens up a number of willing customers looking for another dealer. Finally, as with criminal sanctions, control of supply seems an ineffective deterrent, at least with natural, as opposed to synthetic, drugs. In 1971, the Bureau of Narcotics and Dangerous Drugs confiscated over 21,000 pounds of marijuana, 882 pounds of hashish, 432 pounds of heroin, and 436 pounds of cocaine. At the same time, by all accounts, use of these drugs was increasing parallel to the increase in confiscations (Goode 1993).

To regulate the drug trade through licensing and taxation. This alternative, which involves government legalization and control of certain drugs—making their status similar to the present status of tobacco and alcohol—would ensure high standards of purity and safety; allow the state to collect revenues from sales and other taxes; impose greater limitations on distribution and black-market selling (minors, for example, might be prohibited from purchasing the drug); and limit involvement by criminal elements, thus lowering the cost of law enforcement. This approach might also remove the stigma from drug users, undermine drug subcultures, and reduce the attractiveness of drugs that are defined as forbidden fruit. This approach focuses on harm reduction. Possible negative consequences include government acceptance of drugs, which may be individually or socially dangerous, and the likely outcry from citizens angered by government endorsement of such activity.

To treat the drug user as sick. The therapeutic approach may involve use of a substitute drug, similar to the way that methadone is currently used to help heroin addicts control their addiction; individual and group psychotherapy, with the encouragement of voluntary abstinence; and the establishment of drug-free residential settings where the addict may gain total freedom from drug dependence while resolving personal problems. Public education would attempt to discourage drug use or to tell users how or where they can obtain help. For users to quit, their attitudes and values about drugs must change, with drugs defined in more negative terms.

To ignore drugs and do little or nothing to control their use. An example of this approach is the decriminalization of the possession of small amounts of marijuana. This perspective assumes that the state should not punish or interfere with adult behavior that causes no harm to others. Though it is often difficult to distinguish between what is harmful to oneself and what is harmful to others, and between what is harmful and what is safe, any clear antisocial behavior resulting from drug use is subject to sanction under this strategy.

Intervention strategies aimed at helping people stop smoking have received a lot of media attention lately. The federal government recently announced a $135 million anti-smoking program, to be combined with $30 million from the American Cancer Society. Their goal is to help 5 million smokers stop during a seven-year program and to keep at least 2 million teenagers from starting. Unfortunately, this expenditure does not compare to the billions of marketing dollars spent by the tobacco industry.

President Clinton has made a proposal that calls for the tobacco industry to stop marketing and promoting tobacco to children. He supports legislation to provide a nationwide public education and counter-advertising campaign to deglamorize tobacco; to warn young people of its addictive nature and deadly consequences; and to help parents discourage children from smoking (American Lung Association 1998).

Nancy Rigotti and her colleagues (1997) argue that enforcing laws banning tobacco sales to minors may be an effective way to reduce young people's access to tobacco and tobacco use. In a two-year controlled study, these researchers assessed sales of tobacco to minors in six Massachusetts communities. Three communities enforced tobacco-sales laws (intervention group) while three matched communities did not (control group). Minors working for the study attempted to purchase tobacco in each community every six

months. When the study began, 68 percent of 487 vendors sold tobacco to minors. By the study's end, 82 percent of the merchants in the intervention communities complied with the law, as compared with 45 percent in the control
communities. However, minors reported only a small drop in their ability to
purchase tobacco regardless of the community. Enforcing tobacco-sales
laws improved merchant's compliance and reduced illegal sales to minors
but did not alter adolescents' perceived access to tobacco or their smoking.

The Future of Substance Abuse

In the coming years, most adult Americans will continue to drink alcohol
and to express concern about alcoholism. As states allow eighteen-year-olds
to purchase alcoholic beverages, more and more teenagers will drink, with
some becoming abusers; as economic and social stress increases, adults, too,
may increase their use, and abuse, of the drug. With the failure of Prohibition
and the decreasing use of the criminal law to control drunkenness, medical
treatment will remain the primary intervention. The private sector will likely
assume greater responsibility for the problem, with large corporations either
providing direct services or contracting services through private psychiatric
and social agencies. The company motivation is to assist its employees, as
well as to control absenteeism, equipment damage, and lessened productivity; but many problem drinkers on the executive or managerial level will escape identification, with program benefits going to those on the bottom
rungs of the corporate ladder.

America is a drug-taking culture. The medicine cabinet, filled with prescription and over-the-counter medications, eases a host of physical and psychological problems. The 1960s saw the beginning of the widespread use of illegal drugs, first as a symbol of protest and then for their own sake, to get
high. By the 1980s, more than one-fourth of the population had smoked marijuana at least once, with many people considering a joint no worse than, and
maybe preferable to, a drink. Some illicit drugs are now almost commonplace and easily found, while large quantities of prescription drugs such as
Valium and Percoset are sold illegally for profit.

Agencies such as the Drug Enforcement Administration of the U.S. Department of Justice have attempted to fight the illegal drug trade without
great success. The bust strategy, in which undercover agents buy drugs and
arrest the sellers, has not led to the demise of big-time traffickers. Attempts to
stop the growth of opium poppies in Colombia, Turkey, and Mexico only increased production of high-purity heroin in Southwest Asia and the Middle
East's "golden crescent" of Iran, Afghanistan, and Pakistan. Hawaii and California market quality marijuana as a major cash crop, while in southern
Florida the drug trade may have surpassed tourism as the biggest industry.

Prevention and treatment programs on the federal, state, and local levels
are suffering from a shortage of funds. And yet, along with the widespread
use and ineffective control of drugs, there is a growing concern about the
health consequences and psychological hazards of drug abuse. Some people
are using smaller amounts of drugs for shorter periods of time; others are
avoiding drugs like PCP (angel dust), which are clearly dangerous; while still
others are less likely to mix a variety of drugs to get high, fearing that the
multi-drug usage will create a collapse of the central nervous system. Given

present patterns, however, the use and abuse of both legal and illegal drugs will surely continue.

Summary

Alcoholics have difficulty controlling the amount and frequency of their drinking. Unable to manage without alcohol, they soon find that their family life, job, and social relationships are disrupted by an obsession over which they may be powerless.

Though the causes of alcoholism are unclear, alcoholics seems to view drinking differently from the way the normal drinker does. To them alcohol is a way, perhaps the only way, of relieving stress or of proving manhood. They give it a special meaning and use it to cope with unresolved personal problems. Most adult Americans drink, and alcoholic beverages are readily available to any consumer. Given these facts, and the difficulty of distinguishing between normal and problem drinking, society views alcohol addiction with more tolerance than addiction to illegal drugs such as heroin or cocaine. Though alcoholism is seen as a disease requiring treatment rather than punishment, the very commonness of drinking makes it difficult for alcoholics to recognize that they are uniquely dependent upon a dangerous substance.

Alcoholics Anonymous has had some success in getting alcoholics to recognize their dependency and to begin a life of sobriety. Instead of using professionals to treat patients, AA has alcoholics helping alcoholics. AA members, with the support of fellow members, attempt to redefine themselves and gain the strength necessary for control. However, some research suggests that other approaches may be equally successful.

Despite the growing awareness of the problem of alcoholism, its causes and effective treatment remain unclear. There are no cures and no widely accepted techniques of prevention. The incidence of alcoholism, despite intervention efforts by government and industry, continues to increase—especially among young people attracted to drink because of its accessibility, low cost, and pleasurable sensation.

Psychotropic drugs affect the functioning of the human mind, altering individual perception and mood. They include stimulants, sedatives, tranquilizers, antidepressants, narcotics, and hallucinogens. Some of these drugs are legal and have legitimate medical functions, while others, used for recreation and pleasure, can only be obtained through an illegal black market. Drugs such as nicotine, caffeine, and alcohol are so widely used that users do not even define them as drugs. Some illegal substances, such as marijuana, and other legally available drugs such as amphetamines and barbiturates, also have wide distribution and use.

Americans live in a drug-oriented culture, where people take substances for everything from a headache to anxiety. Not only are drugs often seen as a source of relief for various emotional and physical problems, but the culture and its values may produce individual stress and tension requiring relief. Drugs are pushed on us by suppliers, both corporate and individual, who wish to profit from the drug habit. Most people first take drugs in a group setting, learning about them from parents or peers. Our associations, then, are the most important determinant of drug use; techniques, attitudes, and contacts are developed and maintained through a drug subculture. One's personality type does not seem significant in determining drug abuse, though abuse of drugs can certainly influence personality and individual functioning.

The consequences of drug taking depend on such factors as the type of drug, user personality and prior drug experience, method of administration (such as sniffing or injection), drug quality, social context, and expectations. Users have widely different responses and reactions, even when taking the same drug.

There is little or no relationship between our attitudes toward drugs and the harm they produce. Cigarettes and alcohol are very harmful yet are easily available, whereas marijuana, perhaps less detrimental, is illegal. Moreover, much of the harm allegedly caused is due less to the drug's characteristics than to the social context of drug use and the societal policy toward it. Heroin is less harmful than the conditions forced upon most heroin users: dirty needles, overdose because of uncertainty about drug purity, and crimes committed for money to support an expensive habit.

The most common intervention strategies are the prohibition of certain drugs and criminal prosecution for their distribution and use, the curtailing of drug supply and sources, legalization of drugs and their regulation through licensing and taxation, the defining of users as sick so that they may receive subsequent treatment, and nonintervention so long as the drug use is not socially harmful or dangerous. Which policy is selected depends on such factors as the extent of the drug's use, the characteristics of the users, and the interests of those who make and enforce our nation's drug policies.

Discussion Questions

1. What do you see as the major substance problems facing U. S. society? On what do you base your views?

2. Are there any drugs that are legal that you believe should be illegal? Why?

3. How widespread is alcohol use and abuse on your campus? Is binge drinking common? What kinds of policies would you implement to control binge drinking, if any?

4. Should the tobacco industry take responsibility for the medical consequences of smoking or are individuals solely responsible for any health problems resulting from their decision to smoke?

5. Do you think that some illegal drugs, such as marijuana, for example, should be legalized? What do you see as the possible benefits and problems of legalization?

References

Akers, Ronald. 1996. *Criminological Theories*. Los Angeles: Roxbury Publishing.

American Lung Association. 1998. *Smoking Section Index*, American Lung Asociation Website. http://www.lungusa.org/tobacco/index2.html.

Barendregt, Jan J., Luc Bonneux, and Paul van der Mass. 1997. "The Health Care Costs of Smoking." *New England Journal of Medicine* 337 (October 9): pp.1052-1057.

Brecher, E. M. 1972. *Licit and Illicit Drugs*. Boston: Little, Brown and Co.

Duster, Troy. 1970. *The Legislation of Morality: Law, Drugs, and Moral Judgement*. New York: Free Press.

Fingarette, Herbert. 1988. *Heavy Drinking: The Myth of Alcoholism as a Disease*. Berkeley: University of California Press.

Goode, Erich. 1993. *Drugs in American Society*. Fourth edition. New York: McGraw-Hill.

Gover, Tzivia. 1997. "UMass Contends with a 4th R—Reveling." *Boston Sunday Globe*, October 12, B1, B10.

Grinspoon, Lester, and James B. Bakalar. 1997. *Marihuana, the Forbidden Medicine*. Revised and Expanded Edition. New Haven: Yale University Press.

Hatsukami, Dorothy K., and Marian W. Fischman. 1996. "Crack Cocaine and Cocaine Hydrochloride: Are the Differences Myth or Reality?" *Journal of American Medical Association* 276(19):1580–88.

Holmes, Steven A. 1997. "People Can Claim One or More Races on Federal Forms." *New York Times*, October 30, A1, A26.

Inciardi, James A., Dorothy Lockwood, and Anne E. Pottienger. 1993. *Women and Crack-Cocaine*. New York: Macmillan

Jackson, Derrick Z. 1997. "A Halfhearted Fix for Crack Laws." *Boston Globe*, July 25.

Kappeler, Victor E., Mark Blumberg, and Gary W. Potter. 1996. *The Mythology of Crime and Criminal Justice*. Second edition. Prospect Heights, Illinois: Waveland Press.

Kulnis, Greg. 1997. "Teenagers and Tobacco Equals Trouble. "In *American Cancer Society*. http://www.hcrhs.hunter.

Males, Mike A. 1996. *The Scapegoat Generation: America's War on Adolescents*. Monroe, Maine: Common Courage Press.

Meier, Robert F., and Gilbert Geis. 1997. *Victimless Crime? Prostitution, Drugs, Homosexuality, Abortion*. Los Angeles: Roxbury Publishing.

Merton, Robert K. 1968. *Social Theory and Social Structure*. Enlarged edition. New York: Free Press.

Mothers Against Drunk Driving. 1999. MADD Online, http://www.madd.org.

Musto, David F. 1991. "Opium, Cocaine and Marijuana in American History." *Scientific American*, July, 40–47.

Nadelman, Ethan A. 1997. "Foreword." Pp. ix-xi in *Marijuana Myths, Marijuana Facts*, edited by Lynn Zimmer and John P. Morgan. New York: Lindesmith Center.

National Center for Injury Prevention and Control. 1997. "National Center for Injury Prevention and Control (NCIPC) Homepage." http://www.cdc.gov/ncipc/default.htm.

National Center on Addiction and Substance Abuse. 1996. *Costs of Substance Abuse*. New York: Columbia University. http://www.casacolumbia.org/cost/menu1.htm.

Peele, Stanton. 1998. "All Wet: The Gospel of Abstinence and Twelve-Steps, Studies Show, Is Leading American Alcoholics Astray." *The Sciences*, 38 (March/April, Number 2):17-21.

Philips, Joel L., and Ronald D. Wynne. 1980. *Cocaine: The Mystique and the Reality*. New York: Avon.

Reinarman, Craig, and Harry G. Levine, eds. 1997. *Crack in America: Demon Drugs and Social Justice*. Berkeley: University of California Press.

Rigotti, Nancy A., Joseph R. DiFranza, Yu Chiao Chang, Thelma Tisdale, Becky Kemp, and Daniel E. Singer. 1997. "The Effect of Enforcing Tobacco-sales Laws on Adolescent Access to Tobacco and Smoking Behavior." *New England Journal of Medicine* 337 (October 9):1044-1051.

SAMHSA. 1997. *1996 National Household Survey on Drug Abuse*. Washington, D.C.: Substance Abuse and Mental Health Services Administration, Department of Health and Human Services.

Shea, Christopher. 1997. "In Drug-Policy Debates, a Center at Columbia U. Takes a Hard Line." *Chronicle of Higher Education*, October 3, A15–17.

Wechsler, Henry, et al. 1996. "Binge Drinking on Campus: Results of a National Study." *Bulletin Series: Alcohol and Other Drug Prevention*, The Higher Education Center for Alcohol and Other Drug Prevention, U.S. Department of Education. http://www.edc.org/hec/pubs/binge.htm.

Zimmer, Lynn, and John P. Morgan. 1997. *Marijuana Myths, Marijuana Facts: A Review of the Scientific Evidence*. New York: Lindesmith Center.

Websites

http://ash.org

Action on Smoking and Health. This website includes a wide variety of information on smoking and tobacco. You will find some of the internal tobacco corporation documents on this site.

http://www.edc.org/hec/pubs/binge.htm

The Higher Education Center for Alcohol and Other Drug Prevention, U.S. Department of Education. This site includes a lot of information, the report on binge drinking is among the most significant.

http://www.samhsa.gov/index.htm

The Substance Abuse and Mental Health Services Administration, Department of Health and Human Services. This is one of the most comprehensive sites dealing with substance abuse. To find information on substance abuse, this is the best place to start.

CHAPTER NINE

Child Abuse

In the News: Dead and Abandoned Children

A Boston man was held without bail after being charged with brutally beating his girlfriend's 6-year-old son to death. Apparently he became enraged at the boy for soiling his pants. The prosecutor for the case said a medical examiner found that the child had been struck at least 81 times—including three severe punches or kicks to the stomach that caused his death. The accused claimed that he did not kill the boy. The boy's mother told investigators that her boyfriend had "disciplined" the child six days earlier, but they both tried to cover up the beating by telling friends the boy was sick. A day before the child's death, he was unable to hold down his food and complained to his mother of headaches and stomachaches.

Police sources said the mother gave the child aspirin but never sought medical treatment for him. By the next morning, the youngster was unconscious. A neighbor visiting the home called paramedics despite the boyfriend's objections. Before the ambulance arrived, the boyfriend fled out the back door, but he later called Boston City Hospital several times checking on the child's condition. Police said it was unclear whether charges would be brought against the boy's mother. In these kinds of situations, those who work with abusive parents often wonder how culpable the nonabusing parent or partner might be. In many cases, if a nonabusing parent had intervened or had sought help, the child might have lived.

In another notorious case, a state agency in Massachusetts allowed a woman with a history of child neglect to retain custody of her 2-year-old and 8-month-old sons despite having left them home alone for more than eight hours one evening. After the woman had regained custody of the children, police went to her apartment in response to a report of children being left home alone. The police found the 8-month-old sitting on the kitchen floor amidst a pile of debris and eating garbage from the floor. When the police arrived, the front door was wide open and the 2-year-old was standing just inside the threshold. The police found no adults in the apartment. Both children were unkempt and their clothes were disheveled. While the police were at the apartment, the mother returned home. She told the police she had left the children around 3:00pm to go to the store. She did not return until 11:30pm. She stated that she had asked a neighbor to check on the kids. The neighbor had been checking, but assumed the mother would return soon. The neighbor fell asleep and did not wake up until the police arrived. Even after this incident, the mother was allowed to keep custody of her children. Several state politicians were dismayed; they do not believe the children's safety can be guaranteed (Boston Herald 1996).

Definition and Prevalence

A young mother brings her infant into the emergency room of a large pediatric hospital. Doctors quickly discover that the child has a leg fracture. Longbone x-rays reveal other older and healing fractures. The mother says she does not know how the injuries occurred but speculates that they might have resulted from a fall from a changing table. The physicians suspect child abuse.

Child abuse usually refers to nonaccidental physical injuries inflicted on a child by its parents or guardians. In this sense, abuse is synonymous with broken bones, burns, or serious bruising. In the United States, child abuse has gained recognition from four groups of practitioners: lawyers, pediatricians, social workers, and the police, as well as from criminologists, psychologists, sociologists, and other social scientists. The medical community sees abused children by virtue of the bruises, welts, and broken bones present in a medical setting. Medical professionals define abuse in terms of a child's ailments, which must be healed and the parents' "illness" which must be treated. The legal community defines abuse in terms of intent. Parents have certain legal and moral responsibilities, and failure to comply is to defy the statutes set up by society and is therefore punishable. The child is the victim and the parent is the perpetrator or the accomplice. The legal definition focuses almost exclusively on the debate over individual rights. The debate concerns both the right to privacy in the family as well as the right to use physical discipline on children without societal scrutiny. Although the right to use physical discipline on children is not a legal right, many parents believe it is useful and necessary in some cases. Most children in the United States are spanked and many people believe this is not harmful to the child's well being despite research to the contrary (Straus, Sugarman and Giles-Sims 1997). It is becoming clearer that the legal system is having difficulty determining an adequate definition of child abuse. The social worker, on the other hand, views the family as the system in trouble. Child abuse is defined with respect to anticipated outcome—to restore the balance of family continuity so that the nurturing of children can continue. If this is not possible, the child may be removed from the family. These three approaches have aided in creating a somewhat common definition of abuse that focuses generally on nonaccidental injury to children inflicted by a caregiver (Tower 1996).

Child abuse, however, may take other forms such as emotional abuse, sexual abuse, or neglect. **Emotional abuse** may entail verbal abuse, lack of affection, or lack of attention by the parent or guardian. The most widely used definition is presented by J. Garbarino, F. Guttman, and J. Seeley (1986). They conclude that emotional maltreatment is not an isolated event but rather a pattern of psychologically destructive behaviors that may include any of the following:

1. *Rejecting*—the child's needs and worth are not acknowledged.

2. *Isolating*—the child is cut off from normal social experiences, prevented from forming friendships, and made to believe that he or she is alone in the world.

3. *Terrorizing*—the child is verbally assaulted and lives in a climate of fear.

4. *Ignoring*—the child is deprived of essential stimulation and responsiveness thus stifling the child's emotional growth and intellectual development.

5. *Corrupting*—the child is socialized to engage in destructive and antisocial behavior, making the child unfit for normal social experience.

David Finkelhor defines sexual abuse as any kind of sexual contact between family members. It includes not only intercourse but also "mutual masturbation, hand-genital or oral-genital contact, sexual fondling, exhibition and sexual propositioning" (Finkelhor 1979). As broad as this definition is, there are additional types of sexual abuse, such as peeping tomism, pushing children into prostitution, and forcing children to display themselves for the amusement or stimulation of others. Children who have been sexually abused often show characteristic behavior. Table 9-1 gives an overview of the behavior of sexually abused children.

Table 9-1   The Behavior of Sexually Abused Children

The behavior of sexually abused children may include the following:

- Unusual interest in or avoidance of all things of a sexual nature
- Sleep problems, nightmares
- Depression or withdrawal from friends or family
- Seductiveness
- Statements that their bodies are dirty or damaged, or fear that there is something wrong with them in the genital area
- Refusal to go to school, delinquency
- Secretiveness
- Aspects of sexual molestation in drawings, games, fantasies
- Unusual aggressiveness
- Suicidal behavior

All children should have the right to happy, healthy lives without fear of abuse and neglect by their primary caretakers.

Child neglect is yet another type of child abuse. According to Elizabeth Englander (1997), child neglect occurs when a custodial adult fails to see that a child's basic needs are provided for. There are two types of neglect. Physical neglect results from failure to adequately feed, clothe, or shelter a child; emotional neglect results from denial of love and contact. It may include persistent degradation and humiliation of a child. Refusing to educate a child or to take the child for medical examinations may also be considered emotional neglect or abuse. (See "A Closer Look: Recognizing Physical Neglect.")

A Closer Look

Recognizing Physical Neglect

Physical neglect generally refers to failure of a caretaker, either deliberately or through negligence or inability, to provide a child with minimally adequate food, clothing, shelter, medical care, supervision, emotional stability, or essential care. This definition is not dependent upon location, as neglect can occur while the child is in an out-of-home or in-home setting. The Massachusetts Department of Social Services has issued a report with signs of neglect to look for. (Massachusetts Department of Social Services 1996). The following are physical signs of neglect:

- Abandonment—children abandoned totally or for long periods of time.

- Lack of supervision—very young children are left unattended; children are left in the care of other children too young to protect them; children inadequately supervised for long periods of time or when engaged in dangerous activities.

- Lack of adequate clothing and hygiene—children are chronically dirty; children are dressed inadequately for the weather or suffering from persistent illnesses like pneumonia or frostbite or sunburn that are associated with excessive exposure; child has a severe diaper rash or other persistent skin disorders resulting from improper hygiene.

- Lack of medical or dental care—children whose medical, dental or needs such as medication and health aids are unmet.

- Lack of adequate education—children who are chronically absent from school.

- Lack of adequate nutrition—children lacking sufficient quantity or quality of food; children consistently complaining of hunger or rummaging for food; children suffering severe developmental lags.

- Lack of adequate shelter—structurally unsafe housing or exposed wiring; inadequate heating; unsanitary housing conditions.

When assessing neglect, it is imperative to be sensitive to issues of poverty versus neglect. For example, some families may not be able to provide adequate heat or food for that matter. It is also important to consider differing cultural expectations and values as well as differing child-rearing practices.

Determining the prevalence of child abuse in general is difficult because data depend on the definition of abuse used. In addition, not everyone agrees on definitions of child abuse. For example, failing to feed or clothe a child adequately may be a function of poverty as opposed to deliberate neglect on the part of a parent or guardian.

Richard Bourne describes a difficult case involving poverty. Suppose that a child is brought into a hospital having swallowed some lead. The child was eating paint chips, which can be fatal. If more ingestion occurs, there could be physical damage. Are the parents neglectful because they have not tried to cut off access to lead particles? What if this family lives in an apartment whose landlord refuses to have the lead paint removed? What if the parents cannot afford to move to another apartment? Can the parents watch their child constantly to ensure there is no more lead ingestion? Parents know that it only takes seconds for a child to put something in his or her mouth. This case might be a function of poverty, rather than neglect (Bourne 1985).

Physical abuse is also difficult to define. Most Americans still condone physical, or corporal punishment of children ("Spare the rod and spoil the child"). How do we distinguish between "acceptable" corporal punishment, such as spanking or slapping, and child abuse? Such a distinction is difficult to make and complicates the problem of definition. Harvey Wallace (1996) suggests relevant considerations such as whether a parent hits with an open hand, a fist or a belt; whether the parent aims at the face or at a less vulnerable part of the child's body; whether the parent is in control; and whether the beatings are rare or frequent. Child abuse may also depend on the seriousness of the harm inflicted; the intent of the parents (abuse is deliberate and nonaccidental) and the frequency of injury.

Bourne argues that applications of child abuse and child neglect labels may depend on the race or social class of the parent or guardian. If an affluent and well-educated parent brings a child into a hospital emergency room, and the youngster has an injury of which the cause is unclear, a diagnosis of inflicted injury is less likely to be made than if poor or minority parents appear with a similar problem. The less the social distance between the professional and those being treated, the more frequent is the diagnosis of accident (Bourne 1985).

Because it is difficult to distinguish between punishment and abuse, the amount of abuse in American society is unclear. Obviously, the broader the definition of abuse, the greater the amount. In 1995, over 3 million children were reported for child abuse and neglect to child protective service (CPS) agencies in the United States. About 46 out of every 1,000 children are reported as victims of some form of abuse. Overall, child abuse reporting levels have increased 49 percent between 1986 and 1995. In 1995, 996,000 children were substantiated by CPS as victims of child maltreatment. This represents 15 out of every 1,000 U.S. children (Lung and Daro 1996). Table 9-2 depicts an increase in all types of abuse from 1986–1997.

Table 9-2 Percentage of Child Abuse and Neglect Cases

	1986	1997
Physical abuse	22	26
Sexual abuse	8	16
Neglect	54	55
Emotional abuse	4	8

Source: National Committee to Prevent Child Abuse. 1998. *Child Abuse and Neglect Statistics*. http://www.childabuse.org/facts97.html.

In 1995, an estimated 1,215 child abuse and neglect related fatalities were confirmed by CPS agencies. Since 1985, the rate of child abuse fatalities has increased by 39 percent. Based on these numbers, more than three children die each day as a result of child abuse or neglect. Almost 82 percent of these children are less than five years old at the time of their death with 41 percent under one year of age. As for the cause of death, 40 percent of deaths resulted from neglect, 49 percent from physical abuse and 11 percent from a combination of neglectful and physically abusive parenting. Approximately 43 percent of these deaths occurred to children known to CPS agencies as current or prior clients (Lung and Daro 1996). Table 9-3 presents child fatalities by various states. Of the states presented, Texas has the highest number of fatalities.

Table 9-3 Child Abuse Related Deaths

State	1993	1994	1995	1996	1997
Arkansas	9	NA	3	9	NA
California	49	63	135	135	NA
Connecticut	5	7	5	7	6
Florida	63	71	68	49	NA
Hawaii	2	2	1	4	1
Illinois	78	82	98	83	91
Maine	7	5	3	2	NA
Massachusetts	10	3	11	5	NA
Rhode Island	5	2	7	4	3
Texas	111	102	98	110	104
Vermont	2	NA	0	1	NA
Washington	30	17	17	9	NA

Source: National Committee to Prevent Child Abuse. 1998. *Child Abuse and Neglect Statistics*. http://www.childabuse.org/facts97.html.

A Closer Look

Child Abuse and Neglect Statistics Website

Located at http://www.childabuse.org, this website has information regarding the number of child abuse and neglect reports nationwide. If you click on NCPCA (National Committee to Prevent Child Abuse) , you will get information on NCPCA and its goals. You can obtain child abuse facts, such as the incidence of child maltreatment in day care centers and in the general population; as well as information about different types of child sexual abuse and child fatalities. If you click on "Programs," information concerning treatment programs for child abusers is available as well as resource locations. You'll find this an excellent, informative website for tracking down information on child abuse.

Sexual abuse seems to be easier to define than to recognize. In most cases of sexual abuse, there are no physical symptoms so physicians and therapists rely on a child's explanation or reporting. According to David Finkelhor (1993), many victims of sexual abuse never report the offense to authorities. His studies indicate that approximately 25 to 33 percent of women recall being sexually abused as children compared to 10 percent of men. Studies of the general population of adults show that anywhere from 6 to 63 percent of females were sexually abused as children. The true extent of sexual abuse is unknown. Jim Hopper (1997) states that approximately one in three girls is sexually abused before age eighteen and one in four by age fourteen. In addition, one in six boys is sexually abused before age sixteen.

No matter what the type of abuse, Finkelhor argues that child abuse is largely underreported, despite claims to the contrary. Those arguing that child abuse is overreported claim that people often overreact to minor incidents of child discipline. Such overreporting causes problems for families and children involved. Finkelhor states that people who argue overreporting are minimizing child maltreatment; they are waiting for serious injury to occur. He claims that the presence of injury should not be a requirement for reporting (Finkelhor 1993).

The rate of substantiation for child abuse cases has not declined nationally. This is one piece of evidence disputing the contention that child abuse is overreported. Family researcher Douglas Besharov (1993) argues that there is a high rate of unsubstantiated child abuse reports. These unsubstantiated cases threaten family privacy and cause unavoidable trauma to those involved. Finkelhor argues that we must be careful about defining family privacy, adding that family privacy maintains child abuse. Investigations may be intrusive for parents but may rescue a child. Furthermore, most cases labeled "unsubstantiated" involve CPS workers who have never contacted the family in question. Unsubstantiated cases do not mean that false allegations of child abuse exist. Some unsubstantiated cases involve situations of abuse that are difficult to prove. Table 9-4 presents the estimated numbers of children reported for abuse and the estimated number of substantiated cases of abuse. As one can see from this table, the rate of reporting has increased since 1994 as has the number of substantiated cases.

Table 9-4 Child Abuse and Neglect Reports in the United States

	1994	1995	1996	1997
Estimated # of children reported	3,074,000	3,126,000	3,142,000	3,195,000
Estimated # of children confirmed as victims	1,014,000	1,032,000	1,005,000	1,054,000

Source: National Committee to Prevent Child Abuse. 1998. http://www.childabuse.org

There are three primary sources of abuse statistics: official statistics gathered through mandatory reports to state agencies; household surveys of parents who answer questions on childrearing practices; and surveys of community groups involved in protective services. Whatever the source, Finkelhor argues that abuse statistics are unreliable and probably underestimate the extent of the problem. For example, only a fraction of children who are battered are officially reported. Violent parents may refuse to participate in household surveys, while those persons who do respond may choose to give socially acceptable answers.

Though the number of official cases is clearly increasing, it is doubtful that more child abuse and neglect exist now than in the past. What has changed is the fact that abuse is now a salient social problem. Child abuse and neglect have existed for centuries. Child abuse achieved public recognition as a social problem in 1962, when the *Journal of American Medical Association* (JAMA) published "The Battered Child Syndrome" (Best 1990).

Early reports in both the medical literature and the press portrayed the problem as one of extreme physical violence against children. By 1967, all states had laws requiring physicians to report cases of suspected abuse. It was not until 1974 that the issue encompassed a much broader array of conditions threatening children (Best 1990). In 1974, Congress passed Mondale's Child Abuse and Prevention Act. Sexual abuse joined neglect within the domain of child abuse by the time the act was passed.

More important than the difficulty of adequately defining child abuse is the alarming rate of child abuse. Definitions of child abuse may vary, but whatever the definition, children are being hurt and society needs to stop that hurt. A key step in ending child abuse is understanding what causes it.

Levels of Causation

Why do people neglect or abuse children in their care? Explanations can be made on several levels. In the following, we examine three such levels: the individual, the cultural, and the structural.

Individual

Fewer than 10 percent of abusers are clinically psychotic, though many appear anxious and depressed. Among the psychological characteristics observed by professionals are low self-esteem, role reversal, unrealistic expectations, fatalism, or inappropriate affect, and lack of knowledge about child care.

Low self-esteem—Most abusers have a bad self-image, seeing themselves as worthless.

Role reversal—Abusers want their children to nurture and satisfy them rather than the reverse. They often describe their children as "everything that I have," and express a strong need for their presence; they hope their children will make them feel good, give them a sense of completeness.

Unrealistic expectations—Since abusers have low self-esteem, they frequently view children as a potential source of status and admiration. If they produce intelligent and creative children, then they as parents must be more intelligent and creative than they appear. These attitudes lead to the holding of unrealistic expectations for the youngster which, when not fulfilled, create disappointment and anger.

To a certain degree, of course, most parents hope that their children will reflect well on them. The difference between abusers and nonabusers, then, is not the existence of expectations but the possibility of their fulfillment, the intensity with which they are held, the reasons for their presence, and the reactions at disappointment. Abusers often believe that their children are intentionally refusing to satisfy expectations. They attribute to them a meanness or other adult motivation that the children are not capable of holding—a deliberate unwillingness to perform because of antagonism or stubbornness. Abusing parents are often not tuned in to their child's needs and are unaware of how to satisfy these needs. Mothering and fathering are not innate behaviors, and if they are not learned from role models, they are not easily mastered. Often abusers have not had a happy childhood. They have learned violence and neglect, not caring or loving, from their parents (Ethier, Lacharite, and Couture 1995).

Other psychological characteristics may be associated with abuse: sexual repression, unmastered oral aggression, a tendency to project blame onto others, phobic thought patterns. Not all abusers, however, have the psychological characteristics attributed to them. And there is no clear-cut psychological distinction between abusers and nonabusers. Most parents have probably struck their children inappropriately at some time, and those who have not done so have probably felt the desire.

According to many individual perspectives, abuse depends on the relationship between abuser and abused, and in order to understand it, one must focus not only on the psyche of the abuser but also on the child-victim and the child's characteristics. Premature infants and those born with congenital defects, for example, are more likely to be abused. Children who are normal, but are perceived as deficient, and children who are abnormal, and are so perceived, are both potentially at risk. Despite these individual explanations of child abuse, most researchers of family violence focus on cultural values and norms that may affect or determine the manner in which parents interact or respond to their children.

Cultural

Mildred Pagelow (1984) argues that the values of American society contribute to child abuse (Pagelow 1984). Given the pressures and alienation of contemporary life, one might ask why there is so little abuse rather than why it is so prevalent. Pagelow argues that parents believe they own their children. That is, parents in the United States believe they can do whatever they want to their children whether it be good or bad. Parents abuse children because they can. Parents in this society appear to have ultimate power over their children. In fact, many parents may inform other people, such as teachers or caretakers, that they can or cannot do certain things to their children. For example, letting a baby-sitter know that s/he can physically discipline their child. The child has no power to control these decisions (Pagelow 1984).

In attempting to understand child abuse, one must separate the different types of abuses because there appear to be differences among the types. Which parents are more likely to physically abuse and neglect their children? Since mothers are assigned the largest share of the childrearing task, the abuser may be automatically assumed to be the mother. The high visibility of mothers in the literature seems to indicate that mothers are the primary abusers of children. However, Finkelhor argues that men and fathers are more likely to abuse if the time at risk factor is taken into consideration (Finkelhor 1979). The time-at-risk factor refers to the amount of time a parent spends with the child. Although it is assumed that since mothers spend more time with children they are more likely to abuse their children, fathers actually abuse their children more often when they do spend time with them.

Undoubtedly, many mothers abuse their children. Women are the largest category at risk of perpetrating child abuse. Reasons for this include the isolation of the modern nuclear family, the much greater responsibility assigned to mothers for the care, nourishment, and behavior of children, and the greater percentage of time they spend with children. Despite all that, the literature does not provide strong and conclusive evidence that women are the primary abusers (Pagelow 1984). Females are significantly more likely to be reported for neglect than males either because they spend more time with their children or are assumed to be responsible for their well-being. In fact, Judith Milner (1996) argues that women are held responsible for child neglect and abuse in cases when they are not directly responsible. In cases where the father directly abuses his child, the mother is often focused on for not protecting the child (Cooper 1993; Reder, et al. 1993). The differing definitions of mothering and fathering generally serve to minimize the father's responsibility for child care while increasing the mother's. Judith Herman (1981) demonstrates this in her classic work on incest. She states that often the mother is blamed for not protecting her daughter when it is discovered that the daughter is sexually abused. In addition, the mother may be blamed for being frigid or too aggressive in the marriage.

The most common characteristics of reported cases of child physical abuse and neglect involving one or both parents reveal certain patterns: the parents are young; the first child was born to a teen-age mother (frequently an unwanted or premarital pregnancy); parental education level is low; the parent is socially isolated and lacks family support; parent/s have health problems; and the child has health problems (Zuravin and Diblasio 1992).

Sexual abusers of children share different characteristics. While there is confusion or disagreement in determining whether mothers or fathers physically abuse and neglect their children more, most researchers agree that 90 percent of child sexual abusers are male. Why is this so? Finkelhor argues that there are several reasons why males are more likely than females to sexually abuse children. All of the reasons relate to gender socialization. Finkelhor states that women in our society get trained in the distinction between sexual and nonsexual affection partly as preparation for being caretakers of children. With men, physical affection is withdrawn at an earlier age and only given back later on in adolescence through sex. Thus, men tend to seek fulfillment of all affection through sexual channels. Men are also socialized to focus sexual arousal around specific sexual acts removed from any relationship context, whereas women tend to be more focused on the relationship. This makes it easier for men to sexualize relationships with children. Finkelhor refers to attraction gradient as a further explanation. Men are trained to be attracted to persons who are younger, smaller and less powerful than themselves. On the contrary, women are trained to be attracted to persons who are older, bigger, and more powerful than themselves (Finkelhor 1979).

There is no question that cultural values influence interaction between people whether they are parent and child, husband and wife, or friend to friend. We are so culturally conditioned as parents, as females and males, as husbands and wives, etc. that we do not question our everyday behaviors. Often as parents we revert back to the way we were treated as children. This could be healthy or unhealthy depending on our childhood experiences. Structural aspects of society affect our interaction as well. As we will see, factors such as race, gender, and socioeconomic status influence the way we behave.

Structural

Much of the literature on child abuse and neglect links them with poverty. Harvey Wallace (1996) argues that the poor are more likely to be labeled abusers because of the visibility of their behavior and the greater frequency with which agents of social control apply negative definitions to their actions. Child abuse and neglect exist at all socioeconomic levels. Being poor does not automatically mean abuse will exist. Many middle- and upper-class children experience abuse at the hands of their parents. The difference between classes may simply be a matter of reporting. Professionals and service agencies are less likely to report abuse in middle and upper class families (Bourne 1985).

One perspective on child abuse looks at societal causes of child neglect. An ecological perspective looks at how society contributes to neglect. An example would be the welfare system. If a welfare system encourages single parents to get off welfare, it should supply training programs and day-care services. If it does not, it is difficult for parents to find a job because of lack of skills and day-care costs. The system may actually discourage single parents on welfare from working. The result may be the neglect of children's needs. For those who choose to work, the result may be leaving young children alone or inadequately supervised (Tower 1996).

Child abuse and neglect appear to be related to family structure. The more traditional family values are, the more likely for abuse to occur. Traditional family values refer mainly to values concerning traditional gender roles. For example, in a traditional family, the male is usually perceived as head of the family, the main breadwinner and disciplinarian. The female or mother/wife is generally responsible for childcare, nurturing of family members, and domestic labor. She would not be considered a major breadwinner or decision maker. Her role would be subordinate to the father/husband. Pagelow contends that traditional families may have ideas about certain roles that make child abuse probable. As stated earlier, fathers may believe they "own" their children and can discipline them any way they want. With regard to mothers abusing their children, feminists argue that we must look at the role of women in the family. Women's abuse of children stems directly from their oppression in society and within the family. Women are expected to be major caretakers of children, yet they have few supports. It is not surprising that some women displace their anger and frustration onto their children—family members who are less powerful than themselves (Pagelow 1984).

Kirsti Yllo (1993) contends that males perpetrate more abuse against children because they hold the most power in the family. Society gives males this power and also teaches children that they are less powerful than their parents. All social institutions, such as religion, education, and the mass media, communicate these unequal power dimensions in one way or another. The legal system helps perpetuate child abuse by its reluctance to effectively intervene in child abuse matters. The legal system does not get involved unless a child is seriously injured or dead. Feminists, in general, consider the assault of children as stemming from societal values.

It has been observed that child abuse is intergenerational—that abusing parents were frequently abused as children. This tendency might be explained by abusers never learning appropriate childrearing techniques, or by their learning that beatings were a necessary and proper part of disciplining. It might also relate to the lack of self-esteem in abused children and the tendency of such children to become "needy" adults who want infants for their own gratification.

Consequences

Children who are abused often develop certain characteristics. They are self-destructive or have little sense of self-worth; they are negative in their interpersonal relationships; or they appear precocious and adultlike. These characteristics are understandable given the dynamics of abuse (Wallace 1996).

Effects of abuse on children may vary according to the type of abuse inflicted. Physical abuse may result in medical complications due to inflicted injuries. The most common effects of physical abuse are physical aggression and antisocial behavior (Straus et al. 1997). Children who are sexually abused have displayed a wide range of emotional, physical, and behavioral problems. K. A. Kendall-Tackett and colleagues (1993) concluded that sexualized behavior is a common symptom in sexually abused children. Post-traumatic stress disorder is another frequent problem associated with sexual abuse. Symptoms include nightmares, fear, feeling of isolation, and guilt feelings.

Despite the fact that neglect appears to be the most common form of child abuse in the United States, very little research has been conducted on its effects (Barnett, et al. 1997). One of the most cited problems associated with child neglect is difficulty in social skills. For example, neglected children seem to have difficulty forming attachments with others. Intellectual ability seems to be affected by neglect in some cases. Wodarski and colleagues (1990) found that neglected children experience more academic problems, including overall school performance, reading, and math skills, than nonmaltreated children.

The consequences of childhood abuse can extend into adulthood and affect victims throughout their lives. Depression is the most common symptom for adult survivors of sexual abuse. Substance abuse and eating disorders are common as well (Elliott 1994). Substance abuse becomes an issue for many survivors of all types of child abuse.

Death is the most tragic consequence of child abuse. As stated earlier, fatalities related to child abuse have increased since 1985. Severe head trauma is the most common cause of children dying from abuse. Shaken baby syndrome can also be lethal with 20 to 25 percent of its victims dying. Many children who suffer from shaken baby syndrome suffer brain damage resulting in lifelong cerebral palsy, visual defects, or cognitive impairment (Levitt and Alexander 1994). Most perpetrators of shaken baby syndrome are males who become stressed over a baby's crying (Showers 1994).

One question frequently asked by sociologists studying child abuse is "Will abused children become abusers of their own children?" Whether there is a cycle of violence is questionable. According to Pagelow, there is no way the cycle of violence can be proved or disproved (Pagelow 1984). One reason is that we do not have reliable rates of how many adults were abused as children. Also, there is no consensus on the precise definition of abuse or neglect. Some researchers assert that children who witness abuse in the family are more likely to become abusive as adults than children who directly experience abuse. Pagelow argues that this appears to be more applicable to boys who witness their father abusing their mother. Adult males usually serve as role models for male children. If a young boy sees his father being abusive when angry, he is likely to deal with his anger in similar ways. Pagelow clearly

Shaken Baby Syndrome

On September 21, 1998 Gregory Silva died. He was two months old. According to police, Gregory's father had shaken him so hard that his heart stopped beating and his brain and eyes bled. The baby's mother insisted that her husband could not have beaten their baby and that he had only shaken the baby to save him from choking. The father acknowledged shaking the baby "perhaps twice" to stop him from crying (Valdés-Rodríguez and Langner 1998). As horrifying as this case is, even more disturbing is that it happens so often that it has a name—shaken baby syndrome.

Alisa Valdés-Rodríguez notes that the case "is all too eerily familiar" (1998: B1). In February 1997, 8-month-old Matthew Eappen died after being shaken by British au pair Louise Woodward, who was convicted of manslaughter. However, the two cases differ in an important way. Gregory Silva was allegedly shaken by his father. According to child abuse specialists and researchers, this is a more typical case. Shaken baby deaths typically involve "biological fathers in their early 20s, home alone with a colicky male baby" (Valdés-Rodríguez 1998: B1). A study by researchers at the Child Abuse Prevention Center in Utah indicated that in about 70 percent of the cases of shaken baby syndrome, a male caregiver was the suspect; 60 percent of all shaken babies are boys (Valdés-Rodríguez 1998).

What causes this pattern? Researchers suggest that young men are not given adequate training on how to handle crying babies and that "boys must be targeted for education as early as kindergarten, and no later than middle school" (Valdés-Rodríguez 1998:B8). Some hospitals and agencies have developed abuse-education programs for fathers. This will not end all child abuse, but it seems like an important step toward educating young men as fathers. Perhaps babies like Gregory Silva will have a better chance growing up and become parents themselves.

states that a cycle of abuse is not automatic. If appropriate intervention occurs, the cycle can be broken. Intervention seems to play a key role in determining whether or not an abused child will become an abuser as an adult.

Intervention

Child abuse management focuses on intervention after the abuse has occurred rather than on the prevention of the first episode. This is a problem. It is like parking an ambulance at the bottom of a steep mountain rather than building a fence along the edge of the road.

There are several strategies that can be used to prevent the beginning of abuse or neglect such as introducing family and parenting classes into hospitals and public schools. Parents currently receive almost no training to prepare them for the realities of child care. Women are expected to be "natural mothers," to know everything about children. One problem with child-rearing courses is how to decide what values are appropriate for raising children. The criticism is especially common if the teachers belong to a different racial or socioeconomic group.

A second strategy for prevention involves advertising and public relations campaigns. These campaigns make people aware of child abuse and might stimulate political and economic decision making that would benefit troubled families. Abuse-prone parents, however, are unlikely to be deterred by

commercials, though parents who do not abuse might be reinforced in their ❖ ❖ ❖ ❖
positive child-rearing techniques.

Some states are attempting to prevent child abuse with the initiation of "hotlines." These are toll-free telephone numbers that a potential abuser or reporter of abuse can call to identify cases, learn about possible services, receive counseling, or trigger an immediate protective response through emergency outreach.

Some hospitals, moreover, are hoping to prevent reinjury to abused children by sponsoring child abuse intervention teams. These groups, made up of professionals from different disciplines—law, medicine, psychology, and social work—try to assist families by providing services and by referring parents to appropriate community agencies. If an abused or neglected child enters a hospital and the team determines that the child cannot return home, the team may initiate proceedings to remove custody from the parents.

Many feminist social scientists argue that family values must be reexamined in order to end child abuse. The traditional nuclear family sets up children to be inferior to their parents and therefore as having no power in the family. It may sound ludicrous to suggest giving children equal power in a family but many feminists suggest that perceiving children as subjects instead of objects may be one step in preventing child abuse. This does not mean bringing up children with no limits on their behavior. It means not treating children as if they are property, having no choices about their lives (Gelles and Loseke 1993; Pagelow 1984; Yllo 1993).

Traditionally, children have not received much protection under the law. Parents are assumed to have the right of custody and control over the young, such rights being limited only by a demonstration of gross unfitness or neglect. The state has been reluctant to intervene in family matters. Two important legal issues in child abuse are when to intervene and how to intervene. One view is that intervention should be narrowly restricted because of its defects. Criticism has focused on the fact that courts have precipitously removed children from their homes and that foster placement often has detrimental effects on the child. Great deference is given to family autonomy and the right to be free from state interference. Only the protection of a child from serious and specific harm may justify the legal use of coercive alternatives. (See "A Closer Look: Terminating Parents' Rights.")

A contrary view is that outside decision-makers should have discretion in determining the appropriateness of legal intervention. Since not all cases of abuse and neglect are predictable or easily defined, and since the purpose of intervention is to help families and protect children, it should not be narrowly restricted. The law is seen as a positive force fulfilling important needs, not a danger to be limited. Debate also surrounds the manner of intervention—whether criminal or civil law is more appropriate, whether to report a case of abuse to the Department of Public Welfare, or to initiate a neglect petition in juvenile court.

As noted above, Finkelhor argues that child abuse is underreported in the United States. Evidence suggests that large numbers of seriously abused and neglected children are still not coming to the attention of child protective authorities (Finkelhor 1993). To remedy this, more professionals and members of the public need to be sensitized to recognizing and reporting child abuse. If, in concert with these increased reports, child protective authorities improve their investigatory skills and expand their treatment services, society

A Closer Look

Terminating Parents' Rights

The removal of a child from the home of abusing parents is an obvious form of intervention. Some state statutes allow removal from the home and termination of parental rights when a child or children are abused (Wallace 1996). In the California case of *In re Luwanna,* an appeals court upheld the termination of the parental right of Luwanna's parents based on evidence that her younger brother had been repeatedly beaten with a stick. The appeals court affirmed the termination of parental rights over both children even though there was no evidence that Luwanna's father had beaten her.

Numerous courts have attempted to deal with child abuse and the issue of future births of siblings who might suffer the same abuse. Harvey Wallace (1996) states that the use of involuntary sterilization raises the specter of ethnic cleansing and Nazi Germany. Compulsory sterilization is highly emotional and controversial. Additionally, the United States Supreme Court has ruled that parents have a "right to procreate." However, the same court has ruled that in limited situations, the state may involuntarily sterilize someone. In the still controversial decision of *Buck vs. Bell* in 1927, the United States Supreme Court upheld a Virginia statute allowing superintendents of various state mental institutions to order the sterilization of any patient if that sterilization served the best interests of the patient and of society.

Wallace presents several additional cases of terminating parental rights. In 1991, Darlene Johnson, a pregnant twenty-seven year old mother of four was convicted of physically abusing her children. Johnson had prior convictions of burglary, battery and other theft-related crimes. California Superior Court Judge Broadman suspended Johnson's prison sentence on the condition that she use Norplant, a long-term form of birth control, as a condition of her probation. Johnson originally agreed but later recanted and filed an appeal (Wallace 1996).

In 1993, Ronald and Barbara Gross were convicted of sexual abuse of their four children and sentenced to ten years in prison. Judge Lynne Brown of Washington County, Tennessee, offered to suspend the sentence and place the defendants on probation if they would agree to Barbara Gross submitting to a tubal ligation.

According to Wallace, all states provide for the termination of parental rights of parents whose children have been abused, and a number of these states authorize the termination of parental rights based on sibling abuse. Terminating parental rights is one method of preventing further injury to siblings. While many trial court judges have conditioned probation for abusing parents on acceptance of sterilization, no modern appellate court has approved such a remedy (Wallace 1996).

---

may get closer to identifying and helping all children at risk (Gelles and Loseke 1993).

Elizabeth Englander (1997) believes that abuse should be handled as a criminal matter; the beating of a child is assault and battery and the young victim should receive the same legal protection, and the perpetrator the same punishment, as in offenses committed against adults. In other words, child abuse should be treated as a crime. If it is not treated as a crime, abusers will not have to take responsibility for their actions. Others argue that use of criminal sanctions would hurt rather than help the child and that the criminal justice system is unable to respond effectively in abuse or neglect matters.

Those opposed to criminal action argue that it harms the child psychologically by making the child feel responsible for the punishment of a parent for whom, despite abuse or neglect, the child still has positive feelings. The abuser does not usually receive rehabilitation in prison, and after release may be more angry at the youngster. The state must prove criminal cases "beyond a reasonable doubt," a difficult task in child abuse where frequently the child is too young to testify, the spouse has immunity from testimony, and the evidence of abuse is unclear or lacking. Finally, opponents to criminal action feel that the child can be better protected, and the parent more effectively sanctioned, by use of child protection statutes.

An additional suggestion might be to use both the criminal justice system and child protective services in handling abuse cases. Child abuse would be defined as criminal behavior, and the perpetrator would be processed as a criminal with mandatory counseling as part of the sentence. Depending on the severity of the crime, the abuser might or might not have to serve jail time but would certainly receive counseling. The best interests of the child would be of paramount importance. One option might be to remove the abuser from the home as opposed to placing the child in foster care. Protective service workers would evaluate the abuser's progress and make decisions whether or not the abuser and victim could continue a relationship.

All fifty states now have reporting statutes that require certain professionals—medical personnel, social workers, educators, and counselors—to report cases of suspected abuse and neglect to the police or to a Department of Public Welfare. The agency accepting the report investigates the allegation and, if abuse or neglect is found, offers the family whatever services are necessary to care for, or protect, the child. If the child is endangered by remaining in the home, the agency has the ability to file a petition in family court urging temporary foster placement (Wallace 1996).

Most states have an immunity provision that protects individuals from civil and criminal liability if their report of suspected abuse/neglect should not be corroborated. Because of penalty provisions for failure to report, and the lack of sanctions for reports that later prove erroneous, it is legally safer for professionals to file in error than to avoid filing when abuse exists and should have been recognized.

Legal decisions seem to indicate that if a professional encounters abuse, fails to report it, and the child is later reinjured, the failure to report may be defined as an "intervening cause" of the reinjury. The professional, and his/her institution, risk civil liability and a possible assessment of monetary damages. That is, even if a parent directly inflicted the injury, the law assumes that the parent would not have had an opportunity to reinjure had the professional fulfilled their legal responsibility.

In most states child abuse and neglect reports are kept in a central registry so as to facilitate case identification. Civil libertarians often object that access to reports is inadequately controlled; that undocumented and false information is recorded; and that the reports remain on file indefinitely, creating an unfair image of possibly reformed individuals. The reporting statutes have not been as successful in preventing abuse as their advocates had once predicted, for a variety of reasons. First, despite the compulsory phrasing of the obligation, many professionals are still reluctant to report. They feel that their clients or patients will no longer trust them; that intervention by the police or welfare bureaucracy might harm, rather than help, the family; that the manifestation of abuse or neglect is frequently too vague to justify official involvement. Second, some state departments of public welfare receive so many reports that they are unable to process them adequately. Many reports are not investigated or are only superficially examined, the more serious-appearing cases receiving priority. Third, reporting has become an end in itself, rather than a means of identifying and protecting abused children. State legislatures ritualistically passed reporting laws and then refused to appropriate sufficient resources to allow effective implementation. Without an adequately trained and sufficiently staffed protective services group, which can offer support and programs to troubled families, these statutes are a sham. Finally, poor people are more likely to be subjects of reports than are the affluent. Because of its lesser visibility, and the greater reluctance of professionals to stigmatize those with money and status, abuse by middle-class parents rarely triggers state involvement.

Various treatment approaches attempt to rehabilitate abusing parents. The provision of day-care services, for example, offers abusers a break from their child-rearing responsibilities. Parent-child centers teach parents appropriate disciplinary techniques and offer role models whom young and inexperienced parents can emulate. Homemakers may actually enter an abuser's home to instruct in child care; social workers and volunteers may visit periodically to discuss issues relating to child abuse such as stress, as well as methods of alleviation; individual or group therapy may also be helpful depending on the situation.

Many of these treatment approaches adopt a medical model, which perceives abusers as "sick" persons who require individual treatment of a supportive nature—from physicians, psychologists, and social workers. This treatment orientation, according to Englander (1997) is not always a sufficient intervention. One reason is that child abuse is so common it does not make sense to treat it from an individualistic perspective. A common denominator among abusers is that they have too much power over their children or at least feel as if they own their children. When some parents feel they are losing control of a situation or are feeling powerless, one guaranteed way to regain power is to abuse someone with less power. These feelings of entitlement should be re-examined among abusers.

Pagelow (1984) argues that supportive treatment should be available for abusers. Human services and child protection resources are frequently in short supply or of poor quality. If supportive treatment is unavailable or ineffective because of shortages in state funding, then such alternatives cannot be viewed as viable methods of control.

Even if certain treatment strategies are available, some abusing or neglectful parents are unable or unwilling to benefit from them. For example, most therapists and child protective workers agree that intervention with parents who physically abuse children is much more successful than that with parents who sexually abuse their children. This is because parents who physically abuse their children usually want to stop the behavior; they do not enjoy the abuse. Parents who sexually abuse their children usually enjoy doing so; they are receiving sexual gratification as well as feeling powerful (Finkelhor 1979).

According to Wallace, in the management of child abuse cases, any intervention often has detrimental consequences for the child. Professionals usually attempt to act in a way that is the least detrimental, knowing that no alternative allows the child's best interests to be fully realized. If children are removed from their home, they may blame themselves for breaking up the family. If the children are not removed, they are at risk for reinjury (Wallace 1996).

The Future of Child Abuse

Child abuse became an important social issue in the 1960s when concern for civil rights and the poor was ascendant. It is no coincidence that, in an era of protest and social change, the protection of victimized children emerged as a social issue. By the end of the 1960s, all fifty states had passed abuse-reporting statutes and had initiated treatment programs for children and families.

It seems that children who are abused are abused by caretakers who perceive children as subordinate to them or at least feel they should have control over their children. Researchers such as Pagelow, Gelles, and Herman have consistently argued that children need to have more power in families. Children who are abused usually come from traditional family settings in which parents have complete authority over them. Couple this authority with a privatized family institution and children have little if any voice concerning the prevention of abuse. One perspective is to have children become more active rather than being acted upon. The idea is to give them more authority and freedom within families. For many, this may seem radical. There is no question that children need structure and limits in their lives, but they also need to feel able to tell someone if they are being abused.

In the past few years, many supportive programs designed to prevent child abuse have been eliminated. In addition to this, there has been a resurgence in the belief of parental rights. Government intervention in families is seen as undesirable, except under the gravest of circumstances, and parental

---

A Closer Look

The False Allegations Movement

This movement charges that the incidence of some cases of sexual abuse has been greatly exaggerated or even fabricated. This sentiment is formally known as the False Memory Syndrome Foundation. R. A. Gardner (1991) contends that society has become preoccupied with sexual abuse to the point of obsession or hysteria. He goes so far to state that some parents suggest to their child that he or she has been sexually abused by a particular person or persons. A parent may be attempting to take revenge on an ex-partner, for example, within the context of custody disputes.

Gardner characterizes evaluators of sexual abuse allegations as being untrained, with little knowledge or experience. He questions the use of anatomically correct dolls, the assumption that children never lie, and whether indicators of sexual abuse are in fact reliable. He contends that not only do children lie, but they may seek notoriety and want to please certain adult authority figures.

Related to this is what is known as repressed memory syndrome. This was developed to describe those who have no memory of the abuse they suffered. Coughlin (1995) states that it is not uncommon for people who have been traumatized to repress the memories of an abusive experience. Remembering the abuse may be triggered by certain events like the death of the perpetrator or the birth of one's child. There is much controversy over the concept of repressed memories. Some critics, like Gardner, have blamed therapists for leading their clients in "remembering" experiences that never happened and then falsely accusing others of abusing them. The fact that memories return in vague images which may require some interpretation compounds the argument. Despite this, research tells us that survivors of child abuse do repress memories of abuse that are too painful to keep in their conscious minds.

authority is encouraged as a way of ending youth rebellion. There appear to be an unending number of cases of serious child abuse. Intervention strategies, as they exist, do not appear to be lessening the number of serious cases. Under these circumstances, child abuse and neglect may increase. (See "A Closer Look: The False Allegations Movement.")

Summary

Child abuse is usually defined as nonaccidental injury inflicted on a child by a parent or guardian. Neglect is defined as an omission or failure to perform a necessary parental function. It is often difficult to determine whether or not a child has been abused or neglected intentionally. Such factors as the seriousness, frequency, and deliberations of harm influence its classification. The same type of injury, however, may receive different labels (accident or abuse) depending upon such family characteristics as race and socioeconomic status.

It is impossible to determine the true incidence of child abuse and neglect. Official reports clearly underestimate the number of victimized children; in household surveys, family members are reluctant to reveal their violence.

Much of the literature on child abuse and neglect links them with poverty. The poor are more likely to be labeled abusers because of the visibility of their behavior and their higher likelihood of being reported. Being poor does not automatically mean abuse will occur. Professionals and service agencies are less likely to report abuse in middle- and upper-class families.

Children who are abused often develop certain characteristics, such as low self-esteem and having negative outlooks on life. Adult survivors of child abuse may experience depression, increased aggression, and in many cases may become substance abusers. It is often assumed that abused children may become abusers as adults but this transition is not mandatory. Intervention seems to play a key role in whether a child becomes an abuser as an adult.

There are several strategies employed to prevent child abuse. Family and parenting classes may decrease or prevent the likelihood of child abuse. Campaigns against child abuse can make people aware of child abuse which may influence politicians or lay people to get involved in preventing the abuse of children. Many feminists argue that family values should be re-examined in order to end child abuse.

Various treatment programs attempt to rehabilitate abusing parents. Parent-child centers teach appropriate disciplinary techniques and offer role models for young and inexperienced parents. Despite these programs, intervention does not seem to be lessening the number of child abuse cases.

Child abusers are not mentally ill. They are normal people who believe they have the right to abuse their children. Several researchers argue that the traditional family is set up to allow parents to abuse their children because parents are given too much power over their children and because the family is so privatized. People still generally believe that what happens in the family is private; that violence occurring in the family is not really violence. People tend not to get involved until children are seriously harmed or killed. The criminal justice system and social agencies appear to be lacking in effective responses.

Discussion Questions

1. Do you remember the first time you were left home alone? Do you remember how you felt? In general, how old do you think a child should be before being left home alone?

2. Should some people have their parental rights terminated permanently? Under what conditions do you think that would be justified?

3. Is spanking an effective form of discipline or is it a form of abuse?

4. Do you think child abuse is a private family matter or a criminal matter?

5. Why is it so difficult to define child abuse?

References

Barnett, Ola W., Cindy L. Miller-Perrin, and Robin Perrin, 1997. *Family Violence Across the Lifespan: An Introduction*. Thousand Oaks, California: Sage Publications.

Besharov, Douglas J. 1993. "Overreporting and Underreporting Are Twin Problems." In *Current Controversies on Family Violence*, edited by Richard Gelles and Donileen Loseke. Newbury Park, California: Sage Publications.

Best, Joel. 1990. *Threatened Children: Rhetoric and Concern About Child-Victims*. Chicago: University of Chicago Press.

Boston Herald. 1996. February 2.

Bourne, Richard. 1985. "Family Violence: Legal and Ethical Issues." In *Unhappy Families*, edited by Eli Newberger and Richard Bourne. Littleton, Massachusetts: PSG Publishing.

Cooper, D. M. 1993. *Child Abuse Revisited*, Milton Keynes: Open University Press.

Coughlin, Ellen K. 1995. "Recollections of Childhood Abuse." *Chronicle of Higher Education*, January 27, A8-A16.

Elliott, M. 1994. "Impaired Object Relations in Professional Women Molested as Children." *Psychotherapy* 31: 164–180.

Englander, Elizabeth. 1997 *Understanding Violence*. Mahwah, New Jersey: Lawrence Erlbaum Associates Publishers.

Ethier, L.S., C. Lacharite, and G. Couture. 1995. "Childhood Adversity, Parental Stress and Depression of Negligent Mothers." *Child Abuse and Neglect*, 19, pp. 619-632.

Finkelhor, David. 1979. *Sexually Victimized Children*. New York: Free Press.

———. 1993. "The Main Problem Is Still Underreporting, Not Overreporting." Pp. 273-87 in *Current Controversies on Family Violence*, edited by Richard J. Gelles and Donileen Loseke. Newbury Park, California: Sage Publications.

Garbarino, Janis Wilson, Edna Guttman, and James Seeley. 1986. *The Psychologically Battered Child*. San Francisco: Jossey-Bass.

Gardner, R. A. 1991. *Sex Abuse Hysteria: Salem Witch Trials Revisited*. Cresskil, New Jersey: Creative Therapeutics.

Gelles, Richard, and Donileen Loseke. 1993. *The Battered Woman and Shelters: The Social Construction of Wife Abuse*. Albany: State University of New York Press.

Herman, Judith. 1981. *Father-Daughter Incest*. Cambridge: Harvard University Press.

Hopper, Jim. 1997. "Child Abuse: Statistics, Research, and Resources." http://www.jmhopper.com.

Kendall-Tackett, K. A., M. L. Williams, and D. Finkelhor. 1993. "Impact of Sexual Abuse on Children: A Review and Synthesis of Recent Empirical Studies. *Psychological Bulletin*113: 164–180.

Levitt, C., and R. Alexander. 1994. "Abusive Head Trauma." In *Child Abuse: Medical Diagnosis and Management*, edited by Bob Reece. Philadelphia: Lea and Febiger.

Loseke, Donileen R. 1993 *The Battered Woman and Shelters: The Social Construction of Wife Abuse*. Albany: State University of New York Press.

Lung, C. T., and D. Daro. 1996. *Current Trends in Child Abuse Reporting of Fatalities: The Results of the 1995 Annual Fifty State Survey*. Chicago: National Committee to Prevent Child Abuse.

Massachusetts Department of Social Services. 1996. *Don't Shut Your Eyes to Child Abuse and Neglect*. Boston: Massachusetts Department of Social Services.

Milner, Judith. 1996. "Men's Resistance to Social Workers." In *Violence and Gender Relations: Theories and Interventions*, edited by Barbara Fawcett, B. Featherstone, J. Hearn, and Christine Toft. Newbury Park, California: Sage Publications.

Pagelow, Mildred. 1984. *Family Violence*. New York: Praeger.

Reder, P. S., Duncan, M. Gray. 1993. *Beyond Blame: Child Abuse Tragedies Revisited*. London: Routledge.

Showers, J. 1994. "Shaken Baby Syndrome." *Don't Shake the Baby Campaign News*, pp. 1-2.

Straus, Murray A., David B. Sugarman, and Jean Giles-Sims. 1997. "Spanking by Parents and Subsequent Antisocial Behavior of Children." In *Archives of Pediatrics and Adolescents Medicine*151: 761-767.

Tower, Cynthia Crasson. 1996. *Understanding Child Abuse and Neglect. Third edition*. Boston: Allyn and Bacon.

Valdés-Rodríguez, Alisa. 1998. "Shaken Baby Deaths Typically Involve Fathers." *Boston Globe*, September 22, B1, B8.

Valdés-Rodríguez, Alisa, and Paul Langner. 1998. "A Mother's Plea: Father Didn't Beat Their Baby." *Boston Globe*, September 19, A1, A16.

Wallace, Harvey. 1996. *Family Violence: Legal, Social and Medical Perspectives*. Boston: Allyn and Bacon.

Wodarski, J. S., J. M. Gaudin, and P. T. Howing. 1990. "Maltreatment and the School Age Child: Major Academic, Socioemotional, and Adaptive Outcomes. *Social Work* 35: 506-513.

Yllo, Kirsti A. 1993. "Through a Feminist Lens: Gender, Power, and Violence." Pp. 47–62 in *Current Controversies on Family Violence*, edited by Richard Gelles and Donileen Loseke. Thousand Oaks, California: Sage Publications.

Zuravin, S. J., and F. A. DiBlasio. 1992. "Child-Neglecting Adolescent Mothers: How Do They Differ From Their Non-maltreating Counterparts?" *Journal of Interpersonal Violence*7: 471-487.

Websites

http://www.aecf.org/kc1997/kc1997.htm

Annie E. Casey Foundation, 1997 Kids Count Data Online. Kids Count, a project of the Annie E. Casey Foundation, is a national and state-by-state effort to track the status of children in the United States. The Kids Count Data Online page presents you with a map. Click on your state to find out how children are doing there.

http://www.acf.dhhs.gov/programs/cb

Children's Bureau. The Children's Bureau, the oldest federal agency for children, is part of the United States Department of Health and Human Services' Administration for Children and Families. This website provides a wide variety of information on child abuse. It's a good place to look for anything you want to find.

http://www.jimhopper.com/

Jim Hopper's Website: Child Abuse: Statistics, Research, and Resources. Jim Hopper is a psychologist who has provided information on child abuse, information on child abuse substantiation rates, and pieces of his own work. Statistics are broken down by gender.

CHAPTER TEN

Battered Women

In the News: Nancy—A Battered Woman

It's the kind of story you can read about almost any day in a newspaper. Women are beaten, threatened, and often killed by their partners, who are usually males. Shelter Records make it possible to humanize the newspaper stories and gain a deeper understanding of what often happens to battered women. "Nancy," with her three children, came into the shelter with two broken cheekbones, a broken nose, and a broken jaw. She could not talk or eat. She wrote a note saying that her husband had beaten her up because the dishes were not done when he came home. She was terrified of him, as were the children. Having been married for eight years, she was a stay-at-home mother.

Nancy's husband was a police officer. This was the fourth time in two years that he had severely beaten her. Usually he beat her in areas on her body that no one could see. Nancy believed no one knew what was happening because her neighbors and her family never asked questions. This time, Nancy decided to leave him for good. She had left him before, but he had always convinced her to come back. She was terrified because he had threatened to kill her if she ever left him for a long period of time. Nancy had never reported the abuse to the police. She believed that his supervisors knew that "Jim" was abusive, but they did nothing. Jim never lost his job or was suspended because Nancy would not press charges. Everyone at the police department knew how violent Jim could be. Still, no one helped; no one took his gun.

Nancy believed that Jim would eventually kill her whether she left or not. She decided to leave. Nancy stayed in a shelter for six weeks. During that time, the shelter called the police department where Jim worked and filed a verbal complaint with his supervisor. They begged the department to force treatment on Jim. The supervisor claimed that Nancy had to make a formal report. Nancy was terrified at the prospect of going to Jim's department. She decided to get on with her life. Jim was allowed supervised visitation with the children and promised he would never hurt her again. Nancy eventually found an apartment and a waitress job. She was excited about starting over and the children were happy. Jim said he would leave her alone. Two days after Nancy moved out of the shelter, a neighbor found her shot five times in the chest. Jim lay beside her with one bullet to the head. Now their three children have no parents. The police claimed there was nothing they could have done (Shelter Records 1993).

Definition and Prevalence

The scenario above is all too common in this country. An estimated six million women are assaulted by their male partners each year—1.8 million are severely assaulted. A recent survey of divorced women in the Philadelphia area found that 70 percent had been abused by their spouses, with 19 percent citing the violence as their primary reason for leaving the marriage. 54 percent had suffered several incidents of violence and sustained injury from their ex-husbands. Even after separation, nearly one-half of the women experienced violence from their estranged husbands. Not surprisingly, 30 percent feared further violence during child support negotiations, and, of this subset, 66 percent did not receive regular child support payments (Kurz 1996; National Center for Victims of Crime 1997).

Ten women a day are murdered by their male partners in the United States. Every fifteen seconds a woman is physically battered by her male partner. Approximately 97 percent of the victims of domestic violence are women (Office of Women's Health Report 1997). One out of every two women will be involved in a violent relationship in her lifetime. This does not mean that one out of two men is abusive; only that batterers tend to go through many relationships without intervention to stop the violence (Mintz Levin Project 1994). At least 21 percent of all women who use emergency medical services are battered, which means that 1.5 million women seek medical treatment each year because of domestic violence (Office of Women's Health Report 1997). In spite of this level of battering, violence, and murder, social and legal responses to such violence are weak and inconsistent (Browne 1987; Yllo 1993).

Battering by their male partners and lack of shelters have driven some mothers and their children into homelessness. —*Photo: John A. Gagnon.*

Controversy exists over whether family violence should be called spouse abuse or women abuse, as women are more likely to be victimized than men and the word *spouse abuse* connote equal victimization. In discussing the impact of language, Dobash and Dobash (1979) note that,

> words like chairman have been replaced with words like chairperson. But just as such new terms can help overcome the mental images that contribute to inequality, they can also obscure some of the inequalities that continue to exist. The use of neutral, or egalitarian, terms like "marital violence" or "spousal assault" do exactly that. These terms imply that each marital partner is equally as likely to play the part of perpetrator or victim in a violent episode; that the frequency and severity of the physical force used by each is similar and that the social meanings and consequences of these acts are the same. None of this is true. In the case of marital violence,

it is the husband who is most likely to be the perpetrator and his wife the victim. (p. 267)

Violence is not exclusive to marriage, it happens to women living with and dating men. According to the Mintz Levin Project, 95 percent of perpetrators of family violence are male.

Ginny NiCarthy (1987) defines **battering** or **abuse** as:

> Force used by a male against a female to coerce, demean, punish, release tension or to demonstrate power. A battered woman is one who has been subject to battering on more than one occasion. A battered woman can be physically, emotionally and sexually assaulted by her partner. Battering occurs within and outside of marriage. Battering is not limited to any particular ethnic, racial, class or religious group. (p. 12)

Abuse against women comes in three main forms: physical, sexual, and emotional. Physical abuse may include pushing, shoving, hitting, arm twisting, biting, and choking. Sexual abuse may include making a woman perform sexual acts against her will, physically attacking the sexual parts of her body, and treating her like a sex object. Emotional abuse may include demeaning her and making her feel bad about herself, calling her names, and making her think she's crazy.

A Closer Look

A Battered Woman

Tracey was so happy when she married Rick. He seemed to be everything she wanted. He was kind and wanted to take care of her. She worked part-time as a receptionist at a real estate office. Rick did not want her to work full-time. He constantly reminded her that he was the breadwinner as the man should be. At first, Tracey thought this was fine. The first sign of abuse came when Tracey worked overtime at her job. Rick was furious. He told Tracey that he would make the money in their family and she was never to work overtime again. If she did, she would have to quit her job. Tracey was shocked at his behavior but let it pass.

The first time Tracey was physically abused occurred in the presence of her mother. Rick came home from work and began yelling at Tracey for planning a career. Apparently Tracey's boss ran into Rick and told him that Tracey would make a great real estate agent. Rick took this to mean she was planning to do so. He smashed Tracey in the jaw, breaking it instantly. He would have continued to beat her had her mother not intervened. Tracey was taken to the emergency room by Rick and had her jaw wired. No one at the hospital asked any questions. That night Rick apologized profusely and said it would never happen again, but he forced her to quit her job. Tracey wanted to believe he would never hit her again. She thought by staying home full-time, Rick would be happier.

Several weeks later Rick beat her again, this time breaking several ribs. He said she spent too much time on the phone. He begged her to forgive him and even cried. Tracey felt he must be sorry if he cried and she forgave him. Eventually Rick isolated Tracey from her family and friends. He totally controlled her. Tracey felt she had no way out. Once she told her mother about Rick's behavior and her mother told her to work it out, that her place was with her husband. Tracey began to believe she deserved the abuse. She became pregnant and thought everything would now be fine. She loved to talk about her pregnancy and the upcoming birth. She thought she and Rick would make great parents. One day, during her fourth month of pregnancy Rick punched her in the stomach. He said he was sick of hearing about the baby. The next day she miscarried. Rick said he was glad. He no longer said he was sorry. Tracey left him shortly after and eventually divorced him. She has been in therapy ever since (Shelter Records 1993).

Levels of Causation

Individual

Most theories that focus on individual explanations of violence against women focus on the batterer. In other words, theorists focus on why a particular man batters his partner. Psychiatry offers a multitude of explanations. Batterers are presented as weak, insecure, inadequate, or dependent. They suffer from poor impulse control, poorly developed egos, and deprived childhoods. These males may abuse because they are unable to express their feelings. What these explanations fail to address is that males who abuse, abuse a specific target—women. Instead of asking why a man batters, why not ask why he batters this specific target? If a male who batters suffers from poor impulse control, one would expect that he would strike out at anyone or anything. But he does not. In addition, many batterers are very careful about where they batter their female partners. They usually do so in the privacy of their own homes, and they carefully select which area of a woman's body to abuse.

Psychological explanations of abuse seem inadequate. For example, many psychological theories postulate that stress causes battering. Under enormous stress, most men do not batter. In addition, insecure women under stress do not frequently beat up men. Stress may influence a man's decision to batter, but the concept of stress must be placed in a context. The Emerge Collective states that stress might be defined as threats to the ego and the inability to feel in control of one's life. But stress does not cause abuse; males choose to deal with stress in specific ways. The priority again seems to be why abuse is directed at women, not why each individual man abuses.

Individual-level explanations are unable to explain which psychological traits or which abnormal personality traits are directly associated with violence, especially since only a very small proportion of mentally ill persons are violent (Burgess and Draper 1989). Another popular theme in the explanation of violence against women focuses on the correlation between substance abuse and battering. The primary suggestion is that alcohol and drugs act as disinhibitors, thereby releasing violent tendencies within an individual. Again, there is little scientific evidence to support this premise (see "A Closer Look: Substance Abuse and Domestic Violence.")

Cultural

There is so much violence against women in the home, and in America generally, that one might assume that males are socialized to be violent and abusive toward females. Dobash and Dobash (1979) argue that gender roles are imperative to consider when evaluating violence by males against their female partners. They suggest that in American culture a healthy mature male is considered to be very aggressive, dominant, self-confident, independent, active, competitive, and decisive; to know the ways of the world; not to be easily influenced or excitable in minor crisis, and to be able to hide his emotions (Dobash and Dobash 1979). Imagine what it's like for a male to try to live up to that image. This definition of masculinity is fostered directly and indirectly by all social institutions. Parents are proud when their male toddler holds back his tears and picks himself up from a fall. Males are rewarded for

Substance Abuse and Domestic Violence

Do drug and alcohol abuse cause violence? Many believe it does. Sociologist Richard Gelles (1993) a leading domestic violence researcher, argues that alcohol and other drugs are associated with violence but are not its cause.

Alcohol and drug use have long been associated with abuse. Social workers in the 1800s believed that alcohol use was the cause of child maltreatment. The Prohibition movement of the 1920s in the U.S. was partially based on the assumption that drinking led to the abuse of children.

The key to the argument that alcohol causes violent behavior is the proposition that alcohol acts as a disinhibitor to release violent tendencies. Alcohol is viewed by many as a "superego solvent" that reduces inhibitions and allows violent behavior to emerge or elicits violent behavior. Gelles argues that there is little scientific evidence to support the theory that alcohol and drugs directly produce violent behavior. Evidence from cross-cultural studies, lab studies, and blood tests of men arrested for abusing women all indicate that although alcohol and drug use may be associated with intimate violence, they are not primary causes of violence (Gelles 1993).

The best evidence against a causal theory comes from cross-cultural studies of drinking behavior. "If the pharmacological properties of alcohol are the direct causes of behavior after drinking, then there would be very little variation in drinking behavior across cultures" (Gelles 1993:184). MacAndrew and Edgerton (1969) found that drinking behavior varies from culture to culture. In some cultures, individuals drink and become passive; in other cultures individuals drink and become aggressive. The difference in drinking behavior appears to be related to what people in each society believe about alcohol. In U.S. society, the belief is widespread that alcohol and drugs release violent tendencies when people drink or when they are drunk. Because of this belief, people are given a "time-out" from the normal rules of social behavior. Violence in the family may be rationalized when alcohol and drugs are present. So if abusers want to avoid being responsible for their violence, they can either drink before they are violent or at least say they are drunk (Gelles 1993; MacAndrew and Edgerton 1969).

A. R. Lang and his colleagues tested these cross-cultural findings. If drinking behavior is learned, researchers should be able to manipulate a situation to produce "drunken behavior" even if the people involved are not actually drinking alcohol. Lang selected vodka as the alcoholic beverage because taste could not be differentiated from uncarbonated tonic water. College students were randomly assigned to four groups: 2 groups received tonic water and 2 groups received tonic water and vodka. One group receiving tonic water and one group receiving tonic water and vodka were told what they were drinking. The other two groups were misled. The tonic water only drinkers believed they were drinking tonic water and vodka and the vodka and tonic drinkers believed they were only drinking tonic water (Lang, et al. 1975).

The most aggressive subjects turned out to be those who thought they were drinking, regardless of whether their glasses actually contained alcohol. The expectancy of alcohol determined how the subjects behaved when they were drinking or believed that they were drinking (Lang, et al. 1975).

their bravery and physical toughness and are punished if they act like "sissies" or "like a girl." Boys may be given a general message not to fight, but they are also taught as a matter of pride, never to let anyone get away with hitting them. Some males, when they cannot perform up to their standards of masculinity, may lash out verbally or physically, blaming whoever is at hand. The unacceptable feelings of helplessness, weakness, dependency, or incompetence are buried in a safe place. Angela Browne (1987) states that women are less powerful than men. In order for some men to feel masculine, they must be able to control someone or have more power than someone. Abusing women ensures this power.

Traditional female characteristics may not cause abuse of women but may make particular women vulnerable to abuse or lessen their chances of escaping. Such characteristics include being passive, emotional, dependent and indecisive. Women who find themselves in an abusive relationship may not feel confident enough to leave or believe they are too dependent on their male partner to leave. Women are traditionally socialized in American society to take care of people so leaving an abuser may be perceived as uncaring to them and their families.

Cultural support for male-to-female violence exists in the United States. The majority of men do not repeatedly and severely commit violent acts toward women. However, for those who do, this violence benefits all men. Fear of violence tends to keep a woman "in her place" (Barnette and LaViolette 1993). Murray Straus (1976) identified a number of cultural norms that not only permit but encourage male-to-female violence. Although his research is dated, these norms seem relevant today. Some of the norms are: (1) greater authority of men in our culture; (2) male aggressiveness, that is, the notion that aggression positively correlates to maleness and that aggression is not only an acceptable tool for a man but also a way to demonstrate male identity; (3) wife/mother role as a preferred status for women; and (4) male domination and orientation of the criminal justice system, which provides little legal relief for battered women.

Structural

There are two major streams of sociological work on battered women or **domestic violence**. One is generally referred to as the family violence perspective and the other as the feminist perspective. Work in the **family violence** perspective grew out of family scholars' interest in a variety of family conflict issues and is generally traced to the early work of Straus and Gelles. These two researchers developed a research agenda based on the use of interviews to elicit information regarding family violence from large random samples of the adult population of the United States, conducting national surveys in 1975 and 1985. Methodologically, work in this tradition has relied primarily on quantitative analysis of responses to survey questions. Theoretically, the focus has been largely on commonalities among the various forms of family violence (Johnson 1995). A consistent contention by Straus has been that women are as violent as their male partners (see "A Closer Look: Battered Husband Syndrome.")

In contrast, research from the **feminist perspective** began with a narrower focus on violence against women by their male partners. Methodologically, feminists have relied heavily upon data collected from battered women, especially those who have come in contact with law enforcement agencies, hospitals, or shelters. Theoretically, the emphasis has been upon historical traditions of the patriarchal family, contemporary constructions of masculinity and femininity, and structural constraints that make escape difficult for women who are systematically beaten (Johnson 1995).

Patriarchal terrorism has been a focus of the women's movement and of researchers working from a feminist perspective. Patriarchal terrorism, a product of patriarchal traditions of men's rights to control "their" women, is a

Battered Husband Syndrome

Demie Kurz argues that "battered husband syndrome" does not exist. She and other feminist researchers, support their arguments with official crime statistics, data from the criminal justice system and hospitals, interviews with abusers and abused, and historical evidence. Data from hospitals especially indicate that women are overwhelmingly injured by men as opposed to men injured by women. The evidence compels these researchers to reject the concept of "spouse abuse" (Kurz 1993).

Kurz argues that family researchers, such as Murray Straus, who contend that there exists a battered husband syndrome fail to define abuse and violence adequately. In addition, they do not discriminate among different types of violence. For example, one cannot argue that a woman's bite is equal to a man's kick or punch. Self-defense on the part of a woman should not be perceived as violence or abuse. Feminists argue that men use more serious violence than women, and family researchers minimize it and also dismiss sexual and psychological abuse (Kurz 1993).

In Kurz's view, family researchers ignore gender and power, and fail to acknowledge male dominance. Feminists contend that sexism is more than a factor in domestic violence, it is a fundamental organizing principle of society. According to them, family researchers ignore the influence of gender on marriage and heterosexual relationships, seeing power as gender neutral by assuming women have equal power to men. Social scientific data consistently refute the idea that women have equal power to men (Kurz 1993).

form of terroristic control of females by their male partners that involves the systematic use not only of violence but also of economic subordination, threats, isolation and other such tactics (Johnson 1995).

Susan Schechter (1982) argues that men batter women because of a historically created gender hierarchy in which men dominate women. This hierarchy is reinforced and maintained by all social institutions. For example, the church and government assume the male to be the authoritative and financial head of the household; in primary readers, males are pictured as adventurous, strong and brave; high school history textbooks and television depict males as violent and powerful. Only by studying social and historical relationships within the family can we reveal the meaning and purpose behind battering in this country.

The priority is to understand why abuse is directed at women, not why each individual man abuses. Individual men who abuse have varied personalities. Their families' histories, intimacy problems, stress levels, and alcohol intake will affect their behavior. In individual cases, such factors may contribute to abuse or heighten the likelihood of its occurrence, but they do not explain the consistent target—women. We need to discover what social conditions produce this target generation after generation (Schechter 1982).

The historical context within which battering has developed is that of male domination within and outside the family. Domination describes a social structure in which certain groups of people can determine and limit the spheres of activity of other groups. The power that a dominating group exercises carries with it the threat or the use of force to coerce compliance. Historically, male domination of females was supported by all social institutions.

Christianity supported male-headed marriages and the state codified these relations into the law. This law prevailed through the seventeenth, eighteenth, and nineteenth centuries. Males were perceived as heads of families to be obeyed by their wives and children. Women and children were considered property of their husbands and fathers (Schechter 1982).

Although not present in legal statutes in America, the husband's right to chastise his wife was upheld in the Supreme Court of Mississippi in 1824. The court ruled that a husband should be able to chastise his wife without being subject to persecution, which would supposedly shame all parties. In the United States, during this time (nineteenth century), judges would only imprison the most violent men and not until 1871 was wife beating actually declared illegal in two states, Massachusetts and Alabama. Although wife-beating was considered illegal, it persisted. Because of the privatized family and women's secondary status in it, there was little a woman could do to escape violence (Schechter 1982).

Kersti Yllo (1993) argues that tradition is powerful especially with regard to gender roles. Males are still socialized to believe they at least should have more social, economic and political power than females. All males learn to dominate females, but only some males batter females. Battering is only one of the ways in which some males express their socially structured right to control. Males are not necessarily consciously aware of their need to dominate. Rather, they are socialized to feel uncomfortable when not in control, and some turn to violence as a response to this. This behavior is taught in direct and indirect ways by all social institutions. The main message from all institutions is that males should be leaders, they should be in control. This might explain why there has never been a female pope or president of the United States or why most women are expected to take their husbands' names upon marriage (Yllo 1993).

Yllo further argues that violence against women cannot be adequately understood unless gender and power are taken into account. Violence against women grows out of inequality within marriage and other intimate relations that are modeled on marriage. Violence is a tactic of male control. This conceptualization of violence grew out of the day-to-day work of battered women/activists who struggled to make sense of the victimization they saw (Yllo 1993).

James Messerschmidt (1993) spells this out in his argument that violence is available as a resource for the making of gender, and specifically as a strategy for the making of masculinity, or at least particular forms of masculinity. Miedzian also focuses on the socialization of males into violent behavior and attempts to see the construction of masculinity within broader society as intimately interconnected with violence (Miedzian 1992). In this context of socialization, men's violence to women is in large part a development of dominant-submissive power relations that exist in normal family life. Men may resort to violence when men's power and privilege are challenged, and other strategies have failed. Research by Jeff Hearn (1996) documented repeated justifications for violence against women from their male partners. For example, men's violence to women developed in association with feelings of threat when those women did not do what the men expected, in terms of child care, housework, paid work, and sexuality.

Consequences

Traditional gender roles seem to produce and reinforce violence against women in the home, and they effectively prevent many battered women from escaping violence. Many people become frustrated with women who stay with their abusers. Asking why she stays assumes that the abuse will end if she leaves. In fact, the times when a battered woman leaves her abuser or attempts to leave her abuser are the most dangerous for her. This is the time when she is most likely to be killed. Battered women know this, so they may not attempt to leave (Browne 1987). Society does not provide sufficient support for women to leave their abusers. People want women to leave their batterers but also want families to stay together.

Traditional gender roles encourage women to remain in abusive relationships. Females are socialized to nurture and care for their family members. Lenore Walker states that many battered women believe they can change their abuser. Many may blame themselves for the abuse, believing that if they are better wives, housekeepers, or mothers, the abuse will end. If there are children involved, it is even harder to leave because many women think children need their fathers (Walker 1993).

Many battered women may honestly believe that their partners really want to change. Research, however, has consistently shown that the longer a battered woman stays with her partner, the more danger she is in (Browne 1987). Table 10-1 illustrates the ways in which different types of abuse increase in severity.

Table 10-1 Abuse Can Be Physical, Sexual, and Emotional and Increases in Severity

Physical	Sexual	Emotional
slapping	criticizing sexually	ridiculing
hitting	demanding sex	isolating from family and friends
breaking bones	using objects during sex	controlling money
permanent injuries	sex after abuse	threatening abuse
using weapons	rape	abusing pets
death	sexual mutilation	abusing children

Some battered women are trapped by religious beliefs, such as "till death do us part." These women believe in the sanctity of marriage and may even be convinced by clergy to stand by their men. Considering traditional gender roles, leaving is not an option. A woman may be convinced that she can change her husband or boyfriend, or should at least stand by him "for better or for worse."

According to Schechter, women of all classes who do not work for a wage and whose household labor is unpaid, find themselves in particularly vulnerable and needy positions when battered. These women are terrified that they will not survive without their husband's salary. Women who do work for a wage are not necessarily free of their need for financial support. These women may have more resources and are less dependent than their partners, but lower wages still increase the male's power over the woman. If women have children, they have a more difficult time surviving (Schechter 1982).

Besides inadequate financial support, battered women may have no emotional support to leave their abusers. Their families and friends may not want to be involved or may believe the woman's place is with her male partner. Women may feel trapped in an abusive relationship if they believe they have no options. Walker (1993) points to a "cycle of violence" experienced by battered women as producing obstacles for escape. When a woman is in a battering relationship, there usually develops a pattern called the cycle of violence. This cycle is broken down into three phases: tension-building, battering, and the hearts-and-flowers phase.

In the tension-building phase, the woman senses that the batterer is agitated with someone or something. She believes abuse will be forthcoming and she attempts to prevent it. Some of the indications of this tension-building phase are illness, jealousy, drinking, name-calling, friction, and hostility. Usually, there is nothing she can do to prevent abuse and thus the second phase occurs. The woman is abused physically, sexually, or emotionally. The abuse can last several minutes or several hours. The final phase involves apologies. The batterer is sorry for his behavior and swears never to do it again. He may act in loving and compassionate ways to the victim or he may even blame his partner for provoking the abuse. She believes he will never do it again and life goes on. The problem is that he will abuse her again, and over time the woman becomes trapped by his apologies. Eventually, the loving phase will disappear. By this time, the woman has exhausted all avenues of support, especially from family and friends. She feels she has no place to go and remains with him.

The "apology" stage serves to convince the battered woman to remain with her partner. Initially, she believes that he will never harm her again. Abuse of women by their partners is not usually an isolated event. Abuse may change forms from physical to emotional, but the fact remains that she will more than likely experience repeated incidents of abuse. The longer a woman remains with her batterer, the more likely the abuse will increase in frequency and severity. The cycle of abuse continues and in many cases the "apology" stage disappears.

There are many more not so obvious consequences of abuse for women and their children. Violence against women during the last 20 years has been acknowledged as being a rapidly growing health concern in America's communities. More than 1 million women seek medical assistance each year for injuries caused by battering. Violence against women by their male partners is the leading cause of injury to women between the ages of 15-44. Violence against women is the leading cause of low-birthweight babies, making them highly susceptible to birth defects. The March of Dimes found that violence against women is the leading cause of birth defects—more than all other medical causes combined. A disturbingly high number of pregnant women are battered: of every 1,000 pregnant women, 154 are assaulted by their partner during the first four months of pregnancy. In the United States, we spend 2.5 billion dollars annually to keep low-birthweight babies alive during their first year of life. Battered women are also twice as likely to miscarry than women in healthy relationships (Mintz Levin Project 1994).

During the 1970s, the Battered Women's Movement drew attention to the extent of violence against women by their male partners and the need for more resources for battered women. —*Photo: The Denver Post.*

Figure 10-1   General Information About Domestic Violence

- 6 in every 10 women who are victims of homicide are murdered by someone they know: husband, ex-husband, boyfriend, ex-boyfriend.

- Children are involved in 60 percent of domestic violence cases.

- More than three million children witness violence in their homes.

- Up to 50 percent of all homeless women and children in this country are fleeing violence in their homes.

- More than 53 percent of male abusers abuse their children.

- Victims and abusers are found in every social and economic class, race, and religious group.

Source: National Center for Victims of Crime. 1977. "Domestic Violence Statistics." http://www.nvc.org/stats/dosmestic.htm

The United States Public Health Service treats violence as a health issue and consequently uses injuries, both fatal and nonfatal, physical and psychological, to quantify the impact of violence. For example, children who witness violence at home display emotional and behavioral disturbances as diverse as withdrawal, low self-esteem, nightmares, self-blame, and aggression against peers, family members, and property (Newton Domestic Violence Action Committee 1996).

There are other costs associated with violence against women by their male partners. A Bureau of National Affairs report found that the cost of domestic violence to U.S. companies is between 3 and 5 billion dollars annually from lost work time, increased health-care costs, high turnover rates, and lower productivity. Priorities concerning violence in this country are disturbing. The city of Boston spends more money on its zoo than the entire state of Massachusetts spends on all shelters for battered women and children (Mintz Levin Project 1994).

Ten women a day are murdered by their male partners. Another consequence, although not as prevalent, is batterers killed by their female partners. Women comprise only about 12 percent of homicide perpetrators in the United States. The majority of these women kill batterers in self-defense (Browne 1987). Women who are arrested for murder are usually charged with first degree murder but are rarely convicted of such a serious offense. Some researchers of family violence argue that many battered women end up killing their partners because there was insufficient intervention by the criminal justice system (Hilton 1993; Browne 1987; Buzawa and Buzawa 1996). Researchers in this field also argue that when a battered woman kills her partner, she usually does so in self-defense and that the criminal justice system should recognize this defense. In the past, this defense was not accepted because when battered women fought back, it did not appear that many were in lethal danger. Self-defense as a legal defense was permitted only when it was believed that reasonable people would have thought themselves in imminent mortal danger (Kurz 1993).

Battered women who kill their abusers have a history of abuse with their partners. Many times the woman is threatened with abuse or death. Often she expects abuse and comes to know its predictors. In the past, most courts believed that anyone using the self-defense strategy had to be in immediate danger. This criterion would not apply to battered women who might kill their abusers while they sleep. However, in their minds they believe their lives are in lethal danger. Based on this, the **battered woman syndrome** has been used to defend women who fight back and kill their abusers. Lenore Walker coined the term *battered woman syndrome* to refer to a series of characteristics common to women who are abused, psychologically and physically, over a period of time by a dominant male figure in their lives. The battered woman syndrome is composed of three stages which are cyclical. These stages were described earlier in this chapter as the cycle of violence. The battered woman's syndrome is a psychological condition where the victims believe, based on past experiences, that the only way out of the situation is to kill their partners (Browne 1987).

In most states, courts permit testimony on the battered woman syndrome. This does not guarantee that a battered woman's experiences will be validated. As it stands, it is the only allowance the legal system provides for women's unique circumstances.

Stalking has become a consequence of experiencing a battering relationship for many women. Stalking has become so serious that all 50 states have passed antistalking laws that are gender neutral. Stalking generally refers to harassing or threatening behavior that an individual engages in repeatedly such as following a person or making harassing phone calls (Tjaden and Thoennes 1998). Although stalking laws are gender neutral, most victims of stalking are female. One out of every 12 U.S. women have been stalked at some time in their lives. Both men and women who are stalked are usually stalked by men who they know.

When women are stalked by their partners, it usually occurs after the woman attempts to leave the relationship. The National Violence Against Women Survey of 1998 reported that 23 percent of women who had been stalked by their partners stated that the stalking occurred before the relationship ended, 43 percent stated it occurred after the relationship ended, and 36 percent stated it occurred before and after the relationship ended.

Interventions

Because of sexism or ignorance of violence against women, social institutions often intervene in ways that are more harmful than helpful to the abused. The police, the courts and the legal system, and the social welfare system are the most common avenues of help available to battered women.

The attitudes and actions of the police are crucial if victims are to receive protection. According to Zoe Hilton (1993), the police do not consistently intervene in matters of battered women. Although many department policies indicate a strong stance against domestic violence, the policies are not enforced. In other words, police officer behavior goes largely unchecked because the police believe that violence against women is a private matter. Nonintervention by law enforcement or inconsistent arrests of abusers reinforces abuse against women and encourages the women's hopelessness and continued victimization.

Several factors help to explain inconsistent police response to battered women. First, police officers are usually males who may identify with the male perpetrator and accept the view that the matter is private or that males control females. Police officers may even be batterers themselves. This situation is changing as more women become police officers and as male officers receive more education about the nature of violence against women. Second, the police are unable to act because of legal constraints. In some states, for example, simple assault is a misdemeanor. Police may arrest only if a crime occurred in their presence or if it led to a breach of the peace. These issues—the peace of the community, use of a deadly weapon, degree of injury—take precedence over the seriousness of the assault in personal terms.

Critics of police performance contend that the police perceive a beating as simple assault when it really is aggravated assault or assault with a deadly weapon, offenses that can trigger police arrest if "probable cause" exists, with no legal requirement of police presence or breach of the peace. A fist or a foot is often a deadly weapon, making an attack a felony rather than a less serious misdemeanor. Criminal behavior requires interpretation and police usually define violence against women by their male partners in less serious terms.

Hilton (1993) demonstrates how the criminal justice system has failed battered women and even lends support to abuse against women. This failure can be seen in police policies regarding domestic violence where arrest of batterers is not consistent, and in courts where judges routinely deny protection to battered women or extend mild sentences to men who batter women. In 1984, the U.S. Attorney General's Task Force on Family Violence recommended that family violence be treated as "a criminal activity." This recommendation drew on testimony from social science experts, medical and social service professionals, battered women's advocates, and battered women (Hilton 1993). Despite this, abuse against women is still largely treated as a private or family matter. Batterers are not consistently arrested or convicted of abuse or for violating protective orders.

There are two types of courts that might help battered women: civil and criminal. Both courts have the power to dispense restraining orders (barring an abuser from interfering with his partner's freedom), custody orders (giving her alone the right to make decisions about the children), and monetary awards (for any pain or suffering or for compensation of medical and other expenses).

These courts, unfortunately, do not have sessions at night or on weekends when abuse is more likely to occur. In some states, however, emergency restraining orders can be granted via police officers responding to the abuse. The officer simply has to contact the judge on call and request an emergency restraining order. The order is valid throughout the weekend or the night in question. The woman must then appear in court to receive a permanent order. One of the biggest issues that battered women and their advocates have is that restraining orders are not consistently granted or enforced. Batterers commonly violate restraining orders with minimal consequences even though the act of violating is against the law in most states (Hilton 1993).

Brown (1987) argues that the criminal justice system does not treat violence against women in the home as a crime in a consistent manner. Police officers routinely avoid arrest or discourage a battered woman from pressing charges. Judges routinely refuse to grant restraining orders to battered women or give minimal sentences to batterers who violate restraining orders and batter their female partners and their children. In addition, judges continue to grant visitation to abusive men who say they want to see their children only in order to remain in contact with their mother. These judges fail to consider that although the batterer may not be directly abusing his children, he is abusing their mother, which should be perceived as unacceptable. If he abuses her in front of the children, they are being seriously emotionally abused. The problem seems to be that criminal justice officials continue to treat this type of violence as a family matter in many ways (see "A Closer Look: Outlawing Violence Against Women Website.")

Once initiated in a relationship, battering is very difficult to stop. Usually male perpetrators are poor candidates for therapy, refusing to acknowledge

---

A Closer Look

Outlawing Violence Against Women Website

Legislation against domestic violence has been enacted in 44 countries around the world. The UNICEF, Progress of Nations 1997 website includes important information on the progress and disparity in women's positions around the world. This web page, "Outlawing violence against women: A first step," located at http://www.unicef.org/pon97/p48a.htm, includes lists of countries that have enacted legislation against domestic violence, marital rape, sexual harassment, and female genital mutilation. Check out which countries have enacted legislation against domestic violence and marital rape versus those that have not. You will see that some laws are very clear. For example, Ecuador's 1995 law against domestic violence clearly prohibits physical and mental assaults. Other laws are more vague: New Zealand has enacted family violence legislation without reference to women or girls. From this web page you can move around to others related to violence against women and girls (UNICEF 1997).

---

and having no desire to change their abusive behavior. Most are convinced of their right to reprimand and blame their female partners for the abuse. This sense of entitlement has a long history. One suggestion by David Adams

(1991) is for people to become educated about violence and its consequences. It is very difficult to predict who may become a battered woman since any woman is a potential victim of violence. However, there are predictors commonly used to determine if a male is potentially violent (see "A Closer Look: Predictors of Violence.")

Many experts, indeed, are not happy with the traditional therapeutic interventions for battered women. First, if the therapist is male, the therapeutic

---

A Closer Look

Predictors of Violence

According to the National Coalition Against Domestic Violence, there are signs that might serve as clues to potential abuse. The following are questions to ponder regarding potential abusers:

1. Did he grow up in a violent home? Boys have a higher likelihood of becoming abusers if they witnessed abuse in their home or if they have been abused.
2. Does he use force or violence to "solve" his problems? Males who have a criminal record for violence, who get into fights, and who like to act tough are likely to act in the same way with their female partners.
3. Does he abuse alcohol and other drugs? There is a strong association between violence and problems with drugs and alcohol. Be alert to these problems, especially if he refuses to get help.
4. Does he think poorly of himself? He may guard his masculinity by acting tough.
5. Does he have strong traditional ideas about what men and women should be? Traditional males often believe that they should control women.
6. Is he jealous? He could be jealous of male friends and even jealous of his partner's girlfriends and family. Be careful especially if he wants to know his partner's whereabouts at all times, what she is doing and with whom.
7. Does he play with guns, knives, or other lethal weapons? Be especially careful if he threatens to hurt someone. Take it seriously.
8. Does he expect his partner to follow his orders and advice? If he gets angry when someone does not take his advice or fulfill his wishes, be wary.
9. Does he go through extreme highs and lows as though he is almost two different people? He may be extremely kind one time and extremely cruel at another time.
10. Does his partner fear him when he gets angry? If she fears him, he may have hurt her or threatened to do so.
11. Does he treat his partner roughly? If he continues to rough up his female partner against her wishes, this is abuse. It can only get worse. (National Coalition Against Domestic Violence 1995)

---

relationship continues the dominance-submission pattern of most male-female interactions. Second, male therapists are unlikely to understand the woman's predicament. They often argue, for example, that the victim can change her husband's behavior by changing her own. She should adjust to her husband's notion of what it means to be male and female. This stance only continues to victimize the victim (Schechter 1982).

Sometimes social service professionals emphasize the importance of family unity—"staying together for the sake of the children"—to the detriment of the woman and her physical safety. This overriding concern for the children may indeed reflect a hierarchy of worth within the family, with women being unimportant unless their problems affect others.

The disenchantment with traditional therapy and social work has led to the establishment of self-help groups. The emphasis in such groups is on sisterhood and on women helping women (and with men working with other men to raise their consciousness). Most groups believe it is important for the battered woman to separate from the abuser, with little attention given to keeping the family together.

Many of these support groups are located in shelters for battered women. There are 1,200 such shelters across the United States and many more are needed. Battered women and their children are consistently turned away because of lack of space. In the United States, a person is fined ten thousand dollars for killing a bald eagle and may even serve jail time. When a male batters a female, he is given far less punishment (Barnes and Eng 1993). Support groups and refuges appear to be the most successful approach to the prevention and treatment of violence against women in the home. Friends and neighbors ignore or excuse the violence; physicians often limit assistance to the mending of bones; social workers define the problem as a failure to communicate; and police and court officials fail to invoke official sanctions. In other words, violence is meted out by one man but the responsibility for its continuance is shared (Dobash and Dobash 1979).

One interesting and relatively new approach to preventing abuse against women involves the corporate community. Women who are abused cannot leave the effects of abuse at home. Many effects of abuse show up at work in lost productivity, stress, increased health care costs, sick leave, and high turnover rates. Workplace violence may even exist for some women whose batterers follow them to work.

Many corporations have made domestic violence a priority and have funded efforts to prevent abuse. Polaroid Corporation holds seminars to illustrate how to photograph injuries resulting from domestic violence for court records (Family Violence Prevention Fund 1998). Corporations can make a significant impact in preventing abuse by educating the public about its effects. Violence against women should not be a private issue.

The Future of Battered Women

The concern with battered women began with women's liberation. As long as feminists protest male domination and violence, organizations will strive to maintain public interest in these issues.

As with child abuse, however, the availability of governmental funds for shelters and other prevention or treatment programs will probably decrease. Those who deny the realities of female victimization will attempt to impose strict limits on state intervention in family life. Ten women a day die in the United States at the hands of their male partners and still many people consider these deaths private matters. In the short run, violence against females by males will probably increase. As women gain more independence, traditional males will feel threatened and strike out violently. Males whose authority is threatened may use force to keep women "in their place."

Susan Schechter (1982) asks us to imagine for a moment conditions under which males would not abuse females. Only political struggle would create such a possibility and people would have to be willing to re-evaluate traditional gender roles. Material preconditions must also exist to end violence against women. These conditions—shelters, adequate jobs, incomes, health care, and affordable housing and child care—are essential to allow women independence from violent men and to enable all people to live decently.

Feminists argue that violence against women is rooted in patriarchy and male domination. Males are socialized to dominate females and females are socialized to be submissive to males. These gender roles are reinforced by all social institutions. Yllo (1993) argues that one way to prevent future violence against women is to restructure gender role socialization. Since primary socialization begins in the family, gender role changes should begin here. She suggests that parents stop socializing males to believe they are more valued and more powerful than females. Parents should promote gender equality not gender inequality. Males abuse because they want to feel in control, feel powerful. If males were not socialized to need to feel this way, violence against women would cease.

Dobash and Dobash (1992) argue that other social institutions (religion, the legal system, politics, education, the economy) must recognize that males and females should be treated equally. These institutions consistently reinforce the gender inequality that causes women to be abused by men when the women show independence or assume equality. The researchers argue that the criminal justice system must consistently enforce policies designed to prevent abuse against women as well as enforcing prosecution and conviction of male perpetrators.

Education is crucial in ending violence against women. Children should be educated in school and at home that violence is not an appropriate answer to conflicts. This education should begin at a young age, especially before dating age as dating violence is also on the rise. Males are learning when very young to abuse their female partners when they feel threatened and not in control (Browne 1987).

Angela Browne further argues that more funding must be appropriated for shelters for battered women. These women and their children need protection from violent men. This must be taken seriously. It seems that the government never reacts unless women are murdered. Women are being murdered every day by violent men. This should be evidence enough that women need a safe place to go.

Summary

A battered woman is someone who is emotionally, physically, and/or sexually abused by her male partner on more than one occasion. For a woman to be identified as battered there must exist a pattern of abuse. Most statistics on battered women refer to physical abuse. It is clear from both informal and official reports that women are more likely to be victims, and men the perpetrators, of such battering and that abuse occurs across all class and racial lines.

Though no single factor causes violence against women, the primary influence seems to be the patriarchal nature of society in which males are dominant and females submissive. Individual explanations of violence against women fall short of explaining why women are specific targets of violence by men.

Battered women are not only physically abused but emotionally damaged, living in constant fear. These emotions are further exacerbated by the failure of social institutions to respond in sympathetic and supportive ways. Police are unwilling to arrest, prosecutors unwilling to prosecute, and therapists often urge reconciliation and family togetherness as a solution. There are many consequences associated with violence against women. In particular, many women die, and in some cases batterers are killed as women are forced to defend themselves.

Many women are encouraged to remain in abusive relationships. Some women are trapped by religious beliefs and economic dependency. The cycle of abuse plays a significant role in women from escaping abuse.

Violence against women is now recognized as a rapidly growing health concern. Violence against women by their male partners is the leading cause of injury to women. There are corporate costs associated with violence against women in terms of low productivity, absenteeism, increased health care costs, and high turnover rates.

Intervention for battered women has been inconsistent and in most cases ineffective. Most criminal justice systems do not enforce laws consistently and generally fail to protect battered women. Shelters for battered women offer the most consistent and reliable help for battered women, but they are few in number and generally lack adequate funding.

The women's movement has slowly educated the public on this issue and has established self-help and conscious-raising groups for both men and women. Much more work has to be done to prevent violence against women.

Discussion Questions

1. Could Nancy, from the "In the News" section, have been saved by the police department?

2. Do you think romantic traditions influence violence against women by their male partners?

3. Discuss the predictors of abuse.

4. Is it easy for battered women to leave their abusive partners? Why or why not?

5. In what ways can the criminal justice system better deal with violent men?

References

Adams, David C. 1991. "Empathy and Entitlement: A Comparison of Battering and Nonbattering Husbands." Ph.D. dissertation, Department of Sociology and Anthropology, Northeastern University, Boston.

Barnes, Liz and Betty Eng. 1993. "Domestic Violence: Building an Integrated Community Response." Boston: Jane Doe Safety Fund.

Barnette, O. W., and A. D. LaViolette. 1993. *It Could Happen to Anyone: Why Battered Women Stay*. Newbury Park, California: Sage Publications.

Browne, Angela. 1987. *When Battered Women Kill*. New York: Free Press.

Burgess, R. L., and P. Draper. 1989. "The Explanation of Family Violence: The Role of Biological, Behavioral, and Cultural Selection." Pp. 59-116 in *Family Violence*, edited by L. Ohlin and M. Tonry. Chicago: University of Chicago Press.

Buzawa, E. S., and C. G. Buzawa. 1996. *Domestic Violence: The Criminal Justice Response*, second edition. Newbury Park, California: Sage Publications.

Dobash, R. E., and Russell Dobash. 1979. *Violence Against Wives: A Case Against the Patriarchy*. New York: Free Press.

Dobash, R. E., and Russell Dobash. 1992. *Women, Violence, and Social Change*. New York: Routledge, Chapman and Hall.

Family Violence Prevention Fund. 1998. "Violence at Home Has Effect on the Workplace." http://www.igc.org/fund/workplace/home.html.

Gelles, Richard. 1993. "Alcohol and Other Drugs Are Associated With Violence—They Are Not Its Cause," p. 182. *Current Controversies on Family Violence*, edited by Richard Gelles and Donileen R. Loseke. Newbury Park, California: Sage Publications.

Hearn, Jeff. 1996. "Men's Violence Toward Known Women: Historical, Everyday, and Theoretical Constructions by Men," p. 31. *Violence and Gender Relations: Theories and Interventions*, edited by B. Fawcett et al. London: Sage Publications.

Hilton, N. Zoe, ed. 1993. *Legal Responses to Wife Assault*. Thousand Oaks, California: Sage Publications.

Johnson, Allan G. 1995. *The Blackwell Dictionary of Sociology: A User's Guide to Sociological Language*. Oxford: Blackwell.

Kurz, Demie. 1993. "Physical Assaults by Husbands: A Major Social Problem." Pp. 88-103 in *Current Controversies on Family Violence*, edited by Richard J. Gelles and Donileen Loseke. Thousand Oaks, California: Sage Publications.

———. 1996. "Separation, Divorce, and Woman Abuse." *Violence Against Women* 2:63-81.

Lang, A. R., et al. 1975. "Effects of Alcohol on Aggression in Male Social Drinkers." *Journal of Abnormal Psychology* 84:508-18.

MacAndrew, C., and R. B. Edgerton. 1969. *Drunken Comportment: A Social Explanation*. Chicago: Aldine.

Messerschmidt, James W. 1993. *Masculinities and Crime: Critique and Reconceptualization of Theory*. Lanham, Maryland: Rowman and Littlefield.

Miedzan, Myriam. 1992. *Boys Will Be Boys: Breaking the Link Between Masculinity and Violence*. New York: Anchor Books

National Coalition Against Domestic Violence. 1995. "Predictors of Domestic Violence." http://www.ncadv.org/.

National Center for Victims of Crime. 1997. "Domestic Violence Statistics." http://www.nvc.org/ edir/domestic.htm.

Newton Domestic Violence Action Committee. 1996. "Domestic Violence Information."

NiCarthy, Ginny. 1987. *The Ones Who Got Away: Women Who Left Abusive Partners*. Seattle: Seal Press.

Office of Women's Health Report. 1997. "Domestic Violence Facts." Department of Health and Human Service Administration, Bureau of Primary Health Care. http://www.bphc.hrsa.dhhs.gov/amwh/omwh_8.htm.

Schechter, Susan. 1982. *Women and Male Violence: The Visions and Struggles of the Battered Women's Movement*. Boston: South End Press.

Straus, Murray A. 1976. "Sexual Inequality, Cultural Norms, and Wife Beating." *Victimology: An International Journal* 1:54-76.

———. 1993. "Physical Assaults by Wives: A Major Social Problem." Pp. 67-87 in *Current Controversies on Family Violence*, edited by R.J. Gelles and D. R. Loseke. Thousand Oaks, California: Sage Publications.

Tjaden, Patricia and Thoennes, Nancy. 1998. "Stalking in America: Findings From the National Violence Against Women Survey," U.S. Department of Justice.

UNICEF. 1997. *The State of the World's Children:1997*. New York: Oxford University Press.

Walker, Lenore E. 1993. "The Battered Woman Syndrome Is a Psychological Consequence of Abuse." Pp. 133–153 in *Current Controversies on Family Violence*, edited
by R.J. Gelles and D. R. Loseke. Thousand Oaks, California: Sage Publications.

Yllo, Kirsti A. 1993. "Through a Feminist Lens: Gender, Power, and Violence." Pp. 47–
62 in *Current Controversies on Family Violence*, edited by Richard J. Gelles and
Donileen Loseke. Thousand Oaks, California: Sage Publications.

Websites

http://www.nvc.org/

National Center for Victims of Crime. This website provides domestic violence statistics, as well as information on spousal abuse, intimate homicide,
and criminal justice system response.

http://www.usdoj.gov/vawo/

U.S. Department of Justice, Violence Against Women Office. This website
provides information about all aspects of violence against women, including
selected speeches and articles, federal legislation and regulations, and ongoing research.

http://www.bphc.hrsa.dhhs.gov/omwh/omwh_8.htm

Department of Health and Human Services, Health Resources and Services Administration, Bureau of Primary Health Care, Office of Women's
Health Report, Domestic Violence Facts. This fact sheet on domestic violence
provides basic information and data on domestic violence. It is a useful reference.

CHAPTER ELEVEN

Divorce

In the News: Tightening the Bonds of Marriage in Louisiana

The Associated Press *(1997a) article had an interesting headline: "In Louisiana, a Bid to Revive 'Till Death Do Us Part' Concept." Tom Perkins is a Republican legislator who wrote and introduced the "covenant marriage" bill. Perkins and other conservative legislators saw the bill "as a possible antidote to societal ills caused by the disintegration of the family" (A24).*

On June 23, 1997, the Louisiana legislature overwhelmingly passed the covenant marriage bill. The bill sets up a choice of two kinds of marriage contract. Couples can still choose a standard marriage that allows a no-fault divorce. Or couples will now be able to choose a covenant marriage, in which divorce would be allowed only under very narrow circumstances. Those circumstances include adultery, abuse, abandonment, a lengthy separation, or imprisonment for a felony (Associated Press 1997b).

Representative Perkins, the bill's author, thinks that the availability of covenant marriage may lessen the likelihood of some potentially weak marriages. If one partner wants a covenant marriage and the other wants a standard no-fault marriage, the first person may want to rethink the marriage and consider the other's lack of commitment.

Other observers have pointed out various problems with the covenant marriage idea. For example, in a piece in the New York Times, *commentator Katha Pollitt (1997) argues that supporters of covenant marriages have blamed no-fault divorce for numerous problems, including "the impoverishment of families, teen-age pregnancy, even lower S.A.T. scores." Proponents of covenant marriage also argue that divorce has serious negative consequences for children and therefore should be made more difficult. In fact, all of these assumptions are at least arguable and not strongly supported by social science research. Covenant marriage may make it harder for people to leave unhappy marriages. Women may find it more difficult to divorce abusive spouses. Even though abuse is one criterion for ending covenant marriages, it is often difficult to establish that abuse took place.*

Definition and Prevalence

Nearly everyone seems to agree that the family is a basic social institution, first, because it is found almost everywhere, and second, because it serves some basic human functions. Throughout most of history, the family unit has provided the context in which economic, educational, religious, and political activities occurred. An individual's family members governed; family members were religious leaders; older family members taught; and family members produced and distributed goods and services. In many parts of the world, the family continues to dominate the life of a community.

Disagreement regarding the nature of the family usually concerns *definition*—exactly what characteristics must a group possess to be regarded as a family?—and *evolution*—what changes have family structure and function recently undergone?

In 1949, George Murdock defined the family as "a social group characterized by common residence, economic cooperation, and reproduction. It includes adults of both sexes, at least two of whom maintain a socially approved sexual relationship, and one or more children, own or adopted, of the sexually cohabiting adults" (1949:1). Murdock also argued that the family unit performs a number of important functions in every known society; in particular, the family is responsible for reproducing the population, training and caring for the children, regulating sexual relations, and dividing labor by sex and age. Murdock's classic study of 565 societies found many different forms of family. Some practiced monogamy, others polygamy. Whatever the case, divorce and the perception of it depended on a society's view of the family.

Most contemporary sociologists and anthropologists recognize the important position of the family in most societies; they investigate variations in family structure and functions across societies and throughout history. With respect to U. S. society, everybody seems to agree that the American family is changing, but there is much less agreement regarding exactly what that change means and where it will end.

Until 1960 most Americans seemed to share a common set of beliefs about family life. Family should consist of a husband and wife living together with their children. The father should be the head of the household, earn the family's income, and give his name to his wife and children. The mother's main tasks were to facilitate her husband's work, guide her children's development, look after the home, and set a moral tone for the family. Marriage was an enduring obligation for better or for worse (Hamburg 1993). These ideals have been drastically modified over the last three decades across all social classes. Women have joined the labor force, marriage is postponed, single parenthood is on the rise, and most adults believe that couples should not stay married if they are unhappy. People are getting married at later ages. For example, in 1950, the median age for men to marry was 22.8 years and for women it was 20.3. By 1995, age at first marriage was about four years older for men and almost five years older for women.

Table 11-1 Estimated Median Age at First Marriage, by Sex, 1890–1997

Year	Men	Women
1997	26.8	25.0
1995	26.9	24.5
1990	26.1	23.9
1980	24.7	22.0
1970	23.2	20.8
1960	22.8	20.3
1950	22.8	20.3
1940	24.3	21.5
1930	24.3	21.3
1920	24.6	21.2
1910	25.1	21.6
1900	25.9	21.9
1890	26.1	22.0

Source: U.S. Bureau of the Census. 1998. "Estimated Median Age at First Marriage, by Sex: 1890–1997." http://www.census.gov/population/socdemo/ms-la/tabms-2.txt.

Despite these later marriages, most American children spend part of their childhood in a single-parent family. According to Hamburg (1993), by the time they reach sixteen, close to half the children of married parents will have seen their parents divorce. Close to half of all European American children whose parents remarry will see the second marriage dissolve during their adolescence. Most divorced persons remarry: five of six divorced men and three of four divorced women remarry. However, the older a woman at the time of divorce, the lower the chances of her remarrying. Men are more likely to remarry soon after a divorce. African American women tend to marry less often and remarry with less haste than European American and Hispanic women (Dunn 1997).

Table 11-2 Divorce and Marriage Patterns, 1995–1997 (Approximate Numbers)

	1995	1996	1997
Marriages	2,336,000	2,344,000	2,384,000
Divorces	1,169,000	1,150,000	1,163,000
Divorce Rates (per 1,000 population)	4.4	4.3	4.3

Source: National Center for Health Statistics. 1997. "Births, Marriages, Divorces, and Deaths for 1996." *Monthly Vital Statistics Reports*. Vol. 45, No. 12, July 17. Hyattsville, Maryland: Centers for Disease Control and Prevention; National Center for Health Statistics. 1998. "Births, Marriages, Divorces, and Deaths for 1997." *Monthly Vital Statistics Report*. Vol. 46, No. 12, July 28. Hyattsville, Maryland: Center for Disease Control and Prevention.

Some observers of the current American scene suggest that the American family is in its final stages of deterioration and decay. They contend that the once-important family unit is now obsolete; that it serves few, if any, useful functions for the members of our society. No longer does the family unit produce goods and services, socialize its children, or take care of its elderly. Family farms are anachronistic; and many family firms are in bankruptcy. Many of the functions formerly performed by family members have been taken over by schools, corporations, day-care centers, nursing homes, and hospitals. What is left is a family unit devastated by divorce and separation, illegitimacy, and cohabitation outside of legal marriage. In this view, things look bleak for family life. Two opposing views of the state of the family appear in "A Closer Look: The American Family Crisis."

A cross-cultural perspective sheds much-needed light on the character of family life in our society. All societies provide some means of escape out of marriage. Most permit divorce; a few permit only annulments and informal separations. The rules for ending marriage differ from society to society and from one historical period to another. In some societies, couples may end their marriages through very simple procedures, such as a husband saying to his wife, "I divorce thee," or a wife placing her husband's possessions outside the front door of their home where he will see them when he returns (Goode 1993).

In many societies, divorce is regarded as punishment of a spouse for violating the marriage vows. Thus, adultery is often grounds for divorce, but in certain cultures stinginess, physical violence, and laziness are also included. In our own society, the most common ground for divorce is cruel and abusive treatment, which does not necessarily mean physical violence but may mean

❖ ❖ ❖ ❖

A Closer Look

The American Family Crisis

American families of all types face growing problems regarding the development of children, the emotional and physical health of adults, the special care of the sick and the elderly, and the reinforcement of society's values (Popenoe 1993). In order to understand what may have happened to the family, it is necessary to look at the broad cultural changes that have taken place. David Popenoe states that the United States has long been known as the world's most individualistic society. This individualism supposedly has been balanced by a strong belief in the sanctity of religion, the family, community, and the nation as a whole. Popenoe argues that in recent years, the individualism trend has advanced and people are becoming narcissistic or self-oriented. The sense of community has weakened, and people tend to show concern for social institutions only when the institution directly affects their own well-being.

Popenoe argues that people need strong families to provide them with physical and mental well-being. He specifically states that society needs a nuclear family consisting of a male and a female who marry and live together and share responsibility for their children and for each other. He does not think highly of step families or blended families and believes single-parent families are detrimental to the well-being of children. He believes in a strong emphasis on marriage.

Judith Stacey (1993, 1994) disagrees with Popenoe. She does not believe that a family's structure is more important than the quality of the relationships. She argues that social science research does not support the conservative contention that children are better off with a mother and a father living together, married. She believes that the nuclear family's decline is not at the heart of our social decay. The losses in real earnings and in breadwinner jobs, the persistence of low-wage jobs for women, and the corporate greed that has accompanied global restructuring have wreaked far more havoc.

Stacey (1994) suggests that the family alone does not cause all major problems in society. Some couples need to divorce for the sake of their children and themselves. She agrees that single parents need help and support but says that forcing people to marry is not the answer. The quality of family relationships is much more important to Stacey than the family structure alone.

---

verbal and emotional harassment. Throughout the world, mere incompatibility between husband and wife has seldom been sufficient to justify divorce (Goode 1993).

In some societies, divorce is nothing more than an informal separation, requiring no legal action or ceremony whatever. In many other societies, however, divorce consists of a court proceeding in which legal justification is required. In such formal arrangements, the grounds for divorce may take the form of "excuses" which hide the real reasons for a couple wanting to terminate their marriage.

In both England and the United States, divorces were relatively rare until the last half of the nineteenth century, mainly because it was so difficult to obtain a divorce. In the 1880s, one out of every fourteen marriages ended in divorce. The rate of divorce increased in the immediate aftermaths of both World War I and World War II. Interestingly, fewer people divorced after the Depression. The sharpest increase began in the early 1960s, reaching an unprecedented high in 1981 (Talbot 1997). As in many other societies, a large proportion of American divorces occur during the earliest years of marriage and among childless couples. More specifically, the divorce rate peaks during the second year of marriage, after which it drops dramatically. Childlessness

---

A Closer Look

Divorce and Marriage Data—The Census Bureau Website

Located at http://www.census.gov/population/socdemo, the "U.S. Bureau of the Census, Current Population Reports" provides information on marital status and living arrangements. There are several categories of data available. For instance, if you chose to view data concerning the marital status of the population 15 years old and over by sex and race, you will obtain that specific information and much more. For example, data are presented regarding the numbers of people not only married, but those who have been widowed and divorced since 1950.

You can also obtain information concerning the status of children with regard to whether they live with one or two parents. Data are presented according to whether children in the United States live with their father or mother or both. For children who live with one parent, data are further broken down to show whether parents are divorced, widowed, or never married. These data are further broken down by race.

---

seems to be an important factor in explaining the high proportion of divorces during the first years of marriage. Each year about half as many divorces are granted as there are marriages performed.

Levels of Causation

Why divorce rates rise or fall can be explained in a number of ways, depending upon the approach taken. Here we examine explanations at the individual, cultural, and structural levels.

Individual

The affective nature of the family bond gives it a degree of vulnerability that is not characteristic of most other institutions in U. S. society. The family is one of the few locations where the expression of strong feeling is legitimate. As a result, the marital bond may frequently become a focal point for psychological as well as economic and social stresses. For example, divorce and separation rates increase under the impact of poverty and unemployment. Less obviously, perhaps, a marriage may also suffer when children do not fulfill parental expectations, when a mid-life crisis develops, or when major unanticipated changes in life occur.

It has been proposed that people who are depressed or who suffer from personality abnormalities may be less capable of staying married. Such an interpretation may well be true in many cases, but this psychological approach ignores the influence of societal factors on marital expectations and the family institution itself.

Cultural

Some sociologists have argued that family disorganization is only one expression of a more widespread breakdown in cultural norms, which has left its mark in the form of pervasive ambiguities and anomie (normlessness). Cultural traditions no longer control and direct the everyday affairs of the members of American society. Today, people seem to have more options. These options have increased people's freedom but some sociologists suggest at the expense of clear-cut expectations for the relationship between men and women.

Gender-role changes seem to have had an effect on the high divorce rate. The entry of millions of women into the work force has taken women out of the home, reducing their traditional roles. Also, a woman who can support herself is less likely to stay in a troubled marriage. Cultural factors are related to these gender-role changes. Andrew Cherlin (1995) argues that values have shifted from a philosophy of self-sacrifice for the good of the family to an emphasis on self-fulfillment, autonomy, personal happiness, and personal growth. There may be less social and cultural pressure to stay together, even for "the children's sake." Marriage seems to have become deinstitutionalized; it is more a matter of personal preference. Therefore, it is not surprising that divorce rates are so high.

Culture also plays a part in the outcome of divorce. When a man is divorced, his primary role, defined in terms of employment, remains the same. In contrast, women have to work even harder to survive economically. If they have never worked outside the home, they have to enter the work force, maybe for the first time and often at low-paying, entry-level positions. At the same time, they must juggle the responsibilities of work and home.

Researchers have found a number of factors associated with divorce. Age is one factor: Couples who marry under the age of 18 are more likely to divorce than couples who marry at any later age. Males are more likely than females to divorce if they marry at eighteen. One possible explanation for the high divorce rate among couples who marry young is that they are poorly prepared for marriage. Another possible explanation may be the greater likelihood of the marriage following upon a premarital pregnancy. Conceiving or having a child before marriage does seem to increase the likelihood of divorce, perhaps because the couple has to adjust to both a marriage and a baby.

Studies consistently show that African Americans have higher rates of divorce than European Americans; they are also more likely to remain in a separated status (White 1990). Divorce appears to be more frequent among people in the lower socioeconomic strata than among those in the higher. People at higher status levels generally marry later, which is related to lower divorce rates. They also have more to lose from divorce, especially in terms of social status. Lower-status married couples may have higher divorce rates because they may experience more crises in their lives.

Religious affiliation appears to be associated with divorce. Protestants have a slightly higher divorce rate than Catholics, and Jews have lower divorce rates than Catholics. The highest divorce rates are among those who claim no religion. The issue of divorce and Catholicism seems to be most pronounced in Ireland, where divorce has recently become legal. Divorce now has serious cultural and religious implications for those living in Ireland. In 1937, when Ireland wrote its constitution, it incorporated the laws of the Catholic Church into the law of the state, making divorce illegal. For generations, battles were waged in an attempt to separate the church and state. Some battles were won; others, lost. For example, women are now allowed access to information about abortion. The latest battles involved lifting the constitution's ban on divorce.

In the mid-1990s there were some 80,000 people separated in Ireland, living in limbo (Barbash 1995). There were many others in "second relationships," unable to remarry because they could not sever their first marriage. During the debate, many argued that divorce would destroy the Irish family and devalue the institution of marriage. Others stated that Ireland's "family culture" would be replaced with the "divorce culture" of the United States and Britain.

On the other side of the debate were arguments concerning individual rights of free choice. In September of 1995, according to a poll, 61 percent of respondents stated they would vote in favor of lifting the divorce ban, while 30 percent would vote against. A month later, the yes voters had dropped to 52 percent. Divorce rates certainly are influenced by cultural perspectives. In the United States, most people agree that divorce is a solution to an unhappy marriage. The same sentiment obviously does not exist in other cultures, such as that of Ireland (Barbash 1995).

Structural

Family sociologists usually distinguish between the **nuclear family** consisting of the wife, husband, and their children, and the **extended family** unit consisting of all blood relatives and their nuclear families. William Goode (1993) has argued that the forces of industrialization and urbanization are responsible for a growing worldwide emphasis on the nuclear family at the expense of strong, extended kinship ties.

Goode identifies several features of the nuclear family that weaken ties to extended kin: (1) the members of the nuclear family have a **neolocal residence**—they establish a new and independent household upon marriage and do not continue to live with kin; (2) mate selection is based on the mutual attraction between man and woman rather than on the wishes of their kin; (3) intense emotions are likely to be expressed within the small nuclear family unit and not within the larger kinship network; and (4) the family system is bilateral, so that the kin lines of husband and wife are almost equally important.

Goode identifies the following crucial points of pressure from industrialization that foster the development of a nuclear family unit: (1) Industrialization frequently demands physical movement from locality to locality in order to secure or further employment. This moving about reduces the frequency of intimate contacts between nuclear family members and their extended kin. (2) Kin may become separated by social mobility; that is, some kin may move upward and others downward with respect to wealth, prestige, and power. (3) Specialized agencies and organizations perform functions formerly carried out by kinship networks—for example, lending money, protecting a locality, or pooling money to educate children. (4) Under the impact of industrialization, achieved status tends to be valued more highly than ascribed (that is, family) status; this value undermines the power of the kin to control members, because individual members can make their own way without assistance from other family members.

Goode's conception of industrialization and the nuclear family has implications for family instability. It is the specialized focus of the modern family unit to provide a place in which "psychic wounds can be salved or healed." Depending as it does on affection and intense emotion, the relationship between wife and husband may be intrinsically unstable. As a result, the divorce rate is likely to be high. What is more, because there is no extended family unit to care for the children or to prevent the spouses from making a personal decision concerning mate selection, the rate of remarriage is also likely to be great.

Although much of Goode's analysis remains relevant, much research on the historical family has established that before industrialization, in the West at least, most people lived most of their lives in nuclear families. The widespread extended family has turned out to be a myth. In fact, the incidence of extended families actually increased with industrialization. Extended families provided a variety of social support functions for families in the period of early industrialization.

Some sociologists have suggested that changes in divorce laws caused increases in divorce. They argue that changes in law led to changes in attitudes about divorce. However, Margaret Talbot (1997) argues that divorce has always been an expression of idealism about marriage, not a concession to realism about it. Divorce has long been defended with the ennobling rhetoric of freedom. Divorced women might have been thought of as vulgar and divorced men as cads, but divorce itself was regarded as a necessary safety valve that preserved the institution of marriage. Before the introduction of no-fault laws in the 1970s, the only way to get out of a marriage legally was to charge one's spouse with adultery, desertion, bigamy, or impotence.

By mid-century, many states were adding more flexible criteria such as drunkenness, cruelty, and gross behavior. Despite this, the most acceptable rationale for divorce remained the ideal of a good marriage. Rising divorce rates may be due to the rising expectations people hold for marriage. The direction of the causal connection between attitude and law is not easy to assess. In the case of divorce, we do know, however, that recent changes in state laws have made divorce easier to obtain. In some states, the grounds for divorce have been greatly expanded. In others, traditional grounds have been completely eliminated. California and Massachusetts, for example, permit no-fault divorce, which does not require that responsibility for the collapse of the marriage be established.

In the 1970s, many states passed new no-fault divorce laws that made the divorce process easier. States eliminated moralistic grounds required to obtain a divorce and divided up a marriage's assets based on needs and resources, without reference to which party was held responsible for the marriage's failure (Faludi 1992). In 1985, Lenore Weitzman's research suggested that women who sought freedom from unhappy marriages were winding up poorer under the new divorce laws. The women were worse off than if they had divorced under the old laws or if they had stayed married.

Weitzman (1985) argued that because men and women are differently situated in marriage—that is, husbands usually make more money and, upon divorce, the wives usually get the children—treating the spouses equally upon divorce overcompensates the husband and cheats the wife and children. Research shows that on the average, divorced women and their minor children experience a 73 percent decline in their standard of living in the first year after divorce. Their former husbands experience a 42 percent rise in their standard of living.

Faludi (1991) argues that Weitzman's research findings are misleading. Weitzman had only conducted interviews with men and women who had divorced after the 1970 no-fault divorce laws went into effect in California. She had no comparable data on couples who divorced under the old system and so no way of testing her hypothesis. A later study by two law professors reached the opposite conclusion: women and children were found to be slightly better off economically under the no-fault provisions. Faludi further argues that the real source of divorced women's problems was not found in divorce legislation but in the behavior of ex-husbands and judges. She argues that men are not consistently forced to make child support and alimony payments. Judges were also not ordering adequate amounts of child support and alimony payments, even under the new divorce laws. Faludi argues that the most effective way to correct the post-divorce inequities between the sexes is to correct pay inequality in the work force. If the wage gap were wiped out between the sexes, one-half of female households would be instantly lifted out of poverty (Faludi 1992).

A symbolic interactionist approach has frequently been used to explain the high rate of divorce in the United States. Symbolic interactionists may argue that we have unrealistic expectations about love and marriage. Believing that marriage or true love will be a constant source of emotional satisfaction sets people up for false hopes. When dissatisfaction occurs, couples tend to blame one another. The same can be applied to having children. Raising children is fulfilling but also demanding, pushing the family into "emotional overload."

Gender roles have changed. Responsibilities of husbands and wives are not so clear today. Most women work outside the home. With these economic opportunities and easily obtainable divorces, some wives today may see better alternatives than remaining in an unhappy marriage. As divorce becomes more common, its stigma is removed. The law has made it easier to divorce. Where previously divorce was granted only in the most serious of cases (adultery, abuse), now "incompatibility" is grounds for divorce. Eventually states implemented "no-fault" divorce, in which couples could dissolve their marriages without accusations of wrongdoing. Some government agencies even provide do-it-yourself kits.

A functionalist perspective on divorce asserts that the family has lost many of its traditional functions. These changes have weakened the family institution. Functionalists claim that industrialization and urbanization undermine the traditional functions of the family. For example, prior to industrialization, most family members had to cooperate in producing what they needed to survive. Industrialization disrupted this cooperation and weakened the bonds that tied family members together. Amongst these changes, the government took over many family functions, such as schooling. The care of the sick and the elderly also shifted outside of the family to medical specialists. Functionalists even point to reproduction as losing its traditional family functions. A prime example is the greater number of single women having babies.

Functionalists believe that these changes have made an increase in divorce inevitable. Society does not place as much emphasis on marriage and commitment today as in the past: in the past a couple would stay together in spite of the problems they experienced.

On the contrary, conflict theorists see traditional marriages as reflecting society's basic inequalities between males and females. They argue that marriage maintains male domination and exploitation of women. Traditionally, women have been regarded as property, first by their fathers and then passed on to their husbands. Women have traditionally been assigned the role of satisfying the needs of men, but there have been significant changes with regard to traditional gender roles. Today females participate in social worlds beyond the home and are more likely to dissolve a marriage that has become intolerable. Changing relationships of power and inequality are the keys to understanding the current divorce rate (Benokraitis 1997).

Higher divorce rates result from changed male-female power relationships. An increase in divorce is not a sign that marriage has weakened but may be a sign that women are making headway in their historical struggle with men.

Consequences

Since the mid-1960s, the divorce rate has increased sharply. It is estimated that more than half of all recent marriages will end in divorce, whereas only one-sixth of all marriages begun twenty years ago ended in divorce.

The higher divorce rate has had its impact on children. Specifically, the number of children involved in divorce per 1,000 children increased from 8.7 in 1964 to 17.1 in 1976. During the 1970s, almost 1 million children were involved in a divorce each year (Reiss 1980). Surprisingly, the divorce rate has not increased much since the 1970s. Currently, over 1 million children discover that their parents are divorcing (U.S. Bureau of the Census 1995).

There is no question that children are affected by divorcing parents. How they are affected is up for debate. Some family researchers argue that children will be more stable with divorced parents if there has been constant fighting and abuse in the predivorce household (Stacey 1994). Other researchers have discovered lingering consequences of divorce on children. For example, compared with adults who grew up in intact families, grown-up children of divorced parents are less likely to have contact with either their father or their mother.

Divorce is making its way onto the legislative agenda. According to Rob Gurwitt (1996), over the past two years, the number of marriage- and divorce-related bills in state legislatures has skyrocketed, jumping from 500 measures in 1995 to 750 in 1996. Some measures involve stiffening the penalties for failing to pay child support and changing the procedures for determining alimony. Barry Schneider, a presiding domestic relations judge in Phoenix, is taking part in a widespread effort to change the laws to force divorcing parents to pay more attention to the needs of their children. Some states are considering lengthening the waiting period before a couple can get a divorce or requiring couples who file for divorce to get counseling. Some legislators are drawing up bills to encourage, or even require, premarital counseling.

Divorce does exact a social cost in its impact on children. The pioneering work of Judith Wallerstein (1980, 1996) brought about this notion. Wallerstein studied 131 children of divorcing couples over a 15-year period. She found them, on the whole, to be at greater risk than children in two-parent families for a range of problems, from depression to poor grades to substance abuse. Despite her work, there is also a respectable body of research suggesting that divorce need not be a calamity for children. Andrew Cherlin (1995) argues that most children of divorced parents do not exhibit serious reactions to divorce. Divorce is not an inevitable disaster for children; in some cases it is a necessity, as in the case of abuse.

"Divorce education" is one way government agencies try to protect children of divorcing parents. Several states require this education, including Utah, Connecticut, Indiana, Mississippi, and North Carolina. Some states offer voluntary programs for divorcing parents. The programs last from two to six hours and look at how children react to divorce, the best ways to manage conflict, and the long-term psychological benefits of an amicable process.

The higher divorce rate has also meant that more children have spent some period of time in a single-parent family headed by the mother. Specifically, 90 percent of the children involved in divorce subsequently live with their mothers; only 6 percent with their fathers; and the remainder with other relatives (U.S. Bureau of the Census 1996).

Custody issues are crucial in any divorce proceeding. There are three main types of custody available in the United States: sole custody, joint legal custody, and joint physical custody (Maccoby and Mnookin 1992).

Under sole custody, the child lives with one parent but at certain times will visit the noncustodial parent. The parent with whom the child lives has the right and responsibility to provide for the physical, moral, and mental well-being of the child. Joint legal custody gives both parents equal rights to make decisions about the child's welfare, but the child is likely to live with one parent. Joint physical custody gives parents equal rights to make decisions about day-to-day child-care matters, and typically the child lives with each parent an equal amount of time. In a small number of cases, couples split the custody of their children, with the mother having sole custody of some children and the father sole custody of others. This is called split custody. Mothers usually take younger and female children and fathers take older and male children.

Divorce has had a profound impact on the once dominant nuclear family unit. Presently, only one family in four consists of husband, wife, and dependent children living together in a single household. The growing number of one-parent families has become a matter of general concern. Since 1970, the number of one-parent families has tripled, while the number of two-parent families has actually decreased by 250,000. It is not only the divorce rate that is responsible for this trend; there has also been a sharp increase in unwed parenthood. Approximately 30 percent of U.S. children are born to women and men who are not married, a 50 percent increase in just ten years (U.S. Bureau of the Census 1995).

A consequence of major concern regarding one-parent families is that most of these families are poor, primarily because most one-parent families are headed by women. In the case of divorce, 90 percent of children live with their mother, and most divorced women earn less than their former husbands. In the case of unwed mothers, most have little education and few marketable skills. Children of single-parent families are twice as likely to drop out of high school, and if a female, to have a child while still a teenager. Some researchers are very concerned about the growing number of children growing up without fathers. (See "A Closer Look: Fatherless in America.")

Premarital and extramarital cohabitation are frequently cited as evidence of family breakdown. Cohabitation has increased about seven times in just over two decades. About half of the couples who marry have lived together before marriage. Studies also suggest, however, that cohabitation is not a permanent form of heterosexual relationship. Sociologists have found that couples who live together before marriage are more likely to divorce

A Closer Look

Fatherless in America

Sociologist David Popenoe states that in the past thirty years, we have witnessed an enormous increase in absent fathers. He argues that this is one of the main reasons for the decline of marriage and the family in the United States. From 1960 to 1990, the percentage of children living apart from their fathers more than doubled, from 17 percent to 36 percent. If this rate continues, by the turn of the century nearly 50 percent of American children will be living apart from their fathers (Popenoe 1996).

Popenoe goes so far as to argue that the absence of the father is a major force lying behind many issues such as crime and delinquency; premature sexuality and out-of-wedlock teen births; deteriorating educational achievement; depression; substance abuse; and the growing number of women and children living in poverty. Does this mean that if women and children had men in their lives, everything would be problem-free?

Men or women are perfectly capable of raising healthy children by themselves. In addition, many two-parent families are faced with teenage pregnancies, their child's substance abuse problems, or depression. Having a father present will not necessarily remedy all problems in single-parent households. Single-parent families have been unfairly stigmatized.

Disturbingly, women and children are more likely to need protection *from* their male partners, the children's father, than protection *by* him. Presenting a blanket argument that all children need to live with their father misses many of these crucial points. If fatherhood is to be reestablished, it needs to be reevaluated in terms of its meaning. Popenoe himself states that patriarchal fatherhood is unhealthy but nevertheless strongly suggests the need for children to grow up with their fathers.

than couples who do not. The reason cited is that cohabiting couples have a weaker commitment to relationships (Whyte 1992).

Interventions

Ambivalence concerning the legitimacy of divorce is reflected in the absence of cultural or institutional programs designed to reduce the divorce rate. Unlike many other social problems encountered in this text, divorce interventions have occurred almost exclusively at the individual level. Indeed, the impact of institutional changes such as modifications in legal codes has been to ease prohibitions against divorce and therefore to increase the likelihood of its occurrence.

Desertion is another matter. The federal government's growing ability to keep track of American citizens has made it increasingly more difficult for any given individual to evade the law and fail to support his family (Fullerton 1972).

A "patchwork" approach to reducing the rate of divorce is exemplified by the work of marriage counselors—individuals from the fields of social work, psychiatry, psychology, or pastoral counseling who may or may not have received either theoretical instruction or practical experience related to marital problems. In most states, the title "marriage counselor" is unregulated. As of 1974, only five states had specific legal regulations concerning marriage counseling. As a result, some marriage counselors receive excellent training, whereas others have an inadequate clinical background. Another problem is

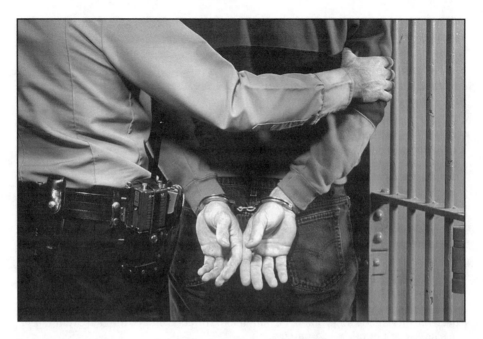

In recent years many states have gotten tougher on "deadbeat dads," fathers who do not pay consistent child support. —*Photo: photostogo.com.*

that couples experiencing marital problems often seek the advice of a counselor only *after* their marriage has effectively been dissolved, at least in any psychological or sociological sense, and the legal divorce is a mere formal step away. A couple may go through the ritualized procedure of seeing a counselor in order to convince themselves that they have "tried everything" before ending their marriage. Frequently, however, it is a judge who orders a couple to seek counseling as a part of the divorce proceedings.

An interesting blend of marriage counseling, religion, and group movement is found in Marriage Encounter, an organization that seeks to make "good marriages even better" by providing a structured opportunity for husband and wife to come together in a relatively nonthreatening situation in order to improve their communication. Thousands of couples have participated in an "encounter weekend," conducted by the clergy, and in subsequent Marriage Encounter group activities, which attempt to reinforce the improved marital relationship.

Organizations also exist to aid an individual in making the adjustment after divorce has occurred. Thousands of single parents in all fifty states and Canada belong to Parents Without Partners, a self-help organization "devoted exclusively to the welfare and interests of single parents and their children." Many of the activities of Parents Without Partners are designed to assist divorced parents in raising their children. Workshops put the members in touch with professionals. Local chapters also frequently hold activities that bring together parents and their children (for example, to participate in a camping weekend). What is more, the monthly calendar of events frequently includes social activities for adult members—dances, book club meetings, and wine-and cheese socials—which provide opportunities for dating.

Proponents of another viewpoint argue for nonintervention, at least at the institutional level. They contend that the American family is in a process of transition rather than of decline or decay. From this standpoint, the family is moving towards new equilibrium, another level of stability at which serial monogamy is normatively sanctioned.

The divorce rate is high, but so is the rate of marriage and remarriage. Apparently, the members of our society—even those experiencing divorce—are not so much disenchanted with the institution of marriage as with their own particular choice of spouse. Otherwise, how do we account for the fact that 75 percent of divorced women and 82 percent of divorced men remarry within three years?

On a broad, cross-cultural basis, the American divorce rate does not appear to be unusually high and may even be leveling off. Moreover, divorce does not necessarily indicate social disorganization. There are many societies—some highly stable and well organized—whose divorce rate is at least as high as ours. And societies experiencing general instability or disorganization nevertheless may have low divorce rates.

Many sociologists, and others, argue that we need more democratic families. Power is a serious factor to consider when discussing families and divorce. The patriarchal family was created so that men could own women and children. Shere Hite (1994) argues that the family is a human creation: humans make it, so humans can change it. There are many family forms, not all have to be nuclear. Hite argues that if families were more democratic, if equality existed for men, women, and children, the rate of divorce would decrease rapidly. Many sociologists would agree with this position.

The Future of Divorce

The family is not likely to disappear from among our important institutions. More likely, the family of the future will continue to develop and change its form and functions in response to modifications in other institutions and changes in cultural values. In the past, divorce was widely regarded as a sign of failure on the part of the divorced individuals, as well as on the part of society as a whole. Those who dissolved their marriages were stigmatized and subject to feelings of shame, guilt, and fear concerning the future.

Despite a continuing negativism associated with the breakup of the family unit, divorce is fast becoming an acceptable aspect of family life in our society. The concept of "a marriage made in heaven," which long supported the nuclear family pattern, is being replaced by the notion of the impermanence of marriage. Most divorced individuals eventually remarry, usually within a few years. Thus, the pattern of marriage-divorce-remarriage is likely to hold, so long as large numbers of American women remain in the labor force and laws continue to make divorce a realistic option.

Summary

Almost everyone agrees that the family is a fundamental social institution. Disagreement regarding the family usually centers on definition and evolution. Murdock's definition of the family includes common residence, economic cooperation, and reproduction. He argues also that in every known society the family unit is responsible for reproducing the population, training the children, regulating sexual relations, and dividing labor by sex and age.

Although there may be a few societies in which Murdock's version of the family does not exist, most contemporary sociologists and anthropologists recognize the importance of the family unit; they investigate variations in family structure and functions.

Some observers contend that the American family is presently in its final stages of deterioration and decay, being devastated by divorce and separation, illegitimacy, and cohabitation outside of marriage. They argue that the once-important family is now obsolete.

A cross-cultural perspective indicates that all societies have provided some means of escape out of marriage, usually divorce. The frequency of divorce ranges widely from culture to culture. In a number of societies, divorce occurs frequently during the early years of marriage until children are born.

Since 1900, divorce has occurred with increasing frequency in American society. A large proportion of these divorces occurs during the earliest years of marriage and among childless couples. Some suggest that family disorganization is only one expression of a much more pervasive breakdown in cultural norms. At the root of the problem are the increased options for individuals, who can decide whether or not to marry, whether or not to have children, whether or not to work, and whether or not to stay married.

At the institutional level of causation, Goode has argued that industrialization is responsible for a growing emphasis on the nuclear family at the expense of strong, extended kinship ties. Also as a result of industrialization, the family's almost exclusive affective bond creates potential instability in the relationship between husband and wife. Divorce is a likely result.

Recent changes in state laws have made divorce easier to obtain. In some states, the grounds for divorce have been completely eliminated, so that "no fault" is established. At the individual level, the marital bond may frequently become a focal point for psychological as well as economic and social stresses, leading to separation and divorce. In addition, people who suffer from personality disorders may be less capable of remaining married.

Since the mid-1960s, the divorce rate has increased dramatically. As a result, the number of children involved in divorce has also grown sharply. Evidence of widespread family disorganization can be found in high rates of illegitimacy and extramarital cohabitation. However, most young people who live together also hope eventually to settle down and marry.

Reflecting society's ambivalence toward divorce, interventions to reduce divorce have occurred almost exclusively at the individual level. The field of marriage counseling has recently shown tremendous growth. In addition, thousands of married couples have participated in organizations such as Marriage Encounter. Thousands more have joined Parents Without Partners, after their marriages have ended.

Some sociologists have argued for nonintervention, at least at the institutional level. They contend that the American family is in a process of transition rather than of decline or decay.

Discussion Questions

1. What is your opinion of "covenant marriage," as it has developed in Louisiana? Do you think it will lead to less divorce? Will it lead to stronger families?

2. You have probably known someone who has gotten a divorce. Perhaps you have. Do you think that some of the people you know went into divorce lightly?

3. What do you think of the view that "fatherlessness" is the major social problem in the United States today? What leads you to that position?

4. In your opinion, should divorce be harder or easier to get? Why?

5. Is the United States a "divorce culture?" Why do you think so?

References

Associated Press. 1997a. "In Louisiana, a Bid to Revive 'Till Death Do Us Part' Concept." *Boston Globe*, June 20, A24.

Associated Press. 1997b. "Antidivorce Bill Advances in Louisiana." *Boston Globe*, June 24, A6.

Barbash, Fred. 1995. "Divorce Bitterly Divides Ireland." *Detroit News*, November 19. http://www.detnews.com/menu/stories/25372.htm.

Benokraitis, Nijole V. 1997. *Marriages and Families: Changes, Choices, and Constraints*. Second edition. Englewood Cliffs, New Jersey: Prentice-Hall.

Blankenhorn, David. 1996. *Fatherless America: Confronting Our Most Urgent Social Problem*. New York: Basic Books.

Cherlin, Andrew. 1995. *Public and Private Families*. New York: McGraw-Hill.

Dunn, Dana, ed. 1997. *Workplace/Women's Place*. Los Angeles: Roxbury Publishing.

Faludi, Susan. 192. *The Undeclared War Against American Women*. New York: Doubleday.

Fullerton, Gail Putney. 1972. *Survival in Marriage*. New York: Holt, Rinehart, and Winston.

Goode, William. 1993. *World Changes in Divorce Patterns*. Connecticut: Yale University Press.

Gurwitt, Rob. 1996. "The Politics of Divorce." *Governing*. Congressional Quarterly.

Hamburg, David. 1993. "The New Family: Investing in Human Capital," *Current* July/August.

Henslin, James. 1997. *Sociology: A Down to Earth Approach*. Third edition. Boston: Allyn and Bacon.

Hite, Shere. 1994. "Bringing Democracy Home." *Ms.* March/April: 54–61.

Maccoby, Eleanor E., and Robert H. Mnookin. 1992. *Dividing the Child: Social and Legal Dilemmas of Custody*. Massachusetts: Cambridge University Press.

Murdock, George. 1949. *Social Structure*. New York: Free Press.

Pollitt, Katha. 1997. "What's Right About Divorce." New York Times, June 27.

Popenoe, David. 1993. "American Family Decline, 1960–1990." *Journal of Marriage and the Family* 55:527–44.

——. 1996. *Life Without Father*. New York: Free Press.

Reiss, Ira L. 1980. *Family Systems in America*, third edition. New York: Holt, Rinehart, and Winston.

Stacey, Judith. 1993. "Good Riddance to 'the Family': A Response to David Popenoe." *Journal of Marriage and the Family*. 55:545–547.

——. 1994. "Scents, Scholars, and Stigma: The Revisionist Campaign for Family Values." *Social Text* 12 (Fall, Number 3): 54–75.

Talbot, Margaret. 1997. "Love, American Style." *New Republic*. April 14: 30–38.

U.S. Bureau of the Census. 1995. *Statistical Abstract of the United States: 1995*. Washington, D.C.: U. S. Government Printing Office.

————. 1996. *Statistical Abstract of the United States: 1996*. Washington, D.C.: U. S. Government Printing Office.

Wallerstein, Judith S., Jean B. Kelly. 1980. *Surviving the Breakup: How Children and Parents Cope With Divorce*. New York: Basic Books.

Wallerstien, Judith S., and Sandra Blakeslee. 1996. *Second Chances: Men, Women, and Children a Decade After Divorce*, revised edition. New York: Basic Books.

Weitzman, Lenore. 1985. *The Divorce Revolution: The Unexpected Social and Economic Consequences for Women and Children in America*. New York: Free Press.

White, Lynn K. 1990. "Determinants of Divorce: A Review of Research in the Eighties." *Journal of Marriage and the Family* 52:904–912.

Whyte, Martin King. 1992. "Choosing Mates the American Way." *Society*, March–April, 71–77.

Websites

http://www.census.gov/population/socdemo/

This website offers statistical information about the estimated age of marriage, number of marriages in the United States, and information concerning divorce.

http://www.legal.net/family/htm

This site offers an overview of family law as it is changing in the United States.

http://www.asanet.org/family.htm

This website contains references to sociologists doing research on the family.

CHAPTER TWELVE

Health and Health Care Issues

In the News: Worrying About Health Care

Are you worried about health care? Can you afford to get sick? Recent news articles indicate that many Americans—and citizens of other countries—have deep concerns about their health care systems. One newspaper headline reported that "being wealthy and wise helps keep one healthy, a U.S. study finds" (Associated Press 1998). The study is mentioned in an annual report that the National Center for Health Statistics compiles on the nation's health (National Center for Health Statistics 1998b). We discuss the study in more detail in the chapter, but want to note some of its highlights here. The overall message of the study seems clear: "From cradle to grave, when it comes to health, money matters. People with less money and less education die younger and suffer more from virtually every health problem than well-off Americans, the government reports" (Associated Press 1998).

Given this situation, it is not surprising that a recent poll indicated that "three-quarters of Americans say that health care reform should be a top priority for Congress" (Reuters 1998). The poll was conducted for Time *and the* Cable News Network *(CNN). Of those responding to the poll, 76 percent listed health care as a top priority for Congress. The only topics the respondents saw as more important were education reform and strengthening Social Security. Only about 40 percent of those surveyed were "very confident" that their health plan would pay for their medical care if they got very sick. This concern, as well as others expressed, suggest that Americans are deeply concerned about their health coverage—increasingly provided by health maintenance organizations (HMOs) through managed care programs. Some large HMOs are now cutting the poor and elderly from their plans or reducing the level of services provided to them (Kilborn 1998a). To make matters worse, "there is a wide gap between the medical procedures that physicians recommend for their patients and what insurers will pay for, according to a new study that begins to fill an information void pervaded by scare stories and lawsuits" (Tye 1998).*

Although many Americans who have health insurance are worried about their coverage, think about how much worse the situation is for those without health insurance. In a recent New York Times *article, Peter Kilborn notes that*

> *despite a decade of steadily rising prosperity, a million more Americans a year are losing the protective umbrella of health insurance. As a result, more than 41 million people, or 15 percent of the population, don't have coverage. (Kilborn 1998b)*

Many people believe that the uninsured do get the care they need, but recent studies indicate that the uninsured are much less likely to get care. In one recent study, the uninsured were over three times as likely as the insured to say they did not receive needed care in the last year. Not surprisingly, the uninsured are over twice as likely to say that the entire American health care system should be rebuilt.

Citizens of the United States are not alone in thinking that major health care reforms are necessary. In fact, fairly large percentages of the populations in many developed, industrialized countries feel that their country's health care systems should be completely rebuilt. The governments of all developed societies are trying to restrain and cut health care costs, and their populations are generally unhappy about the efforts. Even Canadians—generally very proud of their health care system—have become increasingly dissatisfied (Knox 1998). As you

read the rest of this chapter, think about the kinds of changes you would like to
see in the American health care system.

Definition and Prevalence

Have you thought much about health care and health care problems? The "In the News" section focused on health care coverage, the plight of the uninsured, and feelings of discontent with health care systems. Are there other issues related to health and health care that concern you? This chapter examines a variety of health care issues in the United States: what it means to be healthy and sick; what it costs to become or remain healthy; the quality of our health care system; possible alternatives; and why we are unable to provide everyone with equal health care. Because we focus on problems related to health and health care, much of the chapter will take a critical perspective on these issues. Therefore, along with sociologist Peter Conrad we should note that

> by any standard, the American medical system and the American medical
> profession are among the best in the world. Our society invests a great
> amount of its social and economic resources in medical care; has some of
> the world's finest physicians, hospitals and medical schools; is no longer
> plagued by most deadly infectious diseases; and is in the forefront in de-
> veloping medical and technological advances for the treatment of disease
> and illness. (Conrad 1997: 2)

In spite of these achievements and strengths, many people—including social scientists, health care workers, and lay people—argue that American health care is in crisis and that many Americans do not receive the kind of care they need. Because health care should help people achieve health, we first need to define health, which is not as straightforward as it may seem.

The World Health Organization (WHO), a part of the United Nations, defines **health** as a "state of complete physical, mental, and social well-being and not merely the absence of disease or infirmity." This broad definition emphasizes more than just being in good physical shape. It is related to WHO's goal of "Health for All" (HFA) by the year 2000. The objective of HFA is that all the world's people should attain a level of health "that would permit them to lead socially and economically productive lives." At a 1978 conference, WHO and the United Nations Children's Fund (UNICEF) passed a joint resolution stating that primary health care (PHC) was the key to attaining health for all. PHC is defined as "essential health care made universally accessible to individuals and families in the community by means acceptable to them, through their full participation and at a cost that the community and country can afford." Clearly, WHO sees health as a human right that should be available to all (World Health Organization 1998a). Health care would then be the activities intended to sustain, promote, and enhance health.

WHO acknowledges that different countries will choose different paths and means to achieve HFA, which is basically an issue of social justice (World Health Organization 1998a). Others may define health, or the lack of health, in different ways. For example, definitions of sickness vary widely in different cultures. In some cultures, alcoholism is viewed as an illness while in others it is not. People can be diagnosed as physically, mentally and socially ill according to cultural definitions. The authors think that the WHO definition makes sense, but it is clearly not the only definition of health. Although we focus primarily on health and health care issues in the United States, we think that the WHO definitions and ideas about health, including HFA and PHC, provide a useful global framework and context for considering domestic health care issues.

Because health care issues are so fundamental, it is hard to overstate their importance. Numerous sociologists work toward understanding and improving health and healthcare. For example, the Society for the Study of Social Problems' Division of Health, Health Policy, and Health Services studies all aspects of health care in the United States. Some of the most important areas for study include the social causes of disease and disability, how health and illness are socially defined, the delivery of health care, and the study of comparative health care systems and policies (Greil, et al. 1997). Health care problems also include those related to mental health issues, especially the role of social factors in mental disorders (Rosenfield 1997).

Much of this research suggests that American health care is in crisis. Aspects of the crisis include skyrocketing medical costs, barriers to health care for many people, lack of access to primary care as specialization increases, relatively high infant mortality rates, a focus on caring for people after they become sick rather than preventing illness, and a lack of public accountability in the American health care system (Conrad 1997). A survey in 1998 indicates that 33 percent of Americans would like to rebuild the health care system completely. This is an increase of 4 percentage points from 1988 (Knox 1998). Conrad also suggests that the "medicalization of deviance" is one aspect of our health care crisis. By this he means that many social problems, such as drug addiction, and natural life events, such as death, are increasingly seen as medical problems (Conrad 1997).

Perhaps the most serious problems in American health care are linked to continuing disparities in access to health care and well-being. The most recent study of health in the United States—referred to in the "In the News" section—documents pervasive inequalities in health. "Life expectancy is related to family income" (National Center for Health Statistics 1998b:5). Less well educated and lower income Americans have higher death rates for chronic diseases, communicable diseases, and injuries. They also have higher rates of suicide and homicide, and are more likely to report fair or poor health status, rather than good health status. Although infant mortality declined from 1983 to 1995, "substantial socioeconomic disparities remained in 1995" (National Center for Health Statistics 1998b:4). Mothers with more education tend to receive better prenatal care, giving their infants a head start in life. These are just some of the ways in which inequality and health are linked together. Although some of these links are well-known, health researcher Elsie Pamuk, one of the report's co-authors, noted that "we were all somewhat surprised by the strength and persistency of the findings" (Associated Press 1998:A9).

In terms of specific diseases, cancer and diseases of the heart and circulatory system are the most frequent causes of death in the United States, as well as in other industrial societies. These types of diseases affect our physical body. Less dangerous illnesses are also part of living. For example, people commonly become ill from respiratory and intestinal diseases such as colds, flu, and the like. Vaccinations play an important role in keeping people healthy (National Center for Health statistics 1998b; World Health Organization 1998b).

Table 12-1 Mortality Statistics, 1995

Infant Mortality—The 1995 infant mortality rate was 7.6 deaths per 1,000 live births. The death rate from sudden infant death syndrome (SIDS) was down 15 percent between 1994 and 1995.

Life Expectancy—In 1995, life expectancy at birth was 75.8 years. Women currently are expected to outlive men by an average of 6.4 years. The difference between life expectancy for the European American population (76.5 years) and the African American population (69.6) remains at about 7 years.

Deaths and Death Rates—In 1995, a record 2,312,132 deaths were registered. This was an increase of 33,138 over the number in 1994.

Death Rates for Children, Teens, and Young Adults—Death rates decreased substantially from 1994 for those under 5 years of age, primarily death due to accidents decreased. The death rate also declined for those aged 15–24 and 25–34 years, particularly for African American males, and this decline was primarily due to decreases in homicide.

Leading Causes of Death—Heart disease, cancer, and stroke continue as the three leading causes of death.

Source: Center for Disease Control and Prevention. 1996. "Report of Final Mortality Statistics, 1995." *Monthly Vital Statistics Report*, Vol. 45 (No. 11) Supplement 2, June 12. Hyattsville, Maryland: U. S. Department of Health and Human Services, National Center for Health Statistics.

Other illnesses affect a person's mind or emotional health. Mental illness is a serious epidemic in the United States. Although to many it does not appear as real as physical illness, it is a serious social problem affecting many people. Approximately 7 million Americans suffer from some sort of mental disorder each year (National Center for Health Statistics 1998a, 1998b). Most mental illnesses involve anxiety or depression. Defining mental illness is extremely difficult because not everyone agrees on what is appropriate behavior and therefore on what is inappropriate, or abnormal. In other words, it is difficult to arrive at objective standards by which to judge someone's mental state. Mental illnesses can take many forms. They range from personality disorders such as depression or phobias to more severe disorders such as psychoses. Most sociologists are interested in why someone is defined as mentally ill and the social reaction and treatment that follow from such definition.

One interesting recent development in mental health care is the use of computers in diagnosis. Phoned-in interviews with computerized diagnostic programs are spotting psychiatric problems at higher rates than in doctor-patient encounters. Although primary care physicians are the main providers of treatment for such mental disorders as depression, anxiety, substance abuse, and eating disorders, some doctors have had little experience with these disorders and so have difficulty detecting them. A computer-based questionnaire allows people to call a toll-free number to be evaluated. People may be more willing to admit symptoms of certain disorders to the computer than to the primary care physician. There is some skepticism regarding computer accuracy in evaluating mental health (Kobak, et al. 1997).

Men and women seem to receive treatment for mental disorders on a somewhat equal basis, although there are important differences. Men are more likely to be hospitalized while women are more likely to receive outpatient treatment. Women are twice as likely as men to be treated for depression and placed on tranquilizers. (See "A Closer Look: Women and Mental Health Diagnoses.")

A Closer Look

Women and Mental Health Diagnoses

Ronnie Elwell (1989) a sociologist and a psychiatric nurse, carried out research on Borderline Personality Disorder. Elwell, along with other sociologists of health and mental health, noted that mental health diagnoses seemed to be subject to changing medical fashions. The medical construction of reality, in the form of diagnosis, depends on the social and economic conditions under which the diagnosis occurs, the power and status of the persons or institutions defining the problem, and on the relationship of those labeled as "ill" to the power structure of society. Elwell noted that these factors seemed particularly important as they related to "women's illnesses."

Women in the United States visit physicians more frequently than men in all age groups, except for the very old; are more frequently diagnosed with a variety of illnesses, including certain mental illnesses such as Borderline Personality Disorder; and have not traditionally been part of the medical elite that determines diagnoses.

Elwell found that the relationship of women to the medical power structure, the incorporation of social and political values into diagnoses, and political and social negotiating processes determined the emergence of Borderline Personality Disorder as a new diagnosis applied primarily to women. The diagnosis, which was first officially recognized in 1980, seemed to reflect ideas and assumptions about "a women's illness" and women's "hysterical nature."

Overall, the world's population today is healthier and will live longer than people of any other generation in history. In the eighteenth century, the average life expectancy was no more than 35 years. Life expectancy in the industrialized nations is currently about 70 years. With this increase in life expectancy comes a similar increase in expectations for physical health (National Center for Health Statistics 1998b; World Health Organization 1998b).

Social epidemiology is the study of how health and disease are distributed throughout a society's population. Social epidemiologists investigate the origin and spread of epidemic diseases and also contrast the health of various categories of people. For example, almost 80 percent of people in the United States with incomes over $35,000 evaluate their health as excellent or very good. Not quite half of those in families earning less than $10,000 make this claim. Because people of color are three times as likely as whites to be poor, they are more prone to die in infancy and to suffer the effects of violence and illness as adults (National Center for Health Statistics 1998b). (See "A Closer Look: National Center for Health Statistics Website.")

The United States is almost unique among industrialized nations in not having a universal, government-subsidized health care. For the most part, medical care is a private, profit-making industry. In the past, patients generally paid physicians and hospitals directly for services. Starting during the Great Depression of the 1930s and growing rapidly after World War II, health insurance became the primary way to pay for health care. Health insurance

A Closer Look

National Center for Health Statistics Website

The U.S. Department of Health and Human Services (DHHS) and its Center for Disease Control (CDC) maintain the National Center for Health Statistics Website. The site, located at http://www.cdc.gov/nchswww/, provides a wide variety of information about health and related issues in the United States. The site has numerous options. For example, if you click on "News Releases" you can obtain information on the well-being of children in the United States. You can also obtain information on rates of obesity, rates of teenage sexual activity, and general information concerning these, and many other issues. If you click on "Fact Sheets" you can obtain information on trends in child bearing, statistics concerning child abuse, and rates of obesity in the United States. This website offers extensive information on many health-related issues. From it you can link to other useful sites. You can also gain access to *Health, United States, 1998 With Socioeconomic Status and Health Chartbook* (National Center for Health Statistics 1998b.)

in the United States is primarily obtained as a benefit of a full-time job. People who do not have full-time jobs, who work for very small companies, or who work for themselves may not have health insurance at all, unless they pay for it themselves directly. Many Americans stay with jobs they may not like in order to retain their health care coverage. In 1997, an estimated 43.4 million Americans did not have health insurance. This was an increase of 1.7 from 1996. The poor and the near poor are least likely to be covered (U.S. Bureau of the Census 1998). Approximately 70.1 percent of Americans had private health care in 1997, but few programs pay all medical costs. Figure 12-1 shows you what kinds of health insurance Americans in general and poor Americans had in 1997.

Figure 12-1 Types of Health Insurance People Had in the United States: 1997 (Percent of All Persons and Poor Persons)

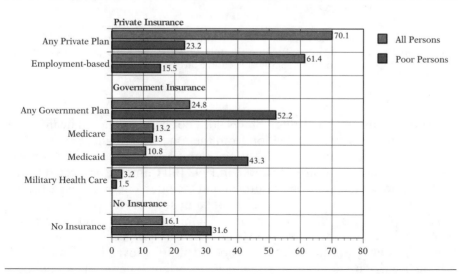

Source: U.S. Bureau of the Census. 1998. "Health Insurance Coverage: 1997." *Current Population Reports*, Consumer Income. Report P60-202. September 1. Washington, D.C.: Department of Commerce, Economics and Statistics Administration.

In 1965, Congress created Medicare and Medicaid, which are government-controlled programs. Medicare pays some of the medical costs for people over 65. However, it does not cover long-term nursing home care for many chronic illnesses that primarily afflict the elderly, such as Alzheimer's Disease. In 1997, 13.2 percent of Americans had Medicare. Medicaid provides benefits for the poor. In 1997, 43.3 percent of poor Americans were covered by Medicaid at some point during the year; 31.6 percent of poor people, and 16.1 percent of the whole population had no health insurance of any kind in 1997 (U.S. Bureau of the Census 1998). You can see from Figure 12-2 that the lower a person's income, the less likely that person is to have health insurance. Those who are most likely to need health coverage are least likely to have it. Many American children do not have health coverage, and you can see from Figure 12-3 that black and Hispanic children are more likely to lack health insurance.

Figure 12-2 Percent of Persons Never Covered by Health Insurance During the Year, by Household Income: 1997

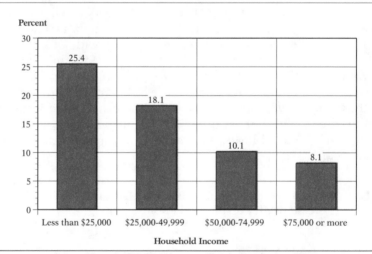

Source: U.S. Bureau of the Census. 1998. "Health Insurance Coverage: 1997." *Current Population Reports*, Consumer Income. Report P60-202. September 1. Washington, D.C.: Department of Commerce, Economics and Statistics Administration.

The reasons why the United States does not have a national health care program include strong opposition from the American Medical Association and the insurance industry. In addition, many people seem to fear government control of health care. However, in 1992 Bill Clinton was elected President. He had campaigned on a platform that include a comprehensive health care reform. In September 1993, Clinton launched his Health Security proposal. Despite apparent public support for some type of universal health care coverage, by September 1994 the Health Security proposal was essentially dead (Skocpol 1996). Clinton then proposed shifting away from traditional private health care to increasing reliance on various types of health maintenance organizations (HMOs) and government-funded programs. The Clinton administration called their Health Security program "managed competition" and claimed it would lower costs because employees and businesses

Figure 12-3 Who Are the Uninsured Children? Percent of Children Without Health Insurance, 1997

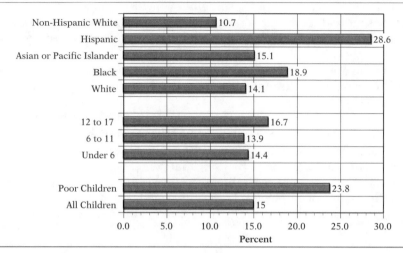

Non-Hispanic White — 10.7
Hispanic — 28.6
Asian or Pacific Islander — 15.1
Black — 18.9
White — 14.1

12 to 17 — 16.7
6 to 11 — 13.9
Under 6 — 14.4

Poor Children — 23.8
All Children — 15

Percent (0.0, 5.0, 10.0, 15.0, 20.0, 25.0, 30.0)

Note: Persons of Hispanic Origin May Be of Any Race.
Source: U.S. Bureau of the Census. 1998. "Health Insurance Coverage: 1997." *Current Population Reports*, Consumer Income. Report P60-202. September 1. Washington, D.C.: Department of Commerce, Economics and Statistics Administration.

would join together to bargain with competing medical providers to provide the greatest value in health care. To make the system universal, the government would ensure that all Americans would have basic health care coverage. The Health Security proposal, which included stringent cost-cutting measures and strict governmental regulation of health care, made a good target for antigovernment forces, who distorted the proposal and played on fears of government regulation (Skocpol 1996). The proposal was far from the kind of universal health care system that many social scientists, health policy analysts, and activists had been hoping for. As limited as it was it was soundly defeated.

Many poor people in the United States rely on emergency rooms for their primary medical care. —*Photo: photostogo.com.*

The defeat of the Health Security proposal and the lack of a universal system leave unequal access to health care as a major problem in the United States. There is certainly not a scarcity of medical personnel. The United States has more doctors per person than any other industrialized country as well as an abundance of medical technology and hospitals. In the United States, the "best medical care in the world" is available to those who can pay for it or who are covered by health insurance. But health care resources are unevenly distributed throughout the country with rural areas increasingly underserved.

Soaring medical costs are another serious problem. In 1993, the cost of health care in the United States was $884 billion compared to $75 billion in 1970 (Cockerham 1995). In 1970, health care costs accounted for 7.1 percent of the gross domestic product. By 1995, that percentage had increased to 13.7 (Hacker 1997). There are several reasons for rising costs. The United States has traditionally not emphasized preventive medicine. Doctors are trained to cure illnesses rather than to maintain health. They rely heavily on technology in providing care.

Levels of Causation

There are many issues to be addressed in looking at health and health care. Some issues can best be examined at an individual level. Others are better explained at a cultural or structural level.

Individual

It is a common assumption that we are individually responsible for our physical and mental health. For example, when smokers develop lung cancer, one tends to blame them for making the choice to smoke. When people develop AIDS, some people assume they were either promiscuous, drug addicts, or homosexual. Blame points to the individual. Despite this, people become ill for a variety of reasons, many of which are uncontrollable. The pollutants that industries dump into the environment are killers. Air pollution is related to deaths from bronchitis, heart disease, and emphysema, as well as several types of cancer. There is little doubt that the depletion of the ozone layer caused by atmospheric pollution is a major factor in the increase in skin cancer. For the poor, environmental factors are compounded by the lack of adequate housing, health care, and nutrition.

People seem to be even less sympathetic to those considered mentally ill. They are more apt to blame an individual instead of attempting to determine whether the environment has had any effect on the person's well-being. In the past, mental disorders were seen to be caused by demons, and those "possessed" were flogged or even killed. Today most mental disorders are judged to be still medical matters but are treated generally on an individual basis. Sociologists do not use an individualistic approach, because they realize that environmental, cultural, and structural factors play significant roles in people's well-being.

The attempt to connect mental illnesses with the environment is a relatively new area of study. In the 1950s, there were more than half a million mental patients living in approximately 300 state and county mental hospitals throughout the United States. Mental patients were regarded as incurable and were consigned to spending their entire lives in mental institutions. In the 1960s, a redefinition of mental illness took place. Sociologists and psychologists argued that mentally ill people could function adequately in a community with supervision and assistance. This redefinition of mental illness led to the **deinstitutionalization** of many mental patients (Mechanic 1990). The idea was to move patients from hospitals to the community and to provide supervision and support for them. However, the money did not follow the former patients to the community. Adequate housing, financial assistance, or social support was not provided for most patients, leading to numerous problems that could have been avoided. Deinstitutionalization may have gone too far, too fast, but it was primarily doomed by inadequate resources. Mental health care providers and researchers continue to search for effective ways of treating mental illness.

Despite the recognition of social and cultural factors in mental illness, many clinicians still make diagnoses based on individual traits which are not connected to any structural or cultural factors. For example, many clinicians believe that schizophrenia has a hereditary component. Hare (1988) argues that because schizophrenics have low fertility rates, one would expect the rates of schizophrenia to be decreasing if the hereditary component was strong. This does not seem to be happening. As we learn more about genetic, cultural, and social factors in the causation of schizophrenia, we may halt its progression. Focusing solely on individual factors does not seem promising.

Cultural

Every culture provides sick roles. A **sick role** includes the culturally defined appropriate behavior of a person labeled as sick and the culturally approved responses to people who are sick. Sick roles are culturally and sociologically determined. The sociologist Talcott Parsons contributed greatly to our understanding of sick roles. He suggested that in the United States, the role of the sick person includes the right to be excused from social responsibilities and other everyday social roles. People do expect sick persons to seek help and care, and if they do not do so, they may be blamed for their illness and for becoming sicker (Parsons 1975). For certain kinds of illnesses, people are often blamed for their illness. They may be stigmatized. This stigmatization may lead others to shun them and hold them responsible not only for not seeking care but also for becoming ill in the first place. This is especially true of those suffering from AIDS, mental illness, and sexually transmitted diseases (STD) such as herpes or gonorrhea.

Culturally defined gender roles also affect health and health care. In the United States, women generally live longer than men. However, women go to doctors more often and are sick more often. Women may be more willing to accept the sick role because they find less **role conflict** in doing so (Klonoff and Landrine 1992). Men may see illness and the sick role as signs of weaknesses, but health is a central issue in many women's lives. Women are generally the initiators of health care and the caretakers for their families. Women also make up the majority of health care workers. Little attention is paid to women's paid and unpaid work in caring for the dependent, aged, or ill. Three out of four caregivers are women who are often caring for both aging parents and children at the same time. This care is usually unpaid and includes housekeeping, meal preparation, feeding, dressing, bathing, and other activities (Wooten 1998).

Despite the different health experiences of men and women, until recently, relatively little attention was paid to the importance of gender for issues of health and reproduction. For example, although women tend to outlive men, research has not revealed why women appear to suffer from ill health more than men. In fact, we know little about the patterns of health and disease in women. Another area of concern is related to culturally created pressures to be thin. Young women are especially vulnerable to such pressures, which often lead to serious health care risks and problems with self-esteem (Hesse-Biber 1996). (See "A Closer Look: Girls and Self-Esteem: A Health Crisis.")

A Closer Look

Girls and Self-Esteem: A Health Crisis

A survey by the Commonwealth Fund (1997) of 3,586 girls and 3,162 boys in grades 5 through 12 has documented that more often than not, young girls entering puberty experience a crisis in confidence that renders them vulnerable to risky health behaviors, such as smoking and using drugs or alcohol. They also are at risk for eating disorders and unwanted pregnancies. According to experts working within the field of self-esteem and gender, self-esteem in girls peaks at about age nine, then begins to plummet. Girls become very concerned with how they look, and many begin to think they cannot measure up to the competition, especially the stereotypical waiflike image of the ideal American woman with the tiny waistline (Brody 1997a, 1997b).

According to the Commonwealth Fund survey, 39 percent of girls in grades 5 through 12 reported smoking, drinking, or using drugs. More than two-thirds of high school seniors have had sexual intercourse, and each year there are almost one million pregnancies, 85 percent of them unplanned. A disturbingly high rate of violence against young girls was documented as well, with 18 percent of the girls reporting some form of physical or sexual abuse. More than half the abuse was perpetrated by a family member. Such abuse can lead to risky health behaviors, with those reporting abuse being twice as likely to drink alcohol, smoke cigarettes, or have eating disorders.

Dieting starts as young as nine years old for many girls. Up to 25 percent of adolescents—90 percent of them girls—regularly purge themselves to control their weight. With all this may come depression. An alarming 29 percent of the girls in this survey reported suicidal thoughts. The connection between mental health and body image is clear, according to the Commonwealth Fund survey: young girls feel too much pressure to conform to an unattainable image, and it is making them sick.

AIDS is another area where little attention is paid to women. AIDS in women is increasing faster than it is in men, both in the United States and throughout the world (Bagley and Merlo 1995). AIDS strikes poor women and women of color disproportionately, with over half the cases due to intravenous drug use. An AIDS diagnosis is based on a definition developed by the Centers for Disease Control (CDC), which has followed the progress of the disease since the first cases were reported in the United States in 1981. Neither the first definition, in 1982, nor the second definition, in 1987, included gynecological conditions (Corea 1992).

This quilt was created to commemorate Michael Shall, who died in 1995. AIDS/HIV has become a grave health problem around the world.—*Photo by Courtney Frisse. Panel creators: Basja Samuelson and Gretchen Klotz Westlight.*

As the definition changed, and new diseases and infections have been added, the number of AIDS cases in women has dramatically increased. Invasive cancer of the cervix was added to the list, which raised the number of HIV-positive women counted as AIDS cases. The CDC definition is important for many reasons. Once a condition or disease has been included in the definition, more effort will be made to develop specific treatments for that condition. A person diagnosed with AIDS may become eligible for experimental drug treatments and may be approved for Social Security disability coverage. Many women with AIDS and HIV are not eligible for such treatments because they contracted AIDS through intravenous drug use. This is rather discriminatory for many reasons, including issues of class and race. Women with AIDS or who are HIV-positive are largely ignored unless they are a threat to others, such as male sexual partners or a fetus they are carrying. The average woman with AIDS lives only 27.4 weeks after diagnosis, while the average man lives 39 months. This difference may be the result of later diagnosis and therefore less treatment for women (Corea 1992).

Some feminist scholars argue that the medical profession—which is largely dominated by men—controls women. For example, these scholars argue that women do not feel in control during pregnancy and birth, and that there is little evidence to support the view that technological intervention in childbirth is beneficial to mother or child (Doyal 1995). Some of these scholars suggest that women and doctors have very different views of pregnancy and childbirth. From this point of view, women are seen as having little control over the childbirth process. As sociologist Margaret Andersen summarizes this view,

> health care institutions in the society are dominated by men, even though healing and caring for others have traditionally been defined as the work of women. Because of the sexist structure of health care in this society, women have had little control over their own reproductive lives. (Andersen 1997:188)

One way in which medicine and health care in the United States have harmed women is related to medical research. Medical studies were often carried out using men as subjects and excluding women. The implications of the studies for women's health received little attention. In response to criticisms that women had been excluded from research funded by the National Institutes of Health (NIH), NIH set up the Office of Research on Women's Health in 1990 (Andersen 1997). Andersen notes that

> the exclusion of women from medical research not only obscures our understanding of women's health, it also obscures an important point: physical and mental health are heavily conditioned by social factors like gender, race/ethnicity, and class. (1997:187)

Gender, race and ethnicity, and class are not the only factors affecting health. Life styles also play an important role in health. A rising standard of living and increased agricultural production have meant better food, shelter, and clothing for the average person today. However, most Americans are less active than their predecessors. The amount of physical activity required for daily living has been reduced, even though exercise is essential to good health and has been shown to reduce the risk of heart disease—the leading cause of death in the United States. Diet also has important effects on health. Americans do not eat enough fruits and vegetables. It is important to note that these lifestyles are related to social factors such as race and ethnicity and class. Class in particular plays a crucial role in lifestyle and health.

Poor people have more serious health problems than those who are better off. Lack of adequate clothing, shelter, and food exacerbates already difficult situations. The United States has an extremely high infant mortality rate for an industrialized country, and African American children, in particular, have high rates of infant mortality and death in their first year of life. Poverty is directly implicated in many of these health problems because poor Americans who are not adequately fed are more susceptible to illness. We shall consider these social factors further in looking at structural explanations for health problems.

Structural

Conflict theorists draw a connection between health and social inequality and tie health to the operation of capitalism. Most people who lack health care coverage in the United States have low incomes. Capitalism only provides well for the rich. Some conflict theorists argue that the real problem is not access to medical care but the character of capitalist medicine. Profit making turns hospitals, doctors, and pharmaceutical industries into multibillion-dollar corporations. Health care appears to be motivated by a concern for profit, not people (Pear and Eckholm 1991).

Those who subscribe to the conflict perspective focus on the reasons why such high rates of mental illness are found in our society and how mental illness is linked to class structure. The conflict perspective sees mental illness as the result of the competitive nature of the economic system and the tensions produced by the need to succeed at any cost. Thus, mental illnesses affect the lower classes more since these people bear the greatest burden of inequality. In addition, the labeling of mental illness works as a system of social control. Those who are labeled mentally ill are often the outgroups in society. Labeling theory suggests that mental illness is merely a label applied to those who break the rules dictated by the ruling class. Labeling theorists place responsibility for mental disorders on the social environment rather than on the individual.

Structural functionalists argue that the U.S. health care system is failing to do its job. They argue that the health care system needs to be reorganized in a way that ensures coverage for everyone. They call for reallocating medical personnel, reducing fraud and medical malpractice, and lowering costs. In the nineteenth century, medical knowledge was so limited that an individual doctor could handle most demands for health care. As medical knowledge grew, people began to see health care as a fundamental right, but our society did not seem to adapt adequately. Not everyone is able to acquire adequate health care.

Medicine became professionalized in the 1900s. In 1906, the AMA examined 160 medical schools in the United States and found only 82 acceptable. The Flexner Report of 1910 classified medical schools into A, B, and C categories and recommended that only the class A schools be retained. The class A schools were modeled after the Johns Hopkins University School of Medicine, which required post-graduate training. The class B and C schools did not have this requirement and many were no more than "diploma mills." However, these were also the schools at which minorities and women could receive medical training. Due to the Flexner Report, admission and teaching standards were raised and certain schools were funded to attract more faculty members and students (Duffy 1993). The others were closed. Affluent white males controlled and made up the faculty and students of the class A schools. These schools then either refused to admit women and minorities or placed severe enrollment limits on them (Goode 1960). In combination with the growth of the AMA and licensing boards governed by physicians, the medical profession gained control over medical knowledge, over who would be admitted to the profession, the conditions of practice, and methods of payment (Starr 1982).

Today health care is big business, in fact, it is the largest industry in the United States. People need health care, and health care services are sold at inflated prices. Programs that would help the poor and pay doctors less are consistently opposed in the United States. One suggestion, according to conflict theorists, would be to reduce the medical profession's control over the distribution of health care. The government would become more involved in the health care system.

Major changes in health care are occurring today. Women and minority group members can no longer be prevented from enrolling in medical schools and their numbers are beginning to equal those of white men. There are also changes in paying for health care with the rise of HMOs and managed care, which lessen the autonomy of physicians. The government has become increasingly involved in health care, either directly through Medicare and Medicaid, or indirectly through funding and various quality assurance programs.

Consequences

What are the consequences of unequal access or at least differential access to medical care? What are the consequences of being physically and mentally ill? Before we answer these questions, it is necessary to point out that society has definitely become "medicalized." This means that all aspects of health and illness have been given medical meaning, even things that were not previously considered medical. Examples include balding, weight, wrinkles, and small breasts. Even many criminal behaviors have become matters to be understood and treated as medical conditions (Akers 1996).

Despite the fact that society has become so medicalized, not everyone has access to medical treatment. As mentioned previously, one of the biggest differences between the poor and the nonpoor is their respective levels of health. Not only do the poor receive less health care, but what they do receive is often inferior in kind than that given to the nonpoor.

The relationship between health care and social class shows up in infant mortality rates, stillbirth rates, chronic disease, heart disease, diabetes, cancer, and ar-

The development of managed care in the United States has led many physicians to worry that health care decisions will be based on economic rather than medical criteria. —*Photo: photostogo.com.*

thritis. Reasons for this lie in the diets of the poor, stress in their lives, higher rates of smoking, and most important, the lack of access to adequate health care. The poor remain largely outside the mainstream of private health care. Their sources of health care are mainly hospitals, emergency rooms, and clinics. Many poor people may delay medical treatment because they can't afford it and they lack health benefits. When people delay treatment until their conditions are serious, health care costs are likely to be far greater than with timely care (National Center for Health Statistics 1998b).

Any discussion of poverty inevitably leads to a discussion of race and gender. Racial and ethnic oppression complicate health issues. Economic inequality often prevents people of color, as well as other poor Americans, from gaining access to health care. Racism itself certainly produces discrimination in the health care system. For example, health care workers may resentfully treat people of color on welfare as "charity cases," in contrast to their attitude with paying patients.

Although the health of the African American population has improved over the last few decades, there still exist differences between African Americans and European Americans concerning health matters. For example, three times as many African American men die as European American men in the age 25 to 44 category. The mortality rate for African American men with heart disease is 50 percent higher than for European American men and 85 percent higher in the stroke category. The chances of African American men getting cancer is three and one-half times as great.

African American women are three times as likely to die from reproductive complications as European American women and are more likely to succumb to cancer, heart disease, strokes, and diabetes. Lifestyle differences seem to explain these discrepancies, but African Americans are also less likely to receive adequate health care (National Center for Health Statistics 1998b).

As we noted above, women receive unequal treatment regarding health care as well. For example, they are twice as likely as men to be given prescription tranquilizers, which suggests that women's health complaints are not taken seriously. Women are often excluded from medical research, which results in a lack of knowledge regarding some health conditions for women. For example, most studies on heart disease focused on men, leaving little hard information on the effect or prevalence of heart disease on women.

What are the consequences of being labeled mentally ill? Obviously, there is a social stigma attached to mental disorders. Within our society, there exist norms that are so ingrained in our lives that we think they are part of human nature. When social norms are violated, we assume the violating behavior is abnormal or unnatural. The one who violates the norms is labeled abnormal and even crazy in some cases. There is no question that some people are unfairly labeled. For those who may be truly mentally ill, this label is difficult to shake. A recent Massachusetts study indicates that many people believe that shame is attached to mental illness. Of the 600 people surveyed, 10 percent got information about mental illness from physicians; 27 percent received their information from newspapers and magazines; and 22 percent got it from television. The Department of Mental Health in Massachusetts contends that 40 percent of adults in Massachusetts believe that mental illnesses result from character flaws and personality defects. Nearly half surveyed believe that cycles of the moon affect people who are manic depressive.

According to the National Institute of Mental Health statistics, treatment succeeds in 60 to 80 percent of serious mental illnesses, including schizophrenia and major depression, while the success rate of certain treatments of heart disease is only 41 percent (Driscoll 1997). Despite the success of treating mental illness, the stigma persists. In addition, many insurance companies do not cover mental illness as they do physical illness. Mentally ill people need support. Most do not have to be hospitalized since community-based programs will suffice in treating them. However, a growing number of mentally ill people are homeless, mostly because of poor physical health and little support (see "A Closer Look: Homelessness and Mental Illness.")

A Closer Look

Homelessness and Mental Illness

The National Coalition on Homelessness Fact Sheet on Mental Illness and Homelessness provides valuable information on the relationship between mental illness and homelessness (National Coalition for the Homeless 1997). Research by Kegel and his colleagues suggests that 20 to 25 percent of the single adult homeless population have some sort of severe and persistent mental illness (Kegel, et al. 1996). People often attribute the growth in the number of mentally ill homeless people to deinstitutionalization; however, most patients were released from mental hospitals in the 1950s and 1960s, but the vast increases in homelessness did not occur until the 1980s. That increase was largely due to declining income and fewer housing options, which pushed people into homelessness. ☞

> ☞ Severely mentally ill homeless people now tend to remain homeless for longer periods of time. Many have little contact with family and friends. The main reasons for the longer periods of homelessness include increasing barriers to employment and poor physical health. People with mental illness require ongoing help, although not necessarily hospitalization. Only about 5 to 7 percent of homeless persons with mental illness need to be institutionalized. Community-based treatment is both imperative and scarce. Such community-based treatment can provide the framework necessary to end homelessness for many people.
>
> Deirdre Oakley and Deborah Dennis (1996) indicate that homeless persons with mental disorders are willing to use services that are easy to enter and that meet their perceived needs. The National Coalition for the Homeless (1997) argues that more programs are needed to help the homeless, especially those who are mentally ill. In addition, Supplemental Security Income (SSI) benefit levels must be increased so that mentally ill people are not forced to live in poverty. Benefit levels have not kept up with increases in the cost of rent. Finally, if society is committed to deinstitutionalization of the mentally ill, more community-based services and other supports are crucial.

Interventions

Despite the fact that the United States does not have a national health care system, the government pays the biggest share of the health care bill—about 41 percent. Insurance companies pay about one-third of the cost, and the public pays about one-quarter directly. Most Americans believe that they cannot afford to pay for health care directly. Those lucky enough to have health insurance also usually pay something out of their own pockets. Most policies have limits on coverage. The private insurance system generally offers inadequate coverage and is wasteful and inefficient. Private insurance companies are more expensive than government programs according to one consumer group. *Consumer Reports* puts the administrative cost of the Canadian system at 1 to 2.5 percent and of private insurance at 10 to 11 percent.

In considering interventions to alleviate problems of health and the health care system in the United States, it is useful to look more closely at the Canadian system. Canada has a single-payer health care system, in which most health care "is not *provided* by the government. It is *paid for* by governments" (Armstrong, Armstrong, and Fegan 1998: 2). The Canadian system is based on the Canada Health Act which sets out five principles the provinces must follow to receive funding for their health care services. These principles "require that core medical services be universal, portable, accessible, comprehensive, and publicly administered" (Armstrong, Armstrong, and Fegan 1998: 2). The requirement of universality means that everyone must be covered, while portability means that you can take the coverage with you if you switch jobs. Canadians need not hold on to jobs they dislike in order to keep their health coverage. By accessibility, the Canada Health Act means that there should be no barriers to health care for anyone and comprehensiveness means that all necessary health care services are covered. Public administration of the health care system saves "20–30 percent overhead associated with [the] overhead and profit. . . . [of] for-profit companies" (Armstrong, Armstrong, and Fegan 1998:xiv).

Although some social scientists, policy analysts, and health industry representatives in the United States criticize the Canadian system, it seems to have worked remarkably well at providing high quality health care to all Canadians. In 1993, in a Gallup Poll, 96 percent of Canadians preferred their system to that of the United States (Armstrong, Armstrong, and Fegan 1998). Dissatisfaction with the Canadian system has increased in recent years, as economic problems have led to cutbacks in resources and cost-cutting measures (Knox 1998). Nonetheless, most Canadians are quite satisfied with their system and the United States can learn much from the Canadian experience.

We mentioned Medicare and Medicaid earlier. Medicare buys medical services for people 65 and older while Medicaid helps the poor, the blind, and the disabled. Medicaid is administered by the states and each state has its own standards of eligibility and levels of benefits. These programs have major gaps, and those who suffer most are the increasing number of the poor who are not eligible for Medicaid and cannot afford private insurance. Medicaid was initially established in the mid-1960s, and it covered about 70 percent of those with incomes below the poverty line. Only about 40 percent of the poor are covered today. Medicare is not as restrictive as Medicaid. Almost everyone over 65 is covered. One major drawback is that Medicare does not cover the cost of nursing homes. Many elderly couples with one member in a nursing home are driven into poverty, and many people residing in nursing homes become impoverished quite rapidly (Treas 1995).

A recent trend in the health care field is home care. Home care is becoming more and more common for cancer patients and those who have AIDS (Minton 1997). According to the Centers for Disease Control (CDC), between 650,000 and 900,000 Americans are living with HIV. The number of people who have contracted AIDS has slowed down in recent years, with African Americans representing a high number of cases. The most difficult aspect of treating people with HIV is funding. Most people with AIDS and HIV are not eligible for Medicare because they do not become disabled enough to go on Social Security. For those who have insurance, many elements of treatment are not covered, such as home health care and mental health issues. For those who can cover home health care, it seems to be easier to live with AIDS and HIV. Most home health care aides spend a lot of time working with people on mental health issues. Mental health remains a critical aspect of AIDS and HIV treatment because of the stigma associated with the disease (Minton 1997). Home health care lessens the stigma for many patients since they are cared for more on a personal level, rather than an institutional one.

Deinstitutionalization of the mentally ill led to community-based care for them. Mentally ill people who remain in their community during treatment avoid the shock of being taken out of their normal environment. They also escape the labeling, humiliation, and feelings of powerlessness that may accompany being institutionalized. Community centers offer many services; some involve short-term hospitalization and other outpatient services. There are not enough of these centers in the United States, despite their success in treating the mentally ill.

Preventive medicine would probably create a much healthier society and make intervention with the ill less complicated. Our current health care system places too much emphasis on treatment and not enough on prevention. It would probably be cheaper to educate people about diet and exercise than to perform thousands of heart surgeries each year. Preventive medicine could include courses on healthier living.

The Future of Health and Health Care

The quality of health care has not improved as much as medical advances might lead one to expect. Millions of people continue to live without adequate health care or with none at all. Health costs continue to soar, and social inequalities remaining within society will only continue to exacerbate health care problems. Technological advances in medicine have driven national spending to an all-time high.

Doctors and medical researchers will continue to combat disease and mental disorders, but health care costs will remain a serious national issue. All in all, it seems that our country needs more nurses and general practitioners or family physicians. There seem to be too many specialists and not enough general physicians. Changing this balance would save money and provide more general care to everyone. Nurse practitioners are increasing in numbers but need to obtain more professional authority and higher pay. Having more nurses and nurse practitioners will also save money in the long run.

Whether or not the United States develops a national health care plan is uncertain. Most Americans appear to want a national health care system, but the medical establishment succeeds in delaying this change and maybe even preventing it. The American Medical Association provides the strongest barrier by being the second largest spender among all the political action committees in the country.

Summary

Health can be defined as the extent to which a person experiences a state of mental, physical, and social well-being. Health care can be defined as all those activities intended to sustain, promote, and enhance health. The definition of illness, however, is generally the absence of health. Definitions of illness vary widely and according to different cultures. Cancer and heart disease are the leading causes of death in the United States. Other illnesses affect Americans' minds or emotional health. Mental illness is a serious epidemic in the United States, yet it is difficult to define because not everyone agrees on what is appropriate or inappropriate behavior.

Social epidemiology is the study of how health and disease are distributed throughout a society's population. Social epidemiologists investigate the origin and spread of epidemic diseases, and they also contrast the health of various categories of people.

The United States does not have a universal, government-subsidized health care system. Approximately three-fourths of the population have private insurance. A major problem with the health care system in the United States is unequal access.

In the United States, people have sick roles—sets of norms setting out the appropriate behavior of and response to people labeled as sick. Females are generally healthier than males and live longer. Poor people have more health problems than those who are better off.

Conflict theorists draw a connection between health and social inequality. Structural functionalists argue that the U.S. health care system is failing to do its job. Not everyone has access to medical treatment. This shows up in infant mortality rates as well as among the poor, especially those of color.

A social stigma is attached to mental disorders. Mentally ill people need support. Most do not have to be hospitalized if they have access to community-based programs, the number of which is growing, but is still inadequate.

The government pays the biggest share of the health care bill. Employers also pay a large share of employees' health care. Medicare and Medicaid are government programs set up to assist the elderly and the disabled and the poor, respectively. A recent trend in health care is home health care.

Preventive medicine would probably create a much healthier society and make intervention with the ill less complicated. Our current health care system places too much emphasis on treatment and not enough on prevention.

Discussion Questions

1. Have you or has a member of your family had extensive experience with the U. S. health care system? What kind of experience was it?

2. Do you see health care as a basic human right or a privilege? Why do you take your position?

3. The chapter suggests that women are treated differently from men in the health care system. Have you seen any examples of such differential treatment?

4. If you could make any changes in the U. S. health care system, what would you do? Would you completely rebuild the system or would you make smaller changes? Why?

5. What do you see as some of the most important ways in which inequality and health are related?

References

Akers, Ronald. 1996. *Criminological Theories*. Second edition. Los Angeles: Roxbury.

Andersen, Margaret. 1997. *Thinking About Women*. Fourth edition. Boston: Allyn and Bacon.

Armstrong, Pat, Hugh Armstrong, with Claudia Fegan. 1998. *Universal Healthcare: What the United States Can Learn from the Canadian Experience*. New York: New Press.

Associated Press. 1998. "Being Wealthy and Wise Helps Keep One Healthy, A U.S. Study Finds." *Boston Globe*, July 30: A9.

Bagley, Kate, and Alida V. Merlo. 1995. "Controlling Women's Bodies." Ch. 7 in *Women, Law, and Social Control*, edited by Alida V. Merlo and Joycelyn M. Pollock. Boston: Allyn and Bacon.

Brody, Jane E. 1997a. "Personal Health; Girls and Puberty: The Crisis Years." *New York Times*, Science Section, November 4, C9.

——. 1997b. "Personal Health; Parents Can Bolster Girls' Fragile Self-esteem." *New York Times*, Science Section, November 11, C10.

Cockerham, William C. 1995. *Medical Sociology*. Sixth edition. Upper Saddle River, New Jersey: Prentice Hall.

Commonwealth Fund. 1997. *Commonwealth Fund Survey of the Health of Adolescent Girls*. September. New York: Commonwealth Fund.

Conrad, Peter. 1997. "General Introduction." Pp. 1–5 in *The Sociology of Health and Illness: Critical Perspectives*. Fifth edition, edited by Peter Conrad. New York: St. Martin's Press.

Corea, Gena. 1992. *The Invisible Epidemic: The Story of Women and AIDS*. New York: HarperCollins.

Doyal, Lesley. 1995. *What Makes Women Sick: Gender and the Political Economy of Health*. New Brunswick, New Jersey: Rutgers University Press.

Driscoll, Anne. 1997. "Mental Illness Needs Treatment, Not Shame." *Boston Sunday Globe*, North Weekly Section, November 30:2.

Duffy, John. 1993. *From Humans to Medical Science: A History of American Medicine*. Chicago: University of Illinois Press.

Elwell, Ronnie. 1989. "Women and Diagnoses: Examination of the Attribution of Psychiatric Illness to Women in Modern Society." Massachusetts Sociological Association Fall Conference. Holyoke Community College, November 4.

Goode, William J. 1960. "Encroachment, Charlatanism, and the Emerging Profession: Psychology, Sociology, and Medicine." *American Sociological Review* 25: 902–914.

Greil, Arthur L., Jeanne Calabro, and Jean Elson. 1997. "Health, Health Policy, and Health Services." Pp. 21–23 in *Working Toward a Just World: Visions, Experiences and Challenges*, edited by Pamela Roby. Knoxville, Tennessee: Society for the Study of Social Problems.

Hacker, Andrew. 1997. "The Medicine in Our Future." *New York Review of Books*, June 12:26–31.

Hare, Edward. 1988. "Is Schizophrenia New in the World?" *British Journal of Psychiatry* 153:521–531.

Hesse-Biber, Charlene. 1996. *Am I Thin Enough Yet?* New York: Oxford.

Kegel, Paul. M., Audrey Burnam, and Jim Baumohl. 1996. "The Causes of Homelessness." Pp. 24–33 in *Homelessness in America*, edited by Jim Baumohl. Phoenix: Oryx Press.

Kilborn, Peter T. 1998a. "Largest HMOs Cutting the Poor and the Elderly." *New York Times*, July 6: A1, A9.

——. 1998b. "The Uninsured Find Fewer Doctors in the House." *New York Times*, Week in Review, August 30: 14.

Klonoff, Elizabeth A., and Hope Landrine. 1992. "Sex Roles, Occupational Roles and Symptom-Reporting: A Test of Competing Hypotheses on Sex Differences." *Journal of Behavioral Medicine* 15:355–364.

Knox, Richard A. 1998. "Beyond Borders, Health Unease Festers." *Boston Globe*, October 23: A10–11.

Kobak, Kenneth A., et al. 1997. "A Computer-Administered Telephone Interview to Identify Mental Disorders." *Journal of the American Medical Association* 278:905–10.

Mechanic, David. 1990. "The Role of Sociology in Health Care." *Health Affairs* 9:85–87.

Minton, Eric. 1997. "AIDS Care Comes Home." *Independent Living Provider*, September/October, 40–44.

National Center for Health Statistics. 1998a. *National Center for Health Statistics Website*. Hyattsville, Maryland: U.S. Department of Health and Human Services, Centers for Disease Control and Prevention. http://www.cdc.gov/nchswww/products/pubs/pubd/hus/hus.htm.

——. 1998b. *Health, United States, 1998 With Socioeconomic Status and Health Chartbook*. Hyattsville, Maryland: U.S. Department of Health and Human Services, Centers for Disease Control and Prevention.

National Coalition for the Homeless. 1997. "Mental Illness and Homelessness." NCH Fact Sheet #5, http://ww2.ari.net/home/nch/mental.html.

Oakley, Deirdre, and Deborah L. Dennis. 1996. "Responding to the Needs of Homeless People with Alcohol, Drug, and/or Mental Disorders." Pp. 179–186 in *Homelessness in America*, edited by Jim Baumohl. Phoenix: Oryx Press.

Parsons, Talcott. 1975. "The Sick Role and Role of Physician Reconsidered." *Health and Society*, 53:257–278.

Pear, Robert, and Erik Eckholm. 1991. "When Healers are Entrepreneurs: A Debate Over Costs and Ethics." *New York Times*, June 2, 17.

Reuters. 1998. "Health Care Should be Priority in Congress, Poll Reports." *Boston Globe*. July 6: A3.

Rosenfield, Sarah. 1997. "Psychiatric Sociology." Pp. 32–34 in *Working Toward a Just World: Visions, Experiences and Challenges*, edited by Pamela Roby. Knoxville: Society for the Study of Social Problems.

Skocpol, Theda. 1996. *Boomerang: Clinton's Health Security Effort and the Turn Against Government in U.S. Politics*. New York: W. W. Norton.

Starr, Paul. 1982. *The Social Transformation of American Medicine*. New York: Basic Books.

Treas, Judy. 1995. "Older Americans in the 1990s and Beyond." *Population Bulletin 2*.

Tye, Larry. 1998. "Insurers Overruling Physicians, Study Finds." *Boston Globe*, March 4: A1, A8.

U.S. Bureau of the Census. 1998. "Health Insurance Coverage: 1997." *Current Population Reports*, Consumer Income. No. P60–202. September 1. Washington, D.C.: U.S. Department of Commerce, Economics and Statistics Administration.

World Health Organization. 1998a. "Health for All: Origins and Mandate." World Health Organization Website, http://www.who.int/who50/ed/health4all.htm.

World Health Organization. 1998b. "World Health Report 1998: Life in the 21st Century—A Vision for All." World Health Organization Website, http://www.who.int/whr/1998.whr-en.htm.

Wooten, Jacqueline C. 1998. "Webwatch—Women's Health: Women as Caregivers." *Journal of Women's Health* 7: No. 5.

Websites

http://ethics.acusd.edu/euthanasia.html

Ethics Updates, University of San Diego, Department of Philosophy, Euthanasia, and End-of-Life Decision. Professor Larry Hinman of the University of San Diego's Department of Philosophy maintains this useful site. It includes links to extensive resources on euthanasia, including court decisions, basic documents, statistical information, and other related websites.

http://www.nami.org/

National Alliance for the Mentally Ill (NAMI). This site includes extensive information on mental illness, including basic facts, information about pending legislation, and statistics.

http://www2.ari.net/home/nch/facts.html

National Coalition for the Homeless. This website includes useful fact sheets on mental illness and homelessness and health care and homelessness. The fact sheets are well documented, solidly researched resources.

CHAPTER THIRTEEN

Cities and Urban Decline

In the News: Should We Abolish This City?

According to a New York Times *article, Buffalo, New York, has many financial problems. However, the City Comptroller of Buffalo has a solution to the city's problems: "Why not just do away with the city?" (Glaberson 1997). Miami is also experiencing serious problems. A* Boston Globe *article reported that on September 4, 1997, Miami voters faced a weighty question. "In its 101st year, the city of Miami faces a serious question: Will it survive to 102?" (Mears 1997). The headlines of these stories certainly seem to reflect symptoms of urban decline: "Aging city weighs putting itself out of business" (Glaberson 1997) and "Miami to vote on whether it should still exist" (Mears 1997). Although Buffalo and Miami each have serious problems that led them to consider abolishing themselves, their problems can help us understand the nature of urban decline and why such drastic solutions have been considered.*

Buffalo faces serious problems, but it is not the only upstate New York city to face such decline. "After years of struggling with decaying retail centers and shrinking tax bases, the mayors of Utica, Syracuse and Schenectady have each said their cities will not be able to make it on their own much longer" (Glaberson 1997). Each mayor has suggested that his city ought to merge with a larger metropolitan or county government. Comptroller Joel A. Giambra proposed abolishing Buffalo as a city and merging the city into Erie County. Buffalo's plight has attracted the most attention in upstate New York, "partly because Buffalo, with some 300,000 people, is a classic old urban center with all the attributes and problems of most middle-size cites." But the attention to Buffalo should also focus on Erie County, a suburban county that has drawn many who moved out of Buffalo to escape its urban problems (Glaberson 1997). Miami has experienced corruption scandals and has been close to bankruptcy. By merging with the county, the city would dramatically cut the costs of providing services. The key question for Miami is whether it "has solved its financial problems and rooted out corruption, or whether it will stumble for years, driven by ethnic rivalries and fights for political spoils" (Mears 1997). In Miami, almost all city officials opposed the merger, and so did the voters: 85.1 percent of the voters chose to retain the city (New York Times 1997).

Other cities have merged with their county governments in recent years, so abolishing a city is not as unusual or dramatic as it might first seem. However, it does raise important questions about the survival of cities and their ability to provide the services that their residents expect. These examples also bring up the relationships between cities and their surrounding suburbs, and the possibility that more regional forms of local government might be increasingly necessary. As urban sociologist Mark Gottdiener suggests: such localities have had to face the fact that they can't possibly provide all the services people want any more" (Glaberson 1997).

Definition and Prevalence

How do you feel about cities? Perhaps you grew up in or currently live in a large American city. Or you may have grown up in a medium-size city, a suburb, or a small town. Have you spent much time in large cities? Do you enjoy cities or does an urban environment make you uncomfortable? You might think about these questions while you read this chapter and reflect on how your answers to them may affect your views on city life and urban decline. If you have negative feelings about cities, you are joining a long tradition of anti-urban bias in the United States (White and White 1964).

Before discussing urban problems we should consider some definitions. **Urbanization**, the increasing movement from rural to urban areas is one of the most important trends in world history. The U.S. Bureau of the Census defines an urban population as all persons who live in places with 2,500 or more residents "incorporated as cities, villages, boroughs (except in Alaska and New York), towns (except in the New England States, New York, and Wisconsin)" but excluding those living in rural areas of cities (U.S. Bureau of the Census 1996:4). The definition gets a little more complicated, but these are the central features. In 1790, only 5.1 percent of the population of the United States lived in urban areas; in 1990, that figure was 77.5 percent.

Increasingly important are **metropolitan areas (MAs)**. A metropolitan area is basically a "core area containing a large population nucleus, together with adjacent communities that have a high degree of social and economic integration with that core" (U.S. Bureau of the Census 1996:4). In other words, a metropolitan area is usually a large city with surrounding suburbs and areas closely tied to the city. Again, as with cities, this definition gets more complicated and detailed, but the key point to grasp here is the general idea of a metropolitan area; it is also important to understand why they are so vital for studying urban decline and social problems.

Think about where you live or where you go to school. If you do not live in an urban setting, you may feel that urban social problems are irrelevant to your life. However, we human beings live in an increasingly urban and metropolitan world, so urban social problems and the extent to which they can be solved will have major impacts on U. S. society and many others. In fact, we live in a nested series of social settings. That sounds more complicated than it

Increasing numbers of Americans live in metropolitan areas, which include large cities and their surrounding area. New York City, seen here from across the Brooklyn Bridge, is at the center of one such metropolitan area. —*Photo: Copyright © 1997 NYCVB.*

is. We live in neighborhoods, some urban and some not. Those neighborhoods may be in cities, suburbs, or outlying areas beyond suburbs. They are very likely to lie within metropolitan areas, so even if you do not think of yourself as an urban dweller, you may live within or go to school in a metropolitan area.

To get a better idea of the importance of cities and metropolitan areas in the United States, look at Table 13-1. In 1950, 62.4 percent of the population lived in metropolitan areas, with 35.4 percent in cities and 27.0 percent in suburbs outside of the cities; 37.5 percent of the population lived in nonmetropolitan, often rural, areas. By 1990, 77.7 percent of Americans lived in metropolitan areas, but 47.2 percent lived in suburban areas outside of central cities. Notice that only 22.3 percent lived in nonmetropolitan areas by 1990.

Table 13-1 Where Americans Live, 1950–1990 (percents)

	1950	1960	1970	1980	1990
Total metropolitan	62.4	66.7	68.6	74.8	77.7
In central cities	35.4	33.4	31.4	30.0	30.5
In suburban areas	27.0	33.3	37.2	44.8	47.2
Nonmetropolitan	37.5	33.3	31.4	25.2	22.3

Source: U.S. Bureau of the Census. Various Years. *Statistical Abstract of the United States*. Washington, D.C.: U. S. Government Printing Office.

Table 13-2 helps explain why the pattern of metropolitan growth is so marked. You can see that migration to metropolitan areas was extensive, but so was migration out of metropolitan areas. However, central cities lost population at a much higher rate than the total metropolitan area. This decline in the size of central cities while metropolitan areas continue to grow is illustrated by the example of Buffalo, in which many have left the city to move to Erie County, as noted above.

Table 13-2 Metropolitan Migration, 1994 (Numbers in Thousands)

Type of Migration	Metropolitan Status			
	Total Metropolitan	Central Cities	Suburbs	Nonmetropolitan
In-migrants	1,770	3,516	6,721	1,856
Out-migrants	1,856	6,452	3,871	1,770
Net internal migration	-86	-2,936	2,850	86
Movers from abroad	1,095	447	658	150
Net total migration	1,009	-2,849	3,498	236

Source: U.S. Bureau of the Census. 1995. *Current Population Reports*.

Not only is the United States increasingly an urban and metropolitan society, the world is increasingly urbanized. In 1950, less than one-third of the world's population lived in urban areas. However, it is now projected that by 2005 half of the world's population will live in urban areas, and that proportion will rise to two-thirds by 2025. Most of the increase in urban dwellers will occur in the developing world, and this increase has important implications for urban problems there (Kearl 1998). In particular, many large Third World

A Closer Look

Shantytowns in the Third World

Have you ever seen Michael Jackson's music video *They Don't Care About Us*? Jackson filmed that video in Santa Marta, a hillside slum, or *favela*, outside of Rio de Janeiro, Brazil. The video includes images of Santa Marta as well as of the better-off sections of Rio. Life in Santa Marta is one of devastating poverty and miserable conditions. During a hot summer afternoon "a toddler cools herself under the water dripping from a rag that dangles from a wire stretched high above her head. Raw sewage runs down the hills, sending nauseating odors like curses through the neighborhood. Drug dealers stand at checkpoints along winding alleys" (Schemo 1996).

Many of the residents of Santa Marta welcomed Michael Jackson and the making of the video, but not everyone was happy about it. "The knowledge that the poverty here will be used as an international image of urban misery has sparked an emotional debate dividing the 'Marvelous City,' as Rio likes to be called. Unfortunately, many other such slums could also be used as images of urban poverty in the Third World" (Schemo 1996).

Such slums encircle many large cities in the developing world. They may be called **shantytowns**, **squatter settlements**, or a variety of other names, often depending on who originally colonized the areas in which they are located. For example, in some former French African colonies they are called *bidonvilles*, or "tin-can cities." In Brazil, they are called *favelas*, like Santa Marta. "Almost all Latin American cities are surrounded by *cinturones de miseria*, large belts of extreme poverty often lacking the most basic comforts and infrastructure and social services" (Macionis and Parillo 1998: 305). They go by many other names: *bustees* in India, *barriadas* in Mexico, *poblaciones* in Chile, *villas miseria* in Argentina, and *Kampongs* in Southeast Asia. What they have in common are "frequent public health crises, crime, crushing poverty, and no future for the next generation since few countries provide them with schools" (Gottdiener 1994:254).

These squatter settlements are colonial legacies. Under colonialism large, usually coastal cities were constructed to facilitate trade. Most former colonies have been unable to control urbanization. In many developing countries poor people leave the countryside because of extreme poverty, lack of land and food, and no job opportunities. They migrate to the cities where they often end up in squatter settlements. This process of **hyper-** or **overurbanization**, refers to the unbalanced growth of extremely large cities with no medium-size or small cities. This unbalanced urbanization limits the social and economic development of urban areas in the Third World and consigns many to lives of extreme poverty and deprivation.

In spite of the poverty and lack of resources in many such areas, such squatter settlements have a vibrant, robust social life. The people who live in them are not "marginal," and the shantytowns may be closely tied to the larger urban and national economy (Gottdiener 1994). In her study of urban poverty in three *favelas* in Rio, Janice Perlman found that the *favelas* were socially well organized and cohesive (Perlman 1976). Lobo's study of two squatter settlements in Lima, Peru, revealed closely-knit ties of mutual obligations and attachment to community (Lobo 1982).

While taking their strengths into account, it is important not to romanticize such squatter settlements. Like inner-city neighborhoods in the United States, they were not created by the values or behavior of those who live in them. Residents display great resourcefulness and adaptability in developing survival strategies. Mark Gottdiener suggests that they be viewed "less as slums than as workers' suburbs that require greater attention and services from local government" (1994:257). It is crucial that they get greater attention and services from the government.

Showing the misery in such settlements is an important step to alleviating the conditions, but as the leader of a residents' group in Santa Marta noted when the government tried to prevent the making of Michael Jackson's video, "they really don't care about us" (Schemo 1996).

cities are encircled by huge **shantytowns**, slum areas in which poverty, crime, and disease plague residents. For more on this, see "A Closer Look: Shantytowns in the Third World".

To focus on urban problems in the United States, we can consider what makes a social problem an "urban problem." What do we mean by an urban problem? Many of the social problems we have covered in this text occur in cities and have urban dimensions. Poverty is one example. So in this chapter we will inevitably touch on some social problems that we explore elsewhere in this book; however, here we focus on more specifically or distinctly urban aspects of those problems. We will examine how the relationships between urban areas and metropolitan areas affect social problems, and we will consider social problems in cities of varying sizes. Rather than examining urban social problems as a series of discrete, separate problems, we focus on the process of urban decline, including its causes and consequences. Urban decline has generated a number of linked urban social problems. In fact, the outcomes of the changes that have led to urban decline have been aptly referred to by Stanley Eitzen and Maxine Zinn as "the mugging of U.S. cities" (1997:147). For more on the "mugging" of one American city, see "A Closer Look: The 'Mugging' of Flint".

A Closer Look

The "Mugging" of Flint

Flint, Michigan, once known as Buick City, was the birthplace of both General Motors (GM) and the United Auto Workers union. In the 1980s GM closed the plants and downsized in Flint. The city "became a national symbol of the labor pain behind the corporate party, the city of busted dreams in the documentary *Roger and Me* (Grunwald 1998:A1). Director Michael Moore made *Roger and Me* to draw attention to the plight of Flint (Moore 1989). In the film, Moore pursues Roger Smith, then CEO of GM, to explain the devastation that closing a plant will bring to Flint. Moore suggests that Roger Smith could not have possibly understood the situation or he would not have closed the plant. The film dramatized Flint's situation and portrayed the city as "an industrial wasteland abandoned by faceless corporate greedheads" (Grunwald 1998: A10).

In a broader sense, *Roger and Me* is also about deindustrialization and its impact on America's urban centers, according to Stephen Dandaneau's insightful analysis of the film in his study of Flint's experience with deindustrializatin (1996). Moore's film and Dandaneau's study both suggest that the solutions offered for Flint's decline were essentially public relations efforts doomed in their efforts to make any meaningful changes.

The extent of Flint's decline is indicated by the extent of job loss. In 1978, GM employed 76,900 workers in Flint. Today the figure is 33,000 and it could drop to as low as 15,000 in the next five years. Most of the UAW workers will not be affected too much by the downsizing. They can retire with pensions or move to other plants. Michael Grunwald points out that "the real impact will be felt by the city, where 75 percent of the economy revolves around GM and its suppliers, 68 percent of the students in public schools receive subsidized lunches, and more than 30 percent of black men are unemployed" (1998:A10).

While the national economy booms, Flint faces even further decline. The city needs to diversify its economic base, but so far no one knows how to accomplish that. Some way must be found to link the deteriorating city with the well-off suburbs surrounding it. In other words, some kinds of regional solution may be neccessary. If such solutions are not adopted, the 'mugging' of Flint will continue to be reflected ironically in its current status as the burglary capital of the United States.

The decline of American cities began just after World War II. "City problems were real and well known. Urban decline was widespread, its causes were said to extend rootlike through American society, and few were spared its consequences." Population loss; the physical deterioration of housing, factories, and shops; the collapse of urban land values; rising city property taxes and soaring crime rates; deepening poverty and unemployment; and the concentration of minorities have all, at one time or another, been dominant themes (Beauregard 1996:363).

Urban decline has certainly been evident in the widespread social problems of large central cities, but it is not restricted to them. Urban decline has affected medium-size and small cities. Sociologist Sharon Zukin suggests that the "problems of big cities—crime, drugs, high housing prices, unemployment—are just as familiar in Spokane or Tulsa as in New York City" (1991:245). Zukin notes that

> in 1986, a list of urban trends drawn up for the U.S. Conference of Mayors described a sorry situation: population drain, increased poverty, an income gap between city and suburban residents, gaps among racial groups, long-term unemployment in places where manufacturing has declined and services grow slowly, homelessness, hunger, low education levels, high crime rates, and very high taxes. (1991:245)

In this chapter we focus on urban decline and on major urban problems that reflect it. Such major urban problems include inadequate housing and shelter; poverty; unrest, including crime; poor education; and racial polarization. Before looking more closely at the consequences of urban decline and urban problems, we examine various attempts to explain them.

Levels of Causation

As in other social problems examined in this text, the causes for urban decline can be sought on three separate theoretical levels: the individual level, the cultural level, and the structural level.

Individual

In the nineteenth century, many people believed that inherent character deficiencies caused poverty and thus the urban problems linked to it. Today, few sociologists attribute urban social problems directly to the behavior of individuals. However, in his book *The New Politics of Poverty*, policy analyst Lawrence Mead suggests that poverty is rooted in individuals' deviant values and behaviors (Mead 1992). The importance of this perspective lies less in its validity as an explanation for the extensive poverty at the root of many urban problems and more in the kinds of interventions that follow from it.

This view—that the problems of cities result from individual failings of urban dwellers in terms of their initiative, moral qualities, and willingness to work—is accepted by many Americans. People living in public housing projects, for example, may be blamed for the deterioration of their dwellings when the projects have outlived their planned useful life. Another example of this approach is represented by the spokesperson for the Massachusetts Department of Transitional Assistance who, in discussing welfare recipients, suggested that "It's time for these people to get a crash course called Work 101" (Anand 1998:B1).

This blaming the victim approach is grounded in strong beliefs in individualism and individual responsibility in the United States. In fact, there is a sense in which our strong belief in individualism, or **privatism**, exacerbates urban problems and makes them difficult to solve. According to Mark Gottdiener, "privatism, a legacy of our colonial history, refers to the civic culture that eschews social interests in favor of private pursuit of individual goals" (1994:42). Note that this argument does not *blame* the existence and persistence of urban problems on the individuals who suffer from those problems; it suggests that our extreme emphasis on individualism precludes our solving the problems.

Cultural

Theories such as Mead's also overlap with, and are closely related to, cultural explanations for urban problems. Culture-of-poverty and underclass theories focus on alleged individual and cultural deficiencies of inner-city residents, especially the poor and members of minority groups. According to Eitzen and Zinn,

> this view blames the problems in our cities on urban residents, particularly poor blacks in the inner city. The poor themselves, their families, their culture, and their neighborhoods produce values and behavior that are the essential cause of poverty and of all urban problems connected to it. (1997:178)

This approach assumes that the values and behavior—the culture—of the poor differ from those of the white middle and upper classes. However, the evidence for these differences is weak. Numerous studies have criticized such approaches and have indicated that social and economic policies and social structures create and maintain poverty and other urban social problems (di Leonardo 1992; Kelley 1997; Stack 1974; Susser 1982).

Stereotypes of the poor are also called into question by Peter Medoff and Holly Sklar in their account of the fall and rise of the Dudley Street neighborhood, long the poorest neighborhood in Boston. Discussing the Dudley Street Neighborhood Initiative, a community-based group working to revitalize the area, Medoff and Sklar note that the "DSNI story challenges those who mask disinvestment and discrimination in slanderous stereotypes about an 'underclass culture of poverty'" (Medoff and Sklar 1994:3). Disinvestment and discrimination are structural features of social life and are seen by many social scientists as most useful for understanding urban social problems.

Structural

The major structural approaches to urban social problems include determinist theory, compositional theory, subcultural theory, and urban political economy. The first three approaches are sometimes considered cultural approaches because they examine whether there is a distinctly urban way of life or culture. In fact, they all emphasize the role of social organization and social structures in generating urban problems. We also consider them together because they developed in relation to each other and are thus easier to understand together (Fischer 1984).

The **determinist approach** is also called Wirthian theory, after its originator, University of Chicago sociologist Louis Wirth. The "Chicago School" dominated American sociology from about 1900 to 1930. The Chicago sociologists carried out many ethnographic studies of immigrants and their neighborhoods, and of others considered "disreputable" or "deviant." Wirth suggested that urban living disrupted social life. In his classic analysis of "urbanism as a way of life," Wirth suggested that sociologists of cities needed to "discover the forms of social action and organization that typically emerge in relatively permanent, compact settlements of large numbers of heterogeneous individuals" (Wirth 1938:9). For Wirth, a distinctly urban way of life was associated with three conditions: large population size, high population density, and heterogeneity.

Wirth's view of the urban way of life was pessimistic. He believed that "because of the heterogeneity, density, and size of urban populations, interactions became segmented and transitory, resulting in weakened social bonds" (Mooney, Knox, and Schacht 1997:348). In place of close primary relationships, urban dwellers had more fleeting, limited, **secondary relationships** leading to less social cohesion and solidarity and a breakdown in the moral order. People did not have clear-cut, widely accepted values and norms. Moreover, the prevalence of more instrumental, impersonal secondary relations and the weakened social solidarity and cohesion characteristic of urbanism produced feelings of anonymity, loneliness, depression, and stress and led to increased levels of antisocial behavior. This antisocial behavior contributed to social disorganization and social pathology, including crime, alcoholism, and family breakup. (Gottdiener 1994; Mooney, Knox, and Schacht 1997).

The key to the determinist view is that city structure itself generates urban social problems by destroying **primary groups** and the ties within and among them. Herbert Gans' **compositional approach** suggests that it is not city structure or the urban environment itself that produces negative aspects of urban life. "According to the compositional view, urban problems are the consequence of factors related to the demographic characteristics of the population, such as class standing, marital status, age, poverty, race, and educational level" (Gottdiener 1994:201). It is not the structure of cities that produces certain behaviors; rather, it is the composition of the population and the behaviors associated with certain population groups.

Gans' more optimistic view of urban living was based on his research in the Italian American West End neighborhood of Boston just before it was destroyed by urban renewal. Gans found that rather than being characterized by impersonal, anonymous relations, the West End was a closely knit neighborhood that he called an urban village (Gans 1984[1962]). The compositional theory suggests that urbanism itself does not have any direct social psychological effects on behavior and so urbanism in itself does not generate urban social problems.

Reconciling the determinist and compositional approaches, Claude Fischer suggested that cities did have a direct effect on behavior, not through weakening primary groups and ties, but rather through strengthening and creating such primary groups. Thus, the **subcultural theory** "contends that urbanism does shape social life—not however, by *destroying* social groups as determinism suggests, but instead by *strengthening* them" by promoting the creation and maintenance of diverse subcultures (Fischer 1984:35–36; Fischer 1982). These subcultures can include criminal subcultures. Because of the greater size and diversity of cities, people have more opportunities to find others who have the same interests and thus more opportunity to engage in various kinds of activities (Fischer 1984; Gottdiener 1994).

Research has supported each of these views; especially in recent years, there has been much support for the subcultural theory. However, the increasing significance of metropolitan regions and the presence of problems within those regions has made the distinctions between cities and suburbs less important. Urban social problems can be better thought of as metropolitan social problems. Moreover, many sociologists have turned to approaches that focus on other key aspects of urban and metropolitan life.

The most important new approach to cities is called **urban political economy**, or sometimes the new urban sociology. Although urban political economists differ from each other in the focus of their research and theory, most stress "the use of power, domination, and resources in the shaping of cities" (Kleniewski 1997:23). Urban political economy has burgeoned because of the inability of earlier approaches to answer key questions about cities, especially questions about major social trends.

Nancy Kleniewski names five social trends that she believes contributed to the development of urban political economy. First, accelerating suburban growth and the movement of companies and jobs to suburban areas created a new situation for cities by the early 1960s. A second important trend was increasing racial polarization in urban areas. Many white members of ethnic groups had moved from inner cities; African Americans stayed in the inner cities, so "the inner-city ghettos had become powerful symbols of the lack of social and economic opportunity for African Americans" (Kleniewski 1997:36). The third trend was the changing role of government in cities and metropolitan areas, in particular an increasingly pervasive government role in urban life. The fourth trend was the changing nature of the economy—including the global economy—and its effects on jobs, poverty, and inequality. A restructuring of urban employment occurred in which many jobs moved and others disappeared. Kleniewski suggests that a final trend that led to the reorientation of urban sociology to the urban political economy approach was the "changing trajectory of cities around the world, particularly in the poor, nonindustrialized countries of the third world" (Kleniewski 1997:37). It became increasingly evident that large Third-World cities were very different from cities in developed countries. We mentioned earlier the rise of shantytowns around many large Third-World cities.

Gottdiener has developed a variant of the new urban sociology that he calls the **sociospatial perspective** (SSP). The SSP emphasizes that the spatial environment, as suggested by Wirth, and the compositional or social factors such as race, class, and gender, as suggested by Gans, both play important roles in urban life and problems. "Social problems in particular are caused by poverty, racial exclusion, gender differences, and the uneven development of capitalist economies which results in differential access to resources and life chances" (Gottdiener 1994:202).

This perspective suggests that there are four underlying factors that make social problems more severe in large cities and densely settled suburbs. First, cities are **built environments** that concentrate people and resources. Because of this concentration, "social problems such as drugs and poverty have a greater impact in large central cities and densely populated suburbs than in less dense areas" (Gottdiener 1994:202). Second, urban populations are often greatly affected by social forces originating in other parts of the world, such as large-scale immigration. Third, global economic changes resulting from changes in investments have major impacts on cities. Finally, "social problems are caused by uneven development, and this pattern of differential resource allocation may be accentuated in dense, built environments" (Gottdiener 1994:202). For example, large cities are characterized by great wealth. Symbols of that wealth, such as expensive restaurants, hotels, and luxury housing, are quite visible. Living close by in such cities are also extremely poor people, who may be homeless, unemployed, and malnourished. This contrast tends to exacerbate urban social problems.

We can be more specific about structural explanations for urban decline by focusing on the research of Saskia Sassen and William Julius Wilson, two well-known urban sociologists. Sassen and Wilson, among others, have suggested that American industrial cities began to undergo major restructuring by the early 1970s. This restructuring led to changes in labor markets and in the availability of jobs in the cities. These changes, in turn, had major implications for urban poverty, the racial and ethnic composition of cities, housing and shelter, urban education, and urban unrest and disorder (Orum 1997; Sassen 1990; Sassen 1991; Sassen 1994; Wilson 1987; Wilson 1996).

In the restructuring, large manufacturing firms began to move out of central cities. Some moved to suburbs outside of cities; others moved to other parts of the United States, especially the South; and more often they moved to other countries. New kinds of industries moved into the cities. These were financial services firms, professional firms, and telecommunications industries, which began to reshape urban and national economies. Manuel Castells (1989) suggests that the culmination of this trend was the rise of the "information city," in which the creation and manipulation of information became central to the city. High levels of education were required for the jobs in the information industries, but many of those left in the cities did not have the needed education and thus were not able to take advantage of the new industries.

In his concise overview of these changes, Anthony Orum (1997) suggests that the loss of industry and restructuring of cities had striking and sometimes "devastating" effects on city residents.

> The loss of manufacturing left many people unemployed, eventually creating a large underclass, while the restructuring of the economy created a new kind of polarization, with very rich groups of people, working in the financial, insurance and telecommunications sector at the top, and a very large group of people at the bottom, more or less servicing the needs of those at the top. (1997:1)

Sassen's research focuses on the polarization that results from these changes, especially from the rise of global cities. Wilson examined the impact of deindustrialization on inner-city residents. The impact of these changes was especially devastating for African Americans in inner cities. As you might expect, such major changes had significant consequences for cities.

Consequences

To help understand the causes and consequences of urban decline, Elvin Wyly and his colleagues have thoughtfully provided "a top 10 list of things to know about American cities" (Wyly, Glickman, and Lahr 1998). The trends in the list arise from the uneven growth among and within metropolitan areas (MAs), leading to increasing imbalances within an MA. In other words, uneven development at different levels is a major force leading to urban change and decline. Table 13-3 summarizes the top 10 things to know, divided into three categories: the broader—sometimes global—context of urban change, interregional trends among MAs, and trends within MAs. We can use the list to connect the trends more closely to their consequences.

Table 13-3 Top 10 Things to Know About American Cities and Metropolitan Areas (MAs)

Broader (Global) Trends	Interregional Trends Among MAs	Trends Within MAs

context of urban change
  macroeconomic
  technological
  demographic
	uneven growth
	
	increased *income inequality*
		income inequality and *social polarization*
		
		changing conditions of inner-city *neighborhoods*

effects of *international migration streams*	*decentralization* *interregional migration* and *urban flight*	changes in *housing* *fiscal* issues facing large cities

Source: Wyly, Elvin K., Norman J. Glickman, and Michael Lahr. 1998. "A Top 10 List of Things to Know about American Cities." *Cityscape: A Journal of Policy Development and Research* 3(3):8.

The broad context for understanding the consequences of urban change includes technological change, international and national economic forces, and changes in population distributions. Probably the most important technological change is the growth of information technologies. These technologies have allowed firms to decentralize their operations while controlling those operations from a central location. We have discussed globalization often in this text. Globalization produced deindustrialization, dispersing jobs and people throughout metropolitan regions. "Thus, larger cities now find themselves with fewer jobs and deteriorating tax bases to pay for local services" (Wyly, Glickman, and Lahr 1998:9).

Major demographic, or population, changes also provide the context for understanding urban change and decline. These include decreases in the white population; increases in the Hispanic population; declining numbers of married people; increasing proportion of divorced and single adults; and increasing numbers of single-parent households, usually headed by women. The number of immigrants has increased recently; more women participate in the labor force; and the aging of the American population has continued. Many of these changes have affected the population make-up of cities. Immigrants and single-parent households are more likely to live in central cities, while married-couple households are more likely to reside in suburbs. The former groups are more likely to need support services at a time when cities are less able to provide them (Wyly, Glickman, and Lahr 1998).

Urban poverty increased in the 1980s and early 1990s and has become more concentrated in central cities, which have 43 percent of the poor. Poverty is also concentrated within certain population groups. For example, in 1993, 23 percent of children and 46 percent of African American children were poor, according to conservative official estimates. That poverty remained high during a general boom economic period is a significant puzzle

(Wyly, Glickman, and Lahr 1998). Other important trends pertaining to MAs include their uneven growth, increased income inequality among them, large-scale immigration to them, continuing decentralization, migration between regions, and urban flight. Of course, some MAs have done well as a result of these trends. MAs around the older industrial cities of the Eastern United States did most poorly. Although polarization and income inequality have increased among regions, they have increased even more within cities and neighborhoods. Many members of the middle class left the cities as soon as they could. "The processes leading upwardly mobile families to the suburbs leave those who remain behind in the cities to face the consequences of concentrated poverty, high crime rates, deteriorating home values, and poor schools" (Wyly, Glickman, and Lahr 1998:23). Racial segregation in the cities has remained high.

It is important to remember that the changes that have led to increasing difficulties in cities are not the result of impersonal, automatic economic forces. They are the outcomes of human decisions and policies to support certain kinds of development but not others. Suburbanization, for example, is often seen as having occurred in response to individual consumer demands and impersonal market forces. In fact, government policies helped push people out of cities and drew them into suburbs. These policies included

> highway building policies that opened the hinterlands to speculation and development, housing policies that offered government-insured mortgages to whites in suburbia (but not in cities), and bulldozer urban renewal policies that destroyed working-class neighborhoods, scattering their residents to blue-collar suburbs, to make way for downtown business development. (Dreier 1996:103)

To repeat, these changes and trends did not just happen; they were the result of decisions by those with power and with access to the resources necessary to implement such major policies, including the federal government, banks, and major corporations. Boston's Dudley Street neighborhood is a good example of the processes that lead to urban and neighborhood deterioration. Medoff and Sklar (1994) note that the neighborhood looked as if it had been hit by an earthquake: "Streets crisscross blocks of vacant lots where homes and shops used to be." However, they leave no doubt about the nature of the "earthquake" that devastated a once-thriving area.

> The earthquake that hit Dudley was neither natural or sudden. Instead, in a pattern repeated nationally, a thriving urban community was trashed and burned. It was redlined by banks, government mortgage programs and insurance companies in a self-fulfilling prophecy of white flight, devaluation and decline. While tax money subsidized the building of segregated suburbia and upscale "urban renewal," inner city neighborhoods like Dudley were stripped of jobs, homes, and government services. (Medoff and Sklar 1994:1)

The human-created urban blight has affected all areas of social life in inner cities. We have seen that urban decline has led to increased social polarization, income inequality, and racial segregation in America's large cities. In the poorest neighborhoods, poverty rates are over 40 percent; social services are scarce; and schools have deteriorated markedly, making escape from such neighborhoods exceptionally difficult.

It is also important to note that people trapped in poor, deteriorating neighborhoods do not give in to despair and hopelessness. Ethnographic studies have demonstrated the residents' initiative and adaptive skills in surviving their situation (Stack 1974; Susser 1982). In *King Kong on 4th Street*, anthropologist Jagna Wojcicka Sharff (1998) reported on the years she spent studying a poor, largely Puerto Rican neighborhood on the Lower East Side of New York City. During the period of her study, the Federal War on Poverty ended, and the wars on crime and drugs were started. These changes had devastating effects on the people she studied. For example, during these years deindustrialization caused a loss of manufacturing jobs, making it harder for the people in the city and in the neighborhood to find jobs. In spite of the societal violence visited on the residents, Sharff notes their joy in child raising, and their determined efforts to maintain their humanity and improve their situation. However, we have seen that social, economic, and political trends beyond their neighborhoods have played important roles in shaping their lives. Interventions to reverse urban decline must take such broader changes into account, while at the same time realizing that people affected by inner city malaise and decline must play a central role in changing their own neighborhoods and cities.

Interventions

There are many possible interventions aimed at improving cities and neighborhoods. There have been federal, state, and private policies and programs that aimed at revitalizing cities. Federal policies have included public housing and urban renewal. Public housing policies often did not respond to the needs of the people they were intended to help. Urban renewal often seemed to be a way of displacing low-income residents from valuable downtown real estate that could then be converted into office buildings or luxury residential areas.

Cities have also adopted economic policies that aim to involve private business in urban development. Kleniewski notes two categories of such privatist policies: "policies that subsidize business by making it cheaper to operate and policies of public-private entrepreneurialism, in which the government invests public money in projects that generate private profit" (Kleniewski 1997:244). Subsidizing businesses includes tax abatements, which give private businesses breaks on their tax bills. Other programs have given businesses a low interest rate on money they borrow to finance development. Local governments have also provided cheap land to businesses. Enterprise zones are special areas in which businesses receive special incentives, "including local and state tax reductions, special loans, cheap land, advertising promotion, technical assistance and training, and a reduction in government regulations" (Kleniewski 1997:245).

The catch to these policies is that it is not clear that they actually work. The presumed benefits of such subsidies in terms of economic development and new jobs are seen as long-term gains. Often, the long term does not seem to arrive. By the time a city should begin reaping the benefits of the subsidies, the corporations may begin looking for breaks from other cities. New York City is an example of this. That city's "use of corporate tax breaks has become so pervasive that some of the city's most powerful and profitable companies are getting a second helping of incentives and subsidies at a time when New York's economy appears to be thriving" (Bagli 1997). Although city officials see such incentives as necessary to stimulate economic development, other urban planners and some politicians have suggested that spending the money on such things as roads, public transportation, and job training would help the city more (Bagli 1997).

Public-private entrepreneurialism has been used to build convention centers, arenas, and sports teams. Again, these kinds of programs often sound good, holding out the promise of creating jobs, bringing revenue into the cities, and invigorating local economies. However, these are often very expensive programs that do not actually create many jobs. The costs of the subsidies may be higher than income from the jobs created. Businesses now expect such subsidies, so states and cities may be forced into competing with each other. Kleniewski notes that the businesses are often more powerful than the cities, because the corporations have various cities competing for their facilities. Local governments may give in too easily to corporate demands (Kleniewski 1997).

Many cities have developed more progressive policies to foster economic development. One type of progressive strategy is called equity planning. In this strategy local planners analyze proposals carefully to ascertain who will actually benefit from them. If local residents benefit directly, the plan is approved. Another progressive strategy is called linkage. This strategy links private real estate development to benefits for local communities. Another recent development in fostering urban development has been partnerships between colleges or universities and local communities. Relations between colleges and the cities in which they are located have often been hostile; however, more colleges have begun to realize that they are citizens of their communities and should give something back to those communities. For more on these kinds of partnerships, see "A Closer Look: Cities, Colleges, and Universities".

Community-based development programs have also enjoyed success in recent years. These are usually small-scale grassroots programs designed to

---

A Closer Look

Cities, Colleges, and Universities

There have often been antagonistic relationships between cities and the colleges and universities in them. The conflict between "town and gown" is a cliche. If there was not outright conflict between cities and colleges, there was often a lack of involvement on the part of colleges. However, recently colleges and universities have been forming partnerships with cities to foster social and economic development. This is not so surprising, for as Richard C. Levin, president of Yale University, points out, the movement of manufacturers out of cities has often left colleges and universities as principal employers. For example, Yale is now the largest employer in New Haven (Levin 1997).

Levin points out that recent developments go beyond voluntary efforts on the part of students and faculty. Colleges and universities increasingly realize that as significant institutions in cities, they have obligations and responsibilities to the cities. Levin notes that colleges and universities all over the country have formed partnerships with their cities—"working together with city government, business leaders, clergy, and neighborhood organizations on issues of economic development, neighborhood revitalization, and human development." In New Haven, Yale has sponsored various programs. One is the New Haven Home Buyers Program. This program, initiated in 1994, provides a $20,000 benefit to full-time university employees to purchase a home in the city. This program generated over $28 million in home sales. A new phase of the program targets neighborhoods deemed most in need of home ownership (Levin 1997). ☞

☞Trinity University in Hartford has also taken important steps to form partnerships with the city's government and business community. Trinity's president, Evan Dobelle, has committed the university and its resources to help revitalize the nearby Frog Hollow neighborhood. President Dobelle "rejected the two standard solutions for good schools in bad neighborhoods: Build high walls and spend a fortune on security or buy up the adjoining land and gentrify" (Gross 1997:A1). Instead of these approaches, Trinity has committed its resources to working with other neighborhood institutions, government, and businesses to provide for Frog Hollow "an ambitious program of safe streets, stable home ownership, state-of-the-art schools and jobs" (Gross 1997: A18).

Trinity's efforts are perhaps the best known, but other colleges and universities are also making significant efforts. For example, the University of Pennsylvania has committed $120 million to help combat blight in Philadelphia. The university is renovating the campus and the surrounding district in an effort to combat urban decay (Belkin 1997). These efforts, and many others, are driven by the sense of the "university as an urban citizen" (Levin 1997). President Dobelle of Trinity University puts it well in terms of the mission and obligations of higher education institutions: "Do we continue to presume that it's O.K. to teach liberal arts to students here, and talk about civility, and not be concerned about what's across the street?" (Gross 1997:A1).

improve living conditions in particular communities. Successful cases of community-based development include programs in Cleveland, Boston, and Minneapolis—The Minneapolis Neighborhood Revitalization Program (Keating, Krumholz, and Star 1996). In *Community Builders*, Gordana Rabrenovic (1996) examines programs in Albany and Schenectady. One of the most interesting cases of community-based development is that of the Dudley Street Neighborhood Initiative (DSNI), mentioned earlier. For more information on a grassroots campaign that may be a model for other communities, see "A Closer Look: Dudley Street—The Fall and Rise of an Urban Neighborhood".

One thing that the community-based models emphasize is that the people affected by urban decline must have a say in reversing that decline. The

A Closer Look

Dudley Street—The Fall and Rise of an Urban Neighborhood

The Dudley Street neighborhood has long been Boston's poorest inner-city neighborhood. But the experience of the Dudley Street Neighborhood Initiative (DSNI) shows how residents can organize themselves to promote community development and reverse the decline of low-income urban neighborhoods. In *Streets of Hope: The Fall and Rise of an Urban Neighborhood*, Peter Medoff and Holly Sklar explain how the DSNI is rebuilding the neighborhood "with the power of pride, organizing and a unified vision of comprehensive community development." (1994: 1). Not only is the Dudley Street case interesting in itself, it may also suggest avenues of neighborhood organizing and community development for other neighborhoods. For example, when *The Nation* magazine started a series on development programs that work, they began with an article on the Dudley Street experience (Walljasper 1997). In fact, the DSNI may provide a national model for community development and change. ☞

☞ The Dudley Street renaissance began in 1985 at a meeting in St. Patrick's Church on Dudley Street. A local social service agency, La Alianza Hispana, had convinced the Riley Foundation, a small Boston-based foundation, to help develop the neighborhood. At the first meeting, neighborhood residents objected to their lack of participation in the proposed project. As a result of this meeting, the DSNI model emerged in which the community residents participated in and maintained control over redevelopment of their neighborhood.

In this chaper, we have discussed problems facing the neighborhood—"poverty, poor schools, crime, drugs, neglect by government officials" (Walljasper 1997:12). These are common problems that face inner- city neighborhoods. However, Dudley Street had additional problems: arson, dumping, abandoned cars, and ethnic fragmentation, among them (Medoff and Sklar 1994; Terry 1996; Walljasper 1997). The video *Holding Ground* presents a vivid picture of the rebirth of Dudley Street (Mahan and Lipton 1996).

DSNI has many concrete accomplishments. They organized a successful "Don't Dump On Us" campaign which closed three illegal trash transfer stations. In a very significant achievement, DSNI became the first grassroots community development organization to gain the power of eminent domain to begin transforming vacant lots into housing, parks, and other fruitful uses. The list of accomplishments goes on (Dudley Street Neighborhood Initiative 1996). However, perhaps the most significant achievement of the community is "they found a way to forge a unified vision of the future and institutionalize resident control" (Medoff and Sklar 1994: 287). Because so many of the forces that led to the deterioration of the neighborhood have origins outside of the neighborhood, local efforts will not be enough to completely reverse urban decline. However, the Dudley Street community provides a model for reversing years of decay and deterioration.

residents of inner cities are the experts on their own lives; they know they have to play a lead role in economic development or that development will not improve their situations. Numerous locally based groups have been creating approaches to urban development that take energy use, job creation, and housing development into account. For a sampling of the rich variety of such neighborhood organizations and their programs, see "A Closer Look: The Center for Neighborhood Technology Website."

A Closer Look

The Center for Neighborhood Technology Website

Chicago's Center for Neighborhood Technology (CNT) is devoted to "making cities work." In order to help make cities work the CNT works at "promoting public policies, new resources and accountable authority which support sustainable, just and vital urban communities" (Center for Neighborhood Technology 1998). Although initially focused on Chicago neighborhoods, the CNT now runs projects and programs aimed at linking environmental improvement and urban economic development all over the country. The CNT website (http://www.cnt.org/) gives you access to information on various CNT projects. They include The Metropolitan Initiative, which focuses on metropolitan issues in various cities and regions, the Urban Sustainability project, a study that explores options for urban sustainability; and *The Neighborhood Works* (*TNW*) magazine.

The Neighborhood Works aims to provide readers with information on the "resources urban residents are using to move their neighborhoods toward self-reliance and to stimulate economic growth" (*The Neighborhood Works* 1998). Recent issues of the magazine have carried stories on natural resources and Western boomtowns, the impact of sports stadiums on cities, and educational reform. ☞

☞ *TNW* focuses on grassroots community projects, programs, and organizations and often shows how seemingly separate topics are closely linked. For example, *TNW* has suggested that there are important links between energy costs and public school funding.

The Neighborhood Works website (http://www.cnt.org/tnw/) provides access to many of the magazine's features. To get information on how local communities and organizations are trying to solve many of the urban problems discussed in this chapter, take a look at these websites.

The Future of Cities and Urban Problems

Architect and urban planner Robert Geddes suggests that a "new form of human settlement has emerged in the twentieth century, radically different from the cities of the past. The city has become a city-region" (Geddes 1997:40). If city-regions are a new form of human settlement, they will require new political forms to overcome the fragmentation of political decision-making characteristic of MAs today. One possible future for cities may be such regional settlements, but that does not seem very likely today.

Of course, the future of cities and the likelihood of continued urban decline rest to a large extent on which of the interventions mentioned earlier are chosen. There is not much debate over what has actually happened to produce urban decline. "That cities are key arenas of capital accumulation is not debatable" (Frisbie and Kasarda 1988:629). There is debate over what this means for the future of cities.

If the world city hypothesis is borne out, the future will differ for different sizes and types of cities. Extremely large "world cities" will continue to grow and thrive, but smaller cities may face increasing difficulties. Although some medium and small cities seem to be rebounding from deterioration and decline, it is too early to tell how successful they will be. For example, Brockton, Massachusetts, a former shoe manufacturing center, may be reversing years of decline (Carroll 1989; Grillo 1998). Gittell's study of four medium-size Northeastern cities that suggested "the effectiveness of any development effort will depend in large part on how the effort addresses local needs, opportunities, and vulnerabilities and how it is coordinated with other efforts (Gittell 1992:181).

According to urban sociologist Peter Dreier, reversing the years of disinvestment in America's cities is key to ensuring their future. He suggests three major components to a federal investment strategy to revitalize the cities. The federal government ought to invest in both the physical and human infrastructure of the society. It must also "invest in urban neighborhoods to improve the economic, physical, and social conditions of these communities" (Dreier 1996:111).

Linda Mooney and her colleagues (1997) emphasize the need for a "societal commitment to a 'pro-growth urban policy.'" That policy should address six basic issues. First, it should help reduce conflict between suburbs and inner cities. Some type of regional governance structures might help here. Second, such a policy should emphasize the importance of improving city services. Third, as Dreier and many others have suggested, policy should enhance human capital. Providing solid job training and education for inner-city residents is necessary. Fourth, it is essential to revitalize urban neighborhoods. Community-based grassroots initiatives can play a major role in this. Fifth, public housing should be a priority, but it should be public housing on a human scale and with input from those who will live in it. Finally, the federal government has to reverse its declining support for cities and fund programs that cities are required to undertake. If such a decline continues or is not reversed, the future of cities in the United States is indeed bleak.

Summary

The problems affecting some cities have become so bad that local officials and citizens have considered abolishing the cities and merging them into surrounding counties. The decline of cities is marked by physical deterioration, increased polarization between the rich and poor, racial segregation of cities, deteriorating urban schools, high crime rates, and increasing poverty in inner cities.

Many of the trends that have led to urban decline are both regional and global in scope. In particular, processes such as suburbanization, decentralization, urban flight, deindustrialization, and the rise of global cities have led to a long-term decline in jobs and in upward mobility in cities. Various attempts to explain urban social problems and decline have been developed at individual, cultural, and structural levels. Little evidence supports the individual level of causation, but there continues to be much debate and disagreement over approaches that emphasize culture. Structural models focusing on the national and international changes that have affected cities are most powerful, especially with explanations focusing on globalization, deindustrialization, and—most basically—uneven development.

The consequences of such changes include increasing poverty and inequality among and within MAs, along with numerous other social ills, worsening conditions in inner-city neighborhoods, higher levels of homelessness, and fiscal crises. Inner-city residents nonetheless exhibit considerable ingenuity and skill in coping with their situations.

Interventions to reverse urban decline range from subsidies to private business to public-private partnerships to community-based development. Federal and local policies also have important roles to play. The future of cities depends on which policies are chosen and the reorganization of settlement spaces into more regionally based entities.

Discussion Questions

1. Do you live or attend college in a city? What kind of city is it? If you do not live or attend college in a city, what cities have you visited? Do cities make you anxious or uncomfortable? Why or why not?

2. Before reading the "In the News" section, had you ever heard about the possibility of a city abolishing itself? What solutions can you see to the problems that lead some city officials and people to consider such a move?

3. Try to see either *Roger & Me* or *Holding Ground*. How do you react to either video? Did it make you uncomfortable? Why? If you were making the video, what would you do differently?

4. You read about various explanations for urban decline. Which do you find most convincing and why?

5. Of the interventions you read about, which do you think is most likely to be most effective?

References

Anand, Geeta. 1998. "Leeway Urged on Welfare Work Rule." *Boston Globe*, Metro/Region, May 18, B1, B12.

Bagli, Charles V. 1997. "Tax Breaks Proliferating to Keep Corporations in New York City." *New York Times*, October 17.

Beauregard, Robert. 1996. "Voices of Decline." Pp. 363–91 in *Readings in Urban Theory*, edited by Susan Fainstein and Scott Campbell. Cambridge: Blackwell.

Belkin, Doug. 1997. "An Ivy Battles for Campus Life: $120 m Penn Plan Targets Philadelphia Blight." *Boston Globe*, November 24.

Carroll, Walter F. 1989. *Brockton: From Rural Parish to Urban Center*. Northridge, California: Windsor Publications.

Castells, Manuel. 1989. *The Informational City*. Oxford: Blackwell.

Center for Neighborhood Technology. 1998. http://www.cnt.org/.

Dandaneau, Steven P. 1996. *A Town Abandoned: Flint, Michigan Confronts Deindustrialization*. Albany: State University of New York Press.

di Leonardo, Micaela. 1992. "Boyz on the Hood." *The Nation*, August 17/24, 178–86.

Dreier, Peter. 1996. "America's Urban Crisis: Symptoms, Causes, and Solutions." Pp. 79–141 in *Race, Poverty, and American Cities*, edited by John Charles Boger and Judith Welch Wegner. Chapel Hill: University of North Carolina Press.

Dudley Street Neighborhood Initiative. 1996. *Anything Is Possible: Most Notable Achievements* (September). Flyer. Boston: Dudley Street Neighborhood Initiative.

Eitzen, D. Stanley, and Maxine Baca Zinn. 1997. *Social Problems*. Seventh edition. Boston: Allyn and Bacon.

Fischer, Claude S. 1982. *To Dwell Among Friends: Personal Networks in Town and City*. Chicago: University of Chicago Press.

———. 1984. *The Urban Experience*, second edition. San Diego: Harcourt Brace Jovanovich.

Frisbie, W. Parker, and John D. Kasarda. 1988. "Spatial Processes." Pp. 629–66 in *Handbook of Sociology*, edited by Neil J. Smelser. Newbury Park, California: Sage Publications.

Gans, Herbert. 1984 [1962]. *The Urban Villagers*. Second edition. New York: Free Press.

Geddes, Robert. 1997. "Metropolis Unbound: The Sprawling American City and the Search for Alternatives." *The American Prospect* 35:40–46.

Glaberson, William. 1997. "Aging City Weighs Putting Itself Out of Business." *New York Times*, April 14.

Gottdiener, Mark. 1994. *The New Urban Sociology*. New York: McGraw-Hill.

Grillo, Thomas. 1998. "Brockton's Future Is Beginning to Look Up: City Revitalizing Downtown, Neighborhoods." *Boston Globe*. Real Estate Section, May 16, G1.

Gross, Jane. 1997. "Trinity College Leads Effort to Create Hartford Renewal." *New York Times*, April 14, A1, A18.

Grunwald, Michael. 1998. "Stalled on a Rough Road." *Boston Globe*. May 4, A1, A10.

Kearl, Michael. 1998. "Cities and Urbanization." In *A Sociological Tour of Cyberspace*. http://www.trinity.edu/~mkearl/demograp.html.

❖ ❖ ❖ ❖

Keating, W. Dennis, Norman Krumholz, and Philip Star, eds. 1996. *Revitalizing Urban Neighborhoods*. Studies in Government and Public Policy. Lawrence: University Press of Kansas.

Kelley, Robin D.G. 1997. *Yo's Mama's Disfunktional: Fighting the Culture Wars in Urban America*. Boston: Beacon Press.

Kleniewski, Nancy. 1997. *Cities, Change, and Conflict*. Belmont, California: Wadsworth.

Levin, Richard C. 1997. "The President's Corner: The University as Urban Citizen." *Boston Globe*, June 13, A27.

Lobo, Susan. 1982. *A House of My Own: Social Organization in the Squatter Settlements of Lima, Peru*. Tucson: University of Arizona Press.

Macionis, John, and Vincent Parillo. 1998. *Cities and Urban Life*. Upper Saddle River, New Jersey: Prentice Hall.

Mahan, Leah, and Mark Lipton. 1996. *Holding Ground: The Rebirth of Dudley Street*. Film. New Day Films.

Mead, Lawrence. 1992. *The New Politics of Poverty: The Nonworking Poor in America*. New York: Basic Books.

Mears, Teresa. 1997. "Miami to Vote on Whether It Should Still Exist." *Boston Globe*, September 2.

Medoff, Peter, and Holly Sklar. 1994. *Streets of Hope: The Fall and Rise of an Urban Neighborhood*. Boston: South End Press.

Mooney, Linda A., David Knox, and Caroline Schacht. 1997. *Understanding Social Problems*. Minneapolis/St. Paul: West Publishing.

Moore, Michael. 1989. *Roger & Me*. Film. Dog Eat Dog Productions, released by Warner Brothers, Inc.

The Neighborhood Works. 1998. *The Neighborhood Works*. In Center for Neighborhood Technology. http://www.cnt.org/tnw/.

New York Times. 1997. "By Wide Margin, Miami Voters Preserve City." September 5.

Orum, Anthony M. 1997. "Review of Roger Waldinger 'Still the Promised City? African-Americans and New Immigrants in Postindustrial New York'." *H-Urban, H-Net Reviews* November. http://www.hnet/msu/edu/reviews/showrev.cgi.

Perlman, Janice E. 1976. *The Myth of Marginality: Urban Poverty and Politics in Rio de Janeiro*. Berkeley: University of California Press.

Rabrenovic, Gordana. 1996. *Community Builders: A Tale of Neighborhood Mobilization in Two Cities*. Philadelphia: Temple University Press.

Sassen, Saskia. 1990. "Economic Restructuring and the American City." *Annual Review of Sociology* 16:465–90.

———. 1991. *The Global City: New York, London, Tokyo*. Princeton: Princeton University Press.

———. 1994. *Cities in a World Economy*. Sociology for a New Century. Thousand Oaks, California: Pine Forge Press.

Schemo, Diana Jean. 1996. "Rio Frets as Michael Jackson Plans to Film Slum." *New York Times*, February 11.

Sernau, Scott. 1997. *Critical Choices: Applying Sociological Insight in Your Life, Family, and Community*. Los Angeles: Roxbury Publishing.

Sharff, Jagna Wojicka. 1998. *King Kong on 4th Street: Families and Violence of Poverty on the Lower West Side*. Boulder: Westview Press.

Stack, Carol. 1974. *All Our Kin*. New York: Harper and Row.

Susser, Ida. 1982. *Norman Street: Poverty and Politics in an Urban Neighborhood*. New York: Oxford University Press.

Terry, Sara. 1996. "Urban Self-Renewal." *Boston Sunday Globe*. May 12, 65, 67.

U.S. Bureau of the Census. 1996. *Statistical Abstract of the United States*. Washington, D.C.: U. S. Government Printing Office.

Walljasper, Jay. 1997. "When Activists Win: The Renaissance of Dudley St." *The Nation*, March 3, 11–17.

White, Morton, and Lucia White. 1964. *The Intellectual Versus the City*. New York: New American Library Mentor.

Wilson, William Julius. 1987. *The Truly Disadvantaged: The Inner City, the Underclass, and Public Policy*. Chicago: University of Chicago Press.

——. 1996. *When Work Disappears: The World of the New Urban Poor*. New York: Knopf.

Wirth, Louis. 1938. "Urbanism as a Way of Life." *American Journal of Sociology* 44:1–24.

Wyly, Elvin K., Norman J. Glickman, and Michael Lahr. 1998. "A Top 10 List of Things to Know About American Cities." *Cityscape: A Journal of Policy Development and Research* 3(3):7–32.

Zukin, Sharon. 1991. "The Hollow Center: U.S. Cities in the Global Era." Pp. 245–61 in *America at Century's End*, edited by Alan Wolfe. Berkeley: University of California Press.

Web Sites

http://www.tulane.edu/~rouxbee/urban.htm

City Life Around the World: Professor April Brayfield's Urban Sociology Projects. In her course on urban life at Tulane University, Brayfield has an assignment in which her students work in teams to construct websites focusing on various world cities. For Spring 1997, the students set up sites for eight cities, including Athens, Beijing, Mexico City, and Tokyo. Take a look at these sites to see what your fellow students have accomplished.

http://www.chass.utoronto.ca:8080/guri/Welcome.html

Global Urban Research Initiative. This website at the University of Toronto is the home base for an ambitious research project on cities around the world. In addition it has links to numerous other sites on cities and urbanization. This site is available in English, French, and Spanish.

http://www.yale.edu/socdept/slc

The Social Life of Cities. This site is a collection of photographs prepared by Professor Joseph Soares of the Department of Sociology at Yale University. The photographs illustrate aspects of urban design and public spaces in a number of cities.

http://www.louisville.edu/org/sun

Sustainable Urban Neighborhoods. This site is sponsored by the University of Louisville Center for Sustainable Urban Neighborhoods. It contains a wealth of material on the collaboration between the university and West Louisville.

CHAPTER FOURTEEN

Population and Food

In the News: Wasted Food, Hungry People

The U.S. Department of Agriculture estimates that 96 billion pounds of food are wasted in the United States every year. Those 96 billion pounds represent more than 25 percent of the food produced in the country every year. At the same time, according to the Department of Agriculture, people in 12 million U.S. households worry about getting enough to eat, and that does not even include the homeless. This information appeared in an Associated Press story, which also reported on efforts to reclaim some of the wasted food (Anderson 1997).

According to the Department of Agriculture report on U.S. eating patterns, about 12 percent of the 100 million households "either experienced some hunger or had poor diets because they could not afford better food" (Anderson 1997). Of those 100 million households, about 800,000 suffered from severe hunger during the year. Those 800,000 households included 215,000 children under age six.

In spite of an apparent economic boom in the 1990s, demand for food assistance continues to rise.—Photo courtesy of Union Rescue Mission, Los Angeles, California.

The report was released at a national conference on how to recover, or "glean," more of the food wasted. Vice President Al Gore referred to the amount of waste as an "appalling figure" and noted that "we already have enough food in America to feed everyone" (Anderson 1997). Gore and Agriculture Secretary Dan Glickman emphasized the importance of efforts to reduce waste and introduced several government programs to reduce food waste. They noted that if the amount, recovered or gleaned, rose by one-third, it would feed about 450,000 people a day for a year.

As serious as domestic hunger is, problems of world hunger loom even larger. You will see in this chapter that the world food and hunger situation has improved in recent years, but it is still exceptionally serious. Millions of people worldwide suffer from malnutrition and have uncertain access to adequate food. If a report discussed in a recent New York Times *article is accurate, things could get worse. The article reported on a study saying that "problems from rising consumer demand to falling water tables could create huge food gaps in the poorest countries despite their economic growth" (Crossette 1997b). The study, "The World Food Situation:*

Recent Developments, Emerging Issues, and Long-Term Prospects," suggests that improving living standards in a world where population is increasing by 80 million people a year puts increasing pressure on available food supplies (Pinstrup-Andersen et al. 1997). The demand for meat is rising rapidly in developing countries: "Better living standards and changing tastes that come with urbanization could strain the world's food supplies on a still unpredictable level," according to the report (Crossette 1997b).

Making things potentially even worse is a drop in aid from rich nations to poor nations. A new survey "The Reality of Aid" was released in the United States in October 1997 by Interaction, a Washington coalition of 150 United States agencies. Reporting on the survey for the New York Times, Barbara Crossette notes that "more than 1.3 billion people live in absolute poverty by world measures—on incomes of less than $1 a day" (Crossette 1997a). James Gustave Speth, administrator of the United Nations Development Program, suggests that because many of the poor live in countries with high population growth, "the numbers of the poor people grow even as poverty-reduction programs begin to make headway" (Crossette 1997a). In this chapter we examine the links among poverty, hunger, and population growth.

Definition and Prevalence

Have you ever been really hungry? Not just a little hungry and looking forward to a snack or your next meal, but *really* hungry? For many people in the United States and around the world, hunger is a persistent reality. Have you ever wondered what it would be like to be really hungry and why some people are hungry so often? Some social scientists suggest that there is not enough food in the world. Maybe part of the answer has to do with waste, as the "In the News" piece suggested. Waste refers to more than just discarding food; it may also be related to the types of food people consume. For example, many social scientists, activists, and nutritionists argue that it is wasteful and inefficient to feed grains to animals that are to be consumed. It is far more efficient to eat the grain directly. However, some analysts suggest that the main cause of hunger is that there are just too many people in the world. In this chapter we examine food and population issues, primarily from a global perspective.

Thinking of social problems related to food and population leads us immediately to world hunger and overpopulation. Both problems are closely linked to each other and are also closely linked to global inequality and poverty. Some commentators see these problems as internal to particular societies. This view implies that if people in poorer countries would just have fewer children and adopt more advanced food production technologies, they could overcome the problems. Producing more in itself, some experts argue, is not enough. If the population in a society continues to increase, then gains from increased production will not do much to alleviate a scarcity problem. This is a popular view, but many see it as oversimplified.

The authors think it is important to consider another point of view. Population ecologist William W. Murdoch suggests that population and food problems are symptoms of a single phenomenon and that the same political, economic, and social machinery both drives rapid population growth and constrains food production. That machinery has created and maintained the structural poverty of rural populations in the underdeveloped world. (1980:6)

Thus, Murdoch argues that population growth, widespread hunger, and poverty are closely linked problems, with structural poverty causing both rapid population growth and inadequate food supplies.

Rich and poor nations have always argued over the causes of poverty, whether population growth or underdevelopment was more responsible (Seitz 1995). For example, at the 1974 United Nations World Population conference in Bucharest, a Chinese delegate presented a complex and troubling view of population and food problems.

> What a mass of figures the superpowers have calculated in order to prove that the population is too large, the food supply too small and natural resources insufficient! But they never calculate the amount of natural resources they have plundered, the social wealth they have grabbed and the super-profits they have extorted from Asia, Africa and Latin America. (Huang 1974)

Even though that statement was made about 25 years ago, it can still help us to understand issues related to food and population. Certainly the world has changed dramatically since 1974: the Soviet Union has disintegrated, the former Eastern European socialist countries are transforming themselves into market-based capitalist societies, the Cold War has ended, and the United States reigns as the world's only superpower. In spite of the changes, if we consider Huang's statement as a set of hypotheses, it may still help us to understand global inequality, world hunger, and population issues. We will return to these issues in the "Levels of Causation" section later in the chapter; however, the connections between food and population are so intricate and sometimes confusing that we think it is useful to explore these issues early in this chapter.

She-tse Huang seems to imply that (1) world population may not be too large, (2) the world food supply may be adequate, and (3) the supply of natural resources may be sufficient. He also suggests that (1) poverty and hunger in the less developed countries are the result of the developed world's taking and consuming their resources, (2) the developed world amassed extensive wealth by taking those resources, and (3) the developed world gained super-profits from the resources they "extorted" from Asia, Africa, and Latin America (Huang 1974).

Notice one additional implication of these hypotheses: they suggest that the development and enrichment of part of the world—the developed countries—impoverished other parts of the world—the less developed countries. It also suggests that if natural resources in developing countries are insufficient, it may be because their resources were "plundered" by the developed world. As uncomfortable as these ideas may make readers living in developed countries, they deserve serious consideration because some social scientists argue that substantial evidence supports them.

There is no question that food and population problems are complex and that questions about causes and interventions are very controversial. In recent years, some observers have become more optimistic about solving problems of world inequality. Still, others remain pessimistic for those concerned about overpopulation, poverty, famine, and the environment. Controversial

Close to 200 million children around the world suffer from malnutrition. That amounts to over one-third of the world's children. —*Photo: UNICEF/HQ93-1007 Betty Press*

aspects of these issues even extend to the terms experts use to describe parts of the world. If you look back a few paragraphs, you will see that we used the terms "less developed" and "developing" to characterize the "poor countries" of the world. In addition, the developed countries are often referred to as the **North**; less developed countries are called the **South**. There is a rough geographical distribution of less developed countries in the southern hemisphere. We have also used the term **Third World**. Before the Cold War ended, the "First World" referred to the United States and the Western industrial democracies; the "Second World" referred to the Soviet Union and the other socialist societies; and the "Third World" referred to poorer, less developed countries. The categories were always ambiguous, but many found them useful. Since the end of the Cold War, and the obsolescence of the notions of "First World" and "Second World," many commentators have argued that the term Third World is misleading and demeaning. However, we still find the term useful.

In *Inside the Third World*, Paul Harrison argues that the Third World refers not so much to a precise geographical location as to "a mode of existence of the poor and disadvantaged." More specifically, he suggests that the "Third World is the world inhabited by the poor of the earth" (1993a: 13). Kofi Hadjor acknowledges that the countries which make up the Third World differ significantly from one another in many ways. However, he suggests that despite their historical, political, cultural, economic, or social differences, they have enough in common to make up a separate category: "The social and economic landscape of the Third World is in all its aspects conditioned by the cumulative effect of **colonialism**, **imperialism** and Western domination" (Hadjor 1993:9) [emphasis added]. In examining food and population problems, we must keep in mind the Western role in the Third World, both historically and in the contemporary world.

People in developed societies may ask what problems of hunger and overpopulation have to do with them and why they should care. You may be asking that question yourself. Harrison provides a powerful and compelling
answer:

> The process of development, the fate of the people going through it, is a
> global drama. It is the story, often tragic, of billions of individual lives, their
> hopes and frustrations, their efforts and their failures, their sufferings and
> their conflicts. It is perhaps the central story of our time. One that concerns,
> directly, three quarters of humanity, and ought to concern the other, industri-
> alized quarter much more than it does, if only because its inhabitants live in
> relative comfort on a planet in which there is so much staggering poverty.
> (Harrison 1993a:17)

Harrison suggests that if the ubiquity of poverty and suffering on the
planet does not lead people to care about development problems such as
world hunger and overpopulation, then enlightened self-interest should provide additional reasons. First, one aspect of globalization is the movement of
jobs from the industrialized world to the Third World. Poor people in the
Third World have so little that they will take almost any jobs, including jobs
moved from developed countries. Second, shortages of key resources will
make maintaining control of their resources more important for poorer
countries. They will be less willing to let those resources move to richer countries. Finally, "scarcity and growing polarization in developing countries"
may lead to civil wars and international conflicts, which will inevitably involve industrialized countries. Therefore, it is in everyone's interest to care
and learn about food and population issues in the world (Harrison 1993a).
       One difficulty in examining these issues is the need to learn new terms in
two related but still distinct areas: the study of food issues and the study of
population. We try to keep these new terms to a minimum, but learning some
of them will help you to understand the issues involved. For an overview of
food-related terms see "A Closer Look: Studying Food and Hunger." Because
these sets of terms are in "Closer Look" boxes, you may find it convenient to
refer back to them if necessary.
       In addition to learning new terms related to food issues, we also need to
get a sense of the prevalence of hunger and food shortages. The United Nations Food and Agriculture Organization's (FAO) *Sixth World Food Survey* indicates that in the Third World, food inadequacy has declined over the last
twenty years (Food and Agriculture Organization 1996). Although various organizations, such as the FAO and the World Bank, formerly used differing estimates of the number of hungry people, today FAO estimates are accepted by
virtually all organizations involved with research and policy on food-related
issues (Uvin 1994b). Those estimates indicate that 20 percent of the population in developing countries had inadequate access to food between 1990 and
1992, compared with 35 percent in the early 1970s.
       Despite this improvement, the FAO points out that 20 percent of people—
that is, one out of five—in the Third World still face food inadequacy. This is
clearly exceptionally serious (Food and Agriculture Organization 1996). It is
also important to remember that food shortages, food poverty, and food deprivation are not evenly distributed around the world, or even within the
Third World. For example, famines have now been eliminated almost everywhere except Africa (Seitz 1995). However, there are important successes in

❖ ❖ ❖ ❖

A Closer Look

Studying Food and Hunger

In compiling *The World Hunger Report: 1993*, Peter Uvin used three distinct but related concepts to "estimate the numbers of people affected by hunger and to analyze the global food situation: *food shortage, food poverty,* and *food deprivation*" (1994a: 1). Each concept focuses on a different aspect of hunger.

> *Food shortage* occurs when total food supplies within a designated area— the world as a whole or continents, countries, or regions within countries— are insufficient to meet the need of the population living within that area. *food poverty* refers to the situation in which households cannot obtain enough food to meet the needs of all their members. *Food deprivation* refers to inadequate consumption of food or of specific nutrients, the form of malnutrition known as undernutrition. (Uvin 1994a: 1)

These three concepts are important because they emphasize that food poverty may exist in households within a region that has no food shortage. Food deprivation may occur in households that are not food poor. Some members of those households may not receive adequate food and nutrition.

Another useful concept is food security, which is defined as access by people at all times to the food they need for a healthy life. This is the goal of most programs that aim to end hunger. Food insecurity, then, is a perceived lack of access to food. (Leidenfrost 1993)

producing food and ending poverty in Africa, as well as in other parts of the world (De Silva 1989; Harrison 1987; Harrison 1993; Uvin 1994).

Although things seem to be improving in terms of food and hunger, there is clearly a long way to go. You may still be wondering how far there is to go and unsure about just how many people are hungry. No one actually knows, but the best estimates are that between 500 million and 1 billion people on earth are hungry (Seitz 1995). In spite of improvements in the availability of food, a recent study by the International Food Policy Research Institute (IFPRI) suggests that the food gap is widening in Third World societies and that "if the global community continues with business as usual, prospects for **food security** will be bleak for millions of people and degradation of natural resources will continue" (Pinstrup-Andersen et al. 1997: 5). This study also suggests that if present trends continue, one out of every four children now will be malnourished by 2020. More than 70 percent of the malnourished children in the world live in sub-Saharan Africa and South Asia. The report also notes that enough food will be produced for those who can afford to buy it but that those who cannot afford it face bleak prospects (Pinstrup-Andersen et al. 1997).

Another way of looking at the difference between the nutrition levels of the rich and the poor nations is in terms of average daily calories consumed, the **Dietary Energy Supply** (DES). The DES for sub-Saharan Africa in 1990 was 2099 calories per day. This level has changed little since 1970. For North America the DES in 1990 was 3600. Europe was 3450, South Asia was 2245, South America was 2625, and Central America was 2822. Consider the gap between sub-Saharan Africa and North America, which in these data includes Canada and the United States. The difference is almost 1,500 calories per person per day, an "enormous difference" (Uvin 1994a:5). Between 1988 and 1990, Third World countries with a total population of 802 million people fell below the dietary requirements needed for typical activity levels in those countries. Although not everyone in those countries had inadequate diets, there was not enough food to adequately feed their entire populations (Uvin 1994b).

Hunger and the number of mouths to feed are clearly global, national, regional, and community issues. As social problems, overpopulation and hunger are not the personal troubles of individuals and families but the problems of societies in an increasingly interrelated world. The developed world is not immune from these problems. Even in the United States about 40 million people lived in poverty in 1993. The cutbacks in social welfare programs of the Reagan/Bush administrations pushed 13 million additional people into poverty, raising the percentage of persons in poverty from 11.7 percent in 1979 to 15.1 percent in 1993 (Braun 1997). Among those hurt most severely in the United States are women—especially single mothers of small children—and children. The same is true in the Third World where women and children are "the poorest of the poor" (Harrison 1993a). (See "A Closer Look: Myths About World Hunger.")

A Closer Look

Myths About World Hunger

In their book, *World Hunger: Twelve Myths*, Frances Moore Lappe and Joseph Collins, founders of Food First (The Institute for Food and Development Policy) argue that widely believed myths make it hard for people to understand the causes of and possible solutions for world hunger. They analyze twelve of the most powerful myths, explain why they are myths, and suggest more useful and accurate ways to think about world hunger (Lappe and Collins 1986). Let's take a look at three of the most widespread myths. You might also want to take a look at David Bodnik and Daniel Zalik's discussion of "6 Myths and Facts about Hunger," (1996) which is based on Food First materials and is available on HungerWeb. Consider these ideas as hypotheses and use them to stimulate your own thinking.

Myth 1: There's Simply Not Enough Food
People are hungry because of scarcity. Although many people accept this myth, Lappe and Collins argue that "abundance, not scarcity, best describes the supply of food in the world" (1986: 9). Enough grain is produced every year to provide every person on the earth with enough calories.

Myth 2: Nature's to Blame
Many people believe that droughts and other natural events beyond human control cause famines and food shortages. However, much research suggests that human-made forces increasingly make people vulnerable to natural disasters. In addition, severe famines and food shortages do not necessarily stem from natural disasters, and, conversely, droughts and other natural disasters do not necessarily lead to famine (Sen 1993).

Myth 3: Too Many Mouths to Feed
This myth suggests that overpopulation causes hunger—that there are just too many people for food-producing resources to support. This myth has led to widespread efforts to slow population growth, based on the belief that slowing population growth is a prerequisite for alleviating hunger. Although the possibility of overpopulation is real and serious, Lappe and Collins dispute the idea that hunger is caused by too many people to feed. In fact, population density and hunger do not consistently occur together. Rather, "hunger, the most dramatic symptom of pervasive poverty, and rapid population growth occur together because they have a common cause" (1986: 25). In their view, the powerlessness of the poor is that common cause.

The Universal Declaration on the Eradication of Hunger and Malnutrition of the 1974 World Food Conference recognized hunger as a social problem. Even though many programs have been set up to combat hunger, little has changed since 1975. Although the rate of population growth in the world has slowed from 1.75 percent in 1975 to around 1.34 percent per year in 1997, there are still about 78 million people added each year to the earth's population (Seitz 1995).

In 1994, the UN estimated that the world's population was about 5.6 billion; in 1997, estimated population was about 5.8 billion. By the year 2000, it is estimated that the population will go over 6 billion, perhaps to 6.25 billion. Even more troubling, the UN estimates that the world's population will peak at somewhere between 8 and 28 billion, with about 12 billion by 2150 seen as the most likely estimate (Seitz 1995). To get a better sense of the growth in world population, look at Figure 14-1, which portrays the steady rise in the number of people in the world. The annual rate of growth in world population has steadily declined in recent years (Figure 14-2), but with such a large population base even a lower rate of increase will lead to increasing population size. Figure 14-3 indicates that the actual number of people added to the world's population is lessening. Nonetheless, the projection of 12 billion people by 2150 does seem very possible. Can the planet sustain a population of 12 billion? At this point no one knows for sure, but it seems doubtful. (For a quick overview of key topics and terms for studying population, see "A Closer Look: Population, Demography, and the Demographic Transition.")

This brings us to the concept of the **carrying capacity** of the planet. "Carrying capacity is the number of individuals of a certain species that can be sustained indefinitely in a given area" (Seitz 1995:51). Carrying capacity can vary up or down over time. No one knows what the carrying capacity of the planet is for human beings. Seitz sets out four possible scenarios for the relationships between a growing population and its environment. The first

---

Figure 14-1 World Population: 1950–2050

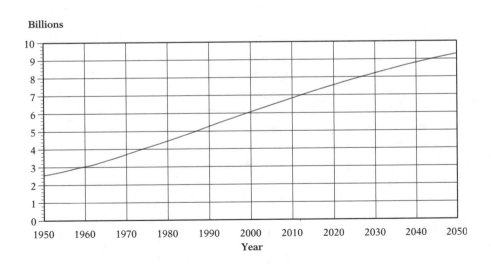

Billions

Source: U.S. Bureau of the Census. 1998. International Data Base. <http://www.census.gov/ ipc/idbnew.html>.

Figure 14-2 World Population Growth Rate: 1950–2050

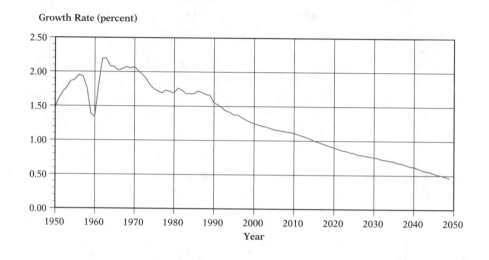

Source: U.S. Bureau of the Census. 1998. International Data Base. <http://www.census.gov/ipc/idbnew.html>

Figure 14-3 Annual World Population Change: 1950–2050

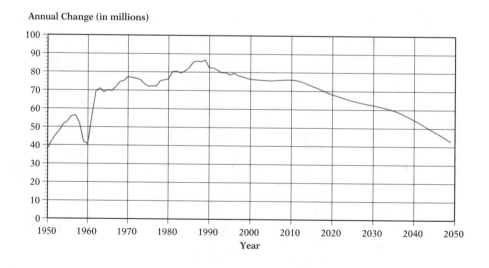

Source: U.S. Bureau of the Census. 1998. International Data Base. <http://www.census.gov/ipc/idbnew.html>.

❖ ❖ ❖ ❖

A Closer Look

Population, Demography, and the Demographic Transition

Demography is the study of human populations. Demographers study numerous aspects of population, but their fundamental concerns are "childbearing and birth rates, dying and death rates, and migration and migration rates" (Kammeyer and Ginn 1986:1). These factors are fundamental because human populations change through births, deaths, and migration. Changing **birth rates**, **death rates**, and **migration rates** affect the growth rate, size, density, and distribution of populations. Birth rates and death rates are also referred to, respectively, as **fertility rates** and mortality rates. Among the most important characteristics of a population are the distribution of people of different ages and genders, often referred to as aspects of **population structure**.

Demographers use **crude birth rates** and **crude death rates** to measure population change. The crude birth rate is the number of births per 1,000 population; the crude death rate is the number of deaths per 1,000 population. For example, a crude birthrate of 15 for a society means that 15 babies will be born for every 1,000 people in the society. The rate of population growth is the difference between the crude birth and death rates. Migration also affects the rate of population growth, but we can leave that aside here to emphasize the impact of fertility and mortality.

One of the most important transformations in world population growth is called the **demographic transition**, which occurred first in northwestern Europe. The demographic transition can be divided into three stages. During the first stage, prior to the demographic transition, death rates and birth rates were both high and produced a fairly stable population size. The high death rates were chiefly the result of malnutrition and disease and fluctuated from year to year because of plagues and harvest failures. Birth rates were high and fairly stable, although some pretransition societies may have engaged in family planning in a conscious effort to prevent excess births. During the second stage of the European demographic transition, which occurred over about 100 years in the eighteenth and nineteenth centuries, death rates decreased by about 60 percent, while birth rates remained high. This is the period—when births exceed deaths—when rapid population growth occurred. In the third stage of a demographic transition, birth rates begin to fall as individuals limit the size of their families. By the end of this stage, birth rates are low, nearly matching the low death rates. This leads to stable population size, or low rates of population growth (Kammeyer and Ginn 1986). Sociologists need to understand the *causes* of declines in fertility and mortality if any of our interventions aimed at moving the whole world population through the demographic transition are to be successful. The demographic transition theory itself is more of a model than a theory. It shows *what* happened, but does not really explain *why* population transformations occur, nor does it prove that all societies must go through a similar transition.

scenario is one of continuous growth: both population and carrying capacity increase together. "The scarcity of only one of the essential resources for humans—which would include air, energy, food, space, nonrenewable resources, heat, and water—would be enough to put a limit on population growth" (Seitz 1995: 51). A second possibility is that population would stabilize at some point below carrying capacity. Third, population may exceed carrying capacity and then oscillate above and below it. Finally, and ominously, population growth may exceed carrying capacity to such an extent and for so long that it leads to a steep decline or even extinction of the population and reduction of carrying capacity (Seitz 1995). Human choices and decisions will determine which scenarios prevail. To understand the possible decisions and their implications, we need to look more closely at population size and structure.

In addition to its size, a population's **age structure**, or age distribution, is important. Population growth is highest in the Third World, and those countries tend to have high proportions of young people. Even if the birth rate drops in a particular society, if most women are in child-bearing years or younger, then that country's population will continue to grow rapidly. Moreover, a high proportion of young children means that they will need to be fed, clothed, and cared for. Demographers study the age structure of countries by using **population pyramids**, which show the distribution of people by gender and age. These can be very valuable for predicting the rate of population growth and the estimated size of the population at various times. The Census Bureau International Data Base provides population pyramids for almost any country. See "A Closer Look: Using Population Pyramids," for more on this.

A Closer Look

Using Population Pyramids

Although the Census Bureau primarily focuses on the United States, it does have valuable international data. The International Data Base (IDB) allows you to create population pyramids for various societies. The pyramids can give you the age structure of the population now, or can give you projections for future years. Located at URL http://www.census.gov/ipc/www/idbpyr.html, this site is a fascinating site and is exceptionally easy to use.

The population pyramids for China for 1997, 2025, and 2050 show a society moving from having a young age composition to an increasingly elderly society. The population pyramid for Ireland shows a predominantly young society in 1997 moving to large numbers of middle-aged people in 2025 and to much larger numbers of older people and a shrinking base of children by 2050. This is a website you really should try. Think about the implications of different age distributions.

Levels of Causation

Individual

Sociology emphasizes the importance of the positions people occupy in social institutions, social structures, and society for shaping their attitudes, beliefs, and behaviors, including those related to population and food. Are people individually responsible for problems related to hunger and overpopulation? Some people would answer yes to this and suggest, for example that certain people should be more responsible for birth control. In order to analyze such a simplistic perspective, one might ask how people make decisions related to reproduction that might help reduce population problems, and, conversely, what causes people to make decisions that worsen food and population problems. Decisions about having children and adopting certain food production technologies are crucially shaped by the cultural, economic, and social contexts within which people live.

Murdoch argues that food and population problems are fundamentally problems of development. In other words, they are inextricably linked to broader social, economic, and political processes of development. Because economic accumulation and development rely on human effort and energy, much development theory emphasizes the psychological and cultural attributes of individuals (Jaffee 1990).

Rather than examining all these theories, we will look at the most influential. This is the individual modernization theory which focuses on the attitudes and values of people in particular countries. David Jaffee notes that this model "argues that Third World development depends on the diffusion and adaptation of modern Western values" (1990: 25). It suggests that values and attitudes precede economic growth and development and that they cause development, in some way. From this point of view, those living in poor countries obviously have the wrong values.

There are variants of this approach. Hagen suggests that innovational personalities enable a society to grow rapidly, as opposed to authoritarian personalities, which hinder development. Lerner's theory of modernization also focused on psychological modernization. The modern person is empathetic and open to change. The traditional personality, according to Lerner, is parochial and resistant to change. David McClelland's approach focuses on the "need for achievement." Societies that are more highly developed usually have greater levels of the need for achievement. Other models also focus on individual psychological modernity as a key to social and economic development (Jaffee 1990). We see these models as flawed in their assumptions about development and in their depiction of both developed and less developed societies. They represent what J. M. Blaut (1993) refers to as **diffusionist** models and seem rooted in **Eurocentric** approaches to world history and development. Diffusionist approaches assume that cultural processes and practices began in Europe and spread —or diffuse—to other parts of the world. The assumption that Europe is the source of cultural innovation is Eurocentric. Blaut also refers to this perspective as the Colonizer's View of the World.

Cultural

There are many cultural causes of fertility and mortality as well as of population growth. Sometimes a single item can have far-reaching consequences on the growth of human populations—for example, the discovery of the potato. Spanish Conquistadors found the potato among the natives of the Andes and brought it back to Europe. Eventually the potato became a staple food for the lower classes. With this more abundant food, fertility increased and the death rate dropped. As a result, Europe's population almost doubled during the 1700s (McKeown 1977).

Obviously, factors other than food availability can affect birth rates. Illness, for example, would interfere with reproduction, as would social attitudes concerning sexual behavior. Despite this, Thomas Malthus (1982 [1798]) argued during the 1700s that people were reproducing at alarming rates and that eventually the population would outstrip its food supply. Contemporary Malthusians still agree with this stance. They point out that the world's population is doubling at equal intervals at an accelerating rate. Soon there will be more and more people with less and less to consume. Many scholars oppose this perspective and argue that no one can infinitely predict the world's future population. Although there is great social pressure for people to reproduce, especially married couples, people do not do so blindly. For example, age at marriage makes a difference as to whether couples will reproduce. Overall, about 11 percent of U.S. married couples never have children, mainly because of age at marriage (U.S. Bureau of the Census 1996).

Populations are increasing in the least industrialized nations, and many reasons are offered to explain this trend. One is the status of parenthood. Motherhood is a highly exalted status in the least developed nations. The more children a woman has, the more she has gained personal and social fulfillment. In addition, a man proves his manhood by fathering children. Also, poor people in the least developed nations may consider children economic assets. When parents become old, they rely on their families to care for them since they do not have social security or medical insurance. In countries such as India, Pakistan, Bangladesh, and in tropical Africa, many births are needed because of high infant mortality rates. The unavailability of birth control devices is also a reason for the high birth rates in developing nations (Seitz 1995).

Although birth rates are high in poorer countries, so are rates of malnutrition and death, especially for children. Why is this happening? Many scholars suggest that there is more than enough food for each person in the world. Although the world's population is high, improved seeds, harvesting techniques, and fertilization have made more food available. Obviously, some countries produce more food than others, so in order to explain why some people die of hunger we must assume that the cause of starvation is an imbalance between supply and demand. Except for Africa, actual starvation is not as common today as in the past, but many people still die of malnutrition. The fact is that millions of people cannot afford to purchase the food they need to survive.

One important cause of early infant malnutrition and death has been the decline in the practice of breastfeeding as a way to nourish infants. This change had little effect on the nourishment of children in the advanced industrialized societies because of improved sanitation and safe water. However, unsanitary conditions in the poor countries of the world has been cited as a major cause of infant mortality since milk formula is mixed with contaminated water. In addition, in the least developed nations, breastfeeding is on the decline partly because of urbanization, the increasing number of women entering the workforce, and the desire to mimic the United States by being "modern" (Harrison 1993a; Seitz 1995).

Historical research in Europe and the United States suggests that in order to lower or even combat infant mortality rates, society must improve food sources as well as access to health care. Another way to look at this is to reduce fertility or at least educate people concerning birth control techniques. For some cultures, this would mean reevaluating some traditional beliefs concerning producing large numbers of children. In countries where women enjoy higher social and economic status in their lives, birth rates are decreasing.

Structural

As a conflict theorist, Marx insisted that problems of overpopulation were caused by the creation of capitalism with its accompanying economic institutions. He argued that capitalism's need to maintain a labor reserve of workers was the factor that directly created population problems. Marx and

Engels both noted the importance of Malthus's ideas and both criticized them in order to go beyond them (Meek 1971). Later Marxist demographers carried these ideas further by investigating the demographic history of Europe (Seccombe 1986). Many contemporary scholars attribute the concentration of population and food problems in less developed countries to the development of a world capitalist economic system that systematically creates poverty and unemployment in the Third World (Braun 1997; Chase-Dunn and Hall 1997; Shannon 1996).

The Agricultural Revolution was the first major event that gave population growth a boost. Food supply greatly increased as people began to domesticate plants and animals. The population continued to grow through the Industrial Revolution, as advances in industry, agriculture, and transportation improved the lives of people. Karl Polanyi's classic book, *The Great Transformation* (1994), suggested that surplus population problems in Europe arose because of the Industrial Revolution. Before much of Europe became industrialized, agriculture was the source of livelihood for many. With industrialization, many agricultural workers became unemployed and consequently became a social problem of eighteenth-century England. Many factories were originally established as welfare agencies to help former agricultural workers.

Scholars formerly believed that although industrialization caused difficulty by disrupting traditional social institutions such as the family, it also contributed to fertility reduction (Goode 1963). Fertility reduction was supposedly a direct result of removing people from the traditional rural norms of reproduction, which encouraged large families. As a result, it was thought, more modern family values developed. In fact, nuclear families were predominant in Western Europe for several hundred years before the Industrial Revolution. Extended families actually became more common in newly industrialized cities.

Changes in educational and political institutions had important effects on population growth. Despite the fact that capitalism encouraged population growth, the establishment of democracy as a core value encouraged working class people to express their opinions concerning the quality of their lives. The spread of mass education further reinforced people's attitudes about controlling their own futures, especially improving their material welfare (Thompson 1966). The idea and implementation of democracy in North America and Europe helped to raise the standard of living of the poor and provided them with education. The formation of democratic institutions is viewed as an important factor in explaining declining population growth during this time. We should note that the poor and working classes had to fight every step of the way for democratic institutions and improvements in their standards of living.

In contrast, structural conditions of both urban and rural poverty in Third World societies encourage families to have more children to help ensure the family's survival. There are several reasons why people in Third World societies wish to have many children. Because many infants die, having many children enhances the likelihood of having surviving children. In addition, rural families need their children to work in the fields, and urban families also rely on children's work to provide added income and resources for them. Urban poor children in Third World societies often engage in small-scale scavenging and selling to bolster their family's well-being. The lack of social security and old age pensions in Third World societies also makes having more children desirable so that aged parents will have someone to provide for them. The unavailability of contraceptive information and devices also leads to high fertility rates (Seitz 1995). Cultural factors such as religion and tradition also play a role in maintaining birth rates, but structural factors seem even more important.

International economic institutions in a capitalist world economy have slowed industrial development in developing countries; also, development is geared to providing international corporations with profits. Coupled with nondemocratic institutions, economic development has had little impact on the widespread poverty in Third World societies (Harrison 1993a). For more information on these topics, see "A Closer Look: The HungerWeb and Food First Websites."

A Closer Look

The HungerWeb and Food First Websites

HungerWeb is a website that aims "to help prevent and eradicate hunger by facilitating the free exchange of ideas and information regarding the causes of, and solutions to, hunger." Sponsored by the World Hunger Program at Brown University, the HungerWeb provides links to other sites that provide relevant information on hunger. The URL for the site is http://www.brown.edu/Departments/World_Hunger_Program/index.html. The Hunger Website provides an introduction to hunger and malnutrition issues. Links to other sites are divided into Research, Field Work, Advocacy and Policy, and Education and Training. This is an extraordinarily valuable set of annotated links.

One of the co-sponsors of HungerWeb is the Institute for Food and Development Policy—better known as Food First—a nonprofit research and education-for-action center, which focuses on the root causes and solutions to hunger and poverty around the world. Food First sees access to adequate food as a basic human right. This think tank produces books, reports, articles, films, and numerous other resources on hunger, poverty, population, and environmental decline. It is an incredibly rich source of information on these topics. The Food First website is at http://www.foodfirst.org. The homepage gives you a variety of options. You can find out more about the organization and what it does. You can also go to the "Director's Letter," in which Peter Rosset, the executive director, explains why Food First sees food as a human right and explains what the organization is doing to make food as a human right a reality. You can also learn how to become a member of or an intern at Food First. One button on the homepage takes you to an extensive list of valuable Food First publications. Included on the website are several important documents, such as the Universal Declaration of Human Rights and the International Covenant on Economic, Social, and Cultural Rights. Another valuable resource on this site is the Food First WWW Links page, which gives you access to about 30 other websites dealing with domestic and international food-related issues. Try out this website; you'll find plenty of useful and thought-provoking information.

The developing countries that have had the greatest declines in birth rates have been those with highly productive agricultural institutions, such as Taiwan and South Korea; socialist political institutions aimed at meeting basic welfare needs, such as Cuba and China; or vigorous, government-supported family planning programs, such as Mexico, Indonesia, and Sri Lanka. However, only in countries whose social institutions provide the circumstances conducive to individual choices for smaller families has the last

phase of the demographic transition been entered and population growth begun to slow down. This has not been the case in most Third World societies.

Consequences

War, famine, disease, and human misery are some of the consequences of
problems related to food and population growth. Infants in poor countries
are more often the victims of malnutrition than adults, and such malnutrition is a major cause of death. The infant mortality rate is beginning to fall in
some developing countries mainly because of medical advancements of the
past eighty years. In many countries, families spend almost half their income
on food, so it becomes difficult to own a decent home or get educated. As a result, many revolutionary wars were waged by people attempting to change
their material lives. Such wars have been waged from Vietnam to El Salvador
(Harrison 1993a).

The United States as well as many other industrialized countries opposed
these revolutions, fearing communism would be the alternative. With the end
of the Cold War this threat to world stability has been eliminated, although
now there is the possibility that conflicts in smaller countries may spill over
into the world area.

The **Green Revolution** was a positive response to the ever-decreasing
food supplies created by rapid population growth. The Green Revolution began in the 1960s and is often defined as the bringing of high agricultural technology to the Third World (Seitz 1995). This advanced technology was basically composed of the use of new seeds, especially for wheat, rice, and corn, as
well as the introduction of fertilizer, irrigation, and pesticides. The new seeds
responded extremely well to the fertilizer and thus produced high yields
(Harrison 1993a; Seitz 1995). For example, over a six-year period, India doubled its wheat production, and impressive increases in rice production occurred in the Philippines, Sri Lanka, Indonesia, and Malaysia.

On the negative side, there were many unfortunate side effects of the
Green Revolution. It tended to benefit rich farmers rather than poor farmers
since the rich ones had the money to purchase these seeds, fertilizers, and
pesticides. In addition, the new seeds were less resistant to diseases and did
not fare well with too much water (from excessive rains) or too little water
(drought).

What happens when a population grows too fast or too slowly? In the
least developed countries, where population growth is fast, a large proportion of the population is very young, often below the age of fifteen. Children
may be considered economic assets in some ways, but they also consume
more than they produce. In addition, they need health care and education to
become productive members of societies. This is a huge burden for some
economies. A population growing at too slow a rate may also incur problems.
For example, countries in need of skilled workers may have to import them,
which happened in Europe during the 1950s and 1960s.

When a significant proportion of the population is aging, unique problems surface. The United States is experiencing what has been called the
"graying of America." The Social Security system in the United States is undergoing serious scrutiny because the number of citizens over sixty-five
keeps growing, relative to the rest of the population. Mainly because of advanced health care and low birth rates, the proportion of working people to

retired people declined. The problem is that payments from workers are supposed to provide for those who are retired. Since the numbers of each group do not even closely match, there is strain on the Social Security system. In addition, there are increasing health care costs as more and more people exceed retirement age.

China implemented a one-child policy to limit its population growth. Families who have only one child receive various benefits. Many have criticized the policy. —*Photo: Mike Dziedzic.*

Interventions

Like the Green Revolution, most interventions formulated to combat dwindling food supplies have focused on advanced agricultural technology. These interventions have basically made the rich richer and the poor poorer since only the rich could afford to purchase advanced technology. As a result, these interventions were relatively unsuccessful in making food available to the least developed countries.

There are many reasons for these failed interventions. First, although most governments do not ignore hunger, developing nations often give low priority to agricultural development and to relieving poverty in rural areas (Seitz 1995). The main reason for this low priority is that public funds usually go to groups with political power, since political leaders want to stay in power. Second, prices paid to farmers in developing countries are low. These low wages are maintained in many ways. First, if there is competition from other farmers, poor farmers will sell at lower prices to keep their heads above water. Second, there is usually political pressure from those living in urban areas to keep prices low. It is difficult for poor farmers to compete with this urban political power.

Modern, mechanized agriculture techniques would seem to be an appropriate intervention to combat food shortages in the Third World. However, many traditional farmers cannot afford advanced technology or simply do not want to change their traditional ways. Anthropologists Peter Farb and George Armelagos (1980) argue that present-day agriculture is much less efficient than traditional agriculture. In traditional agriculture, the amount of energy used to farm is small compared to the yield.

A final reason food shortages persist in the least developed nations is because of **multinational corporations**. These are companies that operate across national boundaries. In many cases, such companies exploit the least developed nations; they actively search for cheap resources and labor. One way to achieve cheap labor is to move manufacturing or harvesting from highly industrialized nations with high labor costs to the least developed nations with low labor costs.

The Institute for Food and Development Policy (Food First) emphasizes the importance of seeing food as a human right. The right to food has been upheld in various international agreements, including the Universal Declaration of Human Rights (UDHR) and the International Covenant on Economic, Social and Cultural Rights (ICESCR), but these covenants have generally been ignored when it comes to actual policies (Institute for Food and Development Policy 1997).

Bread for the World has suggested 10 ways to make the global economy work better for hungry people. These interventions would substantially reorient the way in which economic decisions affecting hungry people are made. Bread for the World recommends: (1) giving priority to the needs of hungry and poor people when making economic decisions; (2) complementing markets with government and civic action to ensure secure livelihoods for all; (3) including hungry and poor people in decisions that affect their lives; (4) coordinating policies among nations to foster full employment and other social goals; (5) promoting international trade—with safeguards for labor rights, the environment, and food security; (6) fostering food security through more liberal agricultural trade coupled with sound agricultural policies and safety nets; (7) encouraging responsible investing through policies that are good for business, workers, and consumers; (8) focusing the World Bank and other international financial institutions on reducing poverty, and making them accountable to the low-income communities they affect; (9) relieving the government debts of poor countries that are committed to reducing poverty, and expanding foreign aid programs that help hungry and poor people; and (10) exercising our influence as responsible citizens, consumers, employers, workers, and investors to make the world economy work for everyone (Bread for the World Institute 1997; Cohen and Rubinstein 1997).

The Bread for the World recommendations seem to apply mainly on an international level, but interventions are also necessary to address domestic hunger. In the United States House of Representatives, 136 representatives sponsored the Hunger Has a Cure Bill (H.R. 1507). Between April 1994 and April 1995, 12 percent of all U.S. households experienced **food insecurity**. Over 34 million Americans live in households where hunger is a threat. The Hunger Has a Cure Bill would begin to address that food insecurity and would reverse the effects of some cutbacks in funding for school-breakfast and other nutrition programs. Among its provisions, the bill would restore food stamps to the most vulnerable legal immigrants—children and the elderly. It would also allow food-stamp recipients to own a car of "reasonable value." This is especially important for enabling recipients to get to work. The bill would also increase funding for various nutrition programs, including school breakfasts and the Special Supplemental Nutrition Program for Women, Infants, and Children (WIC). The bill is not a cure-all, but it would measurably reduce hunger in the United States (Beckmann 1997).

Interventions meant to control population have varied. The current Chinese "one-child family" program is probably the most controversial program enacted to control population growth. The government hopes to limit the population to 1.3 billion by the year 2000. Contraceptives are widely available and abortion is legal and encouraged in order to limit population growth. There are economic incentives to agreeing to have only one child. Couples who have only one child receive better jobs and housing than couples who have more than one child. Couples who have more than one child are taxed more and receive lower-paying jobs (Tien 1991).

At times larger populations have been advocated, such as in sub-Saharan Africa. The belief was generally that a large population was needed for economic development. The United States indirectly promotes large families by offering tax deductions for children. Whatever the case, very few governments have been successful in limiting population or in promoting population growth (Seitz 1995).

The Future of Population and Food

Predicting the future of population and food is difficult. The interventions chosen will largely determine the future. As we indicated earlier in the chapter, current estimates predict world population stabilizing somewhere between 8 and 28 billion people. This is a large interval. The United Nations predicts the world's population will reach around 12 billion by the year 2150 (Haub 1981). Will the world be able to support this population?

The carrying capacity of an environment must be taken into consideration in order to answer this question. By increasing food production, the earth is able to support a growing population. This balance between growing population and carrying capacity affects different geographic areas in different ways. The most industrialized countries will possess the most advanced technology to meet these needs; less developed countries will have problems. In sub-Saharan Africa, population expansion has reached its carrying capacity. Farmland is becoming desert, which is affecting food supply (Seitz 1995). Overpopulation exacerbates already existing hunger problems. Most people do not die of hunger but of malnutrition; that is, they lack adequate amounts of necessary types of food. Immigration is also an issue to many countries. Tensions will be created as more and more people migrate to lands where they are not wanted.

We know that world population will continue to rise and that many people will be malnourished. We do not know when population will stop growing or if enough food will be available for everyone in the world. Future developments in these areas will largely be the consequences of the nature and success of human choices, decisions, and interventions.

Summary

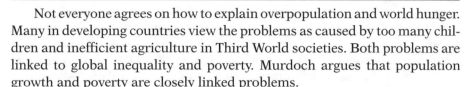

Not everyone agrees on how to explain overpopulation and world hunger. Many in developing countries view the problems as caused by too many children and inefficient agriculture in Third World societies. Both problems are linked to global inequality and poverty. Murdoch argues that population growth and poverty are closely linked problems.

She-tse Huang implies that the world population may not be too large—that the world has adequate food supplies but that the developed world takes resources from less developed, or Third World countries, thus amassing wealth. The issues are obviously debatable and controversial.

The Third World, according to Harrison, is inhabited by the poor of the earth. It is not so much a geographical location as a mode of existence. Hadjor argues that the Third World has been created or is a result of colonialism, imperialism, and Western domination.

The United Nations Food and Agriculture Organization points out that 20 percent of people in the Third World face food shortages. Famine has been eliminated almost everywhere except Africa. Nevertheless, about 500 million to 1 billion people are hungry. Hunger problems and overpopulation problems are the problems of societies. Recognition of hunger as a social problem was shown at the 1974 World Food Conference.

Individual explanations of overpopulation and hunger are inadequate. Individual modernization theory focuses on the attitudes and values of people in particular countries. This theory suggests that those living in poor countries obviously have defective cultural values. Hagen suggests that innovational personalities enable a society to grow rapidly as opposed to authoritarian personalities, which hinder development. There are other variants of this approach.

There are many cultural causes of fertility and mortality, as well as of population growth. Illness and malnutrition affect birth rates, as well as social attitudes concerning sexual behavior. Malthus argued that the world would eventually be overpopulated and lack food supplies. Many scholars oppose this perspective and argue that we cannot infinitely predict the world's population. Populations are increasing in the least developed nations for many reasons. One reason is the high status of parenthood. Another reason relates to the need to reproduce to overcome high infant mortality rates. Rates of malnutrition and related deaths are high in poorer countries. In order to improve this situation, access to health care and adequate food supplies is imperative.

Marx, as well as many present-day theorists, attribute the concentration of population and food problems to the development of capitalism. The argument is that capitalism creates poverty and unemployment in the Third World.

The Agricultural Revolution gave population growth its first boost. Food supplies greatly increased as people began to domesticate plants and animals. Polanyi suggested that surplus population problems arose as a result of the Industrial Revolution; changes in educational and political institutions had important effects on population growth. As more modern family values developed, birth rates lowered.

The opposite effect occurred in the Third World. Here societies encouraged families to have more children to ensure the family's survival. Families need their children to work and take care of elders.

There are many consequences of food and population growth problems. Infant mortality is one. The Green Revolution was a positive response to rapid population growth. This revolution began in the 1960s and is defined as the bringing of high agricultural technology to the Third World. Whether a population grows too fast or too slowly, problems arise. In the least developed countries with fast growth, the proportion of young people is growing, many of them under the age of fifteen. This is a huge burden for some economies since the young consume more than they produce. When growth is slow and populations age, nations with social security systems become strained.

Interventions used to combat food shortages generally focus on introducing advanced agricultural technology. Bread for the World has suggested ways to make the global economy work better for hungry people.

Population control policies have also been at fault. China's one-child policy is not well regarded in rural areas. Most government policies that attempt to promote or discourage population growth have not met with much success.

Discussion Questions

1. Were you surprised by the amount of food wasted in the United States? Do you know anything about food waste on your campus or where you live? Can you think of ways to find out about waste in your area?

2. What changes in lifestyle would you be willing to make to enhance the food security and well-being of people in other parts of the world? What kinds of changes in consumption patterns should Americans begin thinking about?

3. Pick out a Third World country that interests you. Using the Census Bureau IDB Population Pyramids website, at http://www.census.gov/ipc/www/idbpyr.html, get a population pyramid for that society. What implications does the pyramid have for the future development and well-being of the people of that society?

4. Can you think of any cultural influences that may shape your view of whether or not to have children and how many to have?

5. What do you think would be the most effective ways to enhance the supply of food to the Third World?

References

Anderson, Curt. 1997. "Amid Hunger, Ways to Combat Food Waste Explored." *Boston Globe*, September 16.

Blaut, J. M. 1993. *The Colonizer's Model of the World*. New York: Guilford Press.

Beckmann, David. 1997. "Boom Times Don't Stamp out Hunger." *Philadelphia Daily News*, Op-Ed page, December 29.

Bodnick, David, and Daniel Zalik. 1993. "6 Myths and Facts About Hunger."   ❖ ❖ ❖ ❖
In HungerWeb. http://www.brown.edu/Departments/World_Hunger_Program /
hungerweb/intro/6_myths_and_ acts.html.

Braun, Denny. 1997. *The Rich Get Richer: The Rise of Income Inequality in the United
States and the Third World*. Second edition. Chicago: Nelson-Hall.

Bread for the World Institute. 1997. *Hunger in a Global Economy 1998*. Silver Spring
Maryland.

Brown, Lester R. 1981. *World Food Resources and Population: The Narrowing Margin*.
Washington, D.C.: Population Reference Bureau.

Chase-Dunn, Christopher, and Thomas D. Hall. 1997. *Rise and Demise: Comparing
World Systems*. New Perspectives in Sociology. Boulder: Westview Press.

Cohen, Marc J., and Michael Rubinstein. 1997. "Hunger in a Global Economy." *Bread
for the World Newsletter* 9 (8).

Crossette, Barbara. 1997a. "Aid from Rich Nations to Poor Fell in 1996." *New York
Times*, October 17, A10.

——. 1997b. "Study Predicts Food Gap for Poor Countries." *New York Times*, October
27, A7.

De Silva, Donatus, ed. 1989. *Against All Odds: Breaking the Poverty Trap*. Maryland:
Panos Institute/Seven Locks Press.

Farb, Peter, and George Armelagos. 1980. *Consuming Passions: The Anthropology of
Eating*. Boston: Houghton Mifflin.

Food and Agriculture Organization. 1996. *Sixth World Food Survey*. New York: United
Nations Food and Agriculture Organization.

Goode, William J. 1963. *World Revolution and Family Patterns*. New York: Free Press.

Hadjor, Kofi Buenor. 1993. *The Penguin Dictionary of Third World Terms*. London:
Penguin.

Harrison, Paul. 1987. *The Greening of Africa: Breaking Through in the Battle for Land
and Food*. An International Institute for Environment and Development,
Earthscan Study. Harmondsworth, England: Penguin.

——. 1993a. *Inside the Third World*. Third edition. London: Penguin.

——. 1993b. *The Third Revolution: Population, Environment and a Sustainable World*.
London: Penguin.

Haub, Carl. 1981. "Population Pressures Increasing on Less Developed Countries."
Intercom, April 4.

Huang, She-tse. 1974. "Plenary Session Speech." United Nations World Population
Conference. Bucharest, Romania, August.

Institute for Food and Development Policy. 1997. Institute for Food and Development
Policy (Food First) Homepage, http://www.foodfirst.org.

Jaffee, David. 1990. *Levels of Socio-Economic Development Theory*. New York: Praeger.

Kammeyer, Kenneth C. W., and Helen Ginn. 1986. *An Introduction to Population*. Chicago: Dorsey Press.

Lappe, Frances Moore, and Joseph Collins. 1986. *World Hunger: Twelve Myths*. New
York: Grove Weidenfeld.

Leidenfrost, Nancy B. 1993. "Definitions Concerned with Food Security, Hunger,
Undernutrition, and Poverty." In HungerWeb: *Basic Definitions of Hunger-
Related Terms*. http://www.brown.edu/Departments/World_Hunger_Program/
hungerweb/intro/basic_ definitions.html.

Malthus, Thomas. 1982[1798]. *An Essay on the Principle of Population*.
Harmondsworth, England: Penguin.

McKeown, Thomas. 1977. *The Modern Rise of Population*. New York: Academic Press.

Meadows, H. Donella, et al. 1972. *The Limits to Growth*. New York: Universe Books.

Meadows, H. Donella, Dennis L. Meadows, and Jorgen Randers. 1992. *Beyond the
Limits: Confronting Global Collapse, Envisioning a Sustainable Future*. Post Mills,
Vermont: Chelsea Green Publishing.

Meek, Ronald L., ed. 1971. *Marx and Engels on the Population Bomb*. Second edition. Berkeley: Ramparts Press.

Murdoch, William W. 1980. *The Poverty of Nations: The Political Economy of Hunger and Population*. Baltimore: Johns Hopkins University Press.

Pinstrup-Andersen, Per, Rajul Pandya-Lorch, and Mark W. Rosegrant. 1997. *The World Food Situation: Recent Developments, Emerging Issues, and Long-Term Prospects*. 20/20 Vision Food Policy Report. Washington, D.C.: International Food Policy Research Institute. 36 pages.

Polanyi, Karl. 1944. *The Great Transformation*. Boston: Beacon Press.

Seccombe, Wally. 1986. "Marxism and Demography: Household Forms and Fertility Regimes in the Western European Tradition." Pp. 23-55 in *Family, Economy and State: The Social Reproduction Process Under Capitalism*, edited by James Dickinson and Bob Russell. Toronto: Garamond Press.

Seitz, John L. 1995. *Global Issues: An Introduction*. Oxford: Blackwell Publishers.

Sen, Amartya. 1993. "The Economics of Life and Death." *Scientific American*, May, 40–47.

Shannon, Thomas R. 1996. *An Introduction to the World-System Perspective*. Second edition. Boulder: Westview Press.

Thompson, E. P. 1966. *The Making of the English Working Class*. New York: Vintage.

Tien, H. Yuan. 1991. *China's Strategic Demographic Initiative*. New York: Praeger.

U.S. Bureau of the Census. 1996. Statistical Abstract of the United States. Washington, D.C.: U. S. Government Printing Office.

Uvin, Peter, ed. 1994a. *The World Hunger Report 1993*. Annual Reports on Hunger, Alan Shawn Feinstein World Hunger Program, Brown University. Yverda, Switzerland: Gordon and Breach Publishers.

———. 1994b. "The State of World Hunger," pp. 1-48. *The Hunger Report 1993*. Yverda, Switzerland: Gordon and Breach Publishers.

Websites

http://www.bread.org

Bread for the World (BFW). Bread for the World is a Christian movement that "seeks justice for the world's hungry people by lobbying our nation's decision makers." This site provides access to valuable resources on hunger, including fact sheets on domestic and international hunger.

http://www.prb.org/prb/

The Population Reference Bureau (PRB). The PRB, which provides exceptionally useful information on national and international population trends, has been "informing people about population since 1929." Not only does the website provide valuable information itself, it also gives you information about additional resources. PRB's World Population Data Sheet is a well known resource, parts of which are available on the site. From this site you can also access PopNet, "the source for global population information," sponsored and maintained by the PRB.

http://www.Trinity.edu/~mkearl/demograp.html

Sociological Tour Through Cyberspace, Demographic Links. This section of Michael Kearl's Sociological Tour of Cyberspace provides an introduction to demographic issues, useful graphics, and links to many other valuable sites. It is located at the Department of Sociology and Anthropology at Trinity University in San Antonio.

http://www.wri.org/

World Resources Institute. The World Resources Institute provides an incredible range of valuable information. Be sure to try out this website and check out *World Resources 1996–1997*, which is available online here at http://www.wri.org/wr-96-97/.

CHAPTER FIFTEEN

Environmental Problems

In the News: Drug Crops Ravage Colombia's Environment

You probably know that illegal drugs have produced extensive political corruption and violence in Colombia. You may not know that the drug crops have also devastated Colombia's rich, diverse environment. A recent Los Angeles Times *article explains that coffee farming in central Colombia, banana growing on the northern coast, and fishing along the Inirida River near Brazil have all suffered extensive environmental damage. The damage is so great that for government official Hector Moreno, "the war against illegal drugs would be completely justified on environmental grounds alone" (Darling 1997:A1).*

The article draws a stark picture of the impact of the drug crops on coffee production:

> *In the mountains of central Colombia, where the coffee bushes meet the clouds, this country's most famous legal export is dying of thirst. Coffee farmers complain that, for four years, the soil here has gotten progressively drier and that it rains less and less often, leaving their bushes parched and unproductive. The mystery of the climate change clears up along with the morning mist: The uncovered peaks are a blaze of red and purple flowers bordered by the brown dirt of fields that opium poppy farmers have already harvested. (1997:A1)*

By cutting down the lichen-covered trees of the cloud forest, the poppy growers destroy the cloud forest, which played a central role in condensing water from the fog. That water was essential for the coffee crops downhill from the cloud forest. When the poppy growers clear the land to plant poppies, they leave no vegetation to hold the soil when it rains, leading to erosion, which can produce landslides. Without the vegetation and the trees, the coffee farming areas are condemned to devastation.

Luis Eduardo Parra, who heads the government's Environmental Audit of Illegal Crop Eradication, explains that "when you cut down the trees, you change the climate. Coffee growers are going to end up without their water resources, neither streams nor rain" (Darling 1997:A6). Banana growers face the same problems as a result of poppy production. Destruction of the cloud forest is not the only type of environmental destruction caused by the illegal drug crops. Poppy production threatens the mountain environment, but coca, the leaf from which cocaine is made, grows at sea level. Illegal drug crops threaten both environments (Darling 1997).

The effects of illegal drug cultivation are devastating for the people and environment of Colombia. With their livelihoods gone—through loss of coffee or banana cultivation—many Colombians are forced into the cultivation of the illegal crops. The environmental destruction also imperils the inheritance of future generations in the country. As devastating as these developments are for its citizens, the destruction of Colombia's environment has potentially worldwide consequences, for Colombia is a "genetic bank for the world" (Darling 1997). Luis Eduardo Parra notes that "Colombia is considered one of the seven countries with mega-diversity" of plant and animal species. In terms of the number of species relative to the size of the country, Colombia is fourth after Brazil, Madagascar, and Suriname. So poppy and coca production may be destroying species that could be needed for medicines or to end plagues.

Clearly, poppy and coca production have serious consequences environmentally and medically, in addition to those with which people are more famil-

iar. Responding to the seriousness of the problem, Pino Arlacchi, the new head of the United Nations drug agency, intends to follow a program to eliminate poppy and coca cultivation worldwide within 10 years, according to a New York Times *article (Bonner 1997). Although aware of the magnitude of the problem and the difficulty of reaching his goal, Arlacchi is convinced that he can succeed. He suggests that the key is "alternative development—providing peasants with other sources of income, convincing them that it is better to grow legal crops, like onions, so that their income will be steady" (Bonner 1997). The environmental health of Colombia and many other countries may depend on his success.*

Definition and Prevalence

Do you think much about the environment? When you do, what do you think about? You are probably aware of some of the important environmental issues that have been widely discussed in the media. In other classes you may have been introduced to environmental issues such as **global warming**. Many natural scientists argue that—partly as a result of human actions—the earth's temperature is gradually rising to levels that may have serious consequences for people around the world. Other scientists downplay the likelihood of global warming and its consequences. You may have heard about the 1992 Earth Summit in Rio de Janeiro and the 1997 conference on global warming held in Kyoto, Japan. How much significance do these events or processes have for Americans? Perhaps more than we think.

In most public opinion polls, only about 10 percent of Americans choose environmental problems as the most serious ones facing our society (Dunlap, Gallup, and Gallup 1993). But environmental changes and issues may have more of an impact on us than we realize. For example, in the "In the News" section, you just read about the impact that drug crops have on Colombia's environment, including the destruction of species that could be used for making crucial medicines. In fact, a group of doctors and scientists recently told Congress that "human health is directly dependent on a thriving environment, and society must move quickly to preserve it" (Reuters 1997). One scientist noted that of the 157 drugs most often prescribed in the United States in 1993, 57 percent came directly from natural sources. Although not all Americans may be aware of

Toxic wastes create significant health hazards around the world. The effects of such wastes can be physical, social, and psychological. —*Photo: photostogo.com.*

the importance of a healthy environment for human well-being, citizens of many other countries do put more emphasis on environmental issues.

In 1992, environmental sociologist Riley Dunlap and the Gallup International Institute surveyed citizens of 24 countries on their attitudes toward the environment and their assessment of the seriousness of environmental issues. The results showed high levels of awareness and concern. For more on that survey, see "A Closer Look: Who Cares About the Health of the Planet?"

A Closer Look

Who Cares About the Health of the Planet?

Environmental sociologist Riley Dunlap and his colleagues designed and coordinated the *Health of the Planet*, the 1992 George H. Gallup Memorial Survey. This project of the Gallup International Institute, timed to coincide with the 1992 Rio summit, was administered in 24 countries "to give voice to individual citizens around the world concerning the environment and economic development issues affecting their lives" (Dunlap, Gallup, and Gallup 1993:I). The researchers note that in surveys in the United States only about 10 percent of those surveyed indicate that they see environmental problems as the most serious problem in the society. They expected similar results in this international survey. Their expectations were wrong.

The percentages listing environmental problems as their nation's most serious problem range from lows of 1 percent in Poland, Nigeria, and Hungary to a high of 39 percent in the Netherlands. Environmental problems were chosen as most important by citizens in several poorer countries, especially Mexico (29 percent), India (21 percent), and Chile (20 percent). In 16 of the 24 nations surveyed, environmental problems were seen as among the three most serious problems. The survey also found that "when asked directly whether environmental protection or economic growth should be given priority, majorities in all but three nations choose environmental protection" (Dunlap, Gallup, and Gallup 1993:3).

The *Health of the Planet* is a fascinating document in part because the results differed from the researchers' expectations. The authors point out that this survey's results contradicted much of the conventional wisdom about environmental issues. For example, one piece of conventional wisdom suggests that people are "so overwhelmed by daily economic problems that they have little time to worry about the environment." The authors point out that many people are "trapped by environmental problems that directly affect their health—air and water pollution, waste disposal, and the like." Many environmental experts also believed that even if people cared about environmental problems, they would still be unwilling to pay higher prices or taxes to improve the environment. This also proved not to be the case (Dunlap, Gallup, and Gallup 1993:ii).

Several other pieces of conventional wisdom bear on environmental problems in developing countries. For example, it seems to be widely believed that people of developed countries and people of Third World countries blame each other for environmental problems and do not accept any responsibility for those problems. The survey actually found that "to a remarkable degree, citizens of both developing and developed nations accept a share of the responsibility for such problems" (Dunlap, Gallup, and Gallup 1993: iii). Finally, many believe that citizens of developed countries will not support programs to help Third World nations. The survey results did not support this view. The survey results hold out hope that citizens of different countries do see environmental problems as serious and may be willing to support mutually beneficial policies and programs.

Environmental problems are not new to human existence. Several civilizations have destroyed themselves by destroying the environment. The fall of Mesopotamia is one classic example. About 3,000 years ago, this civilization flourished because the people had developed a very sophisticated irrigation system that provided an abundant food supply. The problem was, however, that the people had not developed a drainage system for the water. As a result, water constantly evaporated, and gradually grew saltier. Over the centuries, the land became so salty that crops would not grow (Jacobsen and Adams 1958). Although historians have discovered a number of like problems, the most pressing and dangerous forms of environmental degradation did not begin until industrialization, when people focused on growth at any cost.

Today, America's formerly clean rivers and streams are said to be polluted sewers, and many of our water supplies are unfit to drink. This is evidenced by the growing numbers of people buying bottled water. Air pollution is becoming more and more of a concern to environmental groups, who argue that air quality is becoming dangerous to our lungs. Even if these environmentalists seem too pessimistic, it seems clear that humankind does face serious and escalating environmental challenges.

Some challenges arise from the perfectly understandable desires of people all over the world to achieve a better way of life for themselves and for their children. The media send images of the lifestyles of people in the developed countries all over the world. People in Third World societies see those images and want the lifestyles that they see. However, Helen Caldicott argues that

> because the U.S. population represents only 5 percent of the earth's people but uses 25 percent of the energy, this life-style is not an appropriate model for billions of other people. Such extravagant living is the leading cause of ozone depletion, global warming, toxic pollution of the air, water, and soil, and nuclear proliferation. Each U.S. resident causes twenty to a hundred times more pollution than any Third World resident, and rich American babies are destined to cause a thousand times more pollution than their counterparts in Bangladesh or Pakistan. (Caldicott 1992:13)

People all over the world now demand a more affluent lifestyle, "but 5.4 billion people cannot emulate the life-style of 250 million Americans and expect the planet to survive" (Caldicott 1992:13).

Consider the following developments. Oceans, rivers, lakes, underground water supplies, and even the rain are becoming hazardous to living things, because they contain acid, heavy metallic poisons, and carcinogens. Renewable resources like forests and topsoil are being used faster than they can be replenished, creating an impending crisis in world agriculture's ability to feed people. Nonrenewable resources such as petroleum are being exhausted more rapidly than we can develop alternatives. The possibility looms of a worldwide crisis of water availability.

Let's take a closer look at the range of environmental problems. John L. Seitz examines environmental problems related to the air, water, and land; workplace and home; the use of natural resources; the extinction of species; and the extinction of cultures. Global warming and energy issues are two additional important areas of concern (Seitz 1995). (For an overview of major environmental problems, see "A Closer Look: Major Environmental Problems.")

Environmental issues related to the air include smog, airborne lead, acid rain, ozone depletion, and increased quantities of carbon dioxide in the atmosphere. Although these problems remain serious, some improvements have been made in each of these areas. For example, the 1970 Clean Air Act in the United States has had impressive results. Since the act was passed, "lead was reduced by 95 percent, sulfur dioxide by about 30 percent, and

Major Environmental Problems

This list of major environmental problems appeared in the first edition of this book in 1983. It is sobering to think that although there have been some improvements, the list still remains a useful guide to environmental threats. We have indicated improvements where appropriate.

1. *The Atmosphere*
   Air pollution has decreased but is still a problem in many areas. Atmospheric concentrations of carbon dioxide continue to grow.

2. *Scarcity of Fresh Water*
   Lakes, rivers, and oceans continue to be polluted. This pollution is hazardous to the health of human beings and aquatic species. According to the United Nations, a third of the world's people do not have an adequate supply of clean water, and two-thirds will be deprived of it by 2010 unless action is taken.

3. *Land Degradation*
   Topsoil and productive farmland have been lost.

4. *Solid Waste Disposal*
   Ocean pollution threatens the health of two-thirds of humanity living near coastlines. Toxic chemicals pose significant threats.

5. *Food*
   Food production continues to rise, but these gains are threatened by a growing scarcity of fresh water and a loss of topsoil. Underdeveloped countries are particularly vulnerable.

6. *Fertility Rates*
   Fertility rates are declining more rapidly than expected. The populations of many countries will stabilize within the next generation. But other countries still face high growth rates that will strain their resources.

7. *Species Extinction*
   A large proportion of existing animal and plant species are in danger as a consequence of environmental trends.

particulates (tiny particles in the air) by about 60 percent" (Seitz 1995: 141). The amount of lead in the blood of Americans has dropped by about 80 percent from 1976 to 1991. The ozone layer of the atmosphere is important because it protects the Earth from ultraviolet rays from the sun. Evidence has accumulated that the ozone layer is being depleted, largely through the use of substances produced and used by people. The release of increased amounts of carbon dioxide into the air contributes to global warming, also called the **greenhouse effect** (Seitz 1995). Although improvements have been made in each of these areas, especially in the developed countries, they still remain serious problems for industrial societies and could have devastating impacts on the Third World. See Table 15-1 for sources of air pollution and Figure 15-1 on changing air pollution levels in the United States.

Water is the most essential resource for human health. Access to clean water is crucial for human life and for social development. The United States passed the Clean Water Act in 1972, to "restore and maintain the chemical, physical, and biological integrity of the waterways: by 1985, the discharge of pollutants into the waterways was to cease, and all of the nation's streams, rivers, and lakes were to be fishable and swimmable" (Outwater 1996: xi). The act did help bring about noteworthy improvements: fish kills declined

Table 15-1 Air Pollutant Emissions, by Pollutant and Source: 1996.
(in thousands of tons, except lead in tons)

Source	Particu-lates	Sulfur Dioxide	Volatile Nitrogen Oxides	Organic Compounds	Carbon Monoxide	Lead
Fuel combustion, stationary sources	1,186	16,785	10,493	1,075	5,962	493
Electric utilities	282	12,604	6,034	45	377	62
Industrial	306	3,399	3,170	208	1,072	17
Other fuel combustion	598	782	1,289	822	4,513	414
Residential	472	173	838	758	3,993	NA
Industrial processes	828	1,594	770	1,462	4,584	2,174
Solvent utilization	6	1	3	6,273	6	NA
Storage and transport	109	2	6	1,312	25	NA
Waste disposal and recycling	290	48	100	433	1,203	57
Highway vehicles	274	307	7,171	5,502	52,944	19
Off highway	91	368	4,610	2,426	17,002	545
Miscellaneous	28,018	9	239	601	7,009	NA
Total	31,301	19,113	23,393	19,806	88,822	3,869

Source: U.S. Bureau of the Census. 1998. *Statistical Abstract of the United States: 1998*. Washington, D.C.: Government Printing Office. Table 400, p. 242. <http://www.census.gov/statab/www/>.

Figure 15-1 U.S. Emissions of Selected Pollutants: 1970–1994

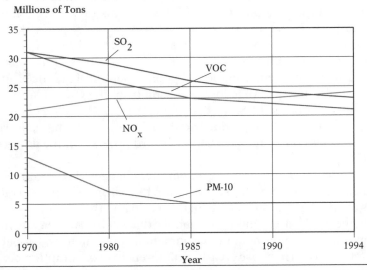

Note: NOx=nitrogen oxides. PM-10=particulate matter with a diameter of 10 microns or less. SO2=sulfur dioxide. VOC=volatile organic compounds.
Source: Council on Environmental Quality. 1996. *Environmental Quality: 25th Anniversary Report*. Wasington D.C.: Council on Environmental Quality. Figure 1.4, p.11. <http://ceq.eh.doe.gov/reports/1994-95.rep_toc.htm>

and the amount of pollutants in rivers and lakes decreased. However, major problems remain. From 1985 to 1995, over a million acres of American wetlands vanished. The loss is one-third less than that of 1975–1985, but it is still serious, especially because the U.S. government imposed new protections for wetlands between 1985 and 1995. Wetlands are important not only as habitats for many species, but also because they filter contaminants from water (Cushman 1997). In *The State of the World 1998*, Lester Brown and his colleagues estimate that about 20 percent of the world's population still does not have access to clean drinking water (1998).

Environmental problems related to the land include the disposal of solid and toxic wastes. Toxic wastes, in particular, have had devastating consequences. The Love Canal disaster is probably one of these disasters. The Love Canal dump site is near Niagara Falls, New York. In the 1970s, the dump site "contained 20,000 tons of more than 200 chemicals" (Gibbs 1998b:A25). Lois Gibbs, now executive director of the Center for Health, Environment and Justice, was a young mother living in Niagara Falls in the late 1970s. Her children had been consistently sick and she wanted to find out if other children were ill. She went door-to-door and "was shocked to hear stories of birth defects, miscarriages, cancers, and the leaking of multicolored chemical ooze into basements." Acknowledging the health hazards of the dump site, on August 2, 1978 the State of New York declared the Love Canal dump site an emergency and President Carter declared the canal a disaster area. Gibbs and other residents of the community carried out a public health survey of the area, organized to close the school that had been built on the site, and managed to secure federal funding for families to relocate out of the area. These organizing efforts were also instrumental in the passage of Superfund legislation to clean up toxic waste sites (Gibbs 1998a, 1998b). Unfortunately, there are still thousands of such toxic waste sites in the United States.

Additional problems related to the land include deforestation and desertification, historically two of the major impacts made by humans on the environment. The destruction of tropical forests seems to be accelerating on a worldwide basis (Seitz 1995). In the last fifty years, about a third of the world's original forest cover has been lost (Brown et al. 1998). A dramatic example of this sort of change in the United States was the dust bowl of the 1930s, during which a combination of poor agricultural practices and natural drought resulted in a huge loss of topsoil from the Great Plains states. A more recent example is the Sahel drought in Africa, which has continued for several years in the countries south of the Sahara Desert. There, overgrazing has for centuries contributed to the southward progress of the desert (Harrison 1993).

The world faces other environmental challenges. For example, China plans to introduce a "people's car" for sale to its citizens. Keeping in mind that China is the most populous society in the world and that one out of every five people in the world are Chinese, you can see that such an increase in numbers of automobiles will have major environmental consequences. Global energy consumption would increase greatly. China's energy consumption per person is now one-sixth that of Japan and one-fourth that of Taiwan. However, if China reaches the "car-to-person ratios of Germany and the United States, then the number of cars in the world would double," leading to huge increases in demand for oil. Competition over oil might lead to conflict and intense rivalries. The people's car would also significantly contribute to air pollution, and that would have effects well beyond China (Zitner 1996). See Table 15-2 on trends in energy production and consumption in the United States.

Table 15-2 U.S. Energy Production and Consumption: 1970–1994

Year	Total Production (quadrillion BTUs)	Total Consumption (quadrillion BTUs)	Consumption/ Production Ratio
1970	62.1	66.4	1.07
1975	59.9	70.6	1.18
1980	64.8	76.0	1.17
1985	64.9	74.0	1.14
1990	70.7	84.1	1.19
1994	70.4	88.5	1.26

Source: U.S. Bureau of the Census. 1996. *Statistical Abstract of the United States: 1996.* Washington, DC: Government Printing Office. Table 913, p. 578.

In fact, in this era of **globalization**, various parts of the world are increasingly connected to one another in ways that amplify the threats posed by environmental problems. Pollution and environmental degradation spread beyond the societies in which they were created.

> Slash-and-burn deforestation in the Amazon affects the ozone layer covering the entire globe; industrial pollutants in the United States cause acid rain to fall on Canada; illegal dumping of industrial waste in Russia deforms the ocean's ecosystem and thus affects South American fisheries. There are no countries that have not contributed to the problems facing the environment. Since the problem is global, so must be the solutions. There is, however, no real supranational entity to date that can tackle this problem. (Rubin 1996:144)

In the absence of a supranational organization that can solve global environmental problems, the United Nations, national governments, and other organizations have tried to reverse the slide toward environmental crisis. For example, at the 1992 Earth Summit in Rio, "the largest gathering of its kind in history, world leaders . . . signed binding agreements designed to prevent dangerous human interference with the earth's climate system and to protect living species" (Stevens 1997). In June 1997, 70 heads of state or government met at the United Nations to assess progress since the Rio summit and to discuss what to do next. Even before the meeting, however, it was clear that environmental trends had changed little (Stevens 1997).

In spite of bright spots in environmental trends since the Rio meeting, the overall trends are not good. Degradation of land, forests, and marine and coastal zones continues, as does loss of plant and animal species. Air and water quality have improved in developed societies but have declined in many parts of the Third World. Urban and industrial contamination and waste have increased in Latin America and the Caribbean, in West Asia, and in the Asia Pacific region. One positive development is that population growth has been increasing at a slower rate (Stevens 1997; Brown, Renner, and Flavin 1997b).

Six years after the Rio Earth Summit, much evidence has suggested that an environmental crisis still exists, a crisis worse for those in the poorer countries of the world. However, some experts disagree with this pessimistic assessment (Bailey 1995; Easterbrook 1995; Ray and Guzzo 1994). In fact, the title of one of Ronald Bailey's books accurately conveys the views of many in the optimistic camp: *Eco-Scam: The False Prophets of Ecological Apocalypse* (Bailey 1993). However, in their *Betrayal of Science and Reason,* (1996) Paul and Anne Ehrlich argue that the optimists use bad science to misrepresent environmental problems. Other respected scientists also support that view (Commoner 1992). Lester Brown and the Worldwatch Institute give us the State of the World every year, while Bailey counters with the *True State of the Planet* (Bailey 1995; Brown et al. 1996; Brown et al. 1997a; Brown et al. 1998). Even people who agree on some basic issues may have major disagreements on other issues. For example, Barry Commoner disagrees with what he sees as the Ehrichs' stress on population growth as the central environmental problem (Ellis 1996).

Levels of Causation

Environmental problems are generally caused by human interaction with the physical world, such as what happened in Mesopotamia. Although human beings are also affected by environmental changes or disruptions, such as volcanoes, earthquakes, and mudslides, which change people's lives forever, this chapter focuses more on the impact of human action on the environment. When looking for the sources of environmental problems, experts may work from individual, cultural, or structural levels of analysis.

Individual

Individual actions can cause environmental problems. For example, the fact that most people litter at least once in their lives causes damage to the environment. If everyone stopped littering, there would no doubt be a cleaner, less polluted environment. Carefully thinking about the choices we make and their environmental impact is a useful step toward global awareness and a healthier planet. David Gershon and Robert Gilman have written the *Household Ecoteam Workbook* (1992) to help people begin to make more environmentally sound choices. They make concrete suggestions for actions people can take in their own households and communities. It is important to note that such individual actions cannot solve the global environmental problems we face; however, they can make a difference at the local level, and they can help people become aware of the need for greater involvement of larger communities of people. They might even contribute to changing the cultural attitudes toward nature and the environment that are dominant in American society.

One interesting individual choice in several countries is whether to use an electric car. There are approximately 7,522 electric cars in use today across the world. Germany has the highest number in use (2,452) followed by the United States (2,306). In the United States, federal, state, and local governments offer a number of tax exemptions for using electric cars. The California Air Resources Board requires that 10 percent of vehicles sold by the seven biggest automobile manufacturers in the state in 2003 be electric (Dunn 1997).

The psychology of environmental problems is a growing field of study (Levy-Leboyer 1982; Sundstrom, et al. 1996). Psychology is generally defined as the study of behavior and mental life (Winter 1996). This discipline has

rarely been seen as an environmental science although it has significant relations to the ways in which we perceive our environment. As a science, psychology can examine our contributions to and destruction of the environment. Deborah Winter (1996) suggests that our perceptions of and responses
to information about the environment depend on psychological needs. We
construct the condition of the environment based on where we live and what
information we are given about its condition. The media in particular affect
our beliefs and influence what conclusions we make about the state of the environment. We may hear about the conditions of the rain forests but may not
react with distress because these forests seem so far away from us. A cognitive psychological approach to environmental problems is that the problems
are a result of inadequate, mistaken, distorted, or missing information about
the consequences of our actions. One example offered by Winter is the fact
that we are seduced into thinking that what is pretty is good. However, a
beautifully landscaped golf course is environmentally harmful because of the
overuse of water and chemicals that are needed to maintain it. In addition,
most of us have very little information about where our food is grown and
how much waste is incurred to bring it to our grocery stores.

Environmental psychology focuses on issues such as why people do not
demand information about their food, where their waste goes, or the rate of
recycling in their community. The main argument within this discipline is
that our values and perceptions of the environment are largely unchallenged
because they are so taken for granted.

Cultural

Even though some cultures, like those of some Native American groups,
created relatively stable balances between people and the natural world, others slowly turned the earth's forests into grasslands, its grasslands into
deserts, and its rivers into sewers. The major difference between modern societies and earlier ones that also devastated the environment is that modern
societies have the means to inflict damage more rapidly and on a worldwide
scale.

Certain societies were able to live in harmony with the physical world. If
we wish to emulate them, we must create a new balance between our culture
and the environment rather than adopting theirs. There are too many people
in the world today for all to survive using the simple technologies of the past.
Some suggest we need what E. F. Schumacher calls, in his classic *Small Is
Beautiful: Economics as if People Mattered* (1973), appropriate technology.
Appropriate technology would meet human needs without disastrous environmental consequences. Schumacher argues that developing countries
need technology that is "intermediate" between the ineffective technology
characteristic of rural areas in the Third World and the technology of the developed world, "which tends to use vast amounts of energy, pollutes the environment, requires imported resources, and often alienates the workers from
their own work" (Seitz 1995:190). Acceptance of such intermediate, or appropriate, technology, would require changes in cultural patterns, among other
things.

In any human culture, there is some discrepancy between ideal ways of
life and real patterns of living. Both have an impact on the environment. People's shared beliefs about what exists in the physical world and what sort of

relationships occur between human beings and the rest of the world are the most important parts of ideal culture insofar as the environment is concerned.

The features of material culture that have the most environmental impact are the technologies people use to convert natural resources into objects for human use. There is no question that many technological advances have destroyed and are destroying the environment. It is difficult to determine whether the state of the environment influences people's technological choices or vice versa. What is contained in an environment is so complicated that no one can see everything. What an individual sees is influenced by what has been consistently pointed out by parents, peers, teachers, etc. At one extreme, people are unable to see the damage being done to the environment as a result of industrialization. At the other extreme are people who believe we must eliminate industrialization and go back to a preindustrial way of living.

One environmental problem that often goes unnoticed is waste. It is taken for granted in two main ways: the idea that we can throw things away and the related idea that things we throw away actually disappear. For example, many believe that what is disposed of in the ocean is actually gone from the environment. The first warning of the dangers of ocean waste came to the United States in the 1970s. The Hooker Chemical Company in Niagara Falls, New York, had been dumping over 20,000 tons of chemical wastes in the 1940s and 1950s into what is known as Love Canal. The results of this dumping surfaced during the 1970s when many people had discovered that a mixture of dangerous chemicals was seeping into their swimming pools and basements (Seitz 1995).

We Americans are raised to believe that we inhabit the earth and should continue to do so through reproduction and production. Because we do not see the earth as an extension of our existence, we believe in conquering the earth, so to speak. The culture of the United States is described as a "melting pot." What this means is that it is a country where immigrants supposedly blend or melt into one dominant culture. A serious consequence is that we are losing unique characteristics of diverse cultures. The teachings of some of these cultures are lost as a result, such as the ability to live in harmony with nature. Tribal people have finally been given credit for their knowledge of natural drugs in rain forests. Connected to this is the recognition that if we want the rain forest to survive, we must help tribal people to survive. In other words, we should be more open-minded with regard to diversity instead of forcing people to give up their culture (Seitz 1995).

Structural

Environmental problems, like so many other social problems examined in this book, can be analyzed using political economy perspectives, stressing social conflict, or by social constructionist perspectives, emphasizing competing claims and social definitions. In addition, two other linked perspectives have been useful: human ecology and the new ecological paradigm.

Some environmental sociologists suggest that in order to understand the environmental crisis, it helps to view the human race as a single biological species living in a single planetary environment. Within that environment there is an enormously complex set of relationships that make life possible. This network of relationships was called the "web of life" by Robert Ezra Park

(1936), one of the first social scientists to study human ecology. **Human ecology** investigates the ways in which human societies achieve and maintain a balance among their populations, their cultures, and the natural world. Because the web of life is governed by scientific laws of nature as well as by socially defined behaviors, human ecology combines social science with biology, chemistry, physics, and geology in order to understand the human-environment interaction.

Although Park borrowed principles from biological ecology, John Hannigan suggests that he tended to emphasize "humans' *exceptional* characteristics (inventiveness, technical capability) rather than their commonality with other species." Focusing on social and cultural factors such as communication and the division of labor rather than biophysical and environmental determinants, Park's approach to human ecology downplayed "the constraints imposed by nature by celebrating the human capacity to master it" (Hannigan 1995: 15).

Sociologists William Catton and Riley Dunlap developed the **new ecological paradigm** (NEP); (Dunlap and Catton 1983; Dunlap 1993). This model identifies three functions that the environment serves for humans: supply depot, living space, and waste repository (Hannigan 1995). As supply depot, the environment provides both renewable and nonrenewable resources, including air, water, and fossil fuels. As living space, it provides shelter and transportation systems. As a waste repository, the environment is a receptacle for garbage, sewage, and industrial pollution. Overusing or exceeding the capacity of the environment in any of these three areas leads to serious problems, such as shortages or scarcity (supply depot), overcrowding or congestion (living space), or health problems from toxic wastes (waste repository). These environmental functions vie with each other, and the competition has become more acute in recent years. Using this model, you can see global warming as the outcome of competition among all three functions (Hannigan 1995). The NEP's focus on the supply and waste disposal functions represents an advance over the human ecology approach. Unlike the human ecology approach, the NEP also takes time into account by looking at environmental trends (Hannigan 1995).

The primary weakness of the model, which it shares with the human ecology approach, is its lack of attention to human actions and decisions. Environmental changes seem to occur without human intervention. "Above all, there is no provision for changing either values or power relationships" (Hannigan 1995:17). Any adequate structural explanation for environmental problems and possible solutions for those problems should take human decisions into account and should examine power and its effects on the environment.

The political economy perspective takes both human decisions and power into account. First in his book *The Environment: From Surplus to Scarcity* and more recently in his co-authored *Environment and Society: The Enduring Conflict*, sociologist Allan Schnaiberg has developed an influential political economy model (Schnaiberg 1980; Schnaiberg and Gould 1994). This model integrates the study of how natural resources are used with the study of social stratification processes. Schnaiberg conceptualizes resource depletion as **ecological withdrawals** and pollution as **ecological additions**. More recently, he has developed the concept of the **treadmill of production**, which refers to a system of social relationships in which production and the extraction of natural resources take place. The treadmill of production in a capitalist world economy pushes the continuing expansion of the world economy and thus requires more incursions into the natural environment—increased use of natural resources—to continually expand production and profits (Schnaiberg 1980; Schnaiberg and Gould 1994).

This expansion and the increasing linkages between different parts of the world economy are often accompanied by a rise in authoritarian governments and increasing inequality between rich and poor. Increasing inequality occurs on both societal and global levels, so there is increasing inequality both within societies and among societies. Even with limited environmental-protection policies and the institution of effective pollution controls, Schnaiberg believes that present inequalities will persist or increase, with a somewhat reduced expansion of present forms of economic production.

This model amplifies and extends the insights of earlier structural approaches to environmental problems. For example, in the early 1970s many environmentalists believed that corporate polluters did not really see the costs of their polluting actions because the polluters were not directly affected by their environmentally destructive decisions. To make clear that there were destructive consequences, a series of legal actions against corporations were initiated. One significant achievement of such litigation was the establishment of the principle that nature—flora, and fauna—had rights and was entitled to the same protection as corporations and oppressed human beings (Dowie 1995).

Environmental regulation in the United States and other industrial societies has reduced pollution and environmental degradation within those societies, but pollution continues on a worldwide scale. Production and investment decisions made by corporations of the industrial world produce external costs that must be borne by Third World societies, usually by the poorest in those societies.

Many of the products Americans use are cited as causes of environmental problems. For example, many of the agricultural products imported into the United States have been sprayed with banned pesticides. In the 1980s, the U.S. Food and Drug Administration estimated that at least 10 percent of the food coming into the country had high levels of pesticides on it (Weir and Schapiro 1981). High residues of pesticides have been found on imported meats, coffee, and beans. Today many people have shifted back to more natural fibers, such as cotton, wool, and linen. Increasing attention has been paid to types of packaging; however, much environmental damage has been done and much of it continues.

Political economy models have been criticized as unidimensional. Hannigan suggests that this model may be more helpful for understanding the "classic cases of resource exploitation by primary producers or toxic dumping by petrochemical firms and other corporate polluters than they are in explaining the more recent transnational problems such as global warming or biodiversity loss" (1995:22). This approach has also been criticized for seeing the role of government as too limited and inflexible. Although there may be some justice to these criticisms, we suggest that understanding environmental problems both within societies and within the global economy requires an understanding of class and political conflict and the operation of a capitalist world economy.

At the same time, the social constructionist model has much to offer, especially in helping us to understand why some environmental problems attract a lot of attention while others seem to be ignored. Social constructionist analysts have demonstrated the reasons for such differential attention and recognition (Hannigan 1995). For example, the hazards of chemical wastes have only slowly come to public attention. Unlike the smoke or odor from a factory, chemicals may lie for years in city dumps or water supplies before scientists recognize them as hazards to human health.

Sociologists and historians who use the social constructionist perspective on environment problems point out that the very concept of "nature" is contested and that nature can have a variety of different, and sometimes incompatible, meanings (Cronon 1996). The definitions of environmental problems are similarly contested and often socially defined. Therefore, the social constructionist perspective focuses on how environmental problems attract public attention and come to be seen as problems. Hannigan suggests that the recognition of social problems and the determination to solve them often has less to do with the real severity of the problems, and more to do with how organized groups present claims about those problems.

Consequences

Industrialization has brought dirtier air to all parts of the world. Although the United States has made progress in reducing air pollution, there is still much to be done. In the early 1990s, nearly 90 million people lived in areas, mainly urban, where the air on occasion, was considered so poor that children were told to stay indoors (Seitz 1995). Children are especially susceptible to respiratory problems caused by smog. The burning of fossil fuels, i.e., coal, oil, and natural gas, is also causing a change in the global climate. A result of this burning is an increase in the levels of carbon dioxide in the air. If it continues, the increase will cause a warming of the earth's surface, called "global warming" or the "greenhouse effect." American scientists warn that with increased warming, there will be major changes in the amount of rainfall and its location. Some areas of the earth will receive more rainfall than others and the changed rainfall pattern will undoubtedly affect climates for growing food. The levels of the oceans may rise as well. This could lead to the evacuation of some coastal cities (Seitz 1995). Warnings about global warming have been criticized as being premature and uninformed. A major criticism is that scientists do not know enough about effects of warming or whether the earth is actually warming at an alarming rate.

Although there have been improvements in care for the environment in recent years, especially in the industrial world, some environmental problems still pose serious risks for humanity. Among the most serious environmental threats are those posed by the effects of water scarcity, man-made chemicals, and toxic waste. On a more global level, Michael Renner (1996) argues that environmental decline and resource loss may lead to social conflicts, generating widespread threats to peace, stability, and security.

It is not only in developing countries that the poor suffer more from the consequences of environmental problems. In the United States, the poor and members of racial and ethnic minority groups bear a disproportionate amount of the burdens of environmental problems. Figure 15-2 shows which groups in the United States are more likely to be exposed to poor air quality.

Water scarcity poses a devastating threat to people all over the world. Sandra Postel examines the policies of waste and mismanagement that have

Figure 15-2 U.S. Populations Exposed to Poor Air Quality, by Race and Ethnicity:1993

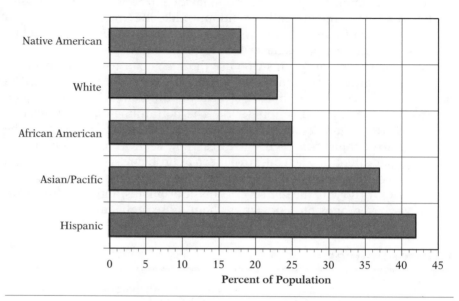

Note: Data refer to percentage of population living in counties with air quality above the primary national air quality standard. Persons of Hispanic origin may be of any race. Source: Council on Environmental Quality. 1996. *Environmental Quality: The 25th Anniversary Report*. Washington D.C.: Council on Environmental Quality. Figure 6.1, p. 111. <http://ceq.eh.doe.gov/reports/1994-95/rep_toc.htm>.

led to increasing shortages of water and that may produce water shortages by early in the twenty-first century: "Sustainedly providing the water needed for an expected population of 8 billion to have adequate and safe drinking water, food for a nutritious diet, and sufficient material goods poses enormous challenges" (Postel 1997:x). Postel argues that we need to develop a water ethic that emphasizes sharing. Such an ethic would demand that all of the world's population should have enough water before a minority of the population has more than enough. For a vivid picture of how the lack of water can affect a people, see "A Closer Look: A River Runs Dry; A People Die."

In 1962, Rachel Carson's *Silent Spring* 1994 [1962] called attention to the threats posed by the pesticide DDT. Many consider this to be one of the most important books of the twentieth century; the book certainly played a major role in spreading environmental awareness. In spite of numerous attacks on the book, Carson's views prevailed and DDT was banned in the United States. Yet this victory was limited. Vice President Al Gore, in an introduction to the re-issue of *Silent Spring*, notes the looseness of the laws regulating pesticides and related chemicals. These man-made chemicals continue to pose serious threats to human life and health. A recent study suggests that synthetic chemicals can disrupt hormonal processes of human beings, possibly leading to birth defects and increasing the incidence of various diseases (Colborn, Dumanoski, and Myers 1997).

Toxic waste disposal poses major public health threats. Love Canal, as mentioned earlier, is one of the best known examples. Phil Brown and Edwin J. Mikkelsen studied a toxic waste crisis in Woburn, Massachusetts and the

❖ ❖ ❖ ❖

A Closer Look

A River Runs Dry; A People Dies

The juxtaposition of the two *Boston Globe* pictures is startling. Inocensia Sainz, a Cocopa Indian, stands on a parched, cracked section of the Colorado River delta. There is no water in the riverbed. On the same page is an aerial view of the Desert Springs Marriott Resort and Spa in Palm Desert, California. The photo caption notes that fifty million gallons of water were required for the lake and waterfalls in the lobby of the hotel. A casual reader might observe the starkly different circumstances of the two situations, might ponder the sad contrast, and might not realize that the two pictures and the two situations are inextricably linked.

Onesimo Sainz, the Cocopa leader, points out that his people lived in this part of Mexico and depended on the river 1,000 years before Christ. "For 2,000 years, this delta was the lifeblood of as many as 5,000 Cocopa Indians living in Baja California" (Grossfeld 1997:A1). Now the river runs dry in Mexico. This is a disaster for these Native Americans, but it is not a *natural* disaster.

Human decisions to dam the Colorado River created the tragedy of the Cocopa Indians. The Colorado River has 49 dams, including the Hoover Dam. Stan Grossfeld notes that the water is "diverted to leaky irrigation channels, pipelines, swimming pools in Los Angeles, golf courses in Palm Springs; to cities like Denver, Salt Lake City, Albuquerque, San Diego, Tucson, Phoenix, and Las Vegas." But "the Cocopa people are dying," says Mexican author Alberto Tapia Landeros. Grossfeld leaves no doubt about the future of the Cocopa: "When the mighty river was dammed in 1935, the Cocopa Indians of Mexico were damned" (Grossfeld 1997:A18).

The plight of the Cocopa illustrates a worldwide problem related to the most basic human need: access to water. In 1992, the Rio Earth Summit drew political leaders from all over the world. These leaders recognized that access to fresh water is one of the most important issues facing people around the world, yet progress on fresh water management since the Earth Summit has been disappointing. The lack of attention to water may be leading to a worldwide crisis of water availability.

According to a 1997 United Nations report, water use has been growing twice as fast as population during the twentieth century, the UN estimates that one-third of the world's people live in countries facing moderate to severe water stress, and that by 2025 the figure may rise to two-thirds. Twenty percent of the world's population may lack access to safe drinking water.

These figures suggest that many other peoples may find themselves in situations similar to that of the Cocopas in the next 20 to 30 years. Unless the world's nations recognize the importance of access to clean, safe water for all their people and begin to work toward it, the devastating experience of the dying Cocopa Indians will be repeated all over the world.

efforts of those affected to cope with the crisis and respond to it (1997[1990]). Several contaminated wells led to increased rates of leukemia among Woburn's children. The citizens of Woburn themselves detected the "leukemia clusters," but it took years before their claims were accepted.

Each of these environmental problems—water scarcity, man-made chemicals, and toxic waste—poses major threats to people in the countries in which they occur. However, as we have seen, environmental problems increasingly have effects beyond the borders of the countries in which they originate. Citizens of Third World societies are often affected by decisions made by transnational corporations headquartered in industrial societies. Michael Renner argues that poverty, unequal distribution of land, and the degradation of ecosystems have the potential to lead to widespread world conflict. He suggests that "humanity is facing a triple security crisis: societies everywhere have to contend with the effects of environmental decline, the repercussions of social inequities and stress, and the dangers arising out of an unchecked arms proliferation that is a direct result of the cold war period" (1996: 17). In a very real way, the ultimate consequences of environmental problems may be increased conflicts within and among nations and world-wide insecurity rooted in those conflicts. The seriousness of these threats points to the need for effective solutions and interventions.

The Exxon Valdez oil spill in Alaska had devastating environmental impacts, as seen in the picture of pools of oil on a rocky beach. —*Photo: NOAA Hazmat.*

Interventions

A multitude of interventions have been brought to bear on various environmental problems. Some interventions have been successful; others, not so successful. Let's review some of them.

When the Cuyahoga River, in Cleveland Ohio caught fire in the 1960s because it was so polluted, serious incentive was given to the U.S. Congress to pass the Clean Water Act of 1972 to deal with pollution. Ten years later many waterways were still not swimmable or fishable. By 1990, 75 million dollars had been spent to improve the nation's waters. This law and the level of spending worked: currently, 75 percent of waters are safe for swimming and 80 percent are safe for fishing. Despite this improvement, a number of rivers still remain unswimmable and unfishable mainly because little progress has been made in reducing pollution from urban and agricultural runoffs (Seitz 1995).

Waste disposal is a serious problem in U. S. society. In the early 1990s, the Environmental Protection Agency (EPA) required that all cities and towns in the United States improve their dumps and landfills so pollutants would not leak from them into waterways. In addition to improved dumps, it appeared necessary to cut down on the amount of solid waste produced. Recycling was one way to get people to reduce trash. One problem in the 1980s was that more material was being recycled than could be resold. Industries began to use recycled materials in the 1990s and were given added incentive when President Clinton ordered all federal government agencies to purchase paper with a minimum of 20 percent recycled fibers in it (Seitz 1995). Even with the recent boom in recycling, the United States does not recycle as much as other countries. In the 1990s the United States was recycling about 15 percent of its trash while Japan was recycling 50 percent of its trash. Recycling is a solution to our waste problem but only a partial one since the process itself creates pollution and uses energy.

Another strategy to cut down on the amount of solid waste is to make citizens pay to dispose of their trash. People may be more likely to reuse or recycle bottles, boxes, and the like if they have to pay to have their trash removed. Also, there is a growing trend for shoppers to use their own cotton grocery bags, which, of course, are reusable and washable, cutting down on the number of plastic bags used and disposed of by consumers. These strategies are in common use today and have been noticeably successful. For some strategies you as a consumer can use, see "A Closer Look: How to Be More Environmentally Sound."

Reducing toxic waste is a more serious and expensive problem than reducing solid waste. Barbara Ward (1979) suggested ways that government can encourage the reduction of toxic waste. One suggestion was to make those who manufacture and dump toxic waste pay for the costs of cleaning and disposal. One important intervention that follows this model is the Superfund. Spurred on by Love Canal and other disasters, Congress passed

---

A Closer Look

How to Be More Environmentally Sound

The following are ways in which individuals can help keep the environment healthy (Gershon and Gilman 1992).

1. Reduce the Amount of Garbage. Everything we throw away costs the environment. Increasing our reduction, reuse, and recycling of materials significantly contributes to keeping the environment clean. In addition, we should replace toxic products with nontoxic ones. One way to reduce the amount of garbage is to avoid excessive packaging of any kind as well as disposable items such as diapers, razors, and plates. Paper, glass, and metal are better than plastics.

2. Improve Home Water Efficiency. Supplies of fresh water are dwindling, not because there is not enough water but because we do not use it efficiently. Using water wisely in our households will make a difference environmentally and economically. Using water wisely can lower water and utility bills since electricity is required to pump the water. Environmentally, we can do a lot to save water resources. Installing water-saving shower heads and faucet aerators makes a difference. Replacing old toilets with those of ultra-low-flow design saves an immense amount of water.

3. Improve Home Energy Efficiency. Most of the energy we use to heat our homes and run our appliances comes from the burning of fossil fuels. These fuels are one of the major sources of acid rain and carbon dioxide; both contribute to global warming. There are many ways we can reduce the use of these fuels. One is to turn down the thermostat on our heating system, particularly at night and when we are not at home. Other ways are to tune-up our heating systems and plug air leaks. Regarding appliances, we can buy energy-efficient ones or tune-up old ones. ☞

> ☞4. Improve Transportation Efficiency. Cars have a significant impact on the environment. They contribute to carbon dioxide levels and cause low-altitude ozone smog (Gershon and Gilman 1992). One way to help reduce or eliminate such pollution is to reduce our need for travel. We can do this by carpooling. Other great fuel savers are walking, biking, and using public transportation.
>
> 5. Be a Wise Consumer. We should change our buying habits because most of what we buy is wasteful. Regarding food, we can buy in bulk, doing away with much packaging; we can eat less meat, eggs, and dairy products since much of these foods comes from factory farms or cleared rainforest land. We can grow our own food. We can also purchase clothing more wisely, making it last longer or reuse it. Generally, we should make a concerted effort to think before we buy and ask ourselves how long this product will last (Gershon and Gilman 1992).

the Comprehensive Environmental Response, Compensation and Liability Act (CERCLA) 1980. CERCLA established the Superfund to identify and clean up the most hazardous waste sites in the country. Superfund was designed so that those who created the problems ended up paying for the cleanups. Since the Superfund law was first passed, the Environmental Protection Agency—charged with enforcing the law—has identified over 35,000 potential hazardous waste sites (Environmental Protection Agency 1996).

Environmental groups initiate actions related to environmental protection. These groups date back to 1892 with the establishment of the Sierra Club. More recent groups include Greenpeace and Friends of the Earth. These groups attempt to educate the public about environmental problems and ways in which to alleviate the problems.

Many people believe, or at least hope, that advancing technology can solve our environmental problems. Dieter Koenig (1995) argues that, on the contrary, technology is not sufficient in responding to environmental issues because it does not address many deep-rooted social causes. Global cooperation appears to be imperative as part of the solution to saving the environment. This will be difficult to attain because developed and underdeveloped nations have different agendas and different economic systems.

The Future of the Environment

The future of the environment and the solution of environmental problems will depend on human decisions. Both within the United States and across the globe, serious environmental problems face humanity. These problems do not threaten everyone equally. Within the United States, "communities at risk believe their neighborhoods were targeted, chosen deliberately by corporations to be sacrificed in the name of economic growth and profits" (Gibbs 1998b:A25) and there is compelling evidence to suggest that they are correct. Globally, inequities are even more pronounced, as indicated in the United Nations *Human Development Report: 1998* (United Nations Development Programme 1998). Industrialization and economic growth have occurred, but the costs have been borne heavily by the poor. "The world's dominant consumers are overwhelmingly concentrated among the well-off— but the environmental damage from the world's consumption falls most severely on the poor" (United Nations Development Programme 1998:4). All over the world people have learned about environmental threats and have mobilized and organized to face the threats. Often they pressure their

Air pollution contributes to the depletion of the Earth's ozone layer. —*Photo: photostogo.com.*

governments to take action. The environment may be in crisis, but the environmental movement is flourishing.

However, while many people in the United States organize to fight air pollution, toxic waste, the use of pesticides, and other environmental threats, they face strong opposition. For example, Gibbs points out that "industry proposes to 'fix' the Superfund law by weakening cleanup standards and eliminating the 'polluter pays' provision. This provision is the primary incentive for corporations to manage and dispose of their waste safely" (1998b:A25). If such "fixes" take effect, the movement to hold polluters responsible for their own pollution will be seriously weakened.

Around the world, corporations have also mounted intensive campaigns to minimize the seriousness of other environmental threats, such as global warming. Paul and Anne Ehrlich refer to such efforts to minimize environmental threats as **brownlash** (Ehrlich and Ehrlich 1996). The writers and scientists who argue about environmental threats, such as global warming, acid rain, and industrial wastes, often portray their opponents as pessimistic doomsayers. The Ehrlichs argue convincingly that these writers often misuse and distort scientific evidence, but the "brownlash" writers often receive extensive and favorable media attention.

The debate over the seriousness of environmental problems and possible solutions to those problems continues. The future of these problems will be shaped by how much people learn and care about environmental problems. What is clear is that people in the United States consume 25-30 percent of the world's natural resources while making up only 5 percent of the world's population. It seems unlikely that people around the world can accept such an imbalance indefinitely.

Summary

Only about 10 percent of Americans choose environmental problems as the most serious facing our society, but environmental issues may have more impact than we realize. Many doctors and social scientists argue that human health is dependent on the environment's thriving. Environmental problems are not new to society.

Pollution is becoming more and more of a concern to society. Our waterways are gradually being cleaned up; still, polluted water is a serious issue for many towns and communities. Renewable resources such as forests and topsoil are being used faster than they can be replenished.

The 1970 Clean Air Act in the United States has improved air quality to some extent. We still have serious air pollution, especially the release of carbon dioxide into the atmosphere, which contributes to global warming. Environmental problems related to the land include the disposal of solid and toxic wastes and deforestation. The destruction of tropical forests seems to be accelerating at an alarming rate.

In this era of globalization, we must be concerned with environmental degradation being spread beyond the societies in which the damage was created. The United Nations, national governments, and other organizations have attempted to deal with this trend but have met with limited success.

Individual actions can cause or help solve environmental problems. It may seem that individuals do not have much control over their environment because of institutional forces. Yet, individual actions can make a difference at local levels. The use of electric cars is one example of individual efforts to reduce pollution from cars using exhaust systems. Over time, certain societies have been able to live in harmony with the physical world; some still do. Americans must create a balance between their culture and the environment. Schumacher suggests we need "appropriate technology." He argues that developing countries need technology "intermediate" between the ineffective technologies of rural areas in the Third World and the technology of the developed world.

Environmental problems can be analyzed using political economy and social constructionist perspectives. Some environmental sociologists suggest that in order to understand the environmental crisis, it helps to view the human race as a single biological species living in a single planetary environment. Catton and Dunlap developed the "new ecological paradigm." This model identifies three functions for the environment: supply depot, living space, and waste repository. These functions compete with one another. This model has several strengths and tends to emphasize settlement space. The primary weakness of the model is its lack of attention to human actions. The political economy perspective takes human decisions and power into account. This model integrates how the use of natural resources depends on social stratification processes. These models have been criticized as unidimensional. This approach has also been criticized for seeing the role of government as too limited and inflexible. Social constructionists point out that even the concept of nature is contested and can have a variety of meanings. It follows that the definitions of environmental problems are also contested. A social constructionist perspective focuses on how environmental problems attract public attention and come to be seen as problems.

Industrialization has brought dirtier air to all parts of the world. Although the United States has made progress in reducing air pollution, there is much to be done. The most serious threats to the environment are posed by the effects of water scarcity, man-made chemicals, and toxic waste, and globally, by global warming.

Various interventions have been attempted to deal with environmental problems. The Clean Air Act of 1972 enforced the cleansing of waterways and was somewhat successful. The Environmental Protection Agency responded to waste disposal and required all cities and towns in the United States to improve their dumps and landfills. Reducing toxic waste is a more serious and expensive problem that requires much more attention.

Discussion Questions

1. Take a moment or so to think about "nature." What images come to your mind? Can you think of any aspects of our culture that have shaped your view of nature? Does this have any consequences for your view of environmental problems?

2. Would you say you are an optimist or a pessimist on environmental problems? Why do you take the position you do?

3. Americans consume many more times than their share of the world's resources, given our population. How do you feel about this? Do you see it as problematic? Why or why not?

4. Would you be willing to cut back on your lifestyle if you knew it would help people in the Third World? Would you be willing to cut back if you thought it would help save the planet?

5. What kinds of ecological awareness programs operate on your campus? Have you had any involvement with them? Why or why not?

References

Bailey, Ronald. 1993. *Eco-Scam: The False Prophets of Ecological Apocalypse*. New York: St. Martins Press.

———, ed. 1995. *The True State of the Planet*. New York: Free Press.

Bonner, Raymond. 1997. "Top U.N. Drug Aid Hopes to Rid Globe of Poppy and Coca Crops." *New York Times*, November 14, A6.

Brown, Lester A., et al. 1996. *State of the World: 1996*. A Worldwatch Institute Report on Progress Toward a Sustainable Society. New York: W. W. Norton.

———. 1997. *State of the World: 1997*. A Worldwatch Institute Report on Progress Toward a Sustainable Society. New York: W. W. Norton.

———. 1998. *State of the World: 1998*. A Worldwatch Institute Report on Progress Toward a Sustainable Society. New York: W. W. Norton.

Brown, Lester, Michael Renner, and Christopher Flavin. 1997. *Vital Signs 1997: The Environmental Trends That Are Shaping Our Future*. New York: W. W. Norton.

Brown, Phil, and Edwin J. Mikkelsen. 1997[1990]. *No Safe Place: Toxic Waste, Leukemia, and Community Action*. Berkeley: University of California Press.

Caldicott, Helen. 1992. *If You Love This Planet: A Plan to Heal the Earth*. New York: W. W. Norton.

Carson, Rachel. 1994 [1996]. *Silent Spring*. Boston: Houghton Mifflin.

Colborn, Theo, Dianne Dumanoski, and John Peterson Myers. 1997. *Our Stolen Future: Are We Threatening Our Fertility, Intelligence, and Survival? A Scientific Detective Story*. New York: Plume/Penguin.

Commoner, Barry. 1971. *The Closing Circle*. New York: Bantam.

———. 1992. *Making Peace with the Planet*. New York: New Press.

Cronon, William, ed. 1996. *Uncommon Ground: Rethinking the Human Place in Nature*. New York: W. W. Norton.

Cushman, John H., Jr. 1997. "Million Wetland Acres Lost in 1985-1995." *New York Times*, September 18.

Darling, Juanita. 1997. "Drug Crops Ravaging Colombia." *Los Angeles Times*, August 11, A1, A6.

Dowie, Mark. 1995. *Losing Ground: American Environmentalism at the Close of the Twentieth Century*. Cambridge: MIT Press.

Dunlap, Riley E. 1993. "From Environmental Problems to Ecological Problems." In *Social Problems*, edited by Craig Calhoun and George Ritzer. New York: McGraw-Hill.

Dunlap, Riley E., and William R. Catton, Jr. 1983. "What Environmental Sociologists Have in Common." *Sociological Inquiry* 33:113–35.

Dunlap, Riley E., George H. Gallup, Jr., and Alec M. Gallup. 1993. *Health of the Planet: A George H. Gallup Memorial Survey; Results of a 1992 International Environmental Opinion Survey of Citizens in 24 Nations*. Princeton: George H. Gallup International Institute.

Dunn, Seth. 1997. "Electric Cars Hit the Road," pp. 118-119. In *Vital Signs* 1997, edited by Lester Brown, Michael Renner, and Christopher Flavin. New York: Norton.

Easterbrook, Gregg. 1995. *A Moment on the Earth: The Coming Age of Environmental Optimism*. New York: Penguin.

Ehrlich, Paul R., and Anne H. Ehrlich. 1996. *Betrayal of Science and Reason*. Washington, D.C.: Island Press/Shearwater Books.

Ellis, Jeffrey C. 1996. "On the Search for a Root Cause: Essentialist Tendencies in Environmental Discourse." Pp. 256–68 in *Uncommon Ground: Rethinking the Human Place in Nature*, edited by William Cronon. New York: W. W. Norton.

Environmental Protection Agency. 1996. "The Superfund Program." Environmental Protection Agency Website, http://www.epa.gov/region09/waste/sfund/superfund.html.

Gershon, David and Robert Gilman. 1992. *Household Ecoteam Workbook*. New York: Global Action Plan for the Earth.

Gibbs, Lois. 1998a. *Love Canal: The Story Continues*. New Haven: New Society Publishers.

———. 1998b. "The Legacy of Love Canal." *New York Times*, August 7, A25.

Grossfeld, Stan. 1997. "A River Runs Dry; a People Wither." *Boston Sunday Globe*, September 21, A1, A18–19.

Hannigan, John A. 1995. *Environmental Sociology: A Social Constructionist Perspective*. Environment and Society. London: Routledge.

Harrison, Paul. 1993. *Inside the Third World*, third edition. London: Penguin.

Jacobsen, Thorkild, and Robert M. Adams. 1958. "Salt and Silt in Ancient Mesopotamian Agriculture." *Science*, November 21, 1251-1258.

Koenig, Dieter. 1995. "Sustainable Development: Linking Global Environmental Change to Technology Cooperation." In *Environmental Policies in the World: A Comparative Analysis*, edited by O. P. Dwivedi and Dhirendra K. Vajpeyi. Westport, Connecticut: Greenwood Press.

Levy-Leboyer, Claude. 1982. *Psychology and the Environment*. Beverly Hills: Sage Publications.

Outwater, Alice. 1996. *Water: A Natural History*. New York: Basic Books.

Park, Robert Ezra. 1936. "Human Ecology." *American Journal of Sociology* 42:1–15.

Postel, Sandra. 1997. *Last Oasis: Facing Water Scarcity*. New edition. Worldwatch Environmental Alert Series. New York: W. W. Norton.

Ray, Dixie Lee, and Ray Guzzo. 1994. *Environmental Overkill: Whatever Happened to Common Sense?* New York: Harper Perennial.

Renner, Michael. 1996. *Fighting for Survival: Environmental Decline, Social Conflict, and the New Age of Insecurity*. Worldwatch Environmental Alert Series. New York: W. W. Norton.

Reuters. 1997. "Humans' Health Held to Depend on Nature's." *Boston Globe*, September 9.

Rubin, Beth A. 1996. *Shifts in the Social Contract: Understanding Change in American Society*. Thousand Oaks, California: Pine Forge Press.

Schnaiberg, Allan. 1980. *The Environment: From Surplus to Scarcity*. New York: Oxford University Press.

Schnaiberg, Allan, and Kenneth Alan Gould. 1994. *Environment and Society: The Enduring Conflict*. New York: St. Martin's Press.

Schumacher, E. F. 1973. *Small Is Beautiful*. New York: Harper and Row.

Seitz, John L. 1995. *Global Issues: An Introduction*. Oxford: Blackwell Publishers.

Stevens, William K. 1997. "5 Years After Environmental Summit in Rio, Little Progress." *New York Times*, June 17, C8.

Sundstrom, Eric, et al. 1996. "Environmental Psychology 1989–1994." *Annual Review of Psychology* 47.

United Nations Development Programme. 1998. *Human Development Report: 1998*. New York: Oxford University Press.

Ward, Barbara. 1979. *Progress for a Small Planet* New York: W. W. Norton.

Weir, David, and Mark Schapiro. 1981 *Circle of Poison*. San Francisco: Institute for Food and Development Policy.

Winter, Deborah Du Nann. 1996. *Ecological Psychology: Healing the Split Between Planet and Self*. New York: HarperCollins.

Zitner, Aaron. 1996. "Building 'People's Car' Next Global Challenge." *Boston Globe*, November 24, A1, A28.

Websites

http://www.earthweek.com

Earthweek. This site is not especially sociological, but it does provide lots of information on the earth and related issues. This is the website for "Earthweek: A Diary of the Planet," a column that appears in many newspapers.

http://www.envirolink.org/

EnviroLink: Community, Ecology, Connection. EnviroLink calls itself "the largest online environmental information resource on the planet." Try EnviroLink. You will find an incredible variety of information related to the environment.

http://www.epa.gov/

U.S. Environmental Protection Agency. This federal agency provides a wide range of information. For example, take a look at the "Plain English Guide to the Clear Air Act." It really is—mostly—in plain English.

CHAPTER SIXTEEN

Mass Media
and Society

In the News: Free Speech on the Internet

Increasing numbers of Americans use the Internet and the World Wide Web to share and discuss ideas and to establish relationships. Increasing web use raises difficult free speech issues which draw much discussion and debate. Two recent articles in the New York Times *illustrate these kinds of issues and debates.*

One article, "Schools Challenge Students' Internet Talk," focuses on Aaron Smith's troubles. Aaron is a thirteen-year-old who attends Dowell Middle School in McKinney, Texas. Apparently, Aaron had made a drawing in the school's computer lab and one of his friends suggested that the drawing looked like a Chihuahua being killed. Aaron and his friends enjoyed the remark so much that they created a "C.H.O.W." (Chihuahua Haters of the World) web page. Aaron created the site on his computer at home. It was unrelated to his school, although he mentioned on the site that he attended the school. When a Fort Worth, Texas, chow breeder visited the site, she threatened an animal-rights protest against the school. Aaron offered to remove mention of the school from the website, but school officials "suspended him for the day; transferred him out of his favorite class, the computer lab where he was an aide; and told him to take down the Website and post an apology" (Lewin 1998).

This case is just one example of growing conflicts between students and schools over student-created web pages, "with students asserting their right to free speech on their personal sites while schools seek to control content that concerns them." The American Civil Liberties Union (ACLU) has defended many of these cases, including Aaron's. He was allowed to return to school, and no mention of the incident was put into his school record. In these cases, and in cases where students criticize school officials and policies, the ACLU has increasingly intervened on the side of the students. The ACLU contends that school officials cannot stop students' off-campus free speech, nor should they unless there is some indication of imminent harm (Lewin 1998).

Straightforward racial dialogue is another type of Internet free speech that has received much recent attention. In another New York Times *story, Michel Marriott referred to comments by a white father lamenting his daughter's relationship with an African American man, a black man commenting on the covert nature of racism in northern cities, and a white man who suggested that African Americans were responsible for most crime in America. Each of these comments on race was made online, in cyberspace (Marriott 1998).*

Marriott notes that "with the increasing popularity of Internet bulletin boards and chat rooms, where typed messages can be posted for millions to see and respond to, no one has to know a person's name, age, sex, sexual orientation, or race." Anonymity on the Internet allows people to "truly express themselves about an issue they would otherwise be reluctant to take up face-to-face with someone of another race on the job, at social events, even on the telephone." The volume of messages dealing with race is heavy. Some critics suggest that the lack of accountability fuels people's willingness to post race-related comments and the critics do not see it as positive. Other commentators take a very different view. Author Alex Kotlowitz argues that, in discussing race, most people don't "'know where in God's name to begin.'" Kotlowitz suggests that maybe the Internet is one place to begin (Marriott 1998).

Definition and Prevalence   ❖ ❖ ❖ ❖

Do you use the Internet or surf the web? Have you seen websites that pushed free speech to the limit or have you encountered frank racial dialogue on the web or in chat rooms? How do you use the Internet, also called the Information Superhighway? What do you think about proposals to regulate and censor the web? How much television do you watch? What kinds of shows do you watch? Where do you get your news—newspapers, radio, or television? Some people insist that they never—or hardly ever—watch television, but most Americans watch at least some of the time. Do you think that watching television affects how people view the world? What do you think about violence on television? Are you familiar with the V-chip or the new television ratings system? As you read this chapter, you might want to reflect on how your own experiences with the mass media affect your views on issues.

In this chapter we discuss social problems related to the media. We distinguish between media behavior and media effects. When we study **media behavior** we look at how the media actually operate, at how they perform. For example, we can examine how the media produce news, which may help us understand why so many Americans today mistrust the news media. Journalist James Fallows' recent study of the news media, *Breaking the News*, is subtitled *How the Media Undermine American Democracy* (1997). Are the media undermining democracy and, if so, how are they doing it? These are especially troubling issues, given the importance of an informed citizenry to a democratic society.

Some researchers have suggested that the highly concentrated ownership of the media affects media behavior (Bagdikian 1997; Croteau and Hoynes 1997; Hazen and Winokur 1997; McChesney, Wood, and Foster 1998). Most of these analysts work within a perspective based on the political economy of communications. A political economy perspective on communications and the media can be very helpful in explaining media behavior and performance, but may not be so useful in understanding media effects (Croteau and Hoynes 1997; McChesney, Wood, and Foster 1998; McChesney 1998b).

In examining **media effects**, a social constructionist

American children watch an average of four hours of television a day. The amount of time children spend watching television and the nature of children's television programs worry many Americans.

approach is helpful. Not everyone responds to a media message the same way. People actively interpret, or "read," media messages. As David Croteau and William Hoynes point out, "an MTV video of a hot new heavy metal band may elicit very different responses from a 15-year old fan of the band and a parent concerned about stereotypically sexist images" (Croteau and Hoynes 1997: 7) People engage in the "social construction of reality" in actively interpreting the messages in media. For example, there has been a lot of research on the impact of media violence on behavior, especially on children's behavior. Occasionally, we read about a murder case in which the perpetrators identify a movie or a television show as their inspiration. However, even though there have been thousands of studies of the effects of television and movie violence, the links between media violence and children's behavior are still unclear (Felson 1996).

The United States was the first country to become "addicted" to television. By the middle 1960s, some 93 percent of all American families had at least one television set. By 1972, the majority of American families owned color sets. By 1994, 98 percent of American households had televisions, with an average of 2.2 sets per home. There were 93 million color televisions. 79 percent of households had at least one VCR and 62 percent had cable television (Croteau and Hoynes 1997). Increasing numbers of Americans have access to the Internet, and software sales continue to grow. Clearly, Americans use mass media such as television and radio heavily and are continuing to expand their use of **new media**, which include cable television, fiber-optic technologies, satellites, and computers. (See Figure 16-1 and Table 16-1 on the extent of media use and consumer spending on media in the United States.) Croteau and Hoynes note that the increasing use of these new media technologies has "resulted in a move away from the mass broadcast audience toward smaller, more specialized niche populations—a process called 'narrowcasting'" (1997:12).

Figure 16-1 Media Usage by Consumers: 1989-1999

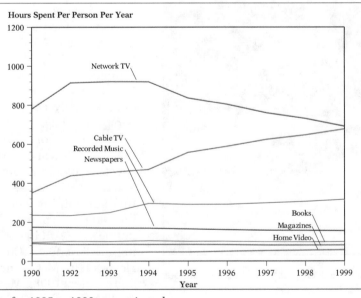

Note: Data for 1995 to 1999 are projected.
Source. U.S. Bureau of the Census. 1996. *Statistical Abstract of the United States: 1996.* Washington, D.C.: Government Printing Office. p. 558.

Table 16-1 Consumer Spending on Selected Media, per Person: 1990-2000   ❖ ❖ ❖ ❖

Type of Media	(Dollars) Years				
	1990	1993	1994	1995	2000*
Basic Cable	88	101	110	122	166
Books	64	75	79	81	102
Home Video	56	69	73	79	97
Recorded Music	37	47	56	57	80
Daily Newspapers	48	52	49	50	59
Magazines	33	35	36	36	43
On-Line/Internet	3	5	7	16	46

*2000—Projections

Source: U.S. Bureau of the Census. 1997. *Statistical Abstract of the United States: 1996.* Washington, D.C.: U. S. Government Printing Office.

Television viewing in the United States ranks just after sleep and work as a consumer of time. On the average, American families watch more than nine hours of television daily. Television viewing crosscuts all population segments including those of age, income, family size, and education; however, the frequency of viewing does vary from one segment of the population to another. College graduates tend to watch less often than high school graduates; poor families less often than wealthy families; younger adults less often than older adults; and families living in Pacific Coast states less often than families in other regions (U.S. Bureau of the Census 1997).

Many Americans believe that television may have undesirable effects on children. Most objections center on the abundance of violent programs, but commentators also express concern about "bad language," sexual suggestiveness, and drugs. George Gerbner, the "man who counts the killings," and his colleagues have been studying violence on network television since 1967 (Stossel 1997). (For more on Gerbner, see "A Closer Look: 'The Man Who Counts the Killings.'") They have examined both the quantity and quality of televised violence on prime-time shows and on children's weekend programs. Although many researchers focus on just the quantity of televised violence, Gerbner has always emphasized that the quality of that violence is also crucial.

Gerbner and his colleagues define violence as "the overt expression of physical force, with or without a weapon, against self or other, compelling action against one's will on pain of being hurt or killed, or actually hurting or killing." Thus, Gerbner records only those violent incidents that are directed against human or humanlike beings and that hurt or kill or threaten to do so (Gerbner, et al. 1978:179).

Gerbner's first analysis indicated that during the 1977 television season, violence occurred in more than two-thirds of all prime-time programs and in nine out of ten weekend morning programs. Violent episodes occurred at the rate of 6.7 episodes per hour. Children's programs on weekend mornings contained the most violence, and prime-time "sitcoms" contained the least. Gerbner also looked at patterns of violence among the 3,651 major characters appearing in television drama from 1969 through 1977: 63 percent of major characters were involved in some type of violence, but involvement in killing was lower. On average, 8.7 percent of the major characters were involved in killing (Gerbner, et al. 1978). These numbers have continued to grow,

A Closer Look

'The Man Who Counts the Killings'

As Scott Stossel points out in his solid piece in *The Atlantic Monthly*, George Gerbner does not just "count the killings." Gerbner and his colleagues in the Cultural Indicators project, "the longest-running continuous media-research undertaking in the world," have, over the past 30 years, studied the quantity *and* the quality of violence on television. Because the quantity of televised violence is so overwhelming, it has been easier to focus on that. However, Gerbner sees the quality of televised violence, and especially "who does what to whom," as extremely significant (Stossel 1997:90).

Gerbner's Cultural Indicators Project dates from 1968, when President Johnson's National Commission on the Causes and Prevention of Violence selected Gerbner to study television violence. This research, along with that by many other scholars, has led to a vast amount of research findings on violence and television. As an example of their findings, the Cultural Indicators Project estimates that "the average American child will have witnessed more than 8,000 murders and 100,000 other violent acts on television by the time he or she leaves elementary school" (Stossel 1997: 90). This kind of research, in which the content of television shows is studied, is called **message system analysis**, and it is very important for understanding the impact that television and televised violence have on people and—especially—on children.

Gerbner believes that another aspect of the Cultural Indicators Project research is even more important: cultivation analysis. **Cultivation analysis** examines how television shapes viewers' conception of the world. Stossels points out that a basic premise of cultivation analysis is that "television violence is not simple acts but rather 'a complex social scenario of power and victimization'" (Stossel 1997: 90). In particular, Gerbner suggests that, given how much violence is on television and the nature of that violence, television viewing leads to a "mean world syndrome" among viewers.

The **mean world syndrome** means that heavy television viewers tend to see the world as more dangerous and hostile. Becoming more fearful, viewers might be more likely to support more draconian social and crime control measures, including capital punishment. Research does support this view.

Gerbner's research has convinced him, and many others, of the need for an organization or social movement to give people a voice in the debate over television. An organized social movement is seen as especially important given the increasing control that a relatively small number of corporations wield over the media. Therefore, Gerbner played a central role in setting up the Cultural Environment Movement (CEM) in 1990. Gerbner explains the challenge to which CEM responds:

> Broadcasting is the most concentrated, homogenized, and globalized medium. The top 100 advertisers pay for two-thirds of all network television. Four networks, allied to giant transnational corporations—our private "Ministry of Culture"—control the bulk of production and distribution, and shape the cultural mainstream. Other interests, minority views, and the potential of any challenge to dominant perspectives, lose ground with every merger. (1996:3)

Even if George Gerbner is only partly correct in his analysis of the media industry, the CEM seems to be an important vehicle for ensuring an industry more responsive to the needs of most people.

although recent research indicates some reduction in network TV violence in the last few years (UCLA Center for Communication Policy 1997).

Gerbner's Cultural Indicators Project has collected a massive database of reports on television programming. Some significant patterns of television watching and violence on television have emerged from this research:

1. Americans spend a third of their free time with television.

2. Women make up less than a third of the characters in samples of all types of shows, except daytime serials.

3. Poor people are underrepresented on television shows. The census bureau classifies about 13 percent of the U.S. population as poor, but poor people make up only 1.3 percent of prime-time characters.

4. For every white male victim of violence, there are seventeen female victims.

5. For every white male victim, there are twenty-two minority female victims.

6. For every ten female aggressors, there are sixteen female victims.

7. Minority women are twice as likely to be victims as they are to be aggressors.

8. Villains tend to be male, lower-class, young, and Latino or foreign.

Much of the concern over violence and the media centers on children, who typically begin watching television at a very early age, as young as six months. American children watch an average of four hours of television a day. They spend more time watching television than doing any other activity, besides sleeping. There are some excellent programs for young children. *Mr. Rogers Neighborhood* and *Sesame Street* teach children numbers, letters, shapes, colors, foreign languages, and more. However, much of children's programming—especially Saturday morning programs—emphasizes violence, consumerism, and stereotypes. Programs specifically designed for children, like cartoons, are the most violent of all programming. The level of violence in prime-time shows is about five violent acts per hour, whereas the violence in children's Saturday morning shows is about twenty to twenty-five violent acts per hour (Sweet and Singh 1994).

Growing concern about the violent content of television has been matched by a substantial increase over the last decade in the portrayal of sexual content and innuendo. Much of television sex is presented in a humorous and light-hearted manner in the context of situation comedies, but increasing numbers of serious movies and dramatic series also treat sexual topics such as prostitution, rape, and child pornography. In the face of higher viewer percentage figures for sexier shows and an absence of evidence that such content has negative effects on viewers, television programs are increasingly likely to make direct references to sexual intercourse.

Problems associated with television may go beyond its sexual and violent content. In suggesting that "the medium is the message," Canadian media scholar Marshall McLuhan (1964) argued that the very existence of the television medium has changed our perspective on living. In this view, television is a "passive medium" to which millions of people routinely "turn on" and "tune in." Even earlier, Paul Lazarsfeld and Robert Merton (1948) wrote about the "narcotizing dysfunction" of the mass media; similarly, C. Wright Mills (1956) asserted that television led to political apathy and alienation, meaning that television information served to narcotize rather than to energize the average viewer.

Many social scientists suggest that television has become the focal point of a pervasive consumer psychology, through which people are socialized to believe that the solutions to their problems will come from consuming goods and services. The content of television also promotes consumption. Some 13 percent of all network television commercials sell drugs such as analgesics (aspirin), antihistamines, antacids, laxatives, and sleeping aids. Many of these ads promise that the consumer who ingests a product will experience not only specific relief but also general relief from pain or discomfort, relaxation, a sense of well-being, or a change in mood. From this viewpoint, there is only a small jump from legal to illegal drugs.

Although many commentators have expressed similar concerns about the Internet, others have pointed to potentially liberating aspects of the Information Superhighway. One attraction of cyberspace is that people can communicate anonymously and even change their sex, race, and sexual orientation online. As we saw in "In the News," people can also engage in frank discussion of sensitive topics, such as race. These interactions have been described as "liberating zones" (Croteau and Hoynes 1997). Some analysts have suggested that the increasing availability of computers and the continuing growth of the Internet have created an Information Society, allowing people access to vast amounts of valuable information online.

Other writers are more skeptical about the Internet. For example, violent content and pornography on the web worry many people. Other analysts are more skeptical about the implications of the Information Society, arguing that it may lead to information overload, which David Shenk refers to as *Data Smog* (Shenk 1998). Astronomer and Internet analyst Clifford Stoll also expresses ambivalence about the Information Superhighway. As the title of his most recent book suggests, some of the glowing acclaim for the Internet, email, and the World Wide Web, may be *Silicon Snake Oil* (1995). Along with Stoll, we need to ask some serious questions about the social implications of the Internet and other new communications technologies. As Stoll suggests, perhaps fascination with information technology leads us away from central issues.

> Perhaps our networked world isn't a universal doorway to freedom. Might it be a distraction from reality? An ostrich hole to divert our attention and resources from social problems? A misuse of technology that encourages passive rather than active participation? (Stoll 1995:2)

We reconsider these questions about the consequences of information technology after examining various explanations for media-related social problems.

Levels of Causation

Individual

Explanations of how media-related social problems arise are plentiful. They range from arguments based on individual characteristics and behavior to cultural approaches to structural explanations. From the individual level of causation, there is not much to say about media behavior. Some observers have argued that people's preoccupation with sex and violence is a result neither of a culture of sex and violence nor of the commercial nature of the media as an institution. They assert instead that violence is an integral part of our human nature—an aspect of an evolutionary survival kit that permits us to defend and protect ourselves both as individuals and as a species (Lorenz 1966). Aggressiveness is viewed as inevitable and universal rather than as a variable of social life that can be diminished or increased in accordance with cultural norms or institutional requirements. In a similar way, sexual desire is regarded as an inborn, universal force of human personality that motivates pathological behavior as well as human productivity (Freud 1953). From this point of view, media sex and violence reflect not cultural values or social structures but our basic nature as human beings. The individual approach has been used to support nonintervention in social policy regarding television and other media.

In regard to media effects, Richard Felson presents a **cognitive priming** approach to the study of film violence and aggressive behavior. According to this approach, violence in films activates aggression in viewers through their memory pathways. The claim seems to be that individuals store violent thoughts in their brains, and, upon viewing violence in a film, these thoughts are activated. Frequent exposure to violence leads individuals, especially children, to store aggressive behaviors (Felson 1996). There is some evidence for this approach, although its effects seem to be short-term.

Perhaps the most important individually based explanations for both media behavior and media effects argue for the centrality and effectiveness of the free market. According to this view, decisions on what media content to create are market driven. In other words, the media industry produces what people want to see. If people are not happy with media content, they will not watch, read, or otherwise consume that content. Although this sounds good, the extent of concentration in the media, also called the Information Industry, is so broad that it makes little sense to even consider the Information Industry as subject to market forces.

Cultural

Cultural approaches suggest that the media serve as windows through which people can observe and reflect upon the prevailing social climate. In this view, the media merely respond to—rather than initiate—changes in our cultural values. From this perspective, problems associated with television and other media must be located within a broad cultural context. Violence and sex are regarded as American values that are also themes of television content. The problem lies in our society rather than specifically in our television sets or in the media industry. Social historians have similarly emphasized cultural aspects of American society in relation to violence: the central role of the military, the history of witch hunting, the unlawful use of violence in intergroup relations, and the widespread use of make-believe weapons for children.

Cultural approaches to media behavior focus on the norms and values of journalists in explaining how news is created. Sociologist Herbert Gans studied journalists at *CBS Evening News*, *NBC Nightly News*, *Newsweek*, and *Time* to understand how journalists' values and norms about professional standards, along with external pressures, shaped their news-making decisions. Gans found that two of the most important values for these journalists were "social order" and "national leadership." The social order they supported was largely that of white, male, upper-middle-class sectors of society. Gans argues that the media are not subservient to or controlled by powerful elites or groups; however, "when all other things are equal, the news pays most attention to and upholds the actions of elite individuals and elite institutions" (Gans 1979: 61).

Cultural approaches to media effects include Michael Morgan's argument that television viewing influences people's images and assumptions about many aspects of life, including violence, gender roles, education, and other issues. Morgan uses a methodology called **cultivation analysis** to examine the relationship between television viewing and behavior (See "A Closer Look: 'The Man Who Counts the Killings.'") Cultivation analysis refers to the relationships between exposure to television's messages and audience beliefs and behavior. Morgan believes that television content is highly political, meaning that it contributes to the structures of social power in society. He argues that television represents ideals that do not contribute to a so-called democratic society. He believes that television presents a very restricted set of choices regarding viewing and provides a "steady stream of politically relevant messages to nearly everyone" (Morgan 1989:116).

Television in the United States has become the primary source of culture for many people. Some commentators have suggested that television tells us what is acceptable and unacceptable about gender roles, political platforms, perceptions of social class, and beliefs about violence, among other topics. Television is not the only powerful medium influencing people's perceptions and behaviors, but it is the most common one.

Structural

In contrast to the cultural approach, structural explanations of media focus on the structure of society and the media. Take television as an example. The commercial nature of television is frequently seen as a key factor in causing social problems. Network television is designed to make money through advertising. Many companies spend millions of dollars a year in order to sell their products on television spot commercials. The prices of spot commercials are influenced by program ratings purporting to measure the number of homes that they reach. Thus, better ratings mean more money for the networks. Violence and sex make money because they represent what mass audiences want to see. This may help explain why children's television, for example, is heavily saturated with *both* violence and advertising.

Television violence and sexual suggestiveness have also been regarded as instruments of political power and manipulation. In 1956, C. Wright Mills argued that the top leadership of American society consisted of a small group of men representing government, business, and the military. According to Mills, members of this unified and coordinated **power elite** gained control of the most important positions in our society—those positions associated with national and international decision making—in order to protect and further their own economic interests.

One aspect of Mills' theory of political power is the role played by the "mass media of distraction." If top decision makers are to continue to control and manipulate for their own benefit without interference from the public, then it is necessary to find a means of mass diversion, "an opiate of the masses" that increases their apathy and indifference. As a result, the mass media, and especially television, have been designed to obscure the individual's connections with political reality ". . . by distracting his [sic] attention and fastening it upon artificial frenzies that are resolved within the program framework, usually by violent action, or by what is called humor" (Mills 1956: 363).

In the realm of media behavior, scholars offer several explanations for how the media portray particular images and ideals. In her book *Thinking About Women* (1997), sociologist Margaret Andersen discusses these explanations in relation to sexism in the media, but they are broader theories that have been applied to media content in general. The **reflection hypothesis** assumes that the media represent dominant ideals within society. These ideals support the existing roles and structure of society and reproduce those roles. For example, advertisements during daytime television viewing focus on issues and items related to housewives. Soap operas have been described as an escape for women and are designed in ways to allow the viewer to identify with characters or issues presented, although some analysts have made much more provocative suggestions about soap operas (see "A Closer Look: Women and Soap Operas").

A Closer Look

Women and Soap Operas

Every day 30 to 40 million people watch the daytime television shows known as soap operas. Every day, Monday through Friday, some 350 soap opera characters are depicted over nine hours of broadcast time on the major networks. The majority of the soap opera audience continues to be housewives aged eighteen to forty-nine years; but as women's position in the work force has increased, more and more retired people and college students have joined the soap opera audience as well.

Since 1950, when the first television soap opera was aired, there have been more and more explicit depictions of sex and violence, somewhat more action, and more attention to social problems such as child abuse, alcoholism, and abortion. On the whole, however, the soaps continue to be dominated by talk; depict predominantly white, upper-middle-class lifestyles; and focus on personal problems and romance.

The world of prime-time television is dominated by male characters. They are more likely than their female counterparts to play heroic roles and they get star billing. By contrast, about one half of soap opera characters are women, many of whom are portrayed in professional careers. On long-running daytime series, women often maintain their roles as heroines, remaining attractive, healthy, and needed despite their advancing age. On the negative side, soap-opera women in careers are frequently also portrayed as suffering from some psychiatric disorder. Moreover, most women who hold jobs are in traditional female occupations, for example, secretaries and nurses.

Soap operas seems to be extremely attractive to women. Following on sociologist Muriel Cantor's pioneering work, feminist social scientists and media analysts have become increasingly interested in the reasons for this (Cantor 1983; Brown 1990; Brown 1994; Van Zoonen 1994). One very commonsense observation concerning why women are so attracted to soap operas is the actual scheduling of soap operas. Women are the main viewers of soap operas during the day because they are more likely than men to be home during this time. Soaps tend to function as an integral part of a housewife's day. Some women may even manage their day around soap opera viewing. Women often use soaps to divide work from leisure, but they are also attracted to what is termed the "narrative structure of the genre" (Van Zoonen 1994). ☞

> ☞ Soap operas generally focus on family and personal lives. This may help account for their appeal to women. In soap operas women are generally portrayed as expressing themselves efficiently and rationally. In fact, Mary Ellen Brown argues that soaps offer a "feminine culture" of themes that women relate to easily. In contemporary society, these themes may not be as highly appreciated as they are in soaps. Brown suggests that soap operas are a part of a women's culture that exists alongside the dominant culture.

Role-learning theory hypothesizes that images in the media encourage role modeling, particularly roles related to race, class, gender, and sexual orientation. For example, women are often depicted in situations defined by men which is why women are predominantly portrayed as sex objects or housewives. Organizational theories of gender inequality attempt to explain sexism in media content by inequality in media organizations. This approach assumes sexism and racism in media content can be traced to the relative lack of women and minorities in media organizations. However, professional norms and organizational culture strongly affect the values, behaviors, and attitudes of those who work in media organizations, including women and members of minority groups (Andersen 1997).

Andersen notes a fourth perspective that emphasizes the role of capitalism in explaining media content. This approach focuses on the capitalist structure of media organizations as well as on the structure of a capitalist society. This approach suggests that sponsors promote images that are consistent with their products, many of which promote certain values.

This political economy of communications perspective—which developed out of Marx's social theory—also emphasizes the importance of the ownership and control of the media by major corporations. From this perspective, the most important trends in social and media change include the increasing role of advertising in the media, the increasing concentration of corporate media ownership, and the emergence of the new electronic media. Those working within this approach are also strongly committed to democratizing the media (McChesney 1998a).

According to Robert McChesney, a leading scholar in the field, there are two main dimensions to the political economy of communications:

Computers and other information technology play an increasingly important role in American society. There is much debate over the social impact of such technology.

First, it addresses the nature of the relationship of media and communications systems to the broader structure of society. In other words, it examines how media (and communication) systems and content reinforce, challenge, or influence existing class and social relations. Second, the political economy of communications looks specifically at how ownership, support mechanisms (e.g. advertising), and government policies influence media behavior and content. This line of inquiry emphasizes structural factors and the labor process in the production, distribution, and consumption of communication. (McChesney 1998a:3)

The political economy approach begins with the process of capital accumulation by which corporations continually expand their profitability.

McChesney identifies three topics that have long been central to the research agenda of this perspective: the extent to which a "professional journalist ideology" has given journalists autonomy from their employers and advertisers; the increasing role of advertising; and the "ever increasing concentration of corporate media ownership, a process flowing from the logic of the market" (1998a:6). The concentration of ownership and control of the media is especially important for understanding contemporary media trends. Such concentration affects all areas of corporate media, including television, films, and newspapers. From the political economy point of view, it is hard to overstate the importance of the consequences of these developments. These consequences include the homogenization of media products, the narrowing of sources of vital information for citizens, and lack of alternative media voices. In a very real sense the increasing corporate concentration of ownership and control of the media represents a monopolization of American culture (Hazen and Winokur 1997).

Consequences

First, we take a look at the most important consequences of the structure of media ownership and control in the United States for media behavior and performance. This will lead us to comment on the globalization of media control. Then we will examine some of the most significant media effects.

One powerful model for explaining how the U.S. media work has been developed by Edward Herman and Noam Chomsky (Chomsky 1989; Herman and Chomsky 1998; Herman 1998). These researchers had "long been impressed with the regularity with which the media operate within restricted assumptions, depend heavily and uncritically on elite information sources, and participate in propaganda campaigns helpful to elite interests." They looked for "structural factors as the only possible root of systemic behavior and performance patterns" (Herman 1998:191). Their **propaganda model** thus explains media content by reference to the structure of media ownership and organization.

The most basic aspects of media organization are "that they are profit-seeking businesses, owned by very wealthy people (or other companies); and they are funded largely by advertisers who are also profit-seeking entities. And who want their ads to appear in a supportive selling environment" (Herman 1998:192). These factors, combined with others such as the reliance of the media on government and business firms for information and the dominant ideology in the society, tend to produce uncritical information reflecting the points of view of those who own and control the resources of

American society, and—increasingly—the world (Herman 1998; Herman and Chomsky 1998).

Herman and Chomsky carried out research on a wide variety of cases, most of which supported their model. For example, the propaganda model does an excellent job of accounting for the nature of reporting on the North American Free Trade Agreement (NAFTA); most media coverage strongly supported the initiative (Herman 1998). The reporting on the Telecommunications Act of 1996 also supports the propaganda model, as does the manner in which American media "cover Islam" (Said 1997). For more on how the news media distort Islam, see "A Closer Look: "Covering Islam."

A Closer Look

Covering Islam

When you first heard about the Oklahoma City bombing in 1995, did you jump to any conclusions about who was responsible for the bombing? Many quickly attributed it to "Arab" or "Islamic" terrorists. Middle Eastern students were threatened on American campuses. Of course, within a few days we learned that the prime suspects were in fact Americans involved in the right-wing militia movement. Why did so many jump to the wrong conclusions?

Reflecting on how the American media cover Islam may help us understand. When you think about Islam, what images come to your mind? When scholar Edward Said first published *Covering Islam* in 1981, he noted that pun in the title. He wrote about how Western news media "covered" Islam in the sense that they cover any story. But the title also conveys the idea that the media also covers Islam in the sense of obscuring it. Specifically, Said argues that the American news media—along with various experts—portray Islam in a way that leads Americans to see Islam in terms of terrorism and religious fundamentalism. In the 1997 second edition of the book, Said notes that

> in the fifteen years since *Covering Islam* first appeared there has been an intense focus on Muslims and Islam in the American and Western media, most of it characterized by a more highly exaggerated stereotyping and belligerent hostility than what [he] had previously described in his book. (1997: xi)

Said concedes that there have been many troubling incidents by Muslims in the Middle East and elsewhere. He does not deny the existence of terrorism and serious social, economic, and political problems in countries in which Islam is the dominant religion.

What concerns Said is the extravagant oversimplifications and stereotypes used to characterize "Islam" and Muslims, so that the "mere use of the label 'Islam,' either to explain or to indiscriminately condemn 'Islam,' actually ends up becoming a form of attack, which in turn provokes more hostility between self-appointed Muslim and Western spokespersons" (1997: xvi). In fact, the stereotyped notion of "Islam" represents only a small proportion of the Islamic world, "which numbers a billion people, and includes dozens of countries, societies, traditions, languages, and, of course, an infinite number of different experiences" (1997: xvi).

The danger of simplistic, distorted, and ethnocentric images of Islam is that they mislead us about such a large number of peoples and countries, making it difficult to deal with and understand them. Instead of carefully investigating the historical background and contemporary significance in the Middle East and many other parts of the world, the media and the experts engage in stereotyping and distortions that ill serve anyone in an increasingly global age.

Herman notes that the propaganda model has also been heavily criticized, but he notes that many criticisms seem to miss the point that it is a "model of *media behavior and performance*, not media *effects*" (1998:193). The model does not suggest that people will uncritically believe what is produced by the media; people can actively analyze and question the outputs of the propaganda system. However,

> the model does suggest that the mainstream media, as elite institutions, commonly frame news and allow debate only within the parameters of elite interests; and that where the elite is really concerned and unified, and/or where ordinary citizens are not aware of their own stake in an issue or are immobilized by effective propaganda, the media will serve elite interests uncompromisingly. (Herman 1998: 194)

The amount of scholarly and popular writing about media effects on social problems is staggering. Consider television as an example. In his *Sociological Tour of Cyberspace* (1998), sociologist Michael Kearl provides a list of twenty five suspected effects of television, divided into three categories: cognitive impacts, affective impacts, and behavioral impacts. The cognitive impacts include responsibility for changing contemporary personality, causing the generation gap, and leading to information overload. Affective impacts include serving as an escape mechanism to relieve societal stress, providing opportunities for emotional release and satisfaction, and communicating life in emotional rather than intellectual or rational terms. In terms of behavioral impacts, Kearl lists four possible ones. For example, some researchers suggest that television watching has a greater impact on adult behavior than it does on that of children.

We look at media effects in several areas. Consider the implications of media representations of gender in our society. Many of these representations are unrealistic. For example, most super models are very thin, beautiful, and well dressed. They do not represent the majority of women in society. Their images are unattainable. Most of these images, whether they exist in the form of photographs or television representations, result from airbrushing and retouching to create artificial beauty (Wood 1994). The media effectively dismiss women once they reach age forty, which is sexist and ageist. Men do not disappear upon reaching forty, but equally unrealistic images are sometimes presented of them. For example, most men are not as bold and strong as they are depicted by the media. Such unrealistic images of men and women contribute to eating disorders, feelings of inadequacy, and the use of cosmetic surgery (Hesse-Biber 1996; Wood 1994).

Mass communication in general is a powerful source of socialization in this culture. Movies may not reflect our day-to-day lives as television does, but we receive important messages and guidance concerning social and political reality. For example, think about all of the movies you have seen centering on a fictional president of the United States. There have been a few with a female or African American president, but not many. A 1964 film *Kisses for My President* starred Polly Bergen and Fred MacMurray. Bergen was president and the comedy revolved around MacMurray's effort to play the "first lady" role. In 1998, the African American actor Morgan Freeman portrayed the president in *Deep Impact*. However, such portrayals are rare.

Communication is essential to society since it enables people to live and work together. Joshua Meyrowitz (1985) states that the "electronic media" influence not only the way people access information but also interpersonal social dynamics. Information available to people, regardless of class, gender, race, and sexual orientation, largely mirrors the status quo or white, middle-

Many sociologists and media scholars argue that the increasing concentration of newspaper ownership in North America restricts access to diverse sources of information and differing points of view on important social and political issues.

class heterosexual male values. The information we receive is homogeneous; actual distinctions become blurred. Electronic media undermine group identity because of this homogenizing effect. They also distort reality.

Think about advertisements directed at women. Women are often portrayed as sex objects or frantic housewives. Also, advertisements portraying food preparation and childrearing usually feature women, which supports the view that these are "women's work," not men's responsibility. Women are also encouraged to buy cosmetic products in order to meet the cultural demand to be attractive. What does this say about the role of women in our society? Many other media materials, such as popular music, advice columns, and Internet information generate ideas about women. Biased depictions of women can be further broken down into racial categories. Very few black women have leading roles on television, and when they do, the roles are rarely serious ones (Benokraitis and Feagin 1986).

In fact, white men and women greatly outnumber people of color on television. In addition, there are limited positive images of people of color. Black women are often portrayed as maids or support staff while black men are portrayed as criminals or athletes. Asian Americans, Native Americans, and Latinos are rarely portrayed at all, and when they are, their roles are specific to their ethnic identity. These distortions have real consequences. For example, surveys tend to show that Americans greatly overestimate the proportion of the poor who are African American and that those who have such misperceptions tend to oppose welfare. Political scientist Martin Gilens (1996) has shown that network TV news and newsmagazines portray the poor as much more African American than is the case. News media distortions have effects.

The presence of television in American homes has helped to change many aspects of family life by introducing new patterns of interaction, activities, and socialization. For one thing, television appears to have reduced the time that family members spend in conversation with one another. Television has also reduced time spent at social events, listening to music, and book reading, to name a few alternative activities. But the most important impact of television may be as an agent of socialization that competes with parents, teachers, and peers in influencing children's beliefs, values, perspectives, and self-concept.

Televised violence is the area of media effects that has been most heavily researched and has received the most attention. Earlier in this chapter, we examined some research related to television and violence. Here we look more closely at its effects. According to much research, the major consequences of televised violence for the attitudes and behavior of individuals in society can be summarized as (1) normative, where television depicts models for appropriate behavior; (2) cognitive, where television defines the parameters of social reality; and (3) self-evaluational, where television provides standards of comparison for abilities and achievements. Television probably does have effects for *some* children in each of these areas. Television does provide children with models of behavior. For example, television dramas frequently depict violence as an effective means to an end—a means employed by most of the star heroes of prime-time dramatic series. Television is not likely to be a primary determinant of behavioral tendencies, but it may reinforce the existing behavioral tendencies of individual audience members (Paik and Comstock 1994). Therefore, a child already predisposed towards aggressive behavior by virtue of his or her family background or other factors may be stimulated to violence by the presence of television heroes being rewarded for their violent actions.

Numerous studies of the effects of media violence have found that prolonged exposure to violence on television does affect some people, particularly children. George Gerbner's research on the mean world syndrome is important here. We must also ask whether television viewing breeds indifference to violence. Some have argued that continued exposure to large amounts of violence on television might lead to an "emotional blunting," which manifests itself in an increased tolerance for aggression in real-life situations. In a classic study, Ronald Drabman and Margaret Thomas (1975) showed, for example, that children who are exposed to television violence are slow to seek adult help when witnessing "real" violence among other children for whom they are baby-sitting. The overall conclusion may seem frightening: TV violence may have the dual effect of exacerbating some children's violent behavior while at the same time teaching the rest to tolerate aggression.

At the same time, it is important to note that for all the thousands of studies of the relationship between television violence and behavior, the results are far from conclusive or clear (Felson 1996). In fact, media sociologist Todd Gitlin summarizes much of the current campaign against violence in the media as supporting a view that "guns don't kill people, picture tubes do" (1994:112). Gitlin makes the serious point that there are more important areas to focus on if people wish to reduce levels of violence in the United States. He acknowledges the profusion of market-driven violence on TV and movie screens but notes that "the necessary condition permitting a culture of aggression to flare into a culture of violence is a lethal weapon" (1994:113). He suggests that there is little political will for actively trying to end poverty or eliminate citizens' access to weapons but that those are the changes that would actually reduce levels of societal violence (1994).

One of the most damaging consequences of media images of men and women is that the media dehumanizes men and women by objectifying them in sexual ways. There is no question that women are consistently portrayed as sex objects through media representation. Men, however, are being increasingly represented this way, which probably accounts for the rise in male cosmetic surgery (Wood 1994). In many ways, the media encourages viewers to live up to unattainable images and standards. They also encourage people to consider normal bodily functions as problems.

Consider the media's construction of menstrual cycles. The message clearly is that it is a negative function. Women should keep it private and this cycle is depicted as making women feel "dirty." Andersen (1997) argues that advertising promotes these images by offering cleansing products or tampons and pads that are so small no one will notice when a woman is menstruating. In relation to this is premenstrual syndrome (PMS). Women who suffer from PMS are supposedly difficult, cranky, and moody. Products are offered to "cure" this condition as well. Positive aspects of menstruating are never promoted, such as the onset of womanhood, or the fact that many women feel more energetic during their menstrual cycle. Advertising seems to effectively convince us that we need products to protect us from such normal developments as aging and baldness. We are told to alter natural processes in order to achieve certain images. A related consequence is that we may be hindered in our ability to enjoy real people and real relationships if they do not live up to the images (Wood 1994).

Some social scientists suggest that the media may have many effects on our behavior. Many of these effects are seen as very powerful, however we may not notice them or we simply take them for granted. The effects of televised violence is one area which has received much attention. Even if one is skeptical about some of the suggestions about media effects, there are other ways the consequences of the social organization of the media are powerful. As we noted above, the increasing concentration of ownership of the media may lead to fewer diverse sources of information. These consequences have led to various interventions aimed at reducing and eliminating damaging effects of the media. The next section reviews such attempts.

Interventions

Most attempts to reduce the harmful effects of television have taken an institutional approach. As established by the Communications Act of 1934, the Federal Communications Commission (FCC) is responsible for granting and revoking licenses to stations for broadcasting in particular geographic areas. The potential of the FCC for regulation of television content lies in its power to periodically renew licenses to broadcast on the basis of a station's attention to "public interest, convenience, and necessity."

In practice, however, the FCC rarely, if ever, exercises its authority in order to influence television content, especially depictions of violence. Instead, the FCC has typically taken a laissez-faire stance with respect to government control of television, arguing that free speech and free press would otherwise be destroyed (Croteau and Hoynes 1997).

The television code of the National Association of Broadcasters (NAB) represents an attempt at self-regulation of television content by the industry itself. The NAB was formed in 1922 as a trade association for the purpose of protecting broadcasters' interests. Its code requires that producers of television fare orient their programs toward "a home audience" and "the special needs of children" through "the highest standards of respect for the American home." With reference to violent content, the code states that the depiction of crime should not "invite imitation" and that violence should not be portrayed in an "attractive manner" or in such a way as to exaggerate its occurrence in life.

The NAB has virtually no power to enforce its rules on its own member stations or networks. Indeed, particular articles of the code involving the depiction of crime and violence are routinely violated on a wide scale (Croteau and Hoynes 1997). This can be seen quite clearly in the case of the Family Viewing Hour, a concept that was included in the NAB Television Code and operationalized for the 1975 television schedule. The Family Viewing Hour was intended to assure that the first hour of network prime-time programming would not include programs considered inappropriate for young children and would be suitable for viewing by the entire family. Later that year, however, television broadcasters filed suit, charging that the Family Viewing Hour was unconstitutional.

A Closer Look

Not in the News: The Project Censored Website

We have started each chapter with an "In the News" section. The Project Censored website provides essential information on important stories that are "not in the news" (http://www.sonoma.edu/ProjectCensored). "The primary objective of Project Censored is to explore and publicize the extent of censorship in our society by locating stories about significant issues of which the public should be aware, but is not, for one reason or another" (Jensen and Project Censored 1997:10). The project hopes that its activities will lead to more media coverage of important issues or will lead people to seek other sources of information. "The essential issue raised by the project is the failure of the mass media to provide the people with all the information they need to make informed decisions concerning their own lives and in the voting booth (Jensen and Project Censored 1997:10).

Created in 1976 by Dr. Carl Jensen, Professor of Communications Studies at Sonoma State University, and now directed by Dr. Peter Phillips, a sociologist at Sonoma State, "Project Censored operates under the principle that since the mass media is the public's primary source of information, any suppression of information—via bias, omission, underreporting, or self-censorship—rates as 'censorship'" (Hazen and Winokur 1997:10). In order to counteract such censorship in American mass media, Project Censored carries out an annual nationwide media research project, the results of which are published in a yearbook *Censored: The News That Didn't Make the News*.

Consider three of the top twenty five censored news stories of 1996. One story was titled "Cashing in on Poverty," and it focused on the astronomical costs of credit for low-income Americans. Another story argued that the teenage drug crisis is a "myth." A third underreported story showed that American corporations have spent large amounts of money on pro-China public relations. Each of these stories has important implications for American decision making and public policy, yet all three were barely reported in the press (Phillips and Project Censored 1997).

Network censors seem to be very much concerned with minimizing violent scenes that might generate negative reactions from viewers. As a result, violence is frequently "cleaned up" and shown "without its consequences."

For example, excessive bloodiness is avoided, dead bodies are not positioned grotesquely, and the consequences of the horror of violence are softened. According to representatives of Action for Children's Television (ACT)—an organization whose members have been outspoken critics of children's television programs and their commercials—television drama gives a child the idea that violence never produces any lasting harm, and that violence doesn't hurt anybody (Chen 1994).

Many researchers believe that the responsibility for controlling children's television exposure belongs not to the government or to the television industry but primarily to parents. In this view, the presence of a parent to monitor, select, and interpret children's viewing can have a significant influence on how children react to television. The same philosophy applies to parents monitoring children using the Internet.

Research supports this viewpoint. Children learn more from such educational programs as *Sesame Street* and *Mister Rogers* when adults involve themselves in the ongoing program (Chen 1994). The implication is clear: the experience of a child who watches television without parental supervision may differ in important ways from the experience of a child who watches the same programs in the presence of an adult. Similar assumptions apply to children who use the Internet.

In 1996, Congress passed the Telecommunications Act of 1996, an update to the Communications Act of 1934. One provision of the act required the installation of a computer chip in television sets to identify programs containing violence or any material inappropriate for children. Homes possessing these "V-chips" television sets were unable to receive such programs. In addition, networks agreed to provide a rating system for their programs to which the V-chip would be keyed (Croteau and Hoynes 1997).

The interventions discussed earlier are important. However, ultimately the resolution of social problems associated with the mass media will require the efforts of citizens organized to influence public policy and to work directly to democratize the media. Grass-roots interventions to work with and to change the media may become increasingly important. The Cultural Environment Movement is one important development. You can also use information sources to find information that is otherwise distorted or unavailable. Project Censored, for example, provides much useful information on distorted, biased, or omitted news stories. For more on Project Censored, see "A Closer Look: Not in the News: The Project Censored Website."

There are also several excellent guidebooks for those who want to learn more about and have an impact on the media. One such resource is Jason Salzman's book *Making the News: A Guide for Nonprofits and Activists* (1998). Going beyond criticizing the irrelevance of much news, Salzman provides information on how to publicize causes in local, national, and international media. Topics covered include staging your own media event, writing news releases, and working with reporters. This book also includes useful lists of resources.

We the Media: A Citizen's Guide to Fighting for Media Democracy (Hazen and Winokur 1997) is another excellent resource for those who wish to understand and democratize the media. *We the Media*, which provides a wealth of information in brief accessible pieces by leading media analysts, is probably the best single source for anyone wishing to understand contemporary mass media. Almost every aspect of the media is covered including

ownership of the media and the increasing concentration of media ownership; the extent and role of commercialization in the media; the media's content; access to media; and new directions for media. In addition to analyzing
the media, *We the Media* provides extensive information on groups working
to democratize the media.

The Future of Mass Media and Society

With varying results, groups such as the FCC, the U.S. Congress, the PTA,
the AMA, and the Christian Right are likely to continue to put pressure on the
television networks in order to reduce the amount of violence and sex. Such
pressure may also occur in connection with videotape recordings, the
Internet, and cable, because their audience pays only for individual programs or a monthly subscriber's fee. For example, a large proportion of prere-
corded cassettes presently consist of X- or R-rated films. A substantial segment of cable movies also have R ratings.

The new technologies also present us with a promise for better quality,
more specialized television—television for smaller audiences that could survive without advertising; television that permits the audience greater control
than does broadcast television. Only time will tell whether the promise of the
new television technologies will actually reduce the troubling aspects of
television.

Although the mass media tend to reflect many traditional images or societal beliefs, some changes have occurred. People still have a long way to go to
change biased images reflected and represented by the mass media. For example, it may take a long time to change images of women in advertising
since the cosmetics industry makes billions of dollars a year. One course of
action would be for people to stop supporting sexist images of women by not
buying products that promote such sexism.

In terms of "electronic media," we have clearly entered a new phase in human history. One concern may be that people will stop communicating with
one another face to face, which may negatively affect our social lives. On the
other hand, we may become a highly efficient society in terms of technology
and communication. Current trends toward increasing concentration of
ownership and control of world media are profoundly troubling, but there
are opportunities to exert leverage to have a more responsive media.

Summary

This chapter examines media behavior and performance and media effects. At least half of all adult Americans believe that television content may
have some undesirable effect on their children. Most of these concerns focus
on the abundance of violent programs and sexual suggestiveness. There has
been a lot of research on the impact of violence in the media, much of it suggesting that viewing violence affects us negatively.

Television coverage crosscuts differences in income, family size, and education. The frequency of viewing varies from one segment of the population
to another. American families watch an average of nine hours of television a
day. Television ranks just after sleep and work as a consumer of time.

On an individual level, observers assert that violence is an integral part of our human nature. Aggressiveness is viewed as universal and inevitable. In this view, television violence and sex are a reflection of our basic nature as human beings.

On the cultural level, problems associated with television may be seen as a reflection of the prevailing social climate. Violence and sex are American values, which are also themes of television content. Gerbner's Cultural Indicators Project has collected a database of reports on television programming. Gerbner attempts to determine how much television contributes to viewers' conceptions of reality. Children spend more time watching television than in any other activity besides sleeping. Similar concerns about violence apply to the Internet.

By contrast, structural explanations focus on the structure of the Information Industries and of society. Also, from the structural perspective, television sex and violence may be regarded as an "opiate of the masses" with which the power elite manipulates public opinion. The propaganda model provides explanations of the nature of media news coverage.

Television has consequences for the attitudes and behavior of individuals in our society. First, it serves a normative function by providing an array of models to imitate, models who are rewarded for their conduct. Second, it defines social reality for millions of children who, for example, overestimate the proportion of whites in the world's population. Finally, it may increase relative deprivation among lower-income members of society who compare their existence with that of relatively affluent television characters.

Discussion Questions

1. Do you use the Internet? How much do you use it and what kinds of information do you get from it? Has using the Internet changed the way you obtain news or information about world events? Do you think you are an Internet addict?

2. Where do you get most of your knowledge of current events? Do you trust the news media? Why or why not?

3. What do you think about the impact of televised violence? Do you think you have been affected by violence in the media? If so, how?

4. Spend a couple of hours some evening monitoring prime-time television shows for gender role portrayals. What did you find? Did it surprise you?

5. How effective do you think the V-chip and the new television rating system will be? Try to design your own rating system for television shows. How would it differ from the new system?

References

Andersen, Margaret. 1997. *Thinking About Women: Sociological Perspectives on Sex and Gender*. Boston: Allyn and Bacon.

Bagdikian, Ben H. 1997. *The Media Monopoly*. Fifth Edition. Boston: Beacon Press.

Benokraitis, Nijole, and Joe Feagin. 1986. *Modern Sexism*. Englewood Cliffs, New Jersey: Prentice Hall.

Brown, Mary Ellen, ed. 1990. *Television and Women's Culture: The Politics of the Popular*. Communications and Human Values Series. Thousand Oaks, California: Sage Publications.

Brown, Mary Ellen. 1994. *Soap Opera and Women's Talk: The Pleasure of Resistance*. Communications and Human Values Series. Thousand Oaks, California: Sage Publications.

Cantor, Muriel G. 1983. *The Soap Opera*. Beverly Hills: Sage Publications.

Chen, Milton. 1994. *The Smart Parent's Guide to Kid's TV*. San Francisco: KQED Books.

Chomsky, Noam. 1989. *Necessary Illusions: Thought Control in Democratic Societies*. Boston: South End Press.

Croteau, David, and William Hoynes. 1997. *Media/Society: Industries, Images, and Audiences*. Thousand Oaks, California: Pine Forge Press.

Drabman, Ronald S., and Margaret H. Thomas. 1975. "Does TV Violence Breed Indifference?" *Journal of Communications* 25:86–89.

Fallows, James. 1997. *Breaking the News: How the Media Undermine Democracy*. New York: Vintage Books.

Felson, Richard B. 1996. "Mass Media Effects on Violent Behavior." *Annual Review of Sociology* 22:103–28.

Freud, Sigmund. 1953. "Three Essays on the Theory of Sexuality." In *Standard Edition of the Complete Psychological Works of Sigmund Freud*. Volume 7, edited by J. Strachey. London: Hogarth.

Gans, Herbert. 1979. *Deciding What's News: A Study of CBS Evening News, NBC Nightly News, Newsweek and Time*. New York: Random House.

Gerbner, George, et al. 1978. "Cultural Indicators: Violence Profile No. 9." *Journal of Communication* 28:176–207.

Gerbner, George. 1996. "Letter From the Founder: Why the Cultural Environment Movement?" Cultural Environment Movement (CRM) Homepage, http://www.cemnet.org.

Gilens, Martin. 1996. "Race and Poverty in America: Public Misperceptions and the American News Media." *Public Opinion Quarterly* 60:515–41.

Gitlin, Todd. 1994. "Imagebusters: The Hollow Crusade Against TV Violence." *The American Prospect* (16) Winter. http://epn/org/prospect/16/16gitl.html.

Hazen, Don, and Julie Winokur, eds. 1997. *We the Media: A Citizen's Guide to Fighting for Media Democracy*. New York: The New Press.

Herman, Edward S., and Noam Chomsky. 1998. *Manufacturing Consent: The Political Economy of the Mass Media*. New York: Pantheon.

Herman, Edward. 1998. "The Propaganda Model Revisited." Pp. 191–205 in *Capitalism and the Information Age: The Political Economy of the Global Communication Revolution*, edited by Robert W. McChesney, Ellen Meiksins Wood, and John Bellamy Foster. New York: Monthly Review Press.

Hesse-Biber, Charlene. 1996. *Am I Thin Enough Yet?* New York: Oxford University Press.

Jensen, Carl, and Project Censored. 1997. *20 Years of Censored News*. New York: Seven Stories Press.

Kearl, Michael. 1998. "Studies of the Mass Mediums." In *A Sociological Tour of Cyberspace*, http://www.trinity.edu/~mkearl/commun.html.

Lazarsfeld, Paul F., and Robert K. Merton. 1948. "Mass Communication, Popular Taste and Organized Social Action." Pp. 95–118 in *The Communication of Ideas*, edited by Lyman Bryson. New York: Harper and Row.

Lewin, Tamar. 1998. "Schools Challenge Students' Internet Talk: ACLU Asserts Pupils' Expressions on the Web Are Free Speech." *New York Times*, March 8, 16.

❖ ❖ ❖ ❖

Lorenz, Konrad. 1966. *On Aggression*. New York: Harcourt Brace Jovanovich.

Marriott, Michel. 1998. "Frank Racial Dialogue Thrives on the Web." *New York Times*, March 8, 1, 28.

McChesney, Robert W. 1998a. "The Political Economy of Global Communication." Pp. 1–26 in *Capitalism and the Information Age: The Political Economy of the Global Communication Revolution*, edited by Robert W. McChesney, Ellen Meiksins Wood, and John Bellamy Foster. New York: Monthly Review Press.

———. 1998b. "The Political Economy of Radio." Pp. 17–24 in *Seizing the Airwaves: A Free Radio Handbook*, edited by Ron Sakolsky and Stephen Dunifer. San Francisco: AK Press.

McChesney, Robert W., Ellen Meiksins Wood, and John Bellamy Foster, eds. 1998. *Capitalism and the Information Age: The Political Economy of the Global Communication Revolution*. New York: Monthly Review Press.

McLuhan, Marshall. 1964. *Understanding Media: The Extensions of Man*. New York: New American Library.

Meyrowitz, Joshua. 1985. *No Sense of Place: The Impact of Electronic Media on Social Behavior*. New York: Oxford University Press.

Mills, C. Wright. 1956. *The Power Elite*. New York: Oxford University Press.

Morgan, Michael. 1989. "Television and Democracy" In *Cultural Politics in Contemporary America*, edited by Ian Angus and Sut Jhally. New York: Routledge, Chapman and Hall.

Paik, Haejung, and George Comstock. 1994. "The Effects of Television Violence on Anti-Social Behavior: A Meta-Analysis." *Communication Research* 21:516–46.

Phillips, Peter, and Project Censored. 1997. *Censored 1997: The News that Didn't make the News—The Year's Top 25 Censored News Stories*. New York: Seven Stories Press.

Said, Edward W. 1997. *Covering Islam: How the Media and the Experts Determine How We See the Rest of the World*. New York: Random House Vintage.

Salzman, Jason. 1998. *Making the News: A Guide for Nonprofits and Activists*. Boulder: Westview Press.

Shenk, David. 1998. *Data Smog: Surviving the Information Glut*, revised and updated. New York: HarperEdge.

Stoll, Clifford. 1995. *Silicon Snake Oil: Second Thoughts on the Information Superhighway*. New York: Doubleday.

Stossel, Scott. 1997. "The Man Who Counts the Killings." *The Atlantic Monthly*, May, 86–104.

Sweet, David, and Ram Singh. 1994. "TV Viewing and Parental Guidance: Consumer Guide Number 10." In *U.S. Department of Education, Office of Educational Research*, http://inet.ed.gov/pubs/OR/ConsumerGuides/tv.html.

U.S. Bureau of the Census. 1997. "Sixty-Five Plus in the United States." *Statistical Brief: Sixty-Five Plus in the United States*, http://www.census.gov/socdemo/ www/ agebrief.html.

UCLA Center for Communication Policy. 1997. *The UCLA Television Violence Report 1996*. Los Angeles: University of California at Los Angeles, Center for Communication Policy.

Van Zoonen, Liesbet. 1994. *Feminist Media Studies*. Media, Culture and Society Series. Thousand Oaks, California: Sage.

Wood, Julia. 1994. *Gendered Lives: Communication, Gender and Culture*. Belmont, California: Wadsworth.

Websites

http://tap.epn.org/cme/index2.html

Center for Media Education (CME). The CME aims to improve the quality of electronic media, "especially on the behalf of children and families." Among their programs are the Campaign for Kids TV; an international debate over online advertising to children; and Interactions, a new research initiative investigating research on children's use of interactive technologies.

http://www.fair.org/fair

Fairness and Accuracy in Reporting (FAIR). FAIR is a leading progressive media watch group that studies and criticizes media bias and censorship. Arguing that the media generally have a conservative, rather than a liberal bias, FAIR suggests that "structural reform is needed to break up the dominant media conglomerates, establish independent public broadcasting, and promote strong, nonprofit, alternate sources of information." You'll find lots of provocative information and resources on this website.

http://www.mediademocracy.org/

Institute for Alternative Journalism (IAJ), Media Democracy. IAJ is dedicated to "strengthening and supporting independent and alternative journalism, and to improving the public's access to independent information sources." If you try this exceptionally useful site, be sure to look at the "MediaCultureReview."

http://www.mrc.org/

Media Research Center (MRC). The MRC is a conservative media research and activist organization dedicated to "bringing political balance to the media." This site gives you access to a wide variety of information and links to other conservative websites.

Glossary

Absolute Poverty   inability to afford the basic necessities of life

Absolute Poverty Line   a government defined level of income that is adequate for meeting the basic needs of living

Abuse   force used to coerce, demean, punish, release tension or to demonstrate power

Activity Theory   argues that the more active an elderly persons is, the greater their satisfaction with life will be

Age Stratification   theory that suggests that the age structure of roles in a society is organized hierarchically

Age Structure   distribution of people in a society by age and gender

Ageism   systematic discrimination toward some group—usually the elderly—based on their age

Alcoholism   a chronic behavioral disorder manifested by a dependence on alcohol

Anomie   a situation in which the norms of a society are weak or inconsistent; normlessness

Attraction Gradient   men are trained to be attracted to persons who are smaller, younger, and less powerful than themselves

Authoritarian Personality   a configuration of interrelated personality traits, including prejudice, conformity, and intolerance

Available Data   data which have already been gathered and are available for use by another researcher

Battered Woman Syndrome   a series of characteristics common to women who are abused psychologically and physically, over a period of time by a dominant male figure in their life. The syndrome consist of three stages and leads the women to expect further battering.

Battering   force used to coerce, demean, punish, release tension, or to demonstrate power

Biological Determinism   the view that human behavior and social phenomena are determined by biology and genetics

Birth Rate   (fertility rates) the number of births annually per some number of people—usually 1,000—in a population

Bisexuality   sexual attraction to members of both sexes

Blaming the Victim   Ryan's term for explanations of social problems which focus on the individual characteristics and alleged defects of groups of people as causes of the problems which affect them, rather than examining structural causes of the problems

Brownlash   arguments that minimize the seriousness of environmental problems

Built Environment   elements of cities that are made by human beings, such as streets and buildings

Capitalism   an economic and social system based on the private ownership of the means of production in which the prime goal is profit

Carrying Capacity the number of individuals of a certain species that can be sustained indefinitely in a given area

Chemicalistic Fallacy the view that a specific drug causes a specific behavior, and that the behavioral effects of a drug are solely a function of the its biochemical properties

Child Abuse nonaccidental physical, sexual, or emotional injuries inflicted on a child by its parents or guardians

Child Neglect failure by a custodial adult to provide for a child's basic needs

Claims in the social constructionist perspective on social problems, the demands made by groups in regard to the conditions they view as problematic

Class used in various ways, but generally refers to a group of people in a similar economic position in society

Cognitive Priming Felson's view that violence in films or television activates aggression in viewers through their memories of violent thoughts

Colonialism establishment of political control by more developed nations over less developed ones

Community Policing a proactive form of crime prevention involving collaboration between the police and members of a community

Compositional Approach this approach, developed by Gans, suggests that urban problems are caused by the characteristics of the urban population, such as their age and class, rather than to innate characteristics of urban living

Compulsory Heterosexuality the socialization to heterosexuality in society

Conflict Perspective sees social problems as socially patterned, harmful, and measurable conditions which result from competition and conflict between groups with differing and often antagonistic interests

Content Analysis a research method based on the systematic analysis of some form of communication

Crime (1) legal definition: an act that violates a law; (2) Gottfredson and Hirschi define crime more sociologically as acts of force or fraud that people commit to further their own self-interest

Crude Birth Rate (crude fertility rate) the number of births annually per 1000 population

Crude Death Rate (crude mortality rate) the number of deaths annually per 1000 population

Cultivation Analysis an analysis, developed by Gerbner, of the relationships between media messages and audience beliefs and behavior

Cultural Level of Explanation explanations of social problems by reference to the values and norms of some group

Culture the way of life which is learned and shared by members of a given society, especially their norms and values

Culture of Poverty theory that suggests that the poor have a separate culture, and that poverty is largely due to the norms and values of that culture

Death Rates (mortality rates) the number of deaths annually per some number of people—usually 1,000—in a population

Deinstitutionalization   the discharge of mental patients from mental hospitals and into the community

Demographic Transition   the process by which a population shifts from an equilibrium based on high birth and death rates to an intermediate stage in which population grows rapidly because of declining death rates to a new equilibrium based on low birth and death rates

Demography   the study of human populations

Dependent Variable   in research a variable that is affected by, or changed by, another variable

Determinist Approach   Wirth's theory that innate characteristics of urban life—primarily the size, density, and heterogeneity of the urban population—produce urban problems

Deviance   violation of the norms of a particular society at a particular time

Deviant Behavior Perspective   view that deviant behavior is learned through the processes of socialization, when individuals are influenced by deviant role models

Dietary Energy Supply   the average daily calories consumed in a particular area

Differential Association   Sutherland's theory of crime and delinquency which suggests that deviance is learned through interaction with others, usually in small groups

Diffusionist   the view that societies develop through the spread of cultural traits from one society to another

Discrimination   unfair treatment and denial of access to social resources to people based on their group membership

Disengagement Theory   a type of functionalist theory which suggests that the disengagement of the elderly from active roles characteristic of middle age is beneficial for society

Division of Labor   the specialization of work tasks and occupations

Domestic Violence   violent behavior used by one member of a household against another, usually to coerce, demean, punish, release tension, or to demonstrate power

Dominant/Subordinate Groups   another set of terms for majority/minority groups, which emphasizes the differential power and access to resources of the groups

Drug   any chemical that affects the structure or functioning of a living organism, usually by affecting body function, mood, perception, or consciousness

Drug Abuse   see substance abuse

Dysfunction   the negative effect of some social practice or institution

Ecological Additions   processes, such as pollution, which cause environmental problems by additions to the environment

Ecological Withdrawals   processes, such as resource depletion, which cause environmental problems by withdrawals from the environment

❖ ❖ ❖ ❖

Emotional Abuse a form of abuse which may entail verbal abuse, lack of affection, or lack of attention by the parent or guardian of a child, or by a partner of an adult

Ethnic Group a group that has a common cultural identity due to shared ancestry

Ethnocentrism judging other cultures by the standards of one's own culture

Eurocentrism the belief that European civilization is superior to other civilizations

Existing Statistics research based on statistical data that has been collected previously

Experiment method of research in which the researcher manipulates the independent variable in order to observe its effect on the dependent variable

Extended Family a family which includes members of more than two generations living together

Family Violence Perspective an approach to domestic violence that views the source of violence within family structure

Feminist Perspective on Domestic Violence explains domestic violence as rooted in the historical traditions of patriarchal societies

Feminization of Poverty the tendency for increasing numbers of women—especially single mothers—to be poor

Field Research a research method involving participation observation of the researcher in a research setting while observing what is happening in that setting

Food Insecurity inadequate access to the food needed for a healthy life

Food Security access by people at all times to the food they need for a healthy life

Gateway Theory the theory that use of some particular drug—marijuana, for example—will lead to use of other drugs

Gay a homosexual label usually referring to a male

Gender a socially and culturally defined status specifying appropriate behavior and roles for men and women

Gender Roles the behaviors and attitudes socially and culturally defined as appropriate according to one's sex

Glass Ceiling invisible barriers limiting the advancement of women and minority group members

Global Warming gradual rise in the earth's temperature due partly to human actions

Globalization the development of extensive worldwide economic and social connections among various parts of the world

Green Revolution development of new breeds of rice, wheat, and other grains—beginning in the 1950s—that led to tremendous increases in agricultural yields

Greenhouse Effect the collection of gases in the atmosphere that trap heat and may lead to global warming

Harm Reduction an approach to substance abuse which, while not condoning substance abuse, recognizes that it will occur, and stresses programs, such as education, which minimize harm to substance abusers

Health a state of complete physical, mental, and social well-being, according to the World Health Organization (WHO) definition

Heterosexism an ideological system that denies, denigrates, and stigmatizes any nonheterosexual form of behavior, identity, relationship, or community

Homophobia fear, misunderstanding, and hatred of homosexuals

Homosexuality sexual preferences for those of the same sex

Human Ecology Park's approach to understanding the relationship of human societies to their environment by investigating how human societies achieve and maintain a balance among their populations, their cultures, and the natural world

Hyperurbanization (overurbanization) extremely rapid urban population growth which outstrips economic development and leads to high unemployment and underemployment

Ideology a set of interrelated, shared ideas and beliefs that legitimate the social distribution of power and resources in a society

Imperialism establishment of political, social, and economic control by more developed nations over less developed ones

Independent Variable a variable that is presumed to bring about, or change the level of some other variable known as the dependent variable

Individual Discrimination intentional discrimination carried out by individuals, or small groups against members of a group and which usually violates the norms of a society

Individual Level Explanation explanations of social problems by reference to the biological or psychological characteristics of individuals

Institution a relatively stable pattern of norms, roles, and values organized around the basic needs of social life

Institutional Discrimination negative treatment of a minority group that is built into society's institutions, including direct institutional discrimination which is built into the social, economic, and political structure of a society, and indirect institutional discrimination, which is unintended discrimination resulting from the normal operation of a society's institution and social structure

Institutional Heterosexism an ideological system that denies, denigrates, and stigmatizes any nonheterosexual form of behavior, identity, relationship, or community and that is built into society's institutions

Interlocking Oppressions the combined effects of the class, gender, and racial hierarchies

Internal Colonialism economic exploitation of a group within a society

Labeling Perspective theory that the cause of social problems lies in one group labeling another group as deviant or manifesting social problems

Learning Theories   theories that propose that behavior is learned through interaction with others, mainly in primary groups

Lesbian   a female homosexual

Life Chances   the standard of living an individual may expect in life, including their education, health, length of life, and overall well-being

Life Expectancy   the number of years a person born into a particular society can expect to live

Macro-Sociology   analysis of social life focusing on large-scale processes and structures

Majority Group   a group which controls access to scarce resources

Mean World Syndrome   tendency for heavy television viewers to see the world as more dangerous and hostile than it truly is

Means of Production   property such as factory, land, and technology that can be used to produce goods and services

Media Behavior   how the media actually operate, how they perform

Media Effects   the effects of media on human attitudes and behavior

Message System Analysis   research, pioneered by Gerbner, into the content of television shows

Metropolitan Area   an area including a central city and surrounding regions linked to the city by economic and social ties

Micro-Sociology   analysis of social life focusing on social interaction

Migration Rate   the rates of movement of people into and out of a specific territory

Minority Group   a group that is denied equal access to power and other social resources based on its physical or cultural characteristics

Modernization Theory   in regard to the elderly, theory that claims that as a society becomes more technologically advanced, the position of the elderly declines

Moral Panic   collective responses which are provoked by conditions of social strain and incited and spread by interest groups to demonize some persons as threats to society and social values

Mores   strongly held norms

Multinational Corporations (MNCs)   large corporations, also called transnational corporations (TNCs) which operate in more than one country

Neolocal Residence   calls for newly married couples in a society to set up their own residence

Net Immigration   the overall number of immigrants to a country when immigrants returning to their country of origin are subtracted from those arriving

New Ecological Paradigm (NEP)   theory developed by Catton and Dunlap which identifies the functions that the environment serves for humans

New Media   new media technology including cable television, fiber-optic technologies, satellites, and computers

Norms   rules of behavior for specific situations and roles

North refers to developed countries, generally in the Northern hemisphere

Nuclear Family a family consisting of a husband, wife, and their dependent children

Objective View (objectivist view) focuses on conditions that sociologists define as social problems, regardless of whether public perception of the problem exists

Occupational Segregation by Sex separation of men and women into separate occupations

Opposite-Sex Eroticism sexual arousal directed at members of the opposite sex

Organized Crime refers to the activities of a group with a hierarchical organization, whose members operate an illegal business or a lawful business using unlawful force

Patriarchal Terrorism a form of terroristic control of females by their male partners that involves the systematic use of not only violence, but economic subordination, threats, isolation, and other tactics

Political Economy of Aging this perspective focuses on the state and its relation to the economy in a capitalist society to explain the plight of the elderly

Population Pyramid a graphic method to show the age structure of a population

Poverty see absolute poverty and relative poverty

Power-Conflict Theory see conflict perspective

Power Elite view that a small group of people at the top of major social institutions have disproportionate control in a society

Prejudice refers to beliefs, ideas, and attitudes about an individual or a group based on stereotypes about that group

Prestige status or honor

Primary Groups/Relationships a small group that has intimate face-to-face relationships and who derive emotional satisfaction from that interaction

Privatism favors the pursuit of private, individual goals over those that are public and social

Productive Property see means of production

Propaganda Model theory that explains media content by reference to the structure of media ownership and organization

Psychoactive Drugs chemicals that change the perceptions or moods of those who take them

Psychological Heterosexism the manifestation of heterosexism in individuals' attitudes and actions

Race a socially and politically defined category of people who appear physically similar

Racial Formation defined by Omi and Winant as the process by which racial categories are created, inhabited, transformed, and destroyed

❖ ❖ ❖ ❖

Racism a system of prejudice and discrimination against a category of people based on their race

Reflection Hypothesis assumption that the mass media reflect the dominant ideals and values within society

Relative Poverty defined by reference to the overall standard of living and expectations in a particular society

Reverse Discrimination belief that programs to aid minority groups have led to less opportunity and resources for members of the majority group

Role the social expectations for behavior attached to a particular social status

Role Conflict incompatible and conflicting expectations for a particular role or being in a state between roles

Same-Sex Eroticism sexual arousal directed towards those of the same sex

Sample a subgroup or smaller number of individuals who are more or less representative of a larger population

Sample Surveys a research method in which a sample of people respond to a series of questions

Scapegoating blaming or stigmatizing some relatively powerless group for problems they did not cause

Secondary Analysis of Sample Surveys surveys designed and carried out by others

Senescence physiological deterioration assumed to occur with aging

Secondary Groups/Relationships a group whose members interact in order to achieve a shared goal or purpose, but who do not have a strong emotional or personal attachment to each other

Sex the biological differences between females and males

Sexism an ideology that holds one sex superior to the other and therefore justifies discrimination on the basis of sex

Sexual Orientation an individual's preference in terms of sexual partners, which often implies that it is biologically determined

Sexual Preference an individual's preference in terms of sexual partners, which often implies that it is a choice

Shantytowns/Squatter Settlements makeshift settlements of the poor located on the outskirts of many Third World cities

Sick Role social expectations of those who are ill

Social Constructionist Perspective argues that social conditions become social problems through a process of collective definition and focuses on how people collectively define social problems

Social Disorganization Perspective locates the source of social problems in the effectiveness or ineffectiveness of the rules which guide and regulate social life

Social Epidemiology the study of how health and disease spread and are distributed through human populations

Social Fact Durkheim's term for social phenomena which are external to individuals, but also constrain them

Social Interaction the main focus of micro-sociology

Social Organization the main focus of macro-sociology

Social Pathology Perspective an organic or biological model applied to the behavior of individuals, institutions, and society as a whole

Social Policy attempts to ameliorate social problems through legislation and political decisions

Social Problem (1) objective definition: a social condition that is patterned, harmful, and measurable; (2) subjective definition: a harmful social condition that is collectively defined as a social problem

Social Stratification a social process through which rewards and resources, such as wealth, power, and prestige are distributed systematically and unequally within and among societies; inequality that has been institutionalized

Social Structure the organized patterns of human behavior in a society

Socialization the process by which people learn the characteristics of their culture

Sociological Imagination Mills' term for the ability to see the connections between one's own life and the broader society

Sociopaths people who are remorseless, lack the capacity to empathize with their victims, and are extremely manipulative in managing others' impressions of them

Sociospatial Perspective (SSP) Gottdiener's perspective which emphasizes the importance of metropolitan areas, the global economy, government policies and real estate, and culture for urban analysis

South refers to less developed countries, generally located in the Southern hemisphere

Split Labor Market Theory suggests that racial and ethnic antagonism and conflict arise from competition over the cost of labor

Stereotype attributing the supposed, usually inaccurate, characteristics of a group to all members of that group

Structural Functionalism social behavior is best understood from the perspective of the equilibrium needs of the social system

Structural Level of Explanation explanations of social problems by reference to social structures and social factors

Structural Strain Theory of Anomie a gap between socially and culturally approved societal goals

Structured Social Inequality patterned, stable inequalities among groups that persist over long periods of time

Subcultural Theory Fischer's theory that cities intensify subcultures

Subculture a group within a society that has a set of distinctive values and norms

Subjective View   (subjectivist view) argues that a social condition only becomes a social problem through a process of collective definition by the people of a society

Subjectivist   sociologist who emphasize social interaction

Substance Abuse   the use of illegal drugs or the excessive or inappropriate use of legal substances so as to produce physical, psychological, or social harm

Survey Research   using interviews or questionnaires to gather data usually for statistical analysis

Symbolic Interactionism   theory that people create a meaningful social world through interaction

Third World   refers to poorer, less economically developed countries

Treadmill of Production   refers to a system of social relationships in which production and the extraction of natural resources take place

Urban Political Economy   (also called new urban sociology) various approaches to urban analysis which emphasize the importance of social class, power, and the distribution of resources

Urbanization   increasing concentration of population into cities

Value-Conflict Perspective   recognizes the United States as a pluralistic society with clashing values and interests

Values   abstract conceptions of what is desirable and undesirable

Wealth   a person's total assets

White-Collar Crime   crimes committed by white-collar or professional workers in the course of the work

White Privilege   a system of privileges that accrue to people by virtue of their being white

World System   an international division of labor in which the countries of the world are linked together in a global economy in which different countries play different roles

Author Index

Subject Index